Time Out
New York

timeout.com/newyork

Penguin Books

PENGUIN BOOKS

Published by the Penguin Group
Penguin Books Ltd, 80 Strand, London WC2R ORL, England
Penguin Books USA Inc., 375 Hudson Street, New York, New York 10014, USA
Penguin Books Australia Ltd, 250 Camberwell Road, Camberwell, Victoria 3124, Australia
Penguin Books Canada Ltd, 10 Alcorn Avenue, Toronto, Ontario, Canada M4V 3B2
Penguin Books (NZ) Ltd, cnr Rosedale and Airborne Roads, Albany, Auckland, New Zealand

Penguin Books Ltd, Registered Offices: Harmondsworth, Middlesex, England

First published 1990
Second edition 1992
Third edition 1994
Fourth edition 1996
Fifth edition 1997
Sixth edition 1998
Seventh edition 1999
Eighth edition 2000
Ninth edition 2001
Tenth edition 2002
10 9 8 7 6 5 4 3 2 1

Printed and bound by Cayfosa-Quebecor, Ctra. de Caldes, Km 3 08 130 Sta, Perpètua de Mogoda, Barcelona, Spain

Let's do the twist Food-cart vendors ply the public with towers of fresh, hot pretzels.

An $89 New York Hotel Room Should Have A Closet, Not Be One.

This year we're cutting our usual room rate by about 25%.

Which means that every day of the week and weekend - all year long - $89 will get you an air-conditioned room right in midtown. At the Hotel Wolcott.

And not some leftover, bottom-of-the-line room, either. Each one is comfortably, spacious, and includes: color TV, in-room movies, internet access, Nintendo, hair dryer, in-room safe, voice mail and: a closet.

Right in midtown means you'll be within easy reach of Greenwich Village, Chelsea, Soho, The United Nations, world-class shopping, the theatre district, everything you come to New York to see.

Of course, there's one other very important thing you'll see in New York this year. How much $89* can buy you.

Affordable never looked so good.

THE **HOTEL WOLCOTT**

Mention booking code #1261 to take advantage of this low price.

4 West 31st Street, New York, NY 10001 (212) 268-2900 Fax: (212) 563-0096
http://www.wolcott.com   sales@wolcott.com   *subject to availability/plus taxes

Contents

Introduction	3

Perspective · 5

History	6
Architecture	18
Green Apple	25
Night Train to Brooklyn	28

Sightseeing · 31

Museums	32
Downtown	46
Midtown	64
Uptown	77
The Outer Boroughs	90
Tour New York	107

Necessities · 113

Accommodations	115
Bars	144
Restaurants	153
Shopping & Services	193

Arts & Entertainment · 233

By Season	235
Art Galleries	244
Books & Poetry	257
Cabaret & Comedy	261
Clubs	265
Film & TV	273
Gay & Lesbian	279
Kids' Stuff	290
Music	299
Sports & Fitness	321
Theater & Dance	335

Trips Out of Town · 349

Trips Out of Town	350

Directory · 357

Getting to and from NYC	358
Getting Around	361
Resources A to Z	364
Further Reference	379
Index	381
Advertisers' Index	390

Maps · 391

Street Index	392
Manhattan	396
Brooklyn	404
Queens	406
Trips Out of Town	407
Manhattan Buses	408
Manhattan Subway	409
New York City Subway	410
Key Sights	412

What a pane! Stained glass depicts a block in Queens at the 7 line's 33rd Street subway stop.

Edited and designed by

Time Out New York Guides
627 Broadway, seventh floor
New York, NY 10012
Tel: 212-539-4444
Fax: 212-253-1174
E-mail: guides@timeoutny.com
www.timeout.com/newyork

Guides/Online Editorial Director Shawn Dahl
Guides Senior Editor Lesa Griffith **Guides Associate Editors** Tom Gogola, Aimee Szparaga **Guides Copy Editor** Ann Lien
Guides/Online Assistant Editors Andrea Delbanco, Jeffrey Whitney **Guides Editorial Coordinator** Angela De Vincenzo

Art Director Shannon Casey **Photo Editor** Anna Kirtiklis
Copy Editor Elizabeth Gall

With

Time Out New York
E-mail: letters@timeoutny.com
www.timeoutny.com

President/Editor-in-Chief Cyndi Stivers
Publisher Alison Tocci
Financial Director Daniel P. Reilly

Production Director Jonathan Bruce
Associate Production Managers Nestor Cervantes, Carly Guarino
Advertising Production Manager Tom Oesau
Advertising Production Coordinator Andrea Dunn **Advertising Designers** Lynda Nardelli, Jamie Dunst, Jay Guillermo

Advertising Director Anne Perton **Advertising Manager** Tony Monteleone
Senior Account Managers Dan Kenefick, Jim Lally, Ridwana Lloyd-Bey, Marianna Shapiro
Account Managers Frances Grant, Emily Kelton, Melissa Norberg, Claudia Pedala, Paula Sarapin
North American Guides Advertising Director Liz Howell **Assistant to the Publisher** Maggie Puddu

Associate Publisher/Marketing Marisa Guillen Fariña
North American Guides Publicity and Marketing Associate Rosella Albanese

For

Time Out Guides Ltd
Universal House
251 Tottenham Court Road
London W1T 7AB
Tel: +44 (0)20 7813 3000
Fax: +44 (0)20 7813 6001
E-mail: guides@timeout.com
www.timeout.com

Editorial Director Peter Fiennes **Series Editor** Ruth Jarvis **Group Art Director** John Oakey **Art Director** Mandy Martin

Group Advertising Director Lesley Gill **Sales Director** Mark Phillips

Publisher Tony Elliott **Managing Director** Mike Hardwick **Group Financial Director** Kevin Ellis
Group Commercial Director Lesley Gill **Marketing Director** Christine Cort **Marketing Manager** Mandy Martinez
Group General Manager Nichola Coulthard **Production Manager** Mark Lamond

Chapters in this guide were written or updated by:

History Tom Gogola **Architecture** Howard Halle **Green Apple** Lesa Griffith **Night Train to Brooklyn** Jeffrey Whitney **Museums** Billie Cohen (non-art museums), Tim Griffin (art museums); *Culture clubbing* Mimi Kriegsman **Downtown** Lesa Griffith; *Isle of might* Tom Gogola **Midtown** Aimee Szparaga **Uptown** Tom Gogola **The Outer Boroughs** Ann Lien (Queens, the Bronx), Jeffrey Whitney (Brooklyn, Staten Island); *All that jazz* Ann Lien **Tour New York** Aimee Szparaga **Accommodations** Lesa Griffith, Aimee Szparaga **Bars and Restaurants** adapted from *Time Out New York Eating & Drinking 2002 Guide*; *Bottoms up!* Tom Gogola, *The next best things* Salma Abdelnour, Katie Hottinger, Brett Martin **Shopping & Services** Angela De Vincenzo, Aimee Szparaga; *Street of dreams* Angela De Vincenzo **By Season** Billie Cohen **Art Galleries** Tim Griffin **Books & Poetry** Tom Gogola **Cabaret & Comedy** Joe Grossman (comedy), H. Scott Jolley (cabaret) **Clubs** Bruce Tantum **Film & TV** Stephen Garrett **Gay & Lesbian** Les Simpson **Kids' Stuff** Barbara Aria **Music** Jay Ruttenberg, Mike Wolf, Elisabeth Vincentelli (pop, rock, electronic music), K. Leander Williams (jazz, world music), Margeaux Watson (hip-hop, R&B), Steve Smith (classical); *A noise grows in Brooklyn* Elisabeth Vincentelli **Sports & Fitness** Brett Martin **Theater & Dance** Gia Kourlas (dance), David Cote (theater); *Raising the bar* Gia Kourlas, *You laughing at me?* David Cote **Trips Out of Town** Tom Gogola; *A toast to Hudson Valley wines* Carole Braden **Directory** Jeffrey Whitney

Cover and inside photographs by Anna Kirtiklis

Additional photographs courtesy of Patrik Rytikangas, 4, 18, 171, 412; Library of Congress, Geography and Map Division, 6; Library of Congress, Prints and Photographs Division, Detroit Publishing Company 11; Brooklyn Public Library's Brooklyn Collection, a national resource that documents the history of Brooklyn from pre-colonial times to the present, containing books, photographs, prints, clippings, movie posters, illustrations, manuscripts and over 500 historic and contemporary maps and atlases and other memorabilia, 7, 14, 16; Madison Bay, 12; Mayor's Photo Unit, 17; Maria Quiroga, 25, 33, 51, 59, 77, 89; Spencer T. Tucker, 27; New Museum of Contemporary Art, 34; Aimee Szparaga, 66; Fiona Smith, 85; Lesa Griffith, 99; David Joseph/Chambers Hotel, 117; The Mansfield, 121; The City Club Hotel, 129; Maryam Sayigh, 145; Sarah-Maria Vischer, 146; Philip Friedman, 155, 173, 181, 186; Graham Morrison, 162, 182; Nara Irigoyen, 175, 176; Deborah Kossman, 188; Michael Luongo, 235; Michal Daniel/The Public Theater/NYSF, 236; Sandra Roa/SCR Design; D. Sheridan/FringeNYC, 240; New York City Ballet, 243; Cathy Carver/Dia Center for the Arts, 253; Nancy Crampton/92nd Street Y, 260; Sesame Workshop, 273; NBC Photo: Mary Ellen Matthews, 277; John Horner/Desgrippes Gobé; Big Apple Circus, 291; John Sann/Knitting Factory, 301; Bob Colton/Black Star/Town Hall, 310; Bargemusic, 319; Jesse D. Garrabrant/WNBA Enterprises, 323; Brooklyn Cyclones, 327; Jivamukti Yoga Center, 332; Joan Marcus, 335; Carol Rosegg, 339; Lois Greenfield/Ballet Tech, 343; Stephanie Berger/BAM, 345; Mark Morris, 347; Tom Gogola, 351; Tom Ligamari, 353; CIA/On Location Studios, 354

Maps by J.S. Graphics, 17 Beadles Lane, Old Oxted, Surrey RH8 9JG, U.K.; maps on pages 408–411 reproduced by kind permission of the Metropolitan Transportation Authority.

Introduction

In a letter dated 1756, a 24-year-old George Washington, then commander of the colonial troops of Virginia, included the term "New Yorker." It's the earliest recorded use of the words. A few decades later, the city became the capital of the country, and Washington was sworn in as the first president of the United States on Wall Street. The city's proud residents recognized him as an honorary New Yorker.

New York has changed a lot since then, but when terrorists steered two jets into the World Trade Center towers on September 11, 2001, the global consensus was that the city, and the world, had changed forever. Yet, people from everywhere responded to the disaster, becoming honorary New Yorkers, and helped this city quickly get back on track. The slogan "I ♥ New York" wasn't just for tourists anymore.

What? Has New York turned warm and fuzzy? This is the city that has made a living out of playing the bad guy—hey, if you never sleep, you can get grumpy. But when even the French, no sentimental softies themselves, proclaim solidarity, as *Le Monde* did with its headline "We Are All Americans" in September, we can't help but want to give some hugs.

While the heart of New York City remains as swollen with pride and good will as it was in Washington's day, this metropolis of 8 million people is constantly transforming in other ways. Look at the pictures in the History section and you can see the physical change: an early Dutch map depicts an almost empty expanse of green; horse-drawn carriages pass in front of a half-built Flatiron Building; passengers sit in a newfangled invention, a bus. Other changes are cultural, as the demographic quilt gets more colorful and diverse with each generation. Brooklyn, once a competing city, then a long-time outer borough backwater, has become a major player again (*see chapter* **Night Train to Brooklyn**).

And just when you think you've got New York sussed out, you find something completely unexpected—like a coyote in Central Park! (*See chapter* **Green Apple**.)

Change. Some think it's good; it makes others nervous. One thing is true: It's inevitable. And while some changes have caused enormous upheavals, New York perseveres. Nothing stays the same, and *that* is New York's constant. September 11 has re-energized, not defeated, the city. New Yorkers may not agree about what will eventually be built at Ground Zero, but they all have an opinion. The shifts in economy and creativity and people have made for a prepped canvas on which to paint the city's future. Now is the time to witness NYC's latest changes.

ABOUT THE TIME OUT CITY GUIDES

The *Time Out New York Guide* is one of an expanding series of Time Out City Guides— now numbering 35—produced by the people behind London and New York's successful weekly listings magazines. All the guides are written and updated by resident experts who strive to provide the most up-to-date information you'll need to explore the city, whether you're a local or first-time visitor.

The staff of *Time Out New York* magazine worked on this tenth edition of the *Time Out New York Guide*. *TONY* has been "the obsessive guide to impulsive entertainment" for all inhabitants of the city (and a few passers-through) for six years. Some chapters have been rewritten from scratch; all have been thoroughly revised; and new feature boxes have been added.

THE LOWDOWN ON THE LISTINGS

While navigating this guide and the city, there are a few facts you should know. All our listings include addresses, telephone numbers, travel directions, opening times, admission prices and credit-card information. We've given up-to-date details on facilities, services and events, all checked and correct at press time. However, owners and managers can—and often do— change their policies. It's always best to call and check the when, where and how much.

> ▶ There is an online version of this guide, including many suggested itineraries, at **www.timeout.com/newyork**.
> ▶ The website for *Time Out New York*, the weekly listings magazine, is at **www.timeoutny.com**.

A lark in the park Central Park's Bethesda Fountain is a destination spot for New Yorkers.

Throughout the book, you'll find bold-faced items (sights or restaurants, for example) for which we give the detailed listings information within that chapter or in one that is cross-referenced. For your convenience, we've included cross-reference boxes throughout (they're outlined in red, like the one on the previous page).

PRICES AND PAYMENT
We have noted whether places such as shops, hotels and restaurants accept credit cards or not, but have only listed the major cards: American Express (**AmEx**), Diners Club (**DC**), Discover (**Disc**), MasterCard (**MC**) and Visa (**V**). Some businesses will also accept other cards. Virtually all shops, restaurants and attractions will accept U.S.-dollar travelers' checks issued by a major financial institution (such as American Express).

The prices we've listed should be treated as guidelines, not gospel. Fluctuating exchange rates and inflation can cause prices—especially in stores and restaurants—to change overnight. While every effort has been made to ensure the accuracy of this guide, the publishers cannot accept responsibility for any errors it may contain. If you find things altered beyond recognition, ask why—and then write to let us know. Our goal is to furnish the most accurate information available, so we always want to know if you've been badly treated or overcharged.

TELEPHONE NUMBERS
All telephone numbers in this guide are written as dialed within the United States. Manhattan's

area codes are 212 and 646; Brooklyn, Queens, the Bronx and Staten Island's are 718 and 347; generally (but not always), 917 is reserved for cellular phones and pagers. If you're calling a number from within the same area code, then dial the seven-digit phone number only. If the area codes differ, you must dial 1, then the area code and the seven-digit phone number (from abroad, dial 00 first as well). Phone numbers beginning with 800, 877 and 888 are free of charge when called from anywhere in the U.S. When numbers are listed as letters for easy recall (e.g. 800-AIR-RIDE), dial the corresponding numbers on the telephone keypad.

ESSENTIAL INFORMATION
For all the practical information you might need for visiting the city—including visa and customs procedures, access for people with disabilities, emergency telephone numbers, a list of helpful websites and how to use the subway system—turn to the **Directory** chapter at the back of this guide. It starts on page 357.

THE LAY OF THE LAND
We've included cross streets in all of our addresses, so you can find your way more easily. And there's a series of fully-indexed **color street maps**, a map of the surrounding metropolitan area and subway and bus maps at the back of the guide, starting on page 391. The very last page is **Key Sights**—a quick list of those places you've heard about; the directions are given so you can quickly get started on your sightseeing.

LET US KNOW WHAT YOU THINK
We hope you enjoy the *Time Out New York Guide,* and we'd like to know what you think of it. We welcome tips on places that you believe we should include in future editions and appreciate your criticism of our choices. There's a reader's reply card at the back of this book. Or please e-mail us at guides@timeoutny.com.

A note about our advertisers

Perspective

History   6
Architecture   18
Green Apple   25
Night Train to Brooklyn   28

Feature box

The march of time   8

Height of achievement The Empire
State Building, 103 floors tall, is once
again the city's loftiest.

History

Here's how New York became the center of the world

THE PROSPECTORS

Before Manhattan ever lured visitors with its skyscrapers and street-corner spectacles— in fact, long before it was even called Manhattan—this lush, forested region offered the finest natural harbor on the East Coast. The island was protected from the elements and strategically located along a vast river—in short, it was the greatest trading post Mother Nature ever created. New York became a natural destination for immigrants seeking their fortunes, and at every stage in its history, the buzzword has been *commerce*.

The first European to get a glimpse of the island was Giovanni da Verrazano, a Florentine sailing under the French flag and searching for the fabled Northwest Passage to China. In 1524, he sought refuge from a storm in what is now called New York Harbor; later, he navigated a small boat into the Upper Bay, where he was greeted by the local Native Americans. Today, Verrazano is remembered by the majestic bridge that links Staten Island with Brooklyn and bears his name.

It would be 85 years before the next European arrived. Henry Hudson, who was employed by the Dutch East India Company, was also looking for the Northwest Passage. He instead found…Albany.

LET'S MAKE A DEAL

In 1613, four years after Hudson's journey, a trading post—the beginning of a Dutch settlement—was established at Albany (then called Fort Orange). In 1621, Holland granted the Dutch West India Company a long-term trade and governing monopoly over New Netherlands (and elsewhere). Soon the first Dutch settlers, about 30 families, arrived in the area. By 1626, when the first director-general (governor), Peter Minuit, took power, about 300 Europeans lived on the southern tip of Manhattan.

In an exchange now regarded as the greatest real-estate swindle in history, Minuit gave a Munsee Indian chief a few trinkets and blankets (which scholars have revalued from the famous $24 to a still bargain-basement $600) and got him to sign an incomprehensible

So where's Soho? This Dutch map of the New York City region dates to 1693.

document. Minuit then assumed the deal was sealed; the Dutch had bought themselves all 13 miles of Manhattan Island. Of course, like all the best real-estate deals, this one was a scam: The Native Americans had very different ideas about property and could not conceive of owning land, let alone in perpetuity.

It also turned out to be a shakedown. Once the Europeans had moved in, they wouldn't move out. The Dutch settlement tried to tax native hunters and keep them from owning firearms, and enforced harsh penalties for petty crimes. It was only a matter of time before a bloody war broke out between the Dutch and the Native Americans; it lasted two and a half years in the 1640s. Guess who won?

Little trace of New York's original inhabitants remains, apart from various Munsee place-names, such as Canarsie ("grassy place"), Rockaway ("sandy place"), Maspeth ("bad water place") and Matinecock ("at the lookout point").

PEG-LEG PETE

After colonists massacred more than 100 Indians in 1643, the Dutch West India Company hired Peter Stuyvesant to keep the peace. Stuyvesant's right leg had been shattered by a cannonball—hence his nickname, Peg-Leg Pete. He ordered a defensive ditch and wall (today's Wall Street) to be built along the northern end of what was by then called New Amsterdam. A commercial infrastructure was built (banks, brokers' offices, wharves), and chandleries and taverns soon lined the waterfront. The city's capitalist culture was born.

And so was its first locally administered government. Stuyvesant founded a municipal assembly, and encouraged the education of the colony's children. In his 17 years as governor, the settlement doubled in size. The town grew more cosmopolitan, expanding to include English, French, Portuguese and Scandinavian settlers, and the area's first African slaves. Both English and Dutch were spoken.

But Peg-Leg was a little too authoritarian. His intolerance of Jewish refugees and Quaker leader John Bowne provoked scoldings from his bosses, who forced Stuyvesant to make the settlement a haven for religious freedom.

THE BRITISH ARE COMING!

Perhaps the Dutch West India Company tried to expand its colony too quickly. By 1661, less than four decades after the Dutch had settled the place, New Amsterdam was nearly bankrupt. When four British warships sailed into the harbor one day in August 1664, the population abandoned the fortifications Stuyvesant had built and welcomed Captain Richard Nicolls and his crew. New Amsterdam was renamed after the British king's brother, the Duke of York.

By 1700, New York's population had reached about 20,000. The colony was a big money-maker for the British, but it was hardly what you would call a stable concern. In 1683, to cut administrative costs, the British tried to consolidate New York, New Jersey and New England into a single dominion. The colonies rebelled, and after nearly two years of battle, ten men were hanged for treason. In the 1730s, John Peter Zenger's *New-York Weekly Journal* provoked gasps by accusing British governor William Cosby's administration of corruption. Zenger's trial on libel charges resulted in a landmark decision: The newspaper publisher was acquitted because, as his lawyer argued, the truth cannot be libelous. The Zenger verdict sowed the seeds for the First Amendment to the Constitution, which established the principle of freedom of the press. This was just the beginning of trouble for the British.

High times At 20 stories, the 1902 Flatiron Building was the architectural marvel of its day.

REVOLUTION—AND THE BATTLE FOR NEW YORK

In British-run outposts in Boston, Philadelphia and Virginia, great thinkers such as John Adams, Benjamin Franklin and Thomas Jefferson spread the ideals of democratic government, while merchants in those settlements chafed under ever-rising British taxes. New York, especially, felt the pinch as the British struggled to pay off debts accumulated in colonial wars against France. The colonies declared independence on July 4, 1776, but the British weren't about to give up New York—because of its economic importance and its strategic position on the Hudson River. That summer, British commander Lord Howe led 200 ships into New York Harbor and occupied the town. New Yorkers vented their fury by toppling a gilded equestrian statue of George III that stood on Bowling Green.

The war's first major battle took place in Brooklyn and on Long Island. It was a complete disaster for the Americans, led by George Washington, who retreated to New Jersey. (While preparing his army, Washington slept at what is now called the Morris-Jumel Mansion in Washington Heights; *see page 88.*) On September 11, 1776, Benjamin Franklin met Lord Howe in Staten Island's Billop Manor House, now known as the Conference House *(see page 106),* but he refused Howe's offer to make all colonists full-fledged British subjects. "America cannot return to the domination of Great Britain," Franklin said firmly.

Life in occupied New York was grim. The town teemed with British soldiers and with loyalists fleeing the American army. Fires destroyed much of the city, and many people starved to death. When the Crown surrendered in 1783, bitter British troops in New York greased the city's flagpole, hoping to make it

The march of time

A recap of key events in New York history

1524 Giovanni da Verrazano is the first European to visit Manhattan.
1609 Henry Hudson sails into New York Harbor.
1624 The Dutch settle New Amsterdam.
1626 First governor Peter Minuit arrives and "buys" Manhattan from the Indians. New Amsterdam's population: 300.
1643 Peter Stuyvesant is made governor.
1661 The Dutch colony nearly goes bankrupt.
1662 Quaker John Bowne's struggle wins the right to religious freedom for the people of New Amsterdam.
1664 The British invade; New Amsterdam is renamed New York.
1733 John Peter Zenger's *New-York Weekly Journal* establishes the right to free speech.
1754 King's College (which will become Columbia University) is founded.
1776 The Declaration of Independence is adopted. The Revolutionary War rages; the British occupy New York.
1783 The defeated British army leaves New York.
1785–90 New York serves as the new nation's capital.
1811 The Commissioners' Plan lays out the grid system for the city's future growth.

1812–14 America fights another war with Britain. New York is isolated from international trade.
1837 Financial panic ruins all but three city banks.
1843 Immigrants flood into the city.
1851 *The New York Times* is first published.
1857 Frederick Law Olmsted and Calvert Vaux lay out plans for Central Park.
1859 Cooper Union, the first American school open to all—regardless of race, religion or gender—is established.
1860 Abraham Lincoln is elected president.
1861 The Civil War erupts.
1863 Conscription causes riots in New York.
1865 The Union wins, and slavery is abolished.
1870 The Metropolitan Museum of Art is founded.
1872 Organized labor strikes for an eight-hour workday.
1883 The Brooklyn Bridge is completed.
1886 The Statue of Liberty is unveiled.
1890 Photojournalist Jacob Riis publishes *How the Other Half Lives,* spurring new housing regulations.
1895 The New York Public Library is founded.
1898 New York City—comprising Manhattan, Brooklyn, Queens, Staten Island and the

harder for the Revolutionaries to raise the banner of the new republic.

But the war was won. On December 4, Washington joined his officers for an emotional farewell dinner at Fraunces Tavern on Pearl Street (now the Fraunces Tavern Museum; *see page 40*), where the general declared his retirement. In 1785, New York became the nation's capital, so when Congress looked to Washington to lead the country, he returned to the city. On April 30, 1789, in the Old Federal Hall (on the same site as the present one, on Wall Street), he took the oath of office as the first president of the United States of America.

THE FIRST U.S. CAPITAL

Before the Revolution, Alexander Hamilton, a young immigrant from the Caribbean island of Nevis, studied at King's College (now Columbia University) and hobnobbed with colonial high society; he married into a powerful merchant family after serving under Washington during the war. Hamilton, who helped create the Bank of New York in 1784, was appointed the first U.S. Treasury secretary in 1789. During his term, Hamilton initiated pro-business measures that nurtured New York's blossoming as a financial center. In 1791, he established the nation's central banking system—much to the horror of Thomas Jefferson, who envisioned a simple, agrarian economy.

Meanwhile, the capital moved to Philadelphia in 1791, then, in 1800, to a new city built on mosquito-infested swampland—Washington, D.C. By that time, with business booming, and the port prospering, New York's financial clout was secured, and it has remained the country's capital of capitalism.

CROWD CONTROL

By 1800, more than 60,000 people lived in what is now lower Manhattan. Rents were high, housing demands were great, and development had been scattershot. The local government

---

Bronx—is incorporated, creating the world's second-largest city.

1902 The world's first skyscraper—the Fuller Building (now called the Flatiron)—is built.

1907 Metered taxicabs are introduced.

1911 The Triangle Shirtwaist factory fire sparks the introduction of workplace-safety regulations.

1917 America enters World War I.

1919 The Volstead Act begins Prohibition; speakeasies open throughout the city.

1920 Women win the right to vote.

1929 The Wall Street stock-market crash on October 29 plunges the nation into the Great Depression. The Museum of Modern Art opens nine days after the crash.

1930s Franklin D. Roosevelt's New Deal funds massive public-works projects. The Empire State Building, the Chrysler Building and Rockefeller Center are built.

1932 Prohibition ends.

1939 Corona Park, Queens, hosts the World's Fair.

1941 America enters World War II.

1946 The United Nations is established in New York.

1947 Brooklyn Dodger Jackie Robinson breaks the color barrier in major-league baseball.

1959 The Guggenheim Museum opens.

1962 Lincoln Center opens.

1965 The entire city endures a 25-hour power blackout.

1968 A student sit-in shuts down Columbia University.

1973 The World Trade Center is completed.

1975 A fiscal crisis puts the city on the verge of bankruptcy.

1977 Another citywide blackout. More than 3,000 people are arrested for looting, rioting and arson.

1978 Mayor Edward Koch presides over an economic turnaround.

1987 Another Wall Street crash.

1990 David Dinkins is inaugurated as the city's first black mayor.

1991 The city's budget deficit hits a record high.

1993 Terrorists bomb the World Trade Center. Rudolph Giuliani is elected as the city's first Republican mayor in 28 years.

1996 TWA Flight 800 crashes off the coast of Long Island, killing all 230 aboard.

1997 The murder rate falls to a 30-year low. Disney arrives on 42nd Street.

1998 New York City falls to 37th on the list of the most dangerous cities in America.

1999 The Dow hits 10,000. The city mourns the death of John F. Kennedy Jr.

2000 Hillary Rodham Clinton is elected as the city's junior senator to Washington.

2001 On September 11, two hijacked jets fly into the Twin Towers, killing thousands and demolishing the World Trade Center. F-16s run combat air patrols over Manhattan. Anthrax-spiked letters are mailed to major media outlets. Giuliani is heralded as a hero for his leadership during the crisis. Voters choose Mike Bloomberg as the city's 108th mayor. New York city's population: 8 million.

decided that the city needed a more orderly way to sell and develop land. A group of city officials, called the Commissioners, came up with a solution: the famous "grid" street system of 1811. It ignored all the existing roads—with the exception of Broadway, which ran the length of Manhattan, following an old Indian trail—and organized New York into a rectangular grid with wide, numbered avenues running north to south and streets running river to river.

When the 362-mile Erie Canal opened in 1825—linking New York to the Midwest via the Hudson River and the Great Lakes—the port city became even more vital to the young country. Along with the new railroads, this trade route facilitated the making of many fortunes, and New York's merchants and traders flourished.

THE ABOLITIONISTS

Today, the African-American Burial Ground near City Hall in lower Manhattan preserves the chilling memory of a time when New York was second only to Charleston, South Carolina, as a slave-trade port. As late as the 1700s, such prominent local families as the Beekmans and Van Cortlandts increased their fortunes by trafficking in human beings.

But as Northern commercial cities became less reliant on manual labor, dependence on slavery waned—and the abolitionist movement bloomed. When New York State abolished slavery in 1827, the city celebrated with two days of fireworks and parades. While the South remained defiant, the antislavery movement flourished in the Northeast.

In New York, the cause was kept alive in the columns of Horace Greeley's *Tribune* newspaper and in the sermons of Henry Ward Beecher, pastor of the Plymouth Church of the Pilgrims on Orange Street in Brooklyn. (He was the brother of Harriet Beecher Stowe, who wrote *Uncle Tom's Cabin*.) Beecher once shocked his congregation by auctioning a slave from his pulpit and using the proceeds to buy back her freedom.

NEW YORK AND THE CIVIL WAR

Preservation of the Union was the hot issue of the 1860 presidential campaign. Abraham Lincoln wavered in his position on slavery—until one fateful trip to New York that year, when he addressed a meeting in the Great Hall of Cooper Union (the first American school open to all, regardless of race, religion or gender). In his speech, Lincoln declared, "Neither let us be slandered from our duty by false accusations against us, nor frightened from it by menaces of destruction to the government nor of dungeons to ourselves. Let

us have faith that right makes might, and in that faith let us, to the end, dare to do our duty as we understand it."

The newly formed Republican Party moved to make Lincoln its presidential candidate. The Southern states promptly seceded from the Union and became the Confederate States of America. The Civil War had begun.

WHITE RIOT

When Lincoln started a military draft in 1863, the streets of New York erupted in rioting. Although New York sided with the Union against the Confederacy, there was considerable sympathy for the South, particularly among poor Irish and German immigrants, who feared that they would lose jobs to freed slaves.

For three days, New York raged. African-Americans were assaulted in the streets; Horace Greeley's office was attacked twice; Brooks Brothers was looted. When the smoke cleared, 100 were dead and 1,000 injured. The violence came to an end only when Union troops returning from victory at Gettysburg subdued the city. The Draft Riots remain the single worst civilian uprising in American history—worse than Watts, beyond Crown Heights, beyond Rodney King.

Apart from the riots, New York emerged from the Civil War unscathed. The city had not seen any actual fighting—and it had prospered as the financial center of the North. As immigration soared, so did the wealth of New York's upper-class captains of industry.

HIGH FINANCE

Jay Gould made enormous profits in the stock market during the Civil War by having the outcome of military engagements secretly cabled to him and trading on the results before they became public knowledge. Gould, together with another master swindler, Jim Fisk, seduced shipping magnate Cornelius Vanderbilt into buying vast quantities of Erie Railroad bonds before the bottom dropped out of the market. (Vanderbilt had the resources to sit out the crisis and the grace to call Gould "the smartest man in America.") Vanderbilt, Andrew Carnegie and banker J.P. Morgan consolidated their fortunes by controlling the railroads. John D. Rockefeller made his money in oil; by 1879, he owned 95 percent of the refineries in the United States.

All of these men—each in his own way representing a blend of capitalist genius and robber baron—erected glorious mansions in New York. Their homes now house some of the city's finest art collections, and their legacies are as apparent on Wall Street as they are along Fifth Avenue. Swindles, panics and

The bus stops here Sightseeing dames and dandies tour the town in style in the early 1900s.

frequent market collapses were cyclical events in the late 19th century, but New York's millionaires weathered the financial disasters, built major cultural institutions, and virtually created high society.

The 1800s saw the birth of the Metropolitan Museum of Art, the Astor Library (now the Public Theater), the American Museum of Natural History, the New-York Historical Society and the Metropolitan Opera. Carnegie gave Carnegie Hall to New York, even though the devoted Pittsburgher never really mingled much among New York's rich (his Fifth Avenue mansion is now the Cooper-Hewitt, National Design Museum). Six years after the New York Public Library was created in 1895, Carnegie donated $5.2 million to establish branch libraries. The nucleus of the library consists of the combined collections of John Jacob Astor, Samuel Jones Tilden and James Lenox (*see chapters* **Museums** *and* **Music**).

MAJOR CAPITAL IMPROVEMENTS

The wealthy also started moving uptown. By 1850, the mansions along Fifth Avenue had indoor plumbing, central heating and a reliable water supply—secured by the 1842 construction of the Croton Reservoir system. In 1857, Frederick Law Olmsted and Calvert Vaux

welcomed crowds to Central Park *(see page 77)*, the nation's first landscaped public green space. A daring combination of formal gardens and rolling hills, the park remains the city's great civilizing force, offsetting the oppressive grid and offering an oasis of sanity in the heart of Manhattan.

Nineteenth-century New York also witnessed many industrial marvels. In 1807, Robert Fulton started the world's first steamboat service on Cortlandt Street. Samuel Morse founded his telegraph company in the 1840s. By the 1860s, Isaac Merritt Singer was producing 13,000 sewing machines a year. In the late 1800s, Thomas Edison formed the world's first electric company in New York; it still carries his name, Consolidated Edison. In 1882, 800 new electric street lamps turned New York into the city that never sleeps (it does, however, take the occasional nap).

Another extraordinary achievement of the era was the construction of the Brooklyn Bridge (1869–83), the longest suspension bridge in the world at the time and the first to use steel cable *(see page 94)*. Designed by John A. Roebling (who died in an on-site accident before construction began) and completed by his son, Washington, the bridge opened up the

Off the rails The destruction of the original Pennsylvania Station still rankles preservationists.

independent city of Brooklyn—and paved the way for its merger with New York.

POLITICAL MACHINATIONS

The 1898 consolidation of all five boroughs into the City of New York assured New York's transition to a crucial world-class force: It became the planet's second-largest city (London was biggest). But the merger happened after several false starts. Local bosses wouldn't give up their power, and most of the metropolis had become mired in corruption. William M. "Boss" Tweed, the young leader of a Democratic Party faction called Tammany Hall (named after a famous Indian chief), had turned city government into a lucrative operation: As commissioner of public works, he collected large payoffs from companies receiving city contracts. Tweed and his ring are estimated to have misappropriated somewhere between $30 and $200 million from various building projects, including the Tweed Courthouse *(52 Chambers St)*. They distributed enough of that money in political bribes to keep a lot of influential mouths shut.

The likes of Tweed ultimately ran up against Theodore Roosevelt, a different kind of New York big shot. The future president drew his power not so much from his wealth and class as from the sheer force of his personality (and from his ability to work the media). As a state assemblyman in the 1880s, Roosevelt turned the town on its ear, accusing capitalist Jay Gould of bribing a judge. Although Gould was exonerated, Roosevelt earned his reputation as a fighter of corruption. And as president of the city's police board in the 1890s, he made friends with news reporters and led a temperance movement—two things that could never be pulled off simultaneously today. (See page 68 for information on the Theodore Roosevelt Birthplace museum.)

COMING TO AMERICA

"Give me your tired, your poor, your huddled masses yearning to breathe free," entreats Emma Lazarus's "The New Colossus," inscribed at the base of Frédéric-Auguste Bartholdi's Statue of Liberty—one of the first sights seen by newcomers to the U.S. as they approached by sea.

The first great waves of immigrants started arriving in America well before the Civil War; the twin ports of welcome were Boston and New York. The Irish population surged after the 1843 potato famine, and German liberals arrived after their failed 1848 revolution. The 1880s saw an influx of Southern Italians and large numbers of immigrants from the old Russian empire—Lithuanians, Poles, Romanians and Ukrainians, many of them Jews. Chinese laborers, who had been brought to America to do backbreaking work on the railroads in California, moved east to New York in droves to escape a violent anti-Chinese movement on the West Coast.

From 1855 to 1890, the immigration center at Castle Clinton in Battery Park processed 8 million people. The Ellis Island center, built in 1892, served the same purpose for roughly the same length of time and handled twice that number. With the introduction of a quota system in 1921, the intake slowed; Ellis Island was closed in 1932 (for information on the Ellis Island Immigration Museum and the Statue of Liberty, see chapters **Downtown** and **Museums**).

HOW THE OTHER HALF LIVES

New immigrants usually ended up in the grim, crowded tenements of the Lower East Side. By 1879, the first of a series of housing laws was passed to improve conditions for the poor, and in 1886, New York established its first settlement house for the underprivileged, at 146 Forsyth Street. In 1890, writer and photographer Jacob Riis published *How the Other Half Lives,* an exposé of sweatshops and squalor in the ghetto; the uptown populace was horrified. The settlement-house movement and a temperance drive would preoccupy New York's philanthropic circles throughout the Great Depression (1929–1939).

The frenetic growth of the city's industries created appalling health-and-safety conditions. Child labor was common. "Nearly any hour on the East Side of New York City, you can see them—pallid boy or spindling girl—their faces dulled, their backs bent under a heavy load of garments piled on head and shoulders, the muscles of the whole frame in a long strain," wrote poet Edwin Markham in 1907. In 1872, about 100,000 workers went on strike for three months until they won the right to an eight-hour workday.

However, it took the horror of the 1911 fire at the Triangle Shirtwaist factory *(23–29 Washington Pl)* in Greenwich Village to stir politicians to action. The fire killed 146 women, because the proprietors had locked the doors to the fire escapes. The state legislature passed more than 50 health-and-safety measures within months of the fire.

THE SUBWAY

If, while staring at a subway map, you wonder why there is no easy connection between such natural depots as Grand Central Terminal and Penn Station, it is because the two were at one time run by different private rail companies. The original names of the subways—the IRT (Interborough Rapid Transit), BMT (Brooklyn-Manhattan Transit Corporation) and IND (Independent Subway System)—are preserved in old subway signage. Many lifelong New Yorkers still use these names to refer to various routes.

The 656-mile subway system, an astounding network of civic arteries that today serves at least 4 million passengers a day, became the 20th century's largest single factor in the growth of the city. The first of the three companies started excavation in 1900, but by the 1940s, the system was consolidated and hasn't changed much since (despite recent reroutings of many lines).

The subway also holds a unique place in the city's imagination: It offers the perfect metaphor for New Yorkers' fast, crowded lives lived among strangers. Most famously, the Duke Ellington Orchestra's signature song, written by Billy Strayhorn, implored its listeners to "Take the A Train," noting, "That's the quickest way to get to Harlem." Subway culture permeates New York life. Tin Pan Alley's songwriters composed such popular ditties as "Rapid Transit Gallop" and "The Subway Glide," and new words and phrases, such as *rush hour,* entered the lexicon.

NEW YORK STORIES

Since the 19th century, New York has consistently sprouted its own artistic and literary movements. Following the seminal figures of New York letters—people such as satirist Washington Irving and Gothic storyteller Edgar Allan Poe, a transplanted Southerner—were Brooklyn poet Walt Whitman and novelists Edith Wharton and Mark Twain. Wharton became an astute critic of old New York society; her most memorable novels, *The Age of Innocence* among them, are detailed renderings of New York life at the turn of the century. Samuel Clemens, a.k.a. Mark Twain, moved in and out of New York (mostly Greenwich Village) during his most prolific

Radio days Chanteuse Lena Horne serenades listeners during the Great Depression.

period, when he published *The Adventures of Tom Sawyer, Life on the Mississippi* and *Huckleberry Finn.*

By the early 1900s, a strain of social consciousness had cropped up in New York literature. Lincoln Steffens (the political muckraker), Stephen Crane ("Maggie: A Girl of the Streets"), Theodore Dreiser *(Sister Carrie)* and O. Henry all pricked the city's conscience with style and fervor.

THE JAZZ AGE

Once World War I had thrust America onto center stage as a world power, New York benefited from wartime commerce. The Roaring '20s brought "looser morals" (women voting and dancing the Charleston!), just as Prohibition provoked a bootleg-liquor culture. Speakeasies fueled the general jazz-age wildness and made many a gangster's fortune. Even Mayor Jimmy Walker went nightclubbing at a casino located in Central Park.

At Harlem's Cotton Club *(see page 86),* Josephine Baker, Duke Ellington and Lena Horne played for white audiences enjoying what poet Langston Hughes called "that Negro vogue." On Broadway, the Barrymore family—Ethel, John and Lionel (Drew's forebears)—were treading the boards between movies. Over at the New Amsterdam Theater on West 42nd Street, the high-kicking Ziegfeld Follies dancers were opening for such entertainers as W.C. Fields, Fanny Brice and Marion Davies.

New York also saw the birth of the film industry: D.W. Griffith's early films were shot in Manhattan, and the Marx Brothers made movies in Astoria. In 1926, hundreds of thousands of New Yorkers flooded the streets to mourn the death of matinee idol Rudolph Valentino.

RADIO DAYS

After the 1929 stock-market crash, when Americans stopped going out and turned instead to their radios for entertainment, New York became the airwaves' talent pool. Unemployed vaudeville players, such as George Burns and Gracie Allen, became stars, as did Jack Benny and Fred Allen. The careers of artists as disparate as Bing Crosby and Arturo Toscanini were launched on New York radio. Italian immigrant Enrico Caruso became one of the first worldwide recording stars here. The Art Deco masterpiece Radio City Music Hall became the industry's Great Depression–era show palace.

Since theatrical productions were tailored for the airwaves, some of the most acclaimed stage directors made their names in radio. In 1938, Orson Welles and John Houseman, who together had already shaken up Broadway with an all–African-American stage version of *Macbeth,* terrified America with their radio adaptation of H.G. Wells's *War of the Worlds.*

LA GUARDIA, FDR AND THE POWER BROKER

The first skyscrapers (including the Woolworth Building) were erected at the turn of the 20th century, and the 1920s saw a second boom in buildings: The Chrysler and Empire State Buildings and Rockefeller Center were all built by the 1930s. Art Deco design was the order of the day (*see chapter* **Architecture**).

In 1932, with the Depression in full swing, the city elected a stocky, short-tempered young congressman, Fiorello La Guardia, as mayor. Boosted by former New York governor Franklin D. Roosevelt's election as president, La Guardia imposed austerity programs that, surprisingly, won wide support. FDR's New Deal, meanwhile, reemployed the jobless on public-works programs and allocated federal funds to roads, housing and parks.

Enter Robert Moses, the city's master builder. As the head of a complex web of governmental authorities and commissions, Moses employed thousands of New Yorkers to build huge public parks (including Long Island's Jones Beach) and recreation centers; he also demolished entire neighborhoods to construct expressways and bridges (including the Verrazano-Narrows). No one since Dutch colonizer Peter Minuit has left a greater stamp on the city. Before his influence ebbed in the 1960s, Moses erected such indelible New York landmarks as Lincoln Center, Shea Stadium and the Flushing World's Fairgrounds.

BUILDING BETTER ARTISTS

The Federal Works Progress Administration (WPA) also made money available to New York's actors, writers, artists and musicians. As the Nazis terrorized the intelligentsia in Europe, the city became a favored refuge. Composer Arnold Schoenberg and architects Ludwig Mies van der Rohe and Walter Gropius (the former director of the influential Bauhaus school of design) were among those who moved to New York from Germany, along with many visual artists.

Arshile Gorky, Piet Mondrian, Hans Hofmann and Willem de Kooning were among the painters welcomed by the fledgling Museum of Modern Art, founded in 1929 by three collectors. By the '50s, MoMA had fully embraced a generation of painters known as the New York School. Critics such as Clement Greenberg hailed Abstract Expressionism as the next step in painting. Willem and Elaine de Kooning, Jackson Pollock, Lee Krasner, Robert Motherwell and Mark Rothko became the stars of a gallery scene that, for the first time, topped that of Paris.

When a young man named Andrew Warhola decided to leave Pittsburgh to become an artist, it was no surprise that he chose to come to New York. Dropping the last letter of his name, Warhol used commercial silk-screening techniques to fuse the city's advertising culture and art world (who can forget those Campbells' soup cans?). At his peak, he was the king of 1960s Pop Art.

MEDIA CENTRAL

Stepping back a bit to the Roaring Twenties literary scene: The monarchs here were Ernest Hemingway and his friend F. Scott Fitzgerald, whose *The Great Gatsby* portrayed a dark side of the 1920s. They worked with editor Maxwell Perkins of the publishing house Charles Scribner's Sons, as did Thomas Wolfe, who constructed enormous semiautobiographical mosaics of small-town life. Dorothy Parker, Robert Benchley, George S. Kaufman and Alexander Woollcott gathered regularly at the famous Round Table at the Algonquin hotel (*see page 124*). Royals of stage and screen, such as Tallulah Bankhead and various Marx Brothers, would show up to pay their respects. Much of the modern New York concept of sophistication and wit took shape in the alcoholic banter of this glamorous clan.

Political discourse was equally scathing. By World War II, the city's socialists were divided over the support some showed for Stalin. The often stormy arguments spawned a generation of intellectuals across the political spectrum, including Norman Podhoretz, Irving Howe, Lionel and Diana Trilling, and William F. Buckley Jr. At the same time, a counterculture emerged: Jack Kerouac and Allen Ginsberg attended Columbia in the 1940s, giving rise to the Beats of the '50s. Throughout the century, Greenwich Village was the lab for alternative culture, from the Bolshevism of the '20s to the '60s New York School of poets (John Ashbery and Kenneth Koch among them).

ENCORES AND HOME RUNS

In the theater, George and Ira Gershwin, Irving Berlin, Cole Porter, Richard Rodgers and Oscar Hammerstein II codified and modified the Broadway musical, adding plots and characters to the traditional follies format. Eugene O'Neill revolutionized American drama in the 1920s, only to have it revolutionized again by Tennessee Williams a generation later. By mid-century, the Group Theater had fully imported Stanislavski acting techniques to America, launching the careers of Actors Studio founder Lee Strasberg, director Elia Kazan and the young stage actor Marlon Brando.

Theater—especially on Broadway—became big business in New York. The Shubert brothers started a national 100-theater empire here in the 1910s. Mid-century, David Merrick pushed modern musicals *(Gypsy, 42nd Street)*. By the '60s, Joseph Papp's Public Theater was bringing Shakespeare to the masses with free performances in Central Park, a tradition that continues to this day.

The theater of the outer boroughs was baseball. The New York Yankees played against either the Brooklyn Dodgers or the New York Giants in 13 World Series ("subway series" to New Yorkers) between 1921 and 1956. The unbeatable Yankees—Babe Ruth, Lou Gehrig, Joe DiMaggio and later, Mickey Mantle—provided as many thrills as any Broadway show. Jackie Robinson integrated baseball in Brooklyn in 1947; when the Dodgers left town a decade later, the borough was devastated. The Giants left the same year.

THE INTERNATIONAL CITY

The affluence of the 1950s allowed many families to head for the suburbs: Towns sprang up around new highways, and roughly a million children and grandchildren of European immigrants—mostly Irish, Italian and Jewish—moved to them. Their places in the city were filled by a wave of newcomers—a million Puerto Ricans and African-Americans, most of the latter relocating from the South. Meanwhile, the United Nations, the international organization supporting global peace and security, established its headquarters overlooking the East River in Manhattan on land donated by John D. Rockefeller Jr. *(see page 73).*

By the mid-1970s, poverty, prejudice and a huge jump in street crime had cast a shadow of fear across the city. Times Square was a drug-infested sleaze scene whose denizens hustled porn and prostitution—an economy that was supported in large part by the invisible hand of organized crime. Many white New Yorkers in working- and middle-class neighborhoods grew disenchanted with the city and its inability to provide safe streets or effective schools and fled to the suburbs in large numbers. To make matters worse, by 1975, the city was all but bankrupt, and the federal government refused to bail it out. The grim situation was immortalized in an infamous *Daily News* headline of the time: FORD TO CITY—DROP DEAD. With a growing population on welfare and a declining tax base, the city resorted to heavy municipal borrowing.

Culturally, New York remained a mecca for music and nightlife, Times Square

Dancing days Brooklyn Dodgers fans were fiercely loyal—until dem bums left for California.

In bloom Billionaire businessman Michael Bloomberg became mayor of NYC in 2002.

notwithstanding. In the 1950s and '60s, the Brill Building gave Carole King, Neil Diamond and Burt Bacharach their starts, and Bob Dylan rose to fame in the Village. In the mid-'70s, CBGB, on the grungy Bowery, launched Blondie, the Ramones and Talking Heads, while midtown's Studio 54 blended disco, drugs and celebrity glamour into a potent, if short-lived, cocktail.

BOOM AND BUST

New York climbed out of its fiscal crisis under Mayor Edward Koch, a onetime liberal from Greenwich Village who wangled state and federal help to ride the 1980s boom in construction and finance. The 1980s and early '90s were the best and worst of times for New York: A new art scene and the booming Wall Street–takeover culture brought money back downtown, fueling the revitalization—some would say gentrification—of the East Village, Soho and Tribeca. But the AIDS and crack epidemics hit the city hard, as did racial politics. David Dinkins became New York's first African-American mayor in 1990. His tenure, however, was marred by racial tensions—incidents in Crown Heights, Brooklyn, and Washington Heights polarized the city and he was not reelected.

Dinkins was succeeded in 1994 by former federal prosecutor Rudolph Giuliani, a tough Italian-American. Crime rates plunged in the late '90s, thanks in part to the mayor's relentless crackdown on petty crime. Wildly unpopular among minorities, mainly over police and housing issues, Giuliani was nevertheless elected to a second term in 1998.

THE 21ST CENTURY

As businesses all over the world surfed the dot-com wave, New York City tourism blossomed again during the Giuliani era, and visitors spent vast sums here. One of Giuliani's major accomplishments was revitalizing Times Square: Disney has replaced the drug culture, and the sex industry has been supplanted by a cornucopia of theme restaurants and attractions—even a Madame Tussaud's wax museum—right on "the Deuce."

A city-budget surplus of more than $2 billion for the year 2000 led to tax cuts—including the elimination of sales tax on clothing items costing less than $110 (another major draw for out-of-towners). But by the end of 2001, due to the recession and the September 11 attack on the World Trade Center, the budget surplus had become a projected $750-million deficit.

As in 1800, real-estate prices have risen beyond affordability for many New Yorkers, although rents have eased somewhat. Formerly dangerous neighborhoods, such as Harlem and Alphabet City, are now sought-after areas where one-bedroom rentals can go for $2,000 a month. The gentrification has led to a displaced class of working homeless, whose earning power can't keep up with real-estate values.

And of course, the events of September 11 put the city at risk of a longer downturn. But the terrorist attacks also unified the city in a way no one alive has ever seen before, as citizens volunteered, donated money and generally put their in-your-face attitude on hold while the city regrouped and rebuilt.

Rudy Giuliani became a hero to the world for his calm leadership throughout the crisis, but was unable to run for mayor in 2001 because of term-limits laws. New mayor Mike Bloomberg, a billionaire businessman, quickly reached out to the minority communities and labor groups Giuliani had spurned during his two terms, showing his own liberal core (a former Democrat, he ran on the Republican ticket with Giuliani's endorsement).

Despite the months of chaos and uncertainty over the "war on terror," New York remains Ground Zero for good reasons as well as sad. Its trailblazing residents are forging ahead into the 21st century with groundbreaking art, literature, music, film and fashion; its stock market may waver a little, but it seems poised for a comeback. New Yorkers demonstrated to the world in the balmy autumn of 2001 that they are a tough, compassionate and not easily intimidated lot. And while their city may not be the capital of the U.S., they like to think it is still the capital of the world.

Architecture

What goes up…keeps on evolving

It's a grim irony, but one of the biggest architectural attractions in New York right now is something that isn't even around anymore. The World Trade Center—whose 110-story Twin Towers were destroyed by terrorists at the tragic cost of 3,000 lives—continues to draw visitors, if only to its footprint, which has been undergoing an agonizing transformation from burial mound to construction site. The towers themselves seem to linger on—both literally, in old postcards or on business signs that used them as logos, and figuratively, in the mind's eye, as a sort of architectural equivalent of the "phantom limb" syndrome experienced by amputees.

Perhaps this is because the collapse of the Twin Towers did more than open a gap in the city's skyline; it ruptured New York's collective memory. The event was so powerful that it defied comprehension—in a few minutes the past and present were destroyed and the future was put into question. The ghosts of the past and the questions of the future will continue to throw shadows over the area that is now known as Ground Zero regardless of what eventually arises on the razed 16 acres (for more on plans

Towers of power The World Trade Center is more evocative than ever, now that it's gone.

for the area, see page 49). As awful as the events of September 11, 2001 were, they were also reminders of some basic truths about the lives of buildings in New York.

The most important of these is that New York architecture has always been vulnerable to the vicissitudes of a metropolis that, for better and worse, exists in a constant churn of reinvention. This city has seen successions of not only immigrant waves, but economic boom and bust cycles, each leaving their distinctive mark on the urban topography.

The original Dutch colony, with its gabled farmhouses and low-ceilinged taverns, gave way to the Georgian elegance of the British trading city that supplanted it. In turn, the American Revolution brought with it the confident Yankee Neoclassicism of the Federal period, when New York was briefly the capital of the nascent republic. Later, a more restrained Greek Revival style characterized the booming "Empire City" of the early 19th century, as the Erie Canal extended New York's power as a trading center deep into the nation's heartland. The Civil War would transform the city yet again, turning it into the Union's armory, and bringing with it dazzling cast-iron buildings— and less-than-dazzling neighborhoods of tenement blocks to house the immigrants who were also pouring in. That conflict's aftermath created the Gilded Age of rich industrial tycoons and a grand new Beaux Arts style to express their outsized tastes. That same sensibility would, thanks to the elevator, reach upwards to create the first spurt of tall buildings colonizing the sky. Later, some of these structures would be cut down for a second growth of modern towers. Building in New York, which typically puts commerce above aesthetic considerations, often seems to take forever, but few structures last very long.

In this respect, the fate of the World Trade Center, which stood a mere 28 years from the time of its completion in 1973, is simply the latest, if deadliest, link in a long chain of memorable casualties that include the Singer Tower, Ebbets Field and the original Pennsylvania Station. In fact, construction of the Twin Towers entailed the destruction of an entire commercial neighborhood: the old "Radio Row," where customers shopped for consumer electronics.

Like the Empire State Building, the Twin Towers and the complex surrounding them were begun at a time of unparalleled prosperity and finished during an economic depression. Yet as originally conceived, they were meant to embody a new sense of permanence. They were a late expression of Corbusier's Radiant City plan, which envisioned an urban future of widely spaced towers separated by plazas, greenbelts and superhighways. This notion influenced urban planners such as Robert Moses for half a century—and indeed, the famously tyrannical Moses, in his role as the city's Parks and Planning Commissioner, acted on these ideas with a vengeance throughout the 1930s, '40s and '50s, tearing down whole sections of Brooklyn, Queens and the Bronx in the process.

Though Moses himself had nothing to do with the towers, the buildings—plunked as they were in the oldest section of Gotham— embodied the purest distillation of Moses's thinking. They were, in fact, a private and public consortium, hatched in the early 1960s by businessman David Rockefeller and his brother Nelson, then governor of New York.

Sleek, self-contained, a city-within-the-city and isolated from the rest of the island, the World Trade Center stood as a kind of rebuke to the urban messiness of lower Manhattan. Their scale was almost impossible to apprehend— except by car, zipping along one of the many expressways Moses had imperiously plowed through various New York neighborhoods. They were never really meant to be a true part of the city; they were meant to symbolize New York's transformation from American conurbation to global megalopolis.

Predictably then, when the towers opened, architecture critics sneered; one even went so far as to describe them as the boxes that the Empire State and Chrysler Buildings had come in. Even an edition of the *AIA Guide to New York City* called them "banal." So how did this monstrosity become beloved? First, there's architect Minoru Yamasaki's understated—and underrated—design. Although boxy and huge, the Twin Towers shimmered in the light, thanks to a stainless-steel exterior corrugated by narrowly spaced columns, which resulted in shoulder-wide mullions. This relationship, between the width of the windows and the height of the towers, imbued them with an elongated grace that was as anthropomorphic as it was aspirational, like a pair of El Greco's saints. Yamasaki also tasseled the fenestration along the top and bottom of each facade with bands of ogival tracery. The pointed archways along the base became hauntingly familiar as charred remnants at Ground Zero.

In their lifetime, the towers inspired dreamers if not critics, and two in particular put their

▶ For an overview of the city's development and past political figures, see chapter **History**.
▶ Other significant architectural sights are listed in the **Sightseeing** section.

stamp on the buildings in ways that would win them a place in the hearts of the public. In 1973, Frenchman Philippe Petit walked a tightrope between the edifices; four years later, an American named George Willig climbed one of the towers with the aid of special rigging that fit into an existing track for window-cleaning scaffolds. Paul Goldberger, architecture critic for *The New Yorker,* once suggested that such acts lent the WTC the romanticism that its original design lacked. But if that quality had really been missing, what inspired these daredevils in the first place? The towers, it would seem, had a knack for defying their detractors, even at the bitter end while under assault by the most virulent sort of hatred: They managed, after all, to stay intact long enough to allow tens of thousands of tenants to be safely evacuated.

RESHAPING THE SKYLINE

As much as the World Trade Center remains a presence in the hearts of New Yorkers, its demise could pave the way for an important new period of rebuilding in New York. Granted, the cost of cleanup and recovery will burden a city budget already threatened by blooming deficits; such eagerly awaited amenities as the Brooklyn Bridge Park could be deferred. And it's also true that even before September 11, the economic downturn, precipitated by the great tech bust of 2000, was having a negative impact on new buildings. A windfall of federal aid dollars should see New York through its greatest difficulties (although federal, state and local politicians will have to fight hard to get the promised money). In any case, a number of important architectural additions to the city that were under way before the attacks have recently been completed and are well worth a visit.

Frank Gehry has realized one small project that is currently open to the public, despite his downtown Guggenheim satellite being stalled: the Tribeca **Issey Miyake boutique** *(119 Hudson St between Franklin and North Moore Sts, 212-226-0100).* The store's 15,000-square-foot interior is dominated by a tornadolike titanium sculpture—perhaps meant to encourage shoppers to buy up a storm? **Prada**'s new Soho store *(575 Broadway at Prince St, 212-234-8888)* designed by Rem Koolhaas as a combination retail and performance space, has been a must-see destination since it opened in January 2002.

Richard Meier, architect of the J. Paul Getty Center in Los Angeles, has added his imprimatur to the skyline. Two sleek apartment towers *(173 and 176 Perry St at West St)*, hard by the West Side Highway, are his first major buildings in New York.

Also a first: Aldo Rossi's posthumous addition to Soho. The Italian architect died in 1997, but 2001 saw the completion of his design for the **Scholastic Books headquarters** *(557 Broadway between Prince and Spring Sts);* the neotraditional building stands out even as it blends in with its cast-iron environs.

More prominent along the skyline are two highly sculptural buildings in midtown that now join Christian de Portzamparc's equally striking **LVMH Tower** *(19 E 57th St between Fifth and Madison Aves)* nearby: Raimund Abraham's design for the new **Austrian Cultural Center** *(11 E 52nd St between Fifth and Madison Aves)* and the newly expanded **American Folk Art Museum** *(see page 38),* by Tod Williams & Billie Tsien. Abraham's creation, which is sandwiched between existing buildings, rises from its narrow site like a soaring Easter Island stone head. While the dark, slanting, louvered facade has a masklike presence, the building as a whole suggests the spinal column of some enormous vertebrate

Ironclad promise Aldo Rossi's Scholastic building fits right in with its cast-iron neighbors.

that's at once prehistoric and futuristic. The American Folk Art Museum, meanwhile, is clad in faceted panels of Tombasil, a white bronze alloy. Its delicately textured surface, which brilliantly captures light, has at once the look of both stone and metal—reflecting the museum's mission of promoting the handcrafted in art, and also lending the block, which is shared by the **Museum of Modern Art** *(see page 35)*, a touch of warmth. MoMA, by the way, will close in June 2002 for two years of reconstruction, which includes Yoshio Taniguchi's seamless contemporary addition, built on the site of the old Dorset Hotel.

Columbus Circle, which was once dominated by the New York Coliseum convention center, is soon to be home to a gleaming new complex across from Central Park: the **AOL Time Warner headquarters** *(1 Central Park at Broadway)*, a soaring mix that will include upscale apartments, a Mandarin Orientel hotel, high-end shops and media-conglomerate offices, plus a new venue for Jazz at Lincoln Center. Just how it got built is indicative of the way things get done in New York. The original Coliseum, another Robert Moses behemoth, closed in 1986 while the city tried to find a private developer to take it off its hands. Proposal after proposal, including one infamous Moshe Safdie plan that would have cast a giant shadow across Central Park, was scotched by various civic groups. The present design finally passed muster and construction began in early 2001. The building's twin-tower motif, which allows for more light in the park, will become as instant a fixture in this neighborhood as the Twin Towers were in theirs.

BUILDINGS OF THEIR TIME

The World Trade Center, which lorded over the oldest part of Manhattan, reflected the city's architecture in a fascinating way. Given their height, design and location at the southern tip of Manhattan, the towers arguably mirrored, more than other Modernist buildings, the city's famous system of streets—a grid plan envisioned by the State Legislature in 1811. The Commissioner's Plan, as it's also known, laid down the crisscross streets that would eventually fill up (like a "thermometer," Rem Koolhaas memorably put it in his book *Delirious New York*) with buildings to create the Gotham we know today. The history of the city's architecture can be followed south to north—plus or minus some detours, starting with the Dutch themselves.

All that's left of Dutch architectural influence in lower Manhattan is the distinctive warren of narrow lanes and streets that cover the lower part of the island (major arteries such as Broadway and the Bowery follow Native American trails).

For actual Dutch buildings, you'll have to make your way uptown or deep into Brooklyn. The **Dyckman Farmhouse Museum** *(see page 88)* was actually built in 1785, well after Dutch rule, but it retains the distinctive characteristics of the Dutch Colonial style, such as a gambrel roof and decorative brickwork. The **Pieter Claesen Wyckoff House Museum** *(5902 Clarendon Rd at Ralph Ave, East Flatbush, Brooklyn)* is the oldest house in New York City. It was built around 1652 by Wyckoff, who had arrived in America in 1637 as an illiterate indentured servant. He later became the wealthiest citizen of what was later called the town of Flatlands. The modest house, with shingled walls, pine floorboards and wide overhanging eaves, was typical of its time. The **Lefferts Homestead** *(see page 292)*, built in the 1780s, combines Dutch Colonial architecture—the bell-shaped gambrel roof— with early Federal details, such as front and back porches set off by slender columns.

In Manhattan, early 19th-century New York buildings are easier to come by. The island's population grew rapidly, and the buildings were designed in the Georgian/Neoclassical styles of the English and Federal periods, starting with **St. Paul's Chapel and Churchyard** *(see page 51)*. Manhattan's only extant pre-Revolutionary structure, the church was begun in 1764 and completed with the addition of a steeple in 1796. It was almost lost in the World Trade Center attack: Although covered by debris from the collapsing towers, the columned and quoined chapel miraculously survived. The more familiar Episcopal landmark, **Trinity Church** *(Wall St and Broadway)*, is actually the third iteration at this site, built in 1846. The original, consecrated in 1698, was destroyed by fire after the Revolutionary War. A second version, completed in 1790, was eventually demolished because of structural problems. **Fraunces Tavern** *(see page 40)*, where George Washington held a victory celebration in 1783 after the British evacuation of New York, is actually a 20th-century renovation of this 1719 building—which was built as a private residence. The largest group of Federal-style houses in New York, dating from the 1820s, can be found in the **Charlton-King-Vandam Historic District** *(9–43, 20–42 Charlton St; 11–49, 16–54 King St; 9–29 Vandam St; and 43–51 MacDougal St)* along the southwestern edge of Greenwich Village. But perhaps the supreme expression of the Federal style, complete with some French Renaissance flourishes, is **City Hall** *(see pages 52 and 53)*. Completed in 1812, this is the mayor's headquarters.

The Greek Revival style, meanwhile, is best exemplified by the 1842 **Federal Hall**

National Memorial *(see page 51),* whose colonnaded facade, carved of Westchester marble, is modeled on the Parthenon (albeit sans sculptured frieze and pediment). George Washington took his oath of office at this site, when the old Federal Hall, built in 1701, stood here. (A statue of Washington graces the spot where the oath was sworn.) **Colonnade Row** *(428–434 Lafayette St between Astor Pl and E 4th St)* is another fine example of the style, although only four of the nine elegant homes that Seth Geer built (1832–1833) still stand. A more complete concentration of Greek Revival housing can be found along **"the Row"** *(1–13 Washington Square North between Fifth Ave and University Pl)* and its neighboring block to the west *(19–26 Washington Square North between Fifth Ave and MacDougal St),* both of which were built in the 1830s. The former **13th Street Presbyterian Church** *(143 W 13th St between Sixth and Seventh Aves)* from 1847, was once the finest Greek Revival church in the city. Unfortunately, its interior was gutted to make way for apartments; the last visible vestige of its pedigree is the impressive, beautifully proportioned portico.

The Empire State Building is New York's most storied, in both senses of the word. It has never diminished in stature, even while existing in the shadows of the World Trade Center.

The cast-iron buildings of the mid- to late-19th century were forerunners of the modern, curtain-wall way of building: cheap, quick and meant to support large expanses of glass, resulting in buildings that were remarkably airy, if not technically lightweight. Often, the cast-iron components—interior columns, exterior sashing and details—were catalog items that could be ordered and bolted together. Although the first buildings to use this technique, such as the 1846 **A.T. Stewart Dry Goods Store** *(280 Broadway between Chamber and Reade Sts),* were located below Canal Street, the Soho neighborhood between Canal and Houston Streets remains the city's preeminent cast-iron domain. There, some of the more remarkable offerings include the Palladian-style **Haughwout Building** *(488–492 Broadway at Broome St),* which had the distinction of including the first Otis elevator in New York when it was built in 1856; and the **"little Singer Building"** of 1902–

1904 *(561 Broadway between Prince and Spring Sts),* with its curly Art Nouveau archways, recessed glass and textured terra-cotta panels.

Chronologically, the cast-iron era overlapped with the grander expressions of the Beaux Arts revival, driven by robber barons who put some of their money (made from rail and steel) to good use by building the city's greatest civic edifices. Supreme among these are **Carnegie Hall** *(see page 316),* completed in 1891; the 1985 **Metropolitan Museum of Art** *(see page 35),* built by the sure hand of architect Richard Morris Hunt; the Carrère & Hastings design for the **New York Public Library** *(see pages 73 and 74),* erected in 1911 next to what was once an Egyptian Revival–style reservoir (now Bryant Park); and the grandest of all, **Grand Central Station** *(see pages 75 and 76),* originally completed in 1913, and recently restored to its full glory after just ducking the wrecking ball a generation ago.

The architectural firm most synonymous with the Beaux Arts period, of course, is McKim, Mead & White. Collectively, they brought forth the 1914 **Municipal Building** *(see page 52),* the 1917 **Morgan Library** *(see page 35)* and the old **Penn Station,** whose design lives on in its sister across Eighth Avenue: the 1913 **General Post Office** *(see page 372),* which straddles the blocks between 31st and 33rd Streets. Another outstanding example of the Beaux Arts style is the **Alexander Hamilton Custom House** *(see National Museum of the American Indian, page 35),* built between 1899 and 1907. Before the national income tax was imposed in 1913, custom duties were the principal means of financing the government. Thus, Cass Gilbert's Italianate design, set off by the *Four Continents,* the group of allegorical sculptures by Daniel Chester French (he did the Lincoln Memorial in Washington, D.C.), is suitably monumental. It also serves as a bridge to the next great period of New York architecture—the skyscraper era.

RISING TO THE OCCASION

To erect skyscrapers, one had to overcome the height limitations imposed by the use of load-bearing masonry walls; happily, the technologies developed in cast-iron building pointed the way. Elevators and steel-frame construction permitted buildings to begin rising above 20 stories, and so the first skyscraper, the **Flatiron Building** *(see page 64),* was born in 1902. Still, aside from its height and narrow triangular footprint, the Flatiron's Renaissance palazzo facade and flat roof had more in common with the loft buildings of lower Broadway than it did with

The glass menagerie The city's glass-box
era began with the UN headquarters.

the Chrysler Building held the title of world's
tallest building for only a few months before
being surpassed in 1931 by the **Empire State
Building** *(see* **Inspired spire,** *page 74).*

The Empire State Building is New York's
most storied, in both senses of the word. It has
never diminished in stature, even while existing
in the shadow of the World Trade Center.
Rising 1,250 feet along a series of incremental
setbacks that are capped by an enormous Art
Deco lantern, its rapid construction during the
aftershock of the 1929 stock market crash
inspired the city as much as the rescue effort
did at Ground Zero after September 11. Like the
WTC, the Empire State was also the scene of an
aircraft disaster: In 1945, an errant bomber on a
training mission slammed into the 80th floor,
killing 14 people but causing no major
permanent damage to the building. The ESB
remained nearly vacant for many years—the
commercial development hoped for by its
owners didn't transpire during the Great
Depression. It stood isolated against the
skyline, "a lighthouse in the harbor of
commerce," as architect Robert A.M. Stern
once put it. Today, it stands alone once again
as Gotham's tallest building.

Like all phases in New York, the Romantic
Age of skyscrapers soon gave way to
something new as economic depression and
war slowed development, and refinements in
curtain-wall construction permitted the purity
of form embodied by the **International Style**.
Many have harped on the so-called sterility of
the glass boxes that sprang up in the years
following the Second World War. But at their
best, buildings such as **The United Nations
Headquarters** *(First Ave at 46th St; see also
page 76)* rival anything else in the skyline.
Designed in 1947 by an A-team of Modernist
architects (including Corbusier, Oscar Niemeyer,
Sven Markelius and Wallace K. Harrison),
the UN's arrangement clearly flows from
Corbusier's Radiant City concept, though the
structure's details are largely by Harrison. The
main building, housing the Secretariat, is a
broad slab of glass, steel and stone 554 feet
high, set perpendicularly between East River
frontage and the swooping, low-slung buildings
of the library and conference hall below.

This play of horizontal and vertical lines was
reprised in New York's first commercial Modern
structure, the **Lever House** *(390 Park Ave
between 53rd and 54th Sts),* built in 1952.
Designed by Gordon Bunshaft of Skidmore,
Owings & Merrill, and recently restored, it was
also the city's first building to be constructed
entirely of steel and glass. The main part of the
building—a slender rectangular slab set at a
right angle to the street—cantilevers over a

what we imagine as skyscrapers today. Gilbert's
Gothic-inflected design for the **Woolworth
Building** *(233 Broadway between Barclay St
and Park Pl)* was a true tower: a sheer shaft,
without setbacks, soaring 792 feet over the city.
When it was finished in 1913, the monument to
wealth was the world's tallest building, a title it
held until the completion in 1930 of its midtown
rival, the **Chrysler Building** *(see page 75).*

William Van Alen's design for the Chrysler
Building is the first pure expression of the
skyscraper vernacular, in that it owed little to
previous historical styles. It is, instead, a paean
to the automobile and the new age of the
machine. Its 1,048 feet culminate in a spired
stainless-steel crown meant to represent a
series of overlapping hubcaps that diminish in
diameter as they climb up the sky. Begun at the
height of the Roaring '20s speculative frenzy,

Color me '80s Philip Johnson's "lipstick building" is the era's over-the-top landmark.

much lower building, which in turn floats above a ground floor that contains only a small lobby. The remaining ground-level space, a large plaza, is a pleasingly luxurious waste of air space—a Manhattan commodity that is just as valuable as real estate. It's an indulgence that wouldn't fit today's maximum-interior-space standards The next major development in the glass-box form, Ludwig Mies van der Rohe's magnificent bronze-clad **Seagram Building** *(375 Park Ave between 52nd and 53rd Sts)*, completed in 1958, is likewise given plenty of breathing room, courtesy of its sizable plaza. The work of another Bauhaus alum, Walter Gropius, is represented by the **Met Life Building**, formerly the Pan Am Building *(200 Park Ave at 45th St)*, which towers dramatically over Grand Central Station. Since it was yet another slab, this time straddling Park Avenue, the building was roundly criticized for being too large and for blocking the straight-shot view up and down the street. Its precast concrete curtain wall, one of the first in New York, can seem, at turns, sinister or warm, depending on the light. It was

in effect a billboard bearing the Pan Am logo until the airline went bankrupt in 1991. In 1992, Met Life affixed it with its own name—over the protests of those who wanted to landmark the original sign. In many respects, the Pan Am building came to symbolize the failure of Modernism in New York.

The "stagflation" and fiscal crisis of the 1970s slowed building once again—with the notable exception of the pennywhistle-shaped **Citicorp Center** of 1977 *(Lexington Ave between 53rd and 54th Sts)*, the last building to noticeably contribute to the city's skyline.

THE POSTMODERN '80S

The '80s brought with them a booming stock market and a sense of irrational exuberance harking back to the 1920s, which manifested itself as a rejection of modern design. Postmodern architecture, with its mix of modern building methods and historicized details, has its detractors (quite rightly, since it spawned a lot of glass-and-stone dreck). But as the style recedes into history, it is naturally becoming burnished by memory. A trio of these midtown buildings were completed in 1983—Philip Johnson's **Sony Building** *(see page 76* and **Sony Wonder Technology Lab**, *page 293)*, which was originally AT&T's headquarters; the former **IBM Building** *(590 Madison Ave between 56th and 57th Sts)*; and **Trump Tower** *(725 Fifth Ave at 56th)*. Together, they express the full emotional palette of postmodern design, from the relatively sober (Edward Barnes's black-granite prism for IBM) past the kitschy signature (Johnson's Chippendale breakfront top for Sony) to the marvelously vulgar (Trump's gold-trimmed pink-granite lobby). Two other buildings, the 1983 Futuro-Egyptian "**lipstick building**" *(885 Third Ave between 53rd and 54th Sts)* by John Burgee and Philip Johnson, and **750 Lexington Avenue** *(between 59th and 60th Sts)*, likewise possess a grandeur that's both awesome and absurd, though the latter has the slight advantage of having a true New York tale behind it.

This cylindrical blue-glass tower, with a finial top, is built around a lone tenement brownstone, a survivor of the block torn down to make way for Helmut Jahn's structure. The story is that one woman occupant of the rent-controlled building refused to move, despite being offered generous financial inducements to do so. By rights, she could stay, so she did—enduring a construction process that included tunneling under her top-floor apartment to create a side entrance for the main lobby. She never left her home, fearing it would be demolished in her absence. She held out on her own patch of ground zero, flying a tiny American flag from her window.

Green Apple

It's a jungle out there, and it's not all concrete. New York City is crawling, flying and swimming with wildlife.

New York may feel like the most unnatural place on earth—heck, even Central Park is man-made—swathed as it is in skyscrapers, asphalt, soot and discarded gum. But nature is a resilient and persistent force. In spring 1999, police captured a coyote in Central Park. Peregrine falcons nest in high-rises and on bridges. And for the first time in living memory, harbor seals have reappeared in New York Harbor. What is going on here?

As humans and animals battle for ever-shrinking patches of undeveloped land near metropolises, there's bound to be occasional crossover—and some species have found that urban life is not too bad. In fact, the city has more than 28,000 acres of parkland, 500 acres of wetlands and 5,000 acres of forest. Granted, they aren't all right in midtown, but all you have to do is hop on the A train to observe osprey hunting for fish in Jamaica Bay Wildlife Refuge. During the last decade, blighted locales such as the

Gowanus Canal and the Bronx River have been cleaned up. Beneath their city-slicker exterior, it seems many New Yorkers are green at heart: An organization called Parks 2001, composed of about 1,000 park-advocacy groups, rallied to make the improvement of the city's 1,704 parks a priority in the 2001 mayoral race.

RETURN OF THE NATIVES

On April Fool's Day, 1999, policemen and dogcatchers chased and caught a renegade coyote that had found its way to Central Park (it now lives in the **Queens Zoo**; *see pages 98 and 99*). How the wild animal, more associated with Midwestern prairies than Fifth Avenue, got to the heart of Manhattan will never be known, but Parks Department officials presume he made his way across the Henry Hudson Bridge, from the Bronx. That's where animals are regularly

Shining path Train and trail lead to world-class bird-watching at Jamaica Bay Wildlife Refuge.

spotted, in **Van Cortlandt Park** *(see pages 102 and 105)* and Woodlawn Cemetery.

Coyotes aren't on the list of species the city is in the process of reintroducing—but a lot of other animals are. Project X (as the program is called), launched by former New York City Parks Commissioner Henry J. Stern in 1997, aims to reintroduce indigenous precolonial animals and plants to the metropolis. By doing so, parks officials hope to create biodiversity—for the benefit of all that live here, people included.

In November 2001, the Urban Park Ranger Biodiversity Team released 18 screech owls in **Central Park** *(see page 77)*. In the 1920s, these little balls of feathers were one of ten bird species that lived in the park year-round; by the 1960s they had disappeared (for unknown reasons). Species reintroduction is still an experiment: The 2001 group is the second round of screech owls—in 1998, six birds were released in the park, and of those, only one remains.

Other Project X reintroductions include 100 bobtail quails in **Pelham Bay Park** in the Bronx *(see pages 104 and 105)*, 75 New England asters in Brooklyn's **Marine Park** *(between Flatbush and Gerritsen Aves, and Ave U and Shore Pkwy)* and 175 wood frogs in Queens' **Cunningham Park** *(between Oceania and 199th Sts, and Long Island Expwy and Union Tpke)*.

Some animals come home on their own: Harbor seals, which once thrived in New York Harbor, have been spotted on tiny man-made Swinburne Island. Located just south of the Verrazano-Narrows Bridge, the island is usually populated entirely by seabirds. Though the seals come and go, Rob DiGiovanni, a marine biologist with the Riverhead Foundation for Marine Research, thinks they may be reestablishing a settlement, helped by "an increased population on the New England coast, due to federally protected status and abundant herring stocks."

THE SKIES ARE ALIVE

The bird-watching is so good in New York City that the Audubon Society *(www.audubon.org)* published a hefty guide on the subject, *Finding Birds in the Metropolitan Area* (Cornell University Press, $17.95). According to authors Marcia Fowle and Paul Kerlinger, the combination of geography and ecosystems has made the area a prime spot for migrating birds and year-round residents since the end of the last ice age, thousands of years ago. New York has back bays, dunes, forests, freshwater marshes, grassland, harbors, rivers, tidal marshes, the ocean and a bunch of other habitats that attract more than 300 different species of bird—you can see up to 100 in a single day if you look hard enough. That's why Central Park is one of the best birding spots in the country. In spring and

fall, its 843 acres are a traffic jam of winged migrators. Bird-watchers come from around the world to spot as many as 30 types of warbler, 15 species of hawk (in autumn), and waterfowl such as loons, grebes and coots making a springtime splashdown at the Jacqueline Kennedy Onassis Reservoir. A pair of calliope hummingbirds, a species that normally winter in Mexico, spent the 2001 holiday season in Fort Tryon Park in northern Manhattan.

Unfortunately, however alluring Manhattan may be, it is also an aerial minefield to birds. Attracted to city lights like tourists to the Empire State Building, migratory birds become disoriented by the electric glare and circle tall buildings until they either drop from exhaustion or smash into a deceptive window. The Twin Towers were particularly challenging for our feathered friends. At the request of the Audubon Society, the crown of colored lights at the top of the Empire State Building is turned off during the heavy migration season.

"Bird-watchers come from around the world to spot loons, grebes and coots."

The other prime area for fowl play is the 9,000-acre **Jamaica Bay Wildlife Refuge** *(see page 98)*. Birds that nest in this haven include the black-crowned night heron, great egret, ibis, osprey and the impressively named boat-tailed grackle. Eurasian wigeons, rough-legged hawks and snow geese are just a few of the winter residents. It can feel surreal to spy on a night heron in a quiet, marshy nook with the Manhattan skyline rising in the distance.

Gotham's most famous feathered residents are the 15 breeding pairs of peregrine falcons scattered throughout the city. Almost poisoned to extinction by DDT in the 1960s, the bird of prey has made a strong comeback. From 1974 to 1988, environmental authorities released peregrines throughout New York State. In 1983, a pair decided to make a home on the Verrazano-Narrows Bridge—the city's first resident peregrines in almost 30 years. Now falcons nest on the 27th floor of New York Hospital, the Brooklyn Bridge and the Met Life Building, among other high-altitude spots. They have no trouble swooping down on food, since their preferred entrée is pigeon. In fact, up until a couple of years ago, some of the same poison that exterminators legally used to kill pigeons (and sparrows and starlings) also killed some falcons—that's life in the big city. The poison, Avitrol, was banned in New York in 2000.

Birds aren't the only airborne creatures that thrive in New York. The city happens to be

They're baaack After a 20-year absence, screech owls once again live in Central Park.

located where the southern edge of the range of northern butterflies overlaps with the northern border of southern butterflies. Members of the New York City Butterfly Club have found more than 100 varieties in the five boroughs. By way of comparison, all of that green and pleasant land known as the United Kingdom has only 57. The rare white M hairstreak can be found at Jamaica Bay Wildlife Refuge and in Staten Island's Conference House Park. Butterfly enthusiasts Harry Zirlin and Jeff Ingraham have compiled a short guide that can be found online *(www.naba.org/pubs/ ab97c/p4.html)*.

RESURRECTION
Little by little, New York's existing natural landscape is being cleaned up. The Hudson River, a mighty open sewer in the 1950s, has undergone a dramatic reclamation: The cleaner water now attracts kayakers and Jet Ski riders and in 1999, for the first time in 20 years, scientists found that chemical contamination in striped bass had dropped enough for the fish to be considered fit to eat (though women of childbearing age and children are still warned to refrain). And environmentalists won a major victory in 2001 when the federal government ordered General Electric to carry out a $480-million cleanup of the river in upstate New York. The company had dumped more than a million pounds of PCBs into the Hudson from the mid-1940s to 1977, and has gone to great lengths to avoid having to dredge the river's contaminated bottom.

Similar, but smaller, projects are going on all over the city. The Bronx River, the city's only freshwater river, has been transformed from a

murky car graveyard to a rediscovered waterway where local residents can now fish, kayak and even swim. Visitors can get an up-close look at the river as it flows through the **New York Botanical Garden** *(see pages 102 and 105)*. Sewage-filled Flushing Bay, in Queens, will be dredged and cleaned as part of the 2002 Energy and Water Development Appropriations Act that President George W. Bush signed in late 2001.

WILD AT HEART
In an effort to improve air quality, the Metropolitan Transportation Authority finally followed the lead of most major U.S. cities and agreed to replace its diesel-fueled buses with natural-gas and hybrid-electric vehicles. Diesel buses will be completely eliminated by 2003.

You don't have to visit the parks to view greenery. Nearly a half-million trees stand tall along the streets of the five boroughs (there are 2.5 million total). The three most common types are Norway maple, London plane and pin oak. Meddling with any of these public-property arbors can bring a fine of up to $1,000—if you're not certified. The city welcomes tree huggers who've had a little training: New Yorkers can take a course that will earn them the right to practice their pruning.

The city is also filled with community gardens—residents have turned neglected empty lots into lush oases, often in the middle of dilapidated blocks. The Lower East Side's **Fireman's Memorial Garden** *(358–364 E 8th St between Aves C and D)* won a 2001 John Deere Seeds of Hope award, which recognizes efforts to breathe some natural goodness into inner cities. Dedicated to firefighter Marty Celic, who lost his life in a blaze where the garden now grows, the garden has taken on new significance since September 11, 2001. In the wake of the attack, firemen and police officers found respite among the cherry trees, lilacs and tulips.

New Yorkers have always had a soft spot for the underdog—just look at the New York Mets baseball team—though the city can be a tough place if you're a tufted titmouse trying to get a little nest together. So it's all the more gratifying when you see a lone osprey gracefully winging against the skyline backdrop, or when a neon-blue dragonfly is spotted, incongruously perched on a car hood. Sightings like these will always bring a thrill to the urban heart—it's only natural.

▶ For information on more green spaces and urban hikes, see **Rest assured**, page 68, and **A walk on the wild (west) side**, page 86.

Night Train to Brooklyn

All you need is $1.50 and a drink to experience your own Kings County nocturne

No! Sleep! Till Brooklyn!—so exclaimed the Beastie Boys in their 1990 road song toasting this boisterous and oft-maligned outer borough. Unfortunately, it took the rest of the city more than a decade to recognize the potential Brooklyn has as a destination worthy of the Beasties' rap.

While it's true that a decent bar, gallery, nightclub or restaurant can be found in nearly all of the borough's neighborhoods—and there are more than two dozen of them—a few hang time havens stand out as paragons of cool. Colonized by struggling artists, **Williamsburg** has a lively gallery scene. Galleries such as **Pierogi 2000** *(see page 254)* began popping up on the main drag, **Bedford Avenue**, about a decade ago. Gallerygoers needed places to go to after the wine and cheese ran out, so savvy entrepreneurs began opening bars, clubs and restaurants in the neighborhood. One of the first was **Galapagos** *(see page 304),* a space that triples as a gallery, performance space and bar. **Bean** *(178 North 8th St at Bedford Ave, 718-387-8222)* is a no-frills Mexican cheapie. A more recent addition is the **Stinger Club** *(241 Grand St between Driggs Ave and Roebling St, 718-218-6662),* a sexy, crimson-lit place featuring local bands that play everything from bluegrass to reggae. Whether you view the avenue's commercial cluster as a welcome development or as cultural imperialism, it's a short L train ride away from Union Square, and is more cutting-edge than, say, the bars and nightclubs of Greenwich Village's Bleecker Street.

Park Slope is more genteel; baby strollers crowd the streets by day, though there are plenty of indigenous inebriates after dark. The stretch of Fifth Avenue from St. Marks Place to 9th Street was, until recent years, lined with pizzerias, Chinese take-out counters, and empty storefronts. Today, the strip is known for some of the best eating and drinking destinations in the city, including **al di là** *(see page 187).* The 2001 opening of **Blue Ribbon Brooklyn** *(see page 168),* the tony chainlet's first foray outside of Manhattan, was evidence that Fifth Avenue had come of age. The restaurant attracts a professional crowd, and on weekends, its bar is packed six yuppies deep. Farther down the street, sophisti-cats file into Reis Goldberg's **Bar Reis** *(375A Fifth Ave between 5th and 6th Sts, 718-832-5716)* to listen to sultry live jazz or a sexy lounge singer. Its garden is filled

Cultural Darwinism Galapagos is the link in Brooklyn's evolution into a party town.

with nuzzling Chianti-sippers; the lower level turns out tapas for delicate snacking.

Down the street, **Great Lakes** *(284 Fifth Ave at First St, 718-499-3710)* is the Brooklyn version of an East Village dive. The crowd tends to be young, the jukebox is filled with indie rock, and there is live music on Monday and Thursday nights. Anyone who gets too hammered here can soak up the poison with fish-and-chips from the **Chip Shop** *(383 Fifth Ave at Sixth St, 718-832-7701)*.

Brooklyn's queer constituency has its evening playgrounds too. **Excelsior** *(see page 251)*, a handsome bar with an outdoor patio and garden, is one of the few places in New York where a roughly equal mix of gays and lesbians commingle. Unpolished **Ginger's** *(363 Fifth Ave between 5th and 6th Sts, 718-788-0924)*, on the other hand, lures mostly lesbians. Unlike other dyke hangouts, which tend to attract specific crowds (for instance, downtown rockers, 40-year-old professionals or Jersey girls), this place draws them all. The jukebox bleats sapphic anthems from the likes of k.d. lang, the Indigo Girls and Ani DiFranco.

Smith Street, Brooklyn's latest destination strip, is west of the Slope, in **Boerum Hill** and **Carroll Gardens**. In the 1940s, most homes, stores and churches were demolished in this area to make way for the Gowanus Expressway (the raised motorway that links the Verrazano-Narrows Bridge with the Brooklyn-Battery Tunnel). The result was that a close-knit Italian community started to unravel. The area slumped until the 1960s, when new settlers began to move in. Today, the neighborhoods are booming, reborn as enclaves for young professionals. **Halcyon** *(see **Halcyon days**, page 270)*—part café, record shop and music lounge—attracts a crowd from all over the city. The space's antique sofas and chairs are packed with musicians, DJs and vinyl collectors, networking and bopping their heads to funky beats. Another multipurpose hangout is **Robin des Bois** *(195 Smith St between Baltic and Warren Sts, 718-596-1609)*, formerly known as the Sherwood Cafe. French owner Bernard Decanali created a space that does quadruple duty—it's a beer-and-wine bar, a café, a gallery and an antiques shop. The merchandise, an array of items that includes religious icons, disco balls and mounted animals, covers the walls and ceiling.

For hooch in a more traditional setting, belly up to **The Bar** *(280 Smith St at Sackett St, 718-246-9050)* and suck down a Brooklyn Lager. Its jukebox is one of the best in the borough, offering everything from hip-hop to punk. Minimalist-chic **Quench** *(see page 152)*

is a little more self-satisfied than its neighbors, but unlike Manhattan hot spots of a similar caliber, the staff is actually concerned about its pretty clientele. Designer drinkers can be spotted sipping apple martinis at the polished cherry bar. Orbicular light fixtures hang overhead like harvest moons, casting lunar hues on the sex-me-up room.

Fort Greene has been home to the **Brooklyn Academy of Music** *(see page 315)* since 1907, drawing the artistically inclined for decades. But until two or three years ago, thespians and other bohos in the area rarely ventured beyond the shadow of BAM. Now Manhattanites are "discovering" a neighborhood rich with black culture that just happens to be lined with stunning brownstones.

As borough-hoppers moved in and locals regained a sense of neighborhood pride, developers and entrepreneurs began to invest in the area. The result is yet another nightlife nucleus. Much of Fort Greene's evening activities are clustered on, but not limited to, Lafayette and DeKalb Avenues. **Loulou** *(222 DeKalb Ave between Adelphi and Clermont Aves, 718-246-0633)* is undoubtedly Brooklyn's only Breton spot. Its rustic digs and covered, candlelit garden make it a good point from which to begin a tour of Fort Greene. Nearby **Butta' Cup Lounge** *(271 Adelphi St at DeKalb Ave, 718-522-1669)* is located on two levels of a restored brownstone. A menu of "global soul food" is found on the ground floor, while the upper level is full of lounge lizards enjoying steel-drum players (Saturdays); other nights, a DJ spins Motown, soul and funk. Across the street, revelers rush into **Liquors** *(219 DeKalb Ave between Clermont Ave and Adelphi St, 718-488-7700)*. On Sundays, rotating jazz trios toot and pluck original tunes and old favorites; on Mondays, a DJ spins classic Haitian *compa* and Cuban salsa.

Believe it or not, there was a time in the not-too-distant past when Brooklyn was a world-class city in its own right—and it deserves to be thought of as one again. The borough can certainly lay claim to being a party-hearty part of "the city that never sleeps."

▶ For more insight into Brooklyn's history and neighborhoods, see chapter **Outer Boroughs**.
▶ To learn about Brooklyn's nascent rock music scene, read **A noise grows in Brooklyn**, page 306.
▶ See **State of the art**, page 250, for more on Brooklyn's rising art community.
▶ Brooklyn has a new baseball team. See **Diamond dogs**, page 326.

See
yourself at
the

Paul McCartney

Henry Kissinger

Tour of Harlem

Hear movers and shakers, history makers, poets, politicians, artists and musicians. Catch a concert, a lecture—whatever your conjecture! Get stock tips. Do back flips. Taste wine. Feel divine. Whoever you are and for all the reasons why, do it all at the 92nd Street Y.

Located at 92nd Street and Lexington Avenue, in the heart of New York City and a few short blocks from historic Museum Mile and Central Park, the 92nd Street Y offers an amazing array of lectures, concerts, literary readings and walking tours. Discover New York with the 92nd Street Y.

Martha Stewart

Kaufmann Concert Hall

Call **212.415.5500** for tickets and information.

92 Y St

"A cultural, spiritual and physical haven"
– The New York Times

Lexington Avenue at 92nd Street
www.92ndsty.org
An agency of UJA-Federation

Sightseeing

Museums	32
Downtown	46
Midtown	64
Uptown	77
The Outer Boroughs	90
Tour New York	107

Feature boxes

Cheap tix	35
Culture clubbing	36
Critics' picks: Museums	40
Isle of might	48
Critics' picks: Chinatown snacks	57
Rest assured	68
Inspired spire	74
A walk on the wild (West) side	86
Let's get lost	97
All that jazz	100
Go to the art of Queens	103
Find your kind	112

Stamping grounds If you don't have time to visit everything in NYC, pick up a postcard.

Museums

Salsa, skyscrapers and sculptures—you can find almost anything in a New York museum

New York's museums are among the best in the world. More than 60 institutions hold collections of everything from Gutenberg bibles (three of them) and ancient Etruscan jewelry to Plains Indians buckskins and salsa records; others feature hands-on science exhibits. The buildings themselves are equally impressive and eclectic. Uptown, the **Guggenheim**'s spiral is a real jaw-dropper, and the granite cube of the **Whitney Museum**, with its cyclops-eye window and concrete moat, is a striking contrast to the surrounding architecture.

It is usually self-defeating to try to cram several museum visits into a single day, or even to try to see every exhibit at major museums, such as the **Metropolitan Museum of Art** or the **American Museum of Natural History**. Pace yourself: Some museums have excellent cafés or restaurants, so you can break for coffee or a complete meal. Café Sabarsky at the **Neue Galerie**, the Museum Café in the **Morgan Library** and the **Jewish Museum**'s Café Weissman are all good reasons to take a breather from the collections. And while it might be traditional to save museum trips for a rainy day, most also offer a gloriously air-conditioned respite from the summer heat.

Although entry usually costs no more than the price of a movie ticket, museum admission prices may still come as a shock to visitors. This is because most New York museums are funded privately and not with government money; in fact, the **New-York Historical Society**, the city's oldest museum, had to close for two years when funding fell short (it is now open again). Even so, most of the city's

major art institutions, including the Whitney, the **Museum of Modern Art** and the **International Center for Photography** *(see page 255),* offer the public at least one evening a week when admission is free or by voluntary donation. And while the city's crown jewel, the Metropolitan Museum, has a suggested $10 donation, it is pay-what-you-wish at all times. That means you can get in for as little as 25 cents!

Many of New York's best-known museums—such as the **Frick Collection**, the Morgan Library, the **Schomburg Center for Research in Black Culture** *(see page 88),* the Whitney and the Guggenheim—began as private collections. **The Cloisters**, at the northern reaches of Manhattan in Fort Tryon Park, was John D. Rockefeller's gift to the city. Its reconstructed medieval monastery houses the Met's beautiful collection of that period's art. When the sun's shining, bring a picnic lunch and inhale the delicate scents of the garden.

Try not to miss the audio tour at the provocative **Ellis Island Museum**, the guided tour at the **Lower East Side Tenement Museum** and the eye-opening exhibitions at the **Museum of Jewish Heritage** *(see pages 40 and 43).* They all give visitors insight into NYC's immigrant history. Across the Hudson River, New Jersey's **Liberty Science Center**, with its interactive exhibits and rooftop terrace overlooking Manhattan and the Statue of Liberty, is an unexpected pleasure. Take the **NY Waterway ferry** *(see page 108)* to get there and admire Lady Liberty during the ride. Don't hesitate to visit the museums if you have kids in tow; most have special events for children, if they aren't already kid-friendly *(see chapter* **Kids' Stuff**).

The prize for most-neglected museum has to go to the **Brooklyn Museum of Art**. Its grandeur is a pleasant surprise as you emerge from the subway station just outside the **Brooklyn Botanic Garden** *(see pages 95 and 96),* yet there's an even greater thrill inside: the excellent exhibits. It's the second-largest museum in New York, but it rarely draws the huge crowds that head for exhibits in Manhattan. And that's a shame, because its Egyptian collection rivals that of the Met, and its recent temporary shows have been first-rate.

▶ See chapter **Art Galleries** for more places to see art.
▶ See chapters **Downtown, Midtown, Uptown** and **The Outer Boroughs** for other sights to see while in the neighborhood.
▶ For reviews and listings of current shows, see *Time Out New York* magazine.
▶ For eating options near museums, see chapter **Restaurants**.
▶ Find out about free museum parties in **Culture clubbing** on page 36.

One of the best features of the city's museums is that they do not rest on their fantastic reputations; they constantly change, expand and enhance themselves. One of the most dramatic examples of this is the American Museum of Natural History's construction of the **Rose Center for Earth and Space**.

Also in expansion mode: MoMA is building a large addition, and has teamed with Queens' hot showcase for young talents, **P.S. 1 Contemporary Art Center**; the **Dia Center for the Arts** plans to open a satellite facility upstate *(see page 255)*.

Most New York museums are closed on New Year's Day, Presidents' Day, Memorial Day, Independence Day, Labor Day, Columbus Day, Thanksgiving and Christmas Day *(see page 363)*. Some change their hours in summer, so it's wise to check before setting out.

Major institutions

American Museum of Natural History

Central Park West at 79th St (212-769-5000, recorded information 212-769-5100; www.amnh.org). Subway: B, C to 81st St–Museum of Natural History; 1, 2 to 79th St. Sun–Thu 10am–5:45pm; Fri, Sat 10am–8:45pm. Suggested donation $10, seniors and students $7.50, children $6. AmEx, MC, V.

The fun begins right in the main rotunda, as a towering barosaur, rearing high on its hind legs, protects its young from an attacking allosaurus. It's an impressive welcome to the largest museum of its kind in the world and a reminder to visit the dinosaur halls on the fourth floor. During the museum's mid-1990s renovation (by the firm responsible for much of the Ellis Island Museum), several specimens were remodeled in light of recent discoveries. The Tyrannosaurus rex, for instance, was once believed to have walked upright, Godzilla-style; now it stalks, head down, with its tail parallel to the ground and is altogether more menacing. The rest of the museum is equally dramatic. The Hall of Biodiversity examines world ecosystems and environmental preservation. The spectacular $210-million Rose Center for Earth and Space is a giant silvery globe where you can learn about the universe through 3-D shows in the Hayden Planetarium and light shows in the Big Bang Theater. The stunning collection of gems includes the obscenely large Star of India blue sapphire. An IMAX theater shows bigger-than-life nature programs *(see pages 274 and 276)*, and there are always innovative temporary exhibitions, in addition to an easily accessible research library with vast photo and print archives and a friendly, helpful staff.

Brooklyn Museum of Art

200 Eastern Pkwy at Washington Ave, Prospect Heights, Brooklyn (718-638-5000; www.brooklynart.org). Subway: 1, 2 to Eastern Pkwy–Brooklyn Museum; weekends only, a free shuttle bus runs hourly between the museum and Grand Army Plaza subway station. Wed–Fri 10am–5pm; Sat, Sun 11am–6pm; first Saturday of each month 11am–11pm. $6, seniors and students $3, under 12 free. Cash only.

The Brooklyn Museum, founded 177 years ago, appended the word *Art* to its name in 1977 to draw wider attention to the world-class collections inside this gorgeous 19th-century Beaux Arts building. The African art and pre-Colombian textile galleries are especially impressive, and the Native American collection is outstanding. There are extensive holdings of American painting and sculpture by such masters as Winslow Homer, Thomas Eakins and John Singer Sargent. Don't miss the Egyptian galleries: The Rubin Gallery's gold-and-silver–gilded ibis coffin, for instance, is sublime. Two floors up, the Rodin sculpture court is further beautified with paintings by French contemporaries such as Degas and Monet. Also, stop by the informal café (which closes at 4pm) and children's museum.

The Cloisters

Fort Tryon Park, Fort Washington Ave at Margaret Corbin Plaza, Washington Heights (212-923-3700; www.metmuseum.org). Travel: A to 190th St, then take the M4 bus or follow Margaret Corbin Dr north (approximately the length of five city blocks) to the museum. Mar–Oct Tue–Sun 9:30am–5:15pm; Nov–Feb Tue–Sun 9:30am–4:45pm. Suggested donation $10 (includes admission to the Metropolitan Museum of Art on the same day), seniors and students $5, under 12 free if accompanied by an adult. Cash only.

The Cloisters houses the Met's medieval art and architecture collections in an unexpectedly tranquil setting. The museum, overlooking the Hudson

Grass appeal Whether you're alone or in a group, the manicured lawns of the Cloisters are primo reading-and-reclining spaces.

Reflective moment The New Museum of Contemporary Art is your window on the cutting edge.

River, is a convincing medieval structure (using elements from five actual cloisters in France), even though it was constructed a mere 60 years ago. Don't miss the famous unicorn tapestries or the *Annunciation Triptych* by Robert Campin.

Cooper-Hewitt, National Design Museum

2 E 91st St at Fifth Ave (212-849-8400; www.si.edu/ndm). Subway: 6 to 96th St. Tue 10am–9pm; Wed–Sat 10am–5pm; Sun noon–5pm. $8, seniors and students $5, under 12 free. Tue 5–9pm free. Cash only.

The Smithsonian's National Design Museum is worth a visit for both its content and architecture. The late 19th-century building once belonged to Andrew Carnegie, and architects responded to his request for "the most modest, plainest and roomy house in New York" by designing a 64-room mansion in the style of a Georgian country house. Recent exhibitions have included the first public viewing of early 20th-century Austrian, Czech and German glass, not to mention a retrospective of Alexander Girard, the father of modern design. This is the only museum in the U.S. devoted exclusively to historical and contemporary design; its changing exhibitions are

always interesting. Sign language interpretation is available upon request *(212-849-8387)*.

Frick Collection

1 E 70th St between Fifth and Madison Aves (212-288-0700; www.frick.org). Subway: N, R, W to Fifth Ave–60th St; 6 to 68th St–Hunter College. Tue–Sat 10am–6pm; Sun 1–6pm. $10, seniors and students $5, children 10–16 must be accompanied by an adult, under 10 not admitted. Cash only.

The opulent residence housing this private, predominantly Renaissance collection is more like a stately home than a museum (the dwelling was built for industrialist Henry Clay Frick). American architect Thomas Hastings designed the 1914 building in an 18th-century European style. The permanent display of paintings, sculptures and furniture are world-class—among them works by Gainsborough, Rembrandt, Renoir, Vermeer, Whistler and the French cabinetmaker Jean-Henri Riesener. The indoor garden court and reflecting pool are especially lovely.

Guggenheim

See **Solomon R. Guggenheim Museum**, page 36.

Metropolitan Museum of Art

1000 Fifth Ave at 82nd St (212-535-7710; www.metmuseum.org). Subway: 4, 5, 6 to 86th St. Tue–Thu, Sun 9:30am–5:30pm; Fri, Sat 9:30am–9pm. Suggested donation $10, seniors and students $5, under 12 free. Cash only. No strollers on Sundays.
It could take days, even weeks, to cover the Met's 1.5 million square feet (139,355 square meters) of exhibition space, so try to be selective. Egyptology fans should head straight for the Temple of Dendur. There's an excellent Islamic art collection, along with more than 3,000 European paintings, including major works by Brueghel, Goya, Manet, Rembrandt, Tiepolo and Vermeer (five of them, including *Young Woman with a Water Jug*). The Greek and Roman halls have received an exquisite face-lift, and the museum has also been adding to its galleries of 20th-century painting. Each year, a selection of contemporary sculptures is installed in the open-air roof garden *(May to October);* have a sandwich there while taking in the panorama of Central Park. On weekend evenings, enjoy a classical quintet performing on the mezzanine overlooking the Great Hall. And don't forget the Costume Institute or the Howard Gilman Photography Gallery. Foreign-language tours are available *(212-570-3711).*

The Morgan Library

29 E 36th St between Madison and Park Aves (212-685-0008; www.morganlibrary.org). Subway: 6 to 33rd St. Tue–Thu 10:30am–5pm; Fri 10:30am–8pm; Sat 10:30am–6pm; Sun noon–6pm. $8, seniors and students $6, under 12 free. Cash only.
This complex houses a museum and an extraordinary literary-research facility. You enter through the Classical Revival building that J.P. Morgan Jr. had built in 1928 (on the site of his father's home) to make J. Pierpont Morgan Sr.'s collection available to the public. Adjacent is the Charles McKim–designed Italianate building that was the famous financier's private library. A subtly colorful marble rotunda with a carved 16th-century Italian ceiling separates the three-tiered library from the rich-red study. Mostly gathered during Morgan's trips to Europe, the collection includes three Gutenberg bibles, original Mahler manuscripts and the gorgeous silver, copper and cloisonné 12th-century Stavelot triptych. Guided tours are available Tuesday through Friday at noon. There's also a modern conservatory, with a tranquil courtyard café.

Museum of Modern Art

11 W 53rd St between Fifth and Sixth Aves (212-708-9400; www.moma.org). Subway: E, V to Fifth Ave–53rd St. Sun–Tue, Thu, Sat 10:30am–5:45pm; Fri 10:30am–8:15pm. $12, seniors and students $8.50, under 16 free. Fri 4:30–8:15pm voluntary donation. Cash only.
The Museum of Modern Art, or MoMA for short, contains the world's finest, most comprehensive holdings of 20th-century art. The permanent collection is exceptionally strong on pieces by Matisse, Miró, Picasso (his *Les Desmoiselles d'Avignon*

hangs here) and later modernists. The photography department has major works by just about every important figure in the medium. The outstanding film-and-video department (it has more than 14,000 films) hosts 20-plus screenings each week *(see page 277)*. A sculpture touch-tour for visually impaired visitors is available by appointment *(212-708-9864)*. MoMA will close in May 2002 for a major renovation and will open a temporary home in Queens *(45-20 33rd St off Queens Blvd; see* **Go to the art of Queens,** *page 102).* The museum will reopen on 53rd Street in 2005.
Other location ● *P.S. 1 Contemporary Art Center, 22-25 Jackson Ave at 46th Ave, Long Island City, Queens (718-784-2084; www.ps1.org). Subway: E, V to 23 St–Ely Ave; G to Court Sq; 7 to 45th Rd–Court House Sq. Wed–Sun noon–6pm. Suggested donation $4, seniors and students $2. Cash only.*
Known for its cutting-edge exhibitions and international studio program, this contemporary-art space was acquired by MoMA in 1999.

National Museum of the American Indian

George Gustav Heye Center, Alexander Hamilton Custom House, 1 Bowling Green between State and Whitehall Sts (212-514-3700; www.nmai.si.edu). Subway: N, R to Whitehall St; 4, 5 to Bowling Green. Mon–Wed, Fri–Sun 10am–5pm; Thu 10am–8pm. Free.
This branch of the Smithsonian Institution's huge organization of museums and research institutes occupies two floors of the grand rotunda in the 1907 Custom House. Located just around the corner from Battery Park, the museum has a permanent collection of documents and artifacts that offers insights into Native American history. Exhibitions are thoughtfully explained, usually by Native Americans. Of special interest is "All Roads Are Good," which reflects the personal choices of storytellers, weavers, anthropologists and tribal leaders. Only 500 of the collection's 1 million objects are on display at any time, which is one reason that, despite the building's lofty proportions, the museum seems

Cheap tix

If you're planning a multimuseum tour over several days that includes the American Museum of Natural History, the Museum of Modern Art, the Guggenheim Museum and the *Intrepid* Sea-Air-Space Museum, it's worth buying a CityPass for $38 ($28 for children ages 12–17); you can go to all four, with the Empire State Building Observatory and a two-hour Circle Line Harbor Cruise thrown in. It's available at the entrance of the participating attractions or online at www.citypass.com.

small. A main branch, on the Mall in Washington, D.C., will open in 2002.

New Museum of Contemporary Art

583 Broadway between Houston and Prince Sts (212-219-1222; www.newmuseum.org). Subway: F, V, S to Broadway–Lafayette St; N, R to Prince St; 6 to Bleecker St. Tue–Sun noon–6pm; Thu noon–8pm. $6, seniors and students $3, under 18 free. Thu 6–8pm free. AmEx, DC, Disc, MC, V.

Since its founding in 1977, this Soho institution has been a magnet for controversy. It quickly became a lightning rod for its fusion of art, technology and political correctness in major group shows that gravitate toward experimental, conceptual and multimedia works. Even its window displays draw crowds. The museum continues to mount important mid-career retrospectives for underrecognized artists, although it has adopted a broader, more international outlook. A retrospective of South African artist William Kentridge in 2001 was particularly successful, and the museum keeps itself on the cutting edge with its new Media Z Lounge, which houses exhibitions of digital art.

Solomon R. Guggenheim Museum

1071 Fifth Ave at 89th St (212-423-3500; www.guggenheim.org). Subway: 4, 5, 6 to 86th St. Sun–Wed 9am–6pm; Fri, Sat 9am–8pm. $15, seniors and students $12, under 12 free and must be accompanied by an adult. Fri 6–8pm voluntary donation. AmEx, MC, V.

Even if you don't want to pay to see the collection inside, visit this uptown museum to admire the white building coiled among the 19th-century mansions on Fifth Avenue. Designed by Frank Lloyd Wright, the Guggenheim is itself a stunning piece of art. In addition to works by Degas, Kandinsky, Manet, Picasso and Van Gogh, the museum owns Peggy Guggenheim's trove of Cubist, Surrealist and Abstract Expressionist works and the Panza di Biumo collection of American Minimalist and Conceptual art from the 1960s and '70s. The photography collection began with the donation of more than 200 works by the Robert Mapplethorpe Foundation. In 1992, a new ten-story tower increased the museum's space, which now includes a sculpture gallery (with views of Central Park) and a café. Since then, the Guggenheim has made news with its ambitious global expansion, its penchant for sweeping historical presentations (such as its overview of 5,000 years of Chinese art) and its in-depth retrospectives of such major American artists as Robert Rauschenberg. The Soho branch opened in 1992 to showcase selections from the permanent collection, as well as to mount temporary exhibitions.

Other location ● *Guggenheim Museum Soho, 575 Broadway at Prince St (212-423-3500). Subway: N, R to Prince St. Call for hours. $5, seniors and*

Culture clubbing

Museum parties give nightspots a run for their money

Are you the kind of visitor who likes some pop with your culture? Are you roaming the galleries all afternoon and haunting the dance clubs until dawn? Well, now you can have your art and party, too. Institutions from Battery Park to Long Island City are opening their doors to carousers and featuring live bands, signature cocktails, exotic munchies and more. Free with museum admission or a small donation, these regular events are perfect for budget travelers with great expectations. So peruse your Picassos, down a Brooklyn Lager and satisfy your low- *and* highbrow cravings.

Fab Fridays

See **Whitney Museum of American Art**, *page 37. Fri 6–9pm. Pay what you wish.*
Descend into the Whitney's Sculpture Court for a night of live jazz, fancy snacks or an infamous Whitney Twist cocktail (actually a Cosmopolitan). You can also stroll through current exhibitions while you mingle with a regular throng of young Upper East Siders. Special evenings may include Broadway themes, with the soundtracks of hit musicals, such as *The Rocky Horror Show* and *Mamma Mia!*, blasting.

First Saturdays

See **Brooklyn Museum of Art**, *page 33. Oct–Aug, first Saturday of the month, 6–11pm. Free.*
Three years old, BMA's First Saturdays party is a hot stop for hip city singles looking for a little action of the cultured kind. Live orchestras, art lectures, wine tastings and dance lessons are just some of the activities visitors can expect. The in-house Mummy's Café offers salads, sandwiches and drinks, while a cash bar serves wine and beer.

Music of the Sea

See **South Street Seaport Museum**, *page 43. Jun–Aug Tue 6–8pm; Oct–May, first Sunday of every month 3–5pm. $3 donation.*

students $3, under 12 free and must be accompanied by an adult. AmEx, MC, V.

Studio Museum in Harlem

144 W 125th St between Malcolm X Blvd (Lenox Ave) and Adam Clayton Powell Jr Blvd (Seventh Ave) (212-864-4500; www.studiomuseuminharlem.org). Subway: 1 to 125th St. Wed, Thu noon–6pm; Fri noon–8pm; Sat, Sun 10am–6pm. $5, seniors $3, under 12 $1. First Saturday of each month free. Cash only.

Opened in 1968, the Studio Museum was the first black fine-arts museum in the country. Today, it shows exhibitions by African-American, African and Caribbean artists, and continues its prestigious artists-in-residence program. And with the recent arrival of a new staff that includes eminent curator Thelma Golden (her major debut, "Freestyle," was a show of important younger artists), the museum is in the forefront of an arts revival on 125th Street.

Whitney Museum of American Art

945 Madison Ave at 75th St (212-570-3600, recorded information 212-570-3676; www.whitney.org). Subway: 6 to 77th St. Tue–Thu, Sat, Sun 11am–6pm; Fri 1–9pm. $10, seniors and students $8, under 12 free. Fri 6–9pm voluntary donation. AmEx, MC, V.

Like the Guggenheim, the Whitney sets itself apart with its unique architecture: a gray granite cube designed by Marcel Breuer. Inside, the Whitney is a world unto itself, one whose exhibitions not only measure the historical importance of American art but also mirror current culture. When Gertrude Vanderbilt Whitney, a sculptor and art patron, opened the museum in 1931, she dedicated it to living American artists; its first exhibition showed the work of eight such talents. Today, the Whitney holds about 12,000 pieces by nearly 2,000 artists, including Jean-Michel Basquiat, Edward Hopper (the museum owns his entire estate), Jasper Johns, Alice Neel, Georgia O'Keeffe, Jackson Pollock and Andy Warhol. The museum is also perhaps the country's foremost showcase for American independent film and video artists. Still, the Whitney's reputation rests mainly on its temporary shows, particularly the show everyone loves to hate: the Biennial. Held every other year, it remains the most prestigious assessment of contemporary American art in the U.S. (It runs March through May in 2002.) There are free guided tours daily. Sarabeth's *(212-570-3670)*, the museum's café, is open daily till 4:30pm and offers an up-from-below view of Madison Avenue, along with excellent—if pricey—food. The Whitney's midtown branch, in a lobby gallery, mounts four shows a year of solo projects by contemporary artists. The space also showcases pieces from the uptown location's permanent collection.

Other location ● *Whitney Museum of American Art at Philip Morris, 120 Park Ave at 42nd St (212-878-2550). Subway: S, 4, 5, 6, 7 to 42nd St–Grand Central. Mon–Wed, Fri 11am–6pm; Thu 11am–7:30pm. Sculpture court Mon–Sat 7:30am–9:30pm; Sun 11am–7pm. Free.*

In the tradition of early American and European sailors who sang as they sailed, the New York Packet maritime music group gathers in one of the museum's three waterside galleries to perform old-fashioned chorus singalongs for audiences of all ages, You can join in on deep-water chanteys, immigrant ballads and songs from New York's early music halls.

Starry Nights: Fridays Under the Sphere

*See **Rose Center for Earth and Space, American Museum of Natural History**, page 33. Fri 5:45–8:15pm. Free with admission: $10, seniors and students $7.50, children $6.*

If the Rose Center's towering moon rocks and psychedelic flat screens don't send you into orbit, this night of live world music, wine and gourmet finger food should do the job. Starry Nights' eclectic musical program, ranging from Brazilian jazz to Baroque chamber quintets, is topped only by the surrounding technology. Glowing star charts, 3-D planet maps and self-contained biospheres keep the steady crowd happy until the real stars come out.

Summer Warm Up

*See **Museum of Modern Art, P.S. 1 Contemporary Art Center**, page 35. Jul–Aug Sat 3–9pm. $5. Jul–Aug Sat 3–9pm. $5.*

The folks at P.S. 1 describe this popular event as a Saturday-night "warm-up," but for most, this energetic dance party is diversion enough for one evening. Each year, the museum chooses an architect to create an environment in the 5,000-square-foot courtyard. Live DJs spin nearby on a sand-filled dance floor, while nonstop barbecue and Brooklyn Brewery lager fuel the revelers.

Worldbeat Jazz

*See **Solomon R. Guggenheim Museum**, page 36. Fri 6–8pm pay what you wish.*

A stamping ground for jazz duos and trios from all over the globe, the Gugg's musical event is often tied to an exhibition. The 2001 season focused on Brazilian jazz (with caipirinhas to boot) while "Brazil: Body and Soul" was on view. Three things that are constant: great music, refreshments and a well-educated under-35 crowd.

Art & design

American Academy of Arts and Letters

155th St between Broadway and Riverside Dr (212-368-5900). Subway: 1 to 157th St. Mid-Mar–mid-Jun Thu–Sun 1–4pm. Free.
This organization honors 250 American writers, composers, painters, sculptors and architects. Henry James, Mark Twain and Edith Wharton were once members; today's list includes John Guare, Alison Lurie, Terrence McNally and Kurt Vonnegut. It's not actually a museum, but there are annual exhibitions open to the public. A magnificent library of original manuscripts and first editions is open to researchers by appointment only.

American Craft Museum

40 W 53rd St between Fifth and Sixth Aves (212-956-3535; www.americancraftmuseum.org). Subway: E, V to Fifth Ave–53rd St. Mon–Wed, Fri–Sun 10am–6pm; Thu 10am–8pm. $7.50, seniors and students $4, under 12 free. Cash only.
This is the country's leading art museum for 20th-century crafts in clay, fiber, glass, metal and wood. There are temporary shows on the four spacious floors, and one or two exhibitions from the permanent collection each year that concentrate on a specific medium. The small gift shop sells some unexpectedly stylish jewelry and ceramics.

American Folk Art Museum

45 W 53rd St between Fifth and Sixth Aves (212-977-7170; www.folkartmuseum.org). Subway: E, V to Fifth Ave–53rd St. Tue–Sun 10am–6pm; Fri 10am–8pm. $9, seniors and students $5, under 12 free. AmEx, MC, V.
Art is everywhere in the new American Folk Art Museum (which got a name change from the Museum of American Folk Art, along with a new address). Designed by architects Billie Tsien and Tod Williams, the eight-floor building is four times larger than the original Lincoln Center location (which is now a second branch of the museum) and includes a café. The exhibits are exquisite; among the more recent breakthrough shows was an influential retrospective of self-taught Chicago-based outsider artist Henry Darger. The range of decorative, practical and ceremonial folk art encompasses pottery, trade signs, delicately stitched log-cabin quilts and even windup toys. There's a schedule of public programs in the auditorium, including lectures, demonstrations and performances, and there's a gift shop next door.
Other location ● *2 Lincoln Sq, Columbus Ave between 65th and 66th Sts (212-595-9533). Subway: 1, 2 to 66th St–Lincoln Ctr. Mon 11am–6pm; Tue–Sun 11am–7:30pm. $3 suggested donation. Cash only.*

Dahesh Museum

601 Fifth Ave between 48th and 49th Sts (212-759-0606; www.daheshmuseum.org). Subway: B, D, F, V to 47–50th Sts–Rockefeller Ctr. Tue–Sat 11am–6pm. Free.
This jewel-box museum houses the private collection of Salim Moussa Achi, a Lebanese philosopher with a consuming passion for European academic art. The collection focuses on Orientalism, landscapes, scenes of rural life, and historical or mythical images painted by artists from the 19th and early-20th centuries whose work you won't see in other public collections.

Forbes Magazine Galleries

62 Fifth Ave at 12th St (212-206-5548). Subway: L, N, Q, R, W, 4, 5, 6 to 14th St–Union Sq. Tue, Wed, Fri, Sat 10am–4pm. Free. Under 16 must be accompanied by an adult. No strollers, no photos.
The late magazine publisher Malcolm Forbes assembled this wonderful private collection of treasures. Besides toy boats and soldiers, the galleries showcase historic presidential letters and—best of all—a dozen Fabergé eggs and other superbly intricate pieces by the famous Russian jeweler and goldsmith Peter Carl Fabergé. Gallery hours are subject to change, so call before visiting.

Isamu Noguchi Garden Museum

36-01 43rd Ave at 36th St, Long Island City, Queens (718-721-1932; www.noguchi.org). Travel: 7 to 33rd St. Wed–Fri 10am–5pm; Sat, Sun 11am–6pm. Suggested donation $4, seniors and students $2. Cash only.
Sculptor Isamu Noguchi designed stage sets for Martha Graham and George Balanchine, as well as sculpture parks and immense works of great simplicity and beauty. The artist's Astoria studios, a showcase for his pieces, are closed for renovation until 2003; meantime, this temporary loft space in Long Island City features selected sculptures from Noguchi's permanent collection. There's a guided tour at 2pm.

Municipal Art Society

457 Madison Ave between 50th and 51st Sts (212-935-3960, tour information 212-439-1049; www.mas.org). Subway: E, V to Fifth Ave–53rd St; 6 to 51st St. Mon–Wed, Fri, Sat 11am–5pm. Free.
This center for urban design, founded in 1980, functions as a gallery, bookshop and lecture forum. It specializes in exhibitions on architecture, public art and community-based projects. The society's greatest attraction may be its location: inside the historic Villard Houses, opposite St. Patrick's Cathedral *(see page 74).*

The Museum at FIT

Seventh Ave at 27th St (212-217-7999; www.fitnyc.edu). Subway: 1, 2 to 28th St. Tue–Fri noon–8pm; Sat 10am–5pm. Free.
The Fashion Institute of Technology houses one of the world's most important collections of costumes and textiles. Recently, many exhibitions have been devoted to showing a single designer's work, although several intriguing ones have had a broader scope: the history of corsets, a look at the importance of the little black dress and the influence of British fashion.

National Academy of Design

1083 Fifth Ave at 89th St (212-369-4880;
www.nationalacademy.org). Subway: 4, 5, 6 to
86th St. Wed, Thu, Sat, Sun noon–5pm; Fri
10am–6pm. $8, seniors and students $4.50,
children 6–16 free. Fri 5–8pm free. Cash only.

Housed in an elegant Fifth Avenue townhouse, the
Academy comprises the School of Fine Arts and a
museum containing one of the world's foremost collections of 19th- and 20th-century American art
(painting, sculpture, architectural renderings and
engraving). The permanent collection includes works
by Mary Cassatt, John Singer Sargent and Frank
Lloyd Wright. Temporary exhibitions are impressive.

Neue Galerie

1048 Fifth Avenue at 86th Street (212-628-6200;
www.neuegalerie.org). Subway: 4, 5, 6 to 86th St.
Mon, Fri, Sat 11am–7pm; Sun 1–6pm. $10,
seniors and students $7, children 12–16 must be
accompanied by an adult, children under 12 not
admitted. AmEx, MC, V.

The city's newest museum is also the only one devoted entirely to 20th-century German and Austrian fine
and decorative arts. The brainchild of the late art dealer Serge Sabarsky and cosmetics mogul Ronald S.
Lauder, the Neue Galerie—housed in a renovated
brick-and-limestone mansion built by the architects
of the New York Public Library—has the largest concentration of works by Gustav Klimt and Egon Schiele
outside of Vienna, along with a bookstore, a design
shop and the popular Café Sabarsky, *(212-288-0665)*.
Have hot chocolate and a piece of Sacher torte, or a
full meal of *tafelspitz*.

Nicholas Roerich Museum

319 W 107th St at Riverside Dr (212-864-7752;
www.roerich.org). Subway: 1 to 110th St–Cathedral
Pkwy. Tue–Sun 2–5pm. Donation requested.

Nicholas Roerich was a Russian-born philosopher,
artist, architect, explorer, pacifist and scenery
painter who collaborated with Diaghilev, Nijinsky
and Stravinsky. The Roerich Peace Pact of 1935,
an international agreement on the protection of
cultural treasures, earned him a Nobel Peace Prize
nomination. Roerich's wife bought this charming
townhouse specifically to house and exhibit her
late husband's possessions. Paintings are mostly
from his Tibetan travels and reveal his interest
in mysticism. It's a fascinating place, although
Roerich's (admittedly intriguing) life story tends to
overshadow the museum.

Queens Museum of Art

New York City Building, park entrance at 49th Ave
and 111th St, Flushing Meadows–Corona Park,
Queens (718-592-9700; www.queensmuse.org).
Subway: 7 to 111th St. Tue–Fri 10am–5pm; Sat,
Sun noon–5pm. Suggested donation $5, seniors
and students $2.50, under 5 free. Cash only.

Located on the site of the 1964–65 World's Fair, the
Queens Museum features art collections and fine, site-
specific temporary exhibitions. The best thing is the
permanent miniature scale model of New York City.
It's fun to search for where you're staying—rent
binoculars for $1 a pair. Dusk falls every 15 minutes,
revealing tiny illuminated buildings and a fluorescent
Central Park. The model is constantly updated; there
had been about 60,000 changes at the last count.

Five Tastes

Nippon nook Bamboo adds a natural Far Eastern touch to the Japan Society.

Sightseeing

Arts & culture

Historical

American Numismatic Society

Audubon Terrace, Broadway at 155th St (212-234-3130; www.amnumsoc.org). Subway: C to 155th St; 1 to 157th St. Tue–Fri 9am–4:30pm. Free.
The collection covers 26 centuries of cash and coins.

Brooklyn Historical Society

128 Pierrepont St at Clinton St, Brooklyn Heights, Brooklyn (718-222-4111; www.brooklynhistory.org). Subway: M, N, R to Court St; 1, 2, 4, 5 to Borough Hall. Mon, Thu–Sat noon–5pm. $2.50. Mondays free. Cash only.
What do Woody Allen, Mel Brooks and Mae West have in common? They were all born in Brooklyn. Thus they merit tributes in this small museum dedicated to Brooklyn's past glories. The society's historic terra-cotta brownstone is undergoing a renovation and is scheduled to reopen in autumn 2002. The society also leads $10 walking tours.

CRITICS' PICKS Museums

You'll find these museums are the best...

...for bare-bones history
American Museum of Natural History, page 33

...for a taste of Harlem
Studio Museum in Harlem, page 37

...for a rainy day
Metropolitan Museum of Art, page 35

...for a Monday (when most museums are closed)
Museum of Modern Art, page 35

...for when you want to have a picnic, too
The Cloisters, page 33

...for a crowd-free experience
The Frick Collection, page 34

...for a reel-informative look at cinema
American Museum of the Moving Image, page 44

...for a day on the waterfront
Intrepid Sea-Air-Space Museum, page 44

...for a tribute to New York's bravest
New York City Fire Museum, page 45

Fraunces Tavern Museum

54 Pearl St at Broad St (212-425-1778). Subway: J, M, Z to Broad St; 4, 5 to Bowling Green. Tue–Fri 10am–5pm; Sat noon–4:45pm. $3, seniors and students $2. Cash only.
This tavern used to be George Washington's watering hole (the renovated restaurant on the ground floor serves upscale American food) and was a prominent meeting place for anti-British groups before the Revolution. Most of its artifacts are displayed in period rooms in the 18th-century building, which is partly reconstructed.

Lower East Side Tenement Museum

90 Orchard St at Broome St (212-431-0233; www.tenement.org). Subway: F to Delancey St; J, M, Z to Delancey–Essex Sts. Visitor center Tue–Fri 1–4pm; Sat, Sun 11am–4:30pm. $9, seniors and students $7. AmEx, MC, V.
This 1863 tenement building, in the heart of what was once Little Germany, is accessible by guided tour only. Tue–Fri 1, 1:30, 2, 2:30, 3, 4pm; Sat, Sun every 30 minutes 11am–4:30pm: "Tour of a 19th-Century Tenement." Hour-long tours of the Baldizzi, Gumpertz and Rogarshevsky apartments tell the true stories of a Sicilian Catholic family, a German-Jewish dressmaker and an Orthodox Jewish brood. Book ahead—the tours sell out. A family-oriented tour runs Saturdays and Sundays every hour from noon to 3pm *(see page 292)*. The museum also has a gallery, shop and video room, and leads a one-hour walking tour of the Lower East Side.

Merchant's House Museum

29 E 4th St between Bowery and Lafayette St (212-777-1089). Subway: F, V, S to Broadway–Lafayette St; 6 to Bleecker St. Thu–Mon 1–5pm. $5, seniors and students $3, children under 12 free. Cash only.
This is the city's only preserved 19th-century family home, fully stocked with the same furnishings and decorations that filled the house when it was inhabited from 1832 to 1933. Seabury Tredwell is the merchant in question. He made his fortune selling hardware and bought this elegant Greek Revival house in 1835, three years after it was built.

Mount Vernon Hotel Museum and Garden

421 E 61st St between York and First Aves (212-838-6878). Subway: N, R, W to Lexington Ave–59th St; 4, 5, 6 to 59th St. Tue–Sun 11am–4pm. $4, seniors and students $3, children under 12 free. Cash only.
Formerly known as the Abigail Adams Smith Museum, this structure, built in 1799 as a carriage house for Smith (daughter of John Adams, the second president of the U.S.) and her husband, Colonel William Stevens Smith, served as a hotel from 1826 to 1833, and is now a designated historic landmark. The house is filled with period articles and furniture. The museum is run by the Colonial Dames of America.

Museum of American Financial History

28 Broadway at Bowling Green (212-908-4110). Subway: 4, 5 to Bowling Green. Tue–Sat 10am–4pm. Suggested donation $2.

The permanent collection, which traces the development of Wall Street and American financial markets, includes ticker tape from the Crash of 1929, a working model stock ticker and the earliest photograph of Wall Street. The museum also hosts a weekly walking tour of the Financial District, which stops inside the New York Stock Exchange.

Museum of the City of New York

1220 Fifth Ave between 103rd and 104th Sts (212-534-1672; www.mcny.org). Subway: 6 to 103rd St. Wed–Sat 10am–5pm; Sun noon–5pm. Suggested admission $7; seniors, students and children $4; families $12. Cash only.

Several ongoing exhibitions showcase the epic, fascinating history of New York City, including its various arts, subcultures and unique personalities. On permanent display is "New York Toy Stories," a look at the city's depiction in countless children's books.

New-York Historical Society

2 W 77th St at Central Park West (212-873-3400; www.nyhistory.org). Subway: B, C to 81st St–Museum of Natural History. Tue–Sun 10am–5pm. $5, seniors and students $3, children under 12 free when accompanied by an adult. Cash only.

New York's oldest museum, founded in 1804, was one of America's first cultural and educational institutions. With the opening of its new 17,000-square-foot gallery space, the Henry Luce III Center for the Study of American Culture, the NYHS can finally display a sizable share of its treasures. Highlights include George Washington's Valley Forge camp cot, the desk at which Clement Clarke Moore supposedly sat when he wrote "A Visit from St. Nicholas" (" 'Twas the night before Christmas…") and the world's largest collection of Tiffany lamps—135 of them, to be exact. On permanent display: "Kid City," a reproduction of the corner of Broadway and West 82nd Street in 1901, in which kids can open doors, look into mailboxes and "shop" from stores to learn more about New York past and present.

Skyscraper Museum

2 West St at Battery Pl (212-968-1961; www.skyscraper.org). Museum to open in mid-2002.

This museum, currently holding temporary exhibitions in other institutions, turned its gallery into a disaster-relief center following the World Trade Center disaster. Its new permanent home in Battery Park City will open in mid-2002, but through May 2002, the museum will mount a show at the New-York Historical Society *(see above)* on the history and construction of the WTC. The permanent location will have two galleries: one for temporary exhibitions and one for the museum's main exhibition "Skyscraper/City," which illustrates the evolution of New York's skyline—past, present and future—through photos, architectural drawings, builders' records and other artifacts.

South Street Seaport Museum

Visitors' center, 12 Fulton St at South St on the East River (212-748-8600; www.southstseaport.org). Subway: A, C to Broadway–Nassau St; J, M, Z, 1, 2, 4, 5 to Fulton St. Apr 1–Sept 30 10am–6pm. Oct 1–Mar 31 Mon, Wed–Sun 10am–5pm. $5, students $4, children under 12 free. AmEx, MC, V.

The museum sprawls across 11 blocks along the East River—an amalgam of galleries, historic ships, 19th-century buildings and a visitors' center. It's fun to wander around the rebuilt streets and pop in to see an exhibition on tattooing before climbing aboard the four-masted 1911 *Peking.* The Seaport itself is pretty touristy, but still a charming place to spend an afternoon. There are plenty of cafés near the Fulton Fish Market building.

The Statue of Liberty and Ellis Island Immigration Museum

See page 47 for listing.

A visit to Liberty and Ellis Islands is practically required. Inside the statue's pedestal is an interesting museum devoted to Lady Liberty's history. On the way back to Manhattan, the tour boat takes you to the Immigration Museum on Ellis Island, through which more than 12 million people entered the country. The exhibitions are an evocative and moving tribute to anyone who headed for America with dreams of a better life. The $3.50 audio tour is excellent, and available in five languages.

Waterfront Museum

Red Hook Garden Pier, 290 Conover St at Pier 45, Red Hook, Brooklyn (718-624-4719; www.waterfrontmuseum.org). Travel: A, C, F to Jay St–Borough Hall; M, N, R to Court St; 1, 2, 4, 5 to Borough Hall, then B61 bus from either Jay St or Atlantic Ave to Beard St; walk one block west to Conover St; barge is two blocks south. Garden Pier open 24 hours; barge open during special events only. Call for schedule. Garden Pier free, barge admission varies with event.

Documenting New York's history as a port city, this museum is located on a 1914 Lehigh Valley Railroad Barge. Listed on the National Register of Historic Places, it's the only wooden barge of its kind afloat today. Summer weekend activities include a music series and circus performances. Views of Manhattan and New York Harbor are superb. The pier is always accessible, but the museum is open only during events, or by appointment. In June 2002, the barge will go to Albany to have a worm problem treated and undergo preservation work. The museum reopens in November 2002, and events will resume in May 2003.

International

Asia Society and Museum

725 Park Ave at 70th St (212-517-2742; www.asiasociety.org). Subway: 6 to 68th St–Hunter

College. Tue–Thu, Sat, Sun 11am–6pm; Fri 11am–9pm. $7, seniors and students $5, children under 16 free. Fri 6–9pm free. Cash only.

The Asia Society plays an important role in fostering Asian-American relations. It sponsors study missions and conferences, and promotes public programs on both continents. The newly renovated headquarters' expanded galleries show major art exhibitions from public and private collections, including the permanent Mr. and Mrs. John D. Rockefeller III collection of Asian art. Asian musicians and performers often entertain here.

China Institute
125 E 65th St between Park and Lexington Aves (212-744-8181; www.chinainstitute.org). Subway: F to Lexington Ave–63rd St; 6 to 68th St–Hunter College. Mon, Wed, Fri, Sat 10am–5pm; Tue, Thu 10am–8pm; Sun 1–5pm. Suggested donation $3, students $2, children under 12 free. AmEx, MC, V.

Consisting of just two small gallery rooms, the China Institute is somewhat overshadowed by the Asia Society. But its exhibitions, ranging from works by Chinese female artists to selections from the Beijing Palace Museum, are impressive. The society also offers lectures and courses on such subjects as calligraphy, Confucianism and cooking.

El Museo del Barrio
1230 Fifth Ave between 104th and 105th Sts (212-831-7272; www.elmuseo.org). Subway: 6 to 103rd St. Wed–Sun 11am–5pm. $5, seniors and students $3, children under 12 free, when accompanied by an adult. AmEx, MC, V.

At the top of Museum Mile, not far from Spanish Harlem (the neighborhood from which it takes its name), El Museo del Barrio is dedicated to the work of Latino artists in the United States, as well as that of Latin Americans. Pepón Osorio was the subject of a recent exhibition. Typical shows are contemporary and consciousness-raising; El Museo also sponsors annual community events such as the celebration of the Mexican Day of the Dead *(November 1).*

French Institute–Alliance Française
22 E 60th St between Madison and Park Aves (212-355-6160; www.fiaf.org). Subway: N, R, W to Fifth Ave–60th St; 4, 5, 6 to 59th St. Mon–Thu 9am–8pm; Fri, Sat 9am–5pm. Free.

This is the New York home for all things French: The institute (a.k.a. the Alliance Française) holds the city's most extensive all-French library and offers numerous language classes and cultural seminars. There are also French film screenings *(see page 277)* and live dance, music and theater performances.

Garibaldi-Meucci Museum
420 Tompkins Ave between Chestnut and St. Mary's Aves, entrance on Chestnut Ave, Staten Island (718-442-1608). Travel: Staten Island Ferry, then S52 bus to Tompkins Ave. Tue–Sun 1–4:30pm. Suggested donation $3. Cash only.

This Gothic Revival home-turned-museum of Italian inventor Antonio Meucci is also the former refuge of Italian patriot Antonio Garibaldi. You'll find memorabilia that commemorates the lives of both men.

Goethe-Institut/ German Cultural Center
1014 Fifth Ave at 82nd St (212-439-8700; www.goethe.de). Subway: 4, 5, 6 to 86th St. Gallery Mon, Wed, Fri 10am–5pm; Tue, Thu 10am–7pm. Library Mon, Wed, Fri noon–5pm; Tue, Thu noon–7pm. Free.

Goethe-Institut New York is just one branch of a German multinational cultural organization founded in 1951. Located across the street from the Metropolitan Museum of Art in a landmark Fifth Avenue mansion, it mounts shows featuring German-born contemporary artists, as well as concerts, lectures and film screenings *(see page 278).* A library offers books in German or English, in addition to German periodicals, videos and audiocassettes.

Hispanic Society of America
Audubon Terrace, Broadway between 155th and 156th Sts (212-926-2234). Subway: 1 to 157th St. Tue–Sat 10am–4:30pm; Sun 1–4pm. Free.

The Society has the largest combined collection of Spanish art and manuscripts outside Spain. Keep an eye out for two portraits by Goya and the striking bas-relief of Don Quixote in the lobby. The collection is dominated by religious artifacts, including 16th-century tombs from the monastery of San Francisco in Cuéllar, Spain.

International Salsa Museum
2127 Third Ave at 116th St (212-289-1368; www.intlsalsamuseum.homestead.com). Subway: 6 to 116th St. Noon–6:30pm. Suggested donation $3.

This museum in Spanish Harlem is dedicated to all aspects of Latin music. The collection includes musical instruments, photographs, personal mementos, recordings and literature.

Jacques Marchais Museum of Tibetan Art
338 Lighthouse Ave between Manor and Terrace Cts, Staten Island (718-987-3500; www.tibetanmuseum.com). Travel: Staten Island Ferry, then S74 bus to Lighthouse Ave and a 15-minute walk up the hill. Wed–Sun 1–5pm. $5, seniors and students $3, children under 12 $2. Cash only.

This mock hilltop Tibetan temple is worth the hour-and-a-half trip from Manhattan. It contains a fascinating Buddhist altar and the largest collection of Tibetan art in the West, including religious objects, bronzes and paintings. In October, the museum hosts an annual Tibetan festival. The landscaped gardens include a zoo of stone animals (with birdhouses and a wishing well); they also offer good views of New York Harbor.

Japan Society
333 E 47th St between First and Second Aves (212-752-3015; www.japansociety.org). Subway: E, V to Lexington Ave–53rd St; 6 to 51st St. Tue–Fri 11am–

Home of the bravest NYC's fire-fighting past is honored at the New York City Fire Museum.

6pm; Sat, Sun 11am–5pm. $5, seniors and students $3. Cash only.
The Japan Society presents performing arts, lectures, exchange programs and special events, plus exhibitions two to three times a year. The gallery shows traditional and contemporary Japanese art. The society's film center is a major showcase for Japanese cinema in the U.S. *(see page 278)*. There's a library and language center in the lower lobby wing.

Jewish Museum
1109 Fifth Ave at 92nd St (212-423-3200; www.jewishmuseum.org). Subway: 4, 5 to 86th St; 6 to 96th St. Mon–Wed 11am–5:45pm; Thu 11am–8pm; Fri 11am–3pm; Sun 10am–5:45pm. $8, seniors and students $5.50, children under 12 free, when accompanied by an adult. Cash only.
The Jewish Museum, housed in the 1908 Warburg Mansion, has a fascinating collection of art, artifacts and media installations. Recent exhibitions have included a Marc Chagall show, and a look at 19th-century Berlin as a Jewish cultural center. The museum commissions a contemporary artist or group of artists to install a new show each year, and the results are always stellar. The permanent exhibition tracks the Jewish cultural experience through exhibits ranging from a filigreed silver circumcision set to an interactive Talmud and even a Statue of Liberty Hanukkah lamp. Most of this eclectic collection was rescued from European synagogues before World War II. You can refuel at the underground Café Weissman.

Museum for African Art
593 Broadway between Houston and Prince Sts (212-966-1313). Subway: F, V, S to Broadway–Lafayette St; N, R to Prince St; 6 to Bleecker St. Tue–Fri 10:30am–5:30pm; Sat, Sun noon–6pm. $5, seniors and students $2.50. Sundays and third Thursday of each month 5:30–8:30pm free. MC, V ($10 minimum).
This tranquil museum was designed by Maya Lin, who created the stark Vietnam Veterans' Memorial in Washington, D.C. Exhibits change about twice a year; the quality of the work—often from amazing private collections—is high. There's an unusually good bookshop with a children's section.

Museum of Chinese in the Americas
70 Mulberry St at Bayard St, second floor (212-619-4785). Subway: J, M, Z, N, Q, R, W, 6 to Canal St; S to Grand St. Tue–Sat noon–5pm. $3, seniors and students $1, children free.
Located in a century-old former schoolhouse on the culturally rich Lower East Side, the two-room museum concentrates on the experience of Chinese immigrants and Chinese-American history.

Museum of Jewish Heritage: A Living Memorial to the Holocaust
Battery Park City, 18 First Pl at Battery Pl (212-509-6130; www.mjhnyc.org). Subway: J, M, Z to Broad Street; N, R to Whitehall; 1, 2 to Wall Street; 4, 5 to Bowling Green. Sun–Wed 10am–5:45pm; Thu 10am–8pm; Fri, eve of Jewish holidays 10am–3pm. Oct–Apr 11. Fri 10am–3pm. $7, seniors and students $5, children under 4 free. Sundays free. Last admission one hour before closing. AmEx, MC, V.
You don't have to be Jewish to appreciate the contents of this institution, built in a symbolic six-sided shape (recalling the Star of David), under a tiered roof. Opened in 1997, it offers one of the most moving cultural experiences in the city. There are 2,000 photographs, hundreds of cultural artifacts and plenty of archival films that vividly detail the crime against humanity that was the Holocaust. The exhibition continues beyond those dark times to days of renewal, ending in an upper gallery that is flooded with daylight and gives meaningful views of Lady Liberty in the harbor. A rotating temporary display (on topics such as forced Jewish labor in Hungary) adds further depth to the experience. Closed-captioned video is available. Advance ticket purchase is recommended; call the museum *(212-945-0039)* or Ticketmaster *(212-307-4007)*.

Scandinavia House: The Nordic Center in America
58 Park Ave between 37th and 38th Sts (212-779-3587; www.amscan.org). Subway: S, 4, 5, 6, 7 to 42nd St–Grand Central. Tue–Sat 11am–5pm. Suggested donation $3, seniors and students $2.
You'll find all things Nordic—from Ikea designs to the latest in Finnish film—at this new $20-million center, the leading cultural link between the United States and the five Scandinavian countries (Denmark, Finland, Iceland, Norway and Sweden). Scandinavia

House features exhibitions, films, concerts, lectures, symposia and readings for all ages. The AQ Café, operated by the renowned NYC restaurant Aquavit, is a hot lunch spot.

Yeshiva University Museum
Center for Jewish History, 15 W 16th St between Fifth and Sixth Aves (212-294-8330; www.yu.edu/museum). Subway: F, V to 14th St; L to Sixth Ave. Tue, Wed, Sun 11am–5pm; Thu 11am–8pm. $6, seniors and children $4, children under 5 free. Cash only.
The museum usually hosts one major exhibition a year and several smaller ones, mainly on Jewish themes.

Media

American Museum of the Moving Image
35th Ave at 36th St, Astoria, Queens (718-784-0077; www.ammi.org). Subway: G, R, V to Steinway St. Tue–Fri noon–5pm; Sat, Sun 11am–6pm. $8.50, seniors and students $5.50, children 5–18 $4.50, children under 5 free. Cash only. No strollers.
About a 15-minute subway ride from midtown Manhattan, AMMI is one of the city's most dynamic institutions. Built within the restored complex that once housed the original Astoria Studios (where commercial filmmaking got its start and continues today), it offers an extensive daily film-and-video program. The core exhibition, "Behind the Screen," will give you interactive insight into every aspect of the mechanics and history of film production—from directing to sound mixing and marketing. Make your own short at a digital animation stand. The museum has a café, but you may want to try one of the great Greek restaurants nearby (*see chapter* **Restaurants, Queens**).

The Museum of Television & Radio
25 W 52nd St between Fifth and Sixth Aves (212-621-6800; www.mtr.org). Subway: B, D, F to 47-50th Sts–Rockefeller Ctr; E, V to Fifth Ave–53rd St. Tue, Wed, Sat, Sun noon–6pm; Thu noon–8pm; Fri noon–9pm. $6, seniors and students $4, children under 12 $3. Cash only.
This is a working archive of more than 100,000 radio and TV programs. Head to the fourth-floor library and use the computerized system to access a favorite *Star Trek* or *I Love Lucy* episode. The assigned console downstairs will play up to four of your choices within two hours. The radio listening room works the same way. There are also special public seminars and screenings. It's a must-see for TV fans and radioheads.

Military

Intrepid Sea-Air-Space Museum
USS Intrepid, 46th St at the Hudson River, Pier 86 (212-245-0072; www.intrepidmuseum.org). Travel: A, C, E to 42nd St–Port Authority, then M42 bus to Twelfth Ave. Oct 1–Mar 31 Tue–Sun 10am–5pm; Apr 1–Sept 30 Mon–Fri 10am–5pm; Sat, Sun 10am–7pm; last admission one hour before closing. $12; seniors, veterans and students $9; children ages 6–11 $6, ages
2–5 $2, children under 2 and servicepeople on active duty free. AmEx, MC, V.
This museum is located on the World War II aircraft carrier *Intrepid*, whose decks are crammed with space capsules and various aircraft. There are plenty of audiovisual shows, as well as hands-on exhibits appealing to children.

New York Public Library

The multitentacled New York Public Library, founded in 1895, comprises four major research libraries and 82 local and specialty branches, making it the largest and most comprehensive library system in the world. The library grew from the combined collections of John Jacob Astor, James Lenox and Samuel Jones Tilden. Today, it holds 52 million items, including more than 18 million books. About a million items are added to the collection each year. Unless you're interested in a specific subject, your best bet is to visit the system's flagship, officially called the Humanities and Social Sciences Library. The newest branch—the Science, Industry and Business Library—opened in 1996. Information on the entire system is at www.nypl.org.

Donnell Library Center
20 W 53rd St between Fifth and Sixth Aves (212-621-0618). Subway: E, V to Fifth Ave–53rd St. Mon, Wed, Fri 10am–6pm; Tue, Thu 10am–8pm; Sat 10am–5pm. Free.
This branch of the NYPL has an extensive collection of records, films and videotapes, with appropriate screening facilities. The Donnell specializes in foreign-language books—in more than 80 languages—and there's a children's section of more than 100,000 books, films, records and cassettes, as well as the original Winnie the Pooh dolls.

Humanities and Social Sciences Library
455 Fifth Ave at 42nd St (recorded information 212-869-8089). Subway: B, D, F, V to 42nd St; 7 to Fifth Ave. Mon, Thu–Sat 10am–6pm; Tue, Wed 11am–7:30pm. Free.
This landmark Beaux Arts building is what most people mean when they say "the New York Public Library." The famous stone lions out front are wreathed with holly at Christmas; during the summer, people sit on the steps or sip drinks at outdoor tables beneath the arches. Free guided tours (11am and 2pm) include the renovated Rose Main Reading Room and the Bill Blass Public Catalogue Room, where you can surf the Internet. Special exhibitions are frequent and worthwhile, and lectures in the Celeste Bartos Forum are always well-attended.

Library for the Performing Arts
Lincoln Center, 111 Amsterdam Ave between 65th and 66th Sts (212-870-1630). Subway: 1, 2 to 66th St–Lincoln Ctr. Free.
After a three-year, $37-million renovation, this facili-

ty is one of the great research centers in the field of performing arts. The library has huge holdings of audio- and videotapes, films, letters and manuscripts. The Rodgers and Hammerstein Archive Collection of Recorded Sound has 500,000 recordings. Visitors can check out books, scores and recordings, or attend concerts and lectures in the Bruno Walter Auditorium.

Schomburg Center for Research in Black Culture

515 Malcolm X Blvd (Lenox Ave) at 135th St (212-491-2200). Subway: 2, 3 to 135th St. Mon–Wed noon–8pm; Thu–Sat 10am–6pm. Free.

This extraordinary trove of vintage literature and historical memorabilia relating to black culture and the African diaspora was founded in 1926 by its first curator, bibliophile Arthur Schomburg. The center hosts jazz concerts, films, lectures and tours.

Science, Industry and Business Library

188 Madison Ave between 34th and 35th Sts (212-592-7000). Subway: 6 to 33rd St. Mon, Fri, Sat 10am–6pm; Tue–Thu 11am–8pm. Free.

The world's largest public information center devoted to science, technology, economics and business occupies the first floor and lower level of the old B. Altman department store. Opened in 1996, the Gwathmey Siegel–designed branch of the NYPL has a circulating collection of 50,000 books and an open-shelf reference collection of 60,000 volumes. Aiming to help small-business owners, the library also focuses on digital technologies and the Internet. Free 30-minute tours are given on Tuesdays at 2pm.

Science & technology

Liberty Science Center

251 Phillip St, Jersey City, NJ (201-200-1000; www.lsc.org). Travel: PATH to Exchange Pl, then the Lafayette-Greenville Bus Company bus to the museum (call 201-432-8046 for bus schedule). 9:30am–5:30pm. $10, seniors and children 2–18 $8; combined entry to center and IMAX movie $14.50, seniors and children 2–18 $12.50. AmEx, Disc, MC, V.

This excellent museum has innovative exhibitions and America's largest, most spectacular IMAX cinema. From the observation tower, you get great views of Manhattan and an unusual sideways look at the Statue of Liberty. The center emphasizes hands-on science, so get ready to elbow your way among the excited kids. On permanent display is E-Quest: Exploring Earth's Energy. On weekends, take the NY Waterway ferry (800-53-FERRY).

New York Hall of Science

47-01 111th St at 46th Ave, Flushing Meadows–Corona Park, Queens (718-699-0005; www.nyhallsci.org). Subway: 7 to 111th St. Jul 1–Aug 31 Mon 9:30am–2pm; Tue–Sun 9:30am–5pm. Sept 1–Jun 30 Mon–Wed 9:30am–2pm; Thu–Sun 9:30am–5pm. $7.50, seniors and children $5. Sept 1–Jun 30 Thu, Fri 2–5pm free. AmEx, MC, V.

Opened at the 1964–65 World's Fair, the New York Hall of Science has a large collection of interactive science exhibits; it's considered one of the top science museums in the country. The emphasis is on education, and exhibits demystify science for the children who usually fill the place. The 30,000-square-foot outdoor science playground is the largest of its kind in the Western Hemisphere.

Rose Center for Earth and Space

See **American Museum of Natural History**, page 33, for listing.

Urban services

New York City Fire Museum

278 Spring St between Hudson and Varick Sts (212-691-1303; www.nycfiremuseum.org). Subway: C, E to Spring St; 1, 2 to Houston St. Tue–Sat 10am–5pm; Sun 10am–4pm. Suggested donation $4, seniors and students $2, children under 12 $1. AmEx, MC, V.

An active firehouse from 1903 to 1954, the museum displays in equal measure the gadgetry and the pageantry associated with New York fire fighting since colonial times. There are a few vintage fire engines and several displays of fire-fighting ephemera dating back 100 years. The museum is also compiling a permanent exhibit about NYC firefighters' heroic work following the World Trade Center attacks.

New York Police Museum

100 Old Slip between South and Water Sts (212-480-3100; www.nycpolicemuseum.org). Subway: 1, 2 to Wall St. Tue–Sun 10am–6pm. Suggested donation $5.

The NYPD's tribute to itself—which moved to a new, larger venue at the end of 2001—features exhibits on the history of the department and the tools (and transportation) of the trade. It's the only place in the city where the public can buy officially licensed NYPD paraphernalia, such as a lovely police-logo golf shirt.

New York Transit Museum

Corner of Boerum Pl and Schermerhorn St, Brooklyn Heights, Brooklyn (718-243-8601; www.mta.info/museum). Subway: A, C, G to Hoyt-Schermerhorn; M, N, R to Court St; 1, 2, 4, 5 to Borough Hall. Tue–Fri 10am–4pm; Sat, Sun noon–5pm. $3, seniors and children under 17 $1.50. Cash only. Museum closed until 2003.

The Transit Museum, underground in an old 1930s subway station, is closed until 2003 for renovation. The museum's gallery at Grand Central Terminal remains open. One recent exhibition looked at the social and transportation history of past Subway Series (matchups between local baseball teams). **Other location ●** *Grand Central Terminal, 42nd St at Park Ave, adjacent to station master's office off the Grand Concourse (212-878-0106). Subway: S, 4, 5, 6, 7 to 42nd St–Grand Central. Mon–Fri 8am–8pm; Sat 10am–6pm. Free.*

Sightseeing

Downtown

From the high-powered finance and history of Wall Street to the nightly party that is the East Village, you'll cover a lot of ground south of 14th Street

Manhattan grew from the bottom up, so the richest and most diverse concentration of neighborhoods and people is below 14th Street. The World Monuments Fund's 2002 list of 100 Most Endangered Sites includes a special "101st Site"—Historic Lower Manhattan. The gesture is more than a nod to the destruction of the World Trade Center: The area has six historic districts and 65 landmarks. Downtown's crooked streets (most of which have names, not numbers) are made for walking. You can wander for hours ogling the architecture of the Financial District and Civic Center, shopping the trendy boutique-lined streets of Soho and Nolita, exploring the ethnic enclaves of the Lower East Side, enjoying the cafés of Greenwich Village or partying in the punk playground of the East Village.

Battery Park

You'll be most aware that you're visiting an island when you explore the southern tip of Manhattan. The Atlantic breeze blows in over New York Harbor, along the same route taken by the hope-filled millions who arrived here by sea. Trace their journey past the golden torch of the **Statue of Liberty**, through the immigration and quarantine center of **Ellis Island** (now a must-see museum), and on to the statue-dotted promenade of Battery Park. Today, few steamships chug in; instead, the harbor is filled during summer with sailboats and Jet Ski riders who jump the wakes left by motorboats. Seagulls perch on the promenade railing, squawking at fishermen, whose lines might snag a shad or a striped bass (although State Health Department officials recommend not eating these fish more than once a month).

The promenade is also a stage for applause-hungry performers, who entertain people waiting to be ferried to the Statue of Liberty and Ellis Island. The park itself often plays host to international touring events such as the Cirque du Soleil as well as free outdoor music on summer evenings. **Castle Clinton**, situated inside the park, was built in 1811 to defend the city against possible attacks by the British. The castle has since been a theater and an aquarium, but now serves as a visitors' center, with historical displays, a bookstore and a

ticket booth for the Statue of Liberty and Ellis Island tours. To the west is **Pier A** *(22 Battery Pl at West St)*, Manhattan's last Victorian-era pier shed; it's being restored and will someday house restaurants and historic vessels.

Whether or not you join the crowds heading for Lady Liberty, you can walk around the shore (going east), where several ferry terminals jut out into the harbor. The 1954 Whitehall Ferry Terminal is where you board the famous—and free—**Staten Island Ferry** *(see page 108)*. The 20-minute ride to Staten Island offers an unparalleled view of the altered downtown Manhattan skyline and, of course, a look at the iconic statue. The terminal, which was damaged by fire in 1991, remains open as it undergoes reconstruction. When it is completed in late 2003, visitors will enter a 75-foot-high hall that will have sweeping views of the Manhattan skyline and New York Harbor. In the years before the Brooklyn Bridge was built, the beautiful **Battery Maritime Building** *(11 South St between Broad and Whitehall Sts)* was a terminal for many ferry services between Manhattan and Brooklyn. Today, in addition to housing Department of Transportation offices, this is where the ferry to **Governors Island** picks up passengers who have signed up for a monthly guided tour *(see **Isle of might**, page 48)*.

At the southeastern end of the Battery Park promenade is **American Park at the Battery** *(see page 153);* the restaurant's outdoor patio overlooking the harbor is a primo spot to sip a cocktail.

Another patch of grass lies north of Battery Park: The triangle of Bowling Green, the city's oldest extant park, is the front lawn of the beautiful 1907 Beaux Arts Alexander Hamilton Custom House, home to the **National Museum of the American Indian** *(see page 35)*. On the north side of the triangle, sculptor Arturo DiModica's muscular bronze bull represents the snorting power of Wall Street (understandably, the city has never commissioned a *bear* statue).

Other historical sights are close by: the rectory of the **Shrine of Elizabeth Ann Seton** (a 1793 Federal-style building dedicated to the first American-born saint) and **New York Unearthed**, a tiny gallery of urban archaeological finds from the area. The

Sweet land of liberty You get an all-American view of New York Harbor from Battery Park.

Fraunces Tavern Museum *(see page 40)* is a restoration of the alehouse where George Washington celebrated his victory over the British. After a bite, you can peruse the Revolution-era relics displayed in the many period rooms.

The **Stone Street Historic District** surrounds one of Manhattan's oldest roads. The once derelict bit of Stone Street between Coenties Alley and Hanover Square was recently resurfaced with granite paving blocks and outfitted with faux-gaslight lampposts. Upscale spots such as the Fragments jewelry store *(see page 209)* and the Stone Street Tavern *(52 Stone St between Coenties Alley and Hanover Sq, 212-425-3663)* have moved in.

Battery Park
Between State St, Battery Pl and Whitehall St. Subway: N, R to Whitehall St; 4, 5 to Bowling Green.
Even though the park faces New York Harbor, the seagulls and folks fishing for bluefish and striped bass are sure signs of the Atlantic's proximity (just beyond the Verrazano-Narrows Bridge). The harbor itself is gorgeous, and one of the most peaceful experiences you can have in the city is to sit on a bench and look toward the Statue of Liberty, Ellis Island, Staten Island and all the boats bobbing on the water.

New York Unearthed
17 State St, behind Shrine of Elizabeth Ann Seton (212-748-8626). Subway: N, R to Whitehall St. Free.
The South Street Seaport Museum's *(see page 41)* tiny archaeology offshoot has 6,000 years' worth of finds that document New York history.

Shrine of Elizabeth Ann Seton
7 State St between Pearl and Whitehall Sts (212-269-6865). Subway: N, R to Whitehall St. Mon–Fri 6:30am–5pm; Saturdays before and after 12:15pm Mass; Sundays before and after 9am and noon Masses. Free.

The Statue of Liberty & Ellis Island Immigration Museum
212-363-3200; www.ellisisland.org. Travel: N, R to Whitehall St; 4, 5 to Bowling Green, then take Statue of Liberty Ferry, departing every half hour from gangway 4 or 5 in Battery Park at the southern tip of Manhattan. 9am–5:30pm; 3:30pm last trip out. Jun 30–Sept 3 8:30am–6:30pm. Purchase tickets at Castle Clinton in Battery Park. $8, seniors $6, children 3–17 $3, under 3 free. Cash only.
"A big girl who is obviously going to have a baby," wrote James Agate about the Statue of Liberty. "The birth of a nation, I suppose." Get up close to the most symbolic New York structure by visiting the island it stands on (as 5.5 million people did in 2000). Frédéric-Auguste Bartholdi's statue was a gift from the people of France (the framework—which can be seen only if you go inside the statue—was designed by Gustave Eiffel), but it took the Americans years to collect enough money to give Liberty her pedestal. The statue stands just over 111 feet toe to crown; there can be an excruciating wait to climb the 354 steps to the observation deck, so go early (in summer, under normal circumstances, only the first ferry

load each day is granted access to the crown). Due to the events of September 11, 2001, security was tightened for all visits to Liberty Island. At press time, the inside of the statue remained closed to the public. On Ellis Island, you can walk through the restored buildings dedicated to the millions of immigrants who passed through there. Ponder the ghostly personal belongings that people left behind in their hurry to become part of a new nation. It's an arresting and moving museum *(see also page 41)*.

Battery Park City & Ground Zero

Forty years ago, lower Manhattan's west coast was a jumble of 20 collapsing piers. By 1976, landfill (from earth excavated to build the World Trade Center) created 92 acres of land where Battery Park City and the World Financial Center would soon be developed. Across West Street soared the Twin Towers and the 16-acre World Trade Center complex. As every New Yorker, American—and probably everyone on the planet—knows, a terrorist attack on September 11, 2001, destroyed many lives and the towers. Miraculously, everyone in nearby buildings and almost all of those in the floors below the planes' impact points survived. The outpouring of concern for the victims' families—especially those of the heroic firefighters, police officers and other uniformed personnel—was a source of strength to New Yorkers. The neighborhood and the city still feel the repercussions.

As of January 2002, the future of Ground Zero was a hotly contested issue. Developer Larry Silverstein, who bought the 99-year lease on the World Trade Center just six weeks before the attack, wants to redevelop the site (which is owned by the Port Authority of New York and New Jersey), combining two new (shorter) towers with a memorial. Advocates for the families of people who died on September 11, backed by former mayor Rudolph Giuliani, are vocal about dedicating the land exclusively to those who perished. Overseeing all the proposals is the Lower Manhattan Redevelopment Corporation, the commission Giuliani charged with rebuilding the neighborhood. Striking the right balance of interests will be critical in the neighborhood's revival as a round-the-clock community.

The World Trade Center was Battery Park City's portal to the rest of Manhattan—residents

Isle of might

Governors Island has a history-rich past—and a possibly lucrative future

Governors Island, the 172-acre parcel located half a mile from Manhattan's southern tip may be the most coveted piece of real estate in the five boroughs. Called Nut Island by the city's original inhabitants, the Munsee Indians, Governors is a genteel swath of green peppered with 19th-century mansions built for the city's governors of yore, which explains, in part, why everyone wants a piece of it.

Big Onion Walking Tours *(see page 109)* offers a free monthly tour of the island, where tour leader and Big Onion founder Seth Kamil treats visitors to the isle's amazing sights and sight lines. Kamil also points out the following little-know facts: The Wright Brothers launched the first-ever over-water flight from the Governors Island airstrip (the plane circled the Statue of Liberty and landed safely); the military barrack that divides the northern and southern halves of the island is the longest building of its kind in the world; thousands of American troops debarked from the island to fight in World War I; Mikhail Gorbachev and

Ronald Reagan held a famous summit there in the 1980s.

In 1997, after Governors Island had been operating for more than 200 years as a military base—for the Army, from 1794 to 1966, then for the Coast Guard—former president Bill Clinton shut it down and offered to sell the island to the state and city for a dollar—provided the city could pay the annual $40 million upkeep costs and devise a development plan "for the people." Otherwise, it would fall to the hands of private developers, at a cost of up to $300 million. A flurry of activity ensued.

Entrepreneurs have presented proposals that would turn the island into a huge amusement park, to be run by the Swiss company Tivoli; a casino complex (championed by former mayor Rudy Giuliani); and a new United Nations headquarters. Mayor Michael Bloomberg has floated the idea of building high schools on it. Others have cried for factories, to rev up New York's once mighty manufacturing machine. Some real estate developers, with visions of the

would walk across two covered pedestrian bridges to take the subways that stopped beneath the WTC. The north bridge was destroyed, and the subway station is slated to be closed for reconstruction until November 2002, although limited service is now available (specifically, the E train to World Trade Center). The complex where people once came to ascend into the sky now attracts crowds that come to pay their respects at Ground Zero. The recovery and cleanup of the area has progressed at breakneck speed—authorities estimate it will be completed by June 2002. To accommodate visitors, a group of architects (Elizabeth Diller, Kevin Kennon, David Rockwell and Ricardo Scofidio), city agencies and private contractors built a 16-foot-high **Viewing Platform** in December 2001. Some people stand in silent wonder, others gasp; all are awed.

Completed in 1988, the **World Financial Center** is an expression of the city-within-a-city concept. Architect Cesar Pelli's four glass-and-granite postmodern office towers—each crowned with a geometric form—surround an upscale retail area, a series of plazas with terraced restaurants and a marina, where water taxis to New Jersey are docked. The glass-roofed **Winter Garden**, a popular venue for concerts

and other forms of entertainment, was badly damaged in the WTC attack and the center closed. But things move quickly in New York; restaurants and shops such as SouthWestNY *(212-945-0528)* and Godiva Chocolatier *(212-945-2174)* started reopening in February 2002. The Winter Garden is slated to resume its performance schedule in autumn 2002.

Battery Park City was devised by then Governor Nelson Rockefeller and Mayor John Lindsay as the site of apartment housing and schools; its public plazas, restaurants and shopping areas were designed to link with the World Financial Center. The most impressive aspects of Battery Park City have turned out to be the esplanade and park, which run north of the Financial Center along the Hudson River, and connect to Battery Park at the south. In addition to offering inspiring views of the sunset behind **Colgate Center** (look for the huge Colgate sign and clock) and Jersey City, New Jersey, across the river, the esplanade is a paradise for bikers, in-line skaters and joggers—although plain old walking is fun, too. A lot of flesh is exposed to the summer sun here on weekends.

The northern end of the park (officially called **Nelson A. Rockefeller Park**) features the

unbelievable views of downtown dancing in their heads, pushed a new Battery Park City–style development. Advocates for the poor called for public housing—in fact, a block of row houses on the island, built in the 1970s for Coast Guard members, was the model for the sort of low-income townhouse-style development that has taken root in the South Bronx and East New York.

Sticky issues to be resolved include the fact that some of the buildings—including several large homes for officers and numerous other well-preserved 19th-century houses—occupy the third of the island that wasn't created with landfill from the construction of the subway system. That portion is protected as a National Historic District, and the buildings there—which have remained unoccupied for the past seven years—would have to be maintained by whomever took control of the island. Several of those are designated New York City landmarks. This part of the island also contains the two imposing forts—Williams and Jay—which were built to fend off a potential British invasion of New York during the War of 1812, an attack that never materialized.

The other two-thirds is not protected; it was part of the Coast Guard's self-contained

community, which included shops, movie theaters and a golf course. Most plans call for this area's five-story apartment complex to be razed.

Governor Pataki and Mayor Bloomberg were to have made a decision on the island's future by January 2002, but the events of September 11, 2001, pushed the deadline back. This gives preservationists and proponents of open access more time to construct a viable plan to keep it out of the hands of private developers. The general consensus among Governors Island's gadflys and fans is that it will almost certainly become the product of a mixed-use equation; a combination of commercial activity, educational facilities, conference centers and—the crucial issue—public access to all New Yorkers.

In September of 2001, following the cataclysmic events at the World Trade Center, the island temporarily assumed its original function when thousands of military personnel were billeted there. The great news is that Big Onion has secured a new contract with the General Services Administration—which means the monthly tours will be back on track, Kamil hopes, by spring 2002. If you'd like to visit Governors Island, check the Big Onion schedule on its website.

large **North Lawn**, which becomes a surrogate beach in summer. Sunbathers, kite flyers and soccer players all vie for a patch of grass. Basketball and handball courts, concrete tables with chess and backgammon boards painted on them, and playgrounds with swings round out the recreational options available on the esplanade. Tennis courts and baseball fields are nearby, just off West Street at Murray Street. The park ends at Chambers Street, but links with piers to the north, which are slowly being claimed for public use and will eventually become the **Hudson River Park**. Where Battery Park City meets Battery Park are the inventively designed **South Cove** area, the **Robert F. Wagner Jr. Park** (an observation deck offers fabulous views of the harbor and the Verrazano-Narrows Bridge) and New York City's Holocaust museum, the **Museum of Jewish Heritage** (see page 43). The entire park area is dotted with fine art. Most notable is Tom Otterness's whimsical sculptural installation *The Real World Behind the North Lawn*. The park hosts outdoor cultural events during the warmer months.

Wealthy Wall Streeters live in the residential area of Battery Park City; a portion of the high rents is supposed to subsidize public housing elsewhere in the city, though the more than $276 million paid since 1992 has largely gone to other city services. To outsiders, the community feels isolated from the rest of Manhattan (it lies *west* of West Street), and its planned-community aspect feels more suburban than urban. Following September 11th, residents were cut off from the rest of Manhattan, but the minicity is making a quick comeback, and even growing—in January 2002, the posh new **Ritz-Carlton** opened its doors (see page 116).

Battery Park City Authority
212-416-5300; www.batteryparkcity.org.
The neighborhood's official website lists events and has a great map of the area.

Lower Manhattan Cultural Council
212-432-0900; www.lmcc.net.
An arts information service for artists and the public, the LMCC offers information on cultural events happening in and around lower Manhattan.

New York Mercantile Exchange
1 North End Ave at Vesey St, World Financial Center (212-299-2499; www.nymex.com). Subway: A, C, 1, 2 to Chambers St. Mon–Fri 9am–5pm. Free.
Watch from the visitors' galleries as the real drama

of the trading floor unfolds. Manic figures in color-coded blazers scream and shout as they buy and sell billions in oil, gas, electric power and gold commodities. The Exchange also houses a museum that traces the roller-coaster history of this American tradition. The trading-floor action ends in the afternoon, so come early.

World Financial Center & Winter Garden
Hudson River to West St and Albany St to Vesey St (212-945-0505; www.worldfinancialcenter.com). Subway: 4, 5 to Wall St; N, R to Rector St. Free.
Phone for information about the free arts events, which range from concerts to flower shows. Note that the Winter Garden is closed for repairs and may reopen by autumn 2002.

World Trade Center Viewing Platform
Church St at Fulton St. Subway: Subway: 4, 5 to Wall St; N, R to Rector St. Free.
At press time, visitors were required to obtain free tickets at the South Street Seaport ticket booth (see page 52). Every day, tickets are distributed for each half-hour block, noon to 8pm the same day, or 9 to 11:30am the next day. Visitors should not arrive at the platform more than 15 minutes before their allotted time.

Wall Street

Since the city's earliest days as a fur-trading post, wheeling and dealing has been New York's prime pastime, and commerce the backbone of its prosperity. **Wall Street** (or just "the Street," if you want to sound like a local) is the thoroughfare synonymous with the world's greatest capitalist gambling den.

Wall Street itself is actually less than a mile long; it took its name from a wooden defensive wall that the Dutch built in 1653, to mark the northern limit of New Amsterdam. The tip of Manhattan in general is known as the Financial District. In the days before telecommunications, financial institutions established their headquarters here to be near the seaport action. This was where corporate America made its first audacious architectural assertions; there are many great buildings built by grand old banks and businesses.

Notable structures include the old **Merchants' Exchange** at 55 Wall Street (now the **Regent Wall Street**; *see page 129*), with its stacked rows of Ionic and Corinthian columns, giant doors and, inside, a rotunda that holds 3,000 people; the **Equitable Building** *(120 Broadway between Cedar and Pine Sts),* whose greedy use of vertical space helped instigate the zoning laws now governing skyscrapers (stand across the street from the building to get a decent view);

▶ For more about the World Trade Center's place in the city's architectural pantheon, see chapter **Architecture**.

Sitting on the dock of the bay South Street Seaport offers a maritime taste of the city.

and **40 Wall Street** (today owned by real-estate tycoon Donald Trump), which in 1929 went head-to-head with the Chrysler Building in a battle for the mantle of "world's tallest building." (The Empire State Building beat them both a year later.)

The Gothic spire of the Episcopalian **Trinity Church** rises at the western end of Wall Street. It was the island's tallest structure when completed in 1846 (replacing the 1698 building that burned down in 1776), but it's now dwarfed by neighboring skyscrapers. Stop in and see brokers praying that the market gets bullish, or stroll through the adjacent cemetery, where cracked and faded tombstones mark the final resting places of dozens of past city dwellers, including signers of the Declaration of Independence and the U.S. Constitution. **St. Paul's Chapel**, a satellite chapel of Trinity, is an oasis of peace modeled on London's St. Martin-in-the-Fields. The chapel is New York City's only extant pre-Revolutionary building (it dates to 1766), and one of the finest Georgian structures in the country. Miraculously, both landmark churches survived the nearby World Trade Center attack. Though mortar fell from their facades, the steeples remained intact—even St. Paul's Waterford crystal chandeliers hung in without a crack.

A block east of Trinity Church, the **Federal Hall National Memorial** is a Greek Revival shrine to American inaugural history—sort of.

This is the spot where Washington was sworn in as the country's first president on April 30, 1789. The original building was demolished in 1812.

The nerve center of the U.S. economy is the **New York Stock Exchange**. The visitors' center is an excellent resource for those clueless about the daily market machinery, and you can look out over the trading floor in action. (For a lesson on Wall Street's influence through the years, check out the **Museum of American Financial History**.) The exchange is computerized these days, so except for quick rises or big drops in the stock market, it's none too exciting as a spectator sport (for the "Buy! Buy! Buy!" action you've seen in the movies, head to the **New York Mercantile Exchange**; *see page 50*). Far more fun is people-watching on the street outside the NYSE. It's an endless pageant of power, as besuited brokers march up and down Broad Street.

The **Federal Reserve Bank**, a block north on Liberty Street, is an imposing structure built in the Florentine Renaissance style. It holds the nation's largest store of gold—just over 9,000 tons—in a vault five stories below street level (you might have seen Jeremy Irons clean it out in *Die Hard 3*).

Federal Hall National Memorial

26 Wall St at Nassau St (212-825-6888). Subway: 1, 2, 4, 5 to Wall St. Mon–Fri 9am–5pm. Free.

Federal Reserve Bank

33 Liberty St between Nassau and William Sts (212-720-6130; www.ny.frb.org). Subway: 1, 2, 4, 5 to Wall St. Tours Mon–Fri on the half hour, 9:30am–2:30pm. Free.
The free one-hour tours through the bank—and the gold vaults—must be arranged at least two weeks in advance; tickets are sent by mail.

Museum of American Financial History

28 Broadway at Beaver St (212-908-4110; www.financialhistory.org). Subway: 4, 5 to Bowling Green. Tue–Sat 10am–4pm. $2 donation.
This tiny museum and gift shop are located on the ground floor of the Standard Oil Building, the original site of John D. Rockefeller's office. Walking tours are every Friday at 10am.

New York Stock Exchange

20 Broad St at Wall St (212-656-5168; www.nyse.com). Subway: J, M, Z to Broad St; 1, 2, 4, 5 to Wall St. Mon–Fri 8:45am–4:30pm. Free.
A third-floor interactive education center overlooks the trading floor, and there are lots of multimedia exhibits.

St. Paul's Chapel

211 Broadway between Fulton and Vesey Sts (212-602-0874). Subway: A, C to Broadway–Nassau St; J, M, Z, 1, 2, 4, 5 to Fulton St. Mon–Sat 9am–3pm; Sun 7am–3pm.

Trinity Church Museum

Broadway at Wall St (212-602-0872;
www.trinitywallstreet.org). Subway: N, R to
Rector St; 1, 2, 4, 5 to Wall St. Mon–Fri 9–11:45am,
1–3:45pm; Sat 10am–3:45pm; Sun 1–3:45pm;
closed during concerts (Thu 1pm). Free.

The small museum inside Trinity Church chronicles
the parish's past and the role it has played in New
York's history.

The Seaport

While New York's importance as a port has
diminished, its initial fortune rolled in on the
salt water that crashes around its natural
harbor. The city was perfectly situated for trade
with Europe—with goods from middle America
arriving via the Erie Canal and Hudson River.
And because New York was the point of entry
for millions of immigrants, its character was
formed primarily by the waves of humanity
that arrived at its docks.

The **South Street Seaport** is the best place
to see this seafaring heritage. Redeveloped in
the mid-1980s, the Seaport is an area of
reclaimed and renovated buildings converted to
shops, restaurants, bars and a museum. It's not
an area that New Yorkers often visit, though it is
rich in history. The Seaport's public spaces are
a favorite with street performers, and the
shopping area of Pier 17 is little more than a
picturesque tourist trap of a mall by day and a
after-work watering hole by night; outdoor
concerts in the summer do attract New Yorkers
from all over the city. Antique vessels are
docked at other piers. The fascinating
Seaport Museum *(see page 41)*—detailing
New York's maritime history—is located within
the restored 19th-century buildings at
Schermerhorn Row *(2–18 Fulton St, 91–92*
South St and 189–195 Front St), which were
constructed on landfill in 1812. At 11 Fulton
Street, the **Fulton Market** building (with
gourmet food stalls and seafood restaurants that
open onto the cobbled streets in summer) is a
great place for slurping oysters and people-
watching. Upscale brand-name shops such as
J. Crew and Abercrombie & Fitch line the
surrounding streets. If you enter the Seaport
area from Water Street, the first thing you'll
notice is the whitewashed *Titanic* **Memorial
Lighthouse**, erected the year after the great
ship went down and moved to its current
location in 1976. The area offers fine views of
the **Brooklyn Bridge** *(see page 94)*. The smell
on South Street is a clear sign that the **Fulton
Fish Market**, America's largest, is nearby.
Opened in 1836, fish came fresh from the sea
until 1930, when fishing boats stopped docking
here. Today, fish is trucked in and out by land.

Go now—the market will move to Hunts Point in
the Bronx when a new facility is completed in 2003.

Fulton Fish Market

South St at Fulton St, Pier 16 (212-487-8476).
Subway: A, C to Broadway–Nassau St; J, M, Z, 1, 2,
4, 5 to Fulton St. 3:30–11:30am.

The Fulton Fish Market's bustling early-morning
scene is worth getting up for (most of the action
occurs before sunrise). But don't ask about the market's long-alleged Mafia ties—you could wind up
"sleeping with the fishes."

South Street Seaport

Water St to the East River, between John St and Peck
Slip (for info about shops and special events, call 212-
SEAPORT; www.southstseaport.org). Subway: A, C
to Broadway–Nassau St; J, M, Z, 1, 2, 4, 5 to Fulton
St. 11am–6pm.

Civic Center & City Hall

The business of running New York takes place
among the many grand buildings of the Civic
Center. This was the budding city's northern
boundary in the 1700s. When **City Hall** was
completed in 1812, its architects were so
confident the city would grow no farther north,
they didn't bother to put any marble on its
northern side. The building, a beautiful blend of
Federal form and French Renaissance details, is
unfortunately closed to the public (except for
scheduled group tours). **City Hall Park**, which
underwent a $30-million renovation in 1999, has
a granite time wheel that displays the park's
history through the ages. For years, the steps of
City Hall and the park have been the site of press
conferences and political protests. Under Mayor
Rudolph Giuliani, the steps were closed to such
activity, although civil libertarians successfully
defied the ban in April 2000. The much larger
Municipal Building, which faces City Hall and
reflects it architecturally, houses other civic
offices, including the marriage bureau, which
can churn out newlyweds at a remarkable clip.

Park Row, east of the park and now lined
with cafés and electronics shops, once held the
offices of 19 daily papers and was known as
Newspaper Row. It was also the site of Phineas
T. Barnum's sensationalist American Museum,
which burned down in 1865.

Facing the park from the west is Cass
Gilbert's famous **Woolworth Building**, a
vertically elongated Gothic cathedral-style
office building that has been called "the Mozart
of Skyscrapers." Its beautifully detailed lobby
is open to the public during business hours.

The houses of crime and punishment are
also located in the Civic Center, around Foley
Square—once a pond and later the site of the
city's most notorious slum of the 19th century,

Five Points. These days, you'll find the State Supreme Court located in the **New York County Courthouse** *(60 Centre St at Pearl St)*, a hexagonal Neoclassical-style building with a beautiful interior rotunda, featuring a mural called *Law Through the Ages*. The **United States Courthouse** *(40 Centre St between Duane and Pearl Sts)* features a golden pyramid-topped tower above a Corinthian temple. Next to City Hall is the old New York County Courthouse, more popularly known as the 1872 **Tweed Courthouse**, a symbol of the runaway corruption of mid–19th-century municipal government. Boss Tweed, leader of the political machine Tammany Hall, pocketed $10 million of the building's huge $14 million cost. But the remainder was still enough to buy a beautiful building; the Italianate detailing is exquisite. It's going to cost a lot more to restore the building: Would you believe $85 million? Once the renovation project is completed, the **Museum of the City of New York** *(see page 41)* will move in at the end of 2003 (it is currently located way uptown). The **Criminal Courts Building and Bernard Kerik Detention Complex** *(100 Centre St between Hogan Pl and Worth St)* is the most intimidating in the district. Built of great slabs of granite with looming towers that guard the entrance, this is NYC justice at its most Kafkaesque. The building is familiarly known

as "the Tombs," a reference not only to the architecture of its predecessor (a long-gone building inspired by a photograph of an Egyptian tomb) but to its once deathly prison conditions; it holds 800 prisoners today. Formerly called the Manhattan House of Detention, it was renamed in honor of former Police Commissioner Bernard Kerik in 2002.

All of these courts are open to the public, weekdays from 9am to 5pm, though only some of the trials allow visitors. Your best bets for courtroom drama are the Criminal Courts, where, if you can't slip into a trial, you can at least observe hallways full of legal wheeler dealers and the criminals they represent. Or, for a twist on dinner theater, check out the all-night parade of pleas at **Arraignment Court**.

A major archaeological site, the **African Burial Ground** *(Duane St between Broadway and Lafayette St)* is a remnant of a five-and-a-half-acre cemetery where 20,000 African men, women and children were buried. The cemetery, which closed in 1794, was unearthed during construction of a federal office building in 1991 and designated a National Historic Landmark.

City Hall

City Hall Park between Broadway and Park Row. (212-788-3000; www.nyc.gov). Subway: J, M, Z to Chambers St; 1, 2 to Park Pl; 4, 5, 6 to Brooklyn Bridge–City Hall. City Hall, at the northern end of the park, contains the mayor's office and the legislative chambers of the

The house that graft built The Tweed Courthouse will become a museum in late 2003.

City Council, and is thus ringed with news vans waiting for "Hizzoner" to appear. Of course, the pretty landscaping and abundant benches make the park a popular lunchtime spot for area office workers. For group tours of City Hall, call two weeks in advance.

Arraignment Court

Criminal Courts Building, 100 Centre St between Hogan Pl and Worth St (212-374-5880). Subway: J, M, Z to Chambers St; 1, 2 to Park Pl; 4, 5, 6 to Brooklyn Bridge–City Hall.
Night court is 6pm to 1am every day. Arraignments occur all night long, Thursday through Saturday.

Tribeca & Soho

Tribeca (Triangle Below Canal Street) today is a textbook example of the process of gentrification in lower Manhattan. It's very much as Soho (South of Houston Street) was 20 years ago: A few pockets are deserted and abandoned—the cobbles dusty and untrodden, and the cast-iron architecture chipped and unpainted—while the rest throbs with arriviste energy. Unlike in Soho, however, the rich and famous have been the pioneers: Harvey Keitel, Ed Burns and Christy Turlington (in JFK Jr.'s old apartment), artist Richard Serra and many other celebrities live in the area. This is a lodestar of haute restaurants, including **Danube** and **Nobu** *(see page 154)*, and swank bars (especially near the corner of North Moore Street and West Broadway). Clubs such as the **Knitting Factory** *(see page 305)* contribute to the culture. The buildings here are generally larger than those in Soho; particularly toward the river, many are warehouses rapidly being converted to condos. There is some fine small-scale cast-iron architecture along White Street and the parallel thoroughfares, including **85 Leonard Street**, the only remaining cast-iron building attributable to James Bogardus, the developer of the cast-iron building method, which prefigured the technology of the skyscraper. On nearby Harrison Street sits a row of well-preserved Federal-style townhouses (although a '70s-era middle-income housing project looms overhead).

As in Soho, you'll find galleries, salons, furniture stores, spas and other businesses that cater to the neighborhood's residents.

> ▶ To further explore Soho's art scene, see chapters **Museums** and **Art Galleries**.
> ▶ Learn more about Soho buildings and other downtown structures in chapter **Architecture**.
> ▶ For the best Soho and Tribeca spots to spend your money, see chapter **Shopping & Services**.

Tribeca is the unofficial headquarters of New York's film industry. Robert De Niro's **Tribeca Film Center** *(375 Greenwich St at Franklin St)* houses screening rooms and production offices in the old Martinson Coffee Building. His **Tribeca Grill** *(212-941-3900)* is on the ground floor. Also in the Film Center are the Queens-bred brothers Bob and Harvey Weinstein and the main offices of their company, **Miramax**. A few blocks away, **The Screening Room** *(see page 275)* shows art-house films in an upstairs theater and serves gourmet food in its elegant dining room.

Soho—New York's glamorous downtown shopping mecca—was once an industrial zone known as Hell's Hundred Acres. In the 1960s, Soho was earmarked for destruction, but the neighborhood's signature cast-iron warehouses were saved by the many artists who inhabited them. (Urban planning theorist Chester A. Rapkin coined the name Soho in a 1962 study on the neighborhood.) Two prime examples of cast-iron architecture are the **"King and Queen of Greene Street"** *(respectively, 72–76 Greene St between Broome and Spring Sts, and 28–30 Greene St between Canal and Grand Sts)*. As loft living became fashionable and the buildings were renovated for residential use, landlords were quick to sniff the profits of gentrification. Today, Soho is a playground for the young, beautiful and rich. Walk around the cobbled streets, among the elegant buildings, boutiques and bistros, and you can try the lifestyle on for size. Many of the galleries that made Soho an art hot spot in the 1980s have made a mass exodus to cheaper (and now cutting-edge) neighborhoods such as West Chelsea and Dumbo in Brooklyn.

Surprisingly, plenty of sweatshops remain, especially near Canal Street—though the buildings also house such businesses as graphic design studios, magazines and record labels.

Upscale hotels, such as the **Mercer, SoHo Grand** and **60 Thompson** *(see page 119)* have opened in the area, and the shop names run from Banana Republic and Old Navy to Marc Jacobs and Cartier. Soho is also the place to go for high-end home furnishings at design stores such as **Kartell** and **Moss** *(see page 226)*. West Broadway, Soho's main shop-lined thoroughfare, is a magnet for out-of-towners—on the weekend, you're as likely to hear French, German and Italian as you are Brooklynese.

Several museums make Soho a destination: the **New Museum of Contemporary Art** *(see page 36)*, **Museum for African Art** *(see page 43)* and **Guggenheim Museum**'s Soho branch *(see page 36)*. Another that has grown very popular is the small **New York City Fire Museum** *(see page 45)*, a former fire station that houses a collection of antique engines dating back to the 1700s.

West of West Broadway, tenement- and townhouse-lined streets contain remnants of the Italian community that once dominated this area. Elderly men and women walk along Sullivan Street up to the **Shrine Church of St. Anthony of Padua** *(at Houston St)*, which was founded by the Franciscan Friars in 1866. You'll still find some old-school flavor in businesses such as **Joe's Dairy** *(156 Sullivan St between Houston and Prince Sts, 212-677-8780)*, **Pino's Prime Meat Market** *(149 Sullivan St between Houston and Prince Sts, 212-475-8134)* and **Vesuvio Bakery** *(160 Prince St between Thompson St and West Broadway, 212-925-8248)*.

Little Italy & Nolita

Little Italy, which once ran from Canal to Houston Streets and Lafayette Street to the Bowery, hardly resembles the insular community portrayed in Martin Scorsese's *Mean Streets*—Italian families have fled to the suburbs, Chinatown has crept north over its southern border, and rising rents have forced mom-and-pop businesses to surrender to the stylish boutiques of Nolita (North of Little Italy, a misnomer since it actually lies within). "It's all restaurants and clothes—and who can fit into them?" moans one lifelong resident on Mott Street. Another telling change in the hood: **St. Patrick's Old Cathedral** *(260–264 Mulberry St between Houston and Prince Sts)* gives services in English and *Spanish*, not Italian. (Built in 1815 and restored after a fire in 1868, this was New York's premier Catholic church until it was demoted, upon consecration of the Fifth Avenue cathedral.) But ethnic pride remains. Italian-Americans flood in from Queens and Brooklyn to show their love for the old neighborhood during the **Feast of San Gennaro** *(see page 241)* in September. In summer, Luca Pizzaroni, a filmmaker from Rome, puts on an open-air Italian-film series in the **De Salvio Playground** *(Mulberry and Spring Sts)*. Aside from the tourist-oriented cafés and restaurants on Mulberry Street *(between Canal and Houston Sts)*, there are pockets of the old lifestyle. The elderly locals still buy olive oils and fresh pasta from venerable shops such as **DiPalo's Fine Foods** *(206 Grand St at Mott St)* and sandwiches packed with Italian meats and cheeses at **Italian Food Center** *(186 Grand St at Mulberry St)*.

Naturally, Little Italy is the site of several notorious Mafia landmarks. The **Ravenite Social Club** *(247 Mulberry St between Prince and Spring Sts)*, now occupied by the accessories boutique **Amy Chan** *(see page 208)*, was celebrity don John Gotti's

headquarters from the mid-1980s until his arrest in 1990. Mobster Joey Gallo was shot to death in 1972 while eating with his family at **Umberto's Clam House**, which has since relocated around the corner *(386 Broome St at Mulberry St)*. The Italian eateries in the area are mostly undistinguished, overpriced grill-and-pasta houses, but two good choices are **Il Cortile** *(125 Mulberry St between Canal and Hester Sts, 212-226-6060)* and **Benito One** *(174 Mulberry between Broome and Grand Sts, 212-226-9171)*. Drop in at one of the many small cafés lining the streets, such as **Caffè Roma** *(385 Broome St at Mulberry St, 212-226-8413)*, which opened in 1891, for an Italian soda or dessert and coffee. For a real drink, head to the bar **Mare Chiaro** *(see page 146)*, once a favorite of Frank Sinatra. A new generation of stylish youth has discovered it, but some old-timers (including a few portrayed in the Frank Mason painting on the wall) still visit.

Chichi restaurants and boutiques seem to open daily in Nolita *(see chapter* **Shopping & Services***)*. Elizabeth, Mott and Mulberry streets—between Houston and Spring streets in particular—are now the source of everything from groovy jeans to handblown glass. The young and the social congregate

Last bastion This butcher shop is a Little Italy relic in a sea of boutiques and cafés.

Sightseeing

outside eateries such as **Cafe Habana** *(17 Prince St at Elizabeth St, 212-625-2001)* and **Cafe Gitane** *(242 Mott St at Prince St, 212-334-9552)*. Long before the Nolita boom, the former **Police Headquarters Building** *(240 Centre St between Broome and Grand Sts)*, was converted into luxe co-op apartments in 1988.

Chinatown

Manhattan's Chinatown is the largest Chinese-immigrant community outside Asia. Even though some residents decamp to four other Chinatowns in the city (two in Queens and two in Brooklyn), a steady flow of new arrivals keeps the original expanding. The tenements and high-rise buildings around East Canal Street house about 150,000 legal (and approximately 100,000 illegal) Chinese. Many work here and never leave the neighborhood. You won't hear much English spoken on Chinatown's busy streets—which get even wilder during the Chinese New Year festivities in January or February, and around the Fourth of July, when the area is the city's best source of (illegal) fireworks.

Food is everywhere. The markets on **Canal Street** sell some of the best fish, fruits and vegetables in the city—you'll see buckets of live eels and crabs, neatly stacked greens and piles of hairy rambutans. Street vendors sell snacks, such as bags of sweet egg pancakes. There are countless restaurants. Mott Street—from Worth to Kenmare Streets—is lined with Cantonese and Szechuan places, as is East Broadway. Adding to the mix are increasing numbers of Indonesian, Malaysian, Thai and Vietnamese eateries and stores. For some suggestions, see page 157, and **Chinatown snacks**, page 57.

Canal Street is also a bargain-hunter's paradise: it's infamous as a source of knock-off designer items, such as "brand-name" handbags. The area's gift shops are stocked with inexpensive Chinese products, from good-luck charms to kitschy pop-culture paraphernalia. One of Chinatown's best shops is the bi-level **Pearl River Mart** *(see page 228)*. It brims with food, dishware, dresses, traditional musical instruments and videos.

Historical sites of interest include **65 Mott Street** *(between Bayard and Pell Sts)*, the city's first building erected specifically as a tenement. It went up about 1824, when the neighborhood was known as the notorious slum Five Points. Chinatown's oldest continuously run shop, **32 Mott Street General Store** *(between Chatham Sq and Pell St)*, has been owned by the Lee family for three generations. The store, founded in 1891, has been at this location since 1899—note the carved-wood arch and peeling tin ceiling. Locals come to buy housewares and porcelain figurines and to pay bills. The antiques shop **Chu Shing** *(12 Mott St between Chatham Sq and Mosco St, 212-227-0279)* was once the New York office of the Chinese revolutionary Dr. Sun Yat-sen *(1866–1925)*, known as the father of modern China.

Explore **Wing Fat Shopping**, a strange little underground mall. Enter the doors at Chatham Square (to the right of the OTB parlor at No. 8) and descend the stairs to your left—you'll find businesses such as the Foot Reflexology Center and Tin Sun Metaphysics, a well-known feng shui agency. The tunnel is rumored to have been a stop on the Underground Railroad, 25 years before the Chinese began populating this area in the 1880s. In 1906, the tunnel connected the Chinese Opera house at 5 Doyers Street with an actors' residence on the Bowery. Members of two rival *tongs* (Chinese organized-crime groups) staged a savage gun battle during an opera. At least four people were killed, and the gunmen escaped down the tunnels.

A statue of the Chinese philosopher marks **Confucius Plaza** at the corner of Bowery and Division Streets. **Columbus Park** at Bayard and Mulberry Streets is where elderly men and women gather around card tables to play mah-jongg and dominoes (you can hear the clacking tiles from across the street), while younger folks practice martial arts. On weekends, the place is jam-packed with families taking a break from shopping. The **Museum of Chinese in the Americas** *(see page 43)* hosts exhibitions and events that explore the Chinese immigrant experience in the Western hemisphere. In the **Eastern States Buddhist Temple of America**, you'll notice the glitter of hundreds of Buddhas and the smell of incense. Near the entrance to the Manhattan Bridge, **Mahayana Temple Buddhist Association** is a larger Buddhist temple.

For a different angle on Chinatown culture, there's the noisy, dingy **Chinatown Fair**, an amusement arcade where some of the East Coast's best *Street Fighter* players congregate. Older kids hit Chinatown for liquid entertainment: The **Double Happiness** bar *(see page 144)* and the club **Fun** *(see page 268)* are popular nightspots for downtown scenesters of all ethnic groups.

Chinatown Fair

8 Mott St at Chatham Sq (www.chinatownfair.com). Subway: J, M, Z, N, Q, R, W, 6 to Canal St.

**CRITICS'
PICKS** # Chinatown snacks

Green tea with tapioca at Saint's Alp
*51 Mott St between Bayard and Canal Sts
(212-766-9889).* This Hong Kong chain's
Taiwanese-style flavored green tea draws
crowds. Try the passion fruit with giant beads
of black tapioca.

**Ice cream at Chinatown Ice
Cream Factory**
*65 Bayard St between Elizabeth and Mott
Sts (212-608-4170).* Chill out with anything
from fresh lychee sorbet to green-tea
ice cream.

Jung at May May
*35 Pell St between Doyers and Mott Sts
(212-267-0733).* Bakery owner John Hung

calls *jung,* which consist of stuffed rice
balls wrapped in bamboo leaves,
"Chinese tamales." The Taiwanese
version is a tasty mix of dried shrimp,
shiitake, peanuts and pork.

Malaysian beef jerky at Wong Kee
*95A Elizabeth St between Grand and
Hester Sts (212-965-0796).* Thin slices of
sweet 'n' spicy pork, chicken and beef jerky
make for easy-eating, meaty snacks.

Roasted-pork buns at Mei Lai Wah
*64 Bayard St at Elizabeth St (212-925-
5435).* Ask for *char siu bao* (steamed or
baked)—fist-size puffs of dough stuffed
with sweet meat, for just 60 cents each.

Sightseeing

Eastern States Buddhist Temple of America

64B Mott St between Bayard and Canal Sts (212-966-6229). Subway: J, M, Z, N, Q, R, W, 6 to Canal St. 9am–7pm.

Mahayana Temple Buddhist Association

133 Canal St at Bowery, No. 33 (212-925-8787). Subway: J, M, Z, N, Q, R, W, 6 to Canal St; S to Grand St. 8am–6pm.

Lower East Side

The Lower East Side tells the story of New
York's immigrants: One generation makes good
and moves to the suburbs, leaving space for the
next wave of hopefuls. The area is busy and
densely populated, a patchwork of strong
ethnic communities, and great for dining and
exploration. Today, Lower East Side residents
are largely Asian and Latino families, with an
increasing number of fresh-from-college kids
sharing small apartments. The early settlers
were mostly Jews from Eastern Europe. Mass
tenement housing was built to accommodate
the 19th-century influx of immigrants, which
included many German, Hungarian, Irish and
Polish families. Unsanitary, overcrowded
conditions prompted the introduction of
building codes. To appreciate how these
immigrants lived, visit the **Lower East Side
Tenement Museum** *(see page 40).*

Between 1870 and 1920, hundreds of
synagogues and religious schools were
established here. Yiddish newspapers were
published, and associations for social reform
and cultural studies flourished, along with
vaudeville and Yiddish theaters. (The Marx

Brothers, Jimmy Durante, Eddie Cantor, and
George and Ira Gershwin were just a few of the
entertainers who lived in this district.) Today,
only 10 percent of the current population
is Jewish; the **Eldridge Street Synagogue**
finds it hard to round up the ten adult males
required to conduct a service. Despite a
shrinking congregation (known as K'hal Adath
Jeshurun with Anshe Lubz), the synagogue has
not missed a Sabbath or holiday service in 115
years. Remarkably, in October 2001, a white-tiled
mikvah (a small pool that collects rainwater used
to cleanse Orthodox Jewish women after their
menstrual cycles), was unearthed behind the
synagogue; it is believed to be the oldest one of
its kind in New York, dating back to 1887. **First
Shearith Israel Graveyard** has gravestones
that date back to 1683.

Puerto Ricans and Dominicans began to
move to the Lower East Side after World War II.
Colorful awnings characterize the area's
bodegas (corner groceries). Many restaurants
serve Caribbean standards, such as rice and
beans with fried plantains. In the summer, the
streets throb with the sounds of salsa and
merengue as residents hang out, slurping ices,
drinking beer and playing dominoes.

Beginning in the 1980s, the most recent cycle
of immigrants started to move in: young artists,
musicians and other rebels attracted by low
rents. Bars, boutiques and music venues that
catered to this crowd sprang up on Ludlow
Street and the surrounding area, creating an
annex of the East Village *(see* **Bottoms up!***,
page 148),* and this scene is still thriving. For
live music, check who's playing at **Arlene
Grocery** *(see page 300),* **Tonic** *(see page 309),*
and the **Bowery Ballroom** *(see page 301).*

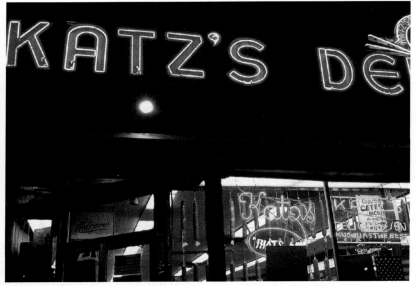

Earl of sandwich When it comes to pastrami, Katz's Deli is Lower East Side royalty.

Many small boutiques have opened near the clubs—or within them, as in the case of the **Short Waves** *(212-254-0787)*, an indie-lit bookstore and press inside Tonic.

The Lower East Side's reputation as a haven for political radicals lives on at the squat **ABC No Rio** *(156 Rivington St between Clinton and Suffolk Sts; www.abcnorio.org)*, which also houses a gallery and performance space. (The arts organization is in the process of legally taking ownership of the building from the city.

Despite the trendy shops that have cropped up along the block, Orchard Street below Stanton Street remains the heart of the **Orchard Street Bargain District**, a row of stores selling utilitarian goods. This is the place for cheap hats, luggage, sportswear and T-shirts. In the 1930s, Mayor Fiorello La Guardia forced pushcart vendors off the streets into large, indoor marketplaces. Although many of these structures are now a thing of the past, **Essex Street Markets** *(120 Essex St between Delancey and Rivington Sts)* is still going strong as a purveyor of all things Latino, from chorizo to religious icons.

Some remnants of the neighborhood's Jewish roots remain. One of the Lower East Side's most famous eateries is the shabby **Sammy's Roumanian** *(157 Chrystie St between Delancey and Rivington Sts, 212-673-*

0330), where hearty servings of Eastern European fare are served with a jug of chicken fat and a bottle of vodka. If you prefer "lighter" food, **Katz's Deli** *(see page 155)* sells some of the best pastrami in New York, and the ensuing orgasms are pretty good too—Meg Ryan's famous "I'll have what she's having" scene in *When Harry Met Sally...* was filmed here. People come from all over for the vinegary cucumbers at **Guss' Pickles** *(see page 223)*, another Lower East Side landmark. **Ratner's** *(138 Delancey St between Norfolk and Suffolk Sts, 212-677-5588)*, a former full-time dairy restaurant, is a 97-year-old institution that also illustrates the collision of the past and present Lower East Side: On Sundays, from 8am to 8pm, it still serves borscht and blintzes (no longer kosher) to the general public; the other six days, it's booked for private parties. Ratner's shares its space with the **Lansky Lounge & Grill** *(104 Norfolk St between Delancey and Rivington Sts, 212-677-9489)*, a swinging speakeasy-style club named for the late Jewish mobster Meyer Lansky; it has its own American menu.

Eldridge Street Synagogue

12 Eldridge St between Canal and Division Sts (212-219-0888; www.eldridgestreet.org). Subway: F to East Broadway. Tours Tue, Thu 11:30am, 2:30pm *and by appointment; Sun 11am–3pm on the hour. $5, seniors and students $3.*

This beautifully decorated building was the pride of the Jewish congregation that once filled it. Services are conducted in the *beth hamedrash* (house of study) on the ground floor.

First Shearith Israel Graveyard

55–57 St. James Pl between James and Oliver Sts. Subway: J, M to Bowery; S to Grand St.

This is the burial ground of the oldest Jewish community in the United States—Spanish and Portuguese Jews who escaped the Inquisition.

The Village

Greenwich Village

The middle section of "the Village" has been the scene of some serious partying throughout its history. Stretching from 14th Street to Houston Street, and from Broadway to Sixth Avenue, Greenwich Village's leafy streets—lined with coffeehouses, theaters, townhouses and tiny bars and clubs—have witnessed and inspired bohemian lifestyles for almost a century. It's a place for idle wandering, for people-watching from sidewalk cafés, for candlelit dining in secret restaurants, or for hopping between bars and cabaret venues. The Village gets overcrowded in summer, and it has lost some of its quaintness as the retail center of lower Broadway has spread west, but much of what attracted creative types to New York still exists. The jazz generation lives on in smoky clubs. Sip a fresh roast in honor of the Beats—Jack Kerouac, Allen Ginsberg and their ilk—as you sit in their former haunts. Kerouac's favorite was **Le Figaro Café**, at the corner of Bleecker and MacDougal Streets. Although it has moved from its original location at the corner of 8th Street, the **Cedar Tavern** on University Place *(between 11th and 12th Sts)* is worth a visit: It's where the leading figures of Abstract Expressionism discussed how best to throw paint: Franz Kline, Jackson Pollock and Larry Rivers drank here in the 1950s.

The hippies who tuned out in **Washington Square** are still there in spirit, and often in person: The park hums with musicians and street artists (although the once-ubiquitous pot dealers have become victims of strict policing and hidden surveillance cameras). Chess hustlers and students from **New York University** join in, along with today's new generation of idlers: hip-hop kids who drive down to West 4th Street in their booming Jeeps, and Generation Y skaters/ravers who clatter around the fountain and the base of the **Washington Square Arch** (a miniature Arc de Triomphe built in 1892 in honor of George Washington). Renovation of the arch started ten years ago, but the money ran out

and the structure is *still* fenced off. The project will take about two more years.

The Village has been fashionable since the 1830s, when the wealthy built handsome townhouses around Washington Square. Some of these properties are still privately owned and occupied; many others have become part of the New York University campus. Literary figures, including Henry James, Herman Melville, Mark Twain and Edith Wharton, lived on or near the square. In 1871, the local creative community founded the **Salmagundi Club**, America's oldest artists' club, which is now situated above Washington Square on Fifth Avenue (No. 47). The landmark building hosts exhibitions, lectures and demonstrations. Take advantage of the evening and weekend sketch classes.

Greenwich Village continues to change with the times. The latest adaptation: The house at West 3rd Street between Sullivan and Thompson Streets, where Edgar Allan Poe

Pipe dream Performers of all stripes do their thing in Washington Square Park.

lived for approximately six months from 1845 to 1846, was razed, so a law school could be built on the site. Fortunately, after a battle with community preservation groups, NYU has agreed to retain and incorporate portions of the building's historic facade.

Eighth Street is presently a long procession of cheap-jewelry vendors, piercing parlors, punky boutiques and shoe shops; in the '60s, it was the closest New York got to San Francisco's Haight Street. Jimi Hendrix's **Electric Lady Studios** are still here at No. 52; Bob Dylan lived at and owned 94 MacDougal Street through much of the 1960s, performing in Washington Square Park and at clubs such as **Cafe Wha?** on MacDougal Street, between Bleecker and West 3rd Streets. Once the stamping ground of Beat poets and hipster jazz musicians, **Bleecker Street** *(between Sixth Ave and La Guardia Pl)* is now a dingy stretch of poster shops, cheap ethnic restaurants and music venues that showcase local talent and cover bands for the college crowd. The famed **Village Gate** jazz club used to be at the corner of Bleecker and Thompson Streets; it's now a CVS pharmacy. but the old sign is still there.

In the triangle formed by Sixth Avenue, Greenwich Avenue and 10th Street, you'll see the Victorian neo-Gothic **Jefferson Market Library** (a branch of the New York Public Library), which has served as a courthouse and a women's prison. Enjoy its lovely flower-filled garden facing Greenwich Avenue. Wander into **Balducci's** *(see page 222)*, across the street, to be tempted by one of the city's most popular food stores. Down Sixth Avenue at 4th Street, you'll stumble upon "the Cage," outdoor basketball courts where you can witness hot hoop action *(see page 325)*.

Jefferson Market Library

425 Sixth Ave between 9th and 10th Sts (212-243-4334). Subway: A, C, E, F, V, S to W 4th St. Library open Mon, Wed noon–8pm; Tue, Fri noon–6pm; Thu 10am–6pm; Sat 10am–5pm; Sun 1–5pm. Free. Built on the site of what was a market until the present structure was completed in 1877, this library has served the Greenwich Village community for 30 years. The landmark building is based on a Bavarian castle.

Salmagundi Club

47 Fifth Ave at 12th St (212-255-7740; www.salmagundi.org). Subway: L, N, Q, R, W, 4, 5, 6 to 14th St–Union Sq. Open for exhibitions only; phone for details. Free. The club, which has an elegant 19th-century interior, is home to artistic and historical societies.

Literary light For a quiet read, you can go to the ex-courthouse Jefferson Market Library.

Washington Square Park

Between Waverly Pl and 4th St, from Fifth Ave to MacDougal St. Subway: A, C, E, F, V, S to W 4th St. Washington Square Park, in the middle of Greenwich Village, is the city's most famous park below 14th Street. Drug dealers were once a dime-bag a dozen here; nowadays, musicians ring the park's center and street performers work around (and in) the fountain, while the southwest corner is home to die-hard chess players. Park yourself on a bench for some of the best people-watching on earth.

West Village & Meatpacking District

Most of the West Village, roughly the area west of Sixth Avenue to the Hudson River, below 14th Street to Houston Street, still retains the features that molded the Village's character and gave it shape. Only here could West 10th Street cross West 4th Street, and Waverly Place with Waverly Place. While this neighborhood harbors plenty of celebrities (from Gwyneth Paltrow to Ed Koch), it has managed to retain a humble, everyone-knows-each-other feel. Denizens fill the bistros and bars that line Bleecker and Hudson Streets, the area's main thoroughfares.

The northwest corner of this area is known as the **Meatpacking District**—it's primarily been a wholesale meat market since the 1930s. Until the 1990s, it was also a prime haunt for prostitutes, many of them transsexual. In recent years, the atmospheric cobblestoned streets have seen the arrival of a new type of tenant: The once lonely **Florent** *(see page 168)*, a 24-hour French diner that opened in 1985, is now part of a chic scene that includes swinging watering holes **APT** *(see page 269)* and **Pastis** *(9 Ninth Ave at Little West 12th St, 212-929-4844)*, as well as designer boutiques **Jeffrey** *(see page 194)* and **Jussara Lee** *(11 Little West 12th St between Ninth Ave and Washington St, 212-242-4128)*. As building owners, happy to cash in on the neighborhood upgrades, raise rents, the meat dealers are moving out. Ten years ago, there were about 100 companies in the area; today the number is down to about 30. In spring 2001, Master Purveyors (which supplies the legendary steak house Peter Luger; *see page 189*) moved to Hunts Point Terminal Market *(see page 103)* in the Bronx because the landlord wouldn't renew the company's lease. Local residents, including designer Diane von Furstenberg, have started the Save Gansevoort Market campaign to obtain landmark status for the neighborhood.

Other charming cobblestoned streets stretch south and west of Hudson Street. At Bethune and Washington Streets is **Westbeth**, a block-long building formerly owned by Bell Telephone (it's where the vacuum tube and the transistor were invented); the 1900 structure was converted to lofts for artists in 1965. Around the corner is the **Westbeth Theatre Center** *(151 Bank St between West and Washington Sts, 212-741-0391)*, which often has fine rock shows, as well as stand-up by Sandra Bernhard and Eddie Izzard, among others. Luxury condos along Washington Street—beyond the historic landmark district—have led to griping that the neighborhood's charm is diminishing. Yet several historic nightlife spots are alive and well: The **White Horse Tavern** *(see page 147)* is where poet Dylan Thomas spent the better part of the 1940s. Earlier in the century, John Steinbeck and John Dos Passos passed time at **Chumley's** *(see page 144)*, a Prohibition-era speakeasy, still unmarked at 86 Bedford Street. On and just off Seventh Avenue South are jazz and cabaret clubs, including **Small's** and the **Village Vanguard** *(see pages 311 and 312)*.

The West Village is also a renowned gay area (although much of the scene has moved to Chelsea; *see page 66*). **The Stonewall** *(see page 285)* on Christopher Street was originally the Stonewall Inn, the sight of the 1969 Stonewall Rebellion, which marked the birth of the gay liberation movement. There are as many same-sex couples strolling along Christopher Street as straight ones, and plenty of shops, bars and restaurants that are out and proud.

East Village

Scruffier than its western counterpart, the East Village has a long history as a countercultural mecca. Originally considered part of the Lower East Side, the neighborhood first took off in the 1960s when writers, artists and musicians moved in and turned it into the hub for the '60s countercultural revolution. (Allen Ginsberg lived at 437 East 12th Street between First Avenue and Avenue A, until his death in 1997.) Many famous clubs and coffeehouses thrived, including the Fillmore East rock theater on Second Avenue between 6th and 7th Streets (now demolished), and the Dom, where the Velvet Underground was a regular headliner, at 23 St. Marks Place (now a community center). In the '70s, the neighborhood took a dive as drugs and crime prevailed—but that didn't stop the influx of artists and punk

▶ More information on downtown nightlife can be found in chapters **Bars** and **Music**.
▶ A complete review of the Stonewall and other gay establishments can be found in chapter **Gay & Lesbian**.
▶ **Street of dreams**, page 218, highlights East Village boutiques on 9th Street.

rockers. In the early '80s, area galleries were among the first to display the work of hot young artists Jean-Michel Basquiat and Keith Haring.

Today, the area east of Broadway between Houston and 14th Streets is no longer quite so edgy, though remnants of its spirited past live on. Now you'll find a generally amiable population of punks, yuppies, hippies, homeboys, homeless and trustafarians—would-be bohos who live off trust funds. This motley crew has crowded into the area's tenements—along with older residents, who tend to be holdouts from previous waves of immigration. They support the area's record shops, bargain restaurants, grungy bars, punky clubs and funky, cheap clothing stores (check for quality before forking over any cash).

St. Marks Place *(8th St between Lafayette St and Ave A)* is the main drag (in more ways than one). Poet W.H. Auden lived at 77 St. Marks Place *(between First and Second Aves)* from 1953 to 1972. Now it's more lowbrow. Lined with bars squeezed into tiny basements and stores overflowing onto the sidewalks, St. Marks is packed until the wee hours with crowds browsing for bargain T-shirts, records and books. The more interesting places are to the east; you'll find cafés and shops on and around Avenue A between 6th and 10th Streets. Since tattooing became legal in New York City in 1997 (it had been banned since 1961), a number of parlors have opened up, including the famous **Fun City** *(see page 232)*, whose awning advertises CAPPUCCINO & TATTOO.

Astor Place, with its revolving cube sculpture, is always swarming with young skateboarders. It is also the site of Peter Cooper's recently refurbished **Cooper Union**, the city's first free educational institute. Opened in 1859, today it's a design and engineering college (and still free). In the 19th century, Astor Place marked the boundary between the ghettos to the east and some of the city's most fashionable homes, such as **Colonnade Row**, on Lafayette Street. Facing these was the distinguished Astor Public Library, which theater legend Joseph Papp rescued from demolition in the 1960s. Today it's the **Public Theater**—a haven for first-run American plays, the producer of the **New York Shakespeare Festival** *(see page 336)* and the home of trendy nightspot **Joe's Pub** *(see page 305)*.

East of Lafayette Street on the Bowery are several missionary organizations that cater to the downtrodden, the sole vestiges of the Bowery's notorious past. In recent years, a few restaurants have also set up shop. At 315 Bowery is the hallowed **CBGB** *(see page 303)*, the birthplace of American punk. CB still packs in guitar bands, both new and used. Many other local bars and clubs successfully apply the formula of cheap

Sacred and profane St. Mark's Church in-the-Bowery, built in 1799, is an arts center.

beer and loud music, including **Brownies**, the **Continental** and the **Mercury Lounge** *(see pages 301, 303 and 307).*

East 7th Street is a Ukrainian stronghold; the focal point is the Byzantine-looking **St. George's Ukrainian Catholic Church**, built in 1977 but appearing considerably older. Across the street, there is often a long line of beefy fraternity types waiting to enter **McSorley's Old Ale House** *(see page 146),* one of the oldest pubs in the city; it still serves just one kind of beer—its own brew. Eclectic items in the boutiques of young designers and vintage clothing dealers that dot 7th, 8th and 9th Streets will also help you deplete your funds *(see **Street of dreams**, page 218).*

On 6th Street between First and Second Avenues is **Curry Row** (one of several "little Indias" in New York). Roughly two dozen Indian restaurants sit side by side, the long-running joke being that they all share a single kitchen. (Not many are commendable except for those on an extremely tight budget.) And if you're wondering about the row of shiny Harleys on 3rd Street between First and Second

Avenues, the New York chapter of the **Hell's Angels** is headquartered here.

Avenues A through D, an area known as **Alphabet City**, stretch toward the East River. The largely Latino population is being overtaken by a group willing and able to pay higher rents. Avenue C is known as "Loisaida Ave," the phonetic spelling of "Lower East Side" when pronounced with a clipped Spanish accent. The neighborhood's long, rocky romance with heroin is pretty much a thing of the past.

Though it's rough around the edges, Alphabet City has its attractions. Two churches on 4th Street are built in the Spanish-colonial style: **San Isidro y San Leandro** *(345 4th St between Aves C and D)* and **Iglesia Pentecostal Camino Damasco** *(289 4th St between Aves B and C).* **The Nuyorican Poets Cafe** *(see page 260),* a 28-year-old clubhouse for espresso-drinking beatniks, is famous for its slams, in which performance poets do battle before a score-keeping audience. **Tompkins Square Park**, now well maintained and landscaped, has historically been the site of demonstrations and rioting. The last uprising was a decade ago, when the city decided to evict the park's squatters and renovate it to suit the tastes of the area's increasingly affluent residents.

North of Tompkins Square, around First Avenue and 11th Street, are remnants of earlier communities: discount fabric shops, Italian cheese shops, Polish restaurants and two great Italian patisseries. Visit **DeRobertis** *(176 First Ave at 11th St, 212-674-7137)* for delicious cakes and **Veniero's Pasticceria and Caffe** *(342 11th St at First Ave, 212-674-7264)* for wonderful pastries and butter biscuits.

St. Mark's Church in-the-Bowery
131 E 10th St at Second Ave (Danspace Project, 212-674-8194; Ontological at St. Mark's, 212-420-1916; Poetry Project, 212-674-0910). Subway: 6 to Astor Pl.
St. Mark's was built in 1799 on the site of Peter Stuyvesant's farm. Stuyvesant, one of New York's first governors, is buried here, along with many of his descendants. Today the church is the East Village's unofficial cultural center, its space rented by arts groups.

Tompkins Square Park
Between Aves A and B, from 7th to 10th Sts. Subway: 6 to Astor Pl.
The community park of the East Village, Tompkins Square is one of the liveliest layabout zones in the city. Latino bongo beaters, hippie types with acoustic guitars, punky squatters, mangy dogs, the neighborhood's yuppie residents and its homeless mingle on the grass under huge old trees. In summer, the park's southern end is often the site of musical performances, while the north is the province of basketball, hockey and handball enthusiasts.

Midtown

Between uptown's posh avenues and downtown's hip enclaves lies the flash
and industry of central Manhattan—and there's nothing middling about it

Midtown, roughly 14th to 59th Streets, is the city's engine room, powered by the hundreds of thousands of commuters who pour in each day. During working hours, the area is all business. The towering office buildings are home to international corporations, book and magazine publishers, record companies and advertising agencies. Garment manufacturers have long clustered in the area on and around Seventh Avenue (a.k.a. Fashion Avenue) . Midtown is also where you'll find most of the city's large hotels (and the legions of tourists and traveling execs who occupy them), department stores, classy retailers of Fifth Avenue and Rockefeller Center, and landmarks such as the Empire State Building and Carnegie Hall. By night, locals and visitors gravitate to the *Blade Runner*–like voltage of Times Square to see movies and Broadway shows, to eat in the many restaurants, or to do some late-night shopping for music and home electronics.

Flatiron District

Running along Sixth Avenue from 14th to 30th Streets and bounded on the east by Park Avenue South, the Flatiron District is on the edge of downtown—and not just in the geographical sense. It's now known as a style enclave and what's left of new-media companies.

As Broadway cuts diagonally through Manhattan, it creates a public square wherever it intersects an avenue. Two such places, Union Square at 14th Street and Madison Square at 23rd, once marked the limits of a ritzy 19th-century shopping district known as **Ladies' Mile**. Extending along Broadway and west to Sixth Avenue, this collection of huge retail palaces (the first Macy's store was on Sixth Avenue between 13th and 14th Streets) attracted the "carriage trade"—wealthy ladies buying the latest fashions and household goods from all over the world. By 1914, most of the department stores had moved farther north, leaving behind the proud cast-iron buildings that had housed them. Today, the area is again a shopping destination. The upscale home-design store **ABC Carpet & Home** *(see page 224)* is in a beautiful old building at the corner of Broadway and 19th Street. **Emporio Armani, Paul Smith** and many other clothing shops

showcase the season's latest designs on lower Fifth Avenue, while Sixth Avenue (which borders the Chelsea neighborhood; *see page 66)* is dotted with such large chain stores as Old Navy and Bed, Bath & Beyond.

Union Square is named after neither the Union of the Civil War nor the lively labor rallies that once took place here, but simply for the union of Broadway and Bowery Lane (now Fourth Avenue). From the 1920s until the early 1960s, it had a reputation as a political hot spot, a favorite location for rabble-rousing oratory. Drug dealers ruled the park until the 1980s, when a renovation paved the way for gentrification. These days, the square is surrounded by a giant **Barnes & Noble** bookstore (in a handsome 1881 redbrick and terra-cotta building that was once home to the popular magazine *Century; see page 217)*, the hotel **W Union Square** *(see page 123)*, the giant Zeckendorf Towers residential complex, a **Virgin Megastore** *(see page 228)* and many restaurants, including the touted **Union Square Cafe** *(21 E 16th St between Park Ave South and Union Sq East, 212-243-4020)* and **Olives NY** *(see page 173)*. While the square itself is now best known as the site of the **Union Square Greenmarket**—an excellent farmers' market—civilians still congregate here to protest or to make a statement, as after the World Trade Center disaster in September 2001, when thousands of mourners gathered for candlelight vigils, and later, for antiwar marches. In summer, the outdoor **Luna Park** bar beckons cocktailers, while skateboarders practice wild tricks on the steps and railings of the square's southern edge.

At the northern end of the neighborhood, just south of **Madison Square** *(between 23rd and 26th Sts, from Fifth to Madison Aves)* is the famously triangular Renaissance palazzo **Flatiron Building**. Originally named the Fuller Building after its first owners, it's the world's first steel-frame skyscraper. The Flatiron provides the name for the neighborhood, an area peppered with boutiques, bookshops, photo studios and labs, not to mention wandering minds. In the mid-'90s, big Internet-related companies, such as Doubleclick, began colonizing the lofts on Fifth

Out on a limb Stop in Madison Square to get a peek of the Flatiron Building through the trees.

Fountain of couth Only the privileged residents of Gramercy Park get a key to its eponymous park.

Avenue and Broadway, earning the neighborhood a new nickname: **Silicon Alley.** Even though many dot-coms went bust and others have decamped to surrounding neighborhoods, the moniker remains in use.

Madison Square is also rich in history. It was the site of P.T. Barnum's Hippodrome and the original Madison Square Garden—the scene of prize fights, lavish entertainment and a scandalous society murder. After years of neglect, statue-filled Madison Square finally got a face-lift, and the area bordering the park's east side is a hot spot. For years, it was notable only for the presence of such imposing buildings as the gold-topped **Metropolitan Life Insurance Company Building**, the **New York Life Insurance Company Building** and the **Appellate Court**, but upscale restaurants, such as **Tabla** *(see page 174),* have injected some leisure-time chic into this once-staid area.

Flatiron Building
175 Fifth Ave between 22nd and 23rd Sts. Subway: N, R, 6 to 23rd St.
Built in 1902, the Flatiron was one of the earliest buildings to use an interior steel cage for support. Its exterior echoes the traditional Beaux Arts facades of the time. Unfortunately, tours of the interior are not available, but for more information on the building's history, see chapter **Architecture**.

Union Square Greenmarket
North end of Union Square, 17th St between Union Sq West and Union Sq East (212-477-3220). Subway: L, N, Q, R, W, 4, 5, 6 to 14th St–Union Sq. Mon, Wed, Fri, Sat 8am–6pm.

Chelsea

Chelsea is the region between 14th and 30th Streets west of Sixth Avenue. Inhabited by professionals of all ages and a large Latino community, the area is probably best known for its flourishing gay life. You'll find all the trappings of an urban residential neighborhood on the upswing: countless stores (some dull) and a generous assortment of lively bars and restaurants, mostly clustered on Eighth Avenue. Chelsea's western warehouse district, currently housing a host of swank lounges and nightclubs, is being developed for residential use. Pioneering galleries, such as the **Dia Center for the Arts** at the west end of 22nd Street, have led the art crowd westward, and the whole area has become the hot gallery zone.

Cushman Row *(406–418 W 20th St between Ninth and Tenth Aves),* in the **Chelsea Historic District**, is a good example of how Chelsea looked when it was developed in the mid-1800s—a grandeur that was destroyed 30 years later when noisy elevated railways were built, dominating the area and stealing the sunlight. Just north, occupying the entire block between Ninth and Tenth Avenues and 20th and 21st Streets, is the **General Theological Seminary**; its garden is a sublime retreat. The seminary's land was part of the estate known as Chelsea, owned by Clement Clarke Moore, a wealthy biblical scholar best recognized as the author of *A Visit from Saint Nicholas.* On Tenth Avenue, the 1929 Art Deco **Empire Diner** *(210 Tenth Ave at 22nd St, 212-243-2736),* was once a lonely eating outpost for pre- and postclubbers. Today, it's been joined by such spots as the beautiful-people mecca **The Park** *(see page 271)* and **The Red Cat** *(see page 170),* an American bistro.

Head east to Sixth Avenue around 27th Street and you might think you're in a tropical forest— the pavement disappears beneath the palm leaves, decorative grasses and colorful blooms of Chelsea's **flower district**. Sixth Avenue in the mid-20s is full of antiques showrooms, which sell everything from old posters to classic furniture, and the **Annex flea market** *(see page 221)* operates year-round on weekends in an empty parking lot on 25th Street (it used to spread across many more lots, but several of those have been replaced with large apartment buildings). Like other pockets of Chelsea, the area is also attracting media: Minimalists with a modern aesthetic will appreciate the stark interior and soaring ceilings of the new **Art Directors Club**, a nonprofit organization and gallery serving the visual communications industry. It's just downstairs from the indie-music dispatcher Caroline Distribution, which makes sure records from labels such as Astralwerks (the Chemical Brothers, Air) and Plan 9 (the Misfits) make it to music stores.

On 23rd Street, between Seventh and Eighth Avenues, is the **Chelsea Hotel** *(see page 131)*, where many famous people checked in—some of whom never checked out, such as Sid Vicious' girlfriend Nancy Spungen. It's worth a peek for its weird artwork and ghoulish guests, and a drink at the lavish lounge Serena *(see page 149)* in the basement. On Eighth Avenue, you'll find the **Joyce Theater** *(see page 343)*, a stunning renovated Art Deco cinema now devoted to dance; and on 19th Street, the **Bessie Schönberg Theater** *(219 W 19th St between Seventh and Eighth Aves, 212-691-6500)*, where poets recite and mimes do…well, whatever mimes do. Farther toward the river on 19th Street is **The Kitchen** *(see page 344)*, the experimental arts center with a penchant for video.

On Ninth Avenue is **Chelsea Market**, a former Nabisco plant where the first Oreo cookie was made in 1912. The block-long building is actually a conglomeration of 17 structures built between the 1890s and 1930s. An upscale food arcade on the ground floor offers meat and fish, wine, tempting cheesecakes and imported Italian foods, among other things. But the building has also become a media center: The Food Network tapes shows in a glassed-in street-level kitchen and studio, and Oxygen Media and NY1 News have installed offices on the floors above.

The **Starrett-Lehigh Building** *(601 W 26th St at Eleventh Ave)* is the perfect barometer of the high-pressure real estate market. Until 1999, the 1930s structure—acclaimed as a masterpiece of the International Style—was a neglected $6-a-square-foot industrial loft and warehouse. Today, companies such as Martha Stewart Living Omnimedia and Hugo Boss pay more than $30 a square foot for raw space.

After you hit some of the art galleries that have colonized the area, keep heading west along 22nd Street to watch the sunset from the **Hudson River Piers**. These were originally

the terminals for the world's grand ocean liners (the *Titanic* was scheduled to dock here). Most are in a state of disrepair, though development has transformed the four between 17th and 23rd Streets into a sports center and TV-studio complex called **Chelsea Piers** *(see page 328)*.

Art Directors Club
106 W 29th St between Sixth and Seventh Aves (212-643-1440; www.adcny.org). Subway: 1, 2 to 28th St. Mon–Fri 10am–6pm.
This nonprofit organization has been providing encouragement, support and resources to visual communications artists since 1920, but its new gallery-like space and calendar of events are anything but antiquated. Recent events have included "Smile i-D," a multimedia installation celebrating *i-D* magazine's 20th anniversary and a speaker series with style pioneers such as Kate and Andy Spade.

Chelsea Historic District
Between Ninth and Tenth Aves from 20th to 22nd Sts. Subway: C, E to 23rd St.
You'll find a range of architecture: Greek and Gothic Revival, Italianate and 1800s apartment buildings.

Chelsea Market
75 Ninth Ave between 15th and 16th Sts. Subway: A, C, E to 14th St; L to Eighth Ave. Mon–Sat 8am–7pm; Sun 10am–6pm.

General Theological Seminary
175 Ninth Ave between 20th and 21st Sts (212-243-5150; www.gts.edu). Subway: C, E to 23rd St. Mon–Fri noon–3pm; Sat 11am–3pm. Free.
Walk through the grounds of the seminary or take a guided tour in summer (call for details).

Gramercy Park

You need a key to get past the gates of Gramercy Park, a tranquil square at the bottom of Lexington Avenue between 20th and 21st Streets. Who gets a key? Only those who live in the beautiful townhouses and apartment buildings that surround the park—or who stay at the **Gramercy Park Hotel** *(see page 133)*. Anyone, however, can enjoy the charm of the neighboring district, between Park Avenue South and Third Avenue. Gramercy Park was developed in the 1830s, copying the concept of a London square. **The Players**, at 16 Gramercy Park, is housed in an 1845 brown-stone that was once owned by actor Edwin Booth; the 19th-century superstar was

► Contemporary art lovers should plan on exploring the far western area of Chelsea. See chapter **Art Galleries** for listings.
► For more information on Chelsea's gay nightlife, see chapter **Gay & Lesbian**.

Sightseeing

the brother of Abraham Lincoln's assassin, John Wilkes Booth. He had it remodeled as a club for theater professionals. (Winston Churchill and Mark Twain were members.) At No. 15 is the Gothic Revival **National Arts Club**, whose members have often donated impressive works in lieu of annual dues. Its bar features perhaps the only original Tiffany stained-glass ceiling left in New York City.

Irving Place, leading south from the park to 14th Street, is named after Washington Irving. Although the author of *The Legend of Sleepy Hollow* didn't actually live on this street, it does have a literary past: **Pete's Tavern** *(129 E 18th St at Irving Pl, 212-473-7676)*, which insists that it and not **McSorley's** *(see page 146)* or the Ear Inn, is the oldest bar in town, is where wit O. Henry wrote *The Gift of the Magi*. Near the corner of 15th Street, **Irving Plaza** *(see page 305)*, a medium-sized live-music venue, hosts big-name acts (everything from Stereolab to Willie Nelson). West of Irving Place, at the corner of 17th Street and Park Avenue South, is the last headquarters of the once omnipotent Tammany Hall political machine. Built in 1929, the building now houses the **Union Square Theater** and the **New York Film Academy**.

West of Gramercy Park is the **Theodore Roosevelt Birthplace**, now a small museum. The low, fortresslike **69th Regiment Armory** *(Lexington Ave at 25th St)*, now used by the New York National Guard, was the site of the sensational 1913 Armory Show, which introduced Americans to the modern forms of Cubism and Fauvism, the precocious Marcel Duchamp and other artistic outrages.

National Arts Club
15 Gramercy Park South between Park Ave South and Irving Pl (212-475-3424). Subway: 6 to 23rd St. Open for exhibitions only.

Theodore Roosevelt Birthplace
28 E 20th St between Broadway and Park Ave South (212-260-1616). Subway: 6 to 23rd St. Wed–Sun 9am–5pm. $2, under 17 free. Cash only.
The president's actual birthplace was demolished in 1916 but has since been fully reconstructed, complete with period furniture and trophy room.

Rest assured
These public spaces promise to ease the strain of midtown madness

Unlike Manhattan's upper and lower reaches, midtown suffers from a lack of pastoral scenery. Ironically, it's the section of the city most in need of designated breathing space. Just the thought of places like Macy's and Times Square, which throb with mobs, is enough to drive pooped-out visitors to the nearest restaurant for a pit stop. But there is respite for weary feet that won't cost you a cup of unwanted coffee. You may not get the rolling lawns of Central Park, but you'll find plenty of public places where you can set down your shopping bags and get a second wind.

For those of you taking on the area above 14th Street and below 23rd Street, there are quite a few alternatives to **Union Square** *(see page 64)*. In the event you're ambling west toward Chelsea, the best spots to take a break are city playgrounds peppered about (however, be forewarned: Many playgrounds bear signs that say NO ADULTS UNACCOMPANIED BY CHILDREN.). Among the neighborhood's most accessible are the **Dr. Gertrude B. Kelly Playground** *(17th St between Eighth and Ninth Aves)*, where you'll find well-muscled youths playing fast-paced handball, and the more upscale **Clement Clarke Moore Park** *(22nd St at Tenth Ave)*, which features manicured landscaping and room for people to spread out.

On the east side of town, the options are more scenic. Just around the corner from the private Gramercy Park, along Second Avenue between 15th and 17th Streets is **Stuyvesant Square Park**. In the 1980s, this green swath was restored to its mid-19th–century splendor, including ornate benches and the city's longest and tallest freestanding cast-iron fence. Bisected by Second Avenue, the park is most easily located by following the scrubs-clad medical professionals who make their way to Beth Israel Medical Center, one of the main buildings bordering the park. Close by is **Stuyvesant Town**, a redbrick high-rise complex that stretches from 14th to 20th Streets, between First Avenue and FDR Drive. At its core is a sprawling park furnished with benches, fountains, footpaths, basketball courts and black squirrels (most of the squirrels in the city's parks are brown). The area is meant for residents, but visitors won't be kicked out.

Kips Bay & Murray Hill

Running from 23rd to 42nd Streets between Park Avenue (and Park Avenue South) and the East River, this area is dominated by large apartment buildings and hospitals. Though the area has its own historical past (Herman Melville wrote *Billy Budd* at 104 East 26th Street), it was, until recently, considered a nondescript neighborhood. But the slightly below-market rents and explosion of restaurants on nearby Park Avenue South have attracted fashionable residents such as designer John Bartlett, not to mention a new name: Nomad (North of Madison Square Park). The southern portion, known as **Kips Bay** (after Jacobus Kip, whose 17th-century farm used to occupy the area) is populated mainly by young professionals. Third Avenue is the main thoroughfare, and it's where you'll find ethnic restaurants representing a variety of mainly Eastern cuisines, including Afghan, Turkish and Tibetan, along with nightspots such as **Spread**, a sleek restaurant and lounge in the hotel **Marcel** *(see page 134)*, and the **Rodeo Bar** *(see page 313)* a Texas-style roadhouse that offers food and live roots music. Lexington Avenue between 27th and 30th Streets is called **Curry Hill** because of the many Indian restaurants and grocery stores offering inexpensive food, spices and imported goods. Other than a complex that includes the multiscreen theater **Loews Kips Bay** *(see page 274)* and a **Borders** bookstore *(see page 218)* at 30th Street, Second Avenue is home to a collection of pubs and small, undistinguished restaurants. First Avenue in the 20s is hospital row: **New York University Medical Center**, the city-run **Bellevue Hospital** and the city's chief medical examiner's office are all here.

Between 30th and 40th Streets is **Murray Hill**. Townhouses of the rich and powerful were once clustered around Park and Madison Avenues. While it's still a fashionable neighborhood, only a few streets retain the elegance that once made it such a tony address. **Sniffen Court** *(150–158 E 36th St between Lexington and Third Aves)* is an unspoiled row of 1864 carriage houses, located within spitting

Above 23rd Street, pedestrians are treated to **Madison Square** *(between Fifth and Madison Aves, from 23rd to 26th Sts)*, which was rededicated in June 2001. The park's views of the Empire State Building and Flatiron Building make it a destination spot for tourists and residents alike (canine-lovers congregate near the dog run). East of here is Bellevue Hospital *(462 First Ave at 27th St)*, which offers a tranquil resting spot in the main entrance courtyard.

After letting your inner spendaholic loose in and around Macy's, you can step off the consumer treadmill into the **Herald Square** or **Greeley Square** commons, located on the north and south sides of the junction of Broadway and Sixth Avenue at 34th Street, and often blooming with flowers. Take a seat at one of the green tables scattered about. If all the chairs are occupied (which they often are by lunching employees of local businesses, roaming nannies and the occasional substance abuser), head west on 34th Street just beyond Seventh Avenue. There, behind **One Penn Plaza**, you'll find a small courtyard that extends to 33rd Street. It isn't glamorous, but it does have plenty of granite tree planters with built-in benches.

Farther uptown, behind the New York Public Library, is the popular **Bryant Park** *(between 40th and 42nd Sts, from Fifth to Sixth Aves)*, a football field–size lawn surrounded by perennial gardens, promenades, monuments and movable chairs. This area, which is lined with towering skyscrapers, has its share of plazas and "vest-pocket" parks, but they're not easy to spot. Keep an eye out for man-made waterfalls, café-style seating with food and beverage kiosks, and beautifully maintained grounds. Two such oases are the islandlike **Greenacre Park** *(north side of 51st St between Second and Third Aves)*, a tri-level paradise of granite, water sculpture and honey locust trees, and **Paley Park** *(53rd St at Fifth Ave)*, poet Frank O'Hara's rest spot of choice, complete with a 20-foot waterfall.

If you're out amid the bright lights and big-city action of the Theater District, take refuge in **Hell's Kitchen Park** *(Tenth Ave between 47th and 48th Sts)*, more than half an acre dotted with benches, monkey bars and basketball and racquetball courts. The cap-wearing denizens look like old Jimmy Cagneys.

While New York doesn't have anything to compete with Rome's Spanish Steps, for quick sits there are the steps (and pews) of **St. Patrick's Cathedral** *(see page 74)* and those of the **New York Public Library** *(see page 74)*. You may not look quite as stately as the great stone lions, Patience and Fortitude, but you can get up and leave whenever you want.

distance of the Queens-Midtown Tunnel's ceaseless traffic.

The charming **Morgan Library** *(Madison Ave between 36th and 37th Sts; see page 35)* is the reason most visitors come to the area. Two elegant buildings (one of which was J. Pierpont Morgan's personal library), linked by a modern glass cloister, house the silver and copper collections, manuscripts, books and prints owned by the notorious banker.

Herald Square & the Garment District

Seventh Avenue in the 30s has a stylish moniker: Fashion Avenue. The surrounding area is the **Garment District**, where midtown office buildings stand amid the buzzing activity of a huge manufacturing industry that's been centered here for a century. Its streets are permanently gridlocked by delivery trucks. Shabby clothing stores and fabric shops line the streets (especially 38th and 39th Streets), along with specialty shops exclusively selling lace, buttons or Lycra swimsuits. Most are wholesale only, although some sell to the public. At Seventh Avenue and 27th Street is the **Fashion Institute of Technology** *(see page 38)*, a state college where aspiring Calvin Kleins and Anna Suis (both FIT graduates) dream up the fashions of tomorrow. The school's gallery features excellent exhibitions.

Plunked at the corner of Broadway and 34th Street, and stretching all the way to Seventh Avenue, **Macy's** *(see page 194)* is still impressive as the biggest—and busiest—department store in the world. Across the street is **H&M** *(see page 194)* department store located in the **Marbridge Building**, which underwent a recent $24-million makeover. **Herald Square**, this retail wonderland's home, is named after a long-gone newspaper. The southern part is known as **Greeley Square**, after the owner of the *Herald*'s rival, the *Tribune*, a paper for which Karl Marx wrote a regular column. *Life* magazine was based around the corner on 31st Street, and its cherubic mascot can still be seen over the entrance of what is now the **Herald Square Hotel** *(see page 138)*. Worth avoiding only a few years ago, the squares now offer bistro chairs

---

▶ To find a place to stay while visiting midtown, see chapter **Accommodations**.
▶ The area's museums are all detailed in the chapter **Museums**.
▶ For information on a multi-museum discount package, see **Cheap tix**, page 35.

---

and rest areas for weary pedestrians looking to take a break *(see **Rest assured**, page 68)*. East of Greeley Square, a bustling district of Korean shops and restaurants lines 32nd Street.

The giant doughnut of a building one block west, on Seventh Avenue, is the sports and entertainment arena, **Madison Square Garden** *(see pages 300 and 322)*. It occupies the site of the old Pennsylvania Station—the McKim, Mead & White architectural masterpiece that was foolishly destroyed by 1960s city planners, an act that brought about the creation of the Landmarks Preservation Commission. The railroad terminal's name has been shortened (as if in shame) to **Penn Station**, and it now lies beneath the Garden, where it serves some 600,000 people daily—more than any other station in the country. The aesthetic tides turned in 2000, with the approval of a $788-million restoration and development project to move Penn Station back home, so to speak, to the **General Post Office** *(421 Eighth Ave between 31st and 33rd Sts, 212-967-8585; see page 372)*, which was designed by the same architects in 1913 to complement the old station. Financial strain on the city has delayed the initiative, which would connect the post office's two buildings with a soaring glass-and-nickel–trussed ticketing hall and concourse. When finally realized, the new Penn Station will offer Amtrak service and rail links to Newark, La Guardia and JFK airports; the current Penn Station will continue to house New Jersey Transit, the Long Island Rail Road and subways.

Herald Square

Junction of Broadway and Sixth Ave at 34th St. Subway: B, D, F, V, N, Q, R, W to 34th St–Herald Sq.

Broadway & Times Square

Around 42nd Street and Broadway, often called "the Crossroads of the World," the night is illuminated not by the moon and stars but by acres of glaring neon. Even native New Yorkers can't help but be electrified by the larger-than-life light show of this buzzing core of entertainment and tourism. Few places represent New York's collective power and noisy optimism as well as **Times Square**.

Originally called Long Acre Square, Times Square was renamed after *The New York Times* moved to the site in the early 1900s, announcing its arrival with a spectacular New Year's Eve fireworks display. Around its building, 1 Times Square, the *Times* erected the world's first zipper sign, on which the paper posted election returns in 1928. The *Times* is now on 43rd Street between Seventh and Eighth Avenues (and has an $84-million plan to build a new tower on Eighth

Big bang The 1913 Armory Show caused a stir at Gramercy's 69th Regiment Armory.

Avenue between 40th and 41st Streets), but the sign and New Year's Eve celebrations remain at the original locale. Times Square is really just an elongated intersection, where Broadway crosses Seventh Avenue. This part of town is the epicenter of the **Theater District**. More than 30 grand stages used for dramatic productions are situated on the streets that cross **Broadway**—which is also another name for the area (see chapter **Theater & Dance**). The peep shows—what's left of Times Square's once-famous sex trade—are now relegated to Eighth Avenue.

The area's transformation began in 1990, when the city condemned most of the properties along **42nd Street** between Seventh and Eighth Avenues (a.k.a. "the Deuce"). A few years later, the city changed its zoning laws, making it harder for adult-entertainment establishments to continue operating legally. The few remaining video supermarkets now sell kung fu films next to skin flicks (thanks to a city ordinance that requires 40 percent of their stock to be nonpornographic), and the live peep shows of yore have been replaced by X-rated video booths. Times Square's XXX days were officially numbered when the Walt Disney Company moved in and renovated the historic **New Amsterdam Theatre**, lair of the long-running musical *The Lion King.* Other corporations followed. The dodgy, grimy Times Square of the 1970s and '80s is now undeniably safer and cleaner. To see how much things have changed, stop by **Show World**, a former porn emporium that now sells tourist trinkets and hosts short (nonporn) film series and (fully clothed) Off-Off Broadway performances.

The streets west of Eighth Avenue are filled with eateries catering mainly to theatergoers. West 46th Street between Eighth and Ninth

Avenues—**Restaurant Row**—has an almost unbroken string of them (see chapter **Restaurants, Theater District**, *page 176).*

As you'd expect, office buildings in the area are filled with entertainment companies: recording studios, theatrical management companies, record labels, screening rooms and so on. **The Brill Building** *(1619 Broadway at 49th St)* has the richest history, having long been the headquarters of music publishers and arrangers. The strip it's on is known as **Tin Pan Alley** (though the original Tin Pan Alley was on West 28th Street). Such luminaries as Cole Porter, George Gershwin, Rodgers and Hart, Lieber and Stoller, Phil Spector and Carole King produced their hits here. Visiting rock royalty and aspiring musicians drool over the selection of new and vintage guitars and countless other instruments in a string of shops on 48th Street, just off Seventh Avenue.

At the southwestern end of the square is the headquarters of **MTV** *(1515 Broadway at 44th St; see* **Crowd pleasers**, *page 276),* which often sends camera crews into the streets to tape segments. Especially during warmer months, crowds of screeching teens congregate under the windows of the network's second-floor studio, hoping for a wave from visiting celebrities inside.

Across the street from MTV, at 4 Times Square, is the glass home of magazine-publishing giant **Condé Nast** *(Broadway at 43rd St).* Completed in 1999, it was the first office tower to be built in Manhattan since the late-'80s recession. The structure's skin features tiny sunlight-capturing cells that generate some of the energy needed for the building's day-to-day operations. In the same building is the **Nasdaq MarketSite** *(877-627-3271; www.nasdaq.com).* Opened in 2000, the multimedia "electronic stock market" dominates Times Square with its eight-story-tall, 9,800-square-foot cylindrical video screen.

Madame Tussaud's New York, a Gothamized version of the London-based wax museum chain, has an "Opening Night Party" room featuring New York personalities such as Woody Allen and Barbra Streisand, along with the glamorous likes of Brad Pitt and RuPaul. Check out the museum's latest inductees: Barbara Walters, Bela Lugosi and President George W. Bush.

Nightlife in the square is dominated by theaters and theme restaurants. For a shot of vein-popping adrenaline—and entertainment at its most outrageous—stop by the **WWF New York** *(1501 Broadway between 43rd and 44th Sts, 212-398-2563)* complex for some burgers and wrestling. An amazing view

Sightseeing

Walk this way At FIT, budding fashionistas strut to class with runway attitude and style.

and more genteel experience can be had at celebrated chef Larry Forgione's **Restaurant Above** *(see page 176)*.

Make a brief detour uptown on Seventh Avenue, just south of Central Park, for a glimpse of the great classical-music landmark **Carnegie Hall** *(see pages 311 and 316)*. Across the street is the celebrated sandwich shop **Carnegie Deli** *(see page 177)*.

West of Times Square, past the curious steel spiral of the **Port Authority Bus Terminal** on Eighth Avenue and the knotted entrance to the Lincoln Tunnel, is an area historically known as **Hell's Kitchen**. During the 19th century, an impoverished Irish community lived here amid gangs and crime. Following the Irish were Italians, Greeks, Puerto Ricans, Dominicans and other ethnic groups. It remained rough-and-tumble (and provided the backdrop for the hit musical *West Side Story*) through the 1970s, when, in an effort to invite gentrification, the neighborhood renamed itself **Clinton**, after **De Witt Clinton Park** on Eleventh Avenue between 52nd and 54th Streets. Today, crime has abated and Clinton's pretty, tree-lined streets and neat redbrick apartment houses are filled with a diverse group of old-timers, actors and business types.

Ninth Avenue is the area's main drag, known for its inexpensive restaurants (many of them ethnic) and bars catering to a young crowd. There's also a small Cuban district around Tenth Avenue in the mid-40s, an otherwise desolate stretch of the city.

South of 42nd Street, the main attraction is the **Jacob K. Javits Convention Center** *(Eleventh Ave between 34th and 39th Sts)*; this glass palace, designed by James Ingo Freed of I.M. Pei & Partners, hosts conventions and trade shows. Finally, along the Hudson River piers, you'll find the terminal for **Circle Line** *(see page 107)* on 42nd Street at Pier 83. At the end of 46th Street is the aircraft carrier *Intrepid*, which houses the **Sea-Air-Space Museum** *(see page 44)*.

Madame Tussaud's New York

234 W 42nd St between Seventh and Eighth Aves (800-246-8872; www.madame-tussauds.com). Subway: N, Q, R, W, S, 1, 2, 3, 7 to 42nd St–Times Sq. Sun–Thu 10am–6pm; Fri, Sat 10am–8pm. $12.75–$19.95.

New York City's Official Visitor Information Center

810 Seventh Ave at 53rd St (212-484-1222; www.nycvisit.com). Subway: B, D, E to Seventh Ave; N, Q, R, W to 57th St; 1, 2 to 50th St. Mon–Fri 8:30am–6pm; Sat, Sun 9am–5pm.
New York's effort to define itself as a welcoming tourist destination is underscored at this very useful visitors' center. There's an information desk, hundreds of brochures and maps, and an ATM.

Show World

669 Eighth Ave between 42nd and 43rd Sts (212-247-6643). Subway: A, C, E to 42nd St–Port Authority. 24 hrs.

Times Square

Times Square Visitors' Center, 1560 Broadway between 46th and 47th Sts, entrance on Seventh Ave (212-768-1560). Subway: N, R, W to 49th St; 1, 2 to 50th St. 8am–8pm.

Fifth Avenue

This majestic thoroughfare is New York's Main Street, the route of the city's many parades and marches. It runs through a stretch of chic department stores and past some of the most recognizable buildings and public spaces in town.

The **Empire State Building** is at 34th Street. While it's visible from many parts of the city (and lit up at night in various colors, according to the holiday or special event; *see* **Inspired spire**, *page 74*), only at the corner of Fifth Avenue and 34th Street can you truly appreciate its height. Situated smack dab in the center of midtown, its observatory offers brilliant views in every direction.

Impassive stone lions guard the steps of the **New York Public Library** at 41st Street. This beautiful Beaux Arts building provides an astonishing escape from the noise outside. The **Rose Main Reading Room**, on the library's top floor, is a hushed sanctuary of 23-foot-long tables and matching oak chairs where people busily read, write and research. Behind the library is **Bryant Park**, an elegant lawn filled in the warm months with lunching office workers; the park also houses the ivy-covered American restaurant **Bryant Park Cafe and Grill** (*25 W 40th St between Fifth and Sixth Aves, 212-840-6500*) and hosts a dizzying schedule of free entertainment (specific events are listed in chapter **By Season, Summer**). Across 40th Street at No. 40, **The Bryant Park** (*see* **Small Wonders**, *page 132*) is a new hotel built within the former American Radiator Building. Designed by architect Raymond Hood in the mid-1920s, the building's near-black brick, trimmed in gold leaf, seems to embody the term *Gotham*. The luxurious hotel is home to the **Cellar Bar** (*see page 147*) lounge and **Ilo** (*see page 177*), a French-infused American restaurant. Another notable hotel in the area, **The Algonquin** (*59 W 44th St between Fifth and Sixth Aves; see page 125*) is where scathing wit Dorothy Parker held court at Alexander Woollcott's Round Table.

The city's diamond trade is located along the 47th Street strip known as **Diamond Row**. In front of glittering window displays, you'll see Orthodox Jewish traders, precious gems in their pockets, doing business in the street.

Veer off Fifth Avenue into the 19 buildings of **Rockefeller Center** (*48th to 51st Sts*) and you'll understand why this masterful use of public space is so lavishly praised. As you stroll down the Chanel Gardens, the stately Art Deco **GE Building** gradually appears above you. The sunken plaza in the center is the site of an often-packed ice-skating rink (*see page 330*). A giant Christmas tree looms above it all December (*see*

page 242). Gathered around the plaza's perimeter are the **International Building** and its companions. The center is filled with murals, sculptures, mosaics, metalwork and enamels. Of special note is José María Sert's mural in the GE Building, depicting the theme "New Frontiers and the March of Civilization," and Sol LeWitt's primary-colored mural *Wall Drawing #896 Colors/Curves* in the lobby of **Christie's** auction house at 20 Rockefeller Plaza.

The **NBC** television network's glass-walled ground-level studio (home of the *Today* show), at the southwest corner of Rockefeller Plaza and 49th Street, draws a weekday-morning crowd. When taping ends, the same crowd—along with thousands of other pedestrians—makes its way to the chain stores thriving above and below Rockefeller Center. Over on Sixth Avenue is **Radio City Music Hall**, the world's largest cinema when it was built in 1932. The Art Deco jewel was treated to a $70-million restoration in 1999; it's a stellar example of the benefits of historic preservation.

Across Fifth Avenue from Rockefeller Center is the beautiful Gothic Revival **St. Patrick's Cathedral**, the largest Catholic cathedral in the United States.

Several museums are just a few blocks north of Rockefeller Center: **The Museum of Television & Radio** (*see page 44*) on 52nd Street, and the **Museum of Modern Art** (*see page 35*), **American Craft Museum** (*see page 38*), and the newly built **American Folk Museum** (*see page 38 and chapter* **Architecture**). Note that MoMA will be closing in June 2002 and temporarily moving to Queens (*see page 96*) for several years while a new addition is built. One more bit of culture before you shop: In the 1920s, 52nd Street was "Swing Street," a row of speakeasies and jazz clubs. All that's left is **'21'** (at No. 21; *see page 178*), long a power-lunch spot.

The blocks of Fifth Avenue between Rockefeller Center and Central Park house

Yo, that's wax! Madame Tussaud's New York specializes in off-the-wall figures.

expensive retail palaces offering everything from Rolexes to gourmet chocolate. Along the stretch from **Saks Fifth Avenue** *(at 50th St; see page 194)* and **Bergdorf Goodman** *(at 58th St; see page 193)*, the rents are among the highest in the world, and you'll find such names as Cartier, Gucci, Tiffany and Versace *(see* **Head of the class***, page 200)*, along with the first U.S. outpost of Swedish clothing giant H&M and the National Basketball Association's official store. The pinnacle of this mall trend is the soaring brass spine of **Trump Tower** *(725 Fifth Ave at 56th St)*, an ostentatious pink-marble shopping emporium built by "the Donald."

Fifth Avenue is crowned by **Grand Army Plaza** at 59th Street. A statue of General Sherman presides over this public space; to the west is that most elegant château, the **Plaza Hotel** *(see page 117)*, while to the east you'll find the famous **FAO Schwarz** toy store *(see page 221)*.

NBC

30 Rockefeller Plaza, 49th St between Fifth and Sixth Aves (212-664-3700; www.nbc.com). Subway: B, D, F, V to 47–50th Sts–Rockefeller Ctr. Tours Mon–Thu 9am–4:30pm; Fri, Sat 9am–5:30pm; Sun 10am–4pm.

Nov 23–Dec 30 Mon–Thu 8:30am–7pm; Fri, Sat 8:15am–8pm; Sun 9:15am–6:30pm. $17.50, seniors and children $15. Children under 6 not admitted. Peer through the *Today* show's studio window with a horde of fellow onlookers, or pay admission for a guided tour of the interior studios.

New York Public Library

Fifth Ave between 40th and 42nd Sts (212-930-0830; www.nypl.org). Subway: B, D, F, V to 42nd St; 7 to Fifth Ave. Mon, Thu–Sat 10am–6pm; Tue, Wed 11am–7:30pm. Some sections closed Mondays.

Radio City Music Hall

See page 308 for listing. Tour tickets are $16 and $10 for children under 12.

Rockefeller Center

48th to 51st Sts between Fifth and Sixth Aves (212-632-3975). Subway: B, D, F, V to 47–50th Sts–Rockefeller Ctr. Free. Guided tours are available for $10 per person at the **NBC Experience Store** *(30 Rockefeller Plaza).* Call 212-664-3700 for more information.

St. Patrick's Cathedral

Fifth Ave between 50th and 51st Sts (212-753-2261). Subway: B, D, F to 47–50th Sts–Rockefeller Ctr; E, V to Fifth Ave–53rd St. Free. 6:30am–9:30pm. Call for tour dates and times. Services Mon–Fri 7, 7:30, 8, 8:30am, noon, 12:30, 1,

Inspired spire

The Empire State Building is a beacon of beauty

More than any other landmark in the metropolis, the Empire State Building *is* New York City (the Statue of Liberty is a national symbol). Built during the devastating Depression on the site of the original Waldorf-Astoria Hotel, the ESB became the most famous skyscraper in the world. Visit it before seeing anything else to get the lay of the land. Expect to wait in line at the 86th floor, where a second elevator takes you to the giddy heights of floor 102. For the curious, here are the facts (and a color decoder) for this Art Deco beauty that has taken on new significance in a post–World Trade Center world.
Architects Shreve, Lamb and Harmon Associates
Date completed May 1,1931. At the time, the Empire State Building was the world's tallest building. It remained so until 1973—when the World Trade Center's twin towers were completed. After the events of September 11, 2001, the Empire State Building once again became the tallest structure in Manhattan.

Height 1,250 feet (1,454 if you include the transmitter; 443.2 meters)
Number of floors 103
Number of steps 1,860 from street level to 102nd floor
Number of windows 6,500
Waste management 100 tons of trash removed from the building each month

The Light Stuff

The nightly glow of the Empire State Building's upper 30 floors changes hue regularly and isn't random. The colors signify holidays, events, seasons and worthy causes—and every time the Yankees win a World Series, blue and white light up the night. Here's the building's standard lighting schedule. *Time Out New York* publishes the week's schedule.
Red, white and blue Normally the lights shine from sunset to midnight, but during the days following the WTC tragedy, the red, white and blue bulbs burned from sunset to sunrise at the request of residents and rescue workers,

5:30pm; Sat 8, 8:30am, noon, 12:30, 5:30pm; Sun 7, 8, 9, 10:15am, noon, 1, 4, 5:30pm.

Midtown East

Grand Central Terminal, a 1913 Beaux Arts station, is the city's most spectacular point of arrival (although only commuter trains operate here). Thanks to its much vaunted renovation in 1998, the terminal has itself become a destination, with upscale restaurants and bars such as **Michael Jordan's—The Steak House NYC** *(see page 181)*, star chef Charlie Palmer's **Métrazur** *(East Balcony, 212-687-4600)* and the swish cocktail lounge **Campbell Apartment** *(see page 147)*. There's even the Euro-style food hall **Grand Central Market**, selling gourmet goodies from New York and around the world, and the food court downstairs, offering many great lunch options. A quirky historical note: The constellations of the winter zodiac that adorn the ceiling of the main concourse are backward—a mistake made by the original artist. The station stands at the junction of 42nd Street and Park Avenue, the latter rising on a cast-iron bridge and literally running around the terminal.

East 42nd Street also offers architectural distinction—in the spectacular hall of the former **Bowery Savings Bank** (at No. 110, now a special-events space owned by the Cipriani restaurant family) and the Art Deco detail of the **Chanin Building** (No. 122). Built in 1930, the gleaming chrome **Chrysler Building** (at the corner of Lexington Avenue) pays homage to the automobile. Architect William van Alen outfitted the base of the main tower with brickwork cars, complete with chrome hubcaps and radiator caps enlarged to vast proportions and projected out over the edge as gargoyles. The building's needle-sharp stainless-steel spire was added to the original plans so that it would be taller than 40 Wall Street, which was under construction at the same time. In 2001, Philip Johnson's **Chrysler Trylons**—three blue-gray glass pyramids—were assembled between the Chrysler Building and 666 Third Avenue. The retail pavilion is Johnson's "monument to 42nd Street." **The Daily News Building** (No. 220), another Art Deco gem designed by Raymond Hood, was immortalized in the *Superman* films and still houses a giant globe in its lobby, although its tabloid namesake newspaper no longer has offices there.

The street ends at **Tudor City**, a pioneering 1925 residential development that's a high-rise

who found inspiration in the patriotic glow. These national holidays also have the lights of the flag: Presidents' Day, Memorial Day, Independence Day, Flag Day, Labor Day, Armed Forces Day and Veterans' Day.
Red, black and green Dr. Martin Luther King Jr. Day
Green St. Patrick's Day, March of Dimes, Rainforest Awareness, Earth Day
Red St. Valentine's Day, Fire Department Memorial Day, Big Apple Circus
Red and blue Equal Parents Day/Children's Rights
Yellow and white Spring/Easter Week
Blue, white and blue Israel Independence Day, First Night of Hanukkah
Blue Police Memorial Day, Child Abuse Prevention
Purple and white Alzheimer's Awareness
Red, yellow and green Portugal Day
Lavender and white Stonewall Anniversary/Gay Pride
Purple, teal, white National Osteoporosis Society
Red and white Pulaski Day, Red Cross
Red, white and green Columbus Day
Blue and white Greek Independence Day, United Nations Day
Red and yellow Autumn

Black, yellow and red German Reunification Day
Pink and white "Race for the Cure"/Breast Cancer Awareness
Green, white and orange India Independence Day
Green and white Pakistan Independence Day
Red and green Holiday Season
Dark/No Lights "Day Without Art/Night Without Lights" AIDS Awareness

Empire State Building

350 Fifth Ave between 33rd and 34th Sts (212-736-3100; www.esbnyc.com). Subway: B, D, F, V, N, Q, R, W to 34th St–Herald Sq; 6 to 33rd St. Observatories open Mon–Fri 10am–midnight; Sat, Sun 9:30am–midnight. Last tickets sold at 11:15pm. $9, seniors $7, children 5–11 $4, under 5 free. Cash only. If you're a fan of virtual-reality rides, the Empire State houses NY Skyride *(10am–10pm; $11.50, seniors and children $8.50)*, a big-screen, eight-minute movie that uses flight-simulator technology to give the audience the sensation of swooping through the city. The experience includes the World Trade Center and a near crash into the Financial District (though the owners say it will be edited out in a future version).

Leaf your worries behind Unwind in the pastoral surroundings of Bryant Park.

version of Hampton Court in England. North of here is the **Turtle Bay** area, though you won't see many turtles in the East River these days. This neighborhood is dominated by the **United Nations** and its famous glass-walled **Secretariat** building. Although you don't need your passport, you are leaving U.S. soil when you enter the UN complex—this is an international zone. Optimistic peacemongering sculptures dot the grounds, and the **Peace Gardens** along the East River bloom with delicate roses. The serenity is trumped, however, by Donald Trump's 72-story **Trump World Tower** *(First Ave between 47th and 48th Sts)*, the world's tallest residential building. Even a coalition of high-powered area residents, including the venerated newsman Walter Cronkite, could not stop Trump from constructing it.

Rising behind Grand Central Terminal, the **Met Life Building** (formerly Pan Am) was once the world's largest office tower. Its most celebrated tenants are the peregrine falcons that nest on the roof, living off pigeons that they kill in midair. Directly north of it, is **230 Park Avenue**. Built by Warren & Wetmore, the architects of Grand Central, the building features glittering gold detail.

On Park Avenue itself, amid the blocks of international corporate headquarters, is the **Waldorf-Astoria Hotel** *(see page 117)*. The famed hotel was originally located on Fifth Avenue but was demolished in 1929 to make way for the Empire State Building; it was rebuilt here in 1931. Many of the city's most famous International Style office buildings are also in this area. Built in 1952, **Lever House** *(390 Park Ave between 53rd and 54th Sts)* was the first glass box on Park Avenue. The 1958 **Seagram**

Building *(375 Park Ave between 52nd and 53rd Sts)*, designed by Ludwig Mies van der Rohe and others, is a stunning bronze-and-glass tower that contains the Philip Johnson–designed, landmark restaurant, **The Four Seasons** *(see page 181)*. A postmodern Chippendale crown tops Johnson's '80s-era **Sony Building** *(550 Madison Ave between 55th and 56th Sts)*. Inside is Sony's public arcade and **Wonder Technology Lab** *(see page 293)*, a hands-on thrill zone of innovative technology.

The newest addition to this cluster of stellar architecture is the **LVMH Tower** *(19 E 57th St between Fifth and Madison Aves)*. Designed by Christian de Portzamparc, the youngest architect to be awarded the Pritzker Prize (the Nobel of architecture), the U.S. headquarters for the French luxury-goods company Louis Vuitton Moët Hennessy is a reworked vision of Art Deco.

Taking advantage of what already existed, the **Bridgemarket** complex *(First Ave at 59th St)*, opened in 1999 in what was once a farmers' market under the Queensboro Bridge. The renovated space is now the site of a **Terence Conran Shop** *(see page 226)* and **Guastavino's Restaurant** *(see page 182)*, named for the maker of the tiles that line the gracefully curved ceilings. Spanish builder Rafael Guastavino Y Moreno's legacy can also be seen in places such as the **Oyster Bar** *(see page 181)* at Grand Central and in the Registry Room at **Ellis Island** *(see pages 41 and 46)*.

Grand Central Terminal

42nd to 44th Sts between Vanderbilt and Lexington Aves. Subway: S, 4, 5, 6, 7 to 42nd St–Grand Central. For tour information, see **Grand Central Partnership**, page 109.

United Nations Headquarters

First Ave at 46th St (212-963-7713; www.un.org). Subway: S, 4, 5, 6, 7 to 42nd St–Grand Central. 9:30am–4:45pm. Free. Guided tours every half hour: $7.50, children under 5 not permitted.

▶ For more on the Modernist and Postmodern buildings in midtown, see chapter **Architecture**.

Uptown

North of 59th Street, bucolic Central Park beckons, while the surrounding neighborhoods, Harlem and Washington Heights teem with cultural offerings

Central Park

"Once around the park, driver." It's a request that has been made countless times over the years, whether by lovers canoodling in cabs or snuggling in a romantic horse-drawn buggy on Central Park South. The park is, of course, Central Park, the crown jewel of the city's park system, and those horse rides are legendary for their romantic appeal; you can clop along, enjoying the sylvan splendor, for about $65 an hour *(see page 111)*.

Still, as natural as it may seem, this sensational 843-acre patch of the great outdoors is as prefab as Manhattan's street grid: The arrangement of everything—except the rocks—was planned by man. Make that two men. It took 20 years for journalist and landscape architect Frederick Law Olmsted and architect Calvert Vaux to create their mowable masterpiece. It was long believed that the land on which the park was built had been nothing more than a swamp when construction began in 1840, but it's been established that some 600 free blacks, along with Irish and German

immigrants, occupied an area in the West 80s that was known as Seneca Village.

Close to the West 72nd Street entrance is **Strawberry Fields**. This is where John Lennon, who lived in the nearby **Dakota** *(see page 82)*, is memorialized. Farther in is the **Sheep Meadow**—yes, sheep actually grazed here until the 1930s. Nowadays, you may see kites, Frisbees or soccer balls whiz past, but most people are working on their tans and investigating the throngs of thong-wearing exhibitionists. If you get hungry and are reasonably wealthy, repair to glitzy **Tavern on the Green** *(see page 183)*, or wolf down a hot dog at an adjacent snack bar. Just south, kids line up for a ride on the **Carousel**. (For more park activities for children, see **Central Park**, page 294.) You can jump on too, for a buck, and grab the brass ring. Come winter, ice skaters lace up at the nearby **Wollman Memorial Rink** *(see page 330)*.

North of the Sheep Meadow is the **Mall**, site of a hot-hot-hot roller-disco rink (with not-to-be-missed costumes and acrobatics), in-line skating paths and volleyball courts. To the east, behind the **Naumburg Bandshell**, is the site of the

Span-tastic This ornate bridge is just one of Central Park's many charming features.

Go west The Dakota was once considered to be as far from downtown as...the Dakotas.

Central Park SummerStage *(see page 314)*, a wildly eclectic series of free concerts held throughout the sultry months. **Bethesda Fountain and Terrace**, near the center of the 72nd Street Transverse Road, is one of the more popular meeting places in the park. North of the fountain, you can rent a boat, gondola or bicycle at the **Loeb Boathouse** on the **Lake**, which is crossed by the elegant **Bow Bridge**. The nearby **Boathouse in Central Park** restaurant *(see page 184)* offers a mesmerizing view of Central Park to go with its first-rate surf-and-turf menu. If water isn't your thing, head to the west side of the lake and soak in the acoustic sounds of one of the park's many buskers. Requests are welcome—as are tips.

For sailing on a smaller scale, head east to the **Conservatory Water**, where enthusiasts race model sailboats. The nearby wild and hilly **Ramble** is known for bird-watching by day and gay cruising by night. As a result, this area of the park is often patrolled by plainclothes police, and at night it's best avoided by those without protection (in every sense of the word).

Farther uptown is the popular **Belvedere Castle**, which houses the **Henry Luce Nature Observatory**; the **Delacorte Theater** *(see page 336)*, where the New York Shakespeare Festival mounts performances during the summer; and the **Great Lawn**, a big patch of grass where concerts and other mega-events are held. The **Reservoir**, above 86th Street, was renamed several years ago in honor of the late Jacqueline Kennedy Onassis, who used to jog around it. North of the sports fields and tennis courts, the park is wild and wooded. Kids fish the restored **Harlem Meer** at the northeastern

corner, and strolling gentry stop to smell the roses in the beautiful, formal **Conservatory Garden** *(Fifth Ave at 105th St)*.

The Carousel
Mid-park at 64th St (212-879-0244). Subway: A, C, B, D, 1, 2 to 59th St–Columbus Circle. Apr–Oct 10am–6pm; Nov–Mar 10am–4:30pm; closed on extremely cold days; extended hours during summer months. $1 per ride, $5 for six rides. Cash only.
The park's first carousel, which was powered partly by a blind mule, opened in 1871. Today's motor-driven carousel was installed in 1951. The horses are hand-carved.

Central Park Zoo/Wildlife Center
See page 297.

Charles A. Dana Discovery Center
Entrance on Fifth Ave at 110th St (212-860-1370). Subway: 6 to 110th St. Apr–Oct Tue–Sun 10am–5pm; Nov–Mar Tue–Sun 10am–4pm. Free.
Stop in for weekend family workshops, cultural exhibits and outdoor performances on the plaza.

The Dairy
Mid-park at 64th St (212-794-6564). Subway: A, C, B, D, 1, 2 to 59th St–Columbus Circle. Apr–Oct Tue–Sun 10am–5pm; Nov–Mar Tue–Sun 10am–4pm. Free.
Built in 1872 to show city kids where milk comes from (cows, in this case), the Dairy is now the park's information center, complete with an interactive exhibit and a history video. Milk it for all it's worth, kids.

Henry Luce Nature Observatory
Belvedere Castle, mid-park at 79th St (212-772-0210). Subway: B, C to 81st St; 6 to 77th St. Apr–Oct Tue–Sun 10am–5pm; Nov–Mar Tue–Sun 10am–4pm. Free.
Enjoy the hands-on "Woods and Water" exhibit that surveys the park's variety of plants and animals.

Learn to bird on ranger-led walks that start at the Castle and head into the Ramble every Friday at 7:30 and 9:30am, and Sunday at 9am. You can also pick up a bird-watching kit that includes binoculars, maps and bird-identification guides.

Loeb Boathouse

The Lake, entrance on Fifth Ave at 74th St (212-517-4723). Subway: 6 to 77th St. Mar–Nov 10am–5:30pm. Call for seasonal restaurant hours. Boat rental: $10 per hour plus $30 deposit; $30 per half hour for chauffeured gondola, only at night. AmEx, MC, V.

Urban Park Rangers

888-NY-PARKS or 212-360-2774. 9am–5pm.

Upper East Side

Once Central Park opened in 1859, New York society was ready to move north. By the mid-1800s, the city's most affluent residents had built mansions along Fifth Avenue, and by the beginning of the 20th century, the super-rich had warmed to the (initially appalling) idea of living in apartment buildings—provided they were near the park. Many grand buildings were thus constructed along Fifth Avenue and its surrounding area.

The Upper East Side, especially near Central Park, is where much of New York's power elite is concentrated; billionaire mayor Michael Bloomberg lives here, on East 79th Street. The neighborhood's zip code, 10021, is the wealthiest in the nation—even Beverly Hills' 90210 takes a backseat. The residents of the mansions, townhouses and luxury apartment buildings of Fifth, Madison and Park Avenues between 59th and 96th Streets include those society staples, the ladies-who-lunch, as well as young scions who spend their sinecures in Madison Avenue's upscale boutiques. Meanwhile, well-heeled heads of corporations take advantage of tax write-offs to fund the area's many cultural institutions; the results of these philanthropic gestures, made over the past 100 years, are the art collections, museums and cultural institutions that attract visitors to the area known to natives as **Museum Mile**.

Museum Mile is as much a promotional slogan as it is a geographical description, and since most of the member museums line Fifth Avenue, it is a fitting designation. (For complete listings, see chapter **Museums**). The **Metropolitan Museum of Art**, set just inside Central Park on Fifth between 80th and 84th Streets, is the grandest of them all, offering a staggering selection of permanent exhibitions and rotating shows. A sunset drink in the Met's rooftop sculpture garden offers a sweeping view of Central Park, but more importantly, it's a great place to check out the city's singles scene in all its overperfumed glory. North of the Met is the city's newest art museum, the **Neue Galerie**, at 86th Street; the unmistakable spiral design of Frank Lloyd Wright's **Guggenheim Museum** stands at 88th Street; the **National Academy of Design** is at 89th Street; the **Cooper-Hewitt Museum**, the Smithsonian Institution's design collection set in Andrew Carnegie's mansion, is at 91st Street; and the **Jewish Museum** is at 92nd Street. To the north are two excellent, though under-appreciated collections: the **Museum of the City of New York** and **El Museo del Barrio**, at 103rd and 104th Streets, respectively.

Another cluster of museums exists in the 70s: The **Frick Collection** faces Central Park at 70th Street; the **Whitney Museum of American Art**, home of the occasionally controversial Whitney Biennial, is on the corner of Madison Avenue and 75th Street. Commercial art galleries also abound in the 70s, including **M. Knoedler & Co.** and **Gagosian** (*see chapter* Art Galleries); the works of established mid-career artists are generally what you'll find on view.

Somewhere amid all this art, you're bound to get hungry. Walk east a few blocks (to Lexington or Third Avenue), where many bistros, trattorias and diners can be found.

In addition to bankrolling art museums, the neighborhood's monied class has used its loot to promote the languages and cultures of foreign lands. Founded by David Rockefeller, the recently renovated and expanded **Asia Society** (*725 Park Ave*) now features a garden court and café. Nearby are the **China Institute in America** (*125 E 65th St*) and the **Americas Society** (*680 Park Ave*), which is dedicated to the nations of Central and South America, not to mention Canada and the Caribbean (it was also seeded with Rockefeller money). On Fifth Avenue is the **Ukrainian Institute**, at 79th Street, and the **Goethe-Institut/German Cultural Center**, at 83rd Street.

At Park Avenue and 66th Street, the **Seventh Regiment Armory** has an interior designed by Louis Comfort Tiffany, assisted by a young Stanford White. It has historically housed the Winter Antiques show (*see page 243*), among other events, but is presently being used to billet National Guard troops.

The aura becomes less grand as you make your way east to **Lexington Avenue**, but the

▶ For more information on the museums in this section, see chapter **Museums**.
▶ Check out chapter **Art Galleries** for additional listings on uptown dealers.
▶ Shopping for high fashion? See **Head of the class**, page 200.

area does hum with history. **The Mount Vernon Hotel Museum** *(61st St at First Ave)*, one of only eight 18th-century houses left in the city, was built as a coach house in 1799; it became a country inn in the 1820s. Kim Novak, Montgomery Clift, Tallulah Bankhead and Eleanor Roosevelt all lived west of here, in the tree-lined stretches of brownstones known as the **Treadwell Farm Historic District**, on 61st and 62nd Streets between Second and Third Avenues.

Located in the mid-60s on a bluff overlooking the East River, **The Rockefeller University** is a medical research institution founded a century ago. Its **Founder's Hall**, built in 1906, is a national historic landmark; it can be reached by walking east through the 66th Street entrance at **York Avenue**. The next few blocks of York Avenue are dominated by medical institutions, including the New York Hospital/Cornell Medical Center, into which the city's oldest hospital was incorporated.

The Rockefeller University

1230 York Ave between 63rd and 68th Sts (212-327-8000; www.rockefeller.edu). Subway: 6 to 68th St–Hunter College.
Monthly exhibitions are open to the public.

Seventh Regiment Armory

643 Park Ave at 66th St (212-452-3067). Subway: 6 to 68th St–Hunter College. Call for information about the status of the Winter Antiques show and other events.

Yorkville

The east and northeast parts of the Upper East Side are residential and mostly filled with the city's professional class. There are countless places to eat and drink, including **Elaine's** *(see page 186)* and **The Auction House Bar** *(300 E 89th St between First and Second Aves, 212-427-4458)*. There are also lots of neighborhood Italian and Chinese restaurants, and 86th Street, the main thoroughfare, is lined with chain stores.

The area extending from the 70s to 96th Street, east of Lexington Avenue, has been known historically as Yorkville and was, at one time, a predominantly German neighborhood and quaint riverside hamlet. In the last decades of the 19th century, 86th Street became the Hauptstrasse of Manhattan, filled with German restaurants, *biergartens* and pastry, grocery, butcher and clothing shops. Tensions flared when World War II broke out, as Nazis and anti-Nazis clashed in the streets; a Nazi newspaper was even published here. Those days are thankfully over, but an Old World legacy does remain in the area. **Schaller & Weber** *(Second Ave between 85th and 86th Sts, 212-879-3047)*,

a homey grocery, has been selling 75 different varieties of German sausage and cold cuts since 1937. Another treasure is the **Elk Candy Company** *(1628 Second Ave between 84th and 85th Sts, 212-585-2303)*, which sells numerous varieties of marzipan.

On East End Avenue at 86th Street is the **Henderson Place Historic District**, where two dozen handsome Queen Anne row houses stand. Commissioned by furrier John C. Henderson, its turrets, double stoops and slate roofs remain intact, and the block looks much as it did in 1882—minus the horse-drawn carriages. Across the street is **Gracie Mansion**, New York's official mayoral residence since 1942 and the only Federal-style mansion in Manhattan still used as a home (except by the present mayor, Michael Bloomberg, who resides in his townhouse and uses the mansion only for special events). The house, built in 1799 by Scottish merchant Archibald Gracie, is the focal point of tranquil **Carl Schurz Park**, named in honor of the German immigrant, U.S. senator and newspaper editor. Linger here for spectacular views of the swift-moving East River. The park's long promenade, the **John H. Finley Walk**, is a beautiful place for a stroll, especially in the early morning and at dusk; a multimillion-dollar spiffing-up is also in the works. During the Revolutionary War, George Washington built a battery on this strategic site.

The **92nd Street Y** *(Lexington Ave at 92nd St; see page 111)* offers the city's most extensive walking-tour program, as well as concerts and lectures. While you're in the neighborhood, be sure to check out the rare wood-frame home at **160 East 92nd Street** between Lexington and Third Avenues. Built in the mid-1800s, the house has retained its historic shutters and Corinthian-columned front porch. The founders of *The New Republic* housed its staff here in the early 1900s; Eartha Kitt once lived in this building as well.

Gracie Mansion

Carl Schurz Park, 88th St at East End Ave (212-570-4751). Subway: 4, 5, 6 to 86th St. Mar–Nov tours by appointment only. Call for details.
The tour takes you through the mayor's living room, a guest suite and smaller bedrooms.

Roosevelt Island

Roosevelt Island, a submarine-shaped East River isle, was called Minnehannonck ("island place") by the Indians, who sold it to the Dutch (who then made a vast creative leap and renamed it Hog's Island). The Dutch farmed the island, as did Englishman Robert Blackwell, who moved there in 1686. His family's old clapboard farmhouse is in **Blackwell Park**, adjacent to

Main Street (the one and only commercial strip on which you can find several restaurants—and keep an eye peeled for Roosevelt Island resident "Grandpa" Al Lewis, star of *The Munsters*). In the 1800s, a lunatic asylum, a smallpox hospital, prisons and workhouses were built on what was by that point known as Welfare Island. On the southern tip are the weathered neo-Gothic ruins of the **Smallpox Hospital** and the burned-out shell of **City Hospital**. The **Octagon Tower**, at the island's northern end, is the remaining core of the former New York City Lunatic Asylum (all of these features are technically off-limits to the public). Charles Dickens visited during the 1840s and was disturbed by its "lounging, listless, madhouse air." In an early example of investigative journalism, reporter Nellie Bly feigned insanity and had herself committed to the asylum for ten days in 1887, then wrote a shocking exposé of the conditions in what she described as a "human rat trap."

Roosevelt Island has been a reasonably sane residential community since the state began planning its development in 1971 (people started moving into apartments in 1975, and 9,500 people now live there). A huge new residential development broke ground on the island in early 2001, and there is also a new sports complex for amateur baseball and soccer teams. The best way to see Roosevelt Island—and to enjoy the sweeping views of the East Side—is to take the tram that crosses the East River from Manhattan. The cable cars have appeared in a host of films, including *City Slickers*. You can also take the F train for a nonscenic (but faster) ride. When you arrive, you'll have to ride up three escalators (the equivalent of ten stories) to get out of the subway stop, one of the deepest in the system. The riverfront promenades afford fabulous panoramas of the skyline and East River. On the East Side, wander down the **Meditation Steps** for river views (located just north of the tram stop), or take one of the river-hugging paths around the island.

Roosevelt Island Operating Corporation

591 Main St (212-832-4540; rioc.com). Mon–Fri 9am–5pm.
Call for details of events and free maps of the island.

Roosevelt Island Tramway

Embark at Second Ave and 60th St in Manhattan. $1.50. Subway tokens only.

Upper West Side

The Upper West Side, it has been observed, is as much a state of mind as it is a geographic appellation. The state of mind? Its residents have long been thought of as intellectually and politically liberal. But that spirit has waned somewhat, as rents have been ratcheted up. European immigrants were attracted here in the late 19th century by the building boom sparked by Central Park, as well as by Columbia University's relocation to the area. Nowadays, the neighborhood, whose main artery is Broadway, is crowded with restaurants, bars, bookstores—and liberal celebrities, such as the progressive gadfly Michael Moore of *Roger & Me* fame, and *Doonesbury* creator Garry Trudeau.

Sightseeing

High wire You get a bird's-eye view of the Upper East Side from the Roosevelt Island tram.

The Upper West Side begins at **Columbus Circle**—a rare rotary in a city of right angles—where Broadway meets 59th Street, Eighth Avenue, Central Park South and Central Park West. To the south, across from a 700-ton statue of Christopher Columbus, is 2 Columbus Circle, an odd, almost windowless building that was built as a modern-art gallery by Huntington Hartford in 1964; its future is uncertain as the circle undergoes massive redevelopment. Donald Trump may gain control of the site to build a hotel. He has already made his sun-blocking imprint on the north side of the circle with his conversion of the old Gulf & Western Building into the pricey **Trump International Hotel and Tower** *(see page 119)*, which features the acclaimed restaurant **Jean-Georges** *(see page 183)*. To the west, on the former site of the New York Coliseum (torn down in 2000), the $1.7 billion **Columbus Centre** (*see chapter* **Architecture**) is going up. It will house the headquarters of AOL Time Warner, an auditorium for Jazz at Lincoln Center, a Mandarin Oriental Hotel, and shops, shops and more shops.

The center of culture in this part of the Upper West Side is **Lincoln Center** *(see page 316),* a complex of concert halls and auditoriums that together are the heart and soul of classical music and highbrow culture in the city. Its buildings are linked by sweeping public plazas and populated by sensitive-looking musical types or, in the summer, amateur dancers who gather in the plaza to dance alfresco at Midsummer Night Swing *(see page 238).*

Just north, on Broadway at 68th Street, is the popular 12-screen **Sony Lincoln Square & IMAX Theatre** *(see page 274),* an example of a multiplex done right. The nearby **Lincoln Plaza Cinemas** *(see page 275)* show the latest in art-house films.

While not as immediately fashionable as Fifth Avenue, the Upper West Side did catch on quickly once the park was built. Magnificent apartment buildings promptly rose on Central Park West. The **Dakota**, on 72nd Street, now has the awful distinction of being the building where John Lennon was murdered, but as one of New York's great early apartment buildings, it did accelerate the westward migration. (When it was completed in 1884, New Yorkers commented that it was so far away from the center of town that it might as well be in the Dakotas.) Yoko Ono and other famous residents can be seen popping in and out. The Art Deco building at **55 Central Park West** *(at 66th St)* is best remembered for its role in *Ghostbusters.* It was the first Art Deco building on the block; within two years, five others had joined it: **The Century** *(at 62nd St),* **The Majestic** *(between 71st and 72nd Sts),*

241 Central Park West *(at 84th St),* **The Eldorado** *(between 90th and 91st Sts),* and **The Ardsley** *(at 92nd St).* The massive twin-towered **San Remo** at 74th Street dates from 1930 and is so exclusive that even Madonna had to settle for the waiting list.

The New-York Historical Society *(see page 41)* is the oldest museum in the city. Across the street, the **American Museum of Natural History** *(see page 33)* attracts visitors with its IMAX theater (which shows Oscar-winning documentary nature films) and permanent rain forest exhibit, as well as such standbys as stuffed and mounted creatures, dinosaur skeletons and ethnological collections. The 2000 opening of the museum's **Rose Center for Earth and Space**, which includes the retooled Hayden Planetarium, meant an astronomical leap in visitors—but it's well worth suffering the crowds to marvel at this installation.

Columbus and Amsterdam, the avenues west of Central Park West, experienced a renaissance when Lincoln Center was built in the '60s. The neighborhood has long been settled by urban professionals and is now full of restaurants, gourmet food shops and boutiques, though many of the old, and mainly Latino, inhabitants and shops remain. A popular Sunday outing is still the Columbus Avenue stroll, which usually starts at the **Flea Market** *(Columbus Ave and 77th St; see page 221)* and continues either up or down Columbus. If you head south, be sure to stop at **Pug Bros. Popcorn** *(265 Columbus Ave between 72nd and 73rd Sts, 212-595-4780)* for a bag of crispy caramel corn, handmade in old-fashioned copper kettles, or an iced cappuccino in the back garden at **Café La Fortuna** *(69 W 71st St between Central Park West and Columbus Ave, 212-724-5846),* a neighborhood favorite for more than 70 years.

On Broadway, the notoriously crowded **72nd Street subway station**, which opened in 1904, is notable for its Beaux Arts entrance. It's undergoing a $53 million renovation and expansion, though when the project is completed in 2003, its platforms will still be a claustrophobic 15∏ feet wide (due to the surrounding bedrock). The station is on **Sherman Square**, named after the general. The opposite triangle, at the intersection of Broadway and 73rd Street, is called **Verdi Square**. It's a fitting name, geometry notwithstanding: Along with Arturo Toscanini and Igor Stravinsky, Enrico Caruso lived in the nearby **Ansonia Hotel** *(Broadway between 73rd and 74th Sts, 212-724-2600)* and kept other inhabitants entertained and awake with renditions of his favorite arias. The Ansonia, a vast Beaux Arts apartment building with exquisite detailing, was also the location for the 1992 thriller *Single White Female*. Bette Midler got her break at the long-gone Continental Baths, a gay spa and cabaret that occupied the Ansonia's lower floors in the 1970s. The **Beacon Theatre** *(see page 301)*, on Broadway at 75th Street, was once a fabulous movie palace and is now a concert venue, hosting annual multinight stands by the Allman Brothers, among others. The interior is a designated landmark. Across the street, the gourmet markets **Fairway** *(2127 Broadway at 74th St, 212-595-1794)* and **Citarella** *(2135 Broadway at 75th St, 212-874-0383)* vie for shoppers. Fairway is known citywide for its produce, and Citarella is renowned for its seafood and meat departments. A few blocks north are the **Children's Museum of Manhattan** *(see page 292)*; **H&H Bagels** *(2239 Broadway at 80th St, 212-595-8000)*, the city's largest purveyor of that New York staple; the enormous **Zabar's** *(see page 224)*, a community center of sorts, and supplier of more than 250 types of cheese, hand-sliced smoked fish, prepared foods and more; and the legendary **Barney Greengrass—The Sturgeon King** *(see page 184)*, an old-time cafeteria-style restaurant with a marvelous smoked-salmon–and–bagel platter.

Just west of Broadway, on the north side of 94th Street, is the 1920s **Pomander Walk**, a quaint row of townhouses built around a courtyard. **Symphony Space** *(see pages 259 and 318)* features repertory film series and music programs, including the famous "Wall-to-Wall" concerts. Nearby, you can rent horses (they live upstairs!) from the **Claremont Riding Academy** *(see page 330)* to ride in Central Park.

Riverside Park, a sinuous stretch of riverbank, lies between Riverside Drive and the banks of the Hudson River, from 72nd to 158th Streets. You'll probably see yachts berthed at the **79th Street Boat Basin**, along with a few houseboats; there's also an open-air café in the adjacent park (open in the summer). Farther north and overlooking the park is the **Soldiers' and Sailors' Monument**, which honors Union soldiers who died in the Civil War. On 100th Street at Riverside is a memorial to fallen firemen, which was built in 1908. **Grant's Tomb**, in Riverside Park at 122nd Street, is the burial site of Ulysses S. Grant. Behind the mausoleum is a folk-art garden of multicolored mosaic benches, created by about 3,000 volunteers (many of them neighborhood children) in a 1970s antivandalism project launched by Chilean-born artist Pedro Silva.

Soldiers' and Sailors' Monument
Riverside Dr at 89th St. Subway: 1, 2 to 86th St.

The 1902 monument was designed by French sculptor Paul DuBoy and architects Charles and Arthur Stoughton.

Morningside Heights

The area between Morningside Park and the Hudson River from 110th to 125th Streets is called **Morningside Heights**, a neighborhood dominated by **Columbia University**. One of the oldest universities in the U.S., Columbia was chartered in 1754 as King's College; the name changed after the Revolutionary War. It moved to its present location in 1897. Thanks to its large student population and that of its sister school, **Barnard College**, the area has an academic feel, with bookshops and cafés along Broadway and quiet, leafy streets toward the west overlooking Riverside Park. **Morningside Park**, which separates the Heights from Harlem, is a lush, steep park that has seen tremendous improvement over the past few years—new gardens, a dog walk and a noticeable drop in the number of empty glassine bags on the trails. It runs from 110th to 123rd Sts, between Morningside Drive and Morningside Avenue. In its southern section, you'll find ball fields and picnic grounds; in summertime, the fields are filled with Latin fast-pitch softball leagues and the quality of play is quite high. Still, avoid the park at night.

Miss Mamie's Spoonbread Too *(see page 185)* is nearby, and it's *the* place for gumbo and banana pudding. Back toward Columbia, **The West End** *(2911 Broadway between 113th and 114th Sts, 212-662-8830)* is notable for its $6 pitchers of Bud *(Sun–Wed 6–11pm)* and the fact that it was a hangout for the original Beats (there are still occasional poetry readings). For dessert, follow your nose to **Mondel Chocolates** *(2913 Broadway at 114th St, 212-864-2111)*, which has been sating students' sweet teeth since 1944.

The neighborhood also has two immense houses of worship. **Riverside Church**, built with Rockefeller money and containing the world's largest carillon. Ride to the top of the 21-story steel-frame tower for views across the Hudson.

The hammering and chiseling at the **Cathedral of St. John the Divine** (the largest in the U.S.) will continue well into this century. Construction began in 1892 in Romanesque style, was stopped for a Gothic Revival redesign in 1911 and didn't begin again until 1941. Then, after another pause for fund-raising, work resumed in earnest in the 1990s. A fire in late 2001 destroyed the church's gift shop, and delayed construction while repairs were made. When the towers and great crossing are completed, New York will have a church that rivals the grandeur of Paris's Notre Dame. In addition to Sunday services, the cathedral also hosts concerts, tours and, on occasion, memorial services for the rich and/or famous. Be sure to check out late Pop artist Keith Haring's altarpiece, the "Poets Corner" and, in season, the cathedral's rose and herb gardens.

Cathedral of St. John the Divine
1047 Amsterdam Ave at 112th St (212-316-7490; www.stjohndivine.org). Subway: B, C, 1 to 110th St–Cathedral Pkwy. Mon–Sat 7am–6pm; Sun 7am–8:30pm. Services: Mon–Sat 8am, 12:15, 5:30pm; Sun 8, 9, 9:30 (Spanish), 11am, 6pm. Tours Tue–Sat 11am; Sun 1pm. $3.

Columbia University
Between Amsterdam Ave and Broadway, and 114th and 120th Sts (212-854-1754; www.columbia.edu). Enter Barnard College at Broadway, just north of 116th St (212-854-5262). Subway: 1 to 116th St–Columbia University.

General Grant National Memorial
Riverside Dr at 122nd St (212-666-1640). Subway: 1 to 125th St. 9am–5pm. Free.
Who's buried in Grant's Tomb? Well, duh! This memorial is the burial site of Ulysses S. Grant, who is interred with his wife, Julia.

Riverside Church
Riverside Dr at 120th St (212-870-6700; www.theriversidechurchny.org). Subway: 1 to 125th St. 9am–5pm.

Harlem

Harlem is on a roll these days, and not just because Bill Clinton, America's "first black president" (to quote writer Toni Morrison) happens to keep an office here *(55 W 125th St)*. Violent crime is significantly down, and everywhere you turn, long-neglected brownstones are being renovated. And while many locals have vociferously complained about rising rents, the infiltration of superstores, the Caucasian invasion and the simultaneous watering-down of black culture, the neighborhood remains the heart and soul of Black America. Its avenues are filled with Afrocentric culture, its institutions and streets are named after great liberators, teachers and orators, and there are constant reminders—from French-speaking Africans selling trinkets to traditional soul food restaurants serving smothered pork chops and collard greens.

Harlem was originally composed of country estates, but when the subways arrived at the turn of the last century, the area was developed with white middle-class New Yorkers in mind. When the whites failed to fill the townhouses, speculators reluctantly began renting them to African-Americans. The area's population

doubled during the 1920s and '30s, a growth that coincided with a great exodus of blacks from the south, and with a cultural explosion known as the Harlem Renaissance. The poets, writers, artists and musicians living in this bohemian republic helped usher in the Jazz Age. Its center is 125th Street where, despite the incursion of Starbucks, a Body Shop, Bill Clinton and other Middle America signifiers, the strip remains resolutely urban and Afrocentric.

The neighborhood's soundtrack is provided by the jazz of the elders, the rap and reggae of the younger generation, and by the salsa and merengue of the Cubans and Dominicans who have joined the Latin population of **Spanish Harlem**, the section east of Fifth Avenue and above 96th Street. Treat your senses to the colorful fruits, vegetables, spices and meats at **La Marqueta**, Park Avenue's multistore food emporium located between 110th and 116th Streets. **El Museo del Barrio** *(see page 42)*, Spanish Harlem's community museum, is on Fifth Avenue at 104th Street.

The **Graffiti Hall of Fame**, on 106th Street between Madison and Park Avenues, is actually a schoolyard, but you'll see the large-scale work of old-school graffiti artists—it's also the site of impromptu artists' gatherings in the summer months. There are also several casitas, or small houses, which function as communal hangouts for local Puerto Ricans and create a slice of island life amid the high-rise projects. An especially beautiful one is on 110th Street between Lexington and Third Avenues.

At 116th Street and Malcolm X Boulevard (Lenox Avenue) is **Masjid Malcolm Shabazz**, the silver-domed mosque of the late Malcolm X's ministry. Opposite Malcolm X Boulevard (Lenox Avenue) is the **African Market**, where street vendors who once lined Harlem's main drags now hawk T-shirts, tapes and (purportedly) African souvenirs. **Sisters Cuisine** *(1931 Madison Ave at 124th St, 212-410-3000)* balances Guyanese food with such Caribbean favorites as Jamaican jerk chicken and curried goat. **Amy Ruth's** *(113 W 116th St between Malcolm X Blvd [Lenox Ave] and Adam Clayton Powell Jr. Blvd [Seventh Ave], 212-280-8779)* is Al Sharpton's favorite restaurant; join him for his signature dish, fried chicken with waffles. A few blocks north is the storied, glorious **Lenox Lounge** *(see page 311)*, where Malcolm X once worked as a hustler and where you can still hear jazz, not to mention the blues-guitar caterwauling of "The Wizard." Still farther north is **Sylvia's** *(328 Malcolm X Blvd [Lenox Ave] between 126th and 127th Sts, 212-996-0660)*, famous for its soul food gospel brunch, and at 138th Street is the **Abyssinian Baptist Church**, which houses a small museum dedicated to Adam Clayton Powell Jr., the first black member of the New York City Council and Harlem's congressman from the 1940s through the 1960s. Just below 125th Street, on Fifth Avenue, is **Marcus Garvey Park**. It's at the center of a historic district of elegant brownstones; some of the most beautiful are open to the public several times a year. The Mt. Morris Park Community Association has the details *(212-369-4241)*. There are also a few nd-breakfasts around the park, including the **Urban Jem** *(see page 143)*, a renovated brownstone on Fifth Avenue that also hosts jazz shows in its parlor.

The **Studio Museum in Harlem** *(see page 37)* presents exhibitions focusing on the area and its artists—a 2001 show of African-American photography featured amazing works by the likes of Gordon Parks and James VanDerZee. Meanwhile, the **Schomburg Center for Research in Black Culture** (part of the New York Public Library system) is where Harlem's rich history lives on. It's the largest research collection devoted exclusively to African-American culture, and its archives include audio and visual recordings of outstanding black musicians, and speeches by leaders ranging from Marcus Garvey to Jesse Jackson. There is also a growing art-gallery scene in Harlem, which includes **The Project** *(see page 250)*, **Gallery X** *(23 W 129th St between Fifth Ave and Malcolm X Blvd [Lenox Ave], 212-534-7044)* and **Gallery M** *(123 W 135th St between Malcolm X [Lenox Ave] and Adam Clayton Powell Jr. Blvds [Seventh Ave], 212-234-4106)*. They each feature Afrocentric and cutting-edge installations and shows *(see **State of the art**, page 250)*. Many

artisans and craftsmen live in Harlem as well; some of their works are shown by appointment only, while others display their wares exclusively in one or another small shop. You can find, for example, West African textiles at **Djema Imports** *(70 W 125th St at Fifth Ave, 212-289-3842)* and at **The Brownstone** *(2032 Fifth Ave at 126th St, 212-996-7980)*, African artifacts and throw pillows.

Harlem's main commercial drag is 125th Street, and the **Apollo Theatre** *(see page 300)* has historically been its focus. For four decades after it began presenting live shows in the 1930s, the Apollo was the world's most celebrated venue for black music. It has had its ups and downs in the last 30 years or so but continues to present live music; in March 2002, "Harlem Song," a permanent revue celebrating the sounds of Harlem debuted. Tours of the recently renovated theater are given daily *(call 212-531-5337 for details)*. The Theresa Towers office complex *(Adam Clayton Powell Jr. Blvd [Seventh Ave] at 125th St)*, was formerly the **Hotel Theresa**. Fidel Castro stayed here during a 1960 visit to the United Nations; his visitors included Nikita Khrushchev and Gamal Abdel Nasser.

The Apollo has a new across-the-street neighbor in the **Harlem USA Mall**. A **Magic Johnson movie theater** *(see page 273)* and retail megastores, such as Old Navy, Modell's, HMV and a Disney Store, are inside. Nearby, **Mart 1-2-5** *(260 W 125th St between Frederick Douglass Blvd and Manhattan Ave, 212-316-3340)* is a neighborhood retail institution, housing numerous small businesses owned by locals.

Docked and loaded Grab a beer and check out the Hudson River at the Boat Basin Café.

Farther west on 125th Street is another black-music landmark. **The Cotton Club** *(666 W 125th St at Riverside Dr, 212-663-7980),* originally located on 142nd Street, was the neighborhood's premier nightclub from the 1920s to the '50s. Dubbed the Aristocrat of Harlem, the club launched the careers of such entertainment royalty as Duke Ellington, Cab Calloway and Dorothy Dandrige; nowadays, it's a showcase for live blues and jazz. **Showman's** *(375 W 125th St at Frederick Douglass Blvd [Eighth Ave], 212-864-8941),* to the east, remains a smoky house of swing. Plans are in the works for refurbishing three other legendary nightspots: **Minton's Playhouse** *(Cecil Hotel, 206–210 W 118th St between St. Nicholas Ave and Adam Clayton Powell Jr. Blvd [Seventh Ave]);* **Small's Paradise** *(135th St at Adam Clayton Powell Blvd [Seventh Ave]);* and the **Renaissance Ballroom** *(Adam Clayton Powell Blvd [Seventh Ave] at 147th St).* Call the Harlem Business Improvement District for information on the status of these projects *(212-662-8999).*

For real jazz fans, a visit to the stoop at **17 East 126th Street**, between Fifth and Madison Avenues, is good for some spine-tingling sensations. It was here, in 1958, that nearly 60 jazz greats gathered to have a sort of class picture taken for *Esquire* magazine. It's a world-famous photo, and was the subject of a mid-'90s documentary titled *A Great Day in Harlem.*

The area between 125th and 155th Streets, west of St. Nicholas Avenue, is known as **Hamilton Heights**, after Alexander Hamilton, who had a farm here at **Hamilton Grange.** The Federal-style home, designed by the same architect who designed City Hall, may be moved to nearby **St. Nicholas Park**. This is one of the gentrified parts of Harlem, where you'll find the Gothic Revival–style City College, the City University of New York's northernmost outpost in Manhattan. On the City College campus, check out the **Croton Gatehouse** (dubbed the Pump Station by locals), on Convent Avenue at 135th Street. In the 1880s, the Gatehouse was instrumental in

A walk on the wild (West) side
For a hike with great views of the water, head to the west coast—of Manhattan!

Hiking and *Manhattan* aren't words you often see in the same sentence, unless said Manhattan hiking adventure takes you over the city's cement-covered hills and dales in pursuit of some iconic retail or epicurean outpost. But despite its reputation as an overpopulated, overpaved megalopolis, where the only tree that grows, grows in Brooklyn, there are ways for wandering souls to experience a reasonable facsimile of an actual outdoor hike.

One of the best ways to experience a city is from its edge, at the waterline, looking in. This way, you can retain your ironic distance—or whatever distance suits you. And for this, the western shoreline of Manhattan is perfectly configured, offering wild woodlands, crucial cultural stop-ins, snacks and delightful views of the Hudson River. So strap on your hiking boots (okay, sneakers will do) grab your walking stick (optional) and let the hiking begin.

Who said, "All good things begin with a subway ride"? We forget, but it's true. For this trip, you first have to take the A train to its terminus stop, at 207th Street in Inwood. From here, you are but a stone's throw from the Bronx, itself a wild kingdom to be conquered...another day (*see chapters* **Green**

Apple *and* **Outer Boroughs, Bronx**). Leaving the subway, head north on Broadway until you reach 218th Street, and turn left. Soon enough, the pavement gives way to **Isham Park**, a flat section of **Inwood Hill Park** *(see page 88)* used mostly for sports. You'll want to follow the contour of the dug-out boat basin to a trail that leads to the deep woods. The trail hugs the shoreline, and within a few minutes of hiking, you'll pass underneath the Hudson River Bridge. Welcome to the tippy-top of Manhattan! It's all downtown from here. You'll swing around this point and begin heading south, weaving among the American elms, between the Amtrak railroad tracks and Hudson River. If you want to take a side trip to the **Cloisters** *(see page 33),* leave the trail at the end of Dyckman Street and climb the steep hill up to the medieval-arts museum.

Otherwise, you will be hiking between Riverside Drive and the Henry Hudson Parkway until you get to the **George Washington Bridge** *(see page 88).* Once you reach the bridge, you'll cross under it and walk beside the storied **Little Red Lighthouse** *(see page 88).* If you happen to be hiking at low tide, a not-quite-shimmering-but-nevertheless-cool strip of bringing water from the Croton Reservoir to New York City.

While you're in the area, tour **Strivers' Row** *(Adam Clayton Powell Jr. Blvd [Seventh Ave] between 138th and 139th Sts)*, a strip of magnificent neo-Georgian houses developed in 1891 by David H. King (who also constructed the first Madison Square Garden). In the 1920s, prominent members of the black community such as Eubie Blake and W. C. Handy lived here, and you can still see signs on the gates that read WALK YOUR HORSES.

Stop for a bite at **Londel's Supper Club** *(2620 Frederick Douglass Blvd [Eighth Ave] between 139th and 140th Sts, 212-234-6114)*, owned by Londel Davis, a former police officer who now serves some of the best blackened catfish in town. The area hops at night, especially at the legendary **St. Nick's Pub** *(773 St. Nicholas Ave at 149th St, 212-283-9728)*, where you can hear live jazz every night except Tuesday (that's comedy night).

A little farther north, **Audubon Terrace** *(Broadway at 155th St)* contains a double cluster of Beaux Arts buildings, which were part of artist John James Audubon's former estate. Now they're an unusual group of museums: the **Hispanic Society of America**, the **American Numismatic Society** and the **American Academy of Arts and Letters** *(see page 38)*.

Abyssinian Baptist Church

132 W 138th St between Malcolm X Blvd (Lenox Ave) and Adam Clayton Powell Jr. Blvd (Seventh Ave) (212-862-7474). Subway: 2, 3 to 135th St. Mon–Fri 9am–5pm. Services: Sun 9, 11am.

The Abyssinian is celebrated for its history and gospel choir. Arrive a half-hour early on Sunday to be assured of a seat (you'll no doubt find yourself in the balcony and next to a fellow tourist).

American Numismatic Society

Audubon Terrace, Broadway at 155th St (212-234-3130). Subway: 1 to 157th St. Tue–Fri 9am–4:30pm. Free.

The museum is devoted to the history of currency, from wampum to the euro.

Hamilton Grange

Convent Ave at 141st St (212-283-5154). Subway: A, C, B, D, 1 to 145th St. Fri–Sun 9am–5pm.

sand emerges just south of the bridge—it's a beach, and it's in Manhattan! Take off your shoes and wiggle your toes—but watch out for broken glass. At 155th Street, the untamed-wilds section of your jaunt has petered out, and you are officially hiking through **Riverside Park** *(see page 83)*. At this point, the street becomes Audubon Terrace. You can leave the trail and head one block east to the **Hispanic Society of the Americas** *(see page 88)* and the **American Numismatic Society** *(see this page, above)*.

Along this section of the trail you'll see ball fields, the homeless, joggers and dog-walkers. You'll meander down Riverside Park for awhile until the monolithic **Riverfront State Park** emerges at 145th Street. This monstrous outcropping of concrete is actually a sewage treatment plant, on top of which a free-access park was constructed. By now, you've hiked about three miles, and it's time for a break. An elevator will take you to the top, where you can walk around, taking in the extraordinary view. Stop at the snack bar near the ice-skating rink for a Coke and a hot dog.

After your snack, descend back to Riverside Park and continue your long march south. At 125th Street, the park narrows to a mere sliver as a giant bargain-price gourmet food market, Fairway, looms alongside. More snacks! At 122nd Street, you're yards away from **Grant's Tomb** *(see page 84)*; at 112th,

you're but two blocks away from the gigantic **Cathedral of St. John the Divine** *(see page 84)*. Within the park itself, you'll notice an increase in bicycle, in-line and foot traffic in these parts, along with fishermen bold enough to cast their lines into these waters, seeking the wily striped bass. Stay on the east side of the Henry Hudson, and you'll walk past the **Soldiers' and Sailors' Monument** *(see page 83)*, at 89th Street.

You may well be getting a little tired at this point, but in just ten more blocks, you will encounter the Parks Department's boat basin, and its adjacent **Boat Basin Café** at 79th Street (just above the park walkway). You might pop in for a couple of Coronas and a hamburger, or you might not—it can get very crowded, and is not exactly conducive to an afternoon of reflection and quietude. Either way, it's always fun to check out the boats—many of them houseboats occupied by the city's river-lovin' taxpayers. At 72nd Street, the park cuts through land owned by real estate mogul Donald Trump; this egress was opened a couple of years ago to connect the uptown and downtown sections of the **Hudson River Greenway.** You'll soon arrive at 59th Street, the southernmost block of that entity called "uptown," and thus, the end of your journey. Four blocks over is where you can catch the A train (and a few other lines), at Columbus Circle. Destination? Your choice.

Hispanic Society of America

Audubon Terrace, Broadway between 155th and 156th Sts (212-926-2234). Subway: 1 to 157th St. Tue–Sat 10am–4:30pm; Sun 1–4 pm. Free.

The society offers a museum, library and other research facilities for anyone interested in exploring Hispanic culture.

Schomburg Center for Research in Black Culture

515 Malcolm X Blvd at 135th St (212-491-2200; www.nypl.org/research/sc). Subway: 2, 3 to 135th St. Mon–Wed noon–8pm; Thu–Sat 10am–6pm. Free.

Washington Heights & Inwood

The area from 155th Street north to Dyckman Street is called **Washington Heights**; venture any higher than that and you're in **Inwood**, Manhattan's northernmost neighborhood. A growing number of artists and young families are moving to this part of town, attracted by Art Deco buildings, big parks, spacious and hilly streets, and comparatively low rents. Up here, the island shrinks in width, and the parks on either side culminate in the wilderness and forest of **Inwood Hill Park** *(see **A walk on the wild (West) side**, page 86).* Some believe the legendary 1626 transaction between Peter Minuit and the Munsee Indians for the purchase of a strip of land called Manahatta took place here. The 196-acre refuge contains the island's last swath of primeval forest. Largely due to the efforts of landscape architect Olmsted, the area was not leveled in the 1800s—the house-size, glacier-deposited boulders (called erratics) were probably a factor too. Today, with a little imagination, you can hike through this mossy forest and see a bit of the beautiful land the Munsees called home.

High Bridge *(Amsterdam Ave at 177th St)* will give you an idea of how New York used to get its water supply. This aqueduct carried water across the Harlem River from the Croton Reservoir in Westchester County to Manhattan. The central piers were replaced in the 1920s to accommodate passing ships. Washington Heights is dominated by another bridge—the **George Washington Bridge**, which connects New York to New Jersey. A pedestrian walkway allows for stunning views of Manhattan, and it's a popular route for bicyclists, too. Under the bridge on the east side is a diminutive lighthouse—those who know the children's story *The Little Red Lighthouse and the Great Gray Bridge* will recognize it immediately.

The main building of **Yeshiva University** *(186th St at Amsterdam Ave)* is one of the strangest in New York, a Byzantine-style orange-brick structure decorated with turrets and minarets. Equally surprising is the **Cloisters** *(see page 33),* at the northern edge of flower-filled Fort Tryon Park. A reconstructed monastery incorporating several original medieval cloisters that the Rockefeller clan shipped over from Europe, it might have been custom-designed for medieval picnics. Actually, it houses the Metropolitan Museum's medieval collection—illuminated manuscripts, priceless unicorn tapestries, sculptures, old silverware and playing cards. It also offers incredible views of the New Jersey Palisades and the Hudson River.

The neighborhood has two significant American historic sites. **Dyckman House,** a 1783 Dutch farmhouse with a high-shouldered gambrel roof and flared eaves, is the oldest surviving home in Manhattan and something of a lonely sight on busy Broadway. In 1915, when the house was threatened with demolition, the Dyckman family's descendants purchased it and filled it with heirlooms. **Morris-Jumel Mansion** was where George Washington planned for the battle of Harlem Heights in 1776, after the British colonel Roger Morris moved out. The handsome 18th-century Palladian-style villa also has some fantastic views. Cross the street to see **Sylvan Terrace**, between 160th and 162nd Streets, which has the largest continuous strip of old wooden houses in Manhattan.

Dyckman Farmhouse Museum

4881 Broadway at 204th St (212-304-9422). Subway: A to 207th St–Inwood. Tue–Sun 10am–5pm. Free.

George Washington Bridge

Take the A train to 181st St; the entrance to the pedestrian walkway is two blocks to the south, on the south side of the bridge.

Inwood Hill Park

Entrance on 207th St at Seaman Ave; visitors' center at 218th St and Indian Rd (212-304-2365). Subway: A, 1 to 207th St.

Morris-Jumel Mansion

65 Jumel Terrace (which runs from Edgecombe Ave to St. Nicholas Ave) between 160th and 162nd Sts (212-923-8008). Subway: C to 163rd St–Amsterdam Ave. Wed–Sun 10am–4pm. $3, seniors and students $2. MC, V accepted in gift shop and for large group admissions.

Built in 1765, the mansion is Manhattan's only surviving pre-Revolutionary house. Now surrounded by brownstones, it originally sat on a 160-acre estate that stretched from river to river.

Pedal to the meadow Inwood Hill Park contains Manhattan's last remaining patch of virgin forest—and plenty of paths to explore.

The Outer Boroughs

Lofty Manhattan rents prompted an exodus to Brooklyn, Queens, the Bronx and Staten Island. The result? An exciting mix of old and new in the outer boroughs.

The four "outer boroughs" have long been home to the "real" New Yorkers—those blue-collar people who keep the town thrumming. As a result, Brooklyn, Queens, the Bronx and Staten Island have been viewed as a hinterland by Manhattanites. But as Manhattan rents skyrocketed in the 1980s—and even more so during the '90s—people left to homestead in Long Island City, Fort Greene, Richmond Hill and other outer-borough neighborhoods. The frontier mentality has led to a democratization of the city. Suddenly every place seems to be groovy. Artist enclaves in Brooklyn and Queens add contemporary cool to Italian and Greek neighborhoods, salty dogs mix with the new breed in working-class bars, and younger generations are discovering old relics—from fabulous dingy diners to grand buildings. In fact, all four boroughs have their fair share of history, compelling architecture, good food and relaxing places to bike and walk. So go beyond Manhattan to get a taste of how 6 million of the city's 8 million live.

Brooklyn

Since Brooklyn is not connected to Manhattan by land, the most scenic way to get there is to walk 1,595 ½ feet (486 ⅓ meters) across its namesake bridge. The 1883 completion of the **Brooklyn Bridge** transformed the borough from a spacious suburb that still contained areas of farmland into a bustling city with nearly 2.5 million residents. Had Brooklyn remained a separate city (it became a borough of New York in 1898), its nearly 2.5 million residents would make it the fourth largest in the U.S., behind New York, Los Angeles and Chicago. Stroll or bike across the bridge's pedestrian walkway for spectacular views of lower Manhattan, the Statue of Liberty and the New York Harbor as it opens at the Verrazano-Narrows Bridge. The Brooklyn Bridge itself is a mesmerizing feat of engineering and architectural grace. As you walk along it, you'll see plaques detailing the story of its construction.

The **Anchorage** *(see page 313)* of the bridge, a cathedrallike structure with ceilings up to four stories high, holds up the Brooklyn side. In summer, the Anchorage is the site of art exhibits and concerts, and it's a great place to cool off after a walk across the bridge. (The Manhattan side has an anchorage, too, but it's not open to visitors.)

Also under the bridge, at the water's edge, is **Fulton Landing**, a pier jutting into the East River at Old Fulton and Water Streets. It's a prime spot for taking photos of the Manhattan skyline. To the right is the rarefied **River Café** *(see page 189)*, and to the left is **Bargemusic** *(see page 317)*, a refurbished barge that hosts chamber-music concerts.

South of the bridge is the **Brooklyn Heights Promenade**, a pedestrian-only perch that overlooks the East River and runs from Cranberry Street to Remsen Street, with its main entrance at the foot of Montague Street. The plentiful benches make it a good place to sit and observe lunching locals, skating kids and other tourists. The Promenade's view of lower Manhattan was forever altered after the 2001 World Trade Center tragedy. The site instantly became an area where people from all over the world could pay their respects to those whose lives were lost.

Neighborhoods

Once entrepreneur Robert Fulton's first steam-powered ferry connected Manhattan to the village of Brooklyn (in 1814), the development of Brooklyn Heights took off. Its streets, particularly Cranberry, Hicks, Pierrepont and Willow, are lined with Greek and Italianate row houses dating to the 1820s. In 1965, 30 blocks of Brooklyn Heights were designated New York City's first historic district.

At 128 Pierrepont Street, at the corner of Clinton Street, is the the **Brooklyn Historical Society** *(see page 40),* in a landmark George C. Post–designed building. Constructed in 1872, it is the city's earliest surviving example of the use of terra-cotta as a decorative material. A restoration is scheduled to be completed in fall of 2002, when it will house the interactive multimedia exhibit "Brooklyn Works: 350 Years of Making a Living in Brooklyn," through 2005.

Also in the Heights, on Orange Street, is the dignified **Plymouth Church of the Pilgrims**, founded by renowned abolitionist Henry Ward Beecher, brother of Harriet Beecher Stowe.

Mason-Brooklyn line The Civil War Memorial Arch dominates the rotary at Grand Army Plaza.

The waterfront below Brooklyn Heights, between the Manhattan Bridge and Atlantic Avenue, will soon undergo a dramatic change. During the next few years, this little-used stretch of piers is slated to be converted into an 80-acre public park that will include open space, recreational facilities, shops and restaurants.

The remains of Brooklyn's days as a separate municipality still exist in the somewhat fragmented downtown. **Borough Hall** *(209 Joralemon St at Fulton St)*, built in 1851, is at the center. Its renovation in the early 1990s won the Municipal Art Society's top prize for restoration of a public structure. Borough Hall is linked to the **New York County Supreme Court** by a vast plaza, where farmers from the tristate area peddle fresh produce on Fridays and Saturdays. Nearby is a massive **U.S. Post Office** *(271 Cadman Plaza East between Johnson and Tillary Sts)*.

Brooklyn's main business district is across the way, in the **MetroTech Center**. A common provides a shady place to rest between 12 MetroTech and **Polytechnic University**, the second-oldest science-and-engineering school in the country. At the easternmost edge of the commons is **Wunsch Student Center** *(311 Bridge St between Johnson and Tillary Sts)*. Long before it became part of the university campus, the 1846 Greek Revival structure was the home of the Bridge Street African Wesleyan Methodist Church, which was a stop on the Underground Railroad. The congregation moved to Bedford-Stuyvesant in 1938.

Farther east, at the edge of downtown, is the **Brooklyn Academy of Music** *(see page 315)*. BAM, America's oldest operating performing arts center (founded in 1861 and at this site since 1908), offers brand-new or cutting-edge theater, music and performance art. The Brooklyn Philharmonic is the orchestra in residence, and the noted Next Wave Festival showcases contemporary experimental works every fall—Australia was highlighted in 2001. The **BAM Rose Cinemas** *(see page 274)*, is Brooklyn's art-house film center.

As you explore Brooklyn, pay attention to the unique character of each neighborhood. Nearly 100 ethnic groups proudly fly the colors of their respective homelands. For example, south of downtown is **Carroll Gardens**. You can still spot this charming area's Italian roots. Although it's fun to walk through Carroll Park, where old men play bocce and grandmothers watch kids run about, it's even better to stroll on Court Street and stop in the shops for a taste of Italy. Buy a prosciutto loaf from the **Caputo Bakery** *(329 Court St between Sackett and Union Sts, 718-875-6871)*, pick up freshly made buffalo mozzarella at **Caputo's Fine Foods** *(460 Court St between 3rd and 4th Sts, 718-855-8852)*, grab an aged *soppressata* from **Esposito and Sons** *(357 Court St between President and Union Sts, 718-875-6863)*, and then settle down in the park.

▶ For inside info on Brooklyn's bar and music scenes, see **Halcyon days**, page 270 and chapters **Night Train to Brooklyn** and **A Noise Grows in Brooklyn**.
▶ See also chapter **Museums**.
▶ A **Brooklyn map** is on pages 404 and 405.

Red, white and view The Smith Street F and G station is the highest in all of New York.

Like so many Brooklyn neighborhoods, Carroll Gardens is changing. Newer residents congregate on bustling Smith Street; a slew of stylish eateries such as **The Grocery** *(see page 188)* and **Sur** *(232 Smith St between Butler and Douglass Sts, 718-875-1716)* have also made the area a destination for Manhattanites.

Arabs have claimed part of **Atlantic Avenue** as their own, on the border between Brooklyn Heights and Cobble Hill. The epicenter is **Sahadi Importing Company** *(187 Atlantic Ave between Clinton and Court Sts),* a market that carries every imaginable Mediterranean delicacy.

North of downtown is **Williamsburg**. "Billyburg" was quickly industrialized because of its user-friendly waterfront, and it became a bustling port after the Erie Canal linked the Atlantic with the Great Lakes in 1825. Companies such as Domino Sugar and pharmaceuticals giant Pfizer started here. In the 20th century, many companies abandoned enormous industrial spaces in the neighborhood.

Williamsburg is also one of New York's more curious multiethnic amalgams. To the south, Broadway divides a vibrant Latino neighborhood from a quiet community of Hassidic Jews. The northern half is shared by Polish and Italian blue-collar residents, many of whom originally worked the East River docks. Because economic good times in the 1990s made Manhattan loft spaces unaffordable for artists, they packed their paint and clay and hopped across the river, using the ample raw square footage for studios. Following the artists' migration was gentrification—some of the city's trendiest bars and restaurants can be found along Bedford Avenue *(see pages 151* and *187).* The neighborhood also houses several art galleries, such as **Pierogi 2000** *(see page 254),* and on

some weekends, area artists hold group exhibitions in their studios, organize sprawling street fairs or show off their art in **Grand Ferry Park** *(Grand St at the East River).* Check the free neighborhood weekly, *Waterfront Week,* for details. The **Williamsburg Art & Historical Center,** housed in an old bank building, is a repository of local lore; it also displays works by New York and international artists, and hosts a dizzying program of dance, theater, music, digital art, video, film and performance art.

Fort Greene is Brooklyn's bohemian center, with an increasingly multiethnic population of successful creative types: Spike Lee, Chris Rock, Rosie Perez and Branford Marsalis have all called this neighborhood home. **Fort Greene Park** *(between DeKalb and Myrtle Aves at Cumberland St),* was created in 1848 at the instigation of poet Walt Whitman (then the editor of the *Brooklyn Daily Eagle* newspaper); it was redesigned by Frederick Law Olmsted and Calvert Vaux in 1867. At the center of the park stands the **Prison Ship Martyr's Monument,** erected in 1908 as the symbolic tomb for 11,500 American soldiers who died on British prison ships anchored nearby during the Revolutionary War. A block away from the park's southern border, at the corner of South Oxford Street and Lafayette Avenue, is the **Lafayette Avenue Presbyterian Church,** founded by a group of abolitionists. Robert Todd Lincoln, eldest son of Abraham Lincoln, broke ground for the church in 1860. Its subterranean tunnel holds steam pipes and boilers, and once served as an emergency Underground Railroad site. The church will be restoring its stained-glass windows, 13 of which were created by Louis Comfort Tiffany, through 2002.

Bedford-Stuyvesant, just east of Fort Greene, is a predominantly African-American community. Join the annual **Brownstoners of Bedford-Stuyvesant House Tour** *(held the third Saturday in October, 718-574-1979)* for an in-depth look. Also in the area, the **Concord Baptist Church of Christ** allows you to experience some old-time religion and hear fabulous gospel music alongside one of the largest black congregations in the U.S.

On the border between Bed-Stuy and **Crown Heights** is a row of four houses that were part of **Weeksville**, New York's first community of freed slaves, founded by stevedore James Weeks. The remnants of what was a bustling 19th-century hamlet were forgotten behind housing projects until 1968, when they were "discovered" by two men flying overhead in a small plane. One of the houses now displays artifacts found on the site; the pair of leg irons on view is a grim reminder of bleaker days. A full restoration is in progress and once completed, the buildings will become a museum.

Crown Heights and **Flatbush** are primarily West Indian neighborhoods, though both also support large Jewish populations. Calypso and soca music blare out of windows and doors. Each block has at least one carry-out place where you can get spicy jerk chicken or meat patties. Try **Sybil's** *(2210 Church Ave at Flatbush Ave, 718-469-9049),* a cafeteria-style Caribbean restaurant. Service is friendly, and the staff will help you choose between the *escovitch* and the akee. The best day to visit the neighborhood is the first Monday in September—because Labor Day is **Carnival** *(see page 241)* time. Many of the city's roughly 1 million citizens of Caribbean descent—along with thousands of neighbors, day-trippers and tourists—come out for this raucous celebration of over-the-top costumes, fiery food and pulsating music. Beginning early in the morning, the neighborhoods lining Eastern Parkway come alive in a vivid masquerade (or *mas*), vibrating to the jubilant clangor of steel-drum bands.

Brooklyn has the largest population of observant Jews outside Israel, and to get a better understanding of Jewish rituals and beliefs, you can go to the heart of that community in **Borough Park**. Take a Hassidic Discovery tour *(see page 109),* or just wander the streets, grazing on the great food. On Fridays before sundown, the streets are at a fever pitch just before the Sabbath *(Shabbes)* begins; on Saturdays, the neighborhood seems almost abandoned.

South of Borough Park is a band of three neighborhoods—Bay Ridge, Bensonhurst and Gravesend. Populated largely by Italian-American and Jewish residents until the 1970s,

all three are now bustling with multiethnic activity. **Bay Ridge** (along with **Bensonhurst**) was the setting for *Saturday Night Fever.* The disco in which John Travolta strutted his stuff is still there—although it's currently a gay club called **Spectrum** *(802 64th St at Eighth Ave, 718-238-8213).* Before it was a hangout for would-be Tony Maneros, Bay Ridge began as a Dutch settlement in 1652, then became a summer retreat in the 1800s. Along the quiet suburban streets, you can still find grand old homes, such as the **Howard E. and Jessie Jones House** *(8220 Narrows Ave at 83rd St),* an Arts and Crafts mansion known locally as the Ginger-bread House, and the Georgian-style mansion at **131 76th Street** *(between Ridge Blvd and Colonial Rd).* Recent Arab, Chinese, Greek and Russian arrivals mean that you'll find lots of eating options on the main drags of Third, Fourth and Fifth Avenues, between 88th Street and Bay Ridge Parkway. **Karam** *(8519 Fourth Ave between 85th and 86th Sts, 718-745-5227),* a take-out café, serves the city's best Lebanese food. For a taste of old Brooklyn, drop by 87-year-old **Hinsch's Confectionary** *(8518 Fifth Ave between 85th and 86th Sts, 718-748-2854)* for an egg malt, a burger and house-made chocolates. The **Verrazano-Narrows Bridge** *(see page 6)* dominates the neighborhood. Completed in 1964, it connects Brooklyn with Staten Island *(see page 106).* The foot of the bridge is in **Fort Hamilton**. Named after Alexander Hamilton, the country's first Secretary of the Treasury, the fort is the second oldest continuously run federal post in the country.

Moving east, **Bensonhurst** is where the TV show *The Honeymooners* took place. It's also where Paul Sorvino and Larry King grew up. On **Cristoforo Colombo Boulevard** *(18th Ave between 68th and 77th Sts),* you'll find a *real* Little Italy (as opposed to Manhattan's tourist-oriented version)—social clubs, delis stocked with more kinds of pasta than soda, shops selling Italian music, and **Villabate Pasti-cceria and Bakery** *(7117 18th Ave between 71st and 72nd Sts, 718-331-8430),* where crowds order pastries and marzipan in Italian. People stand in line half an hour for the hot roast beef sandwich special at **John's Deli** *(2033 Stillwell Ave at 86th St, 718-372-7481),* served on Wednesdays, Thursdays and Saturdays. In September, the neighborhood hosts the **Festa of St. Rosalia** (Sicily's patron saint), a week-long celebration that rivals Manhattan's **Feast of San Gennaro** *(see page 241).*

Finally, you'll hit **Gravesend**, which was founded in 1643 by Lady Deborah Moody, a rich widow and radical Protestant who was the first woman to charter land in the nascent U.S. The **Hicks-Platt House** *(17 Gravesend Neck Rd* between McDonald Ave and Van Sicklen St), a 17th-century house (marred by a fake-stone veneer), is reputed to be on what was the Moody farm. Lady Moody is buried in the cemetery across the street, though the site of her grave has been lost. Today, locals stop at **Joe's of Avenue U** *(287 Ave U between McDonald Ave and Lake St, 718-449-9285)* for pasta *con sarde* (sardines), and *arancini* (delicious rice balls).

Brighton Beach, on the shore, is known as Little Odessa because of its large population of immigrants from the former Soviet Union. If you get a yen for caviar, vodka and smoked sausage, this is the place to go. You can wander the aisles of **M&I International** *(249 Brighton Beach Ave between Brighton 1st and Brighton 2nd Sts, 718-615-1011),* a huge Russian deli and grocery, or make a reservation at one of the local nightclubs. Dress is formal, food and vodka are plentiful, and dancing goes on until the wee hours.

Brooklyn Bridge

Subway: A, C to High St; J, M, Z to Chambers St; 4, 5, 6 to Brooklyn Bridge–City Hall.
The Brooklyn Bridge is the most beautiful and famous of New York's many bridges. The twin Gothic arches of its towers form a grand gateway, no matter which way you are headed. The span took more than 600 men almost 16 years to build; when completed in 1883, it was the world's largest suspension bridge and the first to be constructed of steel. Engineer John A. Roebling was one of 20 men who

died on the project—before construction even started. His son stayed on the job until he was struck by caisson disease (the bends), and then, with his wife's help, he supervised construction from the window of his Brooklyn apartment. "All that trouble just to get to Brooklyn!" was the vaudeville quip of the day. The walkway is great for an afternoon or sunset stroll; for incredible views, take the A or C train to High Street and walk back to Manhattan.

Brooklyn Heights Promenade

Along the East River between Cranberry and Remsen Sts, Brooklyn Heights. Subway: 1, 2 to Clark St, then walk down Clark St toward the river.

Brooklyn Information and Culture

718-855-7882; www.brooklynx.org
This organization, also known as BRIC, provides information about Brooklyn. To get the quarterly calendar of events, *Meet Me in Brooklyn,* call BRIC, then dial extension 42.

Concord Baptist Church of Christ

833 Marcy Ave between Madison and Putnam Aves, Bedford-Stuyvesant (718-622-1818). Subway: A, C to Nostrand Ave. Call for times of services.

Lafayette Avenue Presbyterian Church

85 South Oxford St at Lafayette Ave, Fort Greene (718-625-7515). Subway: C to Lafayette Ave; G to Fulton St.
Free tours by appointment only.

Keepin' it reel Cats in hats enjoy the view from Coney Island's popular fisherman's pier.

Plymouth Church of the Pilgrims
75 Hicks St between Cranberry and Orange Sts, Brooklyn Heights (718-624-4743; www.plymouth church.org). Subway: A, C to High St; 1, 2 to Clark St.
Free tours by appointment only.

Weeksville Society Hunterfly Road Houses
1698–1708 Bergen St between Buffalo and Rochester Aves, Crown Heights (718-756-5250). Subway: A, C to Utica Ave.
Free tours by appointment only.

Williamsburg Art & Historical Center
135 Broadway at Bedford Ave, Williamsburg (718-486-7372). Subway: J, M, Z to Marcy Ave. Sat, Sun noon–6pm and by appointment.

Destinations

Brooklyn is full of all-day diversions. A good place to start is the Beaux Art **Brooklyn Museum of Art**, the second largest museum in the city *(see page 33)*. Right next door is the tranquil **Brooklyn Botanic Garden**. Feed the ducks at the **Japanese Hill-and-Pond Garden**, one of the finest of its kind outside Japan. In the spring, the **Cherry Blossom Esplanade** trees burst with pink; the **Cranford Rose Garden** is at its best in June, when its 5,000 bushes and nearly 1,200 varieties bloom. Plant lovers can stroll the gardens and the indoor, climate-controlled **Steinhardt Pavilion** year-round. Down the street, the **Central Library** *(Grand Army Plaza between Eastern Pkwy and Flatbush Ave; see page 260)* resembles an open book: its main entrance is the spine, and its wings parallel Eastern Parkway and Flatbush Avenue like leaves. The library's Brooklyn Collection includes thousands of photos, manuscripts and artifacts that catalog the borough's history.

Brooklyn's 526-acre heart of green, **Prospect Park**, is just south of the museum and garden. Although it's smaller than Central Park, it's also more rustic—a wonderful place to bird-watch or rent a pedal boat from the boathouse. Reopened in spring 2001, the park's restored **Ravine** is a landscape of waterfalls, reflecting pools and wildlife habitats. Olmsted and Vaux, who designed Central Park, wanted Prospect Park to be enjoyed on horseback. While it's possible to rent horses at nearby **Kensington Stables** *(see page 330)*, biking is the next best thing. Pedal alongside in-line skaters and runners, past Frisbee-catching dogs and picnicking families scattered in the park's meadows. From mid-May through October, the Congo Square Drummers and Dancers gather on Sundays in a section of the park known as **Drummers Grove**, north of the Parkside–Ocean Avenue entrance; onlookers

are encouraged to join in and dance. Children of all ages enjoy riding the hand-carved horses—as well as goats and lions—of the park's 1912 **carousel**, located at the intersection of Empire Boulevard and Flatbush Avenue. At the **Prospect Park Wildlife Center**, you can learn about animals in their natural habitat. The nearby Lake is where kids can compete in the **R.H. Macy's Fishing Contest**, which has been held at this spot every July since 1947. Other summer traditions are the concert series and events that make up the **Celebrate Brooklyn! Festival** *(see page 237)*. In the southwestern part of the park is the private **Quaker Friends Cemetery**, where actor Montgomery Clift, of all people, is buried.

Ten blocks south of the park is another expanse of green—**Green-Wood Cemetery**. A century ago, the stunning 478 acres vied with Niagara Falls as New York state's greatest tourist attraction. Filled with Victorian mausoleums and monuments, cherubs and gargoyles, Green-Wood is the resting place of politico William "Boss" Tweed, architect Stanford White, Leonard Bernstein and Jean-Michel Basquiat.

Architecture buffs might try a tour through Victorian **Flatbush**, just south of Prospect Park. The homes are extravagant, and no two are alike (the developer wouldn't allow it). In early spring, the Flatbush Development Corporation sponsors a tour of mansions that were once inhabited by the city's elite, including reporter Nellie Bly, silent-film star Mary Pickford and the philanthropic Guggenheims.

Coney Island (which is not an actual island anymore) is a destination in itself. After decades of decay, the weirdly wonderful neighborhood, known for its amusement park, beach and boardwalk, has made a comeback. The biggest improvement is KeySpan Park, home to the Brooklyn Cyclones, a minor-league baseball team *(see Diamond dogs, page 326)*. If you're a thrill-seeker, you can't miss Astroland Amusement Park's Cyclone, the 75-year-old wooden roller coaster for which the ball team is named. The ride lasts only 90 seconds, but the initial drop is nearly vertical, and the dozen or so cars clatter along the 3,000 feet of track at speeds up to 60 miles per hour. It's rated as one of the world's top ten roller-coaster experiences.

After your ride, grab a **Nathan's Famous** hot dog *(1310 Surf Ave at Stillwell Ave, 718-946-2202)*, take in the rather tame **Coney Island Sideshows by the Seashore** and walk out to the beach. Stroll along the boardwalk, perhaps as far as the **New York Aquarium for Wildlife Conservation** *(see page 297)*, where you can marvel at the famous beluga whales.

Coney Island is a gathering place for teens, senior citizens and oddball improvisational

Sightseeing

performers, all attracted by a hard-earned patina that is equal parts nostalgia and strangeness. From July to the first week of September, you can boogie to house music on the boardwalk at 10th Street *(Sat 3–9pm)* at **Black Underground**. See **Mermaid Parade** *(see page 238)*, and **Nathan's Famous Fourth of July Hot Dog–Eating Contest** *(see page 239)*, for two annual Coney Island events.

Brooklyn Botanic Garden
900 Washington Ave between Eastern Pkwy and Empire Blvd, Prospect Heights (718-623-7200; www.bbg.org). Subway: C to Franklin Ave, then S to Botanic Garden; 1, 2 to Eastern Pkwy–Brooklyn Museum. Apr–Sept Tue–Fri 8am–6pm; Sat, Sun, holidays 10am–6pm. Oct–Mar Tue–Fri 8am–4:30pm; Sat, Sun, holidays 10am–4:30pm. $3, seniors and students $1.50, under 16 free. Tue 8am–6pm, Sat 10am–noon, Cash only.

Coney Island Sideshows by the Seashore/Coney Island USA
1208 Surf Ave at W 12th St, Coney Island (718-372-5159; www.coneyisland.com). Subway: F, Q, W to Coney Island–Stillwell Ave. Call for show times and schedules. $5, under 12 $3.

Green-Wood Cemetery
25th St at Fifth Ave, Sunset Park (718-768-7300; www.green-wood.com). Subway: M, N, R to 25th St. Mon–Sun 8am–4pm. Free.
A detailed map is available for $3 at the gate. Walking tours are available through John Cashman's Walking Tours *(718-469-5277)* and Big Onion Walking Tours *(see page 109)*.

New York Aquarium for Wildlife Conservation
Surf Ave at W 8th St, Coney Island (718-265-FISH; www.wcs.org/nyaquarium). Subway: F, Q to W 8th St–NY Aquarium. 10am–4:30pm. $9.75,

Arabian sights Atlantic Avenue is the heart of Brooklyn's Arabic community.

seniors and children 2–12 $6, under 2 free. AmEx, Disc, MC, V.

Prospect Park
Flatbush Ave at Grand Army Plaza, Prospect Heights (events hot line 718-965-8999, carousel 718-282-7789, Leffert's Homestead 718-965-6505, Prospect Park Wildlife Center 718-399-7339; www.prospectpark.org). Subway: 1, 2 to Grand Army Plaza.

Queens

New York City's largest borough has many suburban signifiers—no other borough has as many single-family homes. On a drive through its neighborhoods, you'll see almost every style of American housing, from apartment-house co-ops to bungalows. A relative bounty of affordable housing has led to a huge influx of new immigrants into Queens. A third of its more than 2 million residents are foreign-born, resulting in a tantalizing multiethnic scene.

Once a densely forested area inhabited by the Algonquin tribe, Queens developed as a series of small towns whose names remain as neighborhood appellations, including Forest Hills and Flushing. Because of this patchwork development, it can be difficult to navigate. (To decode Queens addresses, *see* **Let's get lost,** *page 97*.)

The logical first stop in Queens is Long Island City, the neighborhood closest to Manhattan, and the hub of the borough's growing art community. **P.S. 1** *(see* **Museum of Modern Art,** *page 35)*, a former public school converted into a contemporary-art gallery and studio space, is part of the Museum of Modern Art. The art center's open workshops, multimedia galleries and censor-taunting exhibitions attract artists from around the world. You'll find works by Richard Serra and Julian Schnabel on the roof, and a Jocelyn Shipley installation in the basement bathroom (not to be missed). On weekends, you can take the free Queens Artlink bus from Manhattan *(see* **Go to the art of Queens,** *page 103)*.

At the **Isamu Noguchi Garden Museum** *(see page 38)*, more than 300 of his sculptures are on view, including his beautiful Akari (paper lantern) sculptures. The museum is currently undergoing renovation and has set up temporary exhibits in Sunnyside near **MoMA QNS** *(see page 35)*. On the banks of the East River is the 4.5-acre **Socrates Sculpture Park**. The large-scale work of established and lesser-known artists dot the big field, which is also the site of occasional concerts and film festivals.

Long before Hollywood was movieland, there was **Astoria**, adjacent to **Long Island City**. W.C. Fields, Rudolph Valentino, Gloria Swanson and the Marx Brothers all made films at **Kaufman Astoria Studios** *(34-12 36th St between 34th and 35th Aves),* which opened in 1917. It's still in "the biz." The Children's Television Workshop (producers of *Sesame Street*) and the Lifetime Network are based here. At the **American Museum of the Moving Image** *(see page 44)* across the street, aspiring filmmakers can learn about the history and process of making movies and TV shows as well as check out actual props, such as the eerily lifelike, swivel-headed Linda Blair dummy from *The Exorcist.* Long Island City's **Silvercup Studios** *(42-22 22nd St between Queens Plaza South and 43rd Ave),* which opened in 1983, is now the largest independent, full-service film and television production facility in the northeastern United States. *Sex and the City* and *The Sopranos* are produced here, and past movies include *Men in Black, Do the Right Thing* and *When Harry Met Sally….* Sorry fans, tours aren't available.

One of the world's premier piano manufacturers is based in **Astoria**: At the **Steinway Piano Factory,** you can get up close (with goggles) and watch craftsmen assemble pianos piece by piece and tune the finished product in soundproof studios.

Of course, when in Astoria, you must eat Greek; the neighborhood has attracted Greek immigrants since the 1920s and has a solid reputation for outstanding restaurants. Try **S'Agapo** *(34-21 34th Ave at 35th St, 718-626-0303),* **Elias Corner** *(see page 190)* or any of the eateries along 31st Street, 30th Avenue or Broadway.

The 7 train, which runs above ground in Queens and offers views of the Manhattan skyline, is known as the International Express because just about every stop takes you to a different ethnic community. Explore these neighborhoods to see how residents have made their mark on the city—and to eat. The first few stops after Long Island City (40th Street to 61st Street–Woodside stations) are **Sunnyside** and **Woodside,** where you'll find Irish pubs aplenty. If you have a craving for black pudding, you have a wide choice of Irish bakeries, delis and restaurants. But the Emerald Isle isn't the only country represented in the area: **Cornel's Garden Romanian** restaurant *(46-04 Skillman Ave between 46th and 47th Sts, 718-786-7894),* **Dazies** Italian restaurant *(39-41 Queens Blvd at 40th St, 718-786-7013)* and **Nazar Turkish Cuisine** *(42-03 Queens Blvd at 42nd St)* are just a few of the eateries that offer delectable cuisine from around the world at lower-than-Manhattan prices.

Once fed, walk around **Sunnyside Gardens,** a 77-acre district of tree-shaded streets, garden apartments and homes that was built in the 1920s; it begins at Skillman Avenue and 43rd Street. Or take in a flamenco or tango show at the internationally renowned **Thalia Spanish Theater.** It presents dance performances, musical concerts, zarzuela (Spanish operetta) and bilingual productions such as *Picasso's Guernica.*

In **Jackson Heights,** get off the subway at the 74th Street–Broadway stop; you'll be struck by the glittering saris and jewels worn by residents and displayed in store windows. Fill up on curry at **Delhi Palace** *(see page 190).*

Jackson Heights' historic district extends for 30 blocks and encompasses 500 apartment buildings and homes. These English garden–style homes an large apartment complexes were built in the early 1900s as models of suburban planning. Though most are not open to the public, the Jackson Heights Beautification Group *(212-439-8784; www.preserve.org/jhbg)* sponsors tours in June for a look at the interiors. Other organizations that offer tours throughout the year: Cooper Union *(212-353-4000; www.cooper.edu)* and Adventure on a Shoestring *(see page 108).*

Main Street in **Flushing**—the heart of a thriving Asian community—is packed with

Let's get lost

What do those crazy Queens addresses mean, anyway?

What's with the hyphenated addresses in Queens? First of all, you should know that, unlike in Manhattan, the numbered streets here run from north to south; the numbered avenues run from east to west, except when they curve or strike out in diagonal directions. The number before the hyphen indicates the perpendicular avenue or street; the numbers after the hyphen indicate how far along the block the address is. (Of course, there are exceptions—such as cross streets or streets with names instead of numbers.) So, 31-31 31st Street, in the heart of Astoria, is between 30th and 31st Avenues. A confusing example? Maybe, but that's a typical Queens address. Now find 23-23 23rd Street…it's south of 23rd Avenue, near 23rd Road and 23rd Drive, just around the way from 23rd Terrace. Hey, if you lived in Queens, you'd understand perfectly.

Chinese and Korean restaurants and food stores. For dim sum, bring a big appetite to the 595-seat **KB Garden** *(136-28 39th Ave between Main and 138th Sts, 718-961-9088)*; for Korean food, head to **Kum Gang San** *(see page 175)*. Flushing is also where you'll find most of Queens' historic buildings. The **Friends' Meeting House**, built in 1694 by religious activist John Bowne, is still used as a Quaker meeting place, making it the oldest house of worship in continuous use in the United States. Next door is **Kingsland House**, a mid-18th–century farmhouse that is the headquarters of the Queens Historical Society. You can also visit the **Bowne House**, which dates to 1661. **Flushing Town Hall**, an 1862 Romanesque Revival building, houses the **Flushing Council on Culture and the Arts** and presents art exhibits and jazz or classical concerts. It also hosts the **Queens Jazz Trail** tour *(see **All that jazz**, page 100)*.

The **Queens Botanical Garden** offers a quiet reprieve from Main Street's crowds; it was created as a horticultural display for the 1939 World's Fair (the two Atlantic cedars out front were planted then). Although the garden can't compete with its rivals in Brooklyn and the Bronx in size and scope, what sets it apart is its plan to create gardens that reflect the borough's ethnic mix. For example, a Chinese garden might include peonies, considered the flower of love, as well as edible and medicinal plants.

Flushing Meadows–Corona Park, a 1,255-acre spread of fields and lakes, contains **Shea Stadium**, home of the New York Mets, and the **United States National Tennis Center** *(see page 324)*, where the U.S. Open is played every August. The 1939 and 1964 World's Fairs were held in Corona Park (then known as Flushing Meadows Park), and some incredible structures are still standing, including the gigantic stainless-steel Unisphere globe. A 1939 pavilion now houses the **Queens Museum of Art** *(see page 39)*, where the main attraction is the diorama, a scale model (1 inch equals 100 feet) of New York City made for the 1964 fair. The **Queens Theatre in the Park**, designed by Philip Johnson, is a cozy amphitheater that hosts dance, theater and comedy performances (often for half what you'd pay for a show in Manhattan).

► The **Queens street map** is on page 406.
► See **All that jazz**, page 100, for info on Queens' musical past.
► See also chapter **Sports & Fitness**.

On weekends, Corona Park is filled with picnicking families and soccer matches between teams of transplanted South Americans. At the park's eastern edge is the **New York Hall of Science** *(see page 45)*, an interactive museum that encourages you to play mad scientist. If you hear barking sea lions, you're near the **Queens Zoo** (also known as the Queens Wildlife Center). Opened for the 1964 World's Fair, the zoo houses North American animals, such as woolly-headed bison, bald eagles and bears—and a coyote found wandering in Central Park in 1999 *(see chapter **Green Apple**)*.

Southeast of Corona, near the Long Island border, is the **Queens County Farm Museum** in Floral Park. The 1772 farm features exhibits on the city's agricultural history. Near Kennedy Airport, the tidal wetlands of the **Jamaica Bay Wildlife Refuge** are prime spots for bird watching, especially in May and September. Bring your binoculars to spot both birds and planes. (*See also chapter **Green Apple**.*)

If you're a gambler, a great bargain is the **Aqueduct** *(see page 323)* racetrack, site of the winter–spring Thoroughbred racing season. Seats cost $1 to $3 (no kidding!), compared with $50 to $80 at other tracks.

Bowne House

37-01 Bowne St between 37th and 38th Aves, Flushing (718-359-0528). Subway: 7 to Flushing–Main St. Tue, Sat, Sun 2:30–4:30pm. $2.
Nine generations of the descendants of John Bowne—a fighter for religious freedom—lived here until it was turned into a museum in 1945. Only part of the house is original. Due to renovation, Bowne house is closed until 2006.

Flushing Meadows–Corona Park

Between Jewel Ave and Northern Blvd, Corona. Subway: 7 to Willets Point–Shea Stadium.

Flushing Town Hall

137-35 Northern Blvd, Flushing (718-463-7700). Subway: 7 to Flushing–Main St. Mon–Fri 10am–5pm; Sat, Sun noon–5pm. $3, seniors and students $2, children $1.

Friends' Meeting House

137-16 Northern Blvd between Main and Union Sts, Flushing (718-358-9636). Subway: 7 to Flushing–Main St.
Tours by appointment only.

Jamaica Bay Wildlife Refuge

Cross Bay Blvd at Broad Channel, Jamaica (718-318-4340). Travel: A to Broad Channel, then from subway station, walk on Noel Rd to Cross Bay Blvd, cross it and turn right, then walk a half mile until you see the trailhead on your left. 8:30am–5pm. Free.
You can spot pairs of osprey, a fish-eating hawk

House proud In Bay Ridge, you'll find mansions and well-kept row houses with pretty patios.

that has come back from the brink of extinction. Migratory species, including the long-legged curlew sandpiper, can be seen in spring and early fall. Guided walks, lectures and all sorts of nature-centered activities are available.

Kingsland House/ Queens Historical Society/ Weeping Beech Park

143-35 37th Ave at Parsons Blvd, Flushing (718-939-0647). Subway: 7 to Flushing–Main St. Mon–Fri 9:30am–5pm. Tours Tue, Sat, Sun 2:30–4:30pm. $3. Cash only.

Built in 1785 by a wealthy Quaker, Kingsland House was moved to a site beside Bowne House in 1968. The Queens Historical Society now uses it for exhibitions detailing local history.

Queens Botanical Garden

43-50 Main St between Dahlia and Elder Aves, Flushing (718-886-3800; www.queensbotanical. org). Subway: 7 to Flushing–Main St. Apr–Oct Tue–Fri 8am–6pm; Sat, Sun 8am–7pm. Nov–Mar Tue–Fri 8am–4:30pm. Free.

Queens Council on the Arts

79-01 Park Ln South, Woodhaven (718-647-3377, info 718-291-ARTS; www.queenscouncilarts.org). Subway: J to 85th St–Forest Pkwy. Mon–Fri 9am–4:30pm.

This organization provides exhaustive details, updated daily, on all cultural events in the borough.

Queens County Farm Museum

73-50 Little Neck Pkwy, Floral Park (718-347-3276). Travel: E, F to Kew Gardens–Union Tpke, then Q46 bus to Little Neck Pkwy. Mon–Fri 9am–5pm outdoor

grounds only; Sat, Sun 10am–5pm tours of farmhouse and museum galleries. Voluntary donation.

Queens Theatre in the Park

Corona Park, trolley picks up at subway station one hour before each show (718-760-0064; www.queenstheatre.org.) Subway: 7 to Willets Point–Shea Stadium. Show times and prices vary.

Queens Zoo

53-51 111th St in Corona Park (718-271-1500; www.queenszoo.org). Subway: 7 to 111th St. Mon–Fri 10am–5pm; Sat, Sun 10am–5:30pm. $2.50, seniors $1.25, children $.50.

Socrates Sculpture Park

Broadway at Vernon Blvd, Long Island City (718-956-1819). Travel: N to Broadway then Q104 bus to Vernon Blvd; Queens Artlink shuttle, see **Go to the art of Queens,** *page 103. 9am–sunset. Free.*

Steinway Piano Factory

Steinway Pl between 19th Ave and 38th St, Astoria (718-721-2600; www.steinway.com). Subway: N to Ditmars Blvd. Free tours by appointment only.

The four-hour tours fill up quickly.

Thalia Spanish Theatre

41-17 Greenpoint Ave between 41st and 42nd Sts, Sunnyside (718-729-3880; www.thaliatheatre.org). Subway: 7 to 40th St. Show times vary. Tickets $20–$25.

The Bronx

The Bronx is so named because it once belonged to the family of Jonas Bronck, a

Swede from the Netherlands who built his farm here in 1636. (People would say, "Let's go over to the Broncks'.") As Manhattan's rich moved into baronial apartments on Fifth Avenue, a similar metamorphosis took place to the north. Consequently, the Bronx contains some of the city's most important cultural landmarks, including the Bronx Zoo, New York Botanical Garden and Yankee Stadium.

Yankee Stadium *(see page 322)* sits at 161st Street. When there are no day games, tours are given of the clubhouse, dugout and the famous right-field fence, which was deliberately made a "short porch"—314 feet from home plate—so that Babe Ruth could set his home-run records. The coolest way to get to a game is by boat: NY Waterway *(800-53-FERRY, see page 108)* will carry you from Manhattan or New Jersey to the game and back aboard the *Yankee Clipper* .

Walk a couple of blocks past Yankee Stadium to 1005 Jerome Avenue at 162nd Street to see the **Park Plaza Apartments**, with its intricate brick patterns, terra-cotta friezes, gargoyles and squirrel and owl statuettes. Designed by Marvin Fine and Horace Ginsberg, the eight-story landmark building stretches almost two-thirds of a block. If you can sneak a peek into the lobby, you'll see a sunburst-tile floor and elegant archways with recessed lighting leading to each wing of the complex.

For an eyeful of Art Deco buildings, take a walk along the **Grand Concourse**, the West Bronx's six-mile main drag, which stretches from 138th Street to Mosholu Parkway. In the 1930s, when Deco was all the rage, the borough experienced a building boom. At the time, this 12-lane boulevard was known as "the Champs-Élysées of the Bronx," because of its urban vibe and jazzy designs.

At the Concourse's intersection with 161st Street, you'll find the most eye-catching edifices: **888 Grand Concourse** has a concave entrance of gilded mosaic, topped by a curvy metallic marquee (although it could use a good shine). Inside, the mirrored lobby's central fountain and sunburst-patterned floor give any hotel on Miami's Ocean Drive a run for its money. The nearby **Executive Towers** *(1020 Grand*

All that jazz

Louis Armstrong, Dizzy Gillespie, Ella Fitzgerald—Queens has been a crucible of musical geniuses

Along with New Orleans, Kansas City and Chicago, Manhattan lays claim to plenty of jazz lore, but it's a humble outer borough that has long been the true *home* of jazz. Louis Armstrong, Ella Fitzgerald, Dizzy Gillespie, Milt Hinton and Fats Waller, among many others, all settled in Queens. (Some contemporary stars, such as Marcus Miller and Donald Blackman, continue the tradition.) These musical transplants from the South found that the borough's space and greenery reminded them of home—yet they were still close to the city's music studios and jazz clubs.

Jazz royalty has lived throughout the large borough, so a walking pilgrimage isn't easy. The easiest option is to take the **Queens Jazz Trail tour**; but it's offered only once a month, so here are some highlights.

The first stop is **Louis Armstrong's house** *(34-56 107th St between 34th and 37th Aves)* in Corona. The modest, three-story house is closed for renovation through 2002, after which it will reopen to the public with a visitors' center (in the converted garage). From the street, you can see part of the pretty backyard, where the annual Pops Is Tops concerts are held for neighborhood kids *(visit www.satchmo.net for details)*.

Unlike many of Armstrong's peripatetic peers, Satchmo and his wife, Lucille, bought the house in 1943 and lived there for the rest of their lives. Armstrong got his hair cut nearby at the two-chair **Joe's Artistic Barber Shop** *(33-06 106th St between Northern Blvd and 34th Ave)*. Joe is still there, and the place hasn't changed a bit, right down to the old wooden booster seat for kids.

The **Louis Armstrong Archives**, located at the Queens College Benjamin S. Rosenthal Library, maintains the house and grounds. At the archives, you can listen to Armstrong's home audiotapes (including one where he accompanies himself on an old recording), watch videos and view his scrapbooks. Aspiring trumpeters can even take a turn on one of Armstrong's actual horns.

Satchmo had some famous neighbors: **Dizzy Gillespie** *(34-68 106th St at 34th Ave)*,

Concourse at 165th St) is a gleaming 1960s high-rise featuring a landscaped forecourt, wave-shaped balconies, a marble entryway and larger-than-life gilded statues. And **1150 Grand Concourse** at 167th Street is bedecked with sawtooth-patterned windows, a marine-themed mosaic entrance, and a circular lobby with mahogany-paneled elevators and painted murals.

The grandest building on the Grand Concourse is the landmark **Andrew Freedman Home**, a 1924 limestone palazzo between McClennan and 166th Streets. In his will, mysterious millionaire Freedman stipulated that the bulk of his $7 million be used to build a retirement home for wealthy people who had fallen on hard times. Today, it still houses the elderly—but financial ruin is no longer a residency requirement.

The **Bronx Museum of the Arts**, which turned 30 in 2001, is housed in a former synagogue. Peer behind the security counter at the entrance to see a piece of the original wall, with an inscription in Hebrew. The museum showcases the talents of local artists and the area's cultural landscape with exhibits such as "One Planet Under a Groove: Hip-Hop and

Contemporary Art," which included works by Keith Haring and Jean-Michel Basquiat.

The **Hall of Fame of Great Americans**, modeled after Rome's Pantheon, is on the Bronx Community College campus. Designed by Stanford White, it was the country's first-ever hall of fame when it opened in 1901, with the bronze busts of 29 inductees, including George Washington and Ralph Waldo Emerson. The busts are by such famous sculptors as Daniel Chester French and Augustus Saint-Gaudens. The group that elected additions to the hall disbanded in 1976 (due to lack of funds). The hall is a pleasant enough rotunda, but isn't a destination in itself.

A ride north on the Bx1 bus will drop you near the Gothic-style campus of **Fordham University** *(441 E Fordham Rd between Washington and Third Aves),* a Jesuit institution founded in 1841. Some buildings date back to 1836, when this was a private estate, including the Rose Hill Administration Building, a Greek Revival manor. Call security ahead of time *(718-817-2222)* if you want to visit; they'll put your name on a list at the gate.

---

and **Cannonball Adderly, Nat Adderly, Jimmy Heath** and **Clark Terry,** who all lived in the Dorie Miller Houses *(112-19 34th Ave between 96th and 97th Sts).*

St. Albans/Addisleigh Park has seen a high concentration of musicians. Bassist **Milt Hinton** lived with his wife at 173-05 113th Avenue *(at Marine Pl)* until his death in 2000. **Ella Fitzgerald** set up house at 179-07 Murdock Avenue *(between 179th and 180th Sts),* and Linden Boulevard was home to **James Brown** *(175-19 Linden Blvd between 175th St and 175th Pl)* and **Billie Holiday** (exact address unknown). **Count Basie** settled at 174-27 Adelaide Road *(between 174th and 175th Sts),* and **Fats Waller** resided nearby at 173-19 Sayres Avenue *(between 173rd and 174th Sts).*

The utopian garden apartments in the **Jackson Heights** historic district were home to several big-time arrangers and band leaders. **Glenn Miller** *(37-60 88th St between Roosevelt and 37th Aves),* **Woody Herman** *(37-52 80th St between Roosevelt and 37th Aves)* and **Benny Goodman** (exact address unknown) all lived here.

If you're in town during the summer, you might want to stop in Sunnyside. Fans of pioneering cornetist **Bix Beiderbecke** gather every August 6 outside his former apartment

building *(43-30 46th St at 43rd Ave)* to mark the anniversary of his death.

And some of Queens' most famous residents rest in peace in the borough. Ragtime master **Scott Joplin** is buried in **St. Michaels Cemetery** *(72-02 Astoria Blvd at Grand Central Pkwy; grave 5, row 2, plot 5).* Both Armstrong *(plot 12B, division A, section 9)* and Gillespie *(grave 1252, section 31)* are interred at **Flushing Cemetery** *(163-06 46th Ave at 163rd St).*

Queens Jazz Trail

Flushing Town Hall, 137-35 Northern Blvd at Linden Pl (718-463-7700), first Saturday of every month, $15. Call for tickets.

The Flushing Town Hall *(see page 98)* hosts a bus tour that visits the homes and neighborhoods where jazz legends lived. You can pick up a map (of more than 75 musicians' homes) from Town Hall and follow the trail yourself—but then you'd miss out on gravelly voiced guide and singer Cobi Knight, who knew many of the musicians, and his funny, insider anecdotes.

Louis Armstrong Archives

Queens College, 65-30 Kissena Blvd between Melbourne and Reeves Aves, Corona (718-997-3670; www.satchmo.net). Travel: E, J, Z to Jamaica Ctr–Parsons/Archer, then Q25 bus to Queens College. Call before visiting.

The tiny clapboard workman's house at East Kingsbridge Road and Grand Concourse is the **Edgar Allan Poe Cottage**, where the writer lived for a year with his sickly young wife. It was moved from its original location in Fordham village to its present spot and converted to a museum.

The Bronx's population is largely Latino, and nightlife centers around **Jimmy's Bronx Cafe** *(281 W Fordham Rd between Broadway and Cedar Ave, 718-329-2000)*. Jimmy Rodriguez opened the club in an old car dealership off the Major Deegan Expressway. The menu is Caribbean seafood, and weekend salsa nights are a big draw.

Farther north lies Riverdale, perhaps the city's most beautiful neighborhood. It sits atop a hill overlooking the Hudson River, and its huge, rambling homes on narrow, winding streets have offered privacy to the famous and the obscure. **Wave Hill**, originally a Victorian country estate where exotic plants were cultivated, is the best-known home in the area. Its illustrious past tenants include William Thackeray, Theodore Roosevelt, Mark Twain and Arturo Toscanini. The art gallery shows nature-themed exhibits, and the grounds provide amazing views of the river. In summer, Wave Hill presents concerts and performances *(see page 347)*.

Some of Riverdale's other high points— literal and figurative—can be found on **Independence Avenue**. Up here, you'll find the mansion where a young John F. Kennedy lived *(5040 Independence Ave at 252nd St)* from 1926 to 1928 while attending the nearby Riverdale Country School. Just above 252nd Street is a peak that offers one of the best views of the Hudson River Valley and Riverdale's manors.

If you crave a day out on foot or bike, the Hudson River–hugging **Riverdale Park** *(between 232nd and 254th Sts)*, a swath of forest preserve, has quiet pathways. Two starting points are the ends of Palisades and Sycamore Avenues *(near 254th St)*. Both meandering roads are dotted with country estates and old barns that have been converted into homes. **Spaulding Lane**, off 248th Street, is blessed with a gurgling stream and waterfall, and on **Ladd Road**, off Palisades north of 255th Street, three Modernist houses sit like serene Buddhas in the woods.

At the 1,100-acre **Van Cortlandt Park** *(Broadway at 249th St),* cricket teams are a common sight. The **Van Cortlandt House**, a fine example of pre-Revolutionary Georgian architecture, was built by Frederick Van Cortlandt in 1748 as the homestead of his wheat plantation; tours of the luxuriously furnished interior are offered.

For a different view of Bronx life, visit **Van Cortlandt Village** and the **Amalgamated and Park Reservoir Houses** *(between Sedgwick Ave and Van Cortlandt Park South, 718-796-9300)*. Nestled between Van Cortlandt Park and Jerome Park Reservoir, this community was founded on socialist principles in 1927. To this day, the 6,000 residents—a mix of old-timers, young families and singletons—buy apartments for an astonishingly low price (a one-bedroom goes for $8,000, with a monthly maintenance fee of $400 to $500) and sell them back to the development, for no profit, when they leave. The picturesque brick apartment blocks and lively playgrounds have made the village a model for cooperative development, a movement that culminated in the late '60s with the development of the epic **Co-op City** in the northeast Bronx *(see "Parkchester," page 104)*.

The **New York Botanical Garden** is the place to enjoy nature at its flowering best. The 250-acre area includes 48 gardens and plant collections, and the last 50 uncut acres of a forest that once covered all of New York City. You can follow winding trails through the unbelievably quiet forest. The Bronx River flows through and creates a small waterfall. In October and November the "Japanese Autumn Garden" is vibrant with turning Japanese maples and fragrant blooming Korean chrysanthemums. At the 1902 **Enid A. Haupt Conservatory**, the "World of Plants" exhibit takes you on an ecotour through tropical, subtropical and desert environments.

The borough's most famous attraction, the **Bronx Zoo**, opened in 1899 and is still the largest urban zoo in the U.S. The highlight is the **Congo Gorilla Forest**—you won't mind the wait and additional fee. In the Gorilla Encounter Tunnel, a glass-encased walkway, you're bound to get up close to one of the endangered lowland gorillas that live here. The Skyfari tram is the best way to traverse the 265-acre zoo; if you take the Bengali Express Monorail, try to get a seat in a front car; passengers in the back can't see what the guide is pointing out and by the time the train advances, the animals can move away.

Head to nearby **Belmont**, a mostly Italian-American neighborhood, after visiting the garden or zoo. It's mostly residential, but the main street, lively **Arthur Avenue**, is the place to go for every kind of Italian delicacy. Browse and have a bite at the **Arthur Avenue Retail Market** *(Arthur Ave at 187th St)*, a bazaar built in the 1940s by former mayor Fiorello La Guardia to get pushcarts off the street. Inside is **Mike's Deli** *(2344 Arthur Ave between 183rd and 186th Sts, 718-295-5033),* where Italian men ply you with compliments and prosciutto (get the trademark *schiacata* sandwich of grilled vegetables). Take an espresso break at the **Arthur Avenue Café**

(2329 Arthur Ave between 185th and 186th Sts, 718-562-0129), whose coffee blows Starbucks away. (Take note: The street shuts down on Sunday.) The observant eye can still pick out Belmont's old-world traces. A sunken garden peeks from behind the houses on tiny Adams Place between Crescent Avenue and Grote Street, and the shrubs and trees surrounding **Margherita Cafe** *(673 E 187th St at Cambreleng Ave, 718-295-2902)* make the spot more like a Capri cliffside eatery than a pizzeria on a busy Bronx street.

Not far away is New York's own little Lourdes. At **St. Lucy's Roman Catholic Church** *(833 Mace Ave at Bronxwood Ave, 718-882-0710),* people line up to take water from Our Lady of Lourdes Grotto, built in 1939. The faithful believe that the water has healing powers, even though it comes from the city's public water supply. (By the way, the church makes no claims about the water.)

Hunts Point, to the south, may look like an industrial wasteland, but it's where grocers,

butchers and top restaurateurs come to buy wholesale produce and meat. **Terminal Market** *(234–237 Hunts Point Ave at Halleck St, 718-542-4115)* is the city's largest produce emporium and **Hunts Point Cooperative Market** *(355 Food Center Dr at Halleck St, 718-842-7466)* sells meat. Both are open to the public (but you can only buy in bulk). The rest of Hunts Point is accessible by subway, but these markets are best visited by car—one with a big trunk.

A new art movement is also taking hold in Hunts Point. In 1996, artists converted a 12,000-square-foot industrial building to create **The Point** *(940 Garrison Ave at Manida St, 718-542-4139),* a performance space, gallery and business incubator. The arts and advocacy center put on a 2001 exhibition called "The South Bronx Story," and holds a regular spoken-word night called "Verbal Ingredients."

At **BAAD!**, the Bronx Academy of Arts and Dance, creative types stage performances and more than a dozen painters and sculptors work in its studios. In 2001, BAAD! hosted

Go to the art of Queens

Hitch a free ride on the weekend Artlink shuttle from Manhattan to Long Island City, to take the pulse of the borough's high culture

The Queens art scene has heated up so much that the Museum of Modern Art started Artlink, a free shuttle service to hustle you to the cultural spots in this borough. On Saturday and Sunday, the bus leaves from the front of MoMA in Manhattan *(11 W 53rd St between Fifth and Sixth Aves)* every hour on the half, beginning at 11:30am. The ride over the 59th Street Bridge to P.S. 1 takes about 30 minutes. The return bus leaves from P.S. 1 on the hour (the last bus back to Manhattan departs at 5pm).

From P.S. 1, you board a second bus to travel the loop between P.S. 1 *(see page 35)*, the Isamu Noguchi Garden Museum *(see page 38)*, Socrates Sculpture Park *(see page 99)* and the American Museum of the Moving Image *(see page 44)*. This shuttle departs every hour beginning at noon. The entire trip takes less than an hour; each segment is a 15-minute ride.

When MoMA closes its Manhattan doors in summer 2002 for its expansion, it will open MoMA QNS *(45-20 33rd St off Queens Blvd)* in Sunnyside, adding yet another stop to the shuttle route. For schedule information, call Queens Artlink at 212-708-9750 or visit www.queensartlink.org.

My blue heaven The Museum of Modern Art finds temporary refuge in Queens.

Let us spray Open fire hydrants, like this one on Arthur Avenue in the Bronx, keep kids cool.

Out Like That, a gay and lesbian arts festival that featured the one-man show "The Bad Boy Next Door" by Los Angeles sex activist Tony Valenzuela.

For music of a more traditional—and spiritual—kind, visit the **Corpus Christi Monastery** on Sunday morning for Mass or in the afternoon, when the cloistered Dominican nuns sing the office. During the music-filled services, the 1890 church is lit mostly by candles, casting shadows on the mosaic floor.

On the eastern edge of the Bronx are **Parkchester** and **Co-op City**, each, in its time, the largest housing complex ever built. Parkchester is bordered by East Tremont Avenue, Purdy Street, McGraw Avenue and White Plains Road. Completed in the early 1940s, it was the first city within a city. It has easy subway access to Manhattan and lots of shops and movie theaters. The designers included lots of pedestrian pathways and landscaping. In contrast, the behemoth Co-op City (35 towers of 35 stories each), in the Northeast Bronx just east of the Hutchinson River Parkway, has malls, parks and schools, but no real community center.

The Bronx is also home to the city's biggest bucolic playground: **Pelham Bay Park**, a

sprawling wilderness in the northeast corner of the borough. You're best off with a car or bike if you want to explore the 2,765 acres, once home to the Siwonay Indians. Pick up a map at the **Ranger Nature Center** *(near the Bruckner Blvd and Wilkinson Ave entrance)* in the park's southern zone. You can also visit the **Bartow-Pell Mansion** on the southeastern part of the park. Inside this 1835 Federal manor, you can see rooms that are furnished as they were in the 19th century. Maintained by the International Garden Club since 1914, the mansion's grounds include gardens, a fountain and a carriage house.

For shore lovers, the park offers 13 miles of coastline, which wends along the Hutchinson River to the west and Long Island Sound and Eastchester Bay to the east. In summer, locals crowd man-made **Orchard Beach**. Created by city planner **Robert Moses** in the 1930s (the sand came from New Jersey and Queens), this salty crescent has been called the "Riviera of New York." Grills and picnic tables line the woods next to the parking lot (which costs $6 per day).

Perhaps the most unexpected part of the Bronx is **City Island**, a small isle on Long Island Sound that's about 45 minutes by train and bus from midtown Manhattan. Settled in

1685, it was once a prosperous shipbuilding center with a busy fishing industry. Now it offers New Yorkers a slice of New England–style recreation—it's packed with marinas, seafood restaurants and nautical-themed bars. Join the crowds at **Johnny's Famous Reef Restaurant** (*2 City Island Ave at Belden's Pt, 718-885-2086*) for steamed clams, a cold beer and nice views. If you're fishing for maritime history, visit the **North Wind Undersea Institute**. Among the attractions are whale bones, ancient diving gear and a 100-year-old tugboat. City Island still has six yacht clubs and a couple of sail makers.

Though few commercial fishermen are left, you'd hardly know that when walking into the **Boat Livery** (*663 City Island Ave at Sutherland St*), a bait-and-tackle shop and bar that's changed so little over the past decades that the boat-rental price painted next to the door still reads $2 PER DAY. The bar, locally known as the Worm Hole, serves $1 beers (in plastic cups) that you can drink on the dock while you watch rental boats return at sunset.

You'll also find one of the city's best record stores—the two-story **Moon Curser Records** (*229 City Island Ave between Centre and Schofield Sts, 718-885-0302*). Eighty-year-old owner Roger Roberge does a remarkable job of schooling his customers in jazz, Latin jazz, salsa, merengue, soul and funk. You'll likely walk away from the store with hot music you would have never thought to buy.

Bartow-Pell Mansion

895 Shore Rd North at Pelham Bay Park (718-885-1461). Travel: 6 to Pelham Bay Park, then W45 bus (ask driver to stop at the Bartow-Pell Mansion; bus does not run on Sunday), or take a cab from the subway station. Wed, Sat, Sun noon–4pm. $2.50, under 12 free.

Bronx Academy of Arts and Dance (BAAD!)

841 Barretto St between Garrison and Lafayette Aves (718-842-5223). Subway: 6 to Hunt's Pt. Hours and prices vary with events.

Bronx County Historical Society Museum

Valentine-Varian House, 3309 Bainbridge Ave between Van Cortlandt Ave and 208th St (718-881-8900; www.bronxcountyhistorical.com). Subway: D to Norwood–205th St. Mon–Fri by appointment only; Sat 10am–4pm; Sun 1–5pm. $2.
This 1758 fieldstone house is a fine example of the pre-Revolutionary Federal style.

Bronx Museum of the Arts

1040 Grand Concourse at 165th St (718-681-6000). Subway: B, D, 4 to 161st St–Yankee Stadium. Wed noon–9pm; Thu–Sun noon–6pm. $3, seniors and students $2, under 12 free.

Bronx Zoo/Wildlife Conservation Society

Bronx River Pkwy at Fordham Rd (718-367-1010; www.bronxzoo.org). Subway: 2, 5 to E 180th St. Apr–Oct Mon–Fri 10am–5pm; Sat, Sun, holidays 10am–5:30pm. Nov–Mar 10am–4:30pm. $7.75, seniors and under 12 $4. Wednesdays free. Cash only.

City Island

Travel: 6 to Pelham Bay Park, then Bx29 bus to City Island. Call the City Island Chamber of Commerce (718-885-9100; www.cityisland.com) for information about events and activities.

Corpus Christi Monastery

1230 Lafayette Ave at Barretto St (718-328-6996). Subway: 6 to Hunts Point Ave. Morning prayer 6am, Mass 7:15am, evening prayer 4:50pm, night prayer 5–7pm; Sun Mass 8:15am.

Edgar Allan Poe Cottage

Grand Concourse at East Kingsbridge Rd (718-881-8900). Subway: B, D, 4 to Kingsbridge Rd. Sat 10am–4pm; Sun 1–5pm. $2.

Grand Concourse

Between 138th St and Mosholu Pkwy. Subway: 4 to 149 St–Grand Concourse or 161st St–Yankee Stadium.

Hall of Fame of Great Americans

Bronx Community College, University Ave at 181st St, Hall of Fame Terrace. Travel: D, 4 to 183rd St. 10am–5pm. Free.

New York Botanical Garden

200th St at Kazimiroff Blvd (718-817-8700; www.nybg.org). Travel: B, D to Bedford Park Blvd, then Bx26 bus; Metro-North from Grand Central Terminal to New York Botanical Garden. Apr–Oct Tue–Sun, holidays 10am–6pm. Nov–Mar Tue–Sun, 10am–4pm. $3, seniors and students $2, children $1, under 2 free. Wed 10am–6pm; Sat 10am–noon free. Ask about Garden Passport, which includes grounds, tram tour and adventure garden admission. Cash only.

North Wind Undersea Institute

610 City Island Ave, City Island (718-885-0701). Travel: 6 to Pelham Bay Park, then Bx29 bus to City Island. Mon–Fri noon–4pm; Sat noon–5pm. $3. Cash only.

Pelham Bay Park

718-430-1890. Subway: 6 to Pelham Bay Park.

Van Cortlandt House Museum

Van Cortlandt Park, Broadway at 242nd St, Riverdale (718-543-3344). Subway: 1 to 242nd St–Van Cortlandt Park. Tue–Fri 10am–3pm; Sat, Sun 11am–4pm. $2, under 14 free. Cash only.

Wave Hill

249th St at Independence Ave (718-549-2055; www.wavehill.org). Travel: Metro-North from Grand Central Terminal to Riverdale. Tue, Thu–Sun 9am–5:30pm; Wed 9:30am–dusk. $4, seniors and students $2. Tue, Sat 9am–noon free. Cash only.

Staten Island

Staten Island, New York's most rural borough, has a love-hate relationship with the rest of the city—with the emphasis on hate. Residents continue to accuse City Hall of taking their taxes to pay for the rest of New York's problems and giving them nothing in return but garbage. (The infamous Fresh Kills landfill is one of the world's largest man-made structures—it closed in early 2001, only to be reopened to receive tons of rubble from the World Trade Center.) Driving through Staten Island's tree-lined suburbs, with their open spaces and vast parks, you can see why the generally well-to-do inhabitants are so eager to bail out on the other boroughs.

Staten Island was one of the first places in America to be settled. Giovanni da Verrazano discovered the Narrows—the body of water separating the island from Brooklyn—in 1524, and his name graces the suspension bridge that connects the two boroughs today. Henry Hudson christened the island "Staaten Eylandt" (Dutch for "State's Island") in 1609. In 1687, the Duke of York sponsored a sailing competition, with Staten Island as the prize. The Manhattan representatives won the race, and since then it has been governed from Gotham.

You reach the island from Manhattan via the **Staten Island Ferry**. The free ride from lower Manhattan *(see page 108)* passes by the Statue of Liberty before sailing into the St. George ferry terminal, next to which sits the new **Richmond County Bank Ballpark**, home to the **Staten Island Yankees** *(see Diamond dogs, page 326)*. Also like the Bronx, the borough has a zoo, albeit much smaller and less expensive but perfect for families with young children. **The Staten Island Zoo's** Children's Center is modeled after a New England farm and features domestic farm animals from around the globe, as well as an indoor replica of an endangered South American creature, replete with flora and fauna.

The **Snug Harbor Cultural Center**, opened in 1833, was originally a maritime hospital and home for retired sailors. It comprises 26 buildings—grand examples of various periods of American architecture—in an 83-acre park. In 1976, the city took over the site and converted it into a cultural center, which now sponsors exhibitions and hosts arts events. Near the lighthouse at the island's highest point is the **Jacques Marchais Museum of Tibetan Art** *(see page 42)*, a collection of art and cultural treasures from the Far East with an emphasis on Tibetan prayer, meditation and healing. Its Buddhist temple is one of New York's more tranquil places.

Historic Richmond Town is a spacious collection of 39 restored buildings, some dating back to the 17th century. Many of the buildings have been moved here from elsewhere on the island. View the courthouse, general store, bakery and tinsmith, as well as private homes. During the Revolutionary War, Billop House (now **Conference House**) was where a failed peace conference took place between the Americans, led by Benjamin Franklin and John Adams, and England's Lord Howe. The building has been turned into a museum. Combine your visit here with a trip to adjacent **Tottenville Beach**.

Staten Island may not be known for its restaurants, but it has some worthy eating options. **Denino's** *(524 Port Richmond Ave between Hooker Pl and Walker St, 718-442-9401)* in Port Richmond has some of the best pizza in the city. The hip head to **Aesop's Tables** *(1233 Bay St at Maryland Ave, 718-720-2005)* for its eclectic, seasonal cuisine. The **Tottenville Inn** *(74 Arthur Kill Rd at Clarke Ave, 718-351-7879)* offers sedate country dining in an 1855 house.

Conference House (Billop House)

7455 Hylan Blvd at Craig Ave (718-984-2086). Travel: Staten Island Ferry, then S78 bus to Hylan Blvd. Apr 1–Dec 15 Fri–Sun 1–4pm. $2, seniors and children $1.
Built circa 1680, this is the oldest manor house in New York City.

Historic Richmond Town

441 Clarke Ave between Arthur Kill and Richmond Rds (718-351-1611). Travel: Staten Island Ferry, then S74 bus to Richmond Rd–St Patrick's Pl. Sept–Jun Wed–Sun 1–5pm. Jul–Aug Wed–Sat 10am–5pm; Sun 1–5pm. $4, seniors and students $2.50, under 6 free. Cash only.
Seven of the houses are open to the public, including Guyon-Lake-Tysen House, a wooden farmhouse with Dutch and Flemish influences, built around 1740 for a French Huguenot. Actors dressed in 18th-century garb lurk in the doorways (seasonally).

Snug Harbor Cultural Center

1000 Richmond Terr (718-448-2500, 718-815-SNUG for tickets; www.snug-harbor.org). Travel: Staten Island Ferry, then Snug Harbor trolley or S40 bus. 8am–5pm. Tours Sat, Sun 2pm. $2 suggested donation for gallery.
Art exhibitions are held in the Greek Revival Main Hall. The Staten Island Botanical Garden is here; the Art Lab offers classes; and there's also a children's museum. You can hear opera, chamber music and jazz in the 1892 Veterans' Memorial Hall, the city's second-oldest music hall. The John A. Noble Collection showcases maritime history and art.

Staten Island Zoo

614 Broadway between Forrest Ave and Victory Blvd (718-442-3100; www.statenislandzoo.org). Travel: Staten Island Ferry, then S48 bus to intersection of Broadway and Forrest Ave. 10am–4:45pm. $3, under 12 $2, under 3 free. Wednesdays after 2pm, donation only. Cash only.

Tour New York

Whether you're searching for famous landmarks or local lore, a tour awaits you

The masterpiece of diversity that is New York City offers an equally varied assortment of tours to show off its many faces and places. Gaze at the towering silver spires by boat, glide through the Central Park greenery by bicycle, experience the thrills and frustrations of a midtown traffic jam by bus, or explore the nooks and crannies of a Chinese apothecary on foot. It's your choice. Through a telescope, microscope or kaleidoscope, New York will amaze you at every turn.

By bicycle

For more city biking options, see page 325.

Bike the Big Apple
201-941-0100; http://toursbybike.com. Late Mar–late Nov Sat, Sun 10am–1pm. $50–$60; includes bicycle and helmet rental fee. Custom tours by appointment. Call or visit website for schedules and meeting locations. Cash only.
Licensed guides Bruce, Joel and Keith treat cyclists to leisurely paced, half- and full-day rides through New York's neighborhoods, and among its sights. See the leaves change color on the "Foliage Tour" or stop off for the city's best Italian ice on a tour of Queens. Check the website calendar for seasonal tours.

Central Park Bicycle Tours
Meet outside 2 Columbus Circle, Broadway at 59th St (212-541-8759; www.centralparkbiketour.com). Subway: A, C, B, D, 1, 2 to 59th St–Columbus Circle. Apr–Dec 10am, 1 and 4pm. Jan–Mar by appointment only. $35, under 15 $20; includes bicycle rental fee. AmEx, Disc, MC, V.
This leisurely two-hour bicycle tour (in English or Spanish) visits the John Lennon memorial at Strawberry Fields, Belvedere Castle and other Central Park sights. There's plenty of rest time when the guide stops to talk and during refreshment breaks. For the same price, the company offers a two-hour "Movie Scenes" and "Celebrity Trivia Bike Tour," as well as a three-hour Manhattan Island Bicycle Tour ($45, weekends by appointment only).

By boat

Bateaux New York
Chelsea Piers, 23rd St at West Side Hwy, Pier 61 (212-352-2022; www.bateauxnewyork.com). Subway: C, E to 23rd St. 7–10pm; dinner cruise Memorial Day–Labor Day 8–11pm. Weekdays $110, weekends $125; first-class service additional $50; lunch cruise noon–2pm $49. AmEx, DC, Disc, MC, V.

Eat a meal against a skyline backdrop while traveling in a glass-covered vessel. The à la carte American menu has French and Mediterranean influences. After dinner, you can shake it to Broadway, jazz and blues tunes on a dance floor. Tax and service charges are included in the prices. Call for a complete schedule and updated cruise information.

Chelsea Screamer
Chelsea Piers, 23rd St at West Side Hwy, Pier 62 (212-924-6262; www.chelseascreamer.com). Subway: C, E to 23rd St. May–Oct Mon–Fri approximately one tour every two hours; Sat, Sun one tour per hour. $15, under 12 $10. Reservations not required; call for exact cruising times. AmEx, Disc, MC, V.
This narrated speedboat cruise takes you past the Statue of Liberty, Ellis Island, the *Intrepid*, the Brooklyn Bridge and, of course, Manhattan's skyline. This is not for the mild-mannered—the yellow-and-blue powerboats really do scream along the river.

Circle Line
42nd St at Twelfth Ave, Pier 83 (212-563-3200; www.circleline.com). Subway: A, C, E to 42nd St–Port Authority. Three-hour tour $24, seniors $20, under 12 $12; two-hour tour $20, seniors $17, under 12 $10; evening cruise $20, seniors $17, under 12 $10; speedboat $16, children $10. AmEx, DC, Disc, MC, V.
Circle Line's three-hour circumnavigation of Manhattan is one of the best and cheapest ways to take in the city's sights. Watch midtown's urban jungle eventually give way to the forest at the northern tip of the island, and keep an eye out for Columbia University's rowing teams practicing in their sculls. A two-hour cruise sticks to mid- and lower Manhattan (the "harbor lights" version sails at sunset from May to October); it's included in the bargain CityPass (see **Cheap tix**, *page 35*). For a quick adventure (April to September only), there's a roaringly fun 30-minute tour on a speedboat called the *Beast*. Call or check website for departure schedules.

> ► For more information on walking tours of New York, see the Around Town section of *Time Out New York*.
> ► Walk to midtown's free public parks and courtyards in **Rest assured**, page 68.
> ► To see Manhattan's shoreline by kayak, see chapter **Sports & Fitness**.
> ► If you long to follow the paths of your favorite writers, check out the literary walking tours mentioned in chapter **Books & Poetry**.

Other location ● *South Street Seaport, South St between Burling Slip and Fulton St, Pier 16 (212-630-8888). Subway: A, C to Broadway–Nassau St; J, M, Z, 1, 2, 4, 5 to Fulton St. Mid-Mar–Dec one-hour cruise $13, seniors $11, children $7; speedboat $16, children $10. Apr–Sept two-hour evening music cruises. Call for performance schedule. AmEx, DC, Disc, MC, V.*

NY Waterway

38th St at West Side Hwy, Pier 78 (800-533-3779; nywaterway.com). Subway: A, C, E to 42nd St–Port Authority. Call for seasonal schedule. $19, seniors $16, children $9. AmEx, Disc, MC, V.
For a concise and scenic overview of downtown, take this guided 90-minute cruise. What these tours lack in refinement is made up for in Manhattan-centric neighborhood history. The close-up view of Lady Liberty is particularly worth the ride. NY Waterway's two-hour version voyages north. The company also runs a commuter ferry service and offers free buses to and from midtown. From May to September, twilight cruises are offered, as are all-day sightseeing tours up the Hudson.
Other location ● *South Street Seaport, South St at Beekman St, Pier 17 (800-533-3779). Subway: 1, 2 to Wall St. Call for schedule. $19, seniors $16, children $9. AmEx, Disc, MC, V.*

Staten Island Ferry

South St at Whitehall St (718-727-2508; www.siferry.com). Subway: N, R to Whitehall St; 4, 5 to Bowling Green. Free.
The poor man's Circle Line is almost as much fun, provided you bring the one you love. No-cost (and unguided) panoramas of lower Manhattan and the Statue of Liberty turn a trip on this commuter barge into a romantic sojourn—especially at sunset. Staten Island is not as scenic, but it does have a nice personality. Boats depart South Ferry at Battery Park continuously throughout the day. Call for schedules or visit the website for updated information.

By bus

Gray Line

Port Authority Bus Terminal, Eighth Ave at 42nd St (212-397-2600; www.graylinenewyork.com). Subway: A, C, E to 42nd St–Port Authority. 9am–8pm. $26–$75. AmEx, Disc, MC, V.

Keepin' it wheel You won't find crowded bus or ferry tours at the Hub—just good old-fashioned, personalized pedicab rides.

Gray Line offers more than 20 bus tours around the city, from a basic two-hour ride to the monster nine-hour "Manhattan Comprehensive," which includes a three-course lunch. Call for prices and tour destinations.
Other location ● *Times Square Visitors' Center, Broadway between 46th and 47th Sts (212-730-4742; www.graylinenewyork.com). Subway: N, R, W to 49th St; 1, 2 to 50th St. 8:30am–8pm. $26–$75. AmEx, Disc, MC, V.*

By foot—walking & other guided tours

Adventure on a Shoestring

212-265-2663. Sat, Sun. $5. Call for current tours, meeting locations, times and reservations. Cash only.
Adventure on a Shoestring's motto is "Exploring the world within our reach…within our means," and founder Howard Goldberg is undyingly faithful to

"real' New York and to the tour's $5 price tag (it hasn't gone up in 39 years). The 90-minute tours such as "Hell's Kitchen Hike" and "Haunted Greenwich Village" explore New York, neighborhood by charming neighborhood. The "Salute to Jackie O" visits places where the former First Lady lived, worshipped and gave birth to daughter Caroline.

Big Apple Greeter

1 Centre St at Chambers St, 20th floor (212-669-8159; fax 212-669-3685; www.bigapplegreeter.org). Subway: J, M, Z to Chambers St; 4, 5, 6 to Brooklyn Bridge–City Hall. Mon–Fri 9:30am–5pm; recorded information at other times. Free.

If you don't feel like letting a tour company herd you along the New York–by–numbers trail, put in a call to Big Apple Greeter. Since 1992, this program has been introducing visitors to one of 500 carefully chosen volunteer "greeters," giving them a chance to see the New York that lies beyond the tourist traps. Visit Vinny's mom in Bensonhurst or have Renata show you around Polish Greenpoint. The service is free and can be tailored to visitors with disabilities. Visits can also be conducted in multiple languages. Call, fax or write *(1 Center St, Suite 2035, New York, NY 10007)* the office three to four weeks in advance to book yourself a New York friend.

Big Onion Walking Tours

212-439-1090; www.bigonion.com. Tours are scheduled every weekend and holiday. Thu–Sun from Memorial Day to Labor Day. Most are $12, senior and students $10. Cash only.

This business, in partnership with the New-York Historical Society, puts together astoundingly informative tours of New York's historic districts and ethnic neighborhoods. It was founded by Columbia University doctoral candidates in history—and they know what they're talking about. Private tours are also available.

ChinatownNYC.com Walking Tours

Tour meets at Kim Lau Memorial Arch, Chatham Sq (212-571-2016; www.chinatownnyc.com). Subway: J, M, Z to Chambers St; 4, 5, 6 to Brooklyn Bridge–City Hall. Wed 9am. $12. Cash only.

Irrepressible Jami Gong, an aspiring actor-comic and licensed guide, gives an insider's tour of Chinatown (where he was born and raised). He's happy to organize custom group tours that include a feast at one of Chinatown's many restaurants. Register online or call.

Foods of New York
Walking and Tasting Tours

Tour meets on Bleecker St between Sixth and Seventh Aves (212-334-5070; www.foodsofny.com). Subway: 1, 2 to Christopher St–Sheridan Sq. Tue–Sun 11am–2pm. Reservations required. Call for schedule. $35 (all tastings included). AmEx, Disc, MC, V.

On these entertaining tours, your food-savvy guide walks you through some of the most famous and unique restaurants and food shops in Greenwich Village—Rocco's Bakery, Joe's Pizza and the eateries of Cornelia Street are typical destinations. Go on an empty stomach; you'll sample at least seven different foods.

Grand Central Partnership

Tour meets at Philip Morris Building, 120 Park Ave at 42nd St (212-697-1245). Subway: S, 4, 5, 6, 7 to 42nd St–Grand Central. Fri 12:30pm. Free.

For a comprehensive look at the splendors of the restored Grand Central, check out this weekly tour, which covers the terminal and its neighborhood, emphasizing social history and architecture.

Greenwich Village Pub Crawl

New Ensemble Theatre Company (212-613-5796). Tour meets at the White Horse Tavern, 567 Hudson St at 11th St. Subway: 1, 2 to Christopher St–Sheridan Sq. 2pm; $12, seniors and students $9. Reservations requested.

Local actors from the New Ensemble Theatre Company lead the way through the haunts of famous writers. Stops include Chumley's and the Cornelia Street Cafe.

Harlem Heritage Tours

230 W 116th St between Malcolm X Blvd (Lenox Ave) and Adam Clayton Powell Jr. Blvd (Seventh Ave), suite 5C (212-280-7888; www.harlemheritage.com). $10–$65. Call for times and locations. AmEx, MC, V.

Now operating 30 different tours, Harlem Heritage shows visitors the soul of Harlem. On Friday and Saturday evenings, "Jazz Nights in Harlem" features landmarks such as the Apollo Theater and the Hotel Theresa, followed by dinner at Sylvia's and live music at a jazz bar. The Sunday "Harlem Gospel Walking Tour" takes in a Baptist church service with gospel music, a tour of churches and lunch. Want to explore the speakeasy where Billie Holiday got her start? This is the tour company for you.

Harlem Spirituals

690 Eighth Ave between 43rd and 44th Sts (212-391-0900; www.harlemspirituals.com). Subway: A, C, E to 42nd St–Port Authority. Mon–Sat 9am–7pm; Sun 8am–4pm. $30–$95. Book at least one day in advance. MC, V.

Sunday-morning gospel tours take in Sugar Hill, Hamilton Grange and the Morris-Jumel Mansion, as well as a service at a Baptist church. Other tours stop by the Schomburg Center for Research in Black Culture and visit a Baptist service with a church choir. Historical tours include lunch, and you can lounge at cabarets during the evening "Soul Food and Jazz" tours. Foreign-language tours are available by request.

Hassidic Tours

Tour meets at 305 Kingston Ave between Eastern Parkway and Union St, Crown Heights, Brooklyn (718-953-5244; www.jewishtours.com). Subway: 1 to Kingston Ave. Sun 10am–12:30pm except Jewish holidays. $36, under 12 $18 (lunch included). AmEx, Disc, MC, V.

Hassidic Jews conduct these excursions and introduce their way of life to the general population. You visit a synagogue, witness a Torah scroll being written and eat at a kosher deli. Tours include some walking, and

Sightseeing

there's time to shop for Jewish gifts and delectables. Group and private tours are available by reservation.

I'll Take Manhattan Tours

732-270-5277; www.newyorkcitywalks.com. Call or visit website for times, location and schedule. $10, seniors and students $8. Cash only.

New Yorker Tony Grifa leads these two-and-a-half-hour weekend walking tours, which concentrate on neighborhood history, architecture and famous past and present residents. Topics range from literary landmarks to the "Magnificent Millionaires' Mile," a walk past the homes and clubs of Manhattan's wealthiest residents.

Joyce Gold History Tours of New York

212-242-5762; www.nyctours.com. Mar–Dec weekends, some midweek and by appointment. Jan, Feb by appointment only. Call or visit website for tours and meeting locations. $12. Cash only.

Author, history professor and Manhattan expert Joyce Gold has been conducting these informative two- to three-hour weekend tours for more than 20 years. Her talks focus on the evolution of neighborhoods, cultural movements and architecture. She can also customize walks to address the special interests of any group.

The Late Great Pennsylvania Tour

Tour meets at tourist information booth in Penn Station, Seventh Ave at 31st St (212-719-3434; http://members.aol.com/pennsy). Subway: A, C, E, 1, 2, 3 to 34th St–Penn Station. Fourth Monday of the month 12:30pm. Free.

The 34th Street Partnership hosts a 90-minute tour through America's busiest rail station. Get an earful of the building's history (complete with a ghost story) and an eyeful of the artifacts that have remained through its transformations.

Mainly Manhattan Tours

212-755-6199. Fri, Sun 1pm; Sat noon. $10. Cash only. Reservations required.

Anita Baron, a born-and-bred New Yorker, gives three tours each weekend. "Greenwich Village: New York's Left Bank" visits the homes of the neighborhood's most famous writers and artists. "West Side Story" includes Lincoln Center and the Dakota, where John Lennon lived and died. The "42nd Street: Off, Off, Off Broadway" tour takes in architectural wonders such as the Grand Central Terminal and the Chrysler Building.

Municipal Art Society Tours

457 Madison Ave between 50th and 51st Sts (212-935-3960, recorded information 212-439-1049; www.mas.org). Subway: E, V to Fifth Ave–53rd St; 6 to 51st St. Call or visit website for times, prices, locations and schedule. AmEx, MC, V.

The society organizes informative tours, including hikes in Harlem, Greenwich Village and Brooklyn Heights. It also offers a free tour of Grand Central Terminal on Wednesdays at 12:30pm and private tours by appointment.

New York City Cultural Walking Tours

212-979-2388; www.nycwalk.com. Public tour Sun 2pm. $10, private tour $30 per hour for a group of four or more, $20 per hour for a group of three or fewer. Cash only.

Alfred Pommer's tours explore the architecture and history behind New York's neighborhoods— Soho, Little Italy, Gramercy Park, Murray Hill, Upper East Side—through stories and pictures. Call for meeting locations of public tours.

New York Curmudgeon Tours

212-629-881; http://users.erols.com/wawalters/curmudgeon.htm. Mar–Nov Sat, Sun 10am. Call for meeting locations. $15. Cash only.

Bill Walters, a seasoned theater professional, guides you past many of New York's famous Broadway theaters, from those on 42nd Street to the Ed Sullivan. He combines an insider's personal experience with historical tidbits to bring the city's entertainment scene to life.

Lady's man A passenger on NY Waterway's tour of Manhattan sizes up Miss Liberty.

NYC Discovery Tours

212-465-3331. Sat, Sun. Call for schedule and meeting locations. $12–$15. Cash only.

These two-hour weekend walking tours come in six varieties: American history (American Revolution to Civil War), biography (George Washington to John Lennon), cultural (art to baseball), indoor winter tours (e.g.. "The Secrets of Grand Central"), neighborhood (Soho to the Upper West Side) and tasting-and-tavern (food-and-drink landmarks). The company has 75 year-round selections; private tours are available by appointment.

Radical Walking Tours

718-492-0069; www.he.net/~radtours. Two weekend tours each month at 1pm. Call for dates and meeting locations. $10. Cash only.

Bruce Kayton's 15 different tours emphasize left-wing history and include tales of Yippie leader Abbie Hoffman, Bob Dylan in his folkie days, Margaret Sanger and the birth-control movement, and the Black Panthers. Follow Kayton for a glimpse back at a more idealistic New York.

Rock & Roll Walking Tour

Rock Junket Tours (212-696-6578). Meet at the southwest corner of Third Ave and 9th St. Subway: N, R to 8th St–NYU; 6 to Astor Pl. Fri 4pm; Sat 1pm. $20. Cash only.

Rocker tour guides Bobby Pinn and Ginger Ail lead this East Village walking tour of legendary rock, punk and glam sites from the 1960s to the present.

Street Smarts N.Y.

212-969-8262. Sat 2–4pm, 6–8pm; Sun 2–4pm. Call for meeting locations. $10. Cash only.

New York City has a thriving ghost population, and Street Smarts offers a tour that visits several infamously haunted bars, hotels and streets. Other Street Smarts tours include "glorious" Gramercy Park, and an adults-only tour of the Bowery called "Dandies, Dudes and Shady Ladies." Tours are about two hours long and do not require reservations.

Tours with the 92nd Street Y

1395 Lexington Ave at 92nd St (212-996-1100, 212-415-5628; www.92ndsty.org). Subway: 4, 5, 6 to 86th St. Office open Mon–Fri 10am–6pm. Call for schedule. Reservations required. Prices vary. AmEx, MC, V.

The 92nd Street Y offers an impressive array of walking tours, day trips and weekend excursions, including "The Famous Chelsea Hotel" and "Saturday Night Dinner and Music," which treats guests to the culture and cuisine of designated neighborhoods. Walking tours are usually on Sundays.

Urban Park Rangers

212-360-2774, information line 866-NYC-HAWK; www.nyc.gov/parks. Office open 9am–5pm. Places and times vary. Call for dates and locations. Free.

A division of the New York City Department of Parks, the Rangers organize walks and talks in all city parks. Subjects and activities include bird-watching, fishing, Native American history, outdoor recreation and

wildlife. The Kids and Around Town sections of *Time Out New York* list tour locations and schedules.

Wall Street Walking Tour

Tour meets at Alexander Hamilton U.S. Custom House, 1 Bowling Green between State and Whitehall Sts (212-606-4064). Subway: N, R to Whitehall St; 4, 5 to Bowling Green. Thu, Sat noon. Free.

Explore Wall Street's wealth of history on a free 90-minute tour hosted by the Alliance for Downtown New York and Big Onion Walking Tours. The guides and routes change weekly. Usual destinations include the New York Stock Exchange, Trinity Church and, now, Ground Zero.

By helicopter, carriage or pedicab

Liberty Helicopter Tours

VIP Heliport, West Side Hwy at 30th St (212-967-4550, recorded info 212-465-8905). Subway: A, C, E to 34th St–Penn Station. 9am–9pm. Reservations required. $49–$155. AmEx, MC, V.

The Liberty choppers are larger than most, which makes for a fairly smooth ride. Several tours are offered each day, depending upon the weather. Even the shortest ride (five minutes) is long enough to get a thrilling, close-up view of the Statue of Liberty and Ellis Island.

Manhattan Carriage Company

200 Central Park South between Seventh Ave and 59th St (212-664-1149). Subway: B, D, E to Seventh Ave; N, R, Q, W to 57th St. 10am–2am. $40 per 20-minute ride. Extended rides must be prebooked. Hours and prices vary during holidays. AmEx, MC, V.

Put a little romance in your tour of Central Park and the surrounding area by experiencing it all from the seat of a horse-drawn carriage.

Manhattan Rickshaw Company

212-766-9222; www.manhattanrickshaw.com. $20 minimum fare for prearranged pickups. Cash only.

Manhattan Rickshaw's pedicabs operate primarily around the Empire State Building and Times Square, as well as the neighborhoods of Soho and Greenwich Village. If you see an available one, hail the driver. (Fares start at $8 and are determined before the ride.) For a prearranged pickup, you need to call and make reservations at least 24 hours in advance.

Pedicabs of New York/The Hub

517 Broome St at Thompson St (212-PONY-CAB). Subway: C, E to Spring St; 1, 2 to Canal St. Mon–Wed 11am–1am; Thu–Sat 11am–2am; Sun 11am–11pm. 50¢–$1 per minute. Cash only.

A PONY pedicab can pick you up anywhere in Manhattan and take you wherever you want to go (even to Brooklyn). But starting in May 2002, PONY will start offering guided tours of the West Village, the Lower East Side and the Financial District for $40 to $50 (two people per cab). Pickups before 11am can be arranged, and a fleet of 30 cabs mean a group of up to 60 people can be wheeled around.

Find your kind

To fly with your favorite flock, it's important to know where it nests

Here's a ready reference guide to help you seek out the type of people you like to hang around with. See **Index** for the venue page references.

If you like the looks of...	Go to...
Girls in fedoras and tinted Chloé glasses or boys in faded Levi's with bedhead hair	Any corner on Prince Street from Mott to Thompson Streets
The *Friend*ly dress-down Friday crew, à la Monica, Phoebe, Chandler, Ross, Rachel and Joey	The Boathouse at Central Park, Drip Cafe, Von Bar, and just before midnight at Welcome to the Johnsons
Anyone dressed like a member of Weezer	Lakeside Lounge or Max Fish
The new "suit," just out of college, with a hungry platinum card	The bar at Michael Jordan's—the Steak House, NYC; Brooks Brothers for shirt shopping
The Gucci set—sheathed in black threads from head to toe	The Park for cocktails after a gallery opening, Pastis for late-night snacks
International backpackers and assorted college kids on a $25-a-day budget	Anything free—such as Hotel 17's rooftop parties, Monday-night movies in Bryant Park and concerts at SummerStage in Central Park
Suffering artists—paint-splattered jeans and Macy Gray hairdos	Diner, Enid's, any alternative boutique on Bedford Avenue in Williamsburg
Gawky, fresh-faced models with a portfolio in one hand and a subway map in the other	Lotus, Suite 16
Skate punks with pink and blue hair and overstuffed backpacks	Astor Place, Washington Square Park and Union Square during school hours
J. Crew–style families with yellow Lab in tow	Bubby's for brunch, Brooklyn Heights Promenade for afternoon strolls. Chelsea Piers
The buppie and the beautiful	Club New York, Madiba, Nell's, S.O.B.'s
Muscle queens, drag queens and plain old gay guys 'n' gals	The Cock for the adventurous, Excelsior for outer-borough cruising, xl Chelsea for fun fashionistas
Goateed wanna-be DJs with the latest copy of *The Flyer,* chicks with "I'm the bomb" attitude	Other Music, Organic Grooves, Halcyon for head-bobbing Sunday brunch
The espresso-croissant–nouvelle-vague crowd	Le Gamin Café, gavin brown's enterprise
The aspiring producer, with an iBook under one arm and a model on the other	Bond St, man ray, Nobu
The kegger crowd—big bangs and tight jeans on her; a flannel shirt and backward baseball cap on him	McSorley's for the breakfast pint, Hogs & Heifers for afternoon boozing, the Bitter End till dawn and Yankee Stadium for the game, dude
Introverted writers jacked up on caffeine	The Lotus Club, Housing Works Used Books Cafe, bar or lobby of the Gershwin Hotel
Perfectly coiffed matrons and the retired execs who love them	Daniel or Le Cirque 2000 for dinner, opera at Lincoln Center

Necessities

Accommodations   **115**
Bars   **144**
Restaurants   **153**
Shopping & Services   **193**

Feature boxes

Critics' picks: Hotels   125
Small wonders   132
Bottoms up!   148
Critics' picks: Eat out   157
Tax & tipping   161
The next best things   164
Critics' picks: Iron chefs   166
Cheap eats   172
Critics' picks: Landmarks   177
Pulldown menus   185
Restaurants by cuisine   191
Head of the class   200
Critics' picks: Shopping   207
Street of dreams   218

Park place The arrival of the W Union Square hotel capped a decade of development along Park Avenue South.

Accommodations

The price of luxury is falling, and there's no better time to lap it up than now

When it comes to finding a place to stay, New York's pain can be your gain. The record highs of 2000—when it was hard to find *any* room, and rates averaged $250 a night—fell along with the economy in early 2001. Then September 11th helped lower the year's average occupancy rate to 73 percent (which is still high compared to many cities' rates that are in the mid-50s), and the median room rate to $192.

Although bookings started to pick up again by the end of 2001, hotel owners and their staffs are still doing whatever it takes to get you, well, into bed. This means you can find slashed room rates, package deals, special promotions and better service all around. (For example, the famous **Plaza Hotel**'s suites can be half their 2001 starting price of $1,200.)

The rub is that the bargains won't last. Economic forecasters predict that the hotel industry will recover by 2003. Hooray for the hoteliers! But that means the clock is ticking on this year's unprecedented deals.

Start your search for accommodations by choosing an area that interests you. Each neighborhood attracts a different sort of hotel. New York has the greatest proportion of small-chain and independent hotels of any big city in the country, with just under half of its properties unaffiliated with a national or international chain. Spearheaded by stylish boutique hotels such as Ian Schrager's **Morgans** (which opened in 1985), the indie-hotel movement had a big growth spurt in the past two years *(see **Small wonders**, page 132)*. Whatever type of lodging you prefer, hotels are pulling out all the stops to attract guests.

While the current air of competition within the industry is working in your favor, holiday lodging in Manhattan is never easy. There will still be times when getting a room in the city is more difficult than hailing a cab at rush hour. When that's the case, go online, where hotel-reservation agencies offer deals—even when everyone swears the city is booked solid.

One more caveat: The 13.25-percent room tax can cause sticker shock for the uninitiated. There's also a $2-per-night occupancy tax. And ask in advance about unadvertised costs—phone charges, minibars, faxes—or you might not find out about them until you check out.

Telephone tip: The toll-free 800, 877 and 888 numbers listed here work only within the U.S.

HOTEL-RESERVATION AGENCIES

These companies book blocks of rooms in advance and thus can offer reduced rates. Discounts cover most price ranges, from economy upwards; some agencies claim savings of up to 65 percent, although 20 percent is more likely. If you know where you'd like to stay, it's worth calling a few agencies before booking, in case the hotel is on their list. If you simply want the best deal, mention the part of town in which you'd like to stay and the rate you're willing to pay, and see what's available. The following agencies work with selected New York hotels and are free of charge. A few require payment for rooms by credit card or personal check ahead of time, but most let you pay directly at the hotel.

Accommodations Express
801 Asbury Ave, sixth floor, Ocean City, NJ 08226 (609-391-2100, 800-444-7666; www.accommodationsexpress.com).

Central Reservation Service
9010 SW 137th Ave, #116, Miami, FL 33186 (305-408-6100, 800-555-7555; fax 305-408-6111; www.reservation-services.com).

Express Hotel Reservations
3825 Iris Ave, Boulder, CO 80301 (303-440-8481, 800-407-3351; www.express-res.com).

Hotel Reservations Network
8140 Walnut Hill Ln, suite 203, Dallas, TX 75231 (214-361-7311, 800-715-7666; fax 214-363-3978; www.hoteldiscount.com).

HotRes.com
1011 High Ridge Rd, Stamford, CT 06905 (203-329-1130; hotres@hotres.com, www.hotres.com).

> ▶ For more accommodations listings, see chapter **Gay & Lesbian**.
> ▶ For more information, contact the **Hotel Association of New York City**, 437 Madison Avenue, New York, NY 10022 *(212-754-6700; www.hanyc.org)*.
> ▶ **NYC & Company**, the convention and visitors bureau *(800-NYC-VISIT; www.nycvisit.com)*, has a free booklet that includes listings of more than 140 hotels.

Quikbook

381 Park Ave South, New York, NY 10016 (212-779-ROOM, 800-789-9887; fax 212-779-6120; www.quikbook.com).

timeoutny.com

In association with 1-800-USA-HOTELS.com, *Time Out New York's* website offers online reservations to more than 200 hotels.

STANDARD HOTEL SERVICES

All hotels have air-conditioning—a must in summer—unless otherwise noted. In the categories **Deluxe, Stylish, First-class, Business** and **Boutique** *(see* **Small wonders,** *page132),* all hotels have the following services and amenities: alarm clock, cable TV, concierge, conference facility, fax (in business center or in room), hair dryer, in-room safe, laundry, minibar, modem line, radio, one or more restaurants, one or more bars and room service (unless otherwise noted). Additional services are included at the end of each listing.

Most hotels in all categories have disabled access, nonsmoking rooms, and an iron and ironing board in the room or on request. Call to confirm.

"Breakfast included" can translate into coffee and toast, or croissants, fresh orange juice and cappuccino. While many hotels boast a "multilingual" staff, the term may be used loosely.

Deluxe

All hotels in this category have a business center and valet service.

Downtown

Ritz-Carlton New York, Battery Park

2 West St at Battery Pl (212-344-0800; fax 212-344-3801; www.ritz-carlton.com). Subway: 4, 5 to Bowling Green. Single/double $465–$625, suite $750–$4,500. AmEx, DC, Disc, MC, V.

Walk into this hotel and you are offered a choice of mineral waters, served on a silver platter by a white-gloved "water sommelier." A handful of New York hotels may be able to match this Ritz-Carlton for sheer luxury and decadence, but none boasts such a singular location on the tip of lower Manhattan. Upper-story rooms facing south offer wide views of New York Harbor: Watch ferries troll around the Statue of Liberty and barges duck under the Verrazano-Narrows Bridge.

Hotel services *Baby-sitting. Ballrooms. Bath butler. Conference areas. Fitness center. Technology butler.* **Room services** *CD player. Telescope. Water sommelier.*

Other location ● *See Ritz-Carlton, Central Park, page 119.*

Midtown

New York Palace

455 Madison Ave between 50th and 51st Sts (212-888-7000, 800-697-2522; fax 212-644-5750; www.newyorkpalace.com). Subway: E, V to Fifth Ave–53rd St. Single/double $255–$710, suite $900–$7,000. AmEx, DC, Disc, MC, V.

The luxurious New York Palace's room decor ranges from traditional to Art Deco. The main hotel—once the Villard Houses, a cluster of mansions designed by Stanford White—is the home of the acclaimed Le Cirque 2000 *(212-303-7788).* It's nearly impossible to make a last-minute reservation, but guests in the tower don't have to worry—both Le Cirque and the nearby excellent Sushisay *(see page 181)* will deliver straight to your room.

Hotel services *Currency exchange. Fitness center. 24-hour dry cleaning.* **Room services** *Dual-line phones. Fax/copier. Voice mail.*

The Waldorf-Astoria

301 Park Ave at 50th St (212-355-3000, 800-924-3673; www.waldorf.com). Subway: E, V to Lexington Ave–53rd St; 6 to 51st St. Single $295–$450, double $350–$450, suite $400–$900. AmEx, DC, Disc, MC, V.

The famous Waldorf salad made its debut in 1931 at the grand opening of what was then the world's largest hotel. Ever since, the Art Deco Waldorf has been associated with New York's high society (former guests include Princess Grace, Cary Grant, Sophia Loren and a long list of U.S. presidents). It's where visiting dignitaries stay when in town for big United Nations meetings.

Hotel services *Beauty salon. Cell-phone rental. Fitness center with steam rooms. Valet parking.* **Room services** *Kitchenette in some suites. VCR on request. Voice mail. Web TV.*

Uptown

The Carlyle Hotel

35 E 76th St between Madison and Park Aves (212-744-1600, 800-227-5737; fax 212-717-4682; www.thecarlyle.com). Subway: 6 to 77th St. Single/double $495–$795, suite $850–$3,200. AmEx, DC, Disc, MC, V.

The Carlyle is one of New York's most sumptuous hotels, featuring whirlpools in almost every bathroom. The hotel has attracted famous guests for more than 70 years—especially those who want privacy. Service is so legendarily discreet that two members of the recently split-up Beatles stayed here at the same time without either of them knowing about it. In the evening, see a cabaret act at the Cafe Carlyle *(see page 261)* or stop in Bemelmans Bar, named for Ludwig Bemelmans, the creator of the children's book *Madeline*; it's lined with murals he painted in 1947, when he lived at the hotel.

Hotel services *Cell-phone rental. Currency exchange. Fitness center. Spa. 24-hour dry cleaning.*

Lofty idea Soaring ceilings at Chambers are topped only by the space's high design.

Video rental. **Room services** *CD player. VCR. Voice mail.*

Four Seasons Hotel

57 E 57th St between Madison and Park Aves (212-758-5700, 800-332-3442; fax 212-758-5711; www.fourseasons.com). Subway: N, R, W to Lexington Ave–59th St; 4, 5, 6 to 59th St. Single/double $495–$795, suite $850–$3,200. AmEx, DC, MC, V.
Renowned architect I.M. Pei's sharp geometric design (in neutral cream and honey tones) is sleek and modern, befitting this favorite haven of media moguls. The rooms are among the largest in the city, with bathrooms made from Florentine marble and tubs that fill in just 60 seconds. Views of Manhattan from the higher floors are superb, especially if you're looking out from one of the hotel's recently refurbished suites with windows that are three times larger. There are T-1 lines for quick Internet access. **Hotel services** *Baby-sitting. Currency exchange. Fitness center. Gift shop. Parking. Spa. 24-hour dry cleaning. Video rental.* **Room services** *Nintendo. VCR in suites, otherwise on request. Voice mail.*

Hotel Plaza Athénée

See **Small wonders**, page 132, for listing.

Le Parker Meridien

118 W 57th St between Sixth and Seventh Aves (212-245-5000, 800-543-4300; fax 212-708-7471; www.parkermeridien.com). Subway: F, N, Q, R, W to 57th St. Single/double $325–$365, junior suite $395–$425, suite $450–$2,500. AmEx, DC, MC, V.

The big draw at this midtown classic is the rooftop pool. The award-winning breakfasts at Norma's *(212-708-7460),* complete with smoothie shots, red-berry–risotto oatmeal and Hudson Valley duck-confit hash, are a close second. Jack's Bar, decked out in primary colors, makes an excellent third. Other attractions include lobby artwork by Damien Hirst and Charles Long, and the expanded spa in the Gravity fitness center. **Hotel services** *Cell-phone rental. Currency exchange. Fitness center. Parking. Spa.* **Room services** *DVD player. Kitchenettes in some rooms. Voice mail.*

The Mark

25 E 77th St between Fifth and Madison Aves (212-744-4300, 800-843-6275; fax 212-472-5714; www.themarkhotel.com). Subway: 6 to 77th St. Single $525–$600, double $555–$630, suite $725–$2,500. AmEx, DC, Disc, MC, V.
Towering potted palms and arched mirrors line the entranceway to this cheerful European-style Upper East Sider. The marble lobby, decorated with 18th-century Piranesi prints and magnums of Veuve Clicquot, is usually bustling with dressy international guests and white-gloved bellmen. Especially popular are the clubby Mark's Bar and the more elegant restaurant, Mark's. **Hotel services** *Cell-phone rental. Currency exchange. Fitness center. Free shuttle to Wall Street. 24-hour dry cleaning.* **Room services** *Fax. Kitchenette. Printer. VCR. Web TV.*

The Pierre Hotel

2 E 61st St at Fifth Ave (212-838-8000, 800-PIERRE-4; fax 212-826-0319; www.fourseasons.com/pierre). Subway: N, R, W to Fifth Ave–60th St. Single $425–$950, double $475–$995, suite $725–$3,990. AmEx, DC, Disc, MC, V.
The Pierre has been seducing guests since 1930 with its service and discreet, elegant atmosphere. Front rooms overlook Central Park, and some of Madison Avenue's most famous stores are only a block away. The full business service means you can have images scanned and have graphics made for that important presentation. Besides dry cleaning, the hotel offers hand laundering for precious garments. **Hotel services** *Baby-sitting. Beauty salon. Cell-phone rental. Currency exchange. Fitness center. Parking. Public notary. Theater desk. 24-hour dry cleaning.* **Room services** *In-room exercise equipment. PlayStation. VCR on request. Voice mail. Web TV.*

The Plaza Hotel

768 Fifth Ave at 59th St (212-759-3000, 800-759-3000; fax 212-759-3167; www.fairmont.com). Subway: N, R, W to Fifth Ave–60th St. Single $269–$549, double $309–$585, suite $625–$15,000. AmEx, DC, Disc, MC, V.
Perfectly located for a shopping spree, the 93-year-old Plaza Hotel is across the street from Central Park and minutes from Fifth Avenue's most exclusive stores. The hotel is renowned for its Baroque splendor; 200 rooms and suites have their original marble fireplaces. If you're an architecture buff, ask for the

Necessities

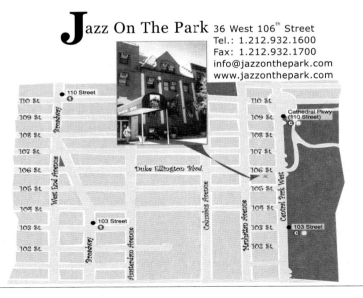

Frank Lloyd Wright suite (room 223), decorated with Wright reproductions. Downstairs, the famous Palm Court has a delightful Tiffany ceiling. After a day of rigorous shopping, unwind at the 8,000-square-foot spa, or with wine and brasserie food at one c.p.s *(212-583-1111),* the restaurant in what was once the Edwardian Room.
Hotel services *Baby-sitting. Fitness center. Salon. Spa. Ticket desk. 24-hour dry cleaning.* **Room services** *PlayStation. VCR on request. Voice mail.*

Ritz-Carlton New York, Central Park

50 Central Park South between Fifth and Sixth Aves (212-308-9100; fax 212-877-6465). Subway: F to 57th St; N, R, W to Fifth Ave–60th St. Single/double $425–$625, corporate/suite $750–$13,500. AmEx, DC, Disc, MC, V.
For other location, see page 116.

Trump International Hotel and Tower

1 Central Park West at Columbus Circle (212-299-1000, 888-448-7867; fax 212-299-1150; www.trumpintl.com). Subway: A, C, B, D, 1, 2 to 59th St–Columbus Circle. Single/double $525–$575, suite $795–$1,650 (call for weekend rates). AmEx, DC, Disc, MC, V.
Donald Trump's glass-and-steel skyscraper towers over Columbus Circle, just steps from Central Park. Inside, all is subdued elegance—from the small marble lobby to the 168 suites equipped with fax machines, Jacuzzis and floor-to-ceiling windows. Each guest is assigned a personal assistant to cater to his or her whims, and a chef will come to the room to cook on request. Better yet, head downstairs to Jean-Georges *(see page 183),* named for its four-star chef, Jean-Georges Vongerichten.
Hotel services *Baby-sitting. Cell-phone rental. Fitness center. Personal attaché service.* **Room services** *CD player. Computer. Kitchenette. Telescope. VCR. Voice mail.*

Stylish

See also **Small wonders,** page 132.

Downtown

The Mercer

147 Mercer St at Prince St (212-966-6060, 888-918-6060; fax 212-965-3820). Subway: N, R to Prince St. Single/double $395–$565, suite $1,100–$2,200. AmEx, DC, Disc, MC, V.
When entrepreneur Andre Balazs bought the site for the Mercer hotel, scenesters were thrilled…though they had to wait five years for its doors to open. The location, in the dead center of Soho, gives this 75-room gem a leg up on its closest competitors, the SoHo Grand and 60 Thompson. Rooms feature techno amenities, furniture made from African woods and oversized bathrooms.
Hotel services *Book-and-magazine library in lobby. CD-and-video library. Free access to nearby gym. Multilingual baby-sitters. Private meeting rooms.*

Room services *Cassette and CD players. Computer on request. Fax machine. Fireplace. VCR.*

60 Thompson

60 Thompson St between Broome and Spring Sts (212-431-0400, 877-431-0400; fax 212-431-0200; www.60Thompson.com). Subway: C, E to Spring St. Single/double $370–$475, suite $575–$700, penthouse suite $3,500. AmEx, DC, Disc, MC, V.
This new Soho entrant has added 100 (slightly cheaper) rooms to the neighborhood. Since it's the tallest building in the vicinity, the views extend from the surrounding low-rise apartment buildings north to the Empire State Building. Guests enter through an outdoor garden café. Thomas O'Brien of Aero Studios designed the "Thompson Chair" (available for purchase) nestled in each guest room. You'll feel pampered with amenities such as down duvets, Philosophy toiletries and a pantry stocked with gourmet goodies from Dean & DeLuca.
Hotel services *Cell-phone rental. DVD library. Fitness center. Laptop computer on request. Parking. Valet.* **Room services** *CD and DVD players. Microwave oven on request. VCR. Voice mail.*

SoHo Grand Hotel

310 West Broadway between Canal and Grand Sts (212-965-3000, 800-965-3000; fax 212-965-3244; www.sohogrand.com). Subway: A, C, E, 1, 2 to Canal St. Single/double $279–$549, suite $1,699–$1,799. AmEx, DC, Disc, MC, V.
When it welcomed its first guests in 1996, this was Soho's first hotel to open since the 1800s. Architecturally, it's one of the city's most striking inns. The unusual design pays homage to Soho's contemporary artistic community and to the area's past as a manufacturing district. A dramatic bottle-glass–and–cast-iron stairway leads up from street level to the elegant lobby and reception desk, where a monumental clock looms. Rooms are decorated in soothing grays and beiges, with photos from local galleries on the walls. In 2000, its sister location, the Tribeca Grand Hotel, was the first major hotel to open in the ultratrendy triangle below Canal Street.
Hotel services *Fitness center. Pets allowed. 24-hour dry cleaning.* **Room services** *VCR. Voice mail.* **Other location ●** *Tribeca Grand Hotel, 2 Sixth Ave between Church and White Sts (212-519-6600, 877-519-6600; fax 212-519-6700; www.tribecagrand.com). Subway: C, E to Canal St. Single/double $399–$599. Suites $849–$1,049. AmEx, DC, Disc, MC, V.*

Midtown

Chambers

15 W 56th St between Fifth and Sixth Aves (212-974-5656; fax 212-974-5657; www.chambershotel.com). Subway: F to 57th St; N, R, W to Fifth Ave–60th St. Single $275–$350, double $350–$400, studio $350–$450, suite $500–$1,200. AmEx, DC, Disc, MC, V.
The vibe at the new Chambers hotel is artist's loft–meets–Fifth Avenue wallet. Rooms are warmer than you'd expect from such a design-oriented hotel:

Rosy glow Sipping cocktails at the Mansfield's M Bar can be an illuminating experience.

Stainless-steel fixtures and track lighting are cozied up by taupe-and-purple bedding, rugs and plenty of textured wood. If all that doesn't give you a warm-and-fuzzy feeling, the American Creative dishes at the hotel's restaurant, Town, should *(see page 180).* **Hotel services** *Baby-sitter. Complimentary passes to New York Sports Club. Computer rental. Valet parking.* **Room services.** *CD-and-DVD library. Cordless telephone. Internet access.*

City Club Hotel

55 W 44th St between Fifth and Sixth Aves (212-921-5500, 888-256-4100; fax 212-575-2758; www.cityclubhotel.com). Subway: B, D, F, V to 42nd St; 7 to Fifth Ave. Single/double $275–$375, duplex suites $600. AmEx, DC, MC, V.
Neither a boutique hotel nor a full-blown luxury palace, City Club aims to be something in between. Guests will find a blend of high fashion and contemporary comfort in the Jeffrey Bilhuber–designed rooms in mahogany, chocolate marble and bronze, and the personalized service characteristic of small European hotels. Rooms also feature original works by contemporary collage artist Richard Giglio. If you prefer edible art, chef Daniel Boulud's db bistro moderne *(see page 178),* the hotel's restaurant, serves American classics with a French twist.
Hotel services *Discount parking. Health club.* **Room services** *CD and DVD players. Cordless phone. Internet access.*

Dylan

52 E 41st St between Madison and Park Aves (212-338-0500, 800-555-DYLAN; fax 212-338-0569; www.dylanhotel.com). Subway: S, 4, 5, 6, 7 to 42nd St–Grand Central. Single/double $295–$395, suite $650–$1,200. AmEx, DC, Disc, MC, V.

Opened in fall 2000 in the former Chemists' Club Building near Grand Central Terminal, the Dylan hotel makes good on its history. The once-crumbling 1903 Beaux Arts brick-and-limestone structure and its grand marble staircase, which spirals up three floors from the lobby, have been restored to the tune of $30 million. Fabrics in rooms and public spaces are soft and rich: velvet, suede, silk, mohair and chiffon.
Hotel services *Complimentary breakfast. Fitness center. Parking.* **Room services** *CD and DVD players. Voice mail.*

The Hudson

356 W 58th St between Eighth and Ninth Aves (212-554-6000; fax 212-554-6001; www.ianschrager hotels.com). Subway: A, C, B, D, 1, 2 to 59th St–Columbus Circle. Single/double $95–$295, suite $350–$425. AmEx, DC, Disc, MC, V.
Ian Schrager's global hotel empire has expanded quickly. He opened the Sanderson in London in April 2000, and six months later came the Hudson, his fourth New York property (Morgans was the first in 1985; the Paramount and Royalton remain as popular as ever). The stylish hotel (yes, those lampshades are by Francesco Clemente) has a lush interior courtyard with enormous potted trees, a rooftop terrace that overlooks the Hudson River, and a glass-roofed lobby that's crawling with imported English ivy and beautiful people. The in-house Hudson Cafeteria and the Hudson Bar instantly attracted the famous and their fans. Those near-mythic $95 rooms barely fit a bed and are hard to come by.
Hotel services *Fitness center.* **Room services** *CD and DVD players. Voice mail.*
Other locations ● *Morgans, 237 Madison Ave between 37th and 38th Sts (212-686-0300, 800-334-*

3408; fax 212-779-8352). Subway: S, 4, 5, 6, 7 to 42nd St–Grand Central. Single $225–$325, double $250–$350, suite $325–$425. AmEx, DC, Disc, MC, V. ● *The Royalton, 44 W 44th St between Fifth and Sixth Aves (212-869-4400, 800-635-9013; fax 212-575-0012). Subway: B, D, F, V to 42nd St; 7 to Fifth Ave. Single $295–$395, double $345–$415, suite $425–$625. AmEx, DC, MC, V.* ● *The Paramount, 235 W 46th St between Broadway and Eighth Ave (212-764-5500, 800-225-7474; fax 212-354-5237). Subway: N, R, W to 49th St. Single $165–$245, double $195–$280, suite $400–$550. AmEx, DC, Disc, MC, V.*

The Mansfield

12 W 44th St between Fifth and Sixth Aves (212-944-6050, 877-847-4444; fax 212-764-4477; www.boutiquehg.com). Subway: B, D, F, V to 42nd St; 7 to Fifth Ave. Single/double $235–$255, suite $415–$485. AmEx, DC, Disc, MC, V.

Popular with the fashion industry, the small and stylish Mansfield offers unique complimentary treats. The espresso and cappuccino flow freely all day, and some rooms have sound-therapy machines so you can listen to the ocean or a running stream. Fashionistas love the minimalist decor; others may find it overly spare. Breakfast is included, and though there's no restaurant, the M Bar serves caviar and a light menu under an uncovered domed skylight. The Mansfield is part of the Boutique Hotels Group, which has four other properties in the city (in midtown, see below; in uptown, see the Franklin and the Hotel Wales).

Hotel services *Access to nearby gym for $15. CD- and- video library. Cell-phone rental. Currency exchange.* **Room services** *CD player. VCR. Voice mail.* **Other locations** ● *The Roger Williams, 131 Madison Ave at 31st St (212-448-7000; fax 212-894-5220). Subway: 6 to 33rd St. Single $265, double $20 per extra person in room, suite $405. AmEx, DC, MC, V.* ● *The Shoreham, 33 W 55th St between Fifth and Sixth Aves (212-247-6700). Subway: E, V to Fifth Ave–53rd St; F to 57th St. Single $275–$295, double $20 per extra person in room, suite $395. AmEx, DC, MC, V.*

The Time

224 W 49th St between Broadway and Eighth Ave (212-320-2900, 877-846-3692; fax 212-245-2305; www.thetimeny.com). Subway: C, E, 1, 2 to 50th St; N, R, W to 49th St. Single/double $199–$409, suite $299–$519, penthouse suite $2,500–$6,000. AmEx, DC, Disc, MC, V.

Designer Adam Tihany says of this stylish Times Square hotel, "The idea is to truly experience a color—to see it, feel it, taste it, smell it and live it." This experience includes guest rooms entirely furnished in the primary color of your choice, complete with artfully placed jelly beans of that color and a color-inspired scent and reading material. Sound like too much? If you're not booked into the vast penthouse triplex, you can always chill out in the hotel's neutral, subdued public spaces.

Hotel services *Cell-phone rental. Fitness center. Shopping services.* **Room services** *CD player. VCR. Video rental. Voice mail. Web TV.*

W New York

541 Lexington Ave at 49th St (212-755-1200, 877-W-HOTELS; fax 212-644-0951; www.whotels.com). Subway: E, V to Lexington Ave–53rd St; 6 to 51st St. Single/double $209–$439, suite $259–$1,700. AmEx, DC, Disc, MC, V.

Designed for executives and leisure travelers, the W New York offers just about every convenience. The attractive, soothing rooms have oversized desks, chaise lounges and luxurious goose-down comforters and pillows. If the atmosphere isn't enough to calm frayed nerves, indulge in craniosacral massage at the Away Spa, or organic tea at Heartbeat *(212-407-2900)*, the hotel's haute but lo-cal restaurant. Expect the same suavity from W's four sister hotels: the Court, the Tuscany, the W Union Square *(see below)* and the newest location in Times Square, which features Rande Gerber's Whisky Blue bar *(212-407-2947)* in the basement, and Blue Fin *(212-918-1400)*, a 400-seat sushi-jazz restaurant.

Hotel services *Fitness center. Spa. Valet parking.* **Room services** *CD player. PlayStation. VCR.* **Other locations** ● *W Union Square, 201 Park Ave South at 17th St (212-253-9119; fax 212-253-9229). Subway: L, N, Q, R, W, 4, 5, 6 to 14th St–Union Sq. Single/double $269–$499, suite $599–$1,600. AmEx, DC, Disc, MC, V.* ● *W New York–The Court, 130 E 39th St between Park and Lexington Aves (212-685-1100; fax 212-889-0287). Subway: S, 4, 5, 6, 7 to 42nd St–Grand Central. Single/double $229–$389, suite $359–$459. AmEx, DC, Disc, MC, V.* ● *W New York–The Tuscany, 120 E 39th St between Park and Lexington Aves (212-686-1600; fax 212-779-7822). Subway: S, 4, 5, 6, 7 to 42nd St–Grand Central. Single/double $249–$389, suite $399–$529. AmEx, DC, Disc, MC, V.* ● *W New York–Times Square, 1567 Broadway at 47th St (212-930-7400). Subway: N, R, W to 49th St; 1, 2 to 50th St. Single/double $269–$339, suites $319–$1,200.*

Uptown

The Franklin

164 E 87th St between Lexington and Third Aves (212-369-1000). Subway: 4, 5, 6 to 86th St. Single $229–$249, double $20 per extra person in room. AmEx, MC, V.

For other locations, see **The Mansfield**, this page and below.

Other location ● *The Hotel Wales, 1295 Madison Ave between 92nd and 93rd Sts. (212-876-6000). Subway: 6 to 96th St. Single $265–$285, double $20 per extra person in room, suite $445. AmEx, MC, V.*

On the Ave Hotel

2178 Broadway at 77th St (212-362-1100, 800-509-7598; fax 917-441-0295; www.ontheave-nyc.com). Subway: 1, 2 to 79th St. Single/double $199–$280, suite $300–$320, penthouse suite $300–$450. AmEx, DC, MC, V.

On the Ave brings some sorely needed style to the Upper West Side's stodgy hotel scene. Its most winning attractions are the canopied "floating beds," the sleek, industrial-style bathroom sinks and the

three recently constructed floors that offer 23 penthouse rooms and suites with fantastic views of Central Park, the Hudson River and beyond. Original artwork and innovative touches, such as individual breakfast trays that can double as laptop desks, help enliven the minimalist decor.
Hotel services *24-hour dry cleaning. Valet.* **Room services** *Refrigerator and VCR rental. Voice mail.*

First-class

Midtown

The Algonquin
59 W 44th St between Fifth and Sixth Aves (212-840-6800, 800-555-8000; fax 212-944-1618; www.camberleyhotels.com). Subway: B, D, F, V to 42nd St; 7 to Fifth Ave. Single/double $269–$389, suite $389–$549. AmEx, DC, Disc, MC, V.
Arguably New York's most famous literary landmark, this was the place where Dorothy Parker, Robert Benchley and other literary lights of the 1920s and '30s gathered to gossip and match wits at the legendary Round Table in the Oak Room *(212-419-9331)*. The rooms are on the small side but cheerful and charming, and the hallways now feature *New Yorker*–cartoon wallpaper. On Monday evenings, there are readings by local authors *(see page 258)*, Tuesday to Saturday nights feature cabaret.
Hotel services *Cell-phone rental. 24-hour dry cleaning. 24-hour fitness center.* **Room services** *CD player and VCR in suites. Complimentary video library. Refrigerator in suites; otherwise on request. Voice mail.*

Fitzpatrick Grand Central Hotel
141 E 44th St between Lexington and Third Aves (212-351-6800, 800-367-7701; fax 212-818-1747; www.fitzpatrickhotels.com). Subway: S, 4, 5, 6, 7 to 42nd St–Grand Central. Single/double $425, suite $600. AmEx, DC, Disc, MC, V.
You can't miss the fact that this family-run East Sider, and its sister property, the Fitzpatrick Manhattan, are New York's only Irish-owned lodgings: There are kelly-green carpets with a Book of Kells pattern in the lobbies…and a Liam Neeson penthouse suite. The Wheel Tapper Pub *(212-351-6800)* serves bangers, rashers, soda bread (what else?) and high tea. Just don't plan to go on St. Patrick's Day; you'll never get a seat.
Hotel services *Cell-phone rental. Free access to nearby gym. In-room massage. 24-hour dry cleaning. Valet. Yogi (who gives private classes).* **Room services** *Computer. DVD rental.*
Other location ● *Fitzpatrick Manhattan, 687 Lexington Ave between 56th and 57th Sts (212-355-0100, 800-367-7701; fax 212-308-5166). Subway: E, V to Lexington Ave–53rd St; N, R, W to Fifth Ave–60th St; 4, 5, 6 to 59th St. Single/double $199–$335, suite $255–$600. AmEx, DC, Disc, MC, V.*

Hotel Elysée
60 E 54th St between Madison and Park Aves (212-753-1066; fax 212-980-9278). Subway: E, V to

Lexington Ave–53rd St; 6 to 51st St. Single/double $295–$345, suite $475–$525. AmEx, DC, MC, V.
This is a charming and discreet hotel with an attentive staff. The quarters feature antique furniture and Italian-marble bathrooms; some rooms have colored-glass conservatories and terraces. It's popular with publishers, so don't be surprised if you see a famous author partaking of the complimentary afternoon tea. You can also eat at the Monkey Bar *(212-838-2600)*, where a well-coiffed clientele dines on American cuisine For its sister hotels, see **Casablanca**, page 133 and **The Library Hotel**, page 134.
Hotel services *Baby-sitting. Free access to nearby gym. Valet parking.* **Room services** *Kitchenette in suites. VCR. Voice mail.*

The Iroquois
49 W 44th St between Fifth and Sixth Aves (212-840-3080, 800-332-7220; fax 212-398-1754;

CRITICS' PICKS

Hotels

Sure, price and room availability are primary factors in picking a hotel, but we think these are the best for…

…stunning views of Lady Liberty
Ritz-Carlton New York, Battery Park, page 116

…landmark status
The Plaza, page 117

…Fifth Avenue shopping
Chambers, page 119

…Morocco in Manhattan
Casablanca Hotel, see **Small Wonders**, page 133

…Broadway lodging that's actually cool
The Time, page 123

…Victorian charm
The Inn at Irving Place, see **Small Wonders**, page 133

…the perfect pillow (from a menu of 11)
The Benjamin, page 129

…a bed with rock & roll history
Chelsea Hotel, page 131

…a Henry James location
The Washington Square Hotel, page 137

…outer-borough inn-clinations
Akwaaba Mansion Bed & Breakfast, page 143

*www.iroquoisny.com). Subway: B, D, F, V to 42nd St;
7 to Fifth Ave. Single/double $199–$395, suite $349–
$695. AmEx, DC, Disc, MC, V.*
The Iroquois, once a budget hostelry, has morphed
into a full-service luxury hotel. A mahogany-paneled library, marble-lined bathrooms and a lobby
furnished in polished stone are just part of a $13-
million renovation that did away with an archaic
barbershop and a photographer's studio. Triomphe,
(212-453-4233) is the hotel's French-accented
American restaurant.
Hotel services *Cell-phone rental. Fitness center.
Parking. 24-hour dry cleaning. Video library.* **Room
services** *CD player. 24-hour room service. Voice mail.*

The Kitano

*66 Park Ave at 38th St (212-885-7000, 800-548-2666;
fax 212-885-7100; www.kitano.com). Subway: S, 4, 5,
6, 7 to 42nd St–Grand Central. Single/double $460–
$605, suite $680–$2,100. AmEx, DC, Disc, MC, V.*
The Kitano has a serene Japanese aesthetic—warm
mood lighting, mahogany paneling, polished stone
floors and complimentary green tea. It is also home
to the Japanese restaurant Nadaman Hakubai *(212-
885-7111)* and an authentic tatami suite. The views
of surrounding Murray Hill are pleasant, and there
are two large terraces for functions and parties.
Hotel services *Baby-sitting. Computer rental. Dry
cleaning and laundry service. Free access to nearby
gym. Gallery. Gift shop. Limousine service to Wall St.*
Room services *CD player. VCR on request. Web TV.*

The Michelangelo

*152 W 51st St between Sixth and Seventh Aves
(212-765-1900, 800-237-0990; fax 212-581-7618;
www.michelangelohotel.com). Subway: B, D, E to
Seventh Ave; N, R, W to 49th St; 1, 2 to 50th St.
Single/double $225–$495, suite $395–$1,200.
AmEx, DC, Disc, MC, V.*
This charming little haven in the Theater District welcomes guests with a cozy lobby full of peach marble,
oil paintings, giant potted palms, and overstuffed
couches in rose and salmon tones. The 178 sizable
rooms are decorated in styles ranging from French
country to Art Deco; each room includes two TVs (one
in the bathroom), a fax machine, a terry-cloth robe and
a giant tub. Complimentary breakfast includes espresso, cappuccino and Italian pastries. The hotel also has
fully equipped apartments for extended stays, with
full or limited hotel service *($3,500–$9,000 per month).*
Hotel services *Baby-sitting. Limousine service to
Wall St (Mon–Fri). 24-hour dry cleaning. 24-hour
fitness center.* **Room services** *CD player.
Complimentary newspaper and shoe shine. Computer
and printer on request.*

The Roger Smith

*501 Lexington Ave between 47th and 48th Sts (212-
755-1400, 800-445-0277; fax 212-758-4061;
www.rogersmith.com). Subway: E, V to Lexington
Ave–53rd St; 6 to 51st St. Single/double $265, suite
$330–$435. AmEx, DC, Disc, MC, V.*
The Roger Smith, which is popular with touring
bands, is owned by the family of sculptor and

painter James Knowles, and some of his work
decorates the lobby. Many of the large rooms have
been recently renovated, and each is uniquely
furnished. The staff is helpful, breakfast is included, and there's a library of free videos for those who
want to stay in for the night.
Hotel services *Baby-sitting. Valet parking. Video
rental.* **Room services** *Coffeemaker. Free local phone
calls. Kitchenette with microwave oven in suites. VCR.
Voice mail.*

The Warwick New York

*65 W 54th St at Sixth Ave (212-247-2700, 800-223-
4099; fax 212-713-1751; www.warwickhotels.com).
Subway: E, V to Fifth Ave–53rd St; F to 57th St.
Single/double $305–$395, suite $365–$1,200.
AmEx, DC, MC, V.*
Built by William Randolph Hearst and patronized by
Elvis and the Beatles in the 1950s and '60s, the
Warwick is still polished and gleaming. It was once
an apartment building, and the rooms are excep-
tionally large by midtown standards. Ask for a view
of Sixth Avenue (double glazing keeps out the noise).
The top-floor Suite of the Stars has a wraparound
balcony and was once the home of Cary Grant.
Hotel services *Baby-sitting. Currency exchange.
Fitness center. Parking. Ticket desk.* **Room services**
Refrigerator on request. VCR on request. Voice mail.

Uptown

Barbizon Hotel

*140 E 63rd St at Lexington Ave (212-838-5700,
800-223-1020; fax 212-223-3287). Subway: N, R,
W to Lexington Ave–59th St; 4, 5, 6 to 59th St.
Single/double $260–$335, suite $425–$530, tower
suites $600–$1,000. AmEx, DC, Disc, MC, V.*
The Barbizon was originally a hotel for women (whose
parents could feel confident that their daughters were
safe in its care). During its years as a women's residence, guests included Grace Kelly, Sylvia Plath and
Candice Bergen, and the rules stated that men could
be entertained only in the lounge. Now it's a good
Upper East Side option—especially for shoppers.
Many of the tower suites (on the 18th floor and above)
feature terraces with great city views. Inside the hotel
is a branch of the Equinox health club (free for guests),
with a 60-by-24-foot pool and full spa. Children under
12 stay for free if sharing their parents' room.
Hotel services *Beauty salon. CD library. Fitness
center. 24-hour dry cleaning. Valet.* **Room services**
*CD player. Laptop computer on request. Minibar. 24-
hour room service. Voice mail.*

Business

Downtown

The Holiday Inn Wall Street

*15 Gold St at Platt St (212-232-7700, 800-HOLIDAY;
fax 212-425-0330; www.HolidayInnWSD.com).
Subway: A, C to Broadway–Nassau St; J, M, Z, 1, 2, 4,*

5 to Fulton St. Single/double $169–$349, suite $500–$700. AmEx, DC, Disc, MC, V.
Slightly cheaper than most of its neighbors, this new Holiday Inn is good for the business exec who brings the family along: It offers special weekend rates and children under 18 stay for free (but a rollaway bed is $25 a night). If you book a single, however, expect one of the smallest rooms in the city—some are only 275 square feet. Keeping up with the e-times, this Holiday Inn has automated check-in and check-out kiosks and "virtual office" rooms that include high-speed Internet access, an eight-foot L-shaped desk, ergonomic office chair and unlimited office supplies.
Hotel services *CD library. Fitness center. Gift shop. Parking.* **Room services** *CD player. Nintendo. Portable phones. Voice mail. Web TV.*

The Regent Wall Street

55 Wall St between Hanover and William Sts (212-845-8600, 800-545-4000; fax 212-845-8601; www.regenthotels.com). Subway: 1, 2 to Wall St. Single/double $350–$550 (weekend rates $245–$495), suite $500–$995. AmEx, DC, Disc, MC, V.
The first five-star hotel in the Financial District, and the first hotel ever on Wall Street, the Regent opened in 2000 after an $80-million remodeling of the historic building it occupies. Built in 1842, 55 Wall Street was originally the Merchants' Exchange. From 1863 to 1899, it was the U.S. Customs House. The 12,000-square-foot ballroom, with 60-foot-high Corinthian columns, marble walls and an elliptical dome, was designated by the Landmarks Preservation Commission as one of the city's most important historic public spaces. Rooms are exquisitely comfortable, offering great views, tubs for two and all the business amenities your broker heart desires. The hotel's 55 Wall Street *(212-699-5555)* restaurant boasts a dramatic stone balcony, where you can eat and drink American cuisine among the soaring columns.
Hotel services *Baby-sitting. Beauty salon. Fitness center. Gift shop. Spa. (212-699-5555) Parking. Valet.* **Room services** *CD and DVD players. Voice mail.*

The Wall Street Inn

9 South William St at 85 Broad St (212-747-1500; fax 212-747-1900). Subway: 1, 2 to Wall St; 4, 5 to Bowling Green. Single/double $249–$450. Call for corporate and weekend rates. AmEx, DC, Disc, MC, V.
This 46-room boutiquelike hotel, tucked into the landmark Stone Street district, is the reincarnation of an old 1830 Lehman Brothers Bank building. To reach beyond the financial-business types who make up 98 percent of the clientele, the hotel offers hefty discounts on weekends. There's no restaurant or room service, though breakfast is included.
Hotel services *Conference facility. Fitness center. Video library.* **Room services** *VCR. Voice mail.*

Midtown

Beekman Tower Hotel

3 Mitchell Pl, 49th St at First Ave (212-355-7300; fax 212-753-9366; www.mesuite.com). Subway: E, V

to Lexington Ave–53rd St; 6 to 51st St. Studio suite $292–330, one-bedroom $319–450, two-bedroom $560–620. AmEx, DC, Disc, MC, V.
Built in 1928, the Beekman's distinctive tower is an Art Deco landmark. The charming hotel is a member of the family-owned Manhattan East Suites, the city's largest all-suite hotel group (it has nine other properties in the city, including the Benjamin, below; *call 800-ME-SUITE for more information*). Rooms include kitchenettes; a grocery service is available, so the refrigerator can be stocked while you're out doing business. The Top of the Tower restaurant *(212-980-4796)* on the 26th floor has a terrace with panoramic views.
Hotel services *Ballroom. Fitness center. Parking. 24-hour dry cleaning. Valet.* **Room services** *Kitchenette. Voice mail.*

The Benjamin

125 E 50th St at Lexington Ave (212-715-2500, 888-4-BENJAMIN; fax 212-465-3697; www.thebenjamin.com). Subway: E, V to Lexington Ave–53rd St; 6 to 51st St. Single/double $420–$530, suite $530–$1,100. AmEx, DC, Disc, MC, V.
Now occupying Emory Roth's famous city landmark the Hotel Beverly (which Georgia O'Keeffe used to paint from her apartment across the street), the Benjamin has reclaimed its historic heritage while evolving into a fully equipped executive-suite hotel, featuring a state-of-the-art communications system and other amenities (such as a pillow menu of 11 varieties, including water-filled, buckwheat and anti-snore). The refurbishment has restored

Join the club City Club Hotel is the latest in a growing group of boutique hotels in NYC.

Roth's original details and brought in noted chef Larry Forgione with his popular restaurant, An American Place *(212-888-5650);* the kitchen also provides the room service. And for the ecoconscious: The Benjamin is the only Ecotel-certified establishment in the city.
Hotel services *Fitness center. Spa.* **Room services** *CD player in suites. Cordless phone. Fax/printer/copier. Kitchenette. VCR. Voice mail. Web TV.*

Metropolitan Hotel
569 Lexington Ave at 51st St (212-752-7000, 800-836-6471; fax 212-753-7253). Subway: E, V to Lexington Ave–53rd St; 6 to 51st St. Single/double $159–$259, suite $229–$399. AmEx, DC, Disc, MC, V.
When this hotel opened as the Summit in 1961, an aquamarine Miami Beach–style swath among midtown's steel-and-glass towers, it was booed by New Yorkers, which prompted a quick toning-down. In 2000, the hotel got a $17-million renovation that returned the building to its Coffeeshop Moderne look, and earned it a new name. Hopefully the style won't be lost on the work-minded clientele. Room toiletries are just like at home: Besides soap and shampoo, guests get cotton balls, Q-tips and a nail file—not luxurious, just thorough.
Hotel services *Baby-sitting. Fitness center. Manicurist. Valet.* **Room services** *CD player. Web TV.*

Sofitel
45 W 44th St between Fifth and Sixth Aves (212-354-8844; fax 212-782-3002; www.sofitel.com). Subway: B, D, F, V to 42nd St; 7 to Fifth Ave. Single/double $209, suite $209–$699. AmEx, DC, Disc, MC, V.
Part of a French chain, Sofitel New York is a 30-story, luxury business hotel with a brasserie, a piano bar, plenty of conference rooms and 52 suites with stunning views of midtown Manhattan. Rooms are contemporary and tasteful, done in warm, earthy colors with mahogany furniture and understated floral bedding—a perfect setting for taking a break from the hustle and bustle of Times Square.
Hotel services *Conference rooms. Parking. Pets allowed.* **Room services** *Dataport. Internet access.*

Uptown

The Bentley
500 E 62nd St at York Ave (212-644-6000, 888-66HOTEL; fax 212-751-7868; www.nychotels.net). Subway: N, R, W to Lexington Ave–59th St; 4, 5, 6 to 59th St. Single/double $135–$245, suite $225–$575. AmEx, DC, Disc, MC, V.
This slender, 21-story glass-and-steel hotel, located as far east as the Upper East Side goes, has unparalleled views of the East River and the Queensboro Bridge. Converted from an office building in 1998, the Bentley is an ideal getaway for tired execs: It has soundproof windows and blackout shades. The mahogany-paneled library has a complimentary cappuccino bar, and there's a nearby spot for sou-

venir shopping—around the corner at designer Terence Conran's shop *(see page 226).*
Hotel services *Complimentary breakfast. Spa. Ticket desk.* **Room services** *CD and DVD players. Nintendo.*

The Phillips Club
155 W 66th St between Broadway and Amsterdam Ave (212-835-8800, 877-854-8800; fax 212-835-8850; www.phillipsclub.com). Subway: 1, 2 to Lincoln Ctr–66th St. Suite $400–$1,000. AmEx, DC, MC, V.
Perhaps the most chic of New York's growing number of extended-stay hotels, the Phillips Club is on the Upper West Side, across from Lincoln Center and two blocks from Central Park. Suites have full kitchens and include access to the Reebok Club. The recent opening of a high-end Balducci's market on the ground floor ensures that all the ingredients for a home-cooked gourmet meal are close at hand.
Hotel services *Baby-sitting. Dry cleaning. Fitness center. Spa.* **Room services** *CD player. Room service.*

Boutique
See **Small wonders**, page 132.

Comfortable
Unless otherwise indicated, all hotels in this category have cable TV, fax service, hair dryers in the room or on request, a safe available at the front desk and 24-hour dry cleaning.

Midtown

Best Western Manhattan
17 W 32nd St between Fifth Ave and Broadway (212-736-1600, 800-567-7720; fax 212-790-2758). Subway: B, D, F, V, N, Q, R, W to 34th St–Herald Sq. Single/double $89–$249, suites $139–$299. AmEx, DC, Disc, MC, V.
This is a good-value hotel with a stylish Beaux Arts facade, a black-and-gray marble lobby and rooms inspired by different neighborhoods—choose between a floral Central Park look or a trendy Soho motif. Curious travelers will enjoy exploring the Korean shops and restaurants on 32nd Street (the hotel lacks its own restaurant).
Hotel services *Fitness center. Laundry.* **Room services** *Modem line. Refrigerator.*

Chelsea Hotel
222 W 23rd St between Seventh and Eighth Aves (212-243-3700; fax 212-675-5531; www.chelseahotel.com). Subway: C, E, 1, 2 to 23rd St. Single/double $150–$285, suite $325–$385. AmEx, DC, Disc, MC, V.
The Chelsea has a reputation to uphold. Built in 1884, the famous redbrick building oozes history. In 1912, *Titanic* survivors stayed here for a few days; other former residents include Mark Twain, Dylan Thomas, O. Henry and Brendan Behan. No evidence remains of the hotel's most infamous association: the murder of Nancy Spungen by Sex Pistol Sid Vicious. The lobby doubles as an art gallery, showing work by past

and present guests, and rooms are large, with high ceilings. Most rooms, but not all, have a private bathroom and air conditioner. The cocktail lounge Serena (see page 149) lures a sleek crowd to the basement. **Hotel services** Beauty salon. Concierge. Laundry. Restaurant. **Room services** Kitchenettes or refrigerators in some rooms. Modem line.

Clarion Hotel Fifth Avenue
3 E 40th St between Fifth and Madison Aves (212-447-1500, 800-228-5151; fax 212-213-0972). Subway: B, D, F, V to 42nd St; 7 to Fifth Ave. Single/double $169–$249. AmEx, DC, Disc, MC, V.
The Clarion is a stone's throw from the New York Public Library, Bryant Park and Lord & Taylor. Request room numbers that end in three to six (the higher the floor, the better) for a street view and

lots of light; back rooms are darker and look into offices. Ask about corporate and weekend rates, and catch a meal at Salmon River (212-481-7887), the hotel's seafood restaurant. **Hotel services** Complimentary newspaper. Restaurant. **Room services** Modem line. Radio. Room service. Voice mail.

Comfort Inn Manhattan
42 W 35th St between Fifth and Sixth Aves (212-947-0200, 800-228-5150; fax 212-594-3047; www.comfortinnmanhattan.com). Subway: B, D, F, V, N, Q, R, W to 34th St–Herald Sq. Single/double $129–$229. AmEx, DC, Disc, MC, V.
This small, family-oriented hotel is around the corner from Macy's and the Empire State Building. Alex at the front desk is a hoot. A hotel fixture for more than a decade, he loves collecting bizarre English

Small wonders
Boutique hotels remain some of Manhattan's hottest properties

Ian Schrager, that visionary hotelier and former Studio 54 impresario, saw an opportunity hiding beneath the lumpy pillows and polyester uniforms dominating New York's hotel scene in the 1980s. His response was **Morgans** (see **The Hudson**, page 121), a 113-room Art Deco hotel with creature comforts galore, and an appeal that reached to the upper echelons of the fashion, art and entertainment industries. The idea was to aim small, do it with style and wit, and make a personal connection with the guest—by entertaining them silly.

To the surprise of many, the formula was a huge success, and Schrager has since opened three other stylish Manhattan hotels—the Philippe Starck–designed **Hudson** (see page 121), **Paramount** and **Royalton**—all of which came to define the concept of "boutique hotel."

In the past decade, Schrager has been joined by a host of enterprising hoteliers who have added their own special flair to the boutique blueprint. These days, a boutique suite has just as much cachet as a hideaway at the Plaza. Fortunately for those who wouldn't dream of a night's sleep under anything but Egyptian cotton, small luxury hotels have become as common as bottled blondes. A slew of newcomers—such as the **Bryant Park**, **Chambers** and **City Club**—are all competing to pamper you, and a wavering economy means all this style can come at a reduced rate.

Below, you'll find a list of the city's finest boutique accommodations. Like most luxury and deluxe hotels, they offer the basics—alarm clock, cable TV, concierge, etc.—plus irresistible extras. (You wouldn't pass up an in-room papaya–and–sea-salt body scrub, would you?)

The Bryant Park
40 W 40th St between Fifth and Sixth Aves (212-642-2200). Subway: B, D, F, V to 42nd St; 7 to Fifth Ave. Single/double from $350, suite from $495, penthouse from $2,500. AmEx, DC, Disc, MC, V.
Former Ian Schrager partner Philip Pilevsky has converted the 1924 American Radiator Building, designed by Raymond Hood, into his first New York property. Sitting across the street from lovely Bryant Park, this luxe spot has a prime location and excellent amenities (not to mention guests such as John Travolta). British designer David Chipperfield created crisp, modern rooms, and celeb chef Rick Laakkonen designed the menus at both Ilo (see page 177), an upscale American Creative restaurant, and Cellar Bar (212-642-2260), the hotel's vaulted lounge. **Hotel services** Boardroom with video conferencing. Fitness center. Screening room. Spa. 24-hour butler service. **Room services** Intrigue System (includes digitally downloaded movies).

place-names, so come prepared if you can. Rates include breakfast.

Hotel services *Continental breakfast. Ticket desk.* **Room services** *Radio. Refrigerator and microwave in some rooms. Voice mail.*

Gramercy Park Hotel

2 Lexington Ave at 21st St (212-475-4320, 800-221-4083; fax 212-505-0535; www.gramercyparkhotel.com). Subway: 6 to 23rd St. Single/double $150–$160, suite $200. AmEx, DC, Disc, MC, V.

This hotel is in a surprisingly quiet location adjoining the small green oasis of Gramercy Park (to which only hotel guests and neighboring residents receive a key). Guests vary from business travelers to rock stars, and though its decor has seen better days, the piano bar is still a favorite local hangout

for young media types and tipsy senior citizens alike. There are no nonsmoking rooms, but there is a roof garden if you wish to catch your breath.

Hotel services *Bar. Beauty salon. Conference facility. Laundry. Newsstand/ticket desk. Restaurant. Valet.* **Room services** *Room service. Voice mail.*

Hotel Edison

228 W 47th St at Broadway (212-840-5000, 800-637-7070; fax 212-596-6850; www.edisonhotelnyc.com). Subway: N, R, W to 49th St; 1, 2 to 50th St. Single $150, double $170 ($15 for each extra person, four-person maximum), suite $175–$220. AmEx, DC, Disc, MC, V.

After a two-year renovation that started in 1998, the Edison looks decidedly spruced-up. The large, high-ceilinged Art Deco lobby is particularly colorful, and even the green-marble–lined corridors

Casablanca Hotel

147 W 43rd St between Sixth Ave and Broadway (212-869-1212, 800-922-7225; fax 212-391-7585; www.casablancahotel.com). Subway: N, Q, R, W, S, 1, 2, 3, 7 to 42nd St–Times Sq; B, D, F, V to 42nd St. Single/double $265, suite $375. AmEx, DC, MC, V.

Run by the same people who own Hotel Elysée (see page 125), the Library Hotel (see page 134) and the Giraffe, this cozy 48-room hotel in the Theater District has a cheerful Moroccan-style charm. Rick's Café (get it?) is on the second floor, serving free wine and cheese on weeknights. A rooftop bar is set to open in summer 2002. Breakfast is included.

Hotel services *Business center. Cybercafé. Free access to nearby gym. 24-hour dry cleaning. Valet. Video library.* **Room services** *VCR. Voice mail.*

Chambers

See page 119.

City Club Hotel

See page 121.

Dylan

See page 121.

The Gorham New York

136 W 55th St between Sixth and Seventh Aves (212-245-1800, 800-735-0710; fax 212-582-8332; www.gorhamhotel.com). Subway: B, D, E to Seventh Ave; F, N, Q, R, W to 57th St. Single/double $220–$420, suite $250–$460. AmEx, DC, MC, V.

In the 115-room Gorham, opposite the City Center theater, the lobby's marble floors, maple walls and slightly worn oriental carpets contribute to the rather European ambience. Rooms, though not luxurious, are furnished in

a contemporary style. A kitchenette in each room is a definite plus for families.

Hotel services *Baby-sitting. Conference facility. Fitness center. Parking. 24-hour dry cleaning.* **Room services** *Kitchenette. Nintendo. VCR on request. Voice mail.*

Hotel Plaza Athénée

37 E 64th St between Madison and Park Aves (212-734-9100, 800-447-8800). Subway: F to Lexington Ave–63rd St. Single/double $490–$665, suite $1,100–$3,600. AmEx, DC, Disc, MC, V.

Hotel Plaza Athénée is one of the few boutique hotels to stray from the Modernist course. Situated steps off of posh Park Avenue on a quiet residential block, this European–style hotel impresses discerning guests from the get go; the lobby features Italian marble floors, French antique furnishings and hand-painted tapestries. The 117 recently renovated guest rooms are just as luxurious: Fresh-cut flowers adorn the bathrooms, plush robes are a courtesy, and most rooms feature pantries with a stove and a refrigerator. Those lucky enough to afford a suite (like the one actor Charlize Theron posed in during a *Vanity Fair* fashion shoot) will be treated to a terrace and solarium. But everyone can enjoy the hotel's American Creative restaurant, Arabelle (212-606-4647)—that is, if red snapper served with black-olive sorbet is your thing.

Hotel services *Fitness center. Overnight shoe shine.* **Room services** *CD player, Complimentary newspaper. Speakerphone. Voice mail.*

The Inn at Irving Place

56 Irving Pl between 17th and 18th Sts (212-533-4600, 800-685-1447; fax 212-533-4611; www.innatirving.com). Subway: L, N, ▶

look good. Rooms are standard, but theater lovers won't find a more convenient location. The coffeeshop (see **Cafe Edison**, *page 177*), just off the lobby, is a longtime favorite of Broadway actors and their fans.

Hotel services *Bar. Beauty salon. Currency exchange. Restaurant. Safe. Travel/tour desk.* **Room services** *Radio. Voice mail.*

Hotel Metro

45 W 35th St between Fifth and Sixth Aves (212-947-2500, 800-356-3870; fax 212-279-1310; www.hotelmetronyc.com). Subway: B, D, F, V, N, Q, R, W to 34th St–Herald Sq. Single/double $155–$300, suite $225–$350. AmEx, DC, MC, V.

It's not posh, but the Metro has good service and a convenient location near the Empire State Building. The lobby has a charming retro feel,

rooms are small but neat and clean, and the roof terrace offers splendid views (not to mention a rooftop bar). The Metro Grill *(212-947-2500)* in the lobby serves Mediterranean and Italian food.

Hotel services *Complimentary breakfast. Fitness center. Library. Restaurant and bar. Ticket desk.* **Room services** *Modem line. Refrigerator. Room service. Voice mail.*

The Marcel

201 E 24th St at Third Ave (212-696-3800; fax 212-696-0077; www.nycityhotels.net). Subway: 6 to 23rd St. Single/double $210–$240. AmEx, DC, Disc, MC, V.

One of the few hotels in this bustling but undistinguished corner of the city, the sleek 97-room Marcel is popular with fashion-industry types for its easy access to Flatiron, Gramercy, downtown and midtown. The compact rooms have nice

---

▶ Small wonders (continued)

Q, R, W, 4, 5, 6 to 14th St–Union Sq. Rates $300–$500. AmEx, DC, MC, V.

For some Victorian charm, book a room at this 19th-century townhouse near Gramercy Park. Offering only a dozen rooms, it's one of Manhattan's smallest inns and also one of its most romantic. Instead of a front desk, there's a parlor with a blazing fireplace. Some rooms are quite small, but each has a fireplace and a four-poster bed. The Madame Wollenska suite has a pretty window seat. The inn is a model mecca and hideaway for chic Hollywood types. Rates include breakfast. Tea at Lady Mendl's (212-533-4466) is an event.

Hotel services Conference facility. Tearoom. 24-hour dry cleaning. Valet. **Room services** CD player. VCR.

The Library Hotel

299 Madison Ave at 41st St (212-983-4500; fax 212-449-9099; www.libraryhotel.com). Subway: S, 4, 5, 6 to 42nd St–Grand Central; 7 to Fifth Ave. Single/double $265–$295, suite $345–$395. AmEx, DC, MC, V.

If you want to bone up on your French lit, you might want to check into the mahogany-rich Library, which is organized according to the Dewey decimal system—each floor is a category, such as math or science, and each room is a subject, such as anthropology, and is stocked with books. The 1912 tapestry-brick building was treated to a $10-million renovation before it opened in mid-2000. Rates include breakfast and evening wine and cheese in the second-floor Reading Room. The Giraffe, one of the Library's sister hotels, offers similar services in an updated European Moderne setting in the up-and-coming Rose Hill area.

Seeing red You'll get hooked on the crisp modern design at the Bryant Park.

design touches (avoid the ones facing noisy Third Avenue). Spread *(212-683-8880)*, the hotel's sexy in-house lounge, serves pricey designer nibbles, but those looking for other dining alternatives will find many options on Park Avenue South, just a short walk away. The Marcel is part of the Amsterdam Hospitality Group, which has six other properties in the city (for more info, visit the website listed above).

Hotel services *Dry cleaning. 24-hour cappuccino bar. Video library.* **Room services** *Alarm clock. CD player. Dataport. Iron and ironing board. Modem line. Nintendo. Radio. VCR on request. Voice mail.*

The Roosevelt Hotel

45 E 45th St at Madison Ave (212-661-9600, 888-TEDDY-NY; fax 212-885-6162; www.theroosevelt hotel.com). Subway: S, 4, 5, 6, 7 to 42nd St–Grand

Central. Single/double $149–$349, suite $500–$3,500. AmEx, DC, MC, V.
Built in 1924, this 1,040-room hotel was a haven for celebs and socialites in the Golden Age (Guy Lombardo did his first New Year's Eve "Auld Lang Syne" broadcast from here). Nostalgic grandeur remains in the lobby, with its 27-foot fluted columns, lots of marble and huge sprays of flowers. The Palm Room serves afternoon tea under a blue-sky mural and the Madison Club Cigar Bar *(212-885-6192)* serves cocktails in a clubby setting adorned with stained-glass windows.

Hotel services *Baby-sitting. Ballroom. Bar. Beauty salon. Concierge. Conference facility. Fitness center. Restaurant. Valet. Valet parking.* **Room services** *Kitchenette and VCR in suites. Modem line. Room service. Voice mail.*

Hotel services *Baby-sitting. Business center. Free access to nearby gym. Parking. Ticket desk.* **Room services** *CD player. VCR. Voice mail.* **Other location** ● *The Giraffe, 365 Park Ave South at 26th St (212-685-7700, 877-296-0009; www.hotelgiraffe.com). Subway: 6 to 28th St. Single/double $325–$425, suite $475–$575. AmEx, DC, MC, V.*

The Lowell Hotel

28 E 63rd St between Madison and Park Aves (212-838-1400, 800-221-4444; fax 212-605-6808). Subway: N, R, W to Lexington Ave–59th St; 4, 5, 6 to 59th St. Single/double $425–$575, suite $775–$1,195. AmEx, DC, Disc, MC, V.
Renovated in 2000, the small, charming Lowell is in a landmark Art Deco building. Rooms feature marble baths and Scandinavian comforters; there are even wood-burning fireplaces in the suites. The gym suite (which has two private baths and a personal gym) has lodged Madonna, Michelle Pfeiffer and Arnold Schwarzenegger, among others.

Hotel services *Baby-sitting. Cellular phone rental. Currency exchange. Fitness center.* **Room services** *CD players in suites. DVD player on request. VCR. Voice mail.*

The Mansfield

See page 123.

The Mercer

See page 119.

The Muse

130 W 46th St between Sixth and Seventh Aves (212-485-2400). Subway: B, D, F, V to 47–50th Sts–Rockefeller Ctr. Single/double $285–$355, suite $450–$600. AmEx, DC, Disc, MC, V.
The new Muse, in the Theater District, is a 200-room converted office building. The concierge-

style hotel aims to anticipate guests' every whim (rooms feature feather beds and Philosophy toiletries), but the real news is the restaurant District *(see First, page 163)*, run by chef Sam DeMarco, well-known for his American cooking. Guests can get in-room spa treatments such as a papaya–and–sea-salt body scrub for $40 to $195.

Hotel services *Business center. Fitness center. Spa. Valet parking.* **Room services** *CD player. VCR on request. Voice mail.*

Park South Hotel

122 E 28th St between Park Ave South and Lexington Ave (212-448-0888, 800-315-4642; www.parksouthhotel.com). Subway: 6 to 28th St. Single/double $225–$245, suite $425. AmEx, DC, Disc, MC, V.
One of the newest boutique hotels, Park South gives a nod to old New York. The restored 1906 building, the mezzanine library crammed with books and photos— all recount historic New York (nearly 100 images depicting early Gotham decorate the walls). The Art Deco rooms—done in warm amber and brown—and the dazzling views of the Chrysler Building really conjure sentimental feelings about the city of yore. The hotel restaurant, Black Duck *(212-204-5240)*, serves Pan-Atlantic cuisine in an adjacent brownstone building.

Hotel services *Dry cleaning. Fitness center. Umbrella loans.* **Room services** *DVD player. Fax/copier. Internet.*

SoHo Grand Hotel

See page 119.

60 Thompson

See page 119.

Wellington Hotel

871 Seventh Ave at 55th St (212-247-3900, 800-652-1212; fax 212-581-1719; www.wellingtonhotel.com). Subway: B, D, E to Seventh Ave; N, Q, R, W to 57th St. Single/double $139–$209, suite $199–$350. AmEx, DC, Disc, MC, V.

This hotel has some fetching old-fashioned touches (like a gold-domed lobby ceiling with a chandelier), though it's a tad frayed around the edges. Still, it's close to Central Park, Broadway and the Museum of Modern Art. Molyvos *(see page 180),* one of the city's best Greek restaurants, is in the building. **Hotel services** *Bar. Beauty salon. Coffeeshop. Restaurant. Transportation desk.* **Room services** *Refrigerator in some rooms. Room service.*

Wyndham Hotel

42 W 58th St between Fifth and Sixth Aves (212-753-3500, 800-257-1111; fax 212-754-5638; www.wyndham.com). Subway: F to 57th St; N, R, W to Fifth Ave–60th St. Single/double $150–$165, suite $195–$240. AmEx, DC, Disc, MC, V.

Popular with actors and directors, the Wyndham has generous-sized rooms and suites with walk-in closets. The decor is a little worn, but homey. This is a good midtown location—you can walk to the Museum of Modern Art, Fifth Avenue shopping and many of the Broadway theaters—but it's reasonably priced, so book well ahead. **Hotel services** *Bar. Beauty salon. Restaurant.* **Room services** *Refrigerator in suites. Voice mail.*

Uptown

The Empire Hotel

44 W 63rd St between Broadway and Columbus Ave (212-265-7400, 888-822-3555; fax 212-315-0349; www.empirehotel.com). Subway: 1, 2 to 66th St–Lincoln Ctr. Single/double $175–$305, suite $300–$650. AmEx, DC, Disc, MC, V.

The Empire sits opposite Lincoln Center and close to a number of decent pretheater restaurants *(see chapter* **Restaurants, Lincoln Center—West Side***).* Wood paneling and velvet drapes make for a surprisingly baronial lobby. The rooms are small—some almost closet-size—but tasteful, with plenty of chintz and floral prints. **Hotel services** *Bar. Conference facility. Currency exchange. Fitness center. Gift shop. Restaurant. Theater/tour ticket desk. Video rental.* **Room services** *Cassette and CD players. Minibar. Modem line. Refrigerator on request. Room service. Two-line phones. VCR. Voice mail.*

Excelsior Hotel

45 W 81st St between Central Park West and Columbus Ave (212-362-9200, 800-368-4575; fax 212-721-9224; www.excelsiorhotelny.com). Subway: B, C to 81st St; 1, 2 to 79th St. Single/double $139–$229, suite $239–$549. AmEx, DC, Disc, MC, V.

On the Upper West Side, where hotels are scarce, the Excelsior offers a prime location just steps from

Piece by piece Americana predominates at Chelsea Lodge, right down to the quilted bedding.

Necessities

Central Park and across the street from the American Museum of Natural History. The rooms are newly renovated but still affordable.
Hotel services *Breakfast room. Cell-phone rental. Conference facility. Fitness center. Library. Valet.*
Room services *Computers in many rooms. Modem line. Nintendo. Radio. Voice mail. Web TV.*

Hotel Beacon

2130 Broadway between 74th and 75th Sts (212-787-1100, 800-572-4969; fax 212-787-8119; www.beaconhotel.com). Subway: 1, 2, 3 to 72nd St. Single/double $180–$225, suite $250–$325. AmEx, DC, Disc, MC, V.
If you're looking for a break from the throngs of tourists clogging Times Square—or if you want to see how Gothamites really live—consider the Beacon. It's in a desirable residential neighborhood and only a short walk from Central Park, Lincoln Center and the famous Zabar's food market. The hallways have been refurbished, and rooms, which vary in decor, are clean and spacious. The Beacon is the tallest building in the area, so rooms are sunny and the windows offer views of the neighborhood.
Hotel services *Laundry (self-service and valet). Safe.* **Room services** *Kitchenette. Microwave oven. Radio. Voice mail.*

The Lucerne

201 W 79th St at Amsterdam Ave (212-875-1000, 800-492-8122; fax 212-721-1179; www.newyork hotel.com). Subway: 1, 2 to 79th St. Single/double $140–$345, suite $170–$635. AmEx, DC, Disc, MC, V.
From the outside, the landmark Lucerne, with its adorned entry columns and elaborate prewar facade, recalls the heyday of high-society New York. The rooftop patio has views of Central Park and the Hudson River, and Lincoln Center is nearby. The Lucerne is part of the Empire Hotel Group and has six sister locations (for more info, visit the website).
Hotel services *Coffeeshop. Concierge. Conference facility. Fitness center. Laundry. Parking. Sundeck.*
Room services *Kitchenette and microwave in suites. Modem line. Radio. Voice mail. Web TV.*

The Mayflower Hotel

15 Central Park West at 61st St (212-265-0060, 800-223-4164; fax 212-265-0227; www.mayflowerhotel .com). Subway: A, C, B, D, 1, 2 to 59th St–Columbus Circle. Single/double $200–$265, suite $335–$1,200. AmEx, DC, Disc, MC, V.
This haven for musicians faces Central Park and is just a few blocks from Lincoln Center. The views of the park are spectacular from the front rooms. The Conservatory Café *(212-581-0896)* on the first floor is a nice spot for a light breakfast.
Hotel services *Bar. Conference facility. Fitness center. Restaurant.* **Room services** *Room service. VCR on request. Voice mail.*

Less than $150

Unless otherwise noted, hotels in this category provide cable TV, a fax machine at the front desk

and hair dryers in the rooms or on request. Most do not have a bar, restaurant or laundry service.

Downtown

Cosmopolitan

95 West Broadway at Chambers St (212-566-1900, 888-895-9400; fax 212-566-6909; www.cosmo hotel.com). Subway: A, C, 1, 2 to Chambers St. Single $119, double $149. AmEx, DC, MC, V.
It's not luxurious by anyone's standards, but this little hotel does have rock-bottom rates and is located within easy walking distance of Chinatown, Little Italy, Soho and the South Street Seaport.
Hotel services *Concierge. Discount parking. Safe.*
Room services *Modem line. Voice mail.*

Larchmont Hotel

27 W 11th St between Fifth and Sixth Aves (212-989-9333; fax 212-989-9496; www.larchmonthotel.com). Subway: F, V to 14th St; L to Sixth Ave. Single $70–$95, double $90–$115, queen $109–$125. AmEx, DC, Disc, MC, V.
This attractive, affordable hotel is housed in a renovated 1910 Beaux Arts building on a quiet side street. Guests enter through a hallway adjacent to the lobby, making the place feel like a private apartment building. Some rooms are small, but all are clean. Each is equipped with a washbasin, robe and a pair of slippers, although not one has a private bath. Rates include breakfast.
Hotel services *Concierge. Kitchenette on some floors. Safe.* **Room services** *Radio. Voice mail.*

Off-Soho Suites Hotel

11 Rivington St between Bowery and Chrystie St (212-979-9808, 800-633-7646; fax 212-979-9801; www.offsoho.com). Subway: F, V to Lower East Side–Second Ave; J, M to Bowery; S to Grand St. Suite with shared bath $119, with private bath $209. AmEx, MC, V.
Off-Soho is a good value for suite accommodations, but the Lower East Side location might not suit everyone. If you're into bars, clubbing and the Soho scene, this spot is perfect. All suites are roomy, clean and bright, with fully equipped kitchens and polished wooden floors.
Hotel services *Café. Fitness room. Laundry. Parking. Safe.* **Room services** *Alarm clock. Microwave. Modem line. Refrigerator. Room service.*

Union Square Inn

209 E 14th St between Second and Third Aves (212-614-0500; www.unionsquareinn.com). Subway: L to Third Ave; N, Q, R, W, 4, 5, 6 to 14th St–Union Sq. Single $139, double $159–$169. MC, V.
For other locations, see **Murray Hill Inn**, page 139.

Washington Square Hotel

103 Waverly Pl between Fifth and Sixth Aves (212-777-9515, 800-222-0418; fax 212-979-8373; www.washingtonsquarehotel.com). Subway: A, C, E, F, V, S to W 4th St. Single $126–$148, double $152–$160, quad $181. AmEx, MC, V.

Necessities

Location, not luxury, is the key here. Bob Dylan and Joan Baez lived in this Greenwich Village hotel when they sang for change in nearby Washington Square Park. Rooms are no-frills, and hallways are so narrow that you practically open your door into the room opposite. A recent renovation has spruced the place up. Rates include breakfast and Tuesday-night jazz at C3 *(212-254-1200)*, the bistro next door. **Hotel services** *Complimentary breakfast. Fitness center.* **Room services** *Modem line. Voice mail.*

Midtown

Broadway Inn

264 W 46th St at Eighth Ave (212-997-9200, 800-826-6300; fax 212-768-2807; www.broadway inn.com). Subway: A, C, E to 42nd St–Port Authority. Single/double $99–$175, suite $199–$250. AmEx, DC, Disc, MC, V.
In contrast to Times Square's megahotels, this inn (a renovated single-room occupancy) feels small and personal—think Off Broadway rather than Broadway. The warm lobby has exposed-brick walls, ceiling fans, shelves loaded with books you can borrow and a hospitable front-desk staff. The 40 basic guest rooms get a lot of natural light and are fairly priced. But beware: The stairs are steep, and the inn has no elevator. Rates include continental breakfast.
Hotel services *Complimentary breakfast. Concierge. Safe.* **Room services** *Kitchenette in suites. Radio.*

Carlton Arms Hotel

160 E 25th St at Third Ave (212-679-0680; www.carltonarms.com). Subway: 6 to 23rd St. Single with shared bath $70, with private bath $85; double with shared bath $80, with private bath $100; triples $99–$111; quads $105–$117. MC, V.
The Carlton Arms is a cheerful, basic budget hotel popular with Europeans (you should reserve at least two months in advance). The themed rooms and corridors are brightly decorated, each by a different artist. Rooms are redesigned every few years—check out the English cottage room, gussied up in a convincing Tudor style. Discounts are offered for students and overseas guests. There is no air-conditioning, cable TV or fax.
Hotel services *Café. Telephone in lobby.* **Room services** *Iron on request.*

Chelsea Lodge

318 W 20th St between Eighth and Ninth Aves (212-243-4499; www.chelsealodge.com). Subway: C, E to 23rd St. Single/double with shared bath $90–$105, deluxe with private bath $135–$150, suite with private bath $195 (each additional person $15; maximum four guests). AmEx, DC, Disc, MC, V.
In the spring of 1998, husband-and-wife team Paul and G.G. Weisenfeld turned a historic landmark brownstone into a European-style inn for budget travelers. Guests can choose from 22 rooms and four suites kitted out in classic Americana. Though most rooms are fairly small, they're so charming you need to book about two months in advance.
Room services *VCR and kitchenette in suites.*

The Chelsea Star Hotel

300 W 30th St at Eighth Ave (212-244-7827; fax 212-279-9018; www.starhotelny.com). Subway: A, C, E to 34th St–Penn Station. Dorm room $26–35, single/double with shared bathroom $69–$91, suite with private bath $129–$175. AmEx, Disc, MC, V.
This theme hotel (the red Madame Butterfly room contains a buddha statue) certainly has a right to its name, considering that it was one of Madonna's first New York homes. Her small room has a rather gritty view of Madison Square Garden, and you can sleep in it for $140 a night. The slight seediness is part of the experience. A roof deck, dorm and common room make the Chelsea Star one of the city's best deals for hostelers. One-bedroom apartments have discounted weekly and monthly rates.
Hotel services *Bicycle and in-line skate rental. Common room. Concierge. Internet access. Kitchenette in apartments. Safe.* **Room services** *Modem line in apartments.*

Clarion Park Avenue

429 Park Ave South between 29th and 30th Sts (212-532-4860, 800-446-4656; fax 212-545-9727; www.bestnyhotels.com). Subway: 6 to 28th St. Single $89–199, double $99–299, quad $159–$450. AmEx, DC, Disc, MC, V.
This tourist-class hotel used to be a Howard Johnson. A complete renovation has dragged the rooms into the present decade, complete with ultramodern TVs, but the hallways still evince a certain cheesy HoJoness. Rates include continental breakfast.
Hotel services *Laundry.* **Room services** *Modem line. Radio. Safe. Voice mail.*

The Gershwin Hotel

7 E 27th St between Fifth and Madison Aves (212-545-8000; fax 212-684-5546; www.gershwinhotel.com). Subway: N, R, 6 to 28th St. $40 per person in 4- to 8-bed dorm, $109–$169 for one to three people in private room, suite $305 ($15 more Thu–Sat). AmEx, MC, V.
The bohemian Gershwin offers extremely reasonable accommodations just off Fifth Avenue. It's popular with young student types who have little need for ambience or amenities. While the lobby pays homage to Pop Art with Lichtenstein and Warhol works, the rooms are spartan.
Hotel services *Bar. Conference facility. Dry cleaning. Gift shop. Lockers. Public telephones. Roof garden. Transportation desk.* **Room services** *Alarm clock. Modem line. TV in private rooms. Voice mail.*

The Herald Square Hotel

19 W 31st St between Fifth Ave and Broadway (212-279-4017, 800-727-1888; fax 212-643-9208; www.heraldsquarehotel.com). Subway: B, D, F, V, N, Q, R, W to 34th St–Herald Sq. Single/double $65–$140, triple $150, quad $160. AmEx, Disc, MC, V.
Herald Square Hotel was the original *Life* magazine building, and it retains its cherub-adorned entrance. All rooms were renovated in 1999, and

most have private bathrooms; corridors are lined with framed *Life* illustrations. As the name suggests, it is near Macy's and the Empire State Building, and it's a good deal, so book well in advance. There are discounts for students.
Hotel services *Safe. Ticket desk.* **Room services** *Modem line. Radio. Voice mail.*

Hotel Grand Union

34 E 32nd St between Madison and Park Aves (212-683-5890; fax 212-689-7397). Subway: 6 to 33rd St. Double $126, triple $143, quad $174 (all taxes included). AmEx, Disc, MC, V.
There's nothing fancy about the Hotel Grand Union, but you will find spacious rooms and clean, private bathrooms for the same price that similar hotels would charge for shared bathrooms. During the busy seasons, the rooms quickly fill with European and Japanese tourists, so reserve at least a month in advance. The helpful staff will book tours for you and provide useful New York advice.
Hotel services *Restaurant. Safe.* **Room services.** *Modem line. Refrigerator. Voice mail.*

Hotel 17

225 E 17th St between Second and Third Aves (212-475-2845; fax 212-677-8178; hotel17.citysearch.com). Subway: N, Q, R, W, 4, 5, 6 to 14th St–Union Sq; L to Third Ave. Single $60–$70, double $75–$85, triple $120–$140, weekly rates $400–$608. Cash and traveler's checks only.
This is the ultimate dive hotel and one of the hippest places to stay if you're an artist, musician or model; everyone in the underground circuit knows the place. Madonna posed here for a magazine shoot, and Woody Allen used the location for *Manhattan Murder Mystery.* The decor is classic shabby chic, with labyrinthine hallways leading to high-ceilinged rooms filled with discarded dressers, gorgeous old fireplaces, velvet curtains and 1950s wallpaper. Ignore the permanent NO VACANCY sign, and expect to share the hallway bathroom with other guests.
Hotel services *Air-conditioning in doubles and triples. Cell-phone rental. Laundry.* **Room services** *Alarm clock. Cable TV in some rooms.*

Murray Hill Inn

143 E 30th St between Lexington and Third Aves (212-683-6900, 888-996-6376; fax 212-545-0103; www.murrayhillinn.com). Subway: 6 to 28th St. Single with shared bath $60–$75, double with shared bath $75–$95, single/double with private bath $95–$125. AmEx, MC, V.
Tucked away on a quiet, tree-lined street in midtown and within walking distance of the Empire State Building and Grand Central Terminal, this 50-room inn is good value for the price. Rooms are basic, but neat and clean, and all have sinks. Discounted weekly rates are available. Book well in advance.
Room services *Complimentary breakfast. Modem line. Voice mail.*
Other locations ● *Union Square Inn, 209 E 14th St between Second and Third Aves (212-614-0500; www.unionsquareinn.com). Subway: L to Third Ave; N, Q, R, W, 4, 5, 6 to 14th St–Union Sq. Single $139,*

double $159–$169. MC, V. ● *Amsterdam Inn, 340 Amsterdam Ave at 76th St (212-579-7500; fax 212-579-6127; www.amsterdaminn.com). Subway: 1, 2 to 79th St. Single $75, double $95–$125. Cash or traveler's checks only.* ● *Central Park Hostel, 19 W 103rd St at Central Park West (212-678-0491; www.central parkhostel.com). Subway: B, C to 103rd St. $25 for a bed, $75 for a room. Cash or traveler's checks only.*

Pickwick Arms

230 E 51st St between Second and Third Aves (212-355-0300, 800-742-5945; fax 212-755-5029; www.pickwickarms.com). Subway: E, V to Lexington Ave–53rd St; 6 to 51st St. Single $75–$110, double $135–$225. AmEx, DC, MC, V.
The rooms may be small at the Pickwick Arms, but they are clean. And although the hotel is in a reasonably quiet district, it's still near restaurants, movie theaters, Radio City Music Hall and the United Nations. Most of the rooms have private bathrooms, but some share an adjoining facility, while others share a bathroom down the hall. There are two restaurants within the hotel, as well as a rooftop garden.
Hotel services *Bar. E-mail access in lobby. Restaurant. Safe.* **Room services** *Radio. Voice mail.*

Quality Hotel and Suites Midtown

59 W 46th St between Fifth and Sixth Aves (212-719-2300, 800-848-0020; fax 212-790-2760; www.hotelchoice.com). Subway: B, D, F, V to 47–50th Sts–Rockefeller Ctr. Single $89–$179, double $99–$189, suite $139–$219. AmEx, DC, MC, V.
This convenient 193-room Theater District hotel, built in 1902, has somehow managed to hang on to its old-time prices. The lobby was renovated at the end of 2000. Rates include breakfast.
Hotel services *Bar. Beauty salon. Conference facility. 24-hour fitness center.*

Red Roof Inn

6 W 32nd St between Fifth Ave and Broadway (212-643-7100, 800-RED-ROOF; fax 212-643-7101). Subway: B, D, F, V, N, Q, R, W to 34th St–Herald Sq; 6 to 33rd St. Single/double $110–$280, king $120–$290. AmEx, DC, Disc, MC, V.
This branch of the U.S. motel chain (a converted office building) is stylish—the black-and-beige lobby is smart and sleek—and it's one of the best deals in town. In the middle of Koreatown, it's centrally located and close to good Korean restaurants (*see chapter* **Restaurants**). Though the rooms are standard chain, the whole place still feels shiny and new (the hotel opened in 2000). Each room that ends in 6 has a minifridge and microwave oven. For quiet, get a room at the back.
Hotel services *Bar. Concierge. Conference room. Safe. 24-hour fitness center.* **Room services** *Refrigerator and microwave oven in some rooms. Web TV.*

ThirtyThirty New York City

30 E 30th St between Madison Ave and Park Ave South (212-689-1900; fax 212-689-0023; www.3030nyc.com). Single $99, double $125–$145, suites $185–$250 Subway: 6 to 28th St. AmEx, DC, Disc, MC, V.
For other location, see **Habitat Hotel**, page 140.

The Wolcott Hotel

4 W 31st St between Fifth Ave and Broadway (212-268-2900; fax 212-563-0096; www.wolcott.com). Subway: B, D, F, V, N, Q, R, W to 34th St–Herald Sq. Single/double $80–$120, suite $80–$150. AmEx, MC, V.

The ornate gilded lobby comes as a surprise in this Garment District hotel, where celebs of another age, such as Edith Wharton and *Titanic* survivor Washington Dodge, once stayed. The rooms are on the small, shabby side, but inexpensive.

Hotel services *Concierge. Conference facility. Fitness center. Laundry.* **Room services** *Modem line. Safe. Voice mail. Web TV.*

Uptown

Habitat Hotel

130 E 57th St at Lexington Ave (212-753-8841, 800-255-0482; fax 212-829-9605; www.stayinny.com). Subway: N, R, W to Lexington Ave–59th St; 4, 5, 6 to 59th St. Single with shared bath $85, double with shared bath $95, single/double with private bath $125–$145, penthouse studio $195. AmEx, DC, Disc, MC, V.

A $20 million overhaul of a dilapidated women's residence has resulted in a fresh-looking "sophisticated budget" hotel with an urban feel. Each room has a sink and mirror, and black-and-white photos of the city grace the walls. Space is tight when you pull out the trundle (which makes the room a double), and the shared bathrooms are tiny, but overall the Habitat makes an ideal resting place for group and budget travelers. Breakfast is included. The Habitat's younger sister, ThirtyThirty, opened in 2001.

Hotel services *Laundry.* **Room services** *Alarm clock. Modem line. Radio. Refrigerator on request. Voice mail.*

Other locations ● *ThirtyThirty New York City, see page 139.* ● *On the Ave, see page 123.*

Malibu Studios Hotel

2688 Broadway at 103rd St (212-222-2954, 800-647-2227; fax 212-678-6842; www.malibuhotelnyc.com). Subway: 1 to 103rd St. Single/double with shared bath $79, private bath $129; triple/quad with shared bath $89, with private bath $149. Cash or traveler's checks only.

Far from the traditional tourist sights, this tidy Upper West Sider offers budget visitors a chance to explore a primarily residential neighborhood that's near Riverside Park and not far from Columbia University. The area is generally safe, but it can get dicey after dark. Rates include breakfast. No cable TV.

Hotel services *Concierge. Safe.* **Room services** *CD player and iron on request.*

Riverside Towers Hotel

80 Riverside Dr at 80th St (212-877-5200, 800-724-3136; fax 212-873-1400). Subway: 1, 2 to 79th St. Single $95, double $100, suite $110–$130. AmEx, DC, Disc, MC, V.

The Riverside offers a good rate for the Upper West Side, and it's one of the very few hotels in Manhattan located on the Hudson River. The views are fine, and

Penny royalty The Wolcott Hotel's gilded lobby contrasts greatly with its bargain prices.

there's a quiet park across the street, but accommodations are basic. This is strictly a place to sleep.

Hotel services *Baby-sitting. Laundry. Safe.* **Room services** *Hot plate. Modem line. Refrigerator.*

Hostels

Bed linens and towels are included in the room rate for the hostels listed here, unless otherwise noted.

Downtown

Bowery's Whitehouse Hotel of New York

340 Bowery between 2nd and 3rd Sts (212-477-5623; fax 212-473-3150; whitehousehotel@aol.com, www.whitehousehotelofny.com). Subway: F, V, S to Broadway–Lafayette St; 6 to Bleecker St. Single/double: $32–$62. AmEx, DC, Disc, MC, V.

Built in 1917 as housing for railroad workers, the Bowery's Whitehouse Hotel is still part flophouse (about 50 permanent residents remain, mainly men in their advancing years) and part hostel. The rooms are glorified horse stalls, but they're clean, the mattresses are decent, and your property is safe. And you won't find anything cheaper downtown—that's why it's popular with European backpackers. Long-staying foreign students work the front desk. A night here is an inside look at a New York that most

New Yorkers haven't seen. And if you sit down with one of the resident old-timers, you'll hear one-of-a-kind stories of the city.
Hotel services *Internet access in lobby. Luggage storage. Safety boxes. Self-service laundry. TV in lobby.*

Midtown

Chelsea Center

313 W 29th St between Eighth and Ninth Aves (212-643-0214; fax 212-473-3945; www.chelsea centerhostel.com). Subway: A, C, E to 34th St–Penn Station. $27 per person in dorm. Cash only.
The Chelsea Center is a small, welcoming hostel with clean bathrooms and a patio garden in the back. It has the feel of a shared student house. Since there are a limited number of beds in each dorm, book at least a week in advance. There's no curfew or air-conditioning, and the price includes continental breakfast. There is also an East Village location, for which bookings should be made through the Chelsea Center.
Hotel services *All rooms nonsmoking. Fax. Garden patio. Kitchen facilities. TV room.*

YMCA (Vanderbilt)

224 E 47th St between Second and Third Aves (212-756-9600; fax 212-752-0210; www.ymcanyc.org). Subway: S, 4, 5, 6, 7 to 42nd St–Grand Central. Single $72, double $86, suite $138. AmEx, MC, V.
This cheerful YMCA's more expensive quarters have sinks, but the rooms aren't very large; the beds barely fit into some of them. Book well in advance by writing to the reservations department and including a deposit for one night's rent. There are almost 400 rooms, but only the suites have private baths.
Hotel services *All rooms nonsmoking. Fax. Fitness facilities. Laundry. Luggage room.* **Room services** *TV. Voice mail.*

Uptown

Central Park Hostel

19 W 103rd St at Central Park West (212-678-0491; www.centralparkhostel.com). Subway: B, C to 103rd St. $25 for a bed, $75 for a room. Cash or traveler's checks only.
For other locations, see **Murray Hill Inn**, page 139.

Hosteling International New York

891 Amsterdam Ave at 103rd St (212-932-2300; fax 212-932-2574; www.hinewyork.org). Subway: 1 to 103rd St. 10- to12-bed dorm room $29, 6- to 8-bed dorm room $35, 4-bed dorm room $32. $3 extra for nonmembers; family room $120, private room with bath $135. AmEx, DC, MC, V.
This gargantuan 624-bed hostel takes up an entire city block. Once a residence for elderly women, the gabled redbrick building retains an institutional, public school feel. Rooms are spare, but immaculately clean and air-conditioned, affording a pleasant stay for those who can abide by the hostel's many rules. There is a large enclosed garden in

the back. Peak-season rates (May to October) are slightly higher.
Hotel services *All rooms nonsmoking. Café. Cafeteria. Conference facility. Fax. Game room. Laundry. Library. Lockers. Shuttles. Travel bureau. TV lounge.*

International House

500 Riverside Dr at 125th St (212-316-8473, in summer 212-316-8436; fax 212-316-1827). Subway: 1 to 125th St. Single $105–$115, double/suite $115–$125. MC, V.
This hostel is on a peaceful block, surrounded by college buildings and overlooking the small but well-tended Sakura Park. A subsidized cafeteria serves main dishes for around $3. Only suites have private bathrooms. The best time to book is summer, when foreign graduate students and visiting scholars check out. Summer single rates drop to as low as $50. Be warned: Though the area around Columbia University is generally safe, you might not want to stroll too far afield after dark if you're new in town.
Hotel services *Bar. Cafeteria. Conference facility. Currency exchange. Fax. Game room. Laundry.*
Room services *TV.*

Jazz on the Park Hostel

36 W 106th St between Central Park West and Manhattan Ave (212-932-1600; fax 212-932-1700; www.jazzhostel.com). Subway: B, C to 103rd St. 4- to 14-bed dorm room $27–$30, 2-bed dorm room $68 (double occupancy). MC, V.
A cozy old-school hostel just off Central Park West, Jazz on the Park has a warm neighborhood staff. The basic rooms can be cramped (use the private lockers) but the price is a bargain. You can occasionally hear live jazz on the weekend, as well as nosh at summer evening barbecues on a second-floor terrace. The new basement lounge hosts local jazz and hip-hop acts twice a week and serves bottled beer out of a cooler. Book in advance.
Hotel services *Bike and in-line skate rental (summer only). Café. Complimentary breakfast. Internet access. Laundry. Private lockers. TV room.*

Park View Hotel

55 W 110th St (Central Park North) at Malcolm X Blvd (Lenox Ave) (212-369-3340; fax 212-369-3046; www.nycityhotels.net). Subway: 2, 3 to 110th St–Central Park North. 4- to 6-bed dorm room $26–$30, private room with shared bath $50–$100. AmEx, DC, Disc, MC, V.
The mod orange-and-yellow lobby is a welcome change from the usual hostel dinginess; rooms and bathrooms are just as colorful and clean. Each floor has a communal kitchen, and there's a downstairs lounge with a pool table and large-screen TV. The rooftop, open during the warmer months, offers a great view of the Harlem Meer across the street in Central Park.
Hotel services *Bicycle and in-line skate rental. Fax. International pay phones. Internet access. Phone-card machine.*

YMCA (West Side)

5 W 63rd St between Central Park West and Broadway (212-875-4100; fax 212-875-1334; www.ymcanyc.org). Subway: A, C, B, D, 1, 2 to 59th St–Columbus Circle. Single $80, with bath $115; double $90, with bath $130. AmEx, MC, V.

A cavernous building close to Central Park and Lincoln Center, this Y has rooms that are simple and clean. Book well in advance. A deposit is required to hold a reservation. Most of the 540 rooms have shared bathrooms.

Hotel services *Cafeteria. Fax. Fitness facilities. Laundry.* **Room services** *Cable TV.*

YMHA (de Hirsch Residence at the 92nd Street Y)

1395 Lexington Ave at 92nd St (212-415-5650, 800-858-4692; fax 212-415-5578). Subway: 6 to 96th St. Single $79, double $49 per person; one-month stay or longer, single with shared bath $945 monthly, double with shared bath $655–$765 per person. AmEx, MC, V.

The Young Men's Hebrew Association is rather like its Christian counterpart, the YMCA, in that to stay there you don't have to be young, male or—in this case—Jewish. The dorm-style rooms are spacious and clean, with two desks and plenty of closet space. There are kitchens and dining facilities on each floor.

Hotel services *Discounted access to fitness center. Laundry. Library. Refrigerator on request. TV lounge. Weekly linen service.*

Bed & breakfast services

New York's bed-and-breakfast scene is deceptively large. There are thousands of beds available, but since there isn't a central B-and-B organization, rooms may be hard to find. Many B-and-Bs are unhosted, and breakfast is usually continental (if it's offered at all). The main difference from a hotel is the more personal ambience. Prices are not necessarily low, but B-and-Bs are a good way to feel less like a tourist and more like a New Yorker. Sales tax of 8.25 percent is added on hosted bed-and-breakfast rooms, but not on unhosted apartments if you're staying for more than seven days. It's always a good idea to ask about decor, location and amenities when booking and, if safety is a concern, ask whether the building has a 24-hour doorman. One caveat: Last-minute changes can be costly; some agencies charge guests for a night's stay if they cancel reservations less than ten days before arriving. Brooklyn B-and-Bs are listed on page 143.

More B-and-Bs are in the chapter **Gay & Lesbian**—and they welcome guests from the straight world too.

A Hospitality Company

247 W 35th St, 4th floor, New York, NY 10001 (212-965-1102; fax 212-965-1149; www.hospitalityco.com).

Studio $99–$165, one-bedroom apartment $125–$225, two-bedroom apartment $275–$325. MC, V.

A Hospitality Company has more than 200 furnished apartments available for nightly, weekly or monthly stays, from East Village walk-ups to Murray Hill doorman buildings, and is popular among visiting artists (one opera diva requested a grand piano during her stay). Every place has cable TV, and many have VCRs and stereos. The nightly B-and-B rate includes continental breakfast.

All Around the Town

150 Fifth Ave, suite 837, New York, NY 10011 (800-443-3800; fax 212-675-6366; aroundtown@worldnet.att.net). Studio $130–$185, one-bedroom apartment $150–$210. AmEx, DC, MC, V.

This agency can arrange accommodations in most Manhattan neighborhoods in unhosted furnished apartments. There is a three-night minimum; ask about reduced rates for monthly stays.

At Home in New York

P.O. Box 407, New York, NY 10185 (212-956-3125, please call only Mon–Fri 9am–6pm, 800-692-4262; fax 212-247-3294; athomeny@erols.com). Hosted single/double $90–$160, unhosted studio $100–$165, unhosted 1-bedroom apartment. $135–$200, Unhosted 2-bedroom apartment $200–$400 Cash only (AmEx, Disc, MC, V can be used to guarantee rooms).

This agency (run from a private residence) has reasonably priced rooms in about 300 properties; most are in Manhattan; a few are in Brooklyn, Queens and Staten Island. There is a two-night minimum.

Awesome Bed & Breakfast

Nassau St at Fulton St (212-528-8492). Subway: A, C to Broadway–Nassau St; J, M, Z, 1, 2, 4, 5 to Fulton St. See other location, page 143.

Bed and Breakfast in Manhattan

P.O. Box 533, New York, NY 10150 (212-472-2528; fax 212-988-9818). Hosted $90–$120, unhosted $125–$400. Cash only.

Each of this organization's 100 or so properties has been personally inspected by the owner, who also helps travelers select a bed-and-breakfast in the neighborhood best suited to their interests.

Bed & Breakfast (& Books)

35 W 92nd St, apartment 2C, New York, NY 10025 (212-865-8740 phone and fax, call only Mon–Fri 10am–5pm; bedbreakfastbook@aol.com). Hosted single $85–$120, hosted double $120–$135, unhosted studio $120–$160, unhosted 1-bedroom apartment from $160, unhosted 2-bedroom apartment from $250. Cash or traveler's checks only (AmEx, DC, Disc, MC, V can be used to guarantee rooms).

Several hosts in this organization are literary types—hence the bookish title. There are 40 hosted and unhosted rooms, and the minimum stay is two nights.

Bed & Breakfast Off the Park

2009-2111 Adam Clayton Powell Blvd (Seventh Ave) between 120th and 121st Sts (917-337-6847;

www.offthepark.com). Subway: 2, 3 to 125th St. Single $55, double $80, triple $115, 3-room suite $260.
Since 1997, François Bovis's 20-room B-and-B in central Harlem has been a refuge for French tourists on holiday. Rooms range from singles to a six-person suite, and many are outfitted with kitchenettes. Only the suite has a private bath. Breakfast is included.

City Lights Bed and Breakfast

P.O. Box 20355, Cherokee Station, New York, NY 10021 (212-737-7049; fax 212-535-2755; www.citylightsbandb.com). Hosted single/double with private or shared bath $95–$135, unhosted single/double $135–$200; monthly hosted $1,200–$1,600, unhosted $2,500–$3,800. DC, MC, V.
This helpful agency lists 300 to 400 properties in Manhattan and Brooklyn. A two-night minimum stay and a 25-percent deposit are required.

CitySonnet

Village Station, P.O. Box 347, New York, NY 10014-0347 (212-614-3034; fax 425-920-2384; mail@ citysonnet.com; www.citysonnet.com). Bed-and-breakfast room $85–$155, studio apartment $135–$175, larger apartment $165–$325. AmEx, MC, V.
This friendly artist-run agency (formerly called West Village Reservations) specializes in downtown locations, but has properties all over Manhattan. The B-and-B rooms and short-term apartment rentals are priced according to room size, number of guests and whether the bathroom is adjacent to the room (i.e., private) or shared with other guests. Hosts provide neighborhood information and continental breakfast. All apartments are private and completely furnished.

The Urban Jem Guest House

2005 Fifth Ave between 124th and 125th Sts (212-831-6029; www.urbanjem.com). Subway: 2, 3 to 125th St. Single/double with shared bath $90–$120, suite for up to four people $200–$220, studio apartment with private kitchen and bath $105–$130; minimum two-night stay on weekends and holidays. AmEx, Disc, MC, V.
Proprietors Jane Mendelson and Oklahoma Simms's renovated 1878 brownstone is just a block from Bill Clinton's 125th Street office. The nearby Synergy Gym offers daily guest passes; Simms runs a car service, and there is also a small library of Harlem-oriented travel, photo, documentary and fiction books. Each of the four rooms is clean and well-appointed, with Afrocentric art on the walls and original marble mantelpieces. The parlor floor, which looks out onto Fifth Avenue, is also the site of regular jazz performances.

Brooklyn lodging

Akwaaba Mansion Bed & Breakfast

347 MacDonough St between Lewis and Stuyvesant Aves, Bedford-Stuyvesant (718-455-5958; fax 718-774-1744; www.akwaaba.com). Subway: A, C to Utica Ave. Weekdays $120–$135, weekends $135–$150. MC, V.
This restored 1860s Italianate mansion, whose name

means "welcome" in Ghanaian, is the handiwork of Glenn Pogue and his wife Monique Greenwood, former editor-in-chief of Essence magazine. Greenwood's decorating sense is meticulous: Akwaaba's four guest suites are furnished with antiques that reflect each room's theme. The spacious Ashante Suite, for example, is accented with African artifacts and textiles. Stays include a hearty Southern-style breakfast and personal touches, such as bedside cookies. There's also the Akwaaba Café (393 Lewis Ave between Decatur and MacDonough Sts, Bedford-Stuyvesant, 718-774-1444) down the street for anyone who can't get enough of that Southern cooking.

Angelique Bed & Breakfast

405 Union St between Hoyt and Smith Sts, Carroll Gardens (718-852-8406; www.sspoerri.com/abb). F, G to Carroll St. Single $75, double $125, triple $150. AmEx, DC, Disc, MC, V.
Housed in an 1889 brownstone in charming Carroll Gardens, Angelique has four rooms done in cozy quasi-Victorian style. The Blue Room has a view of Manhattan. On a warm summer day, you can relax in the back garden or take the F train four stops to Prospect Park. And you can eat like a king (or queen)—the B-and-B is just around the corner from Smith Street, Brooklyn's restaurant scene.

Awesome Bed & Breakfast

136 Lawrence St between Fulton and Willoughby Sts, Downtown Brooklyn (718-858-4859; www.awesome-bed-and-breakfast.com). Subway: A, C, F to Jay St–Borough Hall; M, N, R to Lawrence St; 1, 2, 4, 5 to Borough Hall. Single/double $79–$110, suite $125–$145. MC, V.
One stop from Manhattan on the 4 or 5 train is this eight-room home away from home. It's a nondescript commercial brick building on the outside, but the inside brims with character. Theme rooms include Ancient Madagascar and Aurora Borealis, also known as the "groovy room"—complete with purple walls and lots of daisies. A new lounge hosts live music. Nearby is Montague Street—Brooklyn Heights' main drag—and the Promenade. The Awesome also has a Financial District location—a one-room suite in a loft with a Jacuzzi-size bath is $135. Breakfast is included. **Other location** ● See page 142.

New York Marriott Brooklyn

333 Adams St between Tillary and Willoughby Sts, Brooklyn Heights (718-246-7000; fax 718-246-0563; www.marriott.com). Subway: A, C, F to Jay St–Borough Hall; 1, 2, 4, 5 to Borough Hall. Single/double $169–$229, suite $349–$549. AmEx, DC, Disc, MC, V.
This hotel is what you'd expect from a Marriott, with all the usual amenities, along with a business center and inclusion of dataport phones in every room. Nearby is the landmark Gage & Tollner restaurant (372 Fulton St between Jay and Smith Sts, 718-875-5181); inside is the Archives, which displays local memorabilia and serves American-style food. A five-minute walk will take you to busy Montague Street and the sweeping view of Manhattan from the Brooklyn Heights Promenade.

Necessities

Bars

Whether you're a beer-and-shots boozer or a sophisticated cocktail queen, New York has plenty of places where you can imbibe in style…or squalor

There's no disputing that New York is a damn fine drinking town. The bars here should quench the thirst of any type of drinker, from the polite sipper to the happy-hour hooch hound.

Downtown

APT
419 W 13th St between Ninth Ave and Washington St (212-414-4245). Subway: A, C, E to 14th St; L to Eighth Ave. 6pm–4am. Average drink: $10. AmEx, MC, V.
See page 269.

Baby Doll Lounge
34 White St at Church St (212-226-4870). Subway: A, C, E to Canal St; 1, 2 to Franklin St. Mon–Fri noon–4am; Sat 6pm–4am. Average drink: $8. Cash only.
A red velvet curtain separates the Baby Doll Lounge into two sections: bikini and topless. Mostly, the dancers roll around on a carpeted stage while dollar bills are tossed at them. The place is tiny, dank and dirty, but it is there if you need it.

Baraza
133 Ave C between 8th and 9th Sts (212-539-0811). Subway: L to First Ave; 6 to Astor Pl. 6pm–4am. Average drink: $5. Cash only.
This watering hole was a hit when Avenue C was still slumping, and three years after opening, the party vibe remains a huge draw. You'll have to wait in line to get in on weekends, then wade through wall-to-wall sweaty bodies to order a $5 caipirinha.

Barrow's Pub
643 Hudson St at Barrow St (212-741-9349). Subway: 1, 2 to Christopher St–Sheridan Sq. 11am–4am. Average drink: $5. AmEx.
At Barrow's, Ella Fitzgerald commingles with AC/DC on the jukebox, babes at the bar bewitch old-timers, and not a single soul need be afraid to belly up to the billiards table. Wear jeans, bring smokes.

Botanica
47 E Houston St between Mott and Mulberry Sts (212-343-7251). Subway: F, V, S to Broadway–Lafayette St; 6 to Bleecker St. 5pm–4am. Average drink: $4.50. Cash only.
Botanica is pretty much a beer-gulpin', meet-your-friends bar, with plenty of sticky tables and affable bartenders, and Yuengling on tap.

Chumley's
86 Bedford St between Barrow and Commerce Sts (212-675-4449). Subway: 1, 2 to Christopher St–Sheridan Sq. Mon–Thu 4pm–midnight; Fri 4pm–2am; Sat 10am–4am; Sun 1pm–2am. Average drink: $5. Cash only.
Opened in 1922 by Leland Stanford Chumley—labor organizer, soldier of fortune, waiter, artist, newspaper cartoonist and editorial writer—Chumley's has as many stories as it does brands of suds. The place has hosted its share of literary heavyweights—Upton Sinclair and David Mamet among them.

Church Lounge
Tribeca Grand Hotel, 2 Sixth Ave between Walker and White Sts (212-519-6677). Subway: A, C, E to Canal St; 1, 2 to Franklin St. 7pm–2am. Average drink: $7. AmEx, MC, V.
It's pretty clear from the congested bar and cluttered tables that the sexy masses who descend on this hotel lounge come for one reason: to slurp bartender Marty Vaz's expertly mixed libations. Grab a stiff one and submit to the plush surroundings.

d.b.a.
41 First Ave between 2nd and 3rd Sts (212-475-5097). Subway: F, V to Lower East Side–Second Ave. 1pm–4am. Average drink: $5. AmEx, DC, Disc, MC, V.
You may have a hard time reading the list of beers chalked onto d.b.a.'s blackboards, especially since they come with names such as Stille Nacht Ale and Conistons Bluebird Bitter. But the extra-friendly staff will help you dope it out.

Decibel Sake Bar
240 E 9th St between Second and Third Aves (212-979-2733). Subway: 6 to Astor Pl. Mon–Sat 8pm–3am; Sun 8pm–1:30am. Average drink: $8. AmEx, DC, MC, V.
The tiny bar in this basement space hides a rear cavern furnished with high-backed booths—you can disappear into them for hours. Bring a willing accomplice to tackle the intimidating sake menu.

Double Happiness
173 Mott St between Broome and Grand Sts (212-941-1282). Subway: J, M to Bowery; S to Grand St; 6 to Spring St. Sun–Thu 6pm–3am; Fri, Sat 6pm–4am. Average drink: $5. MC, V.
This Chinatown bar has everything a New York City bar should: mysterious entrance, history (the space allegedly had past lives as a speakeasy and an Italian restaurant), fun and attractive patrons, good tunes and great drinks.

Dylan
62 Laight St between Greenwich and Hudson Sts (212-334-4783). Subway: A, C, E, 1, 2 to Canal St.

C ya on the ave Young lovelies gather at Baraza, located in the heart of Alphabet City.

Mon–Thu 5pm–2am; Fri, Sat 5pm–3am. Average drink: $9. AmEx, DC, Disc, MC, V.
Primo cocktails are why Dylan is the watering hole of choice for Salomon Smith Barney types. Consequently, the place is packed come quitting time. Sample specialties such as the house Manhattan (it has a secret citrus blend).

Fez

Inside Time Cafe, 380 Lafayette St at Great Jones St (212-533-2680). Subway: F, V, S to Broadway–Lafayette St; 6 to Bleecker St. Sun–Thu 6pm–2am; Fri, Sat 6pm–4am. Average drink: $6. AmEx, MC, V.
See pages 150 and 303.

Guernica

25 Ave B between 2nd and 3rd Sts (212-674-0984). Subway: F, V to Lower East Side–Second Ave. 6pm–4am. Average drink: $6. AmEx, MC, V.
See page 269.

The Half King

505 W 23rd St at Tenth Ave (212-462-4300). Subway: C, E to 23rd St. Mon–Fri 9am–5pm, 6pm–4am; Sat, Sun noon–5pm, 6pm–4am. Average drink: $5. AmEx, DC, MC, V.
Since opening Half King with a partner two years ago, Sebastian Junger, author of *The Perfect Storm*, spends some days in this pub (when he's not in Afghanistan, that is). The menu offers Irish eats and there are readings, too *(see also page 258)*.

Halo

49 Grove St between Seventh Ave South and Bleecker St (212-243-8885). Subway: 1, 2 to Christopher St–Sheridan Sq. Tue–Sun 7pm–4am. Average drink: $10. AmEx, DC, Disc, MC, V.
Halo has been attracting the beautiful people for more than two years, and while it is ostensibly open to all, the place seems more like a private club—thanks to hard-nosed doorpersons.

Hell

59 Gansevoort St between Greenwich and Washington Sts (212-727-1666). Subway: A, C, E to 14th St; L to Eighth Ave. Sun–Thu, Sat 7pm–4am; Fri 5pm–4am. Average drink: $7. AmEx, MC, V.
A straight-leaning crowd finds a comfort zone in the plush decor at Hell: crimson walls, retro glass chandeliers and hassocks that can be moved around to accommodate an intimate tête-à-tête or a party of five.

Hogs & Heifers

859 Washington St at 13th St (212-929-0655). Subway: A, C, E to 14th St; L to Eighth Ave. Mon–Fri 11am–4am; Sat 1pm–4am; Sun 2pm–4am. Average drink: $5. Cash only.
After opening in 1992, this Meatpacking District outpost for bikers and sassy babes gained notoriety as tales of striptease brought the A-list (Julia Roberts added her bra to the tangle above the bar). The Jersey crowd followed, but H&H remains the king of the biker bars. Okay, the clown prince.

Joe's Bar

520 E 6th St between Aves A and B (212-473-9093). Subway: F, V to Lower East Side–Second Ave; 6 to Astor Pl. Noon–4am. Average drink: $3. Cash only.
As the smoke swirls languorously between the pool table and the stained-glass overhead lamp, and George Jones sermonizes about hard realities from his jukebox pulpit, you pull your head out of the ashtray and realize that you're safe—safe from subwoofers, safe from all those NYU scenesters.

Joe's Pub

See page 305.

Lakeside Lounge

See page 305.

Liquids

266 E 10th St between First Ave and Ave A (212-677-1717). Subway: L to First Ave; 6 to Astor Pl. 6pm–4am. Average drink: $6. AmEx.
See page 271.

The Lotus Club

35 Clinton St at Stanton St (212-253-1144). Subway: F to Delancey St; J, M, Z to Delancey–Essex Sts.

Mon–Sat 7:30am–4am; Sun 7:30am–2am. Average drink: $5. AmEx, Disc, MC, V.
This earthy-crunchy and somewhat literary bar has a veggie-heavy menu and a full complement of drinks on and off tap.

Mare Chiaro
176½ Mulberry St between Broome and Grand Sts (212-226-9345). Subway: J, M, Z, N, Q, R, W, 6 to Canal St; S to Grand St. Sun–Thu 11am–1am; Fri, Sat 11am–4am. Average drink: $4. Cash only.
No wonder scenes from *Donnie Brasco* and the *Godfather* trilogy were shot here—it's like walking into the Corleones' local. Get whacked or get lost.

McSorley's Old Ale House
15 E 7th St between Second and Third Aves (212-473-9148). Subway: F, V to Lower East Side–Second Ave; 6 to Astor Pl. Mon–Sat 11am–1am; Sun 1pm–1am. Average drink: $1.75. Cash only.
Established in 1854, McSorley's is one of the city's oldest taverns. Chug some beer and watch men pee behind the peekaboo bathroom door. Bring a copy of bartender-poet Geoffrey Bartholomew's *The McSorley Poems* for maximum reverie.

Pressure
110 University Pl between 12th and 13th Sts (212-352-1161). Subway: L, N, Q, R, W, 4, 5, 6 to 14th St–Union Sq. Thu–Sat 7pm–4am. Average drink: $6.
Located upstairs from Bowlmor Lanes *(see page 328)*, Pressure is a huge air-inflated bubble featuring numerous jumbo TVs, movie screens, pool tables, a two-sided bar and—our favorite—a Twister game painted on the carpet.

Puck Fair
298 Lafayette St between Houston and Prince Sts (212-431-1200). Subway: F, V, S to Broadway–Lafayette St; N, R to Prince St; 6 to Bleecker St. 11am–4am. Average drink: $5. AmEx, MC, V.
At this tri-level Irish pub with a rural feel, you can walk in morning or night for Irish sausage, toasties, coffee and, obviously, beer—served from ultramodern, individually chilled, tailor-made taps.

Rhône
63 Gansevoort St between Greenwich and Washington Sts (212-367-8440). Subway: A, C, E to 14th St; L to Eighth Ave. Mon–Sat 6pm–4am. Average drink: $8. AmEx, MC, V.
Rhône, housed in an old garage, serves everything from an aged Côte-Rôtie to your everyday Côtes du Rhône (plus food). Thirty wines are served by the glass and 170 bottles appear on the menu.

▶ For more bar listings, see chapters **Cabaret & Comedy**, **Clubs**, **Gay & Lesbian** and **Music**.

▶ If you want an even larger selection of bar reviews, pick up a copy of the ***Time Out New York Eating & Drinking 2002 Guide***.

Union dues Drink too many single malts at the Lower East Side bar Local 138, and you'll pay for it the next morning.

The Scratcher
209 E 5th St between Bowery and Second Ave (212-477-0030). Subway: F, V to Lower East Side–Second Ave; 6 to Astor Pl. 11am–4am. Average drink: $5. Cash only.
If an Irishman says he's "in the scratcher," he's not in a good way—perhaps on the dole or headed for trouble. But if *you're* in the Scratcher, you must be having fun. This gregarious alehouse offers an endless supply of U.K. rebel tunes, Gaelic sports papers and Guinness, always Guinness.

Suite 16
127 Eighth Ave between 16th and 17th Sts (212-627-1680). Subway: A, C, E to 14th St; L to Eighth Ave. 10pm–4am. Cover: $5–$20. Average drink: $10. AmEx, DC, Disc, MC, V.
Today's hot club could be tomorrow's deli, so to stay in play, this all-star bar cherry-picks the crowd for lively, luscious winners. Improve your chances by being on the right team (three babes, one guy, one celebrity) and wearing the uniform of the moment. The Andrew Kostas–designed space features plush banquettes, stocked minibars and no VIP zone. Spotted on the same night: Hugh Hefner, Derek Jeter and Mark Wahlberg.

Sway
305 Spring St between Greenwich and Hudson Sts (212-620-5220). Subway: C, E to Spring St; 1, 2 to Canal St. 10pm–4am. Average drink: $8. AmEx, DC, MC, V.
Sway is the kind of place where the velvet rope swings wide only when a gaggle of toasted models emerges from a limo at 2am. Still, it's worth check-

ing out, if only to pass out in the plush, mood-of-Morocco room.

Swift Hibernian Lounge

34 E 4th St between Bowery and Lafayette St (212-260-3600). Subway: F, V, S to Broadway–Lafayette St; 6 to Bleecker St. Noon–4am. Average drink: $5. AmEx, DC, Disc, MC, V.
The sign outside urges passersby to stop in for a "Swift one," but you'll want to stay awhile and nurse a pint at this inviting pub. There are 25 beers on tap, 75 in bottles, and lots of murals depicting scenes from the work of satirist Jonathan Swift.

Temple Bar

332 Lafayette St between Bleecker and Houston Sts (212-925-4242). Subway: F, V, S to Broadway–Lafayette St; 6 to Bleecker St. Mon–Thu 5pm–1am; Fri 5pm–2am; Sat 7pm–2am; Sun 7pm–midnight. Average drink: $9. AmEx, DC, MC, V.
Settle into a banquette with your young lovely and sip a strong Old Fashioned—swanky-panky is the rule at Temple Bar. The bar stocks a massive collection of vodkas from around the world, and there's an upper-crust nosh menu.

Von Bar

3 Bleecker St between Bowery and Elizabeth St (212-473-3039). Subway: F, V, S to Broadway–Lafayette St; 6 to Bleecker St. Sun–Wed 5pm–2am; Thu–Sat 5pm–4am. Average drink: $6. AmEx, MC, V.
Brother-and-sister owners Charles and Kaarin Von keep Von stocked with about 20 beers and 40 wines. Romance-seekers can slip past the end of the bar into the seductive second room.

White Horse Tavern

567 Hudson St at 11th St (212-989-3956). Subway: 1, 2 to Christopher St–Sheridan Sq. Sun–Thu 11am–2am; Fri, Sat 11am–4am. Average drink: $5. Cash only.
One night in 1953, Dylan Thomas announced, "I've had 18 straight whiskeys. I think that's the record," and passed out. He woke up the next day, went out for a few beers, and died. His final potation was served at the White Horse. Lovely.

Zum Schneider

107–109 Ave C at 7th St (212-598-1098). Subway: 6 to Astor Pl. Mon–Thu 6pm–2am; Fri, Sat noon–4am; Sun noon–2am. Average drink: $6. Cash only.
The buzz-cut bartender wears his lederhosen with a soccer shirt at Zum Schneider, while a black-turtle-necked smart set mingles with people who knock back mugs of Wartsteiner. Twelve German beers are on tap, and you can get German eats such as sausages—*natürlich.*

Midtown

Aubette

119 E 27th St between Park Ave South and Lexington Ave (212-686-5500). Subway: 6 to 28th St. Mon–Sat 5pm–4am. Average drink: $7. AmEx, MC, V.

If you're longing for that late-'80s industrial aesthetic, hoist yourself onto a barstool at Aubette, a pit stop for packs of pickup-minded young professionals.

Bar Demi

125½ E 17th St between Irving Pl and Third Ave (212-260-0900). Subway: L to Third Ave; N, Q, R, W, 4, 5, 6 to 14th St–Union Sq. Tue–Sat 6pm–midnight. Average drink: $10. AmEx, DC, MC, V.
Demi means "half" in French, but this pint-size charmer has the full measure of style and service. Located around the corner from its parent restaurant, Verbena, Bar Demi serves more than 75 wines and finger food from chef Diane Forley.

Campbell Apartment

Grand Central Terminal, off the West Balcony, 15 Vanderbilt Ave at 43rd St (212-953-0409). Subway: S, 4, 5, 6, 7 to 42nd St–Grand Central. Mon–Sat 3pm–11pm. Average drink: $12. AmEx, DC, Disc, MC, V.
From 1923 to 1941, this was the private office and salon of New York Central Railroad trustee John Campbell, and it was designed to resemble a 13th-century Florentine palazzo. The bar offers wine, champagne, single-malt Scotch and cigars to match the luxe environs.

Carnegie Club

156 W 56th St between Sixth and Seventh Aves (212-957-9676). Subway: F, N, Q, R, W to 57th St. Mon–Fri 4:30pm–1am; Sat 6pm–1am. Cover: $15 (Fri, Sat only). Average drink: $8.50. AmEx, DC, MC, V.
At the Carnegie Club, an inviting faux library makes for a warm spot on a cold block. Friday nights features smokin' biggish-band jazz.

Cellar Bar

The Bryant Park, 40 W 40th St between Fifth and Sixth Aves (212-642-2260). Subway: B, D, F, V to 42nd St; 7 to Fifth Ave. Mon 5:30pm–midnight; Tue–Sat 5:30pm–2am. Average drink: $12. AmEx, DC, Disc, MC, V.
At this hotel's stunning Mediterranean-style bar, you can lounge beneath vaulted ceilings and snack on appetizers from Ilo *(see page 177).* The house cocktails are tempting, too: Try the Razmopolitan, a cool raspberry-flavored vodka concoction.

Enoteca i Trulli

122 E 27th St between Park Ave South and Lexington Ave (212-481-7372). Subway: 6 to 28th St. Mon–Thu noon–10:30pm; Fri noon–11pm; Sat 5–11pm. Average drink: $8.50. AmEx, MC, V.
This wine bar, attached to i Trulli, is a calm retreat. The long list features many Italian vintages, and there are plenty of cheeses to pair with your vino.

The Ginger Man

11 E 36th St between Fifth and Madison Aves (212-532-3740). Subway: B, D, F, V, N, Q, R, W to 34th St–Herald Sq; 6 to 33rd St. Mon–Wed 11:30am–2am; Thu, Fri 11:30am–4am; Sat 12:30pm–4am; Sun 3pm–midnight Average drink: $6. AmEx, DC, MC, V.

Named after a J.P. Donleavy novel, the Ginger Man boasts the kind of extensive beer menu that makes brew geeks giddy and "gimme-a-Bud" guys nervous.

Jimmy's Corner

140 W 44th St between Broadway and Sixth Ave (212-221-9510). Subway: B, D, F, V to 42nd St; N, Q, R, W, S, 1, 2, 3, 7 to 42nd St–Times Sq. 11am–4am. Average drink: $3.50. AmEx, Disc, MC, V.

Any bar with a TV can be a sports bar, but Jimmy's is something rarer and more specialized: a *boxing* bar. Old photos of the greats and posters of fights past cover the walls, and the regulars are punch-drunk.

King Cole Bar

St. Regis Hotel, 2 E 55th St between Fifth and Madison Aves (212-339-6721). Subway: E, V to Fifth Ave–53rd St. Mon–Thu 11:30am–1am; Fri, Sat 11:30am–2am; Sun noon–midnight. Average drink: $14. AmEx, DC, Disc, MC, V.

The King Cole bartenders know how to pour a drink: No need to ask for lots of ice in your Stoli-rocks— they just know. Leather club chairs and the famous Maxfield Parrish mural constitute the decor. The Bloody Mary was reputedly born here; it's referred to by its original name, the Red Snapper.

Landmark Tavern

626 Eleventh Ave at 46th St (212-757-8595). Subway: A, C, E to 42nd St–Port Authority. Mon–Thu noon–11pm; Fri, Sat noon–11:30pm; Sun noon–3:30pm, 5–11pm. Average drink: $6.50. AmEx, DC, Disc, MC, V.

The Landmark hasn't changed much during its 134-year history. Sit in the dark rear dining room and stuff yourself with starchy grub and a pint of Murphy's, or one of the 80 single-malt Scotches.

Metro Grill

Hotel Metro, 45 W 35th St between Fifth and Sixth Aves (212-947-2500). Subway: B, D, F, V, N, Q, R, W to 34th St–Herald Sq. 11am–midnight. Roof open 5:30–10pm. Average drink: $7. AmEx, DC, MC, V.

You can't get out of bed these days without stumbling into a new hotel that hasn't been designed by Philippe Starck. This one has one of the best outdoor bars in the city.

Bottoms up!

If you're looking for a high time on the Lower East Side, just pick a watering hole and go with the flow

LES stands for "Lower East Side," but it might as well mean "Lushes on Every Street." The neighborhood contains dozens of bars: some sleek, some shabby; some featuring flashy mixologists, others manned (and wo-manned) by defiant barkeeps waving the beer-and-shots banner. Pick your poison: It's your call, all the way to last call.

Three main subway stations service the LES; the following bars are closest to the F and V lines' Lower East Side–Second Avenue stop. **Angel** (*174 Orchard St between Houston and Stanton Sts, 212-780-0313*) is a great date place, offering curvy couches (ideal for confidential canoodling), not to mention DJs perched in loftlike hideouts. The DJs rule a roost of their own at **Bar-B** (*188 Allen St between Houston and Stanton Sts, no phone*), where a fun crowd of ethnically diverse rhythm slaves can't get enough of the hip-hop and rock. The music also motivates hips and tushies at **bOb** (*see page 270*), a cramped DJ bar that features some of the best outlaw dance action around. Rest your fatigued feet in a first-class aisle seat at **Idlewild** (*145 E Houston between First and Second Aves, 212-477-5005*), named for the airport that became JFK. Designed to look like a jet airliner, this theme lounge's cocktail waitresses even dress (sort of) like stewardesses. At **Kush** (*183 Orchard St between Houston and Stanton Sts, 212-677-7328*), the theme is resolutely Middle Eastern, putting you in the mood with arch-heavy Moorish decor, hookahs and a bar menu that includes stuffed grape leaves and hummus. **The Living Room** (*84 Stanton St at Allen St, 212-533-7235*) is an aptly named lounge zone furnished with macramé plant hangers and scroll-back kitchen chairs; it also hosts regular performances by local acoustic-guitar troubadours. **Ludlow Bar** (*165 Ludlow St between Houston and Stanton Sts, 212-353-0536*) is a basement-level bar where a mixed crowd gathers on the weekends, united in its love for ill beats and dirty dancing. At the top of the Ludlow strip lies the **Luna Lounge** (*171 Ludlow St between Houston and Stanton Sts, 212-260-2323*), a sure bet for cheap live entertainment any night of the week. **Max Fish** (*178 Ludlow St between Houston and Stanton Sts, 212-529-3959*) is the grandpappy of the Ludlow scene, a second home to rockers and their acolytes for more

Oak Bar

The Plaza Hotel, 768 Fifth Ave at 59th St (212-546-5320). Subway: N, R, W to Fifth Ave–60th St. Mon–Sat 11:30am–1:30am; Sun 11:30am–midnight. Average drink: $10. AmEx, DC, Disc, MC, V.
Everett Shin painted the murals at the Oak Bar, the Plaza's true classic of a hotel bar. Sip a Roze's Tawny 40-year-old port, puff on a Montecristo Churchill cigar and take in the stodgy grandeur of the place: You're bending elbows in a room that was once a favorite of "Diamond" Jim Brady and George M. Cohan.

P.J. Clarke's

915 Third Ave at 55th St (212-759-1650). Subway: E, V to Lexington Ave–53rd St; 6 to 51st St. 11:30am–4am. Average drink: $5.50. AmEx, DC, MC, V.
The oak bar is as solid as a ship at this old timer, and the modest mugs of beer come cheap. The draw is Old New York—alive and open daily.

Rudy's Bar & Grill

627 Ninth Ave between 44th and 45th Sts (212-974-9169). Subway: A, C, E to 42nd St–Port Authority. 8am–4am. Average drink: $3. Cash only.
At Rudy's, the $3 well drinks are strong, the booths are patched with tape, and the resident drunks are merry and friendly. The bar's enduring greatness is not, however, attributable to the wieners occupying the bar stools but to the ones roasting on the grill—you get them free with a drink purchase.

Serena

Chelsea Hotel, 222 W 23rd St between Seventh and Eighth Aves (212-255-4646). Subway: C, E, 1, 2 to 23rd St. Mon–Fri 6pm–4am; Sat, Sun 8pm–4am. Average drink: $8. AmEx, MC, V.
Moderately stylish young things gather here to drink pricey martinis in one of the subterranean club's three rooms, each done up with mirrors and a phenomenal lighting scheme.

Siberia

356 W 40th St between Eighth and Ninth Aves (212-333-4141). Subway: A, C, E to 42nd St–Port Authority. 3pm–4am. Average drink: $4. Cash only.
Forced out of its former subway-station space, Siberia owner Tracy Westmoreland moved his bar to this signless, windowless street-level location next to the Port Authority. He continues to enforce the no-swearing, no-hitting-on-chicks rules.

than a decade—and the juke rules. In business for a dozen years, **Orchard Bar** *(200 Orchard St between Houston and Stanton Sts, 212-673-5350)* is a discreet joint with no signage, so look for the window display that looks like an uninhabited terrarium. **Sapphire** *(see page 268)* is one of the only DJ bars in the neighborhood where dancing is legit, having taken the trouble to obtain a cabaret license. Sapphire paved the way for places like the **Slipper Room** *(167 Orchard St at Stanton St, 212-253-7246)*, which has won over doubters with its offbeat, slightly bawdy character. Big draws include the motley "Bump and Grind" Thursday event. Drink it in.

The Delancey Street F stop and the Essex Street stop on the J, M and Z lines are within stumbling distance of their own assortment of bars and clubs. **Barramundi** *(147 Ludlow St between Rivington and Stanton Sts, 212-529-6900)* is long on seats and short on pretension, and it has one of the best courtyard gardens on the Lower East Side. **The Infrared Lounge** *(210 Rivington St between Pitt and Ridge Sts, 212-254-5043)* is a low-key joint lit with an appropriate dull red glow. Snuggle with your honey at one of the "snugs" (booths) at **Local 138** *(138 Ludlow St between Rivington and Stanton Sts, 212-477-0280)*. This Irish pub's draws are a low tolerance for snootiness and a high one for whiskey shots, followed by pints of Newcastle. Your LES health regime includes

pounding a few more pints at the **Lotus Club** *(35 Clinton St at Stanton St, 212-253-1144)*, a veggie-sandwich outpost that also happens to pour a mean Guinness. The vibe is a touch more rarefied at **Milk & Honey** *(134 Eldridge St between Broome and Delancey Sts)*, a stylish drinkery where you must make a reservation at least 20 minutes before you show up. The ever-changing phone number makes that a challenging, but worthwhile, proposition. You won't have to jump through hoops to drink at nearby **Motor City Bar** *(127 Ludlow St between Delancey and Rivington Sts, 212-358-1595)*, an automotive-themed scuzzhole where you must make a reservation at least 20 minutes before you *throw up*. You can further drown yourself in drink at **Swim** *(146 Orchard St between Rivington and Stanton Sts, 212-673-0799)*, whose decor appears to have come straight from the Salvation Army. Or you can get soused in an old wine cask at **Tonic** *(see page 310)*, a jazz club housed in a former kosher winery (hence the casks, which are in the cellar lounge). It's a welcoming environment, but not as welcoming as…**Welcome to the Johnsons** *(123 Rivington St between Essex and Norfolk Sts, 212-420-9911)*, whose many fine touches include $1.50 cans of that lowbrow American brew, Pabst Blue Ribbon. That's a good thing, because after visiting 20 bars, you'll surely be running short on cash.

Tiki Room

4 W 22nd St between Fifth and Sixth Aves (646-230-1444). Subway: N, R to 23rd St. Mon–Fri 5pm–4am, Sat 6pm–4am. Average drink: $8. AmEx, DC, MC, V.
Tiki Room is a lush lounge where you can sip Honolulu Hangovers and Sneaky Tikis, and munch on skewers of goat cheese and watermelon. Rising through the center of the bar is an 18-foot tiki idol.

Villard Bar & Lounge

New York Palace Hotel, 455 Madison Ave between 50th and 51st Sts (212-869-9397). Subway: N, Q, R, W, S, 1, 2, 3, 7 to 42nd St–Time Sq. 11am–4am. Cover: $5 (Fri, Sat after 10pm). Average drink: $8. AmEx, MC, V.
This cluster of luxurious rooms in the New York Palace Hotel is where you can indulge yourself with a $500 glass of Hardy Perfection cognac. An $8 Jack Daniels works just fine, too.

Uptown

The Bar@Etats-Unis

247 E 81st St between Second and Third Aves (212-396-9928). Subway: 6 to 77th St. Mon–Sat noon–midnight. Average drink: $10. AmEx, DC, MC, V.
The aroma of herbs and olives in the tiny Etats-Unis wine bar will lull you, spa-style, into sweet anticipation—and the long wine list will surely inspire you to sip something new.

The Boat Basin Café

79th St at the Hudson River (212-496-5542). Subway: 1, 2 to 79th St. May–Sept Mon–Fri noon–10:30pm; Sat, Sun 11am–11:30pm. Average drink: $5.50. AmEx, MC, V.
Sip a Corona while you check out the boats in their slips at this outdoor spot along the Hudson River. The place can be packed during peak after-work hours, but is still a fun place to pop a few tops.

Broadway Dive

2662 Broadway between 101st and 102nd Sts (212-865-2662). Subway: 1 to 103rd St. Noon–4am. Average drink: $4. AmEx, MC, V.
A boar's head hangs on the wall and strings of Christmas lights illuminate the way at Broadway Dive. Cretinous trappings aside, taking the plunge is actually pretty fun.
Other locations ● *Dive 75, 101 W 75th St at Columbus Ave (212-362-7518). Subway: B, C, 1, 2, 3 to 72nd St. Mon–Fri 5pm–4am; Sat, Sun noon–4am. Average drink: $5. AmEx, MC, V. ●* *732 Amsterdam Ave between 95th and 96th Sts (212-749-4358). Subway: 1, 2, 3 to 96th St. Mon–Sat 11:30am–4am; Sun noon–4am. Average drink: $4. AmEx, DC, Disc, MC, V.*

Cannon's Pub

2794 Broadway at 108th St (212-678-9783). Subway: 1 to 110th St–Cathedral Pkwy. Mon–Sat 11am–4am; Sun noon–4am. Average drink: $4. AmEx, V.
Cannon's is an Irish place where the TVs are terminally tuned to The Game. But it's not an overwhelming testoster-zone; the gender ratio isn't a disgrace, and female bartenders dress with dignity. Even the Columbia undergrads who pack the place on weekends can't kill the neighborhood-bar vibe.

The Cocktail Room

334 E 73rd St between First and Second Aves (212-988-6100). Subway: 6 to 77th St. Sun–Wed 5pm–2am; Thu, Fri 5pm–4am; Sat 7pm–4am. Average drink: $7. AmEx, MC, V.
South Beach meets Target at this Upper East Side bar, where under-30 females arrive straight from the tanning salon to sip colorful cocktails out of some of the tallest glasses in the known universe.

The Ding Dong Lounge

929 Columbus Ave between 105th and 106th Sts (212-663-2600). Subway: 1 to 103rd St. 4pm–4am. Average drink: $4.50. Cash only.
In early 2001, punk rock arrived on the Upper West Side in the form of the Ding Dong Lounge. Mere months after opening, the owners took over the adjacent space and started hosting live shows.

Fez/Up Over the Time Cafe

2330 Broadway at 85th St (212-579-5100). Subway: 1, 2 to 86th St. Sun–Thu 6pm–2am; Fri, Sat 6pm–4am. Cover $8–$18. Average drink: $6. AmEx, MC, V.
This site went through several rehabs before emerging as the uptown Time/Fez complex. Reversing the downtown arrangement, this Fez is upstairs and feels like EPCOT Center's idea of a Casablanca bordello—red-tasseled lamps, paintings of Moroccan pop stars and a gorgeous waitstaff.

Hogs & Heifers North

1843 First Ave at 95th St (212-722-8635). Subway: 6 to 96th St. Tue–Sat 4pm–4am. Average drink: $5. Cash only.
See page 145.

Lenox Lounge

See page 311.

Saints

992 Amsterdam Ave at 109th St (212-961-0599). Subway: B, C, 1 to 110th St–Cathedral Pkwy. 5pm–4am. Average drink: $5. AmEx, MC, V.
Saints is one of the city's few ecumenical queer bars. Men and women of all sexual preferences, ages, races, neighborhood affiliations and classes mingle: femme undergrads, butch telephone-repair broads, libidinous senior citizens. The mood is set by R&B, funk and throbbing electro-dance sounds.

Soha

988 Amsterdam Ave between 108th and 109th Sts (212-678-0098). Subway: 1 to 110th St–Cathedral Pkwy. 4pm–4am. Average drink: $4.50. AmEx, MC, V.
This spacious bar-lounge sets the tone at chill, using inspired lighting and the hypnotic sounds of funk and R&B to keep both Columbia students and unmatriculated locals grooving.

Booze views The rooftop bar at midtown's Metro Grill has one of the best vistas in town.

Subway Inn
143 E 60th St between Lexington and Third Aves (212-223-8929). Subway: F to Lexington Ave–63rd St; N, R, W to Lexington Ave–59th St; 4, 5, 6 to 59th St. 8am–4am. Average drink: $3. Cash only.
Hidden in plain sight on a busy NYC street, this dark and stinky sanctuary is perfect for dropping in and enjoying a cheap one. Or two. Or three. Or four.

Time Out
349 Amsterdam Ave between 76th and 77th Sts (212-362-5400). Subway: B, C to 81st St; 1, 2 to 79th St. Mon–Fri 5pm–4am; Sat, Sun noon–4am. Average drink: $4.50. AmEx, DC, Disc, MC, V.
Time Out the bar is everything *Time Out* isn't: Whereas we're quiet and thoughtful, this sports bar (28 TVs!) is loud and chaotic. Of course, everyone at both places is completely crocked.

Brooklyn

Angry Wade's
224 Smith St at Butler St, Cobble Hill (718-488-7253). Subway: F, G to Bergen St. Mon–Fri 3pm–4am; Sat, Sun noon–4am. Average drink: $4. AmEx, MC, V.
This is one of the best places in Brooklyn to get a pint of Guinness. Green banquettes further the Eire feeling, but the classic-rock jukebox is pure Americana.

Enid's
560 Manhattan Ave at Driggs Ave, Greenpoint (718-349-3859). Subway: G to Nassau Ave. Sun–Wed 5pm–2am; Thu–Sat 5pm–4am. Average drink: $5. Cash only.

The Williamsburg-artist species has been threatened with extinction, now that its natural habitat—cheap warehouse space—is being snatched by encroaching Manhattanites. Luckily, Enid's has retained its laid-back atmosphere and, consequently, its regulars.

Excelsior
390 Fifth Ave between 6th and 7th Sts, Park Slope, Brooklyn (718-832-1599). Subway: F, M, N, R to Fourth Ave–9th St. Mon–Fri 6pm–4am; Sat, Sun 2pm–4am. Average drink: $5. Cash only.
This Park Slope gay-and-lesbian mainstay features great tap beers (Boddington's, Guinness, Stella), a juke jammed with Hank Williams and the Sex Pistols, and tasty, if tastelessly named, specialty drinks. The Jackmeoff is made with Absolut Citron, Chambourd and pineapple juice. Yummy.

Galapagos
See page 305 for listing.
This former mayonnaise factory sure looks good: You enter via a spooky, darkly lit catwalk, traversing an 800-square-foot antechamber flooded with water. Count on an assortment of DJs and live bands (average drink is $6).

Moe's
80 Lafayette Ave at South Portland Ave, Fort Greene (718-797-9536). Subway: G to Clinton–Washington Aves; M, N, Q, R to DeKalb Ave. 6pm–3:30am. Average drink: $6. Cash only.
This split-level space mixes retro (vinyl stools) and contemporary (a snaking light box inlaid with Japanese rice paper). As for the name: "We wanted something that wasn't pretentious," says co-owner Ruby Lawrence. *Simpsons* fans would approve.

Quench
282 Smith St between Sackett and Union Sts, Carroll Gardens (718-875-1500). Subway: F, G to Carroll St. Mon–Fri 5:30pm–4am; Sat, Sun 4pm–4am. Average drink: $5. Cash only.
At Quench, round light fixtures hang like enormous moons; diffuse orange gels are built into an endless cherry-wood bar; and high-backed, boalike banquettes complete the space's runway vibe. Serious swillers down single-malt Scotch while their lightweight counterparts indulge in designer drinks.

Sparky's Ale House
481 Court St at Nelson St, Carroll Gardens (718-624-5516). Subway: F, G to Smith–9th Sts. Mon 4pm–2am; Tue–Sat 4pm–4am; Sun 12:30pm–2am. Average drink: $4. Cash only.
Sparky's is a popular neighborhood bar where you can choose from a rotating selection of about 30 tap brews, 100-plus bottles and a dozen wines.

> ► For more about Brooklyn nightlife, see chapter **Night Train to Brooklyn**.

Necessities

Restaurants

What's your pleasure—a divey diner for burgers or a posh palace for haute cuisine? New York has plenty of both and lots in between.

Restaurants are central to everyday New York life. Where you eat has a lot to do with how you like, or can afford, to live. To satisfy the spectrum of cravings, there is all manner of eating to be done in New York. Where else can you order Australian kangaroo for lunch, then turn the corner and snack on Italian prosciutto or Malaysian beef jerky?

And if New Yorkers can't find what they want in their own borough, they hop on the subway to another. In fact, food is often a primary motive for exploring unfamiliar corners of the city. The burning desire to try the famous *panelles* (deep-fried chickpea cakes) at Joe's of Avenue U *(see page 94)* will prompt even a staunch Manhattanite to journey to Brooklyn. So do like the locals do, and let your taste buds lead the way to century-old diners and brand-new haute spots.

To snare a table at one of the city's premier eateries, you'll often need to reserve weeks in advance (and then settle for a table at 5:30 or 10pm). We recommend booking ahead at the restaurants listed in the critics' picks boxes **Iron chefs** *(see page 168)* and **Landmarks** *(see page 177)*. Many smaller restaurants and bistros operate on a first-come, first-served basis, and you may have to wait at a crowded bar (or out on the street if there isn't a bar). It's generally a good idea to call ahead and check to see if the place that was sizzling last week is still serving the same kind of food we describe…or is even in business.

Establishments are organized by geography for your convenience. To find restaurants by categories, see the index on page 191. And remember, tipping is a must at New York restaurants *(see **Tax and tipping**, page 161).*

Downtown

Financial District

American Park at the Battery

Battery Park, State St at Water St (212-809-5508). Subway: N, R to Whitehall St; 4, 5 to Bowling Green. Mon–Fri 11am–3pm, 5–10pm; Sat 5–10pm; Sun 11am–3pm. Average main course: $25. AmEx, DC, Disc, MC, V.
A former Battery Park maintenance building at the southern tip of Manhattan, American Park now attracts upscale Wall Streeters. If the weath-

er is even remotely nice, bankers and tourists sit as close to the water as possible (the outdoor terrace gets them pretty damn close), taking in the view of the Statue of Liberty as they get filled to the gills on seafood (though there are entrées such as lamb shank).

Bayard's

1 Hanover Sq between Pearl and Stone Sts (212-514-9454). Subway: 1, 2 to Wall St. Mon–Sat 5:30–10:30pm. Bar 4:30pm–midnight. Average main course: $32. AmEx, DC, MC, V.
Housed in an Italianate 1851 mansion, Bayard's imposing, Gilded Age–style men's club of a room is as disconnected from Wall Street's hustle as a Merchant Ivory movie. (By day, Bayard's is the members-only India Club.) The good news: Here's a great New York restaurant where you can have a quiet conversation and always get a seat. Bayard's vegetables come direct from executive chef Eberhard Müller's Long Island farm, and he uses them in creative American dishes that tend to be unfussy—the better to showcase the flavors of choice ingredients.

Bridge Cafe

279 Water St at Dover St (212-227-3344). Subway: A, C to Broadway–Nassau St; J, M, Z, 1, 2, 4, 5 to Fulton St. Sun, Mon 11:45am–10pm; Tue–Fri 11:45am–midnight; Sat 5pm–midnight. Average main course: $19. AmEx, DC, MC, V.
Lower Manhattan's oldest wooden building (built in 1794) is the weathered setting for the Bridge Cafe's American Creative bistro cuisine. Despite the culinary-school polish, there's a lot of charm and no pretension at this old-timer under the Brooklyn Bridge.

Les Halles Downtown

15 John St between Broadway and Nassau St (212-285-8585). Subway: A, C to Broadway–Nassau St; J, M,

► For reviews of the newest restaurants, see the Eat Out section of *Time Out New York*.
► The *Time Out New York Eating & Drinking 2002 Guide* has more than 3,000 reviews of restaurants and bars; it's on sale at newsstands and bookstores around the city.
► To find the best restaurants that serve your favorite kind of food, check out **Restaurants by cuisine**, page 191.

Z, 1, 2, 4, 5 to Fulton St. Noon–midnight. Average main course: $19. AmEx, DC, MC, V.
See page 172.

Ruben's Empanadas
15 Bridge St between Broad and Whitehall Sts (212-509-3825). Subway: N, R to Whitehall St; 4, 5 to Bowling Green. Mon–Fri 7am–5pm. Average empanada: $3. Cash only. ● 64 Fulton St between Cliff and Gold Sts (212-962-5330). Subway: A, C to Broadway–Nassau St; J, M, Z, 1, 2, 4, 5 to Fulton St. Mon–Fri 8am–7pm; Sat noon–7pm. Average empanada: $3. Cash only.
See page 161.

Sophie's Restaurant
73 New St between Beaver St and Exchange Pl (212-809-7755). Subway: 4, 5 to Bowling Green. Mon–Fri 11am–4pm. Average main course: $7. AmEx, Disc, MC, V.
Sophie Luna has created her own Little Havana in the Financial District with her popular trio of Cuban restaurants. The crowds that wait to take out or eat in are proof that Wall Streeters are starved for cheap ethnic cooking. The huge portions of Cuban classics come with bear-market prices.
Other locations ● *205 Pearl St between Maiden Ln and Platt St (212-809-7755). Subway: 1, 2 to Wall St. Mon–Fri 11am–4pm. Average main course: $7. AmEx, Disc, MC, V. ● 106 Greenwich St between Carlisle and Rector Sts (212-385-0909). Subway: 1, 2 to Wall St. Mon–Fri 11am–4pm. Average main course: $7. AmEx, MC, V.*

Tribeca

Bubby's
120 Hudson St at North Moore St (212-219-0666). Subway: 1, 2 to Franklin St. Mon–Fri 8am–11pm; Sat, Sun 9am–11pm. Average main course: $13. AmEx, DC, Disc, MC, V.
This Tribeca mainstay shares the spotlight with a number of celebs (such as neighborhood resident Harvey Keitel) who fancy its robust American cuisine. Bubby's is jammed for brunch: A crowd waits rain or shine for Eggsadilla (scrambled eggs with a mess of Mexican stuff) and Belgian waffles with bananas and strawberries. For dinner, the homey restaurant is less busy, mainly attracting locals. The plump roasted chicken with macaroni and cheese (so creamy, it's served with a spoon) upstages the famous clientele.

Danube
30 Hudson St at Duane St (212-791-3771). Subway: A, C, 1, 2 to Chambers St. 11:30am–3pm, 5:30–11:30pm. Average main course: $35. Five-course prix fixe: $80. AmEx, DC, MC, V.
The Klimt-style paintings on the walls of Danube's triangular dining room are a hint: You *are* going to swoon—over David Bouley's fantastic dream of Austrian cuisine. Sumptuous lacquered murals, black wood trim and divinely smooth lavender-suede couches help you (and the tastefully attired business types in the dining room) suspend disbe-

lief that one of the most respected chefs of our time is offering Wiener schnitzel every night. Bouley's earthy breaded veal cutlet is one of the menu's best choices. If French is more your style, then plan far enough in advance to get a table at **Bouley Bakery** *(120 West Broadway at Duane St, 212-964-2525).*

The Harrison
353 Greenwich St at Harrison St (212-274-9310). Subway: 1, 2 to Franklin St. Mon–Thu 5:30–11pm; Fri, Sat 5:30–11:30pm; Sun 5:30–10pm. Average main course: $22. AmEx, DC, MC, V.
The Harrison owners, Jimmy Bradley and Danny Abrams, seem to have a fondness for names that sound more like boutique hotels than restaurants. (The duo also owns the Red Cat in Chelsea; *see page 170.*) The elegant interior at the Harrison features white wainscoted walls and brown leather banquettes; the menu has its international moments *(cavatelli* with braised veal cheeks, house-cured *bresaola* on Taleggio toasts, but you'll also find homey fare (chicken with mashed potatoes, shell steak).

Le Zinc
139 Duane St between Church St and West Broadway (212-513-0001). Subway: A, C, 1, 2 to Chambers St. Noon–4am. Average main course: $15. AmEx, DC, Disc, MC, V.
The restaurant's dominating zinc bar is a downtown trendsetter magnet, and the menu is David Waltuck's version of comfort food—an amalgam of French, Asian and American cuisines. The kitchen's at its strongest with classic bistro items, such as the housemade charcuterie and skate with brown butter and capers; the entrées look like your mother plated them. If you're up for it, you can try something more creative, such as Asian-Cajun catfish in ginger-scallion sauce.

Nobu
105 Hudson St at Franklin St (212-219-0500). Subway: 1, 2 to Franklin St. Mon–Fri 11:45am–2:15pm, 5:45–10:15pm; Sat, Sun 5:45–10:15pm. Average hot dish: $16. AmEx, DC, MC, V.
Nobu is the stuff of food lore—it's the most famous Japanese restaurant in America, the place that has no qualms about making you wait a month for a table (unless, of course, you're Gwyneth Paltrow). But here's some heartening news: Instead of setting the phone on speed dial just to reach the reservation line, simply show up. The official house policy is to seat those sans reservation at the sushi bar on a first-come, first-served basis. And it's possible to nab a table due to a last-minute cancellation. The kitchen continues to turn out masterpieces from Japan-by-way-of-Peru. Even the superprofessional waiters will tell you to forgo sushi and concentrate on the chef's small-dish marvels, such as the signature black cod with miso. At Nobu, substance is never sacrificed for style; and you can taste the good life with disposable chopsticks. Next Door Nobu doesn't accept reservations, so while you have to wait, you can be assured of at least getting in.
Other location ● *Next Door Nobu, 105 Hudson St at Franklin St (212-334-4445). Subway: 1, 2 to*

What's the frequency? Locate Mexican Radio at the edge of Little Italy—the tasty eats here aren't just one-hit wonders.

Franklin St. Average sushi meal (8 pieces, 1 roll): $42. AmEx, DC, MC, V.

Odeon

145 West Broadway between Duane and Thomas Sts (212-233-0507). Subway: A, C, 1, 2 to Chambers St. Mon–Thu 11:45am–2am; Fri 11:45am–3am; Sat 11am–3am; Sun 11am–2am. Average main course: $18. AmEx, DC, Disc, MC, V.

The staying power of this legendary Tribeca temple of bistro dining can be attributed to the fact that nothing much changes. For dinner, get the famous steak frites or the familiar roasted free-range chicken and a country garden salad that remains the benchmark by which all other frisée-and-*lardon* mixes are judged. Odeon's art-snob days of Julian Schnabel and *Bright Lights, Big City* may be gone, but when hip-hopper Mos Def strolls in with a foxy lady and grabs a booth, you know the Odeon still has star power—even at brunch.

Lower East Side

aKa Café

49 Clinton St between Rivington and Stanton Sts (212-979-6096). Subway: F, V to Lower East Side–Second Ave. 10:30am–midnight. Average sandwich: $7. AmEx, Disc, MC, V.

aKa Café is one of the most recent arrivals on Clinton Street's restaurant boomlet. The menu is a short list of sophisticated but bargain-priced soups, salads, empanadas and sandwiches. The ceviche of fluke and Scotch bonnet peppers is a knockout.

Congee Village

100 Allen St between Broome and Delancey Sts (212-941-1818). Subway: F to Delancey St; J, M, Z to

Delancey–Essex Sts. 10:30am–midnight. Average main course: $8. AmEx, Disc, MC, V.

There is no bad food at Congee Village. Just about every dish served in this bamboo grotto (complete with plastic vines) is utterly sublime, each seemingly better than the last. The congee, a thick, soupy porridge of rice gruel, can play host to a variety of ingredients, as in the "three-meat version" of pork, chicken and duck. Seafood choices range from whole fish to razor clams. Uninitiated diners might squirm at some of the menu items—pig intestines, steamed fish heads and boiled-live shrimp—but most of the food is accessible.

Katz's Delicatessen

205 E Houston St at Ludlow St (212-254-2246). Subway: F, V to Lower East Side–Second Ave. Sun–Tue 8am–10pm; Wed, Thu 8am–11pm; Fri, Sat 8am–3am. Pastrami sandwich: $9.35. AmEx, MC, V (for catering and shipping only).

This cavernous old dining hall at the invisible portal to the Lower East Side is one of those timeless, unassailable living-history places. Grab a ticket and approach the long station-to-station counter. First, a hot dog. The all-beef crisp-skinned weenies are without peer. Then order your legendarily shareable sandwich. Roast beef goes quickly (steer clear of the late-evening remains). The brisket rates. And the pastrami is the best. Your server will slice you a sample while he carves the hot, juicy hunk of pink meat. For a real New York drink, have a Dr. Brown's soda.

Oliva

161 E Houston St at Allen St (212-228-4143). Subway: F, V to Lower East Side–Second Ave. Sun–Thu 11:30am–3:30pm, 5:30pm–midnight; Fri, Sat 11:30am–3:30pm, 5:30pm–1am. Average main course: $17. AmEx.

The pitchers of sangria are set up early on Oliva's bar, in anticipation of the crush of beautiful blonds and stubbled downtown dudes; and they arrive on schedule (after 9pm). If you come earlier, you can easily get a table and take in the hip, slightly low-rent retro decor before the crowd starts making demands on the kitchen and drowning out conversation. The mostly traditional Basque cuisine is worth a try. The *pintxos* platter is a good sampler of tapaslike selections, and you can choose from a wide range of seafood dishes. When all else fails, there's the familiar filet mignon au poivre.

Paladar

161 Ludlow St between Houston and Stanton Sts (212-473-3535). Subway: F, V to Lower East Side–Second Ave. Sun–Wed 5:30–11:30pm; Thu–Sat 5:30pm–2am. Average main course: $13. Cash only.

Aaron Sanchez, son of restaurateur Zarela Martínez, has brought his Cuban kitchen chops to the Lower East Side with Paladar, a funky, pastel eatery. As consulting chef, Sanchez has created *nuevo* takes on spicy standards, including a ceviche of tangy sea bass and scallops and pan-seared salmon with chayote and

sweet-potato *picadillo* in a saffron-corn sauce. His coconut flan is intoxicating.

Chinatown–Little Italy

Canton
45 Division St between Bowery and Market St (212-226-4441). Subway: F to East Broadway. Sun, Wed, Thu noon–10pm; Fri, Sat noon–11pm. Average main course: $20. Cash only.
Owner Eileen Leong may stop you at the door and insist that you look at a menu before she lets you sit down. She wants you to understand two things: This will not be a budget evening, and she doesn't take credit cards. Canton's short menu of sweet-and-sour standards is a smoke screen. The real menu is mostly in the chef's head; he cooks by the season, using the day's fresh ingredients. For the main course, yield to Leong's suggestions: Her "best" chicken is pieces of golden-brown meat flavored with scallions and ginger.

Goody's
1 East Broadway at Chatham Sq (212-577-2922). Subway: F to East Broadway. Mon–Fri 11:30am–10:30pm; Sat, Sun 11am–10:30pm. Average main course: $13. AmEx, Disc, MC, V.
Goody's has a full menu of decent Shanghai grub, but you'll barely remember what else you ordered once you bite into the little water-balloonlike crab-and-pork steamed buns (a.k.a. soup dumplings). Follow the cartoon directions underneath the table glass, or you might squirt hot, tangy broth across it. Don't panic once they're gone—you can always order more.

Grand Sichuan
125 Canal St at Bowery (212-625-9212). Subway: S to Grand St. 11am–10:30pm. Average main course: $11. Cash only.
See **Grand Sichuan International Midtown**, page 179.

Le Jardin Bistro
25 Cleveland Pl between Kenmare and Spring Sts (212-343-9599). Subway: 6 to Spring St. Noon–3pm, 6–11:30pm. Average main course: $19. AmEx, DC, Disc, MC, V.
This Nolita bistro is a restaurant for all seasons. When snow falls, regulars line the front room's banquettes, digging into hearty cassoulet and checking themselves out in the mirrors. But when spring appears, the place blossoms: The magical garden, lined with lush, curling vines, is the perfect place for wooing. Young French waiters may enjoy a laugh at your expense, but they're a good-natured bunch, always ready to let you close down the place. And that's not hard to do, especially when you're lingering over specialties such as tournedos Rossini, a rosy filet mignon topped with shaved black truffle and a generous slice of seared foie gras.

Lombardi's
32 Spring St between Mott and Mulberry Sts (212-941-7994). Subway: 6 to Spring St. Mon–Thu 11:30am–
11pm; Fri, Sat 11:30am–midnight; Sun 11:30am–10pm. Large plain pizza: $13.50. Cash only.*
Lombardi's endures as a pizza legend because its uniqueness is not overbearing. The famed coal-burning brick oven turns out hot slices of thin, charred-crust pizza, topped with gentle sauce made from San Marzano tomatoes and farm-fresh mozzarella and pecorino. Pizza may not be a panacea, but a slice of Lombardi's sure makes you feel better.

Mexican Radio
19 Cleveland Pl between Kenmare and Spring Sts (212-343-0140). Subway: 6 to Spring St. Noon–11:30pm. Average main course: $12. AmEx, Disc, MC, V.
There's a comforting familiarity to Radio's simple playlist of burritos, enchiladas, tacos and fajitas. For starters, Radio roll-ups rock: Each ingredient—black beans, delicate white cheese and fresh *pico de gallo*

CRITICS' PICKS Eat out

We think these are the best restaurants...

...for a dining epiphany
Craft, page 171

...for a tête-à-tête
Blue Hill (expensive), page 167, or Le Gamin Café (inexpensive), page 168

...to impress a client
The Four Seasons, page 180

...for grown-up grooviness
The Park, page 271

...for a big plate of cheese
Artisanal, page 174

...to take kids
Two Boots Restaurant, page 166

...to go with a large group
Ruby Foo's, page 178

...for postclubbing eats
Florent, page 168

...to eat and smoke
Casimir, page 163

...for brunch
Blue Ribbon Bakery, page 168

...for traditional sushi
Sushisay, page 181

...for outdoor seating
Sushi Samba, page 174

...if you're in Brooklyn
The Grocery, page 188

in a flour tortilla with tomatillo sauce—announces itself without screaming down your throat. The *carnitas*, zesty, soft citrus-marinated shredded pork with genuine, tangy barbecue flavor and refined heat, have the makings of a classic.

New Indonesia & Malaysia Restaurant

18 Doyers St between Bowery and Pell St (212-267-0088). Subway: J, M, Z, N, Q, R, W, 6 to Canal St. 10:30am–11pm. Average main course: $8. Cash only.
The best Malaysian and Indonesian food in the city is found here, at bargain prices. Head to the little boomerang of a street that is Doyers, and at No. 18, walk downstairs into the glare of fluorescent lights. In the kitchen are a guy from Kuala Lumpur and a guy from a tiny Indonesian island, and between them they cook the fragrant staple dishes of both places.

New York Noodle Town

28 Bowery at Bayard St (212-349-0923). Subway: J, M, Z, N, Q, R, W, 6 to Canal St. 9am–4am. Average main course: $9. Cash only.
Although the name would suggest otherwise, the specialty at this Cantonese joint is barbecued meat. As at other Chinatown restaurants, reddish-brown ducks, chickens, loins of pork and sides of crispy baby pig hang in the window—but these have a hard-to-find subtle flavor and succulence. (Arrive early for the suckling pig—this delicacy usually runs out by 8pm.) Noodles are available both wet (in fragrant broths augmented with dumplings) and dry (either panfried until crunchy or stir-fried with vegetables, meat or seafood). When in season, the salt-baked softshell crabs should not be missed.

Nha Trang

148 Centre St between Walker and White Sts (212-941-9292). Subway: J, M, Z, N, Q, R, W, 6 to Canal St. 10:30am–10pm. Average main course: $6. AmEx, MC, V.
At Nha Trang, the menu is huge, the prices dirt cheap and the service agreeable. No wonder the place is full even in the middle of the afternoon. The rice-noodle soup with beef in satay sauce is outstanding; it fills one person for the price of a McDonald's Value Meal. **Other location ●** *87 Baxter St between Walker and White Sts (212-233-5948, 212-962-9149). Subway: J, M, Z, N, Q, R, W, 6 to Canal St. 10am–10pm. Average main course: $7. Cash only.*

Nyonya

194 Grand St between Mott and Mulberry Sts (212-334-3669). Subway: S to Grand St. 11am–11:30pm. Average main course: $9. Cash only.
Part tiki bar, part school cafeteria, Nyonya's bustling atmosphere leaves no time for dawdling. Waiters take your order from the epic menu the minute you sit down, and the open kitchen churns it out almost as quickly. Your conversation will inevitably turn to what's placed before you, whether it's *poh piah* (fluffy steamed spring rolls stuffed with jicama) or a heaping plate of "aromatic crabs" (the crustaceans are cooked in a spicy lemon sauce). In case you're won-

dering, *nyonya* is an archaic term for "Mrs." that now denotes Sino-Malaysian cooking.

Ping's Restaurant

22 Mott St between Mosco and Pell Sts (212-602-9988). Subway: J, M, Z, N, Q, R, W, 6 to Canal St. Mon–Thu 10am–midnight; Fri, Sat 10am–2am; Sun 9am–midnight. Average main course: $11. AmEx, MC, V.
Subtlety is what elevates Ping's Chinese cuisine above the competition. Fresh seafood is the specialty—no surprise, given the tiered tanks of live fish and crustaceans near the door. The ginger-and-scallion lobster is a winner: Tender and pungent with finger-lickin' tanginess, it's easily picked out of the shell with a tiny fork. Even if you don't have the most adventurous palate, summon the courage to try chef-owner Chung Ping Hui's jellyfish appetizer, which balances just-right firmness with a fresh crunch.

Saint's Alp Teahouse

51 Mott St between Bayard and Canal Sts (212-766-9889). Subway: J, M, Z, N, Q, R, W, 6 to Canal St. Average tea: $3. Cash only.
See page 165.

Sosinna's

264 Bowery between Houston and Prince Sts (212-219-9602). Subway: N, R to Prince St; 6 to Spring St. Mon–Fri 8am–11pm; Sat, Sun 11am–11pm. Average main course: $12. AmEx, MC, V.
Someone always has to be first, says owner Sosinna Degefu of her cozy eatery, sandwiched between restaurant-supply stores on the culinary wasteland that is the Bowery. This native of Ethiopia, whose parents own **Ghenet** *(284 Mulberry St between Houston and Prince Sts, 212-343-1888)*, serves Afro-Latin cuisine, which fuses the fiery flavors of Ethiopia and Senegal with tropical notes from the Caribbean and Latin America. The full bar is an extra enticement.

Vietnam Restaurant

11 Doyers St between Bowery and Pell St (212-693-0725). Subway: J, M, Z, N, Q, R, W, 6 to Canal St. Sun–Thu 11am–9:30pm; Fri, Sat 11am–10:30pm. Average main course: $6.50. AmEx.
Hard by a bend on a Chinatown dogleg, this basement spot stands out from other inexpensive Vietnamese places. Even the standards have a little extra: Summer rolls are heady with mint, and a grilled-beef appetizer comes seared in *la lot* leaves (pungent foliage from a relative of the peppercorn plant). *Mi cari vit* (curried-duck and noodle soup) arrives in a steaming bowl, brimming with chunks of duck, potato and eggplant.

Soho

Balthazar

80 Spring St between Broadway and Crosby St (212-965-1414). Subway: N, R to Prince St; 6 to Spring St. Mon–Thu 7:30–11:30am, noon–5pm, 6pm–1:30am; Fri 7:30–11:30am, noon–5pm, 6pm–2:30am; Sat

7:30am–4pm, 6pm–2:30am; Sun 7:30am–4pm, 5:30pm–1:30am. Average main course: $22. AmEx, MC, V.

Keith McNally's brasserie for the beautiful has passed the survival test and entered classic status. After six years, the crowd jostling for Cosmopolitans at the 25-foot zinc-topped bar is still three bodies deep, and the noisy, cavernous room's much-heralded Parisian touches (battered wall mirrors, Art Deco lighting, waiters in white bistro-length aprons) still impress. For all the fabulousness (you might see U2's the Edge at the next table), the brasserie-style food is no afterthought. Reserve in advance—Balthazar may not be the eye of the hipster storm it once was, but it's no walk-in wonderland, either.

Ceci-Cela
55 Spring St between Lafayette and Mulberry Sts (212-274-9179). Subway: 6 to Spring St. Mon–Thu 7am–7pm; Fri, Sat 7am–10pm; Sun 8am–7pm. Average pastry: $2.75. MC, V.

Drop by this hideaway on the edge of Little Italy for pastries, cakes, breads and *croques-monsieurs*. For a light lunch, an almost offensively simple-looking smoked-trout sandwich—a piece of fish on brioche with a slice of lemon and cucumber—is clean and sweet in a way that only a French sense of confidence can pull off. The small back room, filled with slightly fraying rattan tables, is where you can relax and contemplate your madeleines.

Herban Kitchen
290 Hudson St at Spring St (212-627-2257). Subway: C, E to Spring St; 1, 2 to Canal St. Mon–Sat 11am–11pm. Average main course: $17. AmEx, DC, Disc, MC, V.

Classy isn't an adjective that usually comes to mind when thinking about vegetarian restaurants, but Herban Kitchen changes that. The interior has high ceilings, exposed-brick walls, a worn wooden floor and cloth-covered tables. And the food is beautifully plated, creative and organic (including vegan dishes as well as free-range meats). Organic beers and vegan desserts round out the menu, and the garden area (where herbs and tomatoes are grown) is wonderfully romantic.

Honmura An
170 Mercer St between Houston and Prince Sts (212-334-5253). Subway: F, V, S to Broadway–Lafayette St; N, R to Prince St; 6 to Bleecker St. Tue 6–10pm; Wed, Thu noon–2:30pm, 6–10pm; Fri, Sat noon–2:30pm, 6–10:30pm; Sun 6–9:30pm. Average main course: $15. AmEx, DC, MC, V.

Nothing is too big, too rich or too difficult to digest at Honmura An, where the lighting is soft, the table talk hushed and the staff unflappably cool. The pretty salmon *oroshi* appetizer, for example, is a dainty blend of daikon and salmon roe. The main draw is the soba, light buckwheat noodles made in-house. In winter, soba is best served in a hot broth of seaweed, mushrooms or vegetables. In summer, eat the noodles cold out of a bamboo

box, with a side of icy sake. When you're done, don't forget to sip the nutrient-packed water in which the noodles were boiled (the waiter will bring it mid-meal).

Ideya
349 West Broadway between Broome and Grand Sts (212-625-1441). Subway: A, C, E, 1, 2 to Canal St. Mon–Wed 1–11pm; Thu, Fri 1pm–midnight; Sat 11:30am–midnight; Sun 11:30am–11pm. Average main course: $18. AmEx, DC, MC, V.

The mobs and snobs of Soho seem miles away when you kick back with a tart caipirinha at this Latin bistro. The walls are lined with tropical graffiti murals by New York artist Daze, and Brazilian jazz keeps everyone—including the first-rate, guayabera-clad servers—in the groove. Chef Isaac Reyes's food is as spirited as the ambience: Don't miss the juicy Uruguayan-style spinach-stuffed pork chops with apple *pico de gallo* and sherry.

Jean Claude
137 Sullivan St between Houston and Prince Sts (212-475-9232). Subway: C, E to Spring St. Sun–Thu 6:30–11pm; Fri, Sat 6:30–11:30pm. Average main course: $14.50. Cash only.

Just outside the red-trimmed storefront at Jean Claude, beautiful people jostle each other to peer inside and try to gauge how long it will take for one of the dozen tables to open up. Given the satisfying fare and reasonable prices, you can't blame them. But here's a tip for couples: In early evening, the airy, soft-toned dining room exudes the seductive quiet of a modest neighborhood brasserie; it's the perfect backdrop for a tête-à-tête and a fish entrée, such as the divine roasted codfish.

Le Gamin Café
50 MacDougal St between Houston and Prince Sts (212-254-4678). Subway: C, E to Spring St; 1, 2 to Houston St. 8am–midnight. Average main course: $7. Cash only.

See page 168.

Palacinka
28 Grand St between Sixth Ave and Thompson St (212-625-0362). Subway: A, C, E, 1, 2 to Canal St. Mon, Tue 10:30am–11pm; Wed–Sat 10:30am–midnight; Sun 10:30am–6pm. Average crêpe: $7.50. Cash only.

All tin tables and Gauloises-smoking Europeans, this chic little café should be scribbled into the agenda of every boho dreamer in town. Crêpes are Palacinka's pride and joy (that's what the name means, in Czech). The savory crêpes mix ingredients such as chicken with goat cheese and peppers. Sweet crêpes range from the classic lemon and sugar to chestnut paste with crème fraîche.

Pepe Rosso to Go
149 Sullivan St between Houston and Prince Sts (212-677-4555). Subway: C, E to Spring St. 11:30am–11pm. Average main course: $10. Cash only.

See **Pepe Giallo to Go**, page 170.

Raoul's

*180 Prince St between Sullivan and Thompson
Sts (212-966-3518). Subway: C, E to Spring St.
5:30pm–2am. Average main course: $24. AmEx,
DC, MC, V.*

More Left Bank than Soho, this swank joint has
been a celebrity stamping ground since 1975.
Chalkboard menus written in French, a large
aquarium, lived-in bistro digs and a resident palm
reader upstairs are some of the quirks that distinguish Raoul's from its sleek neighbors—that, and
the food. The fish is as flawless as the sirloin, for
which Raoul's is known. Order another cocktail
from the well-schooled bartenders and admit
you're going nowhere. Rock star or not, you'll feel
as if you've arrived.

Ruben's Empanadas

*505 Broome St between Thompson St and West
Broadway (212-334-3351). Subway: A, C, E, 1, 2 to
Canal St. Mon–Fri 8am–8pm; Sat, Sun 9am–7pm.
Average empanada: $3.50. Cash only.*

Ruben's, a minichain of Argentine take-out spots,
has been serving its baked stuffed crusts since
1975. (The other locations are farther downtown,
see page 154.) There are 20 types to choose from
(and a daily "empanada of the moment"), including breakfast (scrambled eggs and Canadian
bacon) and dessert (guava and cheese) versions.
But the best are the spicy, savory varieties, such
as Argentine sausage, beef subtly sweetened with
raisins, and zippy chicken.

Shanghai Tide

*77 W Houston St at Wooster St (212-614-9550).
Subway: C, E to Spring St; N, R to Prince St. 11am–
midnight. Average main course: $13. AmEx, MC, V.*

A righteous Chinese restaurant in Soho? That's
correct. Imported from Flushing, Queens *(see page
190),* this bowling-alley-narrow, block-long eatery
(which used to be called Shanghai Tang, like its parent) serves Shanghai cuisine, including delicately
seasoned soup dumplings and a braised pork shoul-
der so tender and rich, you'll squeal with joy. There's
also a menu of Japanese standards (sushi, sashimi,
tempura and special box lunches).

Zoë

*90 Prince St between Broadway and Mercer St (212-
966-6722). Subway: N, R to Prince St; 6 to Spring St.
Mon 6–10:30pm; Tue–Thu noon–3pm, 6–10:30pm;
Fri noon–3pm, 6–11pm; Sat noon–3pm, 5:30–
11:30pm; Sun 11:30am–3pm, 5:30–10pm. Average
main course: $23. AmEx, DC, MC, V.*

Stewart Woodman, a former sous-chef at Le Bernardin and Alain Ducasse, has breathed new life into
this decade-old Soho favorite. His food isn't flashy;
dishes are sublime combinations of a few choice
ingredients that let nuances emerge. Simple brown
butter ties together barely solid corn-filled ravioli
and garden-fresh peas. Underneath a subtle lobster
sauce, you can taste the citrus of the grilled shrimp's
orange glaze.

Noho

Bond St.

*6 Bond St between Broadway and Lafayette St (212-
777-2500). Subway: F, V, S to Broadway–Lafayette St;
6 to Bleecker St. Mon–Sat 6–11:30pm; Sun 6–11pm.
Lounge Mon–Sat 5pm–2am; Sun 5pm–1am. Average
sushi meal (6 pieces): $25. AmEx, MC, V.*

Now in its fourth year, Bond St. has morphed from
a scorchingly hip downtown hot spot into one of the
city's most respected Japanese restaurants. The
under-30 crowd and fancy cocktails belie the serious-
as-ever creations of Nobu-trained chef Linda
Rodriguez, who displays a masterful hand with
Japanese cuisine, especially seafood; she's able to
twist traditional idioms into playfully modern, continental forms without losing her grip. Meanwhile,
head sushi chef Hiroshi Nakahara knows how to
choose and preserve his fish: The outstanding selection includes *chu toro* (fatty tuna), *kohada* (spotted
sardine) and *botan ebi* (jumbo sweet shrimp).

Five Points

*31 Great Jones St between Bowery and Lafayette St
(212-253-5700). Subway: F, V, S to Broadway–
Lafayette St; 6 to Bleecker St. 5pm–midnight. Average
main course: $21. AmEx, DC, MC, V.*

Three years on, Five Points has settled down and
become perhaps the city's best neighborhood
restaurant. Handsome, vaguely nautical and completely unpretentious, it's the kind of seductive
place where you'd find *Sex and the City*'s Aidan at
the bar, slurping oysters (a buck apiece from 5 to
7pm). Marc Meyer's well-conceived American food
is spiked with Mediterranean accents. The menu
changes daily, but staples include buttermilk-mar-
inated chicken, which has a Middle Eastern tinge
of honey, cinnamon and cardamom, and the nice-

Tax & tipping

Few New York restaurants add a service
charge to the bill (unless your party is of
eight or more), but it is customary to pay
15 to 20 percent of the bill total as a tip.
The easiest way to figure out the amount
is to double the 8.25-percent sales tax.
Complain all you want if you feel service
is under par, but only in the most extreme
cases should you withhold a tip. Remember
that servers receive a paltry minimum
wage ($3.30 an hour), and rely on tips
to pay the rent. Don't forget to tip
bartenders ($1 a drink). The person
who delivers your Chinese food probably
receives no salary at all and relies entirely
on tips ($2 is considered a good amount).
Don't give out-of-towners a bad name.

Morning glory East Villagers hit Café Mogador for brunch specials such as Moroccan eggs.

ly chewy and grilled hanger steak, seasoned with garlic and rosemary.

Jones Diner

371 Lafayette St at Great Jones St (212-673-3577). Subway: F, V, S to Broadway–Lafayette St; 6 to Bleecker St. 6am–6pm. Average main course: $6. Cash only.

This railroad-car diner of brick and (once) gleaming stainless steel has stood watch on this same corner since 1938. For 28 years, George Serkizis has been calling customers "friend" and assembling plates of fresh turkey and pot roast. You'll be hard-pressed to find a better burger. There's an authentic soda fountain and soda jerk. Co-owner Alex Poulos is famous for his old-fashioned lemonade: fresh lemons, seltzer, sugar and ice mixed in a milk-shake canister. Serkizis and Poulos are fighting to keep their lease. If they lose, Jones Diner will be a fond memory come September 2002. Keep your fingers crossed.

Two Boots to Go-Go

74 Bleecker St between Broadway and Crosby St (212-777-1033). Subway: F, V, S to Broadway–Lafayette St; 6 to Bleecker St. Mon–Thu 11:30am–12:30am; Fri, Sat 11:30am–1am; Sun 11:30am–11:30pm. Large plain pizza: $12.95. AmEx.

See page 166.

East Village

Alphabet Kitchen

171 Ave A between 10th and 11th Sts (212-982-3838). Subway: L to First Ave; 6 to Astor Pl. Mon–Thu 6pm–midnight; Fri 6pm–1am; Sat noon–4:30pm,

6pm–1am; Sun noon–4:30pm, 6pm–midnight. Average main course: $19. AmEx, DC, MC, V.

Part Spanish and part Portuguese, just like chef Liz Arana, this upbeat East Village spot serves an Iberian medley of dishes in a relaxed room. Arana wrings complex taste out of simple ingredients, such as *piquillo* pepper stuffed with *bacalhau*. The excellent paella doesn't skimp on saffron or crustaceans. Interesting Portuguese and Spanish selections mark the wine list.

Angelica Kitchen

300 E 12th St between First and Second Aves (212-228-2909). Subway: L to First Ave; N, Q, R, W, 4, 5, 6 to 14th St–Union Sq. 11:30am–10:30pm. Average main course: $10. Cash only.

The community table at this calm, light-filled institution is the place to meet vegetarians. The lunch deal lets you fill up on a thick slice of either whole-wheat, nutty sourdough or sweet corn bread, a cup of soup (miso is a favorite), a house salad and a cup of roasted *kukicha* tea. The highlights are the Dragon or Combo bowls (available for lunch and dinner): Mix and match tempeh, soba noodles, sea vegetables and millet. Like the community table, it's a joyful integration.

Bulgin' Waffles

49½ First Ave at 3rd St (212-477-6555). Subway: F, V to Lower East Side–Second Ave. Tue–Thu 9am–10pm; Fri, Sat 10am–midnight; Sun 10am–4pm. Average waffle: $5. AmEx, MC, V.

At this East Village breakfast nook, the mainstay meal comes in a wide assortment of wheat variations—buckwheat, whole wheat, you name it. But the clincher is the topping: Try seasonal fruit with *dulce de leche.* Eggs, muffins, granola, yogurt and other brekkie items are also available, but the waffles rule.

Café Mogador

101 St. Marks Pl between First Ave and Ave A (212-677-2226). Subway: L to First Ave; 6 to Astor Pl. Sun–Thu 9am–1am; Fri, Sat 9am–2am. Average main course: $12. AmEx, DC, MC, V.
The menu is Moroccan, but the feel is lived-in East Village—Mogador is the kind of place where you won't think twice about showing up with bedhead and mismatched socks. Its Sunday brunch has been a neighborhood fave since Mogador opened in 1983. Couscous and *tagines* are the mainstays, but the menu has guest stars from Mediterranean Europe.

Casimir

103–105 Ave B between 6th and 7th Sts (212-358-9683). Subway: F, V to Lower East Side–Second Ave; 6 to Astor Pl. Mon–Fri 5:30pm–1am; Sat–Sun 11am–4pm, 5:30pm–1am. Average main course: $15. AmEx.
Cheap prices and good steak frites keep Casimir packed. The downtowners always seem to be six deep at the tiny bar. The sashimi-grade salmon tartare is a whale-size portion, and the generous duck, steak and tuna dishes are all cooked *à point.* There's a Moroccan lounge next door when you need a break from the buzz.

Cyclo

203 First Ave between 12th and 13th Sts (212-673-3957). Subway: L to First Ave; N, Q, R, W, 4, 5, 6 to 14th St–Union Sq. Sun–Thu 5:30–10:45pm; Fri, Sat 5:30–11:45pm. Average main course: $12. AmEx, MC, V.
You might find cheaper Vietnamese food in Chinatown, but a few extra bucks here will get you fresh, authentic fare and handsome decor (sconces are made from maps of Saigon). You won't hear any grumbling from the tables of local hipsters dining at Cyclo. The whole snapper swims in a gingery sauce that tastes at once subtle and complex.

Dok Suni's

119 First Ave between St. Marks Pl and 7th St (212-477-9506). Subway: F, V to Lower East Side–Second Ave; 6 to Astor Pl. Sun, Mon 4:30–11pm; Tue–Sat 4:30pm–midnight. Average main course: $14. Cash only.
Dok Suni's might look like a dimly lit haunt for smokers in low-slung denim, but it smells like what it is: a deliciously carnivorous Korean restaurant. The *kalbi* and *bibimbop* are comfort food that's well-thought-out enough to dazzle. Owner Jenny Kwak also serves Korean cuisine at the even slicker **Do Hwa** *(55 Carmine St between Seventh Ave South and Bedford St, 212-414-1224)* in the West Village.

First

87 First Ave between 5th and 6th Sts (212-674-3823). Subway: F, V to Lower East Side–Second Ave; 6 to Astor Pl. Mon–Thu 6pm–2am; Fri, Sat 6pm–3am; Sun 11am–4pm, 5pm–1am. Average main course: $20. AmEx, MC, V.
Sam DeMarco upped the East Village dining ante

when he opened First in 1995. These days, the neighborhood is filled with high-octane restaurant options, but the joint remains a primo place to eat. Just take a look at the jumping crowd of grade-B Charlize Therons in place by 7:30pm on a Saturday. The food—creative versions of American standards—is just so much damn fun, from the seafood tacos stuffed with shrimp, scallops and squid, to grilled hanger steak that gives a nod to the neighborhood with a side of pierogi. Perch at the bar, munch on the famous lollipop buffalo wings and sip on a blood orange Tiny 'Tini. DeMarco has since opened **Merge** *(142 W 10th St between Greenwich Ave and Waverly Pl, 212-691-7757)* and **District** *(130 W 46th St between Sixth and Seventh Aves, 212-485-2999).*

Holy Basil

149 Second Ave between 9th and 10th Sts (212-460-5557). Subway: L to First Ave; 6 to Astor Pl. Sun–Thu 5–11:30pm; Fri, Sat 5pm–1:30am. Average main course: $14. AmEx, Disc, MC, V.
See **Little Basil**, page 168.

Jewel Bako

239 E 5th St between Second and Third Aves (212-979-1012). Subway: 6 to Astor Pl. Tue–Sun 6:30–10:30pm. Average sushi meal (8 pieces, 1 roll): $18. AmEx, DC, MC, V.
A stylish new entry in the East Village's sushi sweepstakes, Jewel Bako is a curvy, tunnellike eatery designed by the firm responsible for Michael Kors Soho. Chef Tatsuya Nagata serves an appealing mix of traditional and contemporary Japanese dishes, such as wild striped sea bass wrapped in cherry leaves, plus a well-edited sushi and sashimi menu. Reservations are a must.

Kate's Joint

58 Ave B between 4th and 5th Sts (212-777-7059). Subway: F, V to Lower East Side–Second Ave. Average main course: $8. AmEx, DC, Disc, MC, V.
A local hot spot for brew-swilling "carniphobes," Kate's Joint is a great place to refuel with some veggie grub. The cigarette smoke and fried-food aromas hanging in the air provide an ironic twist to the stereotypically healthy vegan world. Even ovo-lacto types won't miss the dairy in the popular Caesar salad or the tofu-cheese pizza. Breakfast is served all day long, just in case you get a hankering for dairy-free pancakes at 4pm.

La Focacceria

128 First Ave between St. Marks Pl and 7th St (212-254-4946). Subway: L to First Ave; 6 to Astor Pl. Mon–Thu 10am–10pm; Fri, Sat 10am–11pm. Average main course: $9. Cash only.
At this family-run octogenarian, the smell of tomatoes stewing and garlic roasting makes you feel like you're in a private home—and the food's as reliable as the home-cooked stuff. The menu, scrawled in marker on the wall, largely sticks to Italian-American classics: spaghetti and meatballs, manicotti, chicken marsala. But highlights include huge rice balls filled with ground beef and peas, known

Necessities

as *arancini*; and mozzarella in *carrozza*, a cheese sandwich that is battered in egg, then fried.

Le Gamin Café

536 E 5th St between Aves A and B (212-254-8409). Subway: F, V to Lower East Side–Second Ave; 6 to Astor Pl. 8am–midnight. Average main course: $7. Cash only.
See page 168.

Lucien

14 First Ave between 1st and 2nd Sts (212-260-6481). Subway: F, V to Lower East Side–Second Ave. Mon, Tue 10am–2am; Wed–Sun 10am–4am. Average main course: $20. AmEx, DC, MC, V.

What Lucien Bahaj's eponymous 38-seat restaurant lacks in atmosphere, it more than makes up for with soulful bistro cooking. Sure, the only way to avoid scraping elbows with the people at the next table is to show up at 6pm on a Sunday, but the cheerful staff is attentive, and the solid meals will lift your spirit. Bahaj covers all the bases of French country cooking—frog's legs, bouillabaisse, cassoulet, lamb with flageolets. He serves similar food (with lower prices) at his new Lower East Side spot, the **Pink Pony** *(176 Ludlow St between Houston and Stanton Sts, 212-529-3956).*

Max

51 Ave B between 3rd and 4th Sts (212-539-0111). Subway: F, V to Lower East Side–Second Ave. Noon–midnight. Average main course: $10. Cash only.

Penny-pinching never tasted so good as it does at Max and Max Soha *(see page 187).* A bowl of downy gnocchi with tangy tomato sauce and mozzarella costs less than a movie ticket. As at the movies, you'd better arrive early if you want a seat: Massimo Fortunato's Southern Italian *cucina* is a sliver of a space.

The next best things

If you can't score a table at the big-name eateries, try these alternatives

You're paying $300 for a room in a new boutique hotel that's so "minimalist chic," shampoo didn't make the cut. On your way in from La Guardia, your cabbie took you on a surprise tour of Queens. Your New York trip is not off to an auspicious start, but at least you can return home and brag about your dinners at the city's hottest restaurants. Oops—maybe you can't. If you didn't call ahead for reservations, you may be out of luck. Don't worry; you can still rave about "discovering" these lesser-known alternatives. Sometimes the underdogs try a little harder; you can usually expect food that's just as delicious and service that's probably more personable—plus a clientele of real live New Yorkers.

Instead of Babbo...

Four years after it opened, chef and Food Network personality Mario Batali's restaurant is still ridiculously popular *(see page 166)*, and with good reason: His menu of multiregional Italian cuisine consistently pushes boundaries and succeeds. However, you can skip the table-scoring headache and pamper yourself with this low-hassle, high-satisfaction alternative.

Tappo *(403 E 12th St between First Ave and Ave A, 212-505-0001)*, in the East Village, has scruffy wooden tables, an open kitchen and a counter up front displaying meats and fish. Moody lighting makes for plenty of sexy mystique. The Mediterranean menu approaches Babbo's in its vocabulary-stretching choices. *Seppioline?* It's a type of squid, served here in a bracing salad. *Scamorza?* A creamy Italian cheese served baked. And don't underestimate familiar-sounding items like the gnocchi; Tappo's version is likely to be the fluffiest you've had.

Instead of Union Square Cafe and Gramercy Tavern...

Danny Meyer's Union Square Cafe *(21 E 16th St between Fifth Ave and Union Sq West, 212-243-4020)* and Gramercy Tavern *(see page 171)*—built on the principle of serving fresh, seasonally inspired dishes—have played a significant role in revitalizing New York's American cuisine in the last decade. But some of Manhattan's boldest new contenders are claiming a piece of Meyer's turf.

Annisa Behind floor-to-ceiling front windows, dedicated foodies delve into chef Anita Lo's ever-evolving range of flavors at two-year-old Annisa *(see page 168)*. Fleshy lobster claws come neatly arranged on a pile of fresh rice-noodle spring rolls. Grilled noisette of lamb is peppery, not heavy, served with crunchy Chinese broccoli.

Instead of Le Bernardin...

Siblings Maguy and Gilbert Le Coze revolutionized seafood, elevating fish to a four-star experience—first with their Parisian Le Bernardin in the 1970s, then with its midtown Manhattan offshoot in 1986. Le Bernardin *(see page 178)* remains in the

Moustache

265 E 10th St between First Ave and Ave A (212-228-2022). Subway: L to First Ave; 6 to Astor Pl. Noon–11pm. Average main course: $9. Cash only.
More than just affordable, tiny Middle Eastern Moustache is one of the most enjoyable restaurants in the city. Find a seat in the garden—in winter it's enclosed in plastic tenting and heated—or squeeze behind one of the copper-topped tables at its West Village location *(see page 189).*

Saint's Alp Teahouse

39 Third Ave between 9th and 10th Sts (212-598-1890). Subway: L to Third Ave; 6 to Astor Pl. Mon–Thu 1pm–midnight; Fri, Sat 1pm–1am; Sun 1–11pm. Average tea: $3. Cash only.
Fans know this global Hong Kong–based chain *(see pages 159 and 189)* by its Taiwanese-style tea—ultrasweet, electric-pastel and frothy as a milk shake.

True to the spirit of Asian pop culture, Saint's Alp is Hello Kitty–artificial—and that's what makes it fun. The so-called strawberry milk shake is made with nondairy creamer, strawberry-daiquiri powder mix, cookie crumbs and crushed ice cubes. You will find a few utterly Asian items on the menu, such as flavored tea eggs.

SEA

75 Second Ave between 4th and 5th Sts (212-228-5505). Subway: F, V to Lower East Side–Second Ave. Sun–Thu 11am–11pm; Fri, Sat 11am–midnight. Average main course: $10. AmEx, MC, V.
SEA is not a seafood restaurant; the acronym stands for Southeast Asia. The owners of this small Thai joint eschewed the Bangkok-craft look for a sleek, pared-down room that seems way too nice for such a cheap eatery. You'll invariably have to wait to be seated (reservations are accepted for a minimum of six

highest echelon of New York restaurants, but a slew of brilliant competitors are surfacing.

Cello The mushroom-colored banquettes at Cello *(53 E 77th St between Madison and Park Aves, 212-517-1200)* are full of elder plutocrats and their wives. Sit back and bask in the richness of chef Laurent Tourondel's dishes. His approach is no less French than that of Le Bernardin but tends to yield unexpected results: Witness the warm, creamy and lightly spiced crab gratin, paired with a cool celery salad, or the risotto dotted with lobster and foie gras.

Instead of Peter Luger...

We're not going to lie to you: There is no substitute for the Peter Luger steak house *(see page 189).* Brooklyn's 115-year-old beef stronghold remains one of America's—and the world's—most distinguished culinary institutions. The fabulous meat is dry-aged in-house and charred in massive broilers. But since everybody in the world knows that, you could well find yourself shut out of Luger.

Scopa If it's great beef you're after (as opposed to, say, atmosphere), the Gramercy trattoria Scopa *(27 E 28th St between Madison Ave and Park Ave South, 212-213-2424)* is the place to go. The space is plain and the waitstaff can be overbearing, but all is forgiven when the giant rib steak hits the table. Marbled, tender and glistening with juices, it is a thing of beauty.

Instead of Joe's Shanghai...

In 1996, Joe's Shanghai, in Flushing, Queens, opened a Chinatown branch *(9 Pell St between Bowery and Mott St, 212-233-8888)*, introducing Manhattanites to Shanghai cuisine. Joe's has

been pretty much mobbed ever since. The craze can be summed up in two words: soup dumplings—tender little packages of pork, crab and scalgingly hot broth (alternately known as soup buns or tiny buns). Joe's makes great soup dumplings, but other, far less crowded restaurants have been quick to catch on.

Shanghai Cuisine If Joe's is too packed, head west to the simply named Shanghai Cuisine *(89 Bayard St at Mulberry St, 212-732-8988)*, which offers dumplings stuffed with shrimp and pork, in addition to the traditional varieties. The menu also includes excellent examples of other Shanghai delicacies, such as "drunken crab," a cevichelike appetizer cured in rice wine.

Instead of Pastis...

A celeb-infested scene when it opened in 2000, Pastis *(9 Ninth Ave at Little West 12th St, 212-929-4844)* is now as complacent as many of the city's other faux-French eateries. The dining room and sprawling sidewalk area are still lively, and you might still spot an actor or two, but the food can be disappointing, and the overall experience more hassle than it's worth.

Jules Bistro On Manhattan's numbingly long list of just-like-Paris eateries, precious few combine the electric atmosphere and quality cuisine that's required of a first-rate bistro. Clear across town from Pastis sits one that does: Jules Bistro *(65 St. Marks Pl between First and Second Aves, 212-477-5560)*. This leafy, hidden nook is one of the city's most effortlessly charming restaurants. The menu combines the familiar *(moules frites,* hanger steak, oysters) with enough idiosyncrasy (roasted stuffed quail) to tease bistro habitués.

people). Order the whole fish, which is fried to a delicate crisp and served in a spicy tamarind sauce.

Second Avenue Deli

156 Second Ave between 9th and 10th Sts (212-677-0606). Subway: L to Third Ave; 6 to Astor Pl. Sun–Thu 7am–midnight; Fri, Sat 7am–3am. Pastrami sandwich: $10. AmEx, DC, Disc, MC, V.
Still on the door is a poster offering a $100,000 reward for information leading to the arrest of the killers of Abe Lebewohl, the late owner of New York's most renowned kosher deli. It's been six years since the murder, and the restaurant has been made over with cut glass and shiny new fixtures. You'll find every Jewish old-world classic: luxurious chopped liver slathered on soft rye; dense, raisin-studded noodle

CRITICS' PICKS

Iron chefs

These are some of New York City's top food artistes and the restaurants where they showcase their culinary skills. It can be tough to get reservations at these spots, so call before you arrive in the city (the further in advance the better) or see **The next best things** *(page 164),* for alternatives.

Dan Barber: Blue Hill, page 167
Mario Batali: Babbo, Esca and Lupa, page 166
David Bouley: Bouley Bakery and Danube, page 154
Daniel Boulud: Café Boulud, Daniel and db bistro moderne, page 182
Terrance Brennan: Artisanal, page 174, and Picholine (*35 W 64th St between Central Park West and Broadway, 212-724-8585).*
Floyd Cardoz: Tabla, page 174
Tom Colicchio: Craft and Gramercy Tavern, page 171
Rocco DiSpirito: Union Pacific, page 174
Alain Ducasse: Alain Ducasse at the Essex House, page 179
Todd English: Olives NY, page 172
Rick Laakkonen: Ilo, page 177
Anita Lo: Annisa, page 167
Nobu Matsuhisa: Nobu, page 154
Eberhard Müller: Bayard's, page 153
Alfred Portale: Gotham Bar and Grill, page 167
Eric Ripert: Le Bernardin, page 177
Douglas Rodriguez: Chicama, page 170
Marcus Samuelsson: Aquavit, page 176
Roger Vergé: Medi, page 178
Jean-Georges Vongerichten: Jean-Georges, Jo-Jo and Vong, page 183
Geoffrey Zakarian: Town, page 180

kugel (Yiddish baked pudding). And the corned beef? Try it for yourself and taste what makes a legend.

Siren

12 St. Marks Pl between Second and Third Aves (212-995-9100). Subway: 6 to Astor Pl. Sun, Tue–Fri 6pm–midnight; Sat noon–4pm. Average main course: $17. AmEx, MC, V.
Alternakids are draped along the railings on Siren's front porch, and some nights there's an additional layer of velvet-rope police in front of the door, but inside, you'll find a fine-dining outpost. First, choose between the red-lit main dining hall and the funky Goth-chic bar area. Keeping pace with the high-contrast settings are dishes such as sea bass crusted with ginger and Thai chili in sweet, smoky blood orange sauce. Downstairs, you'll find fashionably disorienting rest-room mirrors and a unisex sink.

Two Boots Restaurant

37 Ave A between 2nd and 3rd Sts (212-505-2276). Subway: F, V to Lower East Side–Second Ave. Mon–Fri 5pm–midnight; Sat 2pm–midnight; Sun noon–11pm. Large plain pizza: $13.95. AmEx, Disc, MC, V.
Two Boots is one of the city's most beloved pizza chains. Devotees flock to its funky locations for crispy cornmeal-crust pizza with spicy Cajun toppings (andouille sausage, crawfish tails) and goofy, film-geek names (Bayou Beast, Mr. Pink, Newman). Two Boots itself is named for the two boot-shaped places—Italy and Louisiana—whose disparate cuisines meld here with spunky results.
Other locations ● *Two Boots Pizzeria, 42 Ave A at 3rd St (212-254-1919). Subway: F, V to Lower East Side–Second Ave. Sun–Thu 11:30am–1am; Fri, Sat 11:30am–2am. Large plain pizza: $12.95. AmEx, Disc, MC, V.* ● *See also pages 162, 169, 175, 178, 189.*

Veselka

144 Second Ave at 9th St (212-228-9682). Subway: L to Third Ave; 6 to Astor Pl. 24hrs. Average main course: $9. AmEx, DC, MC, V.
Come 4am, nothing coats your booze belly like a plate of plump, boiled Veselka pierogi. NYU nightcrawlers and eccentric East Village insomniacs come to this round-the-clock sanctuary for Ukrainian comfort food, burgers and omelettes. Folks who keep regular hours should take advantage of the triangular raspberry-cheese blintzes during the always-busy Sunday brunch.

Greenwich Village

Babbo

110 Waverly Pl between MacDougal St and Sixth Ave (212-777-0303). Subway: A, C, E, F, V, S to W 4th St. Mon–Sat 5:30–11:30pm; Sun 5–11:30pm. Average main course: $27. Average pasta: $19. AmEx, DC, MC, V.
After four years, Mario Batali's famous haute Italian restaurant still requires a reservation made several weeks in advance. Despite Batali's protestations on his TV shows and in his cookbooks, his best dishes are *not* the simple, rustic Italian ones,

Necessities

Lo cuisine Star chef Anita Lo cooks up creative Japanese-American fusion food at Annisa.

but those in which he goes a bit over the top. Creative pastas, such as goose-liver ravioli in a balsamic-vinegar–and–butter sauce, are rich enough to induce tears. Fringe meats, seen in the lamb's-tongue salad (bathed in vinaigrette) and the famous beef-cheek ravioli, show Batali at his very best—giving new twists to traditional preparations. The wine list includes an array of relatively obscure Italian regionals, and many are available by the quarter liter (about a glass and a half), so you can try a few without committing to a bottle. If you can't get a reservation, try one of Batali's other restaurants: casual **Lupa** (170 Thompson St between Bleecker and Houston Sts, 212-982-5089) and midtown seafood haven **Esca** (402 W 43rd St at Ninth Ave, 212-564-7272).

Blue Hill

75 Washington Pl between MacDougal St and Sixth Ave (212-539-1776). Subway: A, C, E, F, V, S to W 4th St. Mon–Sat 6–11pm. Average main course: $24. AmEx, DC, MC, V.
Blue Hill is the rare place that doesn't crumble under the pressure of hyperbolic publicity and impossibly high expectations. You can chalk it up to the gorgeous decor—cocoa-brown banquettes, red chairs, skinny mirrors—and you can point out the dynamic environment and unassailably well-trained waiters. But in the end, dinner at Blue Hill is about the food: Chef-owner Dan Barber and chef Michael Anthony turn out dazzling dishes whose flavors linger for aeons after each bite. Slow-cooked arctic char is magically moist, its salmonlike flavor cut by an assertive Meyer-lemon sauce; pistachios and pancetta add a brilliant textural counterpoint to the fish. Bloodred roasted duck gets a jolt from lime juice. Is there a chance this restaurant is…underrated?

Da Silvano

260 Sixth Ave between Bleecker and Houston Sts (212-982-2343). Subway: A, C, E, F, V, S to W 4th St; 1, 2 to Houston St. Mon–Thu noon–11:30pm; Fri, Sat noon–midnight; Sun noon–11pm. Average main course: $24. Average pasta: $16. AmEx, MC, V.
Since 1975, Silvano Marchetto's restaurant has attracted an A-list crowd—regulars include Vanity Fair editor Graydon Carter, writer Dominick Dunne and screenwriter Paul Schrader. Gwyneth, Brad and Madonna have signed the guest book. Dishes include firm tagliarini alla contadina (noodles with peas, in a silken tomato-cream sauce with sausage) and a tender, grilled veal chop. If you don't feel like waiting, check to see if there's space at Marchetto's more casual **Bar Pitti** next door (268 Sixth Ave between Bleecker and Houston Sts, 212-982-3300).

Gotham Bar and Grill

12 E 12th St between Fifth Ave and University Pl (212-620-4020). Subway: L, N, Q, R, W, 4, 5, 6 to 14th St–Union Sq. Mon–Thu noon–2:15pm, 5:30–10:15pm; Fri noon–2:15pm, 5:30–11:15pm; Sat 5:30–11:15pm; Sun 5:30–10:15pm. Average main course: $35. AmEx, DC, MC, V.
The birthplace of vertical food first opened its doors in 1985, and immediately secured a perennial position near the top of most local foodies' "must-eat" lists. Chef Alfred Portale builds elegant but hearty dishes: The rack of lamb with Swiss chard, roasted shallots and garlicky mashed potatoes actually fills you up. While Gotham is what you'd call a fancy restaurant, it's far from stuffy: Its large, columned dining room remains casual, albeit in a well-heeled sort of way—which also describes the clientele.

Mamoun's Falafel

119 MacDougal St between Bleecker and W 3rd Sts (212-674-8685). Subway: A, C, E, F, V, S to W 4th St. 10am–5am. Average falafel: $2.50. Cash only.
Day or night, this storefront (in the Village since 1971) provides some of the city's best falafel, in pitas stuffed with lettuce, tomatoes and tahini. The lentil soup, lamb shwarma and hummus sandwiches are all high-quality and cheap, making this an ideal stop for people who are ending the evening—or starting the day—with only a few crumpled bucks to spend.

West Village

Annisa

13 Barrow St between Bleecker and W 4th Sts (212-741-6699). Subway: A, C, E, F, V, S to W 4th St; 1, 2 to Christopher St–Sheridan Sq. Mon–Sat 5:30–11pm. Average main course: $26. AmEx, DC, MC, V.
Chef Anita Lo and partner Jennifer Scism, along with the disarmingly warm waitstaff, have created an environment where you can focus your attention on the exquisitely prepared food and whomever you happen to be sharing it with. The menu draws ideas from France, Japan and 21st-century New York, so expect some wild-card action. To wit: seared foie gras with soup dumplings and jicama, and miso-

Necessities

marinated sablefish with crispy deep-fried silken tofu in a bonito-kelp broth.

Blue Ribbon Bakery

33 Downing St at Bedford St (212-337-0404). Subway: A, C, E, F, V, S to W 4th St; 1, 2 to Houston St. Tue–Sun noon–2am. Average main course: $19. AmEx, DC, MC, V.

Blue Ribbon Bakery owners Eric and Bruce Bromberg have assembled an inspired kitchen that doles out small plates of soul-pleasing food. Onion soup, steamed clams and fried-catfish sandwiches are prepared with as much loving skill as the more upscale offerings, such as pigeon in roasted-garlic sauce. No one could leave this brick-walled, turn-of-the-century space unhappy; even vegetarians get their own menu section. Despite such variety, the menu is not overwhelming, and the house favorites are written in red (same with the extensive and affordable wine list). Blue Ribbon Bakery doesn't take reservations, but try to hold out for a seat downstairs in the cellar. Variety is a Bromberg hallmark; their other restaurants are: **Blue Ribbon** *(97 Sullivan St between Prince and Spring Sts, 212-260-8229),* **Blue Ribbon Sushi** *(119 Sullivan St between Prince and Spring Sts, 212-343-0404)* and **Blue Ribbon Brooklyn** *(280 Fifth Ave between Garfield and 1st Sts, Park Slope, Brooklyn, 718-840-0404).*

Corner Bistro

331 W 4th St at Jane St (212-242-9502). Subway: A, C, E to 14th St; L to Eighth Ave. 11:30am–4am. Average burger: $4.50. Cash only.

Corner Bistro consistently tops New Yorkers' best-burger list. After being broiled under an open flame to seal in its juices, the beef is dropped on a toasted sesame-seed bun, draped with lettuce and slices of bacon, tomatoes, pickles and onions, and then rather unceremoniously delivered atop a plate that looks like a coffee filter. Simplicity works: Most nights, the place is packed with diners of all ages, races and creeds, who wait up to an hour for their burgers, further strengthening the eatery's legend.

Florent

69 Gansevoort St between Greenwich and Washington Sts (212-989-5779). Subway: A, C, E to 14th St; L to Eighth Ave. Mon–Fri 9am–5am; Sat 24hrs; Sun 12:01–5am. Average main course: $13.50. Cash only.

Through good times and bad in the Meatpacking District, Florent has been a reliable bistro, a community center of sorts, and a renowned late-night hang zone. Since 1985, regulars have been coming for skirt steak au poivre, always-fresh *moules,* the jumbo burger on a Thomas' English muffin, and the artery choker known as *boudin noir.* During the day, Florent offers a (non-club) kids' menu featuring *beurre de cacahuète et confiture.* Peanut butter and jelly never sounded so sexy.

Hog Pit BBQ

22 Ninth Ave at 13th St (212-604-0092). Subway: A, C, E to 14th St; L to Eighth Ave. Sun–Thu 5–11pm;

Fri, Sat 5pm–1am. Bar 4pm–4am. Average main course: $12. AmEx, DC, Disc, MC, V.

The Hog Pit's expertly prepared homestyle classics, such as fried pickle chips and country-fried steak, are batter-dipped and served hotter than Alabama in August. Fresh coleslaw crunches sweetly and the ribs…well, what can we say? They really do fall off the bone. Honky-tonk women, monstrous bucketmouth bass and the occasional customer displaying two inches of ass-crack complete the picture.

Le Gamin Café

27 Bedford St between Downing and Houston Sts (212-243-2846). Subway: 1, 2 to Houston St. 8am–midnight. Average main course: $7. Cash only.

There's a Gamin in almost every artsy neighborhood in Manhattan. The West Village branch offers the chainlet's familiar menu of crêpes, sandwiches and salads and is also eminently hang-outable. As for the other Gamins…the tiny Soho spot was the first *(see page 160).* The Chelsea branch *(see page 169),* which is a more comfortable size, attracts stylish types from the nearby London Towers apartments and co-ops. Francophiles *à l'est* can take refuge at the one in the East Village *(see page 164).* However, the West Village also gets the full-service kitchen of **Les Deux Gamins** *(see below).*

Les Deux Gamins

170 Waverly Pl at Grove St (212-807-7047). Subway: A, C, E, F, V, S to W 4th St; 1, 2 to Christopher St–Sheridan Sq. 8am–midnight. Average main course: $16. AmEx.

If you're in the mood for self-conscious mugging, Les Deux Gamins should help you scratch that itch. This weathered spot has been adopted by the local Anglo community (regulars include fashion-mag editors, with cameos by the likes of Rupert Everett), but its languid, saucy atmosphere still feels sufficiently French. Order from a rambling menu of dry-aged steaks, charcuterie plates, meal-size salads and staples such as *croque-monsieur,* all served with a laissez-faire attitude.

Little Basil

39 Greenwich Ave at Charles St (212-645-8965). Subway: A, C, E, F, V, S to W 4th St. 5–11:30pm. Average main course: $12. AmEx, DC, MC, V.

Like the baby brother blessed with design sense (**Holy Basil** is the elder, more traditional sibling; *see page 163),* Little Basil flaunts nouvelle presentations of Thai staples such as *tom kha* soup and *yum nuer,* a salad of sliced rare beef and red onion. Every recipe is executed with the confidence of a master: The distinct taste of lemongrass, so often smothered in creaminess, emerges when it's meant to. Little Basil has sidewalk seating for those balmy summer nights.

Mexicana Mama

525 Hudson St between Charles and 10th Sts (212-924-4119). Subway: 1, 2 to Christopher St–Sheridan Sq 5:30–11pm. Average main course: $14. Cash only.

The staff at this tiny 16-seat dining room scurries to deliver earthy dishes from an open kitchen. The bulging *chiles rellenos* (roasted, not fried) are the choicest offering; they're stuffed with Chihuahua cheese, fresh corn and tomato, and served with green rice (made with cilantro and *poblano* chili).

Moustache
90 Bedford St between Barrow and Grove Sts (212-229-2220). Subway: 1, 2 to Christopher St–Sheridan Sq. Noon–11pm. Average main course: $9. Cash only.
See page 165.

Pearl Oyster Bar
18 Cornelia St between Bleecker and W 4th Sts (212-691-8211). Subway: A, C, E, F, V, S to W 4th St. Mon–Fri noon–2:30pm, 6–11pm; Sat 6–11pm. Average main course: $22. MC, V.
The diners packed elbow to elbow on stools at Pearl Oyster Bar are there for one purpose: to swallow fresh, perfect oysters. But briny mollusks aren't the only thing to savor at this minuscule restaurant (it has exactly one real sit-down table). The lobster roll rivals the one made by your favorite dockside joint in Maine. To avoid up to an hour of waiting on the sidewalk, try to arrive near the top of the hour, when much of the restaurant turns over at once. Or better yet, come for lunch, when sunlight floods the narrow space, and it is placidly crowd-free.

Pepe Verde
559 Hudson St between Perry and 11th Sts (212-255-2221). Subway: 1, 2 to Christopher St–Sheridan Sq. 11am–11pm. Average main course: $9. Cash only.
See **Pepe Giallo to Go**, page 170.

Pink Tea Cup
42 Grove St between Bedford and Bleecker Sts (212-807-6755). Subway: 1, 2 to Christopher St–Sheridan Sq. 8am–midnight. Average main course: $11. Cash only.
A well-manicured West Village street isn't the most obvious place for a deliciously greasy soul-food joint, yet legions of devotees have managed to find Pink Tea Cup anyway. The breakfast menu is available all day, but dinner is the real draw. Owner Serretta Ford's smothered pork chops are flavored with lip-smacking gravy that you'll want to sop up with what is some of the best corn bread in town.

Sushi Samba 7
87 Seventh Ave South at Barrow St (212-475-9377). Subway: 1, 2 to Christopher St–Sheridan Sq. Sun–Tue noon–midnight; Wed–Sat noon–2am. Average sushi meal (7 pieces, 1 roll): $22. Average ceviche: $9. AmEx, MC, V.
This outpost of the swinging original Sushi Samba on Park Avenue South *(see page 174)* peddles Brazilian street snacks, such as *anticuchos* (grilled skewers) and *piquillo* peppers stuffed with *bacalhau*. Also on the menu are ceviches and playful sushi rolls (such as the Maya, a spicy package of shrimp, avocado, cilantro, jalapeño and onion). In summer, what Sushi Samba 7 lacks in São Paulo traffic noises, it makes up for with the chaotic sounds of Seventh Avenue, overheard from a sunny roof garden.

Thali
28 Greenwich Ave between Charles and 10th Sts (212-367-7411). Subway: A, C, E, F, V, S to W 4th St. 12:30–9:30pm. Average main course, including rice: $8. Cash only.
This South Indian vegetarian spot offers stuffed *dosa*, dense samosas and vegetable-filled griddle cakes— all at eye-poppingly cheap prices. A platter (or *thali*) filled with an appetizer, two entrées, dal, rice, bread and a sweet changes daily according to what's fresh; but expect regular offerings of healthy, fragrantly spiced entrées, such as stewed eggplant, broccoli with okra, or spinach with sweet corn and peas. Everything is simple, filling and a vast improvement on what's typically offered at local curry houses.

Two Boots to Go West
201 W 11th St at Seventh Ave (212-633-9096). Subway: 1, 2, 3 to 14th St. 11am–1am. Large plain pizza: $12.95. AmEx.
See page 166.

Midtown

Chelsea

Grand Sichuan International
229 Ninth Ave at 24th St (212-620-5200). Subway: C, E to 23rd St. 11:30am–11pm. Average main course: $11. AmEx, MC, V.
See **Grand Sichuan International Midtown**, page 179.

La Chinita Linda
166 Eighth Ave between 18th and 19th Sts (212-633-1791). Subway: 1, 2 to 18th St. 11am–11pm. Average main course: $7. AmEx, MC, V.
This long-standing Chino-Latino, which serves generous plates of good food at 1970s prices, is a welcome change of pace from the nonstop fabulousness of the Chelsea-boy scene. Foodwise, the Chino half of the menu is standard-issue Chinese-American chop suey. Latino is definitely the star, especially the arroz con pollo (chicken and rice); it's good whether your bird is roasted or fried. The aptly named Chicken Crackling— crispy chicken pieces—has a 100-decibel crunch.

Le Gamin Café
183 Ninth Ave at 21st St (212-243-8864). Subway: C, E to 23rd St. 8am–midnight. Average main course: $7. Cash only.
See page 168.

man ray
147 W 15th St between Sixth and Seventh Aves (212-929-5000). Subway: F, V, 1, 2, 3 to 14th St; L to Sixth Ave. Sun–Wed 5:30–11pm; Thu–Sat 5:30–11:30pm. Bar Sun–Wed 5:30pm–1am; Thu 5:30pm–2am; Fri, Sat 5:30pm–3am. Average main course: $25. AmEx, DC, Disc, MC, V.
The French aren't exactly Zen-like, but man ray, Chelsea's newest scenester hangout, pulls off that

tricky Asian-French fusion—a gambit that has failed elsewhere in the city. The restaurant, owned by record producer Thierry Kléméniuk, is an offshoot of the celebrity-crammed original in Paris (the investor list includes Sean Penn, John Malkovich and Johnny Depp). Kléméniuk is both Buddhist and French, which explains the decor: Asia meets Louis XIV.

Old Homestead

56 Ninth Ave between 14th and 15th Sts (212-242-9040). Subway: A, C, E to 14th St; L to Eighth Ave. Mon–Thu noon–10:45pm; Fri noon–11:30pm; Sat 1pm–12:30am; Sun 1–9:30pm. Average main course: $29. AmEx, DC, MC, V.
Look for the big cow above the awning. You come to this 133-year-old legend for aged steaks that are among the best in town. Feast on salt-crusted filet mignon, the venerated prime rib for two, or even fine raw, red slices of carpaccio.

The Park

See page 271 for listing.

Pepe Giallo to Go

253 Tenth Ave between 24th and 25th Sts (212-242-6055). Subway: C, E to 23rd St. Mon–Sat 11am–11pm; Sun 4–11pm. Average main course: $9. AmEx, MC, V.
You've got to like a place with the free-verse motto NO DIET COKE/NO SKIM MILK/NO DECAF COFFEE/ONLY GOOD FOOD. In addition to wit, Giallo serves what is possibly the best-value Italian food in the city. It's part of the four-restaurant Pepe family, all of which serve basically the same menu; Viola in Cobble Hill *(see page 189)* is more of a sit-down place, and Soho's Rosso *(see page 160)* has a liquor license. *(See also* Pepe Verde, *page 169.)* Pepe Giallo's wine list is very short and very cheap—and like its motto, refreshingly to the point.

The Red Cat

227 Tenth Ave between 23rd and 24th Sts (212-242-1122). Subway: C, E to 23rd St. Mon 5:30–11:30pm; Tue–Thu noon–2:30pm, 5:30–11:30pm; Fri, Sat noon–2:30pm, 5:30pm–midnight; Sun 5–10pm. Average main course: $21. AmEx, DC, MC, V.
At this crazy-quilt bistro, barn-red wainscoting cozies up to Moorish candle lanterns. The crowd—a mix of casually chic families, grown-up couples and nubile singletons—can make for a deafening decibel level, but there's no faulting Jimmy Bradley's humble, complex and gently priced food. Dine on crispy skate wing with butternut squash and hedgehog mushrooms, or simple (but no less tasty) roasted chicken and shell steaks.

Wild Lily Tea Room

511 W 22nd St between Tenth and Eleventh Aves (212-691-2258). Subway: C, E to 23rd St. Tue–Sun 11am–10pm. Average main course: $11. MC, V.
An hour at Wild Lily Tea Room will soothe your tattered soul. In the heart of Chelsea's gallery district, painter Ines Sun has created a multilevel stone-floored sanctuary where two koi swim among floating candles and chrysanthemums in a tranquil pond; even the background jazz is serene. Don't worry, you won't fall asleep in your soup. The food is delicate and delicious—edible art on handmade plates (also for sale). And as for that soup, you'll want to lap up every last drop of the puree of butternut squash, coconut and cinnamon-stick. Choose from 50 teas, or from the selection of wines and sakes. You'd be a fool to pass up the chestnut cream cake, which is diabolically rich.

Blue Water Grill

31 Union Sq West at 16th St (212-675-9500). Subway: L, N, Q, R, W, 4, 5, 6 to 14th St–Union Sq. Mon–Thu 11:30am–12:30am; Fri, Sat 11:30am–1am; Sun 10:30am–midnight. Jazz room Mon–Thu 6pm–12:30am; Fri, Sat 6pm–1am; Sun 6:30pm–midnight. Average main course: $20. AmEx, MC, V.
On a Friday night, immense, deafening Blue Water Grill has a lively, crowded bar scene that's unintimidating enough for three European businessmen to connect with three cute local girls, snare a table for six and slurp oysters all night—a good choice, along with sushi and a number of the entrées. Nothing is spectacular, but when you're in the right mood, dining on the wrought iron-accented balcony overlooking East 16th Street can feel a little like Paris. The jazz room downstairs, a louder and smokier venue (cigarettes and cigars are allowed), serves nightly live entertainment along with the food.

Chicama

35 E 18th St between Broadway and Park Ave South (212-505-2233). Subway: L, N, Q, R, W, 4, 5, 6 to 14th St–Union Sq. Mon 6–11pm; Tue–Thu noon–3pm, 6–11pm; Fri, Sat noon–3pm, 5:30pm–midnight; Sun 5:30pm–midnight. Average main course: $27. AmEx, MC, V.
At Chicama, there's a loud, swarming bar, and a 40-minute wait, even *with* a reservation. But chef Douglas Rodriguez makes sure there's no chaos in the kitchen. He carefully combines Latin American ingredients—fresh fish flown in from Chile and rare spices such as *huacatay* (black mint) from Peru—in clever creations. Juicy turkey stewed in a bold sauce of tomato, onion, *aji* (Peruvian yellow peppers) and ground walnuts is a rich, resonant example of what the kitchen does best, and a reminder of why Rodriguez is hailed as the *padrino* of New York's Nuevo Latino cuisine.

City Bakery

3 W 18th St between Fifth and Sixth Aves (212-366-1414). Subway: L, N, Q, R, W, 4, 5, 6 to 14th St–Union Sq. Mon–Sat 7:30am–10pm. Salad bar: $9.50 per pound. AmEx, MC, V.
City Bakery serves fudgy hot chocolate, sinful cookies and super-fresh salads and sandwiches. You'll also find a soda fountain, a closet-size chocolate shop and a beer-and-wine bar. You pay by the pound for many selections at the salad bar, so you may find yourself

Don't be koi Enjoy *shumai* beside the carp pool at Chelsea's Wild Lily Tea Room.

avoiding heavy items (roasted beets, fruit salad) and piling on lighter ones (mesclun, roasted green tomatoes). There's a lot more than salad, though—catfish, jasmine rice with red beans and tofu—but whatever you select, it's worth every penny.

Craft

43 E 19th St between Broadway and Park Ave South (212-780-0880). Subway: N, R, 6 to 23rd St. Tue–Sun 5:30–11pm. Average main course and one side: $33. AmEx, DC, Disc, MC, V.
Craft was the city's most heralded new restaurant in 2001, so make reservations weeks before you arrive in New York. Chef-owner Tom Colicchio has talented artisans in his kitchen using the finest ingredients available. The dining room's Mission-style tables and leather panels lining the walls carry the *craft* theme further. Colicchio's high-concept menu seems like a simple list of food groups (meat, vegetables, fish and shellfish), preparations (raw, cured/marinated, roasted, braised, sautéed) and side dishes (any from the vegetable group, plus potatoes, grains, beans and mushrooms). You choose what you want; how you want it. Does it sound like hard work? Once you experience Craft's pure-tasting, exquisitely prepared food, you'll be planning your return.

Curry in a Hurry

119 Lexington Ave at 28th St (212-683-0900). Subway: 6 to 28th St. 11am–midnight. Average main course, including rice: $8. AmEx, DC, Disc, MC, V.
What's electric blue, salmon pink and sea-foam green all over? Colorful Curry in a Hurry, where you can, as the slogan says, EAT LIKE A KING, PAY LIKE A PAUPER. It churns out solid, no-*nan*sense meals to a multiculti crowd. There are zesty curries for entrées and different veggie dishes daily. All platters come with fluffy basmati rice and fresh, hot nan. Help yourself to salad and condiments, and don't forget to BYOB.

Dano Restaurant

254 Fifth Ave between 28th and 29th Sts (212-725-2922). Subway: N, R, 6 to 28th St. Mon–Fri 11:30am–11pm; Sat 4–11pm; Sun 11:30am–10pm. Average main course: $14. AmEx, DC, Disc, MC, V.
Dano is perfect for a post–Empire State Building lunch or dinner. The small scale of the place means an atmosphere less hectic than the nearby competition. Chef-owner Dan Kobin has designed a menu of light fare with vaguely Southwestern overtones, along with an appealing selection of pastas and salads. On Sundays, Dano serves an attractive brunch for $14.50, drink included. (Try the apple soufflé pancakes.)

Ess-a-Bagel

359 First Ave at 21st St (212-260-2252). Subway: 6 to 23rd St. Mon–Fri 6am–10pm; Sat, Sun 7am–5pm. Plain bagel: 55¢. AmEx, DC, Disc, MC, V.
The ideal bagel should be big as a newborn baby, have a crust that's a little chewy but still breakable, and have no—or almost no—space in the hole. Ess-a-Bagel's original downtown location serves such a bagel. It's perfection at 55 cents a pop. Large chandeliers, faux-wood paneling and a gurgling cauldron of boiling bagels add to the ambience, and the pudgy, doughy rings are just as good at the midtown location (*see page 180*).

Fleur de Sel

5 E 20th St between Fifth Ave and Broadway (212-460-9100). Subway: N, R, 6 to 23rd St. Mon–Thu noon–2pm, 5:30–10:30pm; Fri, Sat noon–2pm, 5–11pm; Sun noon–2pm, 5–9pm. Three-course prix fixe: $62. AmEx, MC, V.
More subdued than stylish, more tasteful than trendy, this compact gem feels like a neighborhood restaurant, but it produces the kind of food that keeps it booked up weeks in advance. Chef-owner Cyril Renaud brings his Breton roots (and his hometown sea salt, for which the restaurant is named) to a seasonal menu that changes daily. One of the few dishes you can always order is seared foie gras with fried-fruit puree and rose water.

Gramercy Tavern

42 E 20th St between Broadway and Park Ave South (212-477-0777). Subway: N, R, 6 to 23rd St. Mon–Thu noon–2pm, 5:30–10pm; Fri noon–2pm, 5:30–11pm; Sat 5:30–11pm; Sun 5:30–10pm. Tavern room

Sun–Thu noon–11pm; Fri, Sat noon–midnight. Prix fixe: $65. AmEx, DC, Disc, MC, V.

After seven years, Danny Meyer's stellar dining room still feels seductive and luxurious enough for festive occasions, while retaining a comfy quotient (and relaxed service) that makes it fine for any old Tuesday—if your budget can support the tab. (Dinner for two is easily $200, even if you take only a few sips from the award-winning wine list. The $36 three-course lunch is a real deal.) Whatever you choose from the prix-fixe menu will be wonderful: Autumn might bring cubes of raw tuna with tomato sorbet; a thick fillet of roasted cod has a delicate, earthy sauce of cèpes. Up front in the Tavern Room, you can enjoy more gently priced dishes—grilled sardines duck confit and cheese boards—without making reservations.

Les Halles
411 Park Ave South between 28th and 29th Sts (212-679-4111). Subway: 6 to 28th St. Noon–midnight. Average main course: $19. AmEx, DC, MC, V

Chef-author Anthony Bourdain still runs the kitchen at this top brasserie, despite his newfound fame as host of a cable-TV show and best-selling author. His latest book is *A Cook's Tour*. Heed Les Halles' motto—AMERICAN BEEF, FRENCH STYLE—and order hanger steak, steak au poivre or the epic, only-to-be-ordered-rare *côte du boeuf.* You can also catch Bourdain's gourmand routine at Les Halles' sister restaurant across the street, **Park Bistro** *(414 Park Ave South between 28th and 29th Sts, 212-689-1360),* or at the new **Les Halles Downtown** *(see page 153)* in the Financial District.

Olives NY
W Union Square Hotel, 201 Park Ave South at 17th St (212-353-8345). Subway: L, N, Q, R, W, 4, 5, 6 to 14th St–Union Sq. 6–10:30am, 11:30am–3pm, 5pm–midnight. Bar menu midnight–2am. Average main course: $23. AmEx, DC, MC, V.

Wunderkind chef-owner Todd English, whose Boston Olives sprouted branches in Las Vegas and elsewhere

Cheap eats
The following restaurants offer main courses (or their equivalent) for $10 or less

Downtown

aKa Café	155
Angelica Kitchen	162
Bulgin' Waffles	162
Ceci-Cela	160
Congee Village	155
Corner Bistro	168
Jones Diner	162
Kate's Joint	163
Katz's Delicatessen	155
La Focacceria	163
Le Gamin Café	160, 164, **168**
Mamoun's Falafel	167
Max	164
Moustache	**165**, 169
New Indonesia & Malaysia Restaurant	159
New York Noodle Town	159
Nha Trang	159
Nyonya	159
Palacinka	160
Pepe Rosso to Go	160
Pepe Verde	169
Ruben's Empanadas	154, **161**
Saint's Alp Teahouse	159, **165**
SEA	165
Second Avenue Deli	166
Sophie's Restaurant	154
Two Boots Restaurant & Pizzerias	162, **166**, 169
Thali	169
Veselka	166
Vietnam Restaurant	159

Midtown

Cafe Edison	177
City Bakery	170
Curry in a Hurry	171
Ess-a-Bagel	**171**, 180
Hallo Berlin	177, **179**
La Chinita Linda	169
Le Gamin Café	169
Los Dos Rancheros Mexicanos	175
Mandoo Bar	175
Margon	178
Market Cafe	175
Menchanko-Tei	181
Pepe Giallo to Go	170
Pongal	173
Republic	173
Sandwich Planet	176
Two Boots	175, 178

Uptown

Awash	184
Bardolino	184
Charles' Southern Style Kitchen	187
Drip Cafe	185
Flor de Mayo	185
Hungarian Pastry Shop	185
Le Pain Quotidien	184
Max Soha	187
M&G Soul Food Diner	187
Miss Mamie's Spoonbread Too	185
Miss Maude's Spoonbread Too	187

The Outer Boroughs

Brooklyn

Ferdinando's Focacceria	187
Joya	188
Karam	188
L-Cafe	188
Pepe Viola	189
Saint's Alp Teahouse	189
Two Boots Park Slope	189

Queens

Delhi Palace	190
Nostalgias	190

Bronx

The Feeding Tree	190

Green party The salad bar at the Flatiron District's City Bakery transcends the usual self-serve offerings.

with Molyvos; *see page 180*). The atmosphere is strictly Aegean: billowing ceiling canopy, white stucco walls and colorful banquettes. Start with assorted dips and grilled octopus with lemon sauce, then move on to the signature grilled lamb chop; it's so tender, you don't need teeth to eat it.

Pipa

ABC Carpet & Home, 38 E 19th St between Broadway and Park Ave South (212-677-2233). Subway: L, N, Q, R, W, 4, 5, 6 to 14th St–Union Sq. Mon–Thu noon–3pm, 6–11pm; Fri noon–3pm, 5:30pm–midnight; Sat 11am–3pm, 5:30pm– midnight; Sun 11am–3pm, 5:30–10pm. Average tapa: $11. AmEx, MC, V.

Celeb chef Douglas Rodriguez's tapas-style Pipa, in a home-furnishing store, is next to his previous hit, Chicama *(see page 170)*. The tapas reveal a crafty interweaving of ingredients and tastes. The veggie *coca* (flatbread) is a prime example, combining the mildness of eggplant, the smokiness of roasted yellow tomatoes and artichokes, the mellowness of *manchego* cheese and the vigor of *piquillo* peppers with a bold, briny olive paste. With each bite, a different ingredient comes to the fore. *Gambas al ajillo* (garlic shrimp), a commonly over-oiled item in tapas bars, has a delightfully light garlic-chili essence.

before blooming on the New York scene, packs a lot of powerful flavors into each dish. The guys at the grill know what they're doing, so the rack of lamb, infused with rosemary, is perfectly cooked.

Patria

250 Park Ave South at 20th St (212-777-6211). Subway: N, R, 6 to 23rd St. Mon–Thu noon–2:45pm, 6–11pm; Fri noon–2:45pm, 5:30pm–midnight; Sat 5:30pm–midnight; Sun 5:30–10:30pm. Average main course: $30. Prix fixe: $45–$79. AmEx, DC, MC, V.

Eight-year-old Patria—the three-tiered, three-star Nuevo Latino sensation—remains an indisputable success. It's obvious why: The upbeat staff, bustling open kitchen and sunny saffron-colored walls prompt even the most irascible sort to discover his inner salsa dancer. Executive chef Andrew DiCataldo makes regular trips to Latin America in search of inspiration and indigenous ingredients. The resulting menu reads like a map: Ecuadoran shrimp tamales, Brazilian seafood stew and Argentine-style beef tenderloin. Practically everything on the menu is extraordinary, bursting with the harmony of sweet and savory flavors.

Periyali

35 W 20th St between Fifth and Sixth Aves (212-463-7890). Subway: F, V, N, R to 23rd St. Mon–Thu noon–3pm, 5:30–10:30pm; Fri noon–3pm, 5:30–11:30pm; Sat 5:30–10:30pm. Average main course: $22. AmEx, MC, V.

Periyali was the first restaurant to introduce fine Greek cuisine to Manhattanites, and 16 years after opening, it remains one of the standards by which all the city's Greek restaurants are judged (along

Pongal

110 Lexington Ave between 27th and 28th Sts (212-696-9458). Subway: 6 to 28th St. Mon–Fri noon–3pm, 5–10pm; Sat, Sun noon–3pm. Average main course, including rice: $9. DC, Disc, MC, V.

Every night, Orthodox Jews and devout Hindus come to Pongal for kosher vegetarian North Indian cuisine. Of course, lots of secular types frequent the place simply for the South Indian food (the place is so popular that the owners opened a second branch down the block. Sample the *thali*, large platters laden with eight items (usually including rice and dal) for less than $15. Just be sure to get one that comes with a *dosa*, a thin, crispy crêpe made of rice flour and lentils.

Republic

37 Union Sq West between 16th and 17th Sts (212-627-7168). Subway: L, N, Q, R,W, 4, 5, 6 to 14th St–Union Sq. Sun–Wed 11:30am–11pm; Thu–Sat 11:30am–midnight. Average main course: $7.50. AmEx, DC, MC, V.

Pan-Asian Republic is a great deal for food *and* scene. For not a lot more than you'd spend at a Chinatown joint, you can sit with a low-budget in-crowd at communal tables and get big a big bowl of noodles laden with tender chicken pieces in a coconut-milk broth, pungent with kafir leaves and lemongrass. Drop by for lunch in the midst of a Flatiron shopping expedition.

Necessities

Sushi Samba

245 Park Ave South between 19th and 20th Sts (212-475-9377). Subway: L, N, Q, R, W, 4, 5, 6 to 14th St–Union Sq. Mon–Wed noon–1am; Thu–Sat noon–2am; Sun 1pm–midnight. Average sushi meal (7 pieces, 1 roll): $22. Average ceviche: $9. AmEx, MC, V.
See **Sushi Samba 7**, page 169.

Tabla

11 Madison Ave at 25th St (212-889-0667).Subway: N, R, 6 to 23rd St. Mon–Fri noon–2pm, 5:30–10:30pm; Sat 5:30–10:30pm; Sun 5:30–9:30pm. Bar Mon–Thu noon–11pm; Fri noon–11:30pm; Sat 5:30–11:30pm; Sun 5:30–10pm. Three-course prix fixe: $54. AmEx, DC, Disc, MC, V.
Owner Danny Meyer's eye for detail is well focused here: widely spaced tables, flattering lighting, original Deco fixtures and perfect service. Situated in this grand room, carved from the lobby of the original 1930s Met Life Building (yes, that's an original nickel-plated bronze Art Deco railing), Tabla is often categorized as upscale Indian, but the food is more reminiscent of Pan-Asian fusion flavors than it is of traditional subcontinental cuisine. Executive chef Floyd Cardoz (born in Goa, trained in France) uses spice in place of butter and cream to create celestial flavors. The multinational wine list is designed to complement the multilayered food.

Tamarind

41–43 E 22nd St between Broadway and Park Ave South (212-674-7400). Subway: N, R, 6 to 23rd St. 11:30am–3pm, 5:30–11:30pm. Average main course: $22. AmEx, DC, Disc, MC, V.
Tamarind's chef Raji Jallepalli-Reiss, whose signature Indian-fusion cuisine wows 'em at her Memphis restaurant, incorporates the namesake fruit into innovative fare, such as *konju pappas* (shrimp cooked in spicy coconut sauce, then flavored with curry leaves and smoked tamarind). In summer 2001, the restaurant opened the adjacent nine-seat **Tamarind Tea Room** *(43 E 22nd St between Broadway and Park Ave South, 212-674-7400),* where you can get Indian-style sandwiches and choose from 17 teas.

TanDa

331 Park Avenue South between 24th and 25th Sts (212-253-8400). Subway: N, R, 6 to 23rd St. Mon–Fri noon–3pm, 6–11pm, Sat, Sun 6–11pm. Average main course: $23. AmEx, MC, V.
The latest posh restaurant-lounge to hit Park Avenue South, TanDa is named after a Vietnamese poet who wrote about food and wine as the essence of life. The Asian motif carries over to the decor and menu. Chef Stanley Wong offers artfully executed dishes, including Balinese roasted duck.

Union Pacific

111 E 22nd St between Park Ave South and Lexington Ave (212-995-8500). Subway: 6 to 23rd St. Mon, Sat 5:30–10pm; Tue–Fri noon–2pm, 5:30–10pm. Three-course prix fixe: $65. AmEx, DC, Disc, MC, V.
After a big opening PR blitz in 1997, chef-proprietor Rocco DiSpirito's bi-level dining palace has quietly settled in for the long haul, and a whole subset of New York food snobs consider Union Pacific their little secret. DiSpirito's inventive fusion menu still succeeds three years on: raw bay scallops, mixed with pieces of *uni* (sea urchin) and drizzled with tomato water and mustard oil, have a harmonious salty-sweet bite. DiSpirito possesses that rare ability to reinvent tastes we thought we already understood.

Veritas

43 E 20th St between Broadway and Park Ave South (212-353-3700). Subway: N, R, 6 to 23rd St. Mon–Sat 5:30–10:15pm; Sun 5–9:30pm. Three-course prix fixe: $68. AmEx, Disc, MC, V.
Three-year-old Veritas's reputation as a wine haven is well established. Wine director Tim Kopec and chef Scott Bryan have made this spare, 55-seat restaurant the definition of epicurean. Part of the reserve list is drawn from the collections of Park Smith and Steve Verlin, two of the owners; the combined market and reserve lists (online at www.veritas-nyc.com) include up to 2,700 types of wine, and while there are rarities, such as a magnum of 1900 Margaux premier cru for $29,000, they also have a number of under-$40 selections. Bryan's refined American food keeps pace with the wines. Barolo-braised veal is as soft as its cushion of mashed potatoes. Budget-conscious diners can order à la carte at the bar.

Zen Palate

34 Union Sq East at 16th St (212-614-9291). Subway: L, N, Q, R, W, 4, 5, 6 to 14th St–Union Sq. Sun–Thu noon–10:30pm; Fri, Sat noon–11:30pm. Average main course: $15. AmEx, DC, MC, V.
See page 179.

Artisanal

2 Park Ave at 32nd St (212-725-8585). Subway: 6 to 33rd St. Mon–Sat 11:30am–midnight. Average main course: $20. AmEx, MC, V.
Terrance Brennan's 3,500-square-foot Artisanal is ostensibly a brasserie, but it has enough surprises to keep the customers guessing. A whopping 150 types of vino are available by the glass. The chicken cooked under a brick is incredibly moist and tender. Yet Artisanal's true mission is to coddle the *fromage*-obsessed. Many dishes involve cheese (including a 100-cheese fondue!); some 200 varieties ripen just so in a climate-controlled cave. Brennan cooks exceptional Mediterranean cuisine at his other restaurant, **Picholine** *(35 W 64th St between Central Park West and Broadway, 212-724-8585)*

Tuscan Steak

622 Third Ave at 40th St (212-404-1700). Subway: S, 4, 5, 6, 7 to 42nd St–Grand Central. Mon–Thu 11:30am–2:45pm, 5:30pm–midnight; Fri 11:30am–2:45pm, 5:30pm–1am; Sat 5:30pm–1am; Sun 5:30–11pm. Average main course: $28. AmEx, DC, MC, V.
At Tuscan Steak, the New York offshoot of the Miami

Beach hot spot, the garlic bread will run you $13.50, a price that's representative of this larger-than-life restaurant. Sure, it's *truffle*-soaked bread, and you get to eat it in a jaw-dropping space. A translucent wine rack soars toward the 30-foot ceiling, while a second-floor lounge allows a panoramic view of the downstairs booths sheltering A-list diners, such as Rachel Hunter and Famke Janssen. The only thing more beautiful than the scene is the slew of artful (and, for the most part, reasonably priced) family-style dishes.

Two Boots

Grand Central Terminal, Lower Concourse, 42nd St at Park Ave (212-557-7992). Subway: S, 4, 5, 6, 7 to 42nd St–Grand Central. Mon–Thu 11am–10pm; Fri, Sat 11am–1pm; Sun 11am–9pm. Large plain pizza: $14. AmEx, DC, Disc, MC, V.
See page 136.

West 30s/Garment District

Kum Gang San

49 W 32nd St at Broadway (212-967-0909). Subway: B, D, F, V, N, Q, R, W to 34th St–Herald Sq. 24hrs. Average main course: $15. AmEx, Disc, MC, V.
See page 130.

Los Dos Rancheros Mexicanos

507 Ninth Ave at 38th St (212-868-7780). Subway: A, C, E to 34th St–Penn Station. 11am–11pm. Average main course: $7. Cash only.
This cafeterialike *taquería*, lined with jungle murals, is superb. Play your favorite mariachi on the jukebox and relax with the mostly Mexican clientele. A small plate of tasty appetizers, such as three chorizo tacos, costs an absurd $2 to $3. Order a half dozen and share with your friends. Follow with the *barbacoa de chivo* (barbecued goat)—it's so good, you'll bleat for more.

Mandoo Bar

2 W 32nd St between Fifth Ave and Broadway (212-279-3075). Subway: B, D, F, V, N, Q, R, W to 34th St–Herald Sq; 6 to 33rd St. 11am–11pm. Average main course: $7. AmEx, MC, V.
A civilized short-order spot in the heart of Korea Town, Mandoo Bar is as cute and accessible as the Korean dumpling for which it is named. Behind the stylish open kitchen are a dozen cool rectangular tables and benches. The *mandoo* is outstanding: tiny and grease-free, all the better to pop and gulp one after another. Get them fried, not steamed, and choose your filling or soup treatment; pork is the classic, but kimchi and beef are also delicious.

Market Cafe

496 Ninth Ave between 37th and 38th Sts (212-564-7350). Subway: A, C, E to 34th St–Penn Station. Mon–Fri 11am–11pm; Sat 5–11pm; Sun 10am–4pm. Average main course: $10. AmEx, DC, Disc, MC, V.
At Market Cafe, you'll find trendies and casual neighborhood types alike lolling on the 1950s-era barstools at the long counter or in blue vinyl booths with Formica-topped tables. The moderately priced menu includes dishes such as steak frites (the classic skirt cut) for under $15. Factor in the great selection of wines by the glass and the unhurried vibe, and you'll always remember Market Cafe.

Modern English Olives NY in Union Square showcases Todd English's creative Mediterranean food.

Manchego of **La Mancha** The Spanish tapas are top-flight at Pipa, just north of Union Square.

Sandwich Planet

534 Ninth Ave between 39th and 40th Sts (212-273-9768). Subway: A, C, E to 42nd St–Port Authority. Mon–Sat noon–9:30pm. Average sandwich: $6.50. Cash only.

At Sandwich Planet, the fresh breads and wide selection of cheeses and home-cured meats add up to some of the best cheap food in the city. Not only are the 78 sandwich selections stellar, but you can send each one in a million directions by adding any of the 41 extras, priced at 75 cents a pop. Talking sides: The peppery arugula in the goat-cheese salad tastes like it was plucked straight from a country garden. Take-out orders pile up until closing time, so drop in during off-peak hours instead, when table space is plentiful.

Theater District

Restaurant Above

Hilton Times Square, 234 W 42nd St between Seventh and Eighth Aves (212-642-2626). Subway: A, C, E to 42nd St–Port Authority; N, Q, R, W, S, 1, 2, 3, 7 to 42nd St–Times Sq. Sun–Thu 6:30–11am, 11:30am–2:30pm, 5:30–10pm; Fri, Sat 5:30–11pm. Average main course: $27. AmEx, MC, V.

Larry Forgione's American–slash–Pan-Asian eatery, perched 202 feet atop Times Square, is a worthwhile pit stop for the culinarily adventurous. The marathon menu is filled with excellent starters (such as spicy yellowfin tuna tartare) and entrées (salmon is framed by silky corn pudding). Impeccable service keeps you feeling coddled from beginning to end.

Aquavit

13 W 54th St between Fifth and Sixth Aves (212-307-7311). Subway: E, V to Fifth Ave–53rd St.
Mon–Sat noon–2:30pm, 5:30–10:30pm; Sun noon–2:30pm, 5:30–9pm. Three-course prix fixe: $68. AmEx, DC, Disc, MC, V.

Known as the "grandest of New York's Scandinavian restaurants," Aquavit is oh-so-much more. For eight years, Swedish-Ethiopian chef Marcus Samuelsson has been seducing diners with his artistic food flights (which end in dreamy détentes). Take the foie gras ganache: Three little bombes of almost-liquid duck liver share a plate with a kumquat tart and a small scoop of truffle ice cream—an amazing play of warm and cold, hard and soft. The space is also a study in contrasts. You enter an 1896 townhouse that once sheltered Rockefellers, then descend into an ultramodern atrium. An adjacent café serves more straight-ahead Swedish food (meatballs, beef Rydberg); Samuelsson also created the menu at the casual **AQ Café** *(Scandinavia House, 58 Park Ave between 37th and 38th Sts, 212-879-9779).*

Baldoria

249 W 49th St between Broadway and Eighth Ave (212-582-0460). Subway: N, R, W to 49th St; 1, 2 to 50th St. Mon–Thu 6–11pm; Fri, Sat 6pm–midnight. Average main course: $24. AmEx, DC, MC, V.

If Frank Sinatra and Dean Martin were still around, Baldoria would be their midtown hangout. This swank operation opened in 2000 when Frank Pellegrino Jr., whose father runs legendary Rao's in East Harlem, decided to take the family act downtown. The result is a low-lit, bi-level restaurant with rich wood paneling and a loud, happy crowd. When it comes to the hearty homestyle food, chef Massimo Cagliari's kitchen delivers, judging by the house-made pastas, smoky *bresaola* (finely sliced, cured filet mignon) and short ribs in balsamic reduction.

Cafe Edison

Hotel Edison, 228 W 47th St between Seventh Ave and Broadway (212-840-5000). Subway: N, R, W to 49th St; 1, 2 to 50th St. Mon–Sat 6am–10pm; Sun 6am–8pm. Average main course: $10. Cash only.
Neil Simon thought so much of the quirky personalities at this longtime hangout for theater folk that it's the setting in his recent Broadway production, *45 Seconds from Broadway*. At Cafe Edison (a.k.a. the Polish Tea Room), decor runs to pink vinyl booths and Broadway show posters. Servings of the straightforward diner-delicatessen food are almost obscenely generous, but the biggest hits are the forgiving prices.

Carnegie Deli

854 Seventh Ave at 55th St (212-757-2245). Subway: B, D, E to Seventh Ave; N, Q, R, W to 57th St. 6:30am–4am. Corned beef sandwich: $10.45. Cash only.
Just *try* to get your mouth around the legendary corned beef on rye, dripping with Swiss, served at this Theater District institution. Visitors and New Yorkers alike find themselves wide-eyed before mountainous piles of sliced meats. The festival of cholesterol, the frenetic waiters and the cramped quarters may leave you feeling a little woozy.

Churrascaria Plataforma

Belvedere Hotel, 316 W 49th St between Eighth and Ninth Aves (212-245-0505). Subway: C, E to 50th St. Noon–midnight. All you can eat: $38.95. AmEx, DC, Disc, MC, V.
If impeccably mannered Brazilian waiters carving prime rib, suckling pig, *linguiça*, lamb, etc., were all this place had to offer, it would still deserve a sterling review. But the salad bar—never before has a restaurant fixture been so inadequately named. Sure, there are greens—if you can find them among the bean-and-sausage *feijão tropeiro*, octopus salad and about ten billion other items. Add an elegant atmosphere, a roving caipirinha cart and live music, and you may not even mind the dining hordes.

db bistro moderne

City Club Hotel, 55 W 44th St between Fifth and Sixth Aves (212-391-2400). Subway: S, 4, 5, 6, 7 to 42nd St–Grand Central. Average main course: $26. AmEx, MC, V.
Amid grim financial forecasts, star chef Daniel Boulud launched db bistro moderne in summer 2001. The intimate, beautifully designed midtown eatery is billed as the casual, more playful version of the uptown Daniel (*see page 182*). But this being Mr. Boulud, you can bet db isn't a cheap steak frites joint. Sit under luscious red flower prints and enjoy the contemporary bistro offerings.

Gallagher's Steak House

228 W 52nd St between Broadway and Eighth Ave (212-245-5336). Subway: C, E, 1, 2 to 50th St. Noon–midnight. Average main course: $30. AmEx, DC, Disc, MC, V.
Now in its 75th year, Gallagher's is still one of the city's premier steak houses. As befits an old-school steak house, all sides are à la carte—and the fried onions are de rigueur. Order the justly famous King Loin; dry-aged, like everything else, for three weeks in the glass-walled meat locker near the entrance, then broiled over hickory logs. It's worth every bit of its $46.75 rib-sticker price.

Hallo Berlin

626 Tenth Ave at 44th St (212-977-1944). Subway: A, C, E to 42nd St–Port Authority. Mon–Sat 11am–11pm; Sun 4–11pm. Average main course: $10. Disc, MC, V.
See page 179.

Ilo

The Bryant Park, 40 W 40th St between Fifth and Sixth Aves (212-642-2255). Subway: B, D, F, V to 42nd St; 7 to Fifth Ave. Mon–Fri 6:30–10:30am, noon–2:30pm, 5:30–11:30pm; Sat 7–11am, 11:30am–2:30pm, 5:30–11:30pm; Sun 7–11am, 11:30am–2:30pm, 5–10pm. Average main course: $31. Six-course greenmarket tasting: $65. AmEx, DC, MC, V.
Rick Laakkonen's elaborate cooking is served in a lively (read: deafening) but spare dining room off the red-leather lobby bar of the Bryant Park *(see* **Small Wonders,** *page 132).* The staff seems to have trained at the Forrest Gump School of Restaurant and Hotel Management—these kids are as chatty and genial as lap dogs. And Laakkonen's creative American food may make you sit up and beg. Try his signature Tidal Pool (oysters and sea urchin in a warm bath) or rabbit with cannelloni of dandelion and sheep's-milk ricotta.

Le Bernardin

155 W 51st St between Sixth and Seventh Aves (212-489-1515). Subway: B, D, F, V to 47–50th Sts–Rockefeller Ctr; N, R, W to 49th St. Mon–Thu noon–2:30pm, 5:30–11pm; Fri noon–2:30pm, 5:30–11:30pm; Sat 5:30–11:30pm. Three-course prix fixe: $77. AmEx, DC, Disc, MC, V.
The setting: equal parts exquisite and understated. The service: beyond gracious. The food: extraordinary. This 250-seat restaurant has been credited with revolutionizing the way fish—particularly tuna and salmon—is prepared and served in this town (medium-rare, with minimal embellishment).

Necessities

CRITICS' PICKS Landmarks

Bamonte's, page 187
Elaine's, page 186
The Four Seasons, page 180
Gallagher's Steak House, page 177
Old Homestead, page 170
Grand Central Oyster Bar & Restaurant, page 181
Peter Luger, page 189
Rainbow Grill, page 178
Tavern on the Green, page 183
'21,' page 178

Deceptively simple entrées, such as steamed halibut with oregano and black-truffle sauce, demonstrate chef Eric Ripert's way with flavors—they're simultaneously delicate and powerful.

Margon

136 W 46th St between Sixth and Seventh Aves (212-354-5013). Subway: B, D, F, V to 47–50th Sts–Rockefeller Ctr. Mon–Fri 6am–4:45pm; Sat 7am–2:30pm. Average main course: $6. Cash only.

During peak weekday lunch hours, the lines at this cramped Cuban cafeteria are out the door. The reason: great, cheap food. In-the-know midtowners squeeze into Margon for heaping plates of *chicharrones de pollo* (fried chicken pieces), steak sandwiches and a succulent roasted pork. Shoot for noon if you want to snag a seat, and remember: Table-sharing is encouraged—so don't hog the hot sauce.

Marseille

630 Ninth Ave at 44th St (212-333-3410). Subway: A, C, E to 42nd St–Port Authority. 5:30–11pm. Average main course: $19. AmEx, MC, V.

A former Hell's Kitchen bank has become a treasure trove of another kind. Chef Alex Urena's menu draws on the cuisines of the Near East and Europe, turning out dishes like lamb *tagine* and black-olive–crusted salmon with savoy cabbage. Those who can't make up their minds can order appetizer tasting plates, like a combo of lamb, sausage and foie gras—named, appropriately, "Yes Meat."

Medi

45 Rockefeller Plaza at 50th St (212-399-8888). Subway: B, D, F, V to 47–50th Sts–Rockefeller Ctr. 11am–11:30pm. Average main course: $26. AmEx, DC, Disc, MC, V.

Medi occupies a patch of prime real estate—overlooking the Rockefeller Plaza skating rink and the Christmas tree—and its yuletide business could probably cover a year's rent. But diners appear all year long: Overseeing the kitchen at the sunny eatery is renowned France-based chef Roger Vergé, whose Mediterranean menu includes spaghetti with wild mushrooms and black truffles, and the Golden Egg, a soft-boiled egg with caviar over ratatouille.

Rainbow Grill

30 Rockefeller Plaza between Fifth and Sixth Aves, entrance on 49th or 50th St, 65th floor (212-632-5100). Subway: B, D, F, V to 47–50th Sts–Rockefeller Ctr. Noon–3pm, 5:30pm–midnight. Bar noon–1am. Average main course: $40. Average pasta: $30. AmEx, DC, MC, V.

No fewer than six members of the Rainbow Grill's waitstaff may alight at your table during a meal—there's no denying that the service is topflight. They'll even pose with you for a picture, with the stunning view of the Empire State Building and panorama of southern Manhattan as the backdrop. Perks such as these explain why, on the top floor of 30 Rock, you'll drop a bundle for well-prepared Italian and continental food. The best time to arrive, of course, is an hour before sundown. Men need to wear a jacket to the dining area; the Grill's jazzy cocktail lounge is more casual, and that's where to go for a smoke, too. Note: The famous adjacent Rainbow Room is mostly used for catered functions these days.

Ruby Foo's

1626 Broadway at 49th St (212-489-5600). Subway: N, R, W to 49th St; 1, 2 to 50th St. Sun–Thu 11:30am–midnight; Fri, Sat 11:30am–1am. Average main course: $19. AmEx, MC, V.

Ruby Foo's is just glam enough to be self-mocking, and the top-notch service and distinctive Sino-Japanese menu have charmed the city's foodies. At both locations *(see page 185),* the design puts a decadent spin on the classic chop suey houses of old. The menu is designed for sharing—the whole table can pick from plates of robust yet delicate *shumai* (shrimp-and-crabmeat dumplings), along with tasty crispy duck. The counter seating is convenient for a spontaneous bite, and the bar tables are smoker-friendly.

Russian Samovar

256 W 52nd St between Broadway and Eighth Ave (212-757-0168). Subway: C, E, 1, 2 to 50th St. Sun, Mon 5pm–midnight; Tue–Thu noon–3pm, 5pm–midnight; Fri, Sat noon–3pm, 5pm–1:30am. Average main course: $22. AmEx, DC, Disc, MC, V.

Co-owned by Mikhail Baryshnikov and once frequented by Joseph Brodsky, the Samovar is amassing a pedigree that rivals the Russian Tea Room. It helps that the food is world-class, from the light salmon *coulibiac* to the intimidating chicken Kiev.

'21'

21 W 52nd St between Fifth and Sixth Aves (212-582-7200). Subway: B, D, F to 47–50th Sts–Rockefeller Ctr; E, V to Fifth Ave–53rd St. Mon–Thu noon–2:30pm, 5:30–10pm; Fri noon–2:30pm, 5:30–11pm; Sat 5:30–11pm. Closed Saturdays Jun–Aug. Average main course: $39. AmEx, DC, Disc, MC, V.

After 73 years, '21' is still a clubby enclave for the powerful. Go even if you don't fancy yourself a mogul, just to experience the aura of 1940s New York—all dark and woody with old *New Yorker* cartoons on the walls and boys' toys hanging from the ceiling. Chef Erik Blauberg, who has worked in the kitchens of Roger Vergé and Alain Ducasse, creates contemporary seasonal plates such as a crisped black sea bass in champagne sauce. But the cool stuff is under the '21' Classics heading. Blauberg ransacked the archives of '21' to revive some dishes that are part of American culinary history. Steak Diane, flambéed tableside, was on the restaurant's very first menu.

Two Boots

30 Rockefeller Plaza, concourse level, between 49th and 50th Sts (212-332-8800). Subway: Subway: B, D, F, V to 47–50th Sts–Rockefeller Ctr. Mon–Fri 11:30am–8pm; Sat 11am–6pm. Large plain pizza: $13.95. AmEx, DC, MC, V.

See page 166.

Fellini cuisine Brasserie 8½ serves rich, satisfying food in a stylish, cinematic setting.

Victor's Cafe 52

236 W 52nd St between Broadway and Eighth Ave (212 586-7714). Subway: C, E, 1, 2 to 50th St. Sun–Thu noon–midnight; Fri, Sat noon–1am. Average main course: $21. AmEx, DC, MC, V.

Paella was an exotic dish to most gringos when Victor del Corral opened his Theater District restaurant in 1963, but thanks to his trailblazing efforts, menus that list the saffron-flavored rice dish are now a dime a dozen. The menu is a crash course in Cuban classics, such as *frijoles negros* soup and seafood stew steeped in cilantro broth.

Virgil's Real BBQ

152 W 44th St between Sixth Ave and Broadway (212-921-9494). Subway: B, D, F, V to 42nd St; N, Q, R, W, S, 1, 2, 3, 7 to 42nd St–Times Sq. Mon 11:30am–11pm; Tue–Sat 11:30am–midnight. Average main course: $16. AmEx, MC, V.

The piles of hickory logs and odor of burning wood attest to the bona fide barbecue smoker, while the globe-trotting collection of foreign currency above the bar reminds you of the key clientele. But don't think "tourist trap"—Virgil's boasts some of the best brisket in the five boroughs. The menu spans Southern favorites—biscuits and gravy, baby back ribs, Texas links and an ample selection of sides. Gluttons and indecisive types should order the Pig Out; it includes five different types of meat. Wear your extra-loose pants, is all we're sayin'.

Zen Palate

663 Ninth Ave at 46th St (212-582-1669). Subway: A, C, E to 42nd St–Port Authority. 11am–10:30pm. Average main course: $15. AmEx, DC, MC, V.

Zen Palate has one of the city's most extensive veg-

etarian menus, which co-owner Sharley Chuang says was inspired by Buddha himself. The 46th Street location *(see page 179)* is a godsend for health-conscious theatergoers, and it's more polished than its Union Square *(see page 184)* and uptown cousins. Dish names—such as Tofu Infinity or Jewel of Happiness—sound like yoga positions, and the flavors will send you that much closer to nirvana.

West 50s/Clinton

Alain Ducasse at the Essex House

155 W 58th St between Sixth and Seventh Aves (212-265-7300). Subway: N, Q, R, W to 57th St. Mon–Wed 7–9pm; Thu, Fri noon–2pm; 7–9pm. Prix fixe: $145–$250. AmEx, DC, Disc, MC, V.

France's Alain Ducasse, the most celebrated chef on the Continent, swooped into the Essex House in summer 2000 and offered what was then the city's most expensive meal. You may feel the effort as Ducasse and his team strive to wring maximum flavor from each ingredient. The effect can range from dazzling to overpowering, and the incredibly gracious service never seems to hover (even when a table for two is attended by more than double that number).

Brasserie 8½

9 W 57th St between Fifth and Sixth Aves (212-829-0812). Subway: N, Q, R, W to 57th St. Mon–Fri 11:30am–3pm, 5:30pm–midnight; Sat 11am–3:30pm, 5:30pm–midnight; Sun 11am–3:30pm, 5:30–10pm. Average main course: $26. AmEx, DC, MC, V.

This sprawling destination (13,000 square feet!) is an exercise in colorful, textural excess. Chef Julian Alonzo, who cut his teeth with David Bouley in New York and Guy Savoy in Paris, deftly updates classics: His frisée salad, for example, comes with poached quail eggs on a tiny brioche; a thick, juicy *côte de boeuf,* with the traditional bone marrow, has a pinot noir glaze. But Alonzo knows there are some dishes you just don't mess with, such as coq au vin.

Grand Sichuan International Midtown

745 Ninth Ave between 50th and 51st Sts (212-582-2288). Subway: C, E to 50th St. Mon–Fri 11am–11pm; Sat, Sun noon–11pm. Average main course: $13. AmEx, MC, V.

On a stretch of Ninth Avenue that's lined with a veritable United Nations of restaurants, Grand Sichuan International looms large. Arguably the best Chinese restaurant outside Chinatown, this is the third outpost of an authentic Szechuan cooking minichain *(see pages 157 and 169).* The part of the menu labeled Mao's Home Cooking features the best dishes, including sour string beans with minced pork, and shredded potatoes in vinegar sauce. You're sure to find something to delight you, even if it takes a lifetime to get through the lengthy menu. It would be a lifetime well spent.

Hallo Berlin

402 W 51st St at Ninth Ave (212-541-6248). Subway: C, E to 50th St. 11am–2am. Average main course: $10. MC, V.

Billed as New York's Wurst Restaurant, Hallo Berlin delivers Teutonic tasties for bargain prices at two no-frills locations (see page 177). Specializing in "German soul food," Berliner Rolf Babiel and his Haitian wife, Bernadette, serve wurst sandwiches on a crusty *brötchen* roll and topped with fresh kraut (red and white), mustard and spicy curry sauce. The daily special of soup, Wiener schnitzel (*mit* fixins) and a mug of Bitburger will have you singing "Liebe Deutschland," or at least "99 Luftballons."

Hell's Kitchen

679 Ninth Ave between 46th and 47th Sts (212-977-1588). Subway: C, E to 50th St. Sun–Wed 5–11pm; Thu–Sat 5pm–midnight. Average main course: $16. AmEx, Disc, V.

A slew of new eateries like Hell's Kitchen are teaching New Yorkers that "Mexican restaurant" doesn't have to mean "let's go have margaritas with rice and beans." The food here, a loose (and refined) interpretation of Mexican, is smothered in flavor, not Monterey Jack cheese. Knowledgeable waiters steer you through tempting choices, such as duck confit empanadas with fig *mole* and crisp cabbage salad. The intimate room, done in warm fire-orange tiles and exposed brick, bucks the usual sombrero style. After 7pm, a wait at the bar is a given—and it's a pleasure, once you taste house concoctions such as the Hell's Kitchen Sink, a loco variation on an old favorite, the Long Island Iced Tea. Ha-cha-cha.

Molyvos

871 Seventh Ave between 55th and 56th Sts (212-582-7500). Subway: B, D, E to Seventh Ave; N, Q, R, W to 57th St. Mon–Thu noon–3pm, 5:30–11:30pm; Fri noon–3pm, 5:30pm–midnight; Sat noon–3pm, 5pm–midnight; Sun noon–11pm. Average main course: $24. AmEx, DC, Disc, MC, V.

Too often, what passes for Greek food in this city is soggy spanakopita and gummy moussaka. Molyvos is out to change all that, presenting sophisticated versions of Greek staples, and adding some twists of its own. Since it's designed to accommodate big groups, Molyvos does tend to get noisy, especially during the pretheater rush.

Town

13 W 56th St between Fifth and Sixth Aves (212-582-4445). Subway: E, V to Fifth Ave–53rd St. Mon–Sat 7:30–10am, noon–2:30pm, 5:30–10:30pm; Sun 11am–2:30pm, 5:30–9:30pm. Average main course: $26. AmEx, DC, Disc, MC, V.

Located in the Euro-rific Chambers hotel, Town has something that separates it from the pack of high-wattage boutique-hotel restaurants: chef Geoffrey Zakarian, whose "dynamic American" menu rarely stumbles. At Balcony, the latest addition to Town, (located high above the restaurant), you'll also find a small menu of Zakarian's upscale snacks (sea scallops with sausage, assorted cheese plates, etc.).

Trattoria dell'Arte

900 Seventh Ave between 56th and 57th Sts (212-245-9800). Subway: N, Q, R, W to 57th St. Mon–Fri

11:45am–11:30pm; Sat 11am–3pm, 5–11:30pm; Sun 11am–3pm, 5–10:30pm. Average main course: $28. Average pasta: $20. AmEx, DC, Disc, MC, V.

High-energy Trattoria dell'Arte features closely packed tables and plates piled with huge portions. Located across the street from Carnegie Hall, this Italian restaurant draws serious pre- and postshow crowds, so reserve well in advance. "New York's largest antipasto bar" has 40 hot and cold antipasti (mostly vegetables and seafood). The celebrated "Etruscan" pizzas cover most of a table for two. The decor has changed little since the restaurant opened in 1988, and the walls remain accented with sketches of giant body parts (including a nose, ear and breast).

Midtown East

Brasserie

100 E 53rd St between Park and Lexington Aves (212-751-4840). Subway: E, V to Lexington Ave–53rd St; 6 to 51st St. Mon–Fri 7–10am, 11:30am–1am; Sat 11am–1am; Sun 11am–10pm. Average main course: $22. AmEx, DC, Disc, MC, V.

Tucked into the basement of the Mies van der Rohe–designed Seagram Building, this 41-year-old eatery reopened in January 2000 after a five-year dormancy, billing itself as "midtown's downtown restaurant" (though it only stays open until 1am on most nights). Redesigned by star architecture team Elizabeth Diller and Ricardo Scofidio, the space now has translucent lime-green tables and a central staircase just made for dramatic entrances. More basic is the menu—brasserie classics such as cassoulet and moist monkfish.

D'Artagnan—The Rotisserie

152 E 46th St between Lexington and Third Aves (212-687-0300). Subway: S, 4, 5, 6, 7 to 42nd St–Grand Central. Sun–Thu noon–10:30pm; Fri, Sat noon–11pm. Average main course: $19. AmEx, MC, V.

D'Artagnan—The Rotisserie is a temple, and meat is its god. Even roasted potatoes are drenched in chicken drippings. Owner Ariane Daguin has dedicated her restaurant to the hearty food of her native Gascony. The cassoulet may well be New York's finest. D'Artagnan serves sandwiches for lunch, but the best way to experience the food is to spend a leisurely evening in one of the high-backed chairs.

Ess-a-Bagel

831 Third Ave between 50th and 51st Sts (212-980-1010). Subway: E, V to Lexington Ave–53rd St; 6 to 51st St. Mon–Fri 6am–10pm; Sat, Sun 8am–5pm. Plain bagel: 60¢. AmEx, DC, Disc, MC, V.
See page 171.

The Four Seasons

99 E 52nd St between Park and Lexington Aves (212-754-9494). Subway: E, V to Lexington Ave–53rd St; 6 to 51st St. Mon–Fri noon–2:15pm, 5–9:30pm; Sat 5–11:30pm. Average main course: $38. AmEx, DC, Disc, MC, V.

The only restaurant in Manhattan that's been grant-

Ice capade A pretheater meal at Aquavit might include such innovative creations as a lobster roll with granité and sorbet.

ed landmark status, the Philip Johnson–designed Four Seasons plays host to power-lunching publishing execs by day and free-spending diners at night. The tycoons gather in the manly Grill Room amid plenty of leather and steel, while civilians repair to the Pool Room, featuring an illuminated reservoir and a collection of seasonal trees. The continental cuisine is consistent, but it's not what draws the crowds: The always-gracious service and spectacular 40-year-old interior make this oasis of calm a perennial favorite.

Grand Central Oyster Bar & Restaurant

Grand Central Terminal, Lower Concourse, 42nd St at Park Ave (212-490-6650). Subway: S, 4, 5, 6, 7 to 42nd St–Grand Central. Mon–Fri 11:30am–9:30pm; Sat 5:30–9:30pm. Average main course: $22. AmEx, DC, Disc, MC, V.
Despite a fire in 1997 and subsequent restoration, little has changed at this 88-year-old Grand Central Terminal institution. The noisy lunch hour still belongs to business titans and budding power brokers, who feast on Manhattan clam chowder and more than two dozen kinds of oysters from the raw bar under the vaulted Guastavino tiled ceilings. The list of market-fresh fish is dizzyingly long (although the kitchen tends to run out of many items by evening), and house specialties such as Maryland crab cakes and *coquilles St. Jacques* (sea scallops in a Parmesan cream sauce), are excellent.

Menchanko-Tei

131 E 45th St between Lexington and Third Aves (212-986-6805). Subway: S, 4, 5, 6, 7 to 42nd St–Grand Central. 11:30am–midnight. Average main course: $10. AmEx, DC, Disc, MC, V.
Menchanko-Tei is part of a Japanese chain, and its

basic ramen menu attracts a slurp-happy salaryman crowd. Ramen is a Japanese adaptation of Chinese wheat noodles, served in a chicken-and-pork stock broth. Menchanko-Tei serves regional ramen preparations—Hakata-style will get you a white-soy broth topped with pork and shredded ginger.

Michael Jordan's— The Steak House NYC

Grand Central Terminal, West Balcony, 23 Vanderbilt Ave at 43rd St (212-655-2300). Subway: S, 4, 5, 6, 7 to 42nd St–Grand Central. Mon–Fri 7–10am, noon–10:45pm; Sat noon–10:45pm; Sun 1–10pm. Average steak: $30. AmEx, DC, MC, V.
Your chances of spotting Michael Jordan at this Grand Central steak house are about zero, but you may feel momentarily like His Airness when you perch here: You're flying high with a massive porterhouse while harried commuters scurry to their trains below you. But look up, and you'll be humbled by the celestial-sky ceiling. Chef David Walzog does stellar work with dry-aged steaks (Jordan helped choose which cuts to serve—expect rib eye, New York strip and filet mignon), and the macaroni and cheese is made from Jordan's mother's recipe. The crisp, salty french-fried potatoes are some of the best in the city.

Sushisay

38 E 51st St between Madison and Park Aves (212-755-1780). Subway: E, V to Lexington Ave–53rd St; 6 to 51st St. Mon–Fri noon–2:15pm, 5:30–10pm; Sat 5:30–9:30pm. Average sushi meal (10 pieces, 1 roll): $25. AmEx, DC, MC, V.
As the New York branch of the landmark Tokyo restaurant Tsukiji Sushisei (located since 1888 in the heart of the world's largest wholesale fish market), Sushisay takes its fish seriously, attracting hordes of free-spending businessmen to its minimalist dining room. Fish is shipped in daily, from Japan or from wherever the catch is best. No seafood is kept overnight. Though the place is casual, you can easily drop $150 for lunch for two. Sushisay prepares unadulterated *edomaesushi*, which means strictly rice and fish (and maybe a *shiso* leaf or other accent here and there). Cooked dishes are available, but it's the raw stuff that's transcendent. After all, the restaurant's name means "pure sushi."

East Side

Ada

208 E 58th St between Second and Third Aves (212-371-6060). Subway: N, R, W to Lexington Ave–59th St; 4, 5, 6 to 59th St. Mon–Sat noon–3pm, 5:30–11pm. Average main course: $20. Prix fixe: $55. AmEx, Disc, MC, V.
A wood-burning fireplace set in a tranquil room creates a languid mood at this high-end Indian restaurant. Prix-fixe meals can include a half-dozen dishes when you factor in all the between-course tastings. But don't expect purebred Indian cuisine—the slow-mounting heat is fueled by flavors from France, Southeast Asia and Italy.

Necessities

Amazon.comidas East Siders love Nascimento for its Brazilian menu and lively atmosphere.

Club Guastavino

409 E 59th St between First and York Aves (212-421-6644). Subway: N, R, W to Lexington Ave–59th St; 4, 5, 6 to 59th St. Tue–Sat 5:30–11pm; Sun 5:30–10:30pm. Three-course prix fixe: $65. AmEx, MC, DC. V.

Located in the balcony area of Guastavino's, the Club feels like the exclusive dining area of a modernized castle (befitting owner Sir Terence Conran). Even though it is far above the main floor, the white-tiled arched ceilings still seem impressively high, and the area is so large that tables have a luxurious amount of space between them. Chef Daniel Orr has a lot to compete with, but he pulls through just fine with well-executed French cooking. You might find pheasant paired with a whiskey reduction; Black Angus, a Burgundy one.

Commissary

1030 Third Ave at 61st St (212-339-9955). Subway: N, R, W to Lexington Ave–59th St; 4, 5, 6 to 59th St. Sun, Mon 11:30am–3pm, 5:30–11:30pm; Tue–Sat 11:30am–3pm, 5:30–11:30pm. Average main course: $22. AmEx, DC, Disc, MC, V.

Commissary marks chef Matthew Kenney's much anticipated return to the neighborhood. The spacious corner spot that used to house Matthew's has been updated in a mod black, white and gray scheme. Kenney uses buzzwords such as "light," "clean" and "refreshing" to describe the menu. Most of the appetizers, such as the seared tuna and crab cakes, are just what you'd expect. However, entrées like grilled lobster with coconut milk, curry leaves and green herb risotto have made Commissary worth the wait.

Daniel

60 E 65th St between Madison and Park Aves (212-288-0033). Subway: F to Lexington Ave–63rd St; 6 to 68th St–Hunter College. Mon–Sat noon–2:30pm,

5:45–11pm. Prix fixe: $82–$145. AmEx, DC, Disc, MC, V.

There's no avoiding it. When talking about Daniel, the premier Upper East Side French restaurant, superlatives must be used. Fantastic. Glittering. Splendid. The dining room's spacious layout somehow fools each guest into thinking that his or hers is the best table in the house—and the impeccable staff does a magnificent job of lending credence to that assumption. Chef Daniel Boulud's flawless cooking technique is irresistibly seductive, from the audacious triple-tiered étagère, laden with *amuses-bouches*, to the fresh-from-the-oven madeleines snuggled in a linen-lined basket, delivered as a parting au revoir (truly "till the next time"). For a (slightly) more relaxed environment, try **Café Boulud** *(20 E 76th St between Fifth and Madison Aves, 212-772-2600)* or **db bistro moderne** *(see page 177).*

Nascimento

1068 First Ave between 58th and 59th Sts (212-755-6875). Subway: N, R, w, to Lexington Ave–59th St; 4, 5, 6 to 59th St. Mon–Thu 8am–2am; Fri, Sat 8am–4am; Sun noon–midnight. Average main course: $20. AmEx, MC, V.

Not only does *nascimento* mean "birth" in Portuguese, but it's also the owner's name. And Paula Nascimento tries hard to make sure her baby is a lively spot. Café society likes to linger in the lounge for espresso and fresh baked goods during the day. At night, an energetic bar crowd sips prize-winning Sambosas (passion-fruit juice, Chambord and brandy) and sways to jazz or Brazilian rhythms. The menu celebrates the proprietor's Brazilian and Italian heritage, and seems as eclectic as the patchwork of patrons. Pastas and Brazilian specialties such as *moqueca* (seafood stew) are aptly executed, but the quality of more unusual dishes can disappoint: *Picanha na tabua*, steak topped with onions and served on a sizzling platter, would benefit from a thicker, more tender cut, not to mention some seasoning. But the culture seekers crowding this spot don't seem to mind. After all, it's the hostess and her élan for entertaining that they really remember.

P.J. Clarke's
915 Third Ave at 55th St (212-759-1650). Subway: E, V to Lexington Ave–53rd St; 6 to 51st St. 11:30am–4am. Average main course: $14. AmEx, DC, MC, V.
Opened in 1890, this saloon is the oldest of its kind uptown (and it was once a second home to Frank Sinatra). The same family has run the place since it was purchased from P.J. himself in 1948. Inside, the carved oak bar seems as solid as a ship, mugs of beer come cheap, the stained-glass windows glow dimly and the jukebox plays strains of history. Selections from the chalkboard menu are hearty (hamburger is ground fresh each day), though plain. The real draw here is Old New York—still alive and open daily.

Shallots NY
550 Madison Ave between 55th and 56th Sts (212-833-7800). Subway: E, V to Fifth Ave–53rd St; N, R, W to Fifth Ave–60th St; F to 57th St. Mon–Thu noon–2pm, 5–10pm; Fri noon–2pm; Sat 1 hour after sundown to midnight; Sun 5–10pm. Average main course: $30. Average Saturday-night grill-menu entrée: $15. AmEx, MC, V.
This kosher haute-cuisine destination in the atrium of the Sony Building offers an array of elegant items, such as porcini-dusted sweetbreads with hazelnut vinaigrette and Moroccan-spiced roasted duck with tamarind sauce. It's pricey, but there's also a cheaper Saturday-night grill menu.

Shun Lee Palace
155 E 55th St between Lexington and Third Aves (212-371-8844). Subway: E, V to Lexington Ave–53rd St; 6 to 51st St. Noon–11:30pm. Average main course: $22. AmEx, DC, MC, V.
Owner Michael Tong has served classic Cantonese, Shanghai and Szechuan cuisines with style and confidence for more than 30 years. The powerful Szechuan wontons, giant moist prawns, tender braised duck and delicate sole are terrific, and served by a professional staff.

Uptown

Lincoln Center–West Side

Epices du Traiteur
103 W 70th St between Columbus Ave and Broadway (212-579-5904). Subway: 1, 2, 3 to 72nd St. Sun–Thu 5:30–10:30pm; Fri, Sat 5:30pm–midnight. Average main course: $15. AmEx, DC, Disc, MC, V.
The food here is distinguished by multitextured, aromatic seasonings. Tunisian, Moroccan and Italian specialties can all be found on the menu at Epices du Traiteur (French for "the caterer's

spices"), where redbrick walls, stark white tablecloths, romantic lighting and a pleasant din create an oasis of warmth.

Jean-Georges
Trump International Hotel and Tower, 1 Central Park West at Columbus Circle (212-299-3900). Subway: A, C, B, D, 1, 2 to 59th St–Columbus Circle. Mon–Fri noon–3pm, 5:30–11pm; Sat 5:30–11pm. Average main course: $31. AmEx, DC, Disc, MC, V.
Jean-Georges Vongerichten is like a one-man Cirque du Soleil: The first time you sit down at one of his restaurants, he performs mesmerizing tricks with food that you've never seen before. And the second time and the third…he continues to fascinate. This is New York's definitive status-symbol meal. Spices give lamb subtle oomph. The luscious beef tenderloin halves are displayed like two uniform, edge-to-edge pink suns. If your patience for making reservations is short, then try for a table in the less formal Nougatine room or, in summer, on the Mistral Terrace (both feature a shorter menu). If you can't swing that, try one of Vongerichten's other restaurants—**Jo-Jo** *(160 E 64th St between Lexington and Third Aves, 212-223-5656)*, **Mercer Kitchen** *(99 Prince St at Mercer St, 212-966-5454)* or **Vong** *(200 E 54th St at Third Ave, 212-486-9592)*.

Shun Lee West
43 W 65th St between Central Park West and Columbus Ave (212-595-8895). Subway: 1, 2 to 66th St–Lincoln Ctr. Mon–Fri noon–midnight; Sat 11:30am–midnight; Sun noon–10:30pm. Average main course: $19. AmEx, DC, MC, V. ● Shun Lee Cafe, 43 W 65th St between Central Park West and Columbus Ave (212-769-3888). Subway: 1, 2 to 66th St–Lincoln Ctr. Mon–Fri 5pm–midnight; Sat 11:30am–2:30pm, 5pm–midnight; Sun noon–2:30pm, 4:30–10pm. Average main course: $12. AmEx, DC, MC, V.
See **Shun Lee Palace**, left.

Tavern on the Green
Central Park West at 67th St (212-873-3200). Subway: B, C to 72nd St; 1, 2 to 66th St–Lincoln Ctr. Mon–Thu noon–3pm, 5:30–10:30pm; Fri noon–3pm, 5–11:30pm; Sat 10am–3:30pm, 5–11:30pm; Sun 10am–3:30pm, 5–10:30pm. Average main course: $30. Pretheater three-course prix fixe: $35. AmEx, DC, Disc, MC, V.
Tavern on the Green, a landmark tourist attraction, is ripe beyond bursting with wedding cake-inspired pastel-colored columns, mirrored hallways, Murano chandeliers and chintz. This is where locals and visitors alike come to celebrate. On a Friday night, you are almost guaranteed to sit through six renditions of "Happy Birthday" by the unjaded staff. The truth is, you and your companions are the stars of the show, not the food. Play it safe: The shrimp cocktail is the perfect lead-in to the thick slice of prime rib. Note: The late owner Warner LeRoy also revamped the **Russian Tea Room** *(150 W 57th St between Sixth and Seventh Aves, 212-974-2111)*, where opulence takes center stage.

Zen Palate

2170 Broadway between 76th and 77th Sts (212-501-7768). Subway: 1, 2 to 79th St. Noon–11pm. Average main course: $15. AmEx, DC, MC, V.
See page 179.

East 70s/Lenox Hill

Bardolino

1496 Second Ave between 77th and 78th Sts (212-734-9050). Subway: 6 to 77th St. 11am–11:30pm. Average main course: $8. AmEx, DC, MC, V.
Italy meets Ipanema at this dimly lit restaurant: Gilberto Gil coos from the sound system, the servers speak with Portuguese-inflected lilts, and a few traditional Brazilian dishes show up on the menu (because of Walaber de Roque Jr., Bardolino's Brazilian-born owner). But it's no culture clash—thin slices of mozzarella wrapped around prosciutto, peppers and basil are a nice break from more standard antipasto plates. Bardolino is worth seeking out for its high-quality dishes at the right prices.

The Boathouse in Central Park

Central Park Lake, Park Drive North at E 72nd St. (212-517-2233). Subway: 6 to 68th St–Hunter College. Mon–Thu noon–3:30pm, 5:30–10pm; Fri noon–3:30pm, 5:30–11pm; Sat 11am–3:30pm, 5:30–11pm; Sun 11am–3:30pm, 5:30–10pm. Average main course: $27. AmEx, DC, MC, V.
Offering a mesmerizing view of Central Park Lake, this place could serve dog food and get away with it. All the more reason to commend new chef Alan Ashkinaze, a Larry Forgione disciple, for his first-rate surf-and-turf menu. Dishes are subtle and sophisticated.

Le Pain Quotidien

1336 First Ave at 72nd St (212-717-4800). Subway: 6 to 68th St–Hunter College. Mon–Fri 7:30am–7pm; Sat, Sun 8am–7pm. Average sandwich: $8.50. Average pastry: $4. Cash only.
There are many reasons to follow your nose into the Upper East Side franchise of Le Pain Quotidien: The sandwiches, such as the Brie with pecans or the *jambon de Paris* (imported Parisian ham with three different kinds of mustard). Then there are the breads—large rye and wheat rounds, baguettes and a small round of wheat with walnuts. But French pastry is reason No. 1 (if you're dubious, there are two locations of the chain bakery in Paris and several in Belgium, home of chef-owner Alain Coumont). For other locations in New York, check the phone book.

Trata

1331 Second Ave between 70th and 71st Sts (212-535-3800). Subway: 6 to 68th St–Hunter College. Sun–Thu noon–3pm, 5–11pm; Fri, Sat noon–3pm, 5pm–midnight. Average main course: $20. AmEx, MC, V.
Trata will make you wonder why anyone has ever felt the need to cook on anything other than a charcoal grill. No matter what you get, it will be tossed

onto the fire, drizzled with Cretan olive oil and squirted with lemon. For a change, try the traditional whole fried *barbounia* (red mullet). This smallish fish can be a challenge to eat, so ask the maître d' for a lesson on deboning.

Upper West Side

Avenue

520 Columbus Ave at 85th St (212-579-3194). Subway: B, C, 1, 2 to 86th St. Mon–Thu 9am–3pm, 5–11pm; Fri 9am–3pm, 5pm–midnight; Sat 10am–3pm, 5pm–midnight; Sun 10am–3pm, 5–11pm. Average main course: $18.50. Three-course prix fixe: $20. AmEx, MC, V.
Avenue is a diplomatic combination of Upper West Side informality and fashionable French taste (in aesthetics and cuisine). And it's a hit—*jour et nuit*, as the sign outside says. In the morning, the place is a veritable *boulangerie*, packed with locals gobbling bread and pastries; later on, in the exposed-brick alcove in the back, patrons gather at the stainless-steel bar and sup on signature dishes such as smoked pork loin and rich roasted duck on creamy mushroom risotto.

Awash

947 Amsterdam Ave between 106th and 107th Sts (212-961-1416). Subway: 1, 2 to 110th St–Cathedral Pkwy. Mon–Fri 1pm–2am; Sat, Sun noon–2am. Average main course: $10. AmEx, MC, V.
Tiny twinkling lights illuminate the crowd of diners, who come from as near as Columbia University and as far as Africa. Glug some honey wine as you hand-to-mouth the light, delicate-yet-filling Ethiopian dishes, and you'll understand why Awash is a favorite of East African expats.

Ayurveda Cafe

706 Amsterdam Ave at 94th St (212-932-2400). Subway: B, C, 1, 2, 3 to 96th St. 11:30am–11pm. Average main course, including rice: $11. AmEx, DC, MC, V.
This snug, calming oasis prides itself on following the 5,000-year-old holistic system of Ayurveda, which incorporates six vital tastes—sweet, sour, salty, bitter, astringent and pungent—into every meal. And while it more or less succeeds at rounding up those varied flavors, the preset vegetable menu du jour is really just your basic *thali*—a routine meal in India—which consists of tiny stainless-steel dishes filled with basmati rice, *raita*, lentils, pickles and various vegetable mixtures.

Barney Greengrass— The Sturgeon King

541 Amsterdam Ave between 86th and 87th Sts (212-724-4707). Subway: B, C, 1, 2 to 86th St. Tue–Fri 8:30am–4pm; Sat, Sun 8:30am–5pm. Average main course (family style): $13. Cash only.
Barney Greengrass is a legendary deli where the food is just too good to pass up. It's half take-out and half restaurant; and although the decor is

pretty schmutzy, the place is a madhouse at breakfast and brunch. Egg platters come with a choice of smoked fish (such as sturgeon or Nova Scotia salmon) and are a relative bargain at $12, since you won't be hungry again for weeks. Ditto the sandwiches, such as silky, salty smoked sablefish on pumpernickel.

Café La Grolla

411A Amsterdam Ave between 79th and 80th Sts (212-579-9200). Subway: 1, 2 to 79th St. Sun–Thu 5:30–11pm; Fri, Sat 5:30pm–midnight. Average main course: $15. AmEx, DC, MC, V.

At Café La Grolla, homemade pastas are the highlight, featuring lots of shapes and gravies, including an excellent veal *ragù*, and ravioli filled with ricotta and spinach in a light butter-and-sage sauce. More adventurous *secondi* include liver and onions with balsamic vinegar and grilled polenta.

Cooke's Corner

618 Amsterdam Ave at 90th St (212-712-2872). Subway: 1, 2 to 86th St. Tue–Thu 5–10pm; Fri, Sat 5–11pm; Sun noon–9pm. Average main course: $15. AmEx.

Judging from the happy locals crowding the small dining room, the need for a tastefully styled eatery on Amsterdam obviously exists. The mix of warm lighting, a decent wine list and an ambitious French-American menu (with plenty of vegetarian-friendly fare) is practically a miracle up here.

Drip Cafe

489 Amsterdam Ave at 83rd St (212-875-1032). Subway: B, C to 81st St; 1, 2 to 79th St. Mon–Thu 8am–1am; Fri 8am–2am; Sat 9am–3am; Sun 9am–midnight. Average drink: $6. MC, V.

Containers of Tang, Cheez Whiz and other American classics salute you from the walls of this coffeehouse-bar-dating service. *Dating service?* Yup, Drip has a for-a-fee system for hooking people up. Although light fare is available (chocolate cake, sandwiches), the drinks, alcoholic and non, are what float this fun lounge: Long Island iced tea for the lushes, the Cap'n Crunch milk shake for those inner children.

Flor de Mayo

484 Amsterdam Ave between 83rd and 84th Sts (212-787-3388). Subway: 1, 2 to 86th St. Noon–midnight. Average main course: $9. AmEx, DC, MC, V.

Hole-in-the-wall Flor de Mayo is far superior to most of the city's Chino-Latino eateries, and it has tucked in its proverbial shirt to fit its growing reputation. It's a spanking-clean, homey place. The front door is plastered with gushing reviews for the Peruvian rotisserie chicken, and those raves are well-deserved: The tender, juicy fowl is flavored with cinnamon and coriander, and served with hot sauce.

Other location ● *2651 Broadway between 100th and 101st Sts (212-663-5520). Subway: 1 to 103rd St. Noon–midnight. Average main course: $9. AmEx, DC, MC, V.*

Hungarian Pastry Shop

1030 Amsterdam Ave at 111th St (212-866-4230). Subway: B, C, 1 to 110th St–Cathedral Pkwy. Mon–Fri 7:30am–11:30pm; Sat 8:30am–11:30pm; Sun 8am–10pm. Average pastry: $2.25. Cash only.

Rigo Janci, Ishler, Goosefoot—no, these aren't the members of a Czech heavy-metal group, but rather some of the desserts at the Hungarian Pastry Shop, a roomy café beloved by generations of Columbia students and professors. The generous slices of cake are knockouts, while the pastries (Linzer tarts, strudels, éclairs et al.) don't lag far behind.

Miss Mamie's Spoonbread Too

366 W 110th St between Manhattan and Columbus Aves (212-865-6744). Subway: B, C, 1 to 110th St–Cathedral Pkwy. Noon–10pm. Average main course: $11. AmEx, DC, MC, V.

See **Miss Maude's Spoonbread Too**, page 187.

Ouest

2315 Broadway between 83rd and 84th Sts (212-580-8700). Subway: 1, 2 to 86th St. Tue–Thu, Sun 5–11pm; Fri, Sat 5pm–midnight. Average main course: $24. AmEx, Disc, MC, V.

Chef-owner Tom Valenti's comfortable, upscale French-inflected American brasserie offers confident cuisine that'll impress food snobs even as it satisfies cravings for hearty home cooking. Convivial crowds pack Ouest's mahogany-and-leather interior, drawn by Valenti's boldly flavorful dishes, such as bacon-wrapped pork tenderloin and the popular Simple Grills (chops, steak and chicken).

Ruby Foo's

2182 Broadway at 77th St (212-724-6700). Subway: 1, 2 to 79th St. Mon–Thu 11:30am–12:30am; Fri, Sat 11:30am–1am; Sun 11:30am–11pm. Average main course: $19. AmEx, MC, V.

See page 178.

Pulldown menus

Find out more than you may want to know about New York's restaurants at these websites.

www.chowhound.com: Obsessive foodie Jim Leff regurgitates everything he's eaten on his homegrown site.
www.nycbeer.org: Chug down this hopping guide to the local brew scene.
www.opentable.com: Make reservations for many of the city's best restaurants.
www.nyc.gov/health, then click on "Restaurant Inspection Information": Get the dirt—for real—on New York restaurants. This is where you'll find a list of health-code violations.

Necessities

Barking Dog Luncheonette

1678 Third Ave at 94th St (212-831-1800). Subway: 6 to 96th St. 8am–11pm. Average main course: $12.50. Cash only.

The Upper East Side's Barking Dog is a place for all seasons and appetites. Quaint details include a soda fountain, tin ceiling, wooden booths and waiters wearing T-shirts bearing the slogan SIT—STAY. The blue-plate special changes daily, but you'll always find staples such as fish-and-chips, crunchy buttermilk-battered chicken and homemade meat loaf.

Dinerbar

1569 Lexington Ave between 100th and 101st Sts (212-348-0200). Subway: 6 to 103rd St. Sun–Thu 7am–11pm; Fri, Sat 7am–2am. Average main course: $28. Average pasta: $10. AmEx, MC, V.

In an area where bodegas and Chinese joints are the culinary mainstay, Dinerbar offers dishes that Spanish Harlem—and possibly the entire city—has yet to see. Its mostly comfort-food menu also features novelties such as ravioli sandwiches (cheese ravioli on semolina-garlic bread). The industrial-chic decor is also a neighborhood rarity. Hang in the lounge or at the bar while DJs spin seven nights a week.

Elaine's

1703 Second Ave between 88th and 89th Sts (212-534-8103). Subway: 4, 5, 6 to 86th St. 6pm–2am. Bar 6pm–3:30am. Average main course: $23. AmEx, DC, Disc, MC, V.

There are two Elaine's, really. There's the classic Elaine's of literary renown: the one where Ms. Kaufman herself sits at your table, conferring legitimacy, and where everyone knows your name, rank and media rating. Then there's Elaine's-for-the-rest-of-us: a shambling Italian-leaning restaurant, where moderately decent food is served to out-of-towners, couples on dates, everyday people.

Etats-Unis

242 E 81st St between Second and Third Aves (212-517-8826). Subway: 6 to 77th St. 6–11pm. Average main course: $26. AmEx, DC, MC, V.

Don't let the French name fool you: *Etats-Unis* means "United States," and the food here is American. This small, popular eatery has no-nonsense decor—lights dangle from an unfinished ceiling above plush, comfortable seats. The kitchen employs fresh ingredients in ingenious combinations (the menu changes daily, based on what the chefs pick up at the greenmarket). Stellar entrées can include delicate gnocchi in a savory veal *ragù*, and oysters baked with crumbled crackers in heavy cream. Etats-Unis has only two seatings each night, between 6 and 7pm, and at 8:30pm.

Totonno Pizzeria Napolitano

1544 Second Ave between 80th and 81st Sts (212-327-2800). Subway: 6 to 77th St. 11am–11:30pm. Large plain pizza: $15. AmEx, DC, MC, V.

See page 189.

A cut above Brooklyn's Peter Luger serves only porterhouse, and it's the best you'll ever eat.

Andy's Colonial

2257 First Ave at 116th St (212-410-9175). Subway: 6 to 116th St. Mon–Fri 11:30am–9pm; Sat 5–10pm. Average main course: $14. Cash only.

Andy's is a corner tavern with no printed menu, just a handful of sturdy wooden tables and warm service. This old-school joint caters mainly to neighborhood locals, and chances are you'll find co-owner/bartender/waiter Joe Medici chatting up his guests and explaining the day's selections. His elderly father, Salvatore, runs the kitchen and has a flair for preparing colossal chops and chicken dishes in any and every Italian style.

Bleu Evolution

808 W 187th St between Fort Washington Ave and Pinehurst Ave North (212-928-6006). Subway: A to 190th St. Mon–Fri 5–11pm; Sat 10am–3pm, 5–11pm; Sun 10am–3pm, 5–10:30pm. Bar 5pm–2am. Average main course: $14. AmEx, Disc, MC, V.

In the quiet, residential swath of Washington Heights, Bleu Evolution makes waves with its loungey velvet-covered chairs and rococo-cum-rock & roll vibe. But the food—a juxtaposition of headstrong yet complementary flavors on a single plate—is what brings locals back. The dishes are mostly American, but the best item is the Moroccan-style fried chicken: Two breasts of poultry, seasoned with cumin and curry, come with sides of Tabasco-flavored collard greens and mashed celeriac.

Charles' Southern Style Kitchen

2841 Frederick Douglass Blvd (Eighth Ave) between 151st and 152nd Sts (212-926-4313). Subway: A, C, B, D to 155th St. Wed–Sun noon–10pm. Average main course: $6. AmEx, Disc, MC, V.

Sandwiched between Charles' all-you-can-eat-buffet dining room and its breakfast counter, this tiny, fluorescent-lit take-out sells the best fried chicken in New York. Charles Gabriel lets his chickens sit in a secret seasoning for eight hours, dips them in batter and flour, then dunks them in a massive skillet. The result—intensely crunchy, well-seasoned poultry—proves that the South ain't got nothing on Harlem.

Max Soha

1274 Amsterdam Ave at 123rd St (212-531-2221). Subway: A, C, B, D, 1 to 125th St. Sun–Thu 11:45am–11pm; Fri, Sat 11:45am–midnight. Average main course: $10 Cash only.

See **Max**, page 164.

M&G Soul Food Diner

383 W 125th St at Morningside Ave (212-864-7326). Subway: A, C, B, D to 125th St. Mon–Thu 24hrs; Fri 12:01am–11pm; Sat, Sun 8:30am–10:45pm. Average main course: $9. Cash only.

The M&G is the very essence of Southern-fried dinners, offering hefty plates of home-style comfort food, not to mention breakfasts of eggs, bacon and morning coffee. The hair-netted waitresses are famously prickly, and their act is just part of the place's charm—speak up and know what side dishes you want, and you'll probably avoid their clucks and barbs. Perennial favorites include the fatty, rich short ribs and the fried chicken with pancakes.

Miss Maude's Spoonbread Too

547 Malcolm X Blvd (Lenox Ave) between 137th and 138th Sts (212-690-3100). Subway: 2, 3 to 135th St. Sun–Thu noon–9:30pm; Fri, Sat noon–10:30pm. Average main course: $10. AmEx, MC, V.

Kissin' cousin to Norma Jean Darden's Miss Mamie's Spoonbread Too *(see page 185)*, farmhouse-cheery Miss Maude's (named for Darden's aunt) is a comfort-food craver's mecca. This Harlem haunt serves generous portions of Southern cuisine—such as tender chicken smothered in peppery gravy, and North Carolina barbecued ribs painted with a sweet and tangy sauce.

Outer Boroughs

Brooklyn

al di là

248 Fifth Ave at Carroll St, Park Slope (718-783-4565). Subway: M, N, R to Union St. Mon, Wed, Thu 5–10:30pm; Fri, Sat 6–11pm; Sun 6–10pm. Average main course: $14.50. MC, V.

Husband-and-wife team Emiliano Coppa and chef Anna Klinger specialize in serious food from Italy's Veneto region. The modern Northern Italian fare,

served with uncommon grace and good nature, includes hard-to-find antipasti such as *baccalà mantecato* (salt cod beaten into a thick cream). The daily-changing menu is matched with a reasonably priced wine list. No wonder such an unpretentious room, decorated with only a few vintage cooking utensils, draws so many families, couples of all ages and solo diners. You'll want to join them *al di là* (over there).

Bamonte's

32 Withers St between Union Ave and Lorimer St, Williamsburg (718-384-8831). Subway: G to Metropolitan Ave; L to Lorimer St. Mon, Wed, Thu noon–10pm; Fri, Sat noon–11pm; Sun 1–10pm. Average main course: $14. MC, V.

The bulk of Bamonte's patrons are vintage New York Italians who all seem to know each other. But this stunning century-old restaurant is one of the friendliest in town. The dark coral walls, gilded chandeliers and aging, tuxedoed waiters are only outpanached by the clientele. Sit at the long tables and feast on the fresh pastas with refreshingly light tomato sauces, knowing that you're dining at a legendary place.

Diner

85 Broadway at Berry St, Williamsburg (718-486-3077). Subway: J, M, Z to Marcy Ave. Mon–Thu 11am–5pm, 6pm–midnight; Fri 11am–5pm, 6pm–1am; Sat 11am–4pm, 6pm–1am; Sun 11am–4pm, 6pm–midnight. Average main course: $15. MC, V.

Don't be fooled by the name. This dark, atmospheric not-so-greasy spoon serves more Cosmos than coffees. While the burgers and fries are cheap and absolutely delicious, the ooh-la-la factor comes through in nightly specials, such as poached oysters or duck rillettes. Be prepared to wait awhile at the bar for a table—mobs are the rule at this scenester magnet.

DuMont

432 Union Ave between Metropolitan Ave and Devoe St, Williamsburg (718-486-7717). Subway: G to Metropolitan Ave; L to Lorimer St. Average main course: $12. MC, V.

Spend an evening at DuMont and you'll have one regret: that you've paid much more money to eat lesser food elsewhere. The restaurant excels at blending down-home style with elegant cuisine. Simply roasted organic chicken gets a slightly reduced white-wine–and–butter sauce. The menu is short, but every day you'll find about five new specials.

Ferdinando's Focacceria

151 Union St between Columbia and Hicks Sts, Carroll Gardens (718-855-1545). Subway: F, G to Carroll St. Average main course: $10. Cash only.

Family-owned Ferdinando's Focacceria, which has held court in Carroll Gardens since 1906, serves homey, Sicilian-style specialties such as *panelli* (deep-fried chickpea-flour pancakes), luscious *caponatina* (sautéed eggplant, olives, celery and capers) and pasta *con le sarde*, a fragrant dish of roasted fennel, pine nuts, dried grapes and sardines over *bucatini*. If you're not a sardine fan, get over it—hand-canned by owner Francesco Buffa, this fish has a subtle flavor.

Necessities

On **Thai ground** Q, a Thai Bistro in Queens serves creative takes on the Southeast Asian cuisine.

The Grocery

288 Smith St between Sackett and Union Sts, Carroll Gardens (718-596-3335). Subway: F, G to Carroll St. Mon–Thu 6–10pm; Fri, Sat 6–11pm. Average main course: $19. MC, V.

This highly touted two-year veteran of Brooklyn's restaurant row exceeds expectations. The no-frills ten-table dining room—featuring two chrome ceiling fans, wall sconces and hardwood floors—fills up fast, as does the backyard garden in warm months. If the lush fig tree out back is in bloom, you're in luck: Owner-chefs Charles Kiely and Sharon Pachter use this very local produce on the menu, as in the foie gras terrine with "Brooklyn figs" appetizer. Winning entrées may include a tender pork chop with tangy peach-tomatillo chutney and yucca fritters.

Joya

215 Court St between Warren and Wyckoff Sts, Cobble Hill (718-222-3484). Subway: F, G to Bergen St. Sun–Thu 5–11:30pm; Fri, Sat 5pm–1am. Average main course: $7. Cash only.

Joya has high ceilings and the type of minimalist furnishings that too many restaurateurs use to prove their place is modern. But don't be fooled: The food is strictly old-world Thai. The green curries are rich, spicy and not too milky. If you try a whole-fish special, such as red snapper with pineapple-curry sauce, its flavor is sure to be more nuanced than whatever the in-house DJ is spinning.

Karam

8519 Fourth Ave between 85th and 86th Sts, Bay Ridge (718-745-5227). Subway: R to 86th St. 6am–12:30am. Average main course: $5. Cash only.

At this tiny spot, offering counter service and a few tables, you'll find unsurpassed shwarma (lamb, chicken, or beef) saturated with garlic sauce, as well as baba ganoush and other top-notch Lebanese dishes.

L-Cafe

187–189 Bedford Ave between North 6th and North 7th Sts, Williamsburg (718-388-6792). Subway: L to Bedford Ave. Mon–Fri 9am–midnight; Sat, Sun 10am–midnight. Take-out Mon–Fri 7am–10pm; Sat, Sun 9am–8pm. Average main course: $7. AmEx, DC, Disc, MC, V.

This Williamsburg pioneer pays homage to its boho legacy by hanging local artists' work on its walls. But the most eye-catching elements of the place are the hipsters who come for the creative but casual food. Try the turkey–and–blue-cheese sub, or one of the various egg dishes. The L's coveted back garden provides a tranquil backdrop for conversation.

Madiba

195 DeKalb Ave between Adelphi and Carlton Sts, Fort Greene (718-855-9190). Subway: C to Lafayette Ave; G to Clinton–Washington Aves. Mon 5:30pm–midnight; Tue–Thu noon–4pm, 5:30pm–midnight; Fri noon–4pm, 5:30pm–1am; Sat 10:30am–4pm, 5:30pm–1am; Sun 10:30am–4pm, 5:30pm–midnight. Average main course: $13. AmEx, DC, Disc, MC, V.

The city's only South African restaurant is a community culture club. Besides serving good, rough-hewn South African cooking (along with a Caribbean menu on Mondays), Madiba has entertainment, special events and a "tuck shop" selling imported dry goods. Trademark dishes are Durban bunny chow (thick curry in a hollowed-out hunk of bread) and *bobotie* (a vaguely Malaysian-spiced meat loaf topped with sweet mango chutney).

Max & Moritz

426A Seventh Ave between 14th and 15th Sts, Park Slope (718-439-5557). Subway: F to 15th St–Prospect Park. 5:30–11pm. Average main course: $15. AmEx, MC, V.

Sophisticated flavors tumble all over each other in Paul Goebert's inventive French-accented American food. He really lets loose with the specials: calf's liver with crunchy *haricots verts* and tapioca pudding with a mango coulis. Come early if you want to sit in the backyard, and make reservations if you want to get in at all. In a nod to his Viennese roots, Goebert opened **Café Steinhof**, an all-Austrian pub down the street *(422 Seventh Ave at 14th St, 718-369-7776).*

Pepe Viola

200 Smith St at Baltic St, Cobble Hill (718-222-8279). Subway: F to Bergen St. Mon–Thu noon–11pm; Sat, Sun noon–midnight. Average main course: $10. Cash only.

See **Pepe Giallo to Go**, page 170.

Peter Luger

178 Broadway at Driggs Ave, Williamsburg (718-387-7400). Subway: J, M, Z to Marcy Ave. Sun–Thu 11:30am–10pm; Fri, Sat 11:30am–11pm. Steak for two: $62.90. Cash only.

Is this the best restaurant in the world? You'd be hard pressed to find any dissenters among those who crowd this landmark. (Expect to wait even if you have reservations, which are a must.) Opened as a German beer hall in 1887, Luger's has evolved into the carnivore's ne plus ultra. Unlike some of Manhattan's fancier meat palaces, this one serves only one cut of dry-aged USDA Prime: porterhouse. It's thick, charbroiled and expertly served by joke-telling waiters, who spoon the beef's juices over the sizzling top.

Rasputin

2670 Coney Island Ave at Ave X, Brighton Beach (718-332-8333). Subway: F to Ave X; Q to Neck Rd. Fri–Sun 7pm–3am. Average main course: $20. AmEx, Disc, MC, V.

Named after czarist Russia's resident bad boy, Rasputin has a cut-rate take on opulence that involves a disco ball and a house band playing Britney Spears and the Gipsy Kings. On the balcony, red-jacketed waiters ply birthday boys with Stoli; on the dance floor, computer engineers dressed like gangsters shake it with gangsters dressed like computer engineers. Arrive with a group—the "banquet" of standard Russian *zakuski* will be all the cheaper.

River Café

1 Water St at Old Fulton St, Brooklyn Heights (718-522-5200). Subway: A, C to High St; F to York St. Mon–Sat noon–3pm, 6–11pm; Sun 11:30am–3pm, 6–11pm. Three-course prix fixe: $70. Tasting menu: $90. AmEx, DC, MC, V.

Come aboard this ritzy landmark, with a knockout panorama of the twinkling Financial District, and you'll find a genteel barge decked out in a nautical motif. Bridging the gap between nouveau Manhattan and staid Brooklyn Heights, the menu combines French, Mediterranean and Latin elements to make classic American recipes sparkle. The wine list is generally pricey, but there are a few affordable offerings and a selection of half-bottles. The spot itself, which sees its share of marriage proposals, is a destination in its own right. And isn't that view worth it?

Saint's Alp Teahouse

5801 Eighth Ave at 58th St, Sunset Park (718-437-6622). Subway: N to Eighth Ave. Sun–Thu 11am–11:30pm; Fri, Sat 11:30am–midnight. Average tea: $3. Cash only.

See page 165.

Totonno Pizzeria Napolitano

1524 Neptune Ave between West 15th and West 16th Sts, Coney Island (718-372-8606). Subway: F, Q, W to Coney Island–Stillwell Ave. Wed–Sun noon–8:30pm. Large plain pizza: $14.50. Cash only.

Totonno's has been open since 1924, and it looks its age: Hey, the staff focuses on pizza, not decor. You won't find a better combination of crispy, black-ened-on-the-edges crust, sweet sauce and fresh cheese. The pizza *bianca* is pretty fabulous too. The Upper East Side offshoot *(see page 186)* cranks out comparable pies, minus the lived-in atmosphere. It also offers Italian-American staples made simply but with care.

Two Boots Park Slope

514 2nd St between Seventh and Eighth Aves, Park Slope (718-499-3253). Subway: F to Seventh Ave. Sun–Thu 10:30am–4pm, 5–11pm; Fri, Sat 10:30am–4pm, 5pm–midnight. Large plain pizza: $12.25. AmEx, DC, MC, V.

See page 166.

Victory Kitchen

116 Smith St between Dean and Pacific Sts, Boerum Hill (718-858-8787). Subway: F, G to Bergen St. Tue–Fri 6–10:30pm; Sat, Sun 11am–3pm, 6–10:30pm. Average main course: $13. AmEx, Disc, MC, V.

Step into Victory Kitchen, located at the north end of Brooklyn's trendy Smith Street, and feel the love. Food offerings are limited, yet clean and lovingly crafted. Marinated hanger steak with potatoes is sliced into tender bite-size morsels. Rich chocolate pudding and berry crisp with a flaky crust are winners. On warmer days, wait for a table in the spacious back garden, which is lit with tiki torches.

Delhi Palace

*37-33 74th St between Roosevelt and 37th Aves,
Jackson Heights (718-507-0666). Subway: E, F, V, G,
R to Jackson Hts–Roosevelt Ave; 7 to 74th St–
Broadway. Mon–Fri noon–10pm; Sat, Sun noon–
10:30pm. Average main course, including rice: $10.
AmEx, DC, MC, V.*

An Indian restaurant filled with Indians is generally
a good sign, and it's one to heed at the Palace. Locals
in jeans and saris gather here to eat flavorful curries,
perfectly prepared rice dishes, warm flatbreads and
huge, crispy *dosas.* You'll be stuffed after dinner, so
take a stroll and check out the windows of the neighborhood's sari vendors and bridal salons.

Elias Corner

*24-02 31st St at 24th Ave, Astoria (718-932-1510).
Subway: N, W to Astoria Blvd. 5–11pm. Average
main course: $13. Cash only.*

Loyalists consider simple Elias to be the best fish
restaurant in the city. Most of the seafood is brushed
with olive oil, rubbed with oregano and slapped whole
onto the grill. What arrives at your table is moist, true-
flavored fish. Appetizers include oysters, clams, mus-
sels…you get the picture. Decor is minimal to the
point of nonexistent: plastic chairs (some on the new
patio), a few pictures of Greece on the walls and, on
display in the cooler, the fish. Because no reservations
are taken, expect to wait.

Kum Gang San

*138-28 Northern Blvd at Union St, Flushing (718-
461-0909). Subway: 7 to Flushing–Main St. 24hrs.
Average main course: $15. AmEx, MC, V.*

On Saturday nights, carfuls of Korean families
from all over the metro area wait outside Kum
Gang San's parking lot for a spot. If you join them
inside, you'll find wood tables, wood-paneled walls
and strummed wooden instruments. Dishes of *ban
chan*—kimchi, sautéed peppers, fried tofu, white
beans, miso soup—are brought to you gratis. Then
the real feast begins. There are rich casseroles such
as *dae gu maewoon tang,* a delectable bubbling
stew starring cod and caviar; and the tenderest,
juiciest *kalbi* in New York. There's also a sizable
Japanese menu here and at the midtown branch
(see page 175).

Nostalgias

*85-09 Northern Blvd between 85th and 86th Sts,
Jackson Heights (718-533-9120, 718-429-8113).
Subway: 7 to 82nd St–Jackson Hts. Sun, Tue–Thu
11am–10pm; Fri, Sat 11am–3am. Average main
course: $9. AmEx, Disc, MC, V.*

Part community center, part supper club, part
sports bar, Nostalgias is NYC's headquarters for
homesick Bolivians. Local expats gather here for live
Andean music, soccer matches on the TV and
karaoke. But the best reason to swing by—no matter where you're from—is the *salteña,* Bolivia's distinct spin on the empanada, which holds a savory,

soupy stew inside a slightly sweet casing. Choose
from beef or chicken, mixed with potato, olives, eggs
and onion. One bite and you'll have a new favorite
snack. But don't miss out on the other meat-and-
potatoes specialties.

Q, a Thai Bistro

*108-25 Ascan Ave between Austin and Burns Sts,
Forest Hills (718-261-6599). Subway: E, F, V, G, R to
Forest Hills–71st Ave. Tue–Thu noon–3pm, 5–
10:30pm; Fri, Sat noon–3pm, 5–11:30pm; Sun noon–
3pm, 5–10:30pm. Average main course: $14. MC, V.*

Named after the uptight weapons inventor from the
007 films, Q the restaurant offers a setting seductive enough for Bond, James Bond: tropical blossoms, soft lighting and a live-and-let-die soundtrack
of Stan Getz, Chet Baker and Patsy Cline. The creative, all-Thai kitchen staff shoehorns strong flavors into light presentations. Stir-fries expertly
balance crunchy greens with tender meat. If you
really want to Thai one on, have a martini—yes, *of
course* it's shaken, not stirred.

Shanghai Tide

*135-20 40th Rd at Main St, Flushing (718-651-
4234). Subway: 7 to Flushing–Main St. Mon–Fri
10:30am–11pm; Sat, Sun 10:30am–11:30pm.
Average main course: $11. MC, V.*
See page 161.

Dominick's

*2335 Arthur Ave between Crescent Ave and 187th St
(718-733-2807). Travel: B, D, 4 to Fordham Rd, then
Bx12 bus to Hoffman St. Mon, Wed, Thu noon–10pm;
Fri, Sat noon–11pm; Sun 1–9pm. Average main
course: $15. Cash only.*

Dominick's has bragging rights: It's the most popular restaurant in what locals proudly call New York's
real Little Italy. You really *are* among family in the
pinewood dining room of proprietor Charlie DiPaolo.
Join the tracksuited guys from the neighborhood at
long, crowded tables. You'll be amazed to see patrons
consume impossibly massive platters of veal parmi-
giana and linguine with white clam sauce—until you
get a taste yourself. There are no menus, so heed your
waiter's suggestions.

The Feeding Tree

*892 Gerard Ave between 161st and 162nd Sts (718-
293-5025). Subway: B, D, 4 to 161st St–Yankee
Stadium. 8am–11pm. Average main course: $7.
AmEx, MC, V.*

The Feeding Tree is just a couple of blocks from
Yankee Stadium, but locals, and those working in
the nearby courts, don't need a Yankees game to
draw them here. The Feeding Tree's dining room
and bustling take-out area are welcoming in
that South Bronx who-needs-decor-when-we've-got-
flavah kind of way. The Jamaican food can get pretty spicy: The jerk chicken and the goat, chicken and
shrimp curries are masterfully made.

Restaurants by cuisine

African
Awash (Ethiopian) 184
Madiba (South African) 188
Sosinna's (Pan-African) 159

American
Barking Dog
  Luncheonette 186
Bleu Evolution 186
Bubby's 154
Corner Bistro 168
Craft 171
Dano Restaurant 171
Diner 187
First 163
Five Points 161
The Grocery 188
Market Cafe 175
P.J. Clarke's 183
The Red Cat 170
Tavern on the Green 183
'21' 178

American Creative
Restaurant Above 176
Annisa 167
Avenue 184
Bayard's 153
Blue Hill 167
Bridge Cafe 153
DuMont 187
Etats-Unis 186
The Four Seasons 180
Gotham Bar & Gril 167
Gramercy Tavern 171
Ilo 177
Max & Moritz 189
Ouest 185
River Café 189
Town 180
Union Pacific 174
Union Square Cafe 164
Veritas 174
Victory Kitchen 189
Zoë 161

American Regional
Charlie's Southern Style
  Kitchen 187
Hog Pit BBQ 168
M&G Soul Food Diner 187
Miss Mamie's
  Spoonbread Too 187
Pink Tea Cup 169
Virgil's Real BBQ 179

Austrian
Danube 154

Baked Goods
Ceci-Cela 160
Hungarian Pastry Shop 185
Le Pain Quotidien 184

Bars
Bond St. 161
Corner Bistro 168
Elaine's 186
First 163
Hog Pit BBQ 168
Rainbow Grill 178

Brazilian
Churrascaria
  Plataforma 177
Sushi Samba 7 169

Cafés & Take-out
Bulgin' Waffles 162

Cafe Edison 177
Ceci-Cela 160
City Bakery 170
Ess-a-Bagel 171
Hungarian Pastry Shop 185
L-Cafe 188
Le Gamin Café 160
Palacinka 160
Ruben's Empanadas 161
Saint's Alp Teahouse 165
Sandwich Planet 176

Chinese
Canton 157
Congee Village 155
Goody's 157
Grand Sichuan International
  Midtown 179
La Chinita Linda 169
New York Noodle Town 159
Ping's Restaurant 159
Shanghai Cuisine 165
Shanghai Tide 161
Shun Lee Palace 183

Cuban
La Chinita Linda 169
Margon 178
Sophie's Restaurant 154
Victor's Cafe 52 179

Delis & Diners
Barney Greengrass—
  The Sturgeon King 184
Carnegie Deli 177
Jones Diner 162
Katz's Delicatessen 155
Second Avenue Deli 166

Eastern European
Hungarian Pastry Shop 185
Veselka 166

Eclectic
aKa Café 155
Blue Ribbon Bakery 168
Dinerbar 186
Siren 166

French
Alain Ducasse at the
  Essex House 179
Artisanal 174
Avenue 184
Balthazar 159
Brasserie 180
Brasserie 8½ 179
Casimir 163
Cello 165
Club Guastavino 182
Cooke's Corner 185
D'Artagnan—The
  Rotisserie 180
Daniel 182
db bistro moderne 177
Fleur de Sel 171
Florent 168
Jean Claude 160
Jean-Georges 183
Jules Bistro 165
Le Bernardin 177
Le Jardin Bistro 157
Le Zinc 154
Les Deux Gamins 168
Lucien 164
man ray 169
Odeon 155
Pastis 165

Raoul's 161

German
Hallo Berlin 179

Greek
Elias Corner 190
Molyvos 180
Periyali 173
Trata 184

Indian
Ada 181
Ayurveda Cafe 184
Curry in a Hurry 171
Delhi Palace 190
Pongal 173
Tabla 174
Tamarind 174
Thali 169

Italian
al di là 187
Andy's Colonial 186
Babbo 166
Baldoria 176
Bamonte's 187
Bardolino 184
Café La Grolla 185
Da Silvano 167
Dominick's 190
Elaine's 186
Ferdiando's Focacceria 187
La Focacceria 163
Max 164
Pepe Giallo to Go 170
Rainbow Grill 178
Tappo 164
Trattoria dell'Arte 180

Jamaican
The Feeding Tree 190

Japanese
Bond St. 161
Honmura An 160
Jewel Bako 163
Menchanko-Tei 181
Nobu 154
Shanghai Tide 161
Sushi Samba 7 169
Sushisay 181

Korean
Dok Suni's 163
Kum Gang San 190
Mandoo Bar 175

Kosher
Shallots NY 183

Latin American
Chicama 170
Flor de Mayo 185
Ideya 160
Nascimento 182
Nostalgias 190
Paladar 155
Patria 173

Malaysian
New Indonesia & Malaysia
  Restaurant 159
Nyonya 159

Mediterranean
Epices du Traiteur 183
Five Points 161
Medi 178
Olives NY 172

Picholine 166
The Red Cat 170

Mexican
Hell's Kitchen 180
Los Dos Rancheros
  Mexicanos 175
Mexicana Mama 168
Mexican Radio 157

Middle Eastern
Karam 188
Mamoun's Falafel 167
Moustache 165

Moroccan
Cafe Mogador 163

Pan-Asian
Republic 173
Ruby Foo's 178
Wild Lily Tea Room 170
Zen Palate 179

Pizza
Lombardi's 157
Totonno Pizzeria
  Napolitano 189
Two Boots Restaurant 166

Portuguese
Alphabet Kitchen 162

Russian
Rasputin 189
Russian Samovar 178

Scandinavian
Aquavit 176

Seafood
American Park at
  the Battery 153
Blue Water Grill 170
The Boathouse in
  Central Park 184
Cello 165
Grand Central Oyster
  Bar & Restaurant 181
Le Bernardin 177
Pearl Oyster Bar 169

Spanish
Alphabet Kitchen 162
Oliva 155
Pipa 173

Steak Houses
Gallagher's Steak House 177
Michael Jordan's—
  The Steak House NYC 181
Old Homestead 170
Peter Luger 189
Tuscan Steak 174

Thai
Holy Basil 168
Joya 188
Little Basil 168
Q, a Thai Bistro 190
SEA 165

Vegetarian
Angelica Kitchen 162
Herban Kitchen 160
Kate's Joint 163
Zen Palate 179

Vietnamese
Cyclo 163
Nha Trang 159
Vietnam Restaurant 159

Necessities

New York has 7.5 million
opportunities for romance.

(We've got everything else you need to set the mood.)
CD, DVD, VHS, Accessories and much more.

Shopping & Services

Great deals and the best of everything make it hard to resist the city's spoils

People may say they come to New York for the museums and culture, but deep down, they're really here for the shopping. After all, NYC is the shopping capital of the world (especially now that the sales tax on clothing applies only to items costing more than $110). Some visitors come for the city's gargantuan department stores, others for the high fashion, and still others for cheap Levi's and good deals on electronics. Regardless of your agenda, as you're making your way through the myriad options, it helps to think like a New Yorker. Below are a few tips on just how that's done.

SHOP TILL YOU DROP

New Yorkers are the smartest kind of shoppers: They wait for end-of-season clearances, shop at discount emporiums such as **Daffy's** and **Century 21** *(see **Head of the class**, page 200)*, and sneak off to sample sales during lunch hour. Designers' sample sales are some of the best sources of low-priced clothes by fashion's biggest names. To find out who's selling where, see the Check Out section in *Time Out New York*. The **S&B Report** *($10 per issue; 877-579-0222; www.lazarshopping.com)* and the **SSS Sample Sales** hot line *(212-947-8748)* are also great discount resources. Sales are usually held in the designer's shops, or a rented loft space. Typically, the loft sales are not equipped with changing rooms, so bring appropriate clothing and a courageous spirit.

Smaller shops carry clothing by smaller designers *(see **Boutiques**, page 197, and **Street of dreams**, page 218)*. To find out who's making waves in New York's fashion scene, visit the *TONY* website at www.timeoutny.com, click on Check Out and peruse the archives.

Downtown shops stay open an hour or two later than those uptown (and open later in the morning too). Thursday is the universal—though unofficial—shop-after-work night; most stores are open till 7pm, if not later. Regardless of which day you choose to spree, make sure you know the rules: Putting an item on hold is allowed, as is returning it should you decide it's not right for you. Just remember to check the store's return policy before making your purchase.

Keep in mind that certain stores listed below have multiple locations. If a shop has more than a few branches, we'll tell you to check the business pages in the phone book for other addresses.

Department stores

Barneys New York

660 Madison Ave at 61st St (212-826-8900).
Subway: N, R, W to Fifth Ave–60th St; 4, 5, 6 to 59th St. Mon–Fri 10am–8pm; Sat 10am–7pm; Sun 11am–6pm. AmEx, MC, V.
All the top designers are represented at this haven of New York style (and at Christmastime, it has the most provocative windows in town). Barneys also sells seductive home furnishings and fancy children's clothes. Its Co-op store in Chelsea carries more affordable merchandise by such hip names as Daryl K and Katayone Adeli, as well as shoes and accessories. Every August and February, Co-op rolls the racks aside to host the Barneys Warehouse Sale, where prices are reduced 50 to 80 percent.
Other location ● *Barneys Co-op, 236 W 18th St between Seventh and Eighth Aves (212-826-8900). Subway: 1, 2 to 18th St. Mon–Fri 10am–8pm; Sat 10am–7pm; Sun 11am–6pm. AmEx, MC, V.*

Bergdorf Goodman

754 Fifth Ave at 57th St (212-753-7300). Subway: E, V to Fifth Ave–53rd St; N, R, W to Fifth Ave–60th St. Mon–Fri, Sat 10am–7pm; Thu 10am–8pm; Sun noon–6pm. AmEx, MC, V.
While Barneys aims for a young, trendy crowd, Bergdorf's is dedicated to an elegant, understated one with lots of money to spare. As department stores go, it's one of the best for clothes and accessories. The famed men's store is across the street.

Bloomingdale's

1000 Third Ave at 59th St (212-355-5900). Subway: N, R, W to Lexington Ave–59th St; 4, 5, 6 to 59th St. Mon–Fri 10am–8:30pm; Sat 10am–7pm; Sun 11am–7pm. AmEx, MC, V.
Bloomie's is a gigantic, glitzy department store, offering everything from handbags and cosmetics to furniture and designer clothes. Brace yourself for crowds—the store is the third most popular tourist attraction in NYC, after the Empire State Building and Statue of Liberty.

Felissimo

10 W 56th St between Fifth and Sixth Aves (212-247-5656). Subway: F to 57th St; N, R, W to Fifth Ave–60th St. Tue–Thu, Sat, Sun noon–6pm; Fri noon–8pm. AmEx, MC, V.
This five-story townhouse is a Japanese-owned, eco-savvy specialty store that stocks a collection of covetable items. Choose from jewelry, travel accessories, clothing, candles and collectibles. Assistance is available in nine languages.

Plum good clothing Calypso epitomizes the stylish boutiques that line the streets of Nolita.

Henri Bendel

712 Fifth Ave at 56th St (212-247-1100). Subway: E, V to Fifth Ave–53rd St; N, R, W to Fifth Ave–60th St. Mon–Wed, Fri, Sat 10am–7pm; Thu 10am–8pm; Sun noon–6pm. AmEx, DC, Disc, MC, V.
Bendel's lavish quarters resemble a plush townhouse—there are elevators, but it's nicer to saunter up the elegant, winding Impulse line and the sporty L.O.G.G. collection. You'll find a large selection of other upscale stores, but things look more desirable here—must be those darling brown-striped shopping bags.

H&M

640 Fifth Ave at 51st St (212-489-0390). Subway: B to 47–50th Sts–Rockefeller Ctr; E, V to Fifth Ave–53rd St. Mon–Sat 10am–8pm; Sun 11am–7pm. AmEx, MC, V.
This trendy, inexpensive Swedish megamart opened in 2000. The three-story, 35,000-square-foot venue is constantly mobbed. Clothes are separated by various "brands," such as the trendy Impulse line and the sporty L.O.G.G. collection. You'll find a large selection of undies and accessories. There's also a makeup line and a plus-size women's collection.
Other locations ● *558 Broadway between Prince and Spring Sts (212-343-2722). Subway: N, R to Prince St. Mon–Sat 10am–8pm; Sun 11am–7pm.*
● *1328 Broadway at 34th (646-473-1165). Subway: B, D, F, V, N, Q, R, W to 34th St–Herald Sq. Mon–Sat 10am–8pm; Sun 11am–8pm. AmEx, MC, V.*

Jeffrey New York

449 W 14th St between Ninth and Tenth Aves (212-206-1272). Subway: A, C, E to 14th St; L to Eighth Ave. Mon–Wed, Fri 10am–8pm; Thu 10am–9pm; Sat 10am–7pm; Sun 12:30–6pm. AmEx, MC, V.
Jeffrey Kalinsky, a former Barneys shoe buyer, has spiced up the Meatpacking District with his namesake shop, a branch of the Atlanta original. Designer clothing abounds—Alexander McQueen,

Ann Demeulemeester, Helmut Lang, Versace and YSL. But the centerpiece is the shoe salon, which includes Manolo Blahnik, Prada and Robert Clergerie.

Lord & Taylor

424 Fifth Ave between 38th and 39th Sts (212-391-3344). Subway: B, D, F, V to 42nd St; 7 to Fifth Ave. Mon–Thu 10am–8:30pm; Fri 9am–8:30pm; Sat 9am–8pm; Sun 10am–7pm. AmEx, Disc, MC, V.
Lord & Taylor is shedding its conservative, rather old-fashioned image by carrying hipper contemporary designs—clothing by designers such as Betsey Johnson can now be found on the racks.

Macy's

151 W 34th St between Broadway and Seventh Ave (212-695-4400). Subway: B, D, F, V, N, Q, R, W to 34th St–Herald Sq; 1, 2, 3 to 34th St–Penn Station. Mon–Sat 10am–8:30pm; Sun 11am–7pm. AmEx, MC, V.
You'll find everything here from designer labels to cheap imitations, a pet-supply shop, a restaurant in the cellar, a Metropolitan Museum of Art gift shop, a juice bar and—gulp—a McDonald's on the kids' floor. The store also offers "Macy's by appointment," a free service that allows shoppers to order goods or clothing over the phone and have it shipped anywhere in the world *(800-343-0121).*

Saks Fifth Avenue

611 Fifth Ave between 49th and 50th Sts (212-753-4000). Subway: B, D, F to 47–50th Sts–Rockefeller Ctr; E, V to Fifth Ave–53rd St. Mon–Wed, Fri, Sat 10am–7pm; Thu 10am–8pm; Sun noon–6pm. AmEx, DC, Disc, MC, V.
Saks is the classic upscale American department store. It features all the big names in women's fashion (and some of the better lesser-known ones), an excellent menswear department, one of the city's best shoe departments, fine household linens and extremely attentive customer service.

Takashimaya

693 Fifth Ave between 54th and 55th Sts (212-350-0100). Subway: E, V to Fifth Ave–53rd St. Mon–Sat 10am–7pm; Sun noon–5pm. AmEx, DC, Disc, MC, V.
The first two floors of this Japanese department store offer 4,500 square feet of art gallery space and a men's and women's signature collection, as well as Japanese makeup and exotic plants; the top floor is devoted to beauty essentials. The basement's Tea Box café is a sanctuary for shoppers craving tea and a light meal.

National chains

Many New Yorkers regard chain stores as a less imaginative (if more expedient) way to shop, but that doesn't mean you won't have to stand behind a whole line of them while you make your way to the register. Stores such as **Banana Republic**, **Express**, **Old Navy** and **Victoria's Secret** are all over the city, including the shopping nexuses of Soho, Rockefeller, and near Macy's and Bloomingdales. To find the nearest locations of your favorites, refer to the phone book.

Fashion

Trendsetters

Catherine

468 Broome St at Greene St (212-925-6765). Subway: C, E to Spring St; N, R to Prince St. Mon–Sat 11am–7pm; Sun noon–6pm. AmEx, MC, V.
Take refuge from chain-store madness at this colorful shop, which showcases everything from tile-topped cocktail tables to beaded silk pillows—not to mention the breathtaking fashions of owner-designer Catherine Malandrino.

Comme des Garçons

520 W 22nd St between Tenth and Eleventh Aves (212-604-9200). Subway: C, E to 23rd St. Sun, Mon noon–6pm; Tue–Sat 11am–7pm. AmEx, MC, V.
This austere store is devoted to Rei Kawakubo's architecturally constructed designs for men and women. It's no surprise that the boutique is in the new art mecca of Chelsea: Kawakubo's clothing is hung like art, and the space is very gallerylike.

D&G

434 West Broadway between Prince and Spring Sts (212-965-8000). Subway: C, E to Spring St; N, R to Prince St. Mon–Sat 11am–7pm; Sun noon–6pm. AmEx, MC, V.
While most of Milan's heavies still prefer the Upper East Side, some (like D&G) are choosing Soho as the home of their more youthful, less pricey lines. Custom-mixed disco, house and opera music play as gals and guys shop for jeans, suits, collection dresses and shoes.

Diane von Furstenberg, the Shop

385 W 12th St between Washington St and West Side Hwy (646-486-4800). Subway: A, C, E to 14th St; L to Eighth Ave. Mon–Wed, Fri 11am–7pm; Thu 11am–8pm; Sat 11am–6pm; Sun noon–5pm. AmEx, MC, V.
Though she's known for her pricey wrap dresses, Diane von Furstenberg has installed quite a bit more at this elegant space. No matter what you try on—ultrafeminine dresses, sporty knits or denim—you'll feel like a princess stepping out of the sateen dressing room, located in the middle of the store.

Diesel

1 Union Sq West at 14th St (646-336-8552). Subway: L, N, Q, R, W, 4, 5, 6 to 14th St–Union Sq. Mon–Sat 10am–9pm; Sun noon–8pm. AmEx, DC, Disc, MC, V.
This 14,000-square-foot emporium will satisfy any denim craving you have. In addition to jeans, stylish accessories and vinyl clothing, there are shoes, underwear and outerwear. Check the phone book for other locations.

Earl Jeans

160 Mercer St between Houston and Prince Sts (212-226-8709). Subway: F, V, S to Broadway–Lafayette St; N, R to Prince St; 6 to Bleecker. Mon–Sat 11am–7pm; Sun noon–6pm. AmEx, Disc, MC, V.
Industrial design meets country comfort at this raw yet homey space. And you could say the same for the perfect-fitting jeans: Dark, light, stretchy or tight, you've got a good shot at scoring your favorite pair. The denim jackets are truly the best around.

Katayone Adeli

35 Bond St between Bowery and Lafayette St (212-260-3500). Subway: F, V, S to Broadway–Lafayette St; 6 to Bleecker St. Tue–Sat 11am–7pm; Sun noon–6pm. AmEx, MC, V.
Katayone Adeli's collection pieces are available at this store, but for those perfect side-slit pants, you'll still have to scour the racks at Barneys, Bergdorf's or Saks. Ditto for the new line, 2 by Katayone Adeli.

Mayle

252 Elizabeth St between Houston and Prince Sts (212-625-0406). Subway: F, V, S to Broadway–Lafayette St; N, R to Prince St; 6 to Bleecker St. Mon–Sat noon–7pm; Sun noon–6pm. AmEx, MC, V.
Mayle, a Nolita-based, model-owned store, epitomizes the neighborhood: The clothes are elegant, and a touch whimsical.

Philosophy di Alberta Ferretti

452 West Broadway between Houston and Prince Sts (212-460-5500). Subway: C, E to Spring St; N, R to Prince St. Mon–Sat 11am–7pm; Sun noon–6pm. AmEx, MC, V.
This three-story shop features mother-of-pearl–tinted walls and cascading water—elements that echo the layering, translucence and craft in Ferretti's collection of delicate women's wear.

Necessities

Plein Sud

70 Greene St between Broome and Spring Sts (212-431-8800). Subway: C, E to Spring St; N, R to Prince St. Mon–Sat 11am–7pm; Sun noon–6pm. MC, V.
This store is as sexy and beautiful as the 13-year-old French line it houses. Madonna, Jennifer Lopez and Mary J. Blige are fans.

Product

71 Mercer St between Broome and Spring Sts (212-274-1494). Subway: N, R to Prince St; 6 to Spring St. Mon–Sat 11am–7pm; Sun noon–6pm. AmEx, MC, V.
Product is a hip clothier for women that features wonderful stretchy fabrics, clean lines and frivolous accessories. Sales are frenzied and frequent.
Other location ● *219 Mott St between Prince and Spring Sts (212-219-2224). Subway: J, M to Bowery; 6 to Spring St. Mon–Sat 11am–7pm; Sun noon–6pm. AmEx, MC, V.*

Boutiques

Bond 07

7 Bond St between Broadway and Lafayette Sts (212-677-8487). Subway: F, V, S to Broadway–Lafayette St; 6 to Bleecker St. Mon–Wed, Sat 11am–7pm; Thu 11am–8pm; Sun noon–7pm. AmEx, MC, V.
Selima Salaun, of **Le Corset** *(see page 200)* and **Selima Optique** *(see page 208)* fame, has branched out from undies and eyewear; this time, offering a carefully edited selection of clothing (Alice Roi, Colette Dinnigan), accessories and 20th-century French furniture.

Calypso on Broome

424 Broome St between Crosby and Lafayette Sts (212-274-0449). Subway: 6 to Spring St. Mon–Sat 11am–7pm; Sun noon–6pm. AmEx, MC, V.
While customers can still shop at the original Calypso on Mott Street, this location (which is about four times larger) features more upscale merchandise (i.e., less resort wear) and totally different vendors. Stop by either shop for gorgeous slip dresses, suits, sweaters and scarves, many from unknown French designers. Check the phone book for other locations. (For children's versions, *see* **Calypso Enfants**, *page 204*.)

DDC Lab

180 Orchard St between Houston and Stanton Sts (212-375-1647). Subway: F, V to Lower East Side–Second Ave. Mon–Sat 11am–7pm; Sun noon–6pm. AmEx, Disc, MC, V.
This airy shop specializes in items you can't get anywhere else in New York, such as Rogan NYC jeans and a pair of U.K.-made Cyclonic shoes.

Dressing Room

49 Prince St between Lafayette and Mulberry Sts (212-431-6658). Subway: N, R to Prince St; 6 to Spring St. Mon–Sat 1–7pm; Sun 1–6pm. AmEx, MC, V.
The Dressing Room, one of Nolita's first clothing boutiques, set the 'hood in motion. It carries girlie goodies such as frilly panties, feather necklaces, nylon skirts, denim duds and vintage shoes.

Hedra Prue

281 Mott St between Houston and Prince Sts (212-343-9205). Subway: F, V, S to Broadway–Lafayette St; N, R to Prince St; 6 to Bleecker St. Mon–Sat 11am–7pm; Sun noon–7pm. AmEx, MC, V.
A shopping trip to Nolita isn't complete unless you check out the wares at Hedra Prue. This shop stocks downtown's latest and greatest young designers (Ulla Johnson, Trosman Churba) and accessories.

Intermix

125 Fifth Ave between 19th and 20th Sts (212-533-9720). Subway: N, R to 23rd St. Mon–Sat 11am–8pm; Sun noon–6pm. AmEx, Disc, MC, V.
The buyers have amazing taste at Intermix: The clothing and shoe designers include Chaiken and Capone, Jimmy Choo, Katayone Adeli, Sigerson Morrison and Tocca.
Other location ● *1003 Madison Ave between 77th and 78th Sts (212-249-7858). Subway: 6 to 77th St. Mon–Sat 10am–7pm; Sun noon–6pm. AmEx, Disc, MC, V.*

Kirna Zabête

96 Greene St between Prince and Spring Sts (212-941-9656). Subway: C, E to Spring St; N, R to Prince St. Mon–Sat 11am–7pm; Sun noon–6pm. AmEx, MC, V.
Founded by 28-year-old fashion veterans (not an oxymoron in NYC) Sarah Hailes and Beth Shepherd, Kirna Zabête includes more than 50 designers from around the globe, such as Hussein Chalayan, Isabel Marant and Olivier Theyskens.

Language

238 Mulberry St between Prince and Spring Sts (212-431-5566). Subway: N, R to Prince St; 6 to Spring St. Mon–Wed, Fri, Sat 11am–7pm; Thu 11am–8pm; Sun noon–6pm. AmEx, DC, Disc, MC, V.
Language is a clothing boutique, furniture store, art gallery and bookstore—a can't-miss for folks who buy into the lifestyle-shopping aesthetic.

Louie

68 Thompson St between Broome and Spring Sts (212-274-1599). Subway: C, E to Spring St. Tue–Sat noon–7pm; Sun noon–6pm. AmEx, MC, V.
Louie is the launching pad for young, unknown cloth-

▶ **Fashion**, starting on page 195, includes everything from "Trendsetters" to places that are "Menswear" shops.
▶ **Fashion Services**, page 206, lists shoe repair places, dry cleaners, etc.
▶ **Accessories**, page 208, includes shops devoted to selling hats, jewelry and the like.
▶ **Health & Beauty**, page 213, lists our recommended places to get good haircuts, massages and other services.
▶ Looking for unique gifts, a camera, or something for your home? See **Objects of Desire**, page 217.

iers, such as Gessous Dessus, Mon Petit and Rozae Nichols. There are scores of bags, hats and jackets too.

Min-K

334 E 11th St between First and Second Aves (212-253-8337). Subway: L to First Ave; 6 to Astor Pl. 2–9pm. AmEx, MC, V.
Unless you shop in Tokyo or Seoul, you probably won't recognize any of the streetwear labels sold at this East Village boutique. Min-K owner Minge Kim designs much of the clothing; the rest is gathered on her frequent trips to Japan and Korea.

Olive & Bette's

252 Columbus Ave between 71st and 72nd Sts (212-579-2178). Subway: B, C, 1, 2, 3 to 72nd St. Mon–Wed 11am–7pm; Thu–Sat 11am–8pm; Sun 11am–6pm. AmEx, MC, V.
Olive & Bette's has all a girl could ever want: underwear, outerwear (Earl Jeans, Rebecca Taylor, Theory), jewelry and itty-bitty decals for your nails.
Other locations ● *158 Spring St between West Broadway and Wooster St (646-613-8772). Subway: C, E to Spring St. Mon–Thu 11am–7pm; Fri, Sat 11am–8pm; Sun noon–6pm. AmEx, Disc, MC, V. ●* *1070 Madison Ave between 80th and 81st Sts (212-717-9655). Subway: 6 to 77th St. Mon–Sat 11am–7pm; Sun 11am–6pm. AmEx, MC, V.*

Patricia Field

10 E 8th St between Fifth Ave and University Pl (212-254-1699). Subway: N, R to 8th St–NYU. Sun–Fri noon–8pm; Sat noon–9pm. AmEx, Disc, MC, V.
Patricia Field is brilliant at working club and street fashion (just check out the costumes that she and partner Rebecca Weinberg have assembled for *Sex and the City*) and her original mix of jewelry, makeup and club gear proves it.
Other location ● *Hotel Venus, 382 West Broadway between Broome and Spring Sts (212-966-4066). Subway: C, E to Spring St. Mon–Fri, Sun noon–8pm; Sat noon–9pm. AmEx, MC, V.*

Scoop

1275 Third Ave between 73rd and 74th Sts (212-535-5577). Subway: 6 to 77th St. Mon–Fri 11am–8pm; Sat 11am–7pm; Sun noon–6pm. AmEx, MC, V.
Scoop is the ultimate fashion editor's closet. Clothing from Daryl K, Diane von Furstenberg, Philosophy and plenty of others are arranged by hue, not label.
Other location ● *532 Broadway between Prince and Spring Sts (212-925-2886). Subway: N, R to Prince St; 6 to Spring St. Mon–Sat 11am–8pm; Sun 11am–7pm. AmEx, MC, V.*

Steven Alan

60 Wooster St between Broome and Spring Sts (212-334-6354). Subway: C, E to Spring St; N, R to Prince St. Mon–Sat 11am–7pm; Sun noon–7pm. AmEx, MC, V.
Steven Alan's stock (American Manufacturing, Moi et Cat, as well as the co-owners' own designs) is coveted by hip girls (Wooster Street location) and boys (the Broome Street shop) from all over town.

Other location ● *558 Broome St between Sixth Ave and Varick St (212-625-2541). Subway: C, E to Spring St. Tue–Sat 11am–7pm; Sun noon–7pm. Disc, MC, V.*

TG-170

170 Ludlow St between Houston and Stanton Sts (212-995-8660). Subway: F, V to Lower East Side–Second Ave. Noon–8pm. AmEx, MC, V.
Terry Gillis has an eye for emerging designers: She was the first to carry Pixie Yates and Built by Wendy. Nowadays, you'll find Jared Gold, Liz Collins and United Bamboo hanging gracefully on the racks.

Tracy Feith

209 Mulberry St between Kenmare and Spring Sts (212-334-3097). Subway: J, M to Bowery; 6 to Spring St. Mon–Sat 11am–7pm; Sun noon–7pm. AmEx, MC, V.
Tracy Feith, known for his darling dresses, has his full women's line on view here.

Trash & Vaudeville

4 St. Marks Pl between Second and Third Aves (212-982-3590). Subway: 6 to Astor Pl. Mon–Fri noon–8pm; Sat 11:30am–9pm; Sun 1–7:30pm. AmEx, MC, V.
This punk clubhouse has two floors of collar tips, jewelry, leathers, snakeskin boots, stretchy tube dresses and other accoutrements.

Zao

175 Orchard St between Houston and Stanton Sts (212-505-0500). Subway: F, V to Lower East Side–Second Ave. 11am–7pm. AmEx, MC, V.
The garden isn't the only thing groundbreaking about Zao—its artfully displayed clothing and jewelry are created by fashion's next big talents.

Leather goods

Carla Dawn Behrle

89 Franklin St between Broadway and Church St (212-334-5522). Subway: 1, 2 to Franklin St. By appointment only. AmEx, MC, V.
Carla Dawn Behrle's Tribeca shop features leather pants, skirts and dresses that can be best described as chic duds for that modern Bond girl (or boy). Just ask devotees Bono and the Edge.

Coach

595 Madison Ave at 57th St (212-754-0041). Subway: N, R, W to Lexington Ave–59th St; 4, 5, 6 to 59th St. Mon–Sat 10am–8pm; Sun 11am–6pm. AmEx, MC, V.
Coach's butter-soft leather briefcases, wallets and handbags have always been exceptional, but this is one of only three Coach stores in Manhattan to stock the label's outerwear collection. Check the phone book for other locations.

Jutta Neumann

158 Allen St between Rivington and Stanton Sts (212-982-7048). Subway: F, V to Lower East Side–Second Ave. Tue–Sat noon–8pm. AmEx, MC, V.
Jutta Neumann designs leather sandals and bags, as well as belts and jewelry. Haven't you always wanted a leather choker?

Necessities

New York City Custom Leather

168 Ludlow St between Houston and Stanton Sts (212-375-9593). Subway: F, V to Lower East Side–Second Ave. By appointment only. Cash only.
Fashion bugs buzz around Agatha Blois's shop to custom-order camouflage-print jackets with rabbit hoods and lace-up corsets with rose inlays.

Lingerie

Enelra

48½ E 7th St between First and Second Aves (212-473-2454). Subway: 6 to Astor Pl. Sun–Thu noon–8pm; Fri, Sat noon–9pm. AmEx, MC, V.
You'll find plenty of imported bras, corsets and slinky slips, as well as fluffy marabou mules, body products and the Shop Girl clothing line here.

La Perla

777 Madison Ave between 66th and 67th Sts (212-570-0050). Subway: 6 to 68th St–Hunter College. Mon–Sat 10am–6pm. AmEx, MC, V.
Every woman deserves the luxury of La Perla, a high-end line of Italian lingerie, but few can afford

it. Bras start at about $200, and lace corsets can run to more than $500.

La Petite Coquette

51 University Pl between 9th and 10th Sts (212-473-2478). Subway: N, R to 8th St–NYU. Mon–Wed, Fri, Sat 11am–7pm; Thu 11am–8pm; Sun noon–6pm. AmEx, MC, V.
Liv, Uma, Cindy and Sarah Jessica all join the throngs who flip through the panels of pinned-up bras and panties at La Petite Coquette. If your selection isn't in stock, owner Rebecca Apsan will order it for you.

Le Corset by Selima

80 Thompson St between Broome and Spring Sts (212-334-4936). Subway: C, E to Spring St. Mon–Sat 11am–7pm; Sun noon–7pm. AmEx, DC, MC, V.
In addition to Selima Salaun's slinky designs, this spacious boutique stocks antique camisoles, Renaissance-inspired girdles and of-the-moment lingerie by Colette Dinnigan and Carine Gilson.

Lingerie & Co.

1217 Third Ave between 70th and 71st Sts (212-737-7700). Subway: 6 to 68th St–Hunter College. Mon–Sat 9:30am–7pm. AmEx, Disc, MC, V.

Head of the class

This A-plus roster lists designers who need little introduction

They're the designers we all know and love, their signature pieces worn by aspiring fashionistas everywhere. Calvin, Donna, Giorgio, Ralph—each has at least one outpost in Manhattan. And like actors and models, they stick together, so you'll find most of your favorite stores clustered in one area. New attention-grabbing stores include Donna Karan's opulent collection palace, Prada's Rem Koolhaas–designed Soho store and the Tribeca flagship of Issey Miyake *(119 Hudson St at North Moore St, 212-226-0100)*, created by Frank Gehry.

Tony upscale labels and couture designers congregate uptown on and around the Fifth Avenue and Madison Avenue strips; younger, trendier brands can be found in Soho. However, there is plenty of crossover, so if you're looking to save yourself a trip in either direction, check the phone book for locations not listed below. You're bound to find a branch in either neighborhood.

Uptown brands

To get uptown, take the N, R or W to Fifth Avenue (it drops you at the corner of Fifth Avenue and 60th Street). The stores listed

below are peppered along the ten-block stretch below 59th Street on Fifth Avenue, or the 20-block stretch above it on Madison Avenue. A handful of shops are on side streets.

Bottega Veneta

635 Madison Ave between 59th and 60th Sts (212-371-5511).

Burberry

9 E 57th St between Fifth and Madison Aves (212-371-5010).

Calvin Klein

654 Madison Ave at 60th St (212-292-9000).

Celine

667 Madison Ave between 60th and 61st Sts (212-486-9700).

Chanel

15 E 57th St between Fifth and Madison Aves (212-355-5050).

Chloé

850 Madison Ave at 70th St (212-717-8220).

Christian Dior

21 E 57th St between Fifth and Madison Aves (212-931-2950).

Sibling team Mark Peress and Tamara Watkins take a look at your body (and ask a few questions) before giving lingerie recommendations. You'll find delicates from Chantelle, Hanro, Lejaby, Le Mystère…and many, many thongs.

Only Hearts

386 Columbus Ave between 78th and 79th Sts (212-724-5608). Subway: B, C to 81st St–Museum of Natural History; 1, 2 to 79th St. Mon–Sat 11am–8pm; Sun 11am–6pm. AmEx, Disc, MC, V.
Lacy and sheer, the undergarments at Only Hearts are the work of a hopeless romantic, designer Helena Stuart. The downtown store focuses on her recently launched ready-to-wear line.
Other location ● *230 Mott St between Prince and Spring Sts (212-431-3694). Subway: 6 to Spring St. Mon–Sat 11am–7pm; Sun noon–6pm. AmEx, MC, V.*

Religious Sex

7 St. Marks Pl between Second and Third Aves (212-477-9037). Subway: 6 to Astor Pl. Mon–Wed noon–8pm; Thu–Sat noon–9pm; Sun 1–8pm. AmEx, Disc, MC, V.

Religious Sex is a playpen for your inner fetishist. The store carries mesh tops with FUCK printed all over them, panties that are smaller than eye patches and rubber corsets that will all but guarantee a dangerous liaison, or a rash.

Swimwear

Malia Mills

199 Mulberry St between Kenmare and Spring Sts (212-625-2311). Subway: 6 to Spring St. Tue–Sun noon–7pm. AmEx, MC, V.
Ever since one of her designs made it onto the cover of *Sports Illustrated's* swimsuit issue a few years ago, Malia Mills's swimwear has become a staple for those who spend their New Year's Eve on St. Barth.

OMO Norma Kamali

11 W 56th St between Fifth and Sixth Aves (212-957-9797). Subway: F to 57th St; N, R, W to Fifth Ave–60th St. Mon–Sat 10am–6pm. AmEx, MC, V.
This 17-year-old store carries new and vintage women's wear, menswear and accessories, plus Kamali's bathing-suit separates and one-piece cutouts.

Necessities

Dolce & Gabbana
816 Madison Ave between 68th and 69th Sts (212-249-4100).

Donna Karan
819 Madison Ave between 68th and 69th Sts (212-861-1001).

Fendi
720 Fifth Ave at 56th St (212-767-0100).

Giorgio Armani
760 Madison Ave at 65th St (212-988-9191).

Givenchy
710 Madison Ave at 63rd St (212-772-1040).

Gucci
685 Fifth Ave at 54th St (212-826-2600).

Issey Miyake
992 Madison Ave between 76th and 77th Sts (212-439-7822).

Joseph
804 Madison Ave between 67th and 68th Sts (212-570-0077).

Louis Vuitton
703 Fifth Ave at 55th St (212-758-8877).

Michael Kors
974 Madison Ave at 76th St (212-452-4685).

Moschino
803 Madison Ave between 67th and 68th Sts (212-639-9600).

Nicole Farhi
10 E 60th St between Fifth and Madison Aves (212-223-8811).

Ralph Lauren
867 Madison Ave at 72nd St (212-606-2100).

Valentino
747 Madison Ave at 65th St (212-772-6969).

Vera Wang
991 Madison Ave at 77th St (212-628-3400).

Versace
647 Fifth Ave between 51st and 52nd Sts (212-317-0224).

Yves Saint Laurent
855 Madison Ave between 70th and 71st Sts (212-988-3821).

Downtown brands

To get to these chic shops, take the N or the R line to Prince Street, or the 6 train to Spring Street. You can also hop on the F, V or S lines to Broadway–Lafayette. Most of these stores are west of Broadway, Soho's main artery.

agnès b.
76 Greene St between Prince and Spring Sts (212-925-4649).

Anna Sui
113 Greene St between Prince and Spring Sts (212-941-8406).

▶

Streetwear

Active Wearhouse

514 Broadway between Broome and Spring Sts (212-965-2284). Subway: N, R to Prince St; 6 to Spring St. Mon–Sat 9am–9pm; Sun 10am–8pm. AmEx, Disc, MC, V.
This is the place to pick up the latest in footwear from Adidas, Nike, Saucony and others. The store also sells clothing; the North Face section is especially strong. Active Wearhouse's sister shop, **Transit** *(see page 211),* stocks the same in its subway-themed store.

alife

178 Orchard St between Houston and Stanton Sts (646-654-0628). Subway: F, V to Lower East Side–Second Ave. Noon–8pm. AmEx, MC, V.
This shop, run by the graphic design team Artificial Life, sells footwear from Dry Shod (plus Nike limited editions), Snipe, Tsubo; one-of-a-kind accessories by Nuflow and Suckadelic; Nixon watches; CDs by club-friendly artists; and rare Japanese action figures.

Canal Jean Company

504 Broadway between Broome and Spring Sts (212-226-1130). Subway: N, R to Prince St; 6 to Spring St. 9:30am–9pm. AmEx, DC, MC, V.
Browse the vast acreage of jeans, T-shirts and other basics, plus new and vintage clothing and accessories. Canal's prices are definitely worth the trip.

Final Home

241 Lafayette St between Prince and Spring Sts (212-966-0202). Subway: 6 to Spring St. Mon–Sat 11am–7pm; Sun noon–6pm. AmEx, MC, V.
Kosuke Tsumura's Final Home shop carries unisex essentials with more pockets, zippers, twists and turns than one of the *Choose Your Own Adventure* books (one coat has 44 pockets).

Memes

3 Great Jones St between Broadway and Lafayette St (212-420-9955). Subway: F, V, S to Broadway–Lafayette St; 6 to Bleecker St. Noon–8pm. AmEx, MC, V.
Tetsuo Hashimoto's shop offers refined men's streetwear, but is not uptight at all. You'll find Adidas

---

▶ Head of the class (continued)

Betsey Johnson
138 Wooster St between Houston and Prince Sts (212-995-5048).

Costume National
108 Wooster St between Prince and Spring Sts (212-431-1530).

Cynthia Rowley
112 Wooster St between Prince and Spring Sts (212-334-1144).

Daryl K
21 Bond St at Lafayette St (212-777-0713).

Helmut Lang
80 Greene St between Broome and Spring Sts (212-925-7214).

Jill Stuart
100 Greene St between Prince and Spring Sts (212-343-2300).

Marc Jacobs
163 Mercer St between Houston and Prince Sts (212-343-1490).

Miu Miu
100 Prince St between Greene and Mercer Sts (212-334-5156).

Prada
575 Broadway at Prince St (212-234-8888).

Vivienne Tam
99 Greene St between Prince and Spring Sts (212-966-2398).

Vivienne Westwood
71 Greene St between Broome and Spring Sts (212-334-5200).

Yohji Yamamoto
103 Grand St at Mercer St (212-966-9066).

Designer discount

Can't afford the top labels at full price? The following stores sell designer goods at a discount. *(See also **Vintage & discounted clothes**, page 205.)*

Century 21
22 Cortlandt St at Broadway (212-227-9092). Subway: A, C to Broadway–Nassau St; J, M, Z, 1, 2, 4, 5 to Fulton St.

Daffy's
111 Fifth Ave at 18th St (212-529-4477). Subway: L, N, Q, R, W, 4, 5, 6 to 14th St–Union Sq.

Woodbury Common Premium Outlets
Central Valley, NY (845-928-4000). Travel: Short Line Bus (800-631-8405, 212-736-4700; www.shortlinebus.com) from Port Authority Bus Terminal, 42nd St at Eighth Ave; round-trip $22.45, children $12.45; ask about special packages. Call for directions by car.

and Kangol goods, as well as Addict, Dope, Soul Rebel, Thunder Thorn and WK Interact.

Mr. Joe

500 Eighth Ave between 35th and 36th Sts (212-279-1090). Subway: A, C, E to 34th St–Penn Station. 9:30am–8pm. AmEx, MC, V.
What started in 1975 as a spot to buy Converse sneakers and Jordache jeans has evolved into a prime destination for hip-hop shoes and clothes. Mark Wahlberg, Memphis Bleek and DJ Clue are patrons.

Nylonsquid

222 Lafayette St between Broome and Spring Sts (212-334-6554). Subway: 6 to Spring St. Mon–Sat 11:30am–7pm; Sun noon–6pm. AmEx, MC, V.
London-based sneaker and clothing distributors Mick Hoyle and John Chatters originally wanted to open a showroom but opted instead for a retail space that doubles as one.

Phat Farm

129 Prince St between West Broadway and Wooster St (212-533-7428). Subway: C, E to Spring St; N, R to Prince St. Mon–Sat 11am–7pm; Sun noon–6pm. AmEx, MC, V.
This store showcases Def Jam Records impresario Russell Simmons's classy and conservative take on hip-hop couture: phunky-phresh oversize and baggy clothing. For gals, there's the Baby Phat line.

Recon

237 Eldridge St between Houston and Stanton Sts (212-614-8502). Subway: F, V to Lower East Side–Second Ave. Tue–Sun noon–7pm. AmEx, MC, V.
This joint venture of famed graffiti artists Stash, Futura and Bleu offers graf junkies a chance to admire the work of their favorite taggers on everything from clothes to accessories.

SSUR

219A Mulberry St between Prince and Spring Sts (212-431-3152). Subway: N, R to Prince St; 6 to Spring St. Mon–Fri noon–7pm; Sat noon–7:30pm; Sun noon–6:30pm. AmEx, MC, V.
Designer Russ Karablin's gallery-turned-shop combines military-surplus antichic with streetwear style.

Stüssy

140 Wooster St between Houston and Prince Sts (212-274-8855). Subway: N, R to Prince St. Mon–Thu noon–7pm; Fri, Sat 11am–7pm; Sun noon–6pm. AmEx, MC, V.
Check out the fine hats, T-shirts and other skate- and surfwear that Sean Stüssy is famous for.

Supreme

274 Lafayette St between Houston and Prince Sts (212-966-7799). Subway: F, V, S to Broadway–Lafayette St; N, R to Prince St; 6 to Spring St. Mon–Sat 11:30am–7pm; Sun noon–6pm. AmEx, MC, V.
This skatewear store is filled mostly with East Coast brands such as Chocolate, Independent, Zoo York and the shop's eponymous line. Of course, there are decks and the necessary skate accessories, too.

Triple Five Soul

290 Lafayette St between Houston and Prince Sts (212-431-2404). Subway: F, V, S to Broadway–Lafayette St; N, R to Prince St; 6 to Bleecker St. Mon–Sat 11am–7:30pm; Sun noon–7pm. AmEx, MC, V.
All the men and women's streetwear clothing and accessories inside this Soho shop are from New York designers.

Union

172 Spring St between Thompson St and West Broadway (212-226-8493). Subway: C, E to Spring St. Mon–Sat 11am–7pm; Sun noon–7pm. AmEx, MC, V.
This store is the exclusive dealer of the Duffer of St. George, the famed streetwear sold at the British shop of the same name. Union also sells Maharishi, 68 and Brothers, as well as the Union label.

X-Large

267 Lafayette St between Prince and Spring Sts (212-334-4480). Subway: N, R to Prince St; 6 to Spring St. Noon–7pm. AmEx, Disc, MC, V.
New Yorkers were thrilled when X-Large graduated from its closet-size shop on Avenue A and moved into these sleek digs, which now house the X-Large label for boys, and Mini and X'elle for girls.

Menswear

Although chic department stores such as Barneys New York and Bergdorf Goodman *(see page 193)* have enormous men's sections (Bergdorf's is even housed in a separate building across the street from the main shop), it's not always easy or comfortable for guys to search for new duds. At many fashion boutiques, the men's collections are either limited or tucked away in the back. The following shops offer stylish clothing for men only. At these stores, it's the women who will find themselves waiting on the couch outside the dressing room. *(See also **Streetwear**, page 202.)*

agnès b. homme

79 Greene St between Broome and Spring Sts (212-431-4339). Subway: C, E to Spring St; N, R to Prince St. 11am–7pm. AmEx, DC, MC, V.
The films of Jean-Luc Godard and his contemporaries are clearly a primary inspiration for agnès b.'s designs. Men's basics include the classic snap cardigan sweater and striped, long-sleeved T-shirts that will make you feel like Picasso in his studio.

Brooks Brothers

346 Madison Ave at 44th St (212-682-8800). Subway: S, 4, 5, 6, 7 to 42nd St–Grand Central. Mon–Wed, Fri, Sat 9am–7pm; Thu 9am–8pm; Sun noon–6pm. AmEx, Disc, MC, V.
This famous store is still where prepsters head for high-quality button-down shirts and chinos, but it's also the place to buy a classic men's tuxedo. There are classy clothes for the ladies, too.

Other location ● *666 Fifth Ave between 52nd and 53rd Sts (212-261-9440). Subway: E, V to Fifth Ave–53rd St. Mon–Fri 10am–8pm; Sat 10am–7pm; Sun 11am–7pm. AmEx, Disc, MC, V.*

D/L Cerney
13 E 7th St between Second and Third Aves (212-673-7033). Subway: 6 to Astor Pl. Noon–8pm. AmEx, MC, V.
This vintage shop specializes in menswear from the 1940s to the 1960s, plus new but timeless original designs for the stylish groom.
Other location ● *222 West Broadway between Franklin and White Sts (212-941-0530). Subway: 1, 2 to Franklin St. Noon–8pm. AmEx, Disc, MC, V.*

INA Men
See **INA**, page 206.

Jack Spade
See **Kate Spade**, page 209.

Paul Smith
108 Fifth Ave between 15th and 16th Sts (212-627-9770). Subway: L, N, Q, R, W, 4, 5, 6 to 14th St–Union Sq. Mon–Wed, Fri, Sat 11am–7pm; Thu 11am–8pm; Sun noon–6pm. AmEx, Disc, MC, V.
Stop by Paul Smith for the relaxed English-gentleman look. These designs and accessories are exemplary for their combination of elegance, quality and wit.

Sean
132 Thompson St between Houston and Prince Sts (212-598-5980). Subway: C, E to Spring St. Mon–Sat 11am–8pm; Sun noon–7pm. AmEx, MC, V.
If you yearn to make a style statement but have a Gap-size wallet, come here. Store owner Sean Cassidy stocks his racks with French designer Pierre Emile Lafaurie's suits, poplin shirts (in 23 colors!) and corduroy jackets.
Other location ● *224 Columbus Ave between 70th and 71st Sts (212-769-1489). Subway: B, C, 1, 2, 3 to 72nd St. Mon–Sat 11am–8pm; Sun noon–7pm. AmEx, MC, V.*

Seize sur Vingt
243 Elizabeth St between Houston and Prince Sts (212-343-0476). Subway: F, V, S to Broadway–Lafayette St; N, R to Prince St; 6 to Bleecker St. Mon–Sat noon–7pm; Sun noon–6pm. AmEx, MC, V.
Men's shirts come in vibrant colors and are made with impeccable touches: mother-of-pearl buttons and square, short collars that look good with the top button undone. And ladies will love the women's line.

Ted Baker London
107 Grand St at Mercer St (212-343-8989). Subway: J, M, Z, N, Q, R, W, 6 to Canal St. Mon–Sat 11:30am–7pm; Sun noon–6pm. AmEx, DC, MC, V.
The Brits behind this label present a modern, restrained line of men's clothing whose focus is short- and long-sleeved shirts in bright colors. Customers should not overlook the rest of the clothing, which has been popular in England for more than a decade.

Thomas Pink
520 Madison Ave at 53rd St (212-838-1928). Subway: E, V to Fifth Ave–53rd St. Mon–Wed, Fri 10am–7pm; Thu 10am–8pm; Sat 10am–6pm; Sun noon–6pm. AmEx, DC, MC, V.
Pink's shirts are offered in bold, dynamic colors that may be paired with more conservative suits. But it's no longer strictly for men: The women's department includes accessories, jewelry and—of course—shirts.
Other location ● *1160 Sixth Ave at 44th St (212-840-9663). Subway: B, D, F, V to 42nd St. Mon–Wed, Fri 10am–7pm; Thu 10am–8pm; Sat 10am–6pm; Sun noon–5pm. AmEx, DC, MC, V.*

Children's clothes

For **Children's toys**, see page 221.

Bonpoint
1269 Madison Ave at 91st St (212-722-7720). Subway: 6 to 96th St. Mon–Sat 10am–6pm. AmEx, MC, V.
Perfect for toddlers with expense accounts, this Upper East Side institution carries frilly white party dresses and starched sailor suits.
Other location ● *811 Madison Ave at 68th St (212-879-0900). Subway: 6 to 68th St–Hunter College. Mon–Sat 10am–6pm. AmEx, MC, V.*

Calypso Enfants
426 Broome St between Crosby and Lafayette Sts (212-966-3242). Subway: F, V, S to Broadway–Lafayette St; 6 to Spring St. Mon–Sat 11am–7pm; Sun noon–6pm. AmEx, MC, V.
Fans of Calypso—and its ultrafeminine women's clothing, bags and accessories *(see* **Calypso on Broome,** *page 197)*—positively adore this francophone children's boutique: The tiny wool coats look as if they leaped from the pages of *Madeline.*

Hoyt & Bond
248 Smith St between DeGraw and Douglass Sts, Carroll Gardens, Brooklyn (718-488-8283). Subway: F, G to Carroll St. Mon–Thu 10am–6pm; Fri–Sun 10am–7pm. MC, V.
Designer Elizabeth Beer's store features her line of hip children's clothing (wool kilts, hand-knit sweaters) and women's pieces (dickeys in every hue, A-line skirts).

Lilliput
240 Lafayette St (212-965-9201) and 265 Lafayette St (212-965-9567) between Prince and Spring Sts. Subway: N, R to Prince St; 6 to Spring St. Sun, Mon noon–6pm; Tue–Sat 11am–7pm. AmEx, Disc, MC, V.
This style source for children sells new and second-hand clothing, plus accessories, bedding and toys.

Space Kiddets
46 E 21st St between Broadway and Park Ave South (212-420-9878). Subway: N, R, 6 to 23rd St. Mon, Tue, Fri, Sat 10:30am–6pm; Wed, Thu 10:30am–7pm. AmEx, MC, V.
This shop strives for a unique combination: clothing that is cool, practical, comfortable and fun for

I feel pretty Diane von Furstenberg's body-skimming dresses come in dozens of patterns.

kics. In addition to one-of-a-kind toys, Space Kiddets features a preteen collection for girls.

Z'Baby Company

100 W 72nd St at Columbus Ave (212-579-2229). Subway: B, C, 1, 2, 3 to 72nd St. Mon–Sat 10:30am–7:30pm; Sun 11am–6pm. AmEx, MC, V.
Uptown yuppies clothe their newborns and kids (up to size seven) in Z'Baby's styles. Sonia Rykiel is among the designers who trim their cuts down to size; others include Cakewalk, Geisswein and Lili Gaufrette. Other location ● *996 Lexington Ave at 72nd St (212-472-2229). Subway: 6 to 68th St–Hunter College. Mon–Sat 10am–7pm; Sun noon–5pm. AmEx, MC, V.*

Maternity wear

Liz Lange Maternity

958 Madison Ave between 75th and 76th Sts (212-879-2191). Subway: 6 to 77th St. Mon–Fri 10am–7pm; Sat 10am–6pm; Sun noon–5pm. AmEx, MC, V.
Liz Lange is the mother of stylish maternity wear. Catering to such high-profile recent moms as Catherine Zeta-Jones and Iman, Lange takes nonpregnant styles and modifies them. Her inspiration in fashion? Jackie O., whose fresh, feminine style she imitates.

Pumpkin Maternity

407 Broome St at Lafayette St (212-334-1809). Subway: 6 to Spring St. Mon–Sat noon–7pm; Sun noon–5pm. AmEx, DC, Disc, MC, V.
At former rocker Pumpkin Wentzel's store, you'll find casual, tailored and machine-washable essentials for the expectant mother, especially one who craves the feel of real denim against her skin. Baby clothing and newborn accessories (strollers, etc) are also available.

Vintage & discounted clothes

The cardinal rule of secondhand-clothes shopping is: The less you browse, the more you have to pay. Although we've included a few in our listings, the shops along lower Broadway tend to ask inflated prices for anything except the most mundane '70s disco shirts. The alternatives, too numerous and ever-changing to list here, are the many small shops in the East Village and on the Lower East Side. These nooks (along with the legendary, but overrated **Domsey's** in Brooklyn) are where real bargains can be found. Salvation Army and Goodwill stores are also worth checking out—as is any place with the word *thrift* in its name. **Flea markets** *(see page 221)* also have a lot of vintage/antique clothing. (For designer labels, *see* **Designer discount**, *page 202.*)

Alice Underground

481 Broadway at Broome St (212-431-9067). Subway: N, R to Prince St; 6 to Spring St. 11am–7:30pm. AmEx, MC, V.
This vintage mainstay houses a good selection of gear from the 1940s through the oughts, in all sorts of fabrics and in varied condition. Prices are high, but it's always worth rummaging through the bins at the front and back.

Allan & Suzi

416 Amsterdam Ave at 80th St (212-724-7445). Subway: 1, 2 to 79th St. Mon–Fri noon–6pm. AmEx, Disc, MC, V.
Models drop off their worn-once Comme des Garçons, Gaultiers, Muglers and Pradas here. The platform-shoe collection is incomparable, and there's a fab selection of vintage jewelry. There's a branch in Asbury Park, New Jersey *(732-988-7373).*

Antique Boutique

712–714 Broadway between Astor Pl and E 4th St (212-995-5577). Subway: N, R to 8th St–NYU. Mon–Thu 11am–9pm; Fri, Sat 11am–10pm; Sun noon–8pm. AmEx, DC, Disc, MC, V.
At Antique Boutique, you'll find countless racks of vintage threads.

Domsey's Warehouse

431 Kent Ave at South 9th St, Williamsburg, Brooklyn (718-384-6000). Subway: J, M, Z to Marcy Ave. Mon–Fri 9am–5:30pm; Sat 9am–6:30pm; Sun 11am–5:30pm. Disc, MC, V.
Domsey's Warehouse has allowed the quality of its preworn duds to drop in recent years. Still, it's usu-

ally easy to turn up something worthwhile. Choose from a huge selection of used jeans, jackets, military and industrial wear, ball gowns, shoes, hats and a wide selection of Hawaiian shirts. There's an outpost in Perth Amboy, New Jersey *(732-376-1551)*.

Filthmart
531 E 13th St between Aves A and B (212-387-0650). Subway: L to First Ave; N, Q, R, W, 4, 5, 6 to 14th St–Union Sq. Sun–Tue 1–7pm; Wed–Sat noon–8pm. Disc, MC, V.
This East Village store (co-owned by *Sopranos* star Drea de Matteo) specializes in white trash and rock & roll memorabilia from the 1960s through the early '80s. Expect lots of leather, denim and T-shirts. Also check out the excellent pinball machine selection and the house jeans line.

INA
101 Thompson St between Prince and Spring Sts (212-941-4757). Subway: C, E to Spring St. Noon–7pm. AmEx, MC, V.
For the past nine years, INA on Thompson Street has reigned supreme over the downtown consignment scene. The cheery Soho location features drastically reduced couture pieces, while the Nolita site carries trendier clothing. And be sure to visit the men's store on Mott Street.
Other locations ● *21 Prince St between Elizabeth and Mott Sts (212-334-9048). Subway: J, M to Bowery; N, R to Prince St; 6 to Spring St. Sun–Thu noon–7pm; Fri, Sat noon–8pm. AmEx, MC, V.* ● *INA Men, 262 Mott St between Houston and Prince Sts (212-334-2210). Subway: F, V, S to Broadway–Lafayette St; 6 to Bleecker St. Sun–Thu noon–7pm; Fri, Sat noon–8pm. AmEx, MC, V.*

Keni Valenti Retro-Couture
247 W 30th St between Seventh and Eighth Aves (212-967-7147). Subway: A, C, E, 1, 2, 3 to 34th St–Penn Station. By appointment only. AmEx, DC, Disc, MC, V.
This appointment-only, retired evening gown showroom caters to models and actresses, but the space is also a mecca for anyone passionate about Balenciaga, Courrèges and Halston. Prices start in the thousands.

Marmalade
172 Ludlow St between Houston and Stanton Sts (212-473-8070). Subway: F, V to Lower East Side–Second Ave. 1–9pm. AmEx, MC, V.
One of the cutest vintage-clothing stores on the Lower East Side, Marmalade also has some of the hottest 1970s- and '80s-era threads below Houston Street. Whether you're in need of a slinky cocktail dress or a ruffled blouse, you'll find it amid the selection of well-cared-for and well-priced items. Accessories, a fantastic array of vintage shoes and a small selection of men's clothing are also available.

Resurrection
123 E 7th St between First Ave and Ave A (212-228-0063). Subway: F, V to Lower East Side–Second Ave; 6 to Astor Pl. Tue–Fri noon–8pm; Sat 1–9pm; Sun 1–8pm. AmEx, MC, V.
This vintage boutique is a Pucci wonderland; Kate

Moss and Anna Sui are regulars. Owner Katy Rodriguez rents the space from the Theodore Wolinnin Funeral Home next door. But don't worry: Rodriguez's shop looks more like a jewel box than a haunted house.
Other location ● *217 Mott St between Prince and Spring Sts (212-625-1374). Subway: N, R to Prince St; 6 to Spring St. Mon–Sat 11am–7pm; Sun noon–7pm. AmEx, MC, V.*

Screaming Mimi's
382 Lafayette St between Great Jones and E 4th Sts (212-677-6464). Subway: N, R to 8th St–NYU; 6 to Astor Pl. Mon–Sat noon–8pm; Sun 1–7pm. AmEx, DC, Disc, MC, V.
This was where Cyndi Lauper shopped in the 1980s. The prices are reasonable for what you're getting, and the selection is more carefully chosen than Ms. Lauper would have had you think.

Fashion Services

Clothing rental

One Night Out/Mom's Night Out
147 E 72nd St between Lexington and Third Aves (212-988-1122). Subway: 6 to 68th St–Hunter College. Mon–Fri 10:30am–6pm; Sat 11am–5pm. AmEx, MC, V.
One Night Out rents brand-new evening wear to uptown socialites and downtown girls who are trying to pass for the same. Across the hall, Mom's Night Out provides the service to expectant mothers for $195 to $375.

Zeller Tuxedos
1010 Third Ave at 60th St (212-355-0707). Subway: N, R, W to Lexington Ave–59th St ; 4, 5, 6 to 59th St. Mon–Fri 9am–6:30pm; Sat 10am–5pm. AmEx, MC, V.
Valentino and Lubiam tuxes are available for those who didn't think to pack theirs. Check the phone book for other locations.

Laundry

Dry cleaners

Madame Paulette Custom Couture Cleaners
1255 Second Ave between 65th and 66th Sts (212-838-6827). Subway: 6 to 68th St–Hunter College. Mon–Fri 7:30am–7pm; Sat 8am–5pm. AmEx, MC, V.
This 42-year-old luxury dry cleaners knows how to treat a society lady's things. Take advantage of free pickup and delivery all over Manhattan, and a worldwide shipping service.

Meurice Garment Care
31 University Pl between 8th and 9th Sts (212-475-2778). Subway: N, R to 8th St–NYU. Mon–Fri 7:30am–7pm; Sat 7:30am–5pm. AmEx, MC, V.

Laundry is serious business here. Meurice's roster of high-profile clients includes Armani and Prada, and the company handles all kinds of delicate stain removal and other repair jobs.
Other location ● *245 E 57th St between Second and Third Aves (212-759-9057). Subway: N, R, W to Lexington Ave–59th St; 4, 5, 6 to 59th St. Mon–Fri 8am–6:30pm; Sat 9am–3pm. AmEx, MC, V.*

Midnight Express Cleaners
212-921-0111, 800-764-3648. Mon–Fri 9am–7pm; Sat 9am–1pm. AmEx, MC, V.
Midnight Express will pick up your dry cleaning anywhere below 96th Street at a mutually convenient time and return it to you the next day (that goes for bulk laundry, too). It costs $6.95 for a man's suit to be cleaned, including pickup and delivery.

Self-service laundry

Most neighborhoods have self-service laundries with coin-operated machines, but in New York it doesn't cost much more to drop off your wash and let someone else do the work. Check the yellow pages for specific establishments.

Ecowash
72 W 69th St between Central Park West and Columbus Ave (212-787-3890). Subway: B, C to 72nd St; 1, 2 to 66th St–Lincoln Ctr. 7:30am–10pm. Cash only.
For the green-minded, Ecowash uses only natural, nontoxic detergent. You can wash your own duds, starting at $1.75, or drop off up to seven pounds for $6.50 (each additional pound is 75 cents).

Repairs

Clothing repair

Ramon's Tailor Shop
306 Mott St between Bleecker and Houston Sts (212-226-0747). Subway: F, V, S to Broadway–Lafayette St; 6 to Bleecker St. Mon–Fri 7:30am–7:30pm; Sat 9am–6:30pm. Cash only.
Ramon's can alter or repair "anything that can be worn on the body." There's also an emergency service, and pickup/delivery is free in much of Manhattan.

R&S Cleaners
212-475-9412. Cash only.
This cash-only pickup-and-delivery service specializes in cleaning, repairing and tailoring leather jackets. Prices start at $35, and cleaning takes about a week.

Jewelry & watch repair

Zig Zag Jewelers
1336A Third Ave between 76th and 77th Sts (212-794-3559). Subway: 6 to 77th St. Mon–Fri 11am–
7:30pm; Sat 10am–6:30pm; Sun noon–5:30pm. AmEx, DC, Disc, MC, V.
These experts won't touch costume jewelry, but they'll restring and reclasp your broken Bulgaris and Harry Winstons. Watch repairs are always trustworthy, and estimates are free.
Other location ● *963 Madison Ave between 75th and 76th Sts (212-472-6373). Subway: 6 to 77th St.*

CRITICS' PICKS # Shopping

We suggest you shop here...

...for high-design home accessories
ABC Carpet & Home, page 224

...for A-list books at bargain prices
Unoppressive Non-Imperialist Bargain Books, page 218

...for remedies that work
C.O. Bigelow Apothecaries, page 215

...for goods of an Asian persuasion
Pearl River Mart, page 228

...for the fasten-conscious
Tender Buttons, page 232

...for the fashion-conscious guy
Sean, page 204

...for gadgets with character
Kar'ikter, page 227

...for that important letter to send back home
Kate's Paperie, page 231

...for Kodak moments
B&H, page 219

...for those who are naughty by nature
Toys in Babeland, page 232

...for the modern jet-setter
Flight 001, page 230

...for bargain antiques
Annex Antiques Fair & Flea Market, page 221

...for when you want to say it with flowers
Gotham Gardens, page 222

...for knishes and other New York delicacies
Russ & Daughters, page 224

Necessities

Mon–Sat 10am–6pm; Sun noon–5pm. AmEx, DC, Disc, MC, V.

Shoe repair

Andrade Shoe Repair

103 University Pl between 12th and 13th Sts (212-529-3541). Subway: L, N, Q, R, W, 4, 5, 6 to 14th St–Union Sq. Mon–Fri 7:30am–7pm; Sat 9am–6:30pm. Cash only.

Andrade is a basic—but reliable—shoe-repair chain. Check the phone book for other locations.

Shoe Service Plus

15 W 55th St between Fifth and Sixth Aves (212-262-4823). Subway: E, V to Fifth Ave–53rd St. Mon–Fri 7am–7pm; Sat 10am–5pm. AmEx, DC, Disc, MC, V.

This shop is bustling with customers, and no wonder: The staff will give just as much attention to your battle-weary combat boots as to your delicate and pricey Manolos.

Accessories

Eyewear emporiums

Alain Mikli Optique

880 Madison Ave between 71st and 72nd Sts (212-472-6085). Subway: 6 to 68th St–Hunter College. Mon–Sat 10am–6pm. AmEx, MC, V.

French frames for the bold and beautiful are available from this 14-year-old Madison Avenue outlet, including specs designed by architect Philippe Starck.

Myoptics

123 Prince St between Greene and Wooster Sts (212-598-9306). Subway: N, R to Prince St. Mon–Sat 11am–7pm; Sun noon–6pm. AmEx, Disc, MC, V.

Plastics are hot at Soho's Myoptics; look for styles by Matsuda, Oliver Peoples and Paul Smith. Check the phone book for other locations.

Selima Optique

59 Wooster St between Broome and Spring Sts (212-343-9490). Subway: C, E to Spring St. Mon–Wed, Fri, Sat 11am–7pm; Thu 11am–8pm; Sun noon–7pm. AmEx, DC, MC, V.

Selima Salaun's wear-if-you-dare frames are popular with such famous four-eyes as Sean Lennon and Lenny Kravitz (both of whom have frames named for them). Salaun also stocks Face à Face, Gucci, Matsuda and others.
Other locations ● Lunettes et Chocolat, 25 Prince St between Elizabeth and Mott Sts (212-334-8484). Subway: F, V, S to Broadway–Lafayette St; N, R, to Prince St; 6 to Bleecker St. Mon–Sat 11am–7pm; Sun noon–7pm. AmEx, MC, V. ● 84 E 7th St between First and Second Aves (212-260-2495). Subway: F, V to Lower East Side–Second Ave; 6 to Astor Pl. Noon–7pm. AmEx, DC, Disc, MC, V.

Sol Moscot Opticians

118 Orchard St at Delancey St (212-477-3796). Subway: F to Delancey St; J, M, Z to Delancey–Essex Sts. 9am–5:30pm. AmEx, DC, Disc, MC, V.

At this 76-year-old family-run optical emporium, expect to find the same big-name designer frames for at least 20 percent less than what they go for uptown. Sol Moscot also carries vintage varieties (starting at $49), wrap-shield sunglasses by Chanel and Gucci, and bifocal contacts.
Other locations ● 69 W 14th St at Sixth Ave (212-647-1550). Subway: F, V to 14th St; L to Sixth Ave. Mon–Fri 10am–7pm; Sat 10:30am–6pm; Sun noon–5pm. AmEx, DC, Disc, MC, V. ● 107-20 Continental Ave between Austin St and Queens Blvd, Forest Hills, Queens (718-544-2200). Subway: E, F, V, G, R to Forest Hills–71st Ave. Mon–Fri 10am–7pm; Sat 10am–5pm; Sun noon–5pm. AmEx, Disc, MC, V.

Zeitlin Optik

40 E 52nd St between Madison and Park Aves (212-319-5166). Subway: E, V to Fifth Ave–53rd St. Mon–Fri 10am–6pm; Sat 10am–5pm. AmEx, DC, MC, V.

Marc Zeitlin's 15-year-old boutique stocks not-so-recognizable brands from around the world: Buvel and Mugen from Japan, Binocle from France and Marwitz from Germany. He specializes in specs for the seriously hard of seeing. And if he doesn't have what you want, Zeitlin will whip up a custom pair (as the store does for films and fashion shows).

Handbags

See also **Leather goods**, page 199.

Amy Chan

247 Mulberry St between Prince and Spring Sts (212-966-3417). Subway: F, V, S to Broadway–Lafayette St; N, R to Prince St; 6 to Spring St. Noon–7pm. AmEx, MC, V.

Designer Amy Chan made her mark a few years back when she launched a collection of handbags made from Chinese silks, sari fabric and feathers; they're now the centerpiece of her Nolita store. She also sells clothing and jewelry for chic rocker-chicks.

Blue Bag

266 Elizabeth St between Houston and Prince Sts (212-966-8566). Subway: F, V, S to Broadway–Lafayette St; 6 to Bleecker St. Mon–Sat 11am–8pm; Sun noon–7pm. AmEx, Disc, MC, V.

Blue Bag is the walk-in handbag closet of your dreams. Its delicious and ever-changing bags (not all blue) are popular with the fashionable likes of Cameron Diaz and Courtney Love. The nearby sister shop, **Minette** (238 Mott St between Prince and Spring Sts, 212-334-7290), sells every accessory except bags.

Jamin Puech

252 Mott St between Houston and Prince Sts (212-334-9730). Subway: F, V, S to Broadway–Lafayette St; 6 to Bleecker St. Mon–Sat 11am–7pm; Sun noon–6pm. AmEx, MC, V.

Necessities

Looking for a precious accessory or two? Make tracks to this tiny boutique, which sells exquisite creations by French partners Benoit Jamin and Isabel Puech. The selection includes flirty sequined bags, large leather totes and colorful boas.

Kate Spade

454 Broome St at Mercer St (212-274-1991). Subway: N, R to Prince St; 6 to Spring St. Mon–Sat 11am–7pm; Sun noon–6pm. AmEx, MC, V.
Popular handbag designer Kate Spade sells her classic boxy tote as well as other smart numbers in this stylish store. Prices range from $80 to $400. Spade also stocks shoes, pajamas and rain slickers. For the new line of luggage, see page 231.
Other location ● *Jack Spade, 56 Greene St between Broome and Spring Sts (212-625-1820). Subway: C, E, 6 to Spring St; N, R to Prince St. Mon–Sat 11am–7pm; Sun noon–6pm. AmEx, MC, V.*

Kazuyo Nakano

223 Mott St between Prince and Spring Sts (212-941-7093). Subway: 6 to Spring St. Mon–Wed 12:30–6pm. AmEx, MC, V.
Straight out of high school, Kazuyo Nakano worked on the assembly line at her father's kimono-bag factory in Kyoto. Now Nakano has her own handbag shop selling her fun, functional designs. She has also launched a leather-heavy clothing collection.

Hats

Amy Downs Hats

227 E 14th St between Second and Third Aves (212-358-8756). Subway: L to Third Ave; N, Q, R, W, 4, 5, 6 to 14th St–Union Sq. Tue–Sat 11am–7pm. Cash only.
Downs's soft wool and felt hats are neither fragile nor prissy. In fact, feel free to crumple them up and shove them in your bag—they just won't die.

Arnold Hatters

620 Eighth Ave between 40th and 41st Sts (212-768-3781). Subway: A, C, E to 42nd St–Port Authority. Mon–Sat 9am–7:15pm; Sun 10am–5pm. AmEx, DC, MC, V.
At 75-year-old family-owned Arnold Hatters (the old sign outside says Knox Hats) the selection includes Kangols (widest array in the USA), Stetsons, fedoras, spitfires and more. Prices range from $6 to $275.

Eugenia Kim

203 E 4th St between Aves A and B (212-673-9787). Subway: F, V to Lower East Side–Second Ave. Noon–8pm; call for appointment. AmEx, MC, V.
This is the source for Eugenia Kim's funky cowboy hats, feather cloches and more.

The Hat Shop

120 Thompson St between Prince and Spring Sts (212-219-1445). Subway: C, E to Spring St. Mon–Sat noon–7pm; Sun 1–6pm. AmEx, MC, V.
Linda Pagan isn't a hat designer—she's a hat junkie, and her boutique is a cross between a millinery shop and a department store. Customers can choose from 40 different designers—plus the house line, Chapeau Château—and get scads of personal attention, too.

Kelly Christy

235 Elizabeth St between Houston and Prince Sts (212-965-0686). Subway: F, V, S to Broadway–Lafayette St; 6 to Bleecker St. Tue–Sat noon–7pm; Sun noon–6pm. AmEx, MC, V.
The selection for men and women is lovely and the atmosphere is relaxed. Try on anything you like (by such designers as Wendy Mink and Jeanine Payer); Christy is more than happy to help and give you the honest truth. There's also a great scarf selection.

Jewelry

Bulgari

730 Fifth Ave at 57th St (212-315-9000). Subway: N, R, W to Fifth Ave–60th St. Mon–Sat 10am–5:30pm. AmEx, DC, MC, V.
Bulgari offers some of the world's most beautiful adornments—everything from watches and chunky gold necklaces to leather goods and stationery.
Other location ● *783 Madison Ave between 66th and 67th Sts (212-717-2300). Subway: 6 to 68th St–Hunter College. Mon–Sat 10am–5:30pm. AmEx, MC, V.*

Cartier

653 Fifth Ave at 52nd St (212-446-3459). Subway: E, V to Fifth Ave–53rd St. Mon–Sat 10am–5:30pm. AmEx, DC, MC, V.
Cartier bought its Italianate mansion, one of the few remnants of this neighborhood's previous life as a classy residential area, for two strands of oriental pearls. All the usual Cartier items—jewelry, silver, porcelain—are sold within. Check the phone book for other locations.

Fragments

107 Greene St between Prince and Spring Sts (212-334-9588). Subway: C, E, 6 to Spring St; N, R to Prince St. Mon–Fri 11am–7pm; Sat noon–7pm; Sun noon–6pm. AmEx, MC, V.
Over the years, Fragments buyers Janet Goldman and Jimmy Moore have assembled an exclusive stable of more than 50 artists. The jewelers first offer their designs (which are never *too* trendy) at the Soho store, before Goldman and Moore sell them to department stores such as Barneys.
Other location ● *53 Stone St between Coenties Alley and Hanover Sq (212-269-3955). Subway: N, R to Whitehall St; 4, 5 to Bowling Green. Mon–Wed, Fri 10am–5:30pm; Thu 11am–7pm.*

Ilias Lalaounis

739 Madison Ave between 64th and 65th Sts (212-439-9400). Subway: F to Lexington Ave–63rd St; N, R, W to Fifth Ave–60th St. Mon–Sat 10am–6pm. AmEx, MC, V.
This Greek jewelry designer's work is inspired by his native country's ancient symbols, as well as by Native American and Arabic designs.

Necessities

Boot camp Walking in a pair of Jimmy Choo heels may require some basic training.

Kara Varian Baker

215 Mulberry St between Prince and Spring Sts (212-431-5727). Subway: N, R to Prince St; 6 to Spring St. Wed–Sat noon–7pm; Sun noon–5pm. AmEx, MC, V.
Kara Varian Baker's store feels more like a New Age living room than a trendy boutique. Famous for her chunky sterling-silver and 18-karat gold lockets, Baker also designs classic pearl necklaces and avant-garde pieces with colorful precious and semi-precious stones.

L'Atelier

89 E 2nd St between First Ave and Ave A (212-677-4983). Subway: F, V to Lower East Side–Second Ave. Mon–Fri 11am–7pm; Sat 1–7pm. AmEx, MC, V.
All of the precious-metal adornments at this small East Village jewel box are made on-site.

Manny Winick & Son

34 W 47th St at Fifth Ave (212-302-9555). Subway: B, D, F, V to 47–50th Sts–Rockefeller Ctr. Mon–Fri 10:30am–5:15pm. AmEx, Disc, MC, V.
Traditional jewelry made from precious stones is sold alongside more sculptural, contemporary pieces.

Me & Ro

239 Elizabeth St between Houston and Prince Sts (917-237-9215). Subway: F, V, S to Broadway–Lafayette St; 6 to Bleecker St. Mon–Sat 11am–7pm; Sun noon–6pm. AmEx, MC, V.
Michele Quan and Robin Renzi, the dynamic duo behind Me & Ro jewelry, are inspired by ancient Chinese, Tibetan and Indian traditions (such as tying bells around the wrist as a form of protection).

Piaget

730 Fifth Ave at 57th St (212-246-5555). Subway: N, R, W to Fifth Ave–60th St. Mon–Fri 10am–6pm; Sat 10am–5:30pm. AmEx, DC, MC, V.
This giant boutique full of glittering jewels would surely make anyone swoon—especially the person *paying* for that perfect diamond.

Push

240 Mulberry St between Prince and Spring Sts (212-965-9699). Subway: 6 to Spring St. Tue–Sat noon–7pm; Sun 1–6pm. AmEx, DC, MC, V.

Karen Karch's charming rings, most of which are simple, narrow diamond settings, make spending two months' salary on an engagement band an obsolete gesture. If you're not getting hitched, the store still has plenty to offer.

Reinstein/Ross

122 Prince St between Greene and Wooster Sts (212-226-4513). Subway: N, R to Prince St. Mon–Sat 11:30am–7pm; Sun noon–6pm. AmEx, MC, V.
Most of the sleek, handmade engagement rings and wedding bands at Reinstein/Ross are made with the store's custom alloys, such as 22-karat "apricot" gold. **Other location ●** *29 E 73rd St between Fifth and Madison Aves (212-772-1901). Subway: 6 to 77th St. Mon–Sat 11am–6:30pm. AmEx, MC, V.*

Robert Lee Morris

400 West Broadway between Broome and Spring Sts (212-431-9405). Subway: C, E to Spring St; N, R to Prince St. Tue–Fri 11am–6pm; Sat 11am–7pm; Sun noon–6pm. AmEx, Disc, MC, V.
Robert Lee Morris is one of the foremost contemporary designers; his bright Soho gallery is the only place where you can view his entire line of strong, striking pieces.

Ted Muehling

27 Howard St between Broadway and Lafayette St (212-431-3825). Subway: C, E to Spring St; N, R to Prince St. Tue–Sat noon–6pm. AmEx, MC, V.
Ted Muehling creates beautiful organic shapes in the studio behind his store, where he also sells the work of other artists. He also carries porcelain vases, cups, lanterns and other items for the home.

Tiffany & Co.

727 Fifth Ave at 57th St (212-755-8000). Subway: N, R, W to Fifth Ave–60th St. Mon–Fri 10am–7pm; Sat 10am–6pm. AmEx, DC, MC, V.
Tiffany's heyday was around the turn of the last century, when Louis Comfort Tiffany, son of store founder Charles Lewis Tiffany, took the reigns and began designing his famous lamps and sensational Art Nouveau jewelry. Today, the big stars are Paloma Picasso and Elsa Peretti. Three stories are stacked with precious jewels, silver accessories, chic watches, stationery and porcelain.

Luggage

Need more luggage because you bought too much stuff? Before you head for the nearest Samsonite dealer, check out the many shops on Canal Street that sell cheapo luggage, or suss out the few that remain on Orchard Street. None of them stand out, but they are good for quick fixes. Other, more expensive options are listed below.

Bag House

797 Broadway between 10th and 11th Sts (212-260-0940). Subway: L, N, Q, R, W, 4, 5, 6 to 14th St–Union Sq. Mon–Sat 11am–6:45pm; Sun 1–5:45pm. AmEx, DC, MC, V.

All sorts of bags, from the tiniest tote to something you could stow a small family in, are available here.

Flight 001
See page 230 for listing.

Innovation Luggage
300 E 42nd St at Second Ave (212-599-2998). Subway: S, 4, 5, 6, 7 to 42nd St–Grand Central. Mon–Fri 10am–8pm; Sat 11am–7pm; Sun 11am–5pm. AmEx, Disc, MC, V.
This chain carries the newest models of top-brand luggage, including Andiamo, Dakota, Samsonite and Tumi. Check the phone book for other locations.

Shoes

Shoe stores line both sides of West 8th Street *(between Broadway and Sixth Ave)*. Don't want to shop-hop? For high-style shoes, swing by **Barneys New York** *(see page 193)* or **Jeffrey New York** *(see page 194)*. For sheer variety, **Saks Fifth Avenue** *(see page 194)* wins, toes down. Below, you'll find sneakers, boots and designer knockoffs. *(For **Shoe repair**, see page 208.)*

Billy Martin's
220 E 60th St between Second and Third Aves (212-861-3100). Subway: F to Lexington Ave–63rd St; N, R, W to Lexington Ave–59th St; 4, 5, 6 to 59th St. Mon–Fri 10am–7pm; Sat 10am–6pm; Sun noon–5pm. AmEx, DC, MC, V.
Founded in 1978 by the late, great New York Yankees manager Billy Martin, this Western store features heaps of cowboy boots in all colors and sizes.

Camper
125 Prince St at Wooster St (212-358-1842). Subway: N, R to Prince St; 6 to Spring St. Mon–Sat 11am–8pm; Sun noon–6pm. AmEx, DC, MC, V.
This large corner store stocks dozens of styles of the legendary Spanish sneakers.

Christian Louboutin
941 Madison Ave between 74th and 75th Sts (212-396-1884). Subway: 6 to 77th St. Mon–Sat 10am–6pm. AmEx, MC, V.
Serious shoe hounds should plan to drop several hundred dollars on Louboutin's sexy, superpricey red-soled shoes.

Chuckies
399 West Broadway between Broome and Spring Sts (212-343-1717). Subway: C, E to Spring St. Mon–Sat 11am–7:30pm; Sun noon–7:30pm. AmEx, MC, V.
An alternative to department stores, Chuckies carries an exhaustive supply of high-profile labels for men and women—Calvin, Jimmy Choo, etc. Stock ranges from old-school Fendis to up-and-coming Ernesto Espositos.
Other location ● *1073 Third Ave between 63rd and 64th Sts (212-593-9898). Subway: F to Lexington Ave–63rd St. Mon–Fri 10:45am–7:45pm; Sat 10:45am–6:30pm; Sun 12:30–5:30pm. AmEx, MC, V.*

Jimmy Choo
645 Fifth Ave, entrance on 51st St (212-593-0800). Subway: E, V to Fifth Ave–53rd St. Mon–Sat 10am–6pm. AmEx, MC, V.
Jimmy Choo, famed for conceiving Princess Diana's custom shoe collection, is conquering America with his five-year-old emporium. The plush space features Choo's chic boots, sexy pumps and kittenish flats—not one pair of which sells for less than $350.

J.M. Weston
812 Madison Ave at 68th St (212-535-2100). Subway: 6 to 68th St–Hunter College. Mon–Wed, Fri 10am–6:30pm; Sat 10am–6pm. AmEx, MC, V.
Weston shoes, exquisitely handmade in 34 styles, appeal to a range of men from Woody Allen to Yves Saint Laurent. The shop also stocks women's shoes.

Manolo Blahnik
31 W 54th St between Fifth and Sixth Aves (212-582-3007). Subway: E, V to Fifth Ave–53rd St. Mon–Sat 10:30am–6pm. AmEx, MC, V.
Made by the high priest of glamour, these timeless shoes will put style in your step and a dent in your wallet.

McCreedy & Schreiber
213 E 59th St between Second and Third Aves (212-759-9241). Subway: N, R, W to Lexington Ave–59th St; 4, 5, 6 to 59th St. Mon–Sat 9am–7pm; Sun 12:30–5:30pm. AmEx, DC, Disc, MC, V.
This well-known high-quality men's shoe store is good for traditional American styles: Bass Weejuns, Sperry Topsiders, Frye boots and the famous Lucchese boots.

Otto Tootsi Plohound
137 Fifth Ave between 20th and 21st Sts (212-460-8650). Subway: N, R to 23rd St. Mon–Fri 11:30am–7:30pm; Sat 11am–8pm; Sun noon–7pm. AmEx, DC, Disc, MC, V.
One of the best places for the latest shoe styles, Tootsi has a big selection of trendy (and slightly overpriced) imports for women and men. Check the phone book for other locations.

Sigerson Morrison
28 Prince St between Elizabeth and Mott Sts (212-219-3893). Subway: F, V, S to Broadway–Lafayette St; N, R to Prince St; 6 to Bleecker St. Mon–Sat 11am–7pm; Sun noon–6pm. AmEx, MC, V.
Stop by this cultish women's shoe store for delicate styles in the prettiest colors: baby blue, ruby red and shiny pearl.

Transit
655 Broadway between Bleecker and Bond Sts (212-358-8726). Subway: F, V, S to Broadway–Lafayette St; 6 to Bleecker St. Mon–Sat 9am–9pm; Sun 10am–8pm. AmEx, DC, Disc, MC, V.
In addition to Adidas, New Balance and Nike, this store carries designer kicks from DKNY and Polo Ralph Lauren.

Health & Beauty

Bath, body & beauty booty

Alcone

235 W 19th St between Seventh and Eighth Aves (212-633-0551). Subway: 1, 2 to 18th St. Mon–Sat 11am–6pm. AmEx, MC, V.

Frequented by makeup artists, Chelsea's Alcone offers brands and products you won't find elsewhere in the city, such as Visiora foundation and the German brand Kryolan. It's full of items that might belong on a horror-movie set (kits of fake blood and bruises, for instance), but mere mortals shop for its premade palettes (trays of a dozen or more eye, lip and cheek colors). Not to be missed: Alcone's own sponges.

Aveda

233 Spring St between Sixth Ave and Varick St (212-807-1492). Subway: C, E to Spring St; 1, 2 to Houston St. Mon–Fri 10am–9pm; Sat 10am–7pm; Sun 10am–6pm. AmEx, DC, MC, V.

This is a spacious, tranquil boutique filled with an exclusive line of hair- and skin-care products, make-up and massage oils made from flower and plant extracts. Check the phone book for other locations.

The Body Shop

714 Lexington Ave at 58th St (212-755-7851). Subway: N, R, W to Lexington Ave–59th St; 4, 5, 6 to 59th St. Mon–Fri 10am–9pm; Sat 10am–8pm; Sun 11am–6pm. AmEx, Disc, MC, V.

The Body Shop, as most people know, is the premier place for natural beauty products in no-nonsense, biodegradable plastic bottles. Check the phone book for other locations.

Face Stockholm

110 Prince St at Greene St (212-966-9110). Subway: N, R to Prince St. Mon–Sat 11am–7pm; Thu–Sat 11am–8pm; Sun noon–6pm. AmEx, MC, V.

Along with a full line of shadows, lipsticks, blushes and tools, Face offers two services: makeup applications and lessons.

Other locations ● *687 Madison Ave at 62nd St (212-207-8833). Subway: F to Lexington Ave–63rd St; N, R, W to Fifth Ave–60th St. Mon–Wed, Fri 10am–6pm; Thu, Sat 10am–7pm; Sun noon–6pm. AmEx, MC, V.* ● *226 Columbus Ave between 70th and 71st Sts (212-769-1420). Subway: B, C, 1, 2, 3 to 72nd St. Mon–Wed 11am–7pm; Thu–Sat 11am–8pm; Sun noon–6pm. AmEx, MC, V.*

Fresh

1061 Madison Ave between 80th and 81st Sts (212-396-0344). Subway: 6 to 77th St. Mon–Sat 10am–7pm; Sun noon–6pm. AmEx, MC, V.

Fresh is a Boston company that bases its soaps, lotions and other products on natural ingredients such as honey, milk, soy and sugar.

Other locations ● *57 Spring St between Lafayette and Mulberry Sts (212-925-0099). Subway: 6 to Spring St. Mon–Sat 10am–8pm; Sun noon–6pm.*

AmEx, MC, V. ● *388 Bleecker St between Perry and W 11th Sts (917-408-1850). Subway: A, C, E to 14th St; L to Eighth Ave; 1, 2 to Christopher St–Sheridan Sq. Mon–Sat 11am–8pm; Sun noon–7pm. AmEx, MC, V.*

Kiehl's

109 Third Ave between 13th and 14th Sts (212-677-3171). Subway: L to Third Ave; N, Q, R, W, 4, 5, 6 to 14th St–Union Sq. Mon–Wed, Fri 10am–6:30pm; Thu 10am–7:30pm; Sat 10am–6pm; Sun noon–6pm. AmEx, MC, V.

Kiehl's is a New York institution; it has called this Third Avenue shop home since 1851, and it's still a mob scene. Try the company's luxurious face moisturizer, lip balm or Creme with Silk Groom, and you'll be hooked for life. The staff is knowledgeable and generous with free samples.

L'Occitane

1046 Madison Ave at 80th St (212-396-9097). Subway: 6 to 77th St. Mon–Sat 10am–7pm; Sun noon–6pm. AmEx, DC, Disc, MC, V.

Fans of L'Occitane, a line of bath and beauty products made in Provence, flock to this shop to pick up brick-size soaps, massage balm and shea-butter hand cream. Check the phone book for other locations.

M•A•C

14 Christopher St at Gay St (212-243-4150). Subway: A, C, E, F, V, S to W 4th St. Mon–Sat 11am–7pm; Sun noon–6pm. AmEx, Disc, MC, V.

Makeup Art Cosmetics is committed to the development of cruelty-free products and is famous for its lipsticks and eyeshadows in otherwise unobtainable colors. The enormous Soho branch is a bit like an art gallery and features nine makeover counters.

Other location ● *113 Spring St between Greene and Mercer Sts (212-334-4641). Subway: N, R to Prince St; 6 to Spring St. Mon–Sat 11am–8pm; Sun noon–6pm. AmEx, Disc, MC, V.*

Make Up Forever

409 West Broadway between Prince and Spring Sts (212-941-9337). Subway: C, E to Spring St; N, R to Prince St. Mon–Sat 11am–7pm; Sun noon–6pm. AmEx, MC, V.

Make Up Forever, a French line, is popular with women and drag queens alike. Colors range from bold purples and fuchsias to muted browns and soft pinks. The mascara is a must-have.

Ricky's

718 Broadway at Washington Pl (212-979-5232). Subway: N, R to 8th St–NYU. Mon–Thu 8:30am–10pm; Fri 8:30am–11pm; Sat 10am–11pm; Sun 11am–9pm. AmEx, DC, Disc, MC, V.

Stock up on tools and extras such as Tweezerman tweezers, cheap containers for traveling, and empty palettes and makeup cases that look like souped-up tackle boxes. Ricky's in-house makeup line, Mattése, offers fake lashes, glitter, nail polish and other items in colors and packaging similar to those of M•A•C. Check the phone book for other locations.

Necessities

Sephora

555 Broadway between Prince and Spring Sts (212-625-1309). Subway: N, R to Prince St. Mon–Wed 10am–8pm; Fri, Sat 10am–8:30pm; Sun 11am–7pm. AmEx, Disc, MC, V.

Sephora, the French beauty chain that is slowly working its way across America, has given downtown gals a reason to stay put: It has everything. The 8,000-square-foot makeup library looks like the first floor of a department store, but no one is standing behind the display cases (staffers hang back until you seek them out). The flagship store is at Rockefeller Center *(636 Fifth Ave between 50th and 51st Sts, 212-245-1633)*. Check the phone book for other locations.

Shiseido Studio

155 Spring St between West Broadway and Wooster St (212-625-8820). Subway: C, E to Spring St. Sun, Mon noon–6pm; Tue 11am–6pm; Wed–Sat 11am–7pm. Free.

A beauty store that doesn't sell anything? It may sound crazy, but Shiseido has opened a 3,800-square-foot consumer learning center to educate shoppers. Visitors can take free skin-care classes and test more than 330 items—cosmetics, fragrances and more.

Shu Uemura

121 Greene St between Houston and Prince Sts (212-979-5500). Subway: C, E to Spring St; N, R to Prince St. Mon–Sat 11am–7pm; Sun noon–6pm. AmEx, MC, V.

The entire line of Shu Uemura Japanese cosmetics is for sale at this stark, well-lit Soho boutique. Most hit Shu Uemura for its blushes, brushes, eye shadows and lipsticks, but for a real eye-opening experience, check out the best-selling eyelash curler.

Perfumeries

Creed

9 Bond St between Broadway and Lafayette St (212-228-1940). Subway: F, V, S to Broadway–Lafayette St; 6 to Bleecker St. Mon–Sat 11:30am–7:30pm; Sun noon–6pm. AmEx, MC, V.

In this city, you'd be hard-pressed to find many affordable items that are two-and-a-half centuries old. But the arrival of 242-year-old English perfume house Creed in 1999 brought many pedigreed items—and they smell good too. Customers are encouraged to create fragrance blends of their own. **Other location ● ** *897 Madison Ave between 72nd and 73rd Sts (212-794-4480). Subway: 6 to 77th St. Mon–Sat 10am–7pm; Sun noon–6pm. AmEx, MC, V.*

Demeter Fragrances

83 Second Ave between 4th and 5th Sts (212-505-1535). Subway: F, V to Lower East Side–Second Ave. Mon–Fri 10am–6pm; Sat noon–7pm; Sun noon–6pm. MC, V.

If you smell dirt, gin and tonic, and tomato along lower Second Avenue, it doesn't necessarily mean you're near a restaurant dumpster. Your nose could have led you to Demeter Fragrances' anything-but-chichi boutique. In addition to its famous single-note scents such as Crème Brûlée, Holy Water, Mushroom, Prune and Riding Crop, the shop carries Demeter's full range of bath and body products.

Pharmacists

For 24-hour pharmacies, see page 367.

C.O. Bigelow Apothecaries

414 Sixth Ave between 8th and 9th Sts (212-533-2700). Subway: A, C, E, F, V, S to W 4th St. Mon–Fri 7:30am–9pm; Sat 8:30am–7pm; Sun 8:30am–5:30pm. AmEx, DC, Disc, MC, V.

One of the grand old New York pharmacies, Bigelow is the place to find creams, hair accessories, hygiene products, makeup, over-the-counter remedies, perfumes, soaps—you name it.

Zitomer

969 Madison Ave between 75th and 76th Sts (212-737-4480). Subway: 6 to 77th St. Mon–Fri 9am–8pm; Sat 9am–7pm; Sun 10am–6pm. AmEx, DC, Disc, MC, V.

Zitomer has every bath, beauty and health product under the sun. The second floor has children's clothing, and there are toys on the third. The store also sells panty hose, socks and underwear.

Salons & spas

Salons

Some swanky salons free up their $200 chairs one night a week for those willing to become cut or color guinea pigs for trainees. Not to worry—there's much supervision, and the results are usually wonderful. Best of all, it costs a fraction of the usual price. All of the following have model nights, with prices starting at $30 (usually payable in cash only). Phone for details about the next model night, but know that you may well have to join a three-month waiting list at places such as **Frédéric Fekkai Beauté de Provence** *(212-753-9500)*, **Louis Licari** *(212-758-2090)* and **Peter Coppola Salon** *(212-988-9404)*. The salons below are also standouts.

John Masters Salon and Spa

79 Sullivan St between Broome and Spring Sts (212-343-9590). Subway: N, R to Prince St; 6 to Spring St. Mon–Fri 11am–6:30pm; Sat 9am–6:30pm; Sun noon–5pm. AmEx, MC, V.

This salon has been inspired by nature, from its interior woodwork and waterfall, right down to the Organics skin and haircare products used in the shop (Masters' own line). Cuts start at $80, and the salon doubles as a spa—book an appointment for reflexology or a shiatsu.

Miano Viel Salon and Spa

16 E 52nd St between Fifth and Madison Aves, second floor (212-980-3222). Subway: E, V to Fifth

Necessities

Ave–53rd St. Tue 9am–7pm; Wed 9am–6pm; Thu, Fri 9am–8pm; Sat 9am–5pm. MC, V.

You could pay more than $300 in one sitting, but Damien Miano and Louis Viel know how to treat tresses.

Parlor

102 Ave B between 6th and 7th Sts (212-673-5520). Subway: F, V to Lower East Side–Second Ave; L to First Ave. Tue–Fri noon–9pm; Sat 9am–5pm; Sun 10am–6pm. AmEx, MC, V.

Cuts range from $50 to $85 at this East Village beauty parlor for downtown glamour-pusses.

Privé

310 West Broadway between Canal and Grand Sts (212-274-8888). Subway: A, C, E to Canal St. Tue, Wed, Fri 10am–7pm; Thu 10am–9pm; Sat 10am–7pm; Sun 11am–6pm. AmEx, MC, V.

No need to go uptown for luxe locks. Laurent D., famous for tending to the tresses of such celebs as Gwyneth and Blink 182 members, scored prime retail space in the SoHo Grand Hotel for his first New York salon. Haircuts with Laurent cost $185; cuts with other stylists range from $90 to $150. Highlights start at $125.

Suite 303

Chelsea Hotel, 222 W 23rd St between Seventh and Eighth Aves (212-633-1011). Subway: C, E, 1, 2 to 23rd St. Tue–Fri 10am–7pm; Sat noon–5pm. MC, V.

Owned by three ex-Racine stylists, Suite 303 is located in the wonderfully spooky Chelsea Hotel. Haircuts start at $60. Highlights start at $110.

Ultra

233 E 4th St between Aves A and B (212-677-4380). Subway: F, V to Lower East Side–Second Ave. Tue, Wed, Fri 11am–8pm; Thu noon–9pm; Sat 10am–4pm. AmEx, DC, Disc, MC, V.

It's no wonder the music industry flocks to Ultra. This tiny salon's anonymous, mint-green storefront has the feel of a low-profile club. Cuts start at $75 and color at $60, while highlights are $85 and up.

Cheap cuts & blow-drys

Astor Place Hair Stylists

2 Astor Pl at Broadway (212-475-9854). Subway: N, R to 8th St–NYU; 6 to Astor Pl. Mon–Sat 8am–8pm; Sun 9am–6pm. Cash only.

This is the classic New York hair experience. An army of barbers does everything from neat trims to shaved designs, all to pounding music—usually hip-hop. You can't make an appointment; just take a number and wait outside with the crowd. Sunday mornings are quiet. Cuts start at $12, blow-drys at $15, dreadlocks at $75.

Jean Louis David

1180 Sixth Ave at 46th St (212-944-7389). Subway: B, D, F, V to 47–50th Sts–Rockefeller Ctr. Mon–Fri 10am–7pm. MC, V.

Everything happens fast at this chain. Models flick-

er in and out of view on a television screen. Stylists scurry about in white lab coats. Best of all, a shampoo, trendy cut (with clippers) and blow-dry can be yours, without an appointment, for $22.49. Check the phone book for other locations.

Nails

Rescue

21 Cleveland Pl between Kenmare and Spring Sts (212-431-3805). Subway: 6 to Spring St. Mon–Fri 11am–8pm; Sat 10am–6pm. AmEx, MC, V.

Are your hands in a state of emergency? Run to Rescue. This charming garden-level space has been open for four years—and neighbors are still discovering its intensive treatments. The Ultra TLC manicure ($30) is worth every penny.

Other location ● *Rescue Beauty Lounge, 8 Centre Market Place between Broome and Grand Sts (212-431-0449). Subway: 6 to Spring St. Tue–Fri 11am–8pm; Sat, Sun 10am–6pm. AmEx, MC, V.*

Spas

Feeling frazzled? After long days of battling vicious city crowds while schlepping about, you may want to pamper your weary body with a spa visit. Most treatments start at $60, and no matter how ridiculously relaxed you feel when you're done, don't forget to leave a tip (15 to 20 percent).

Avon Salon & Spa

Trump Tower, 725 Fifth Ave between 56th and 57th Sts, sixth floor (212-755-2866, 888-577-AVON). Subway: E, V to Fifth Ave–53rd St; N, R, W to Fifth Ave–60th St. Mon, Tue, Sat 9am–6pm; Wed, Thu, Fri 9am–8pm. AmEx, MC, V.

Forget Skin-So-Soft Avon: This is just the type of place you'd expect to find in glitzy Trump Tower. It offers not only face and body treatments but also highlights with top colorist Brad Johns, and the famous eyebrow waxings of Eliza Petrescu.

Bliss 57

19 E 57th St between Fifth and Madison Aves, third floor (212-219-8970). Subway: F to 57th St; E, V to Fifth Ave–53rd St. Mon, Tue, Thu, Fri 9am–8:30pm; Wed noon–8:30pm; Sat 9:30am–6:30pm. AmEx, MC, V.

This uptown sister of Soho's hippest spa is the ultimate in pricey retreats. The sleekly designed Bliss 57 brings indulgence to a new level, offering multiple services at once, to compress the time that your necessary coddling requires. Want a manicure in tandem with your facial? Done. The new "simultanebliss" offers an oxygen facial combined with a hot-cream manicure and pedicure. Just prepare to plop down—and max out—the plastic.

Other location ● *Bliss, 568 Broadway between Houston and Prince Sts, second floor (212-219-8970). Subway: F, V, S to Broadway–Lafayette St; N, R to Prince St; 6 to Bleecker St. Mon–Fri 9:30am–8:30pm; Sat 9:30am–6:30pm. AmEx, MC, V.*

Magic potions C.O. Bigelow is a Greenwich Village favorite for remedies and more.

Carapan

5 W 16th St between Fifth and Sixth Aves, garden level (212-633-6220). Subway: L, N, Q, R, W, 4, 5, 6 to 14th St–Union Sq. 10am–9:45pm (retail store open until 8pm). AmEx, MC, V.
Carapan, which means "a beautiful place of tranquillity where one comes to restore one's spirit" in the language of the Pueblo Indians, offers reiki, craniosacral therapy and manual lymphatic drainage.

Helena Rubinstein

135 Spring St between Greene and Wooster Sts (212-343-9963). Subway: C, E, 6 to Spring St. Mon–Fri 11am–8pm; Sat 11am–7pm; Sun noon–6pm. AmEx, MC, V.
In HR's spacious and bright street-level Beauty Gallery you can dabble with the superb makeup line. Then retreat downstairs to a plush oasis. Sink into the elegant lounge (in your terry robe and slippers) browse a magazine and snack on nuts, berries and fresh juice. Choose any one of the perfected "Art of Spa Rituals" (like the body soufflé wrap). To prepare for reentry into the real world, take a steam shower and indulge in the skin-care and perfume samples in the bathroom.

Ling Skin Care

105 W 77th St between Amsterdam and Columbus Aves (212-877-2883). Subway: B, C to 81st St–Museum of Natural History; 1, 2 to 79th St. Mon–Thu 10am–9pm; Fri 10am–7pm; Sat 9:30am–5:30pm; Sun 11am–5pm. AmEx, MC, V.
There's a reason that beauty queen Ling has been in the skin-care biz for 40 years: Her triple-peel facial removes impurities and dead skin, leaving you with…a new face! Ling also has her own product line.

Other locations ● *128 Thompson St between Houston and Prince Sts (212-982-8833). Subway: A, C, E, F, V, S to W 4th St. Mon–Thu 8am–9pm; Fri 8am–7pm; Sat 8am–5:30pm; Sun 11am–5pm. AmEx, MC, V.* ● *12 E 16th St between Fifth Ave and Union Sq West (212-989-9833). Subway: L, N, Q, R, W, 4, 5, 6 to 14th St–Union Sq. Mon–Thu 10am–9pm; Fri 10am–7pm; Sat 9:30am–5:30pm; Sun 11am–5pm. AmEx, MC, V.*

The Mezzanine Spa at Soho Integrative Health Center

62 Crosby St between Broome and Spring Sts (212-431-1600). Subway: 6 to Spring St. Tue, Wed noon–8pm; Thu, Fri 9am–8pm; Sat 10am–6pm. AmEx, MC, V.
The brainchild of dermatologist Dr. Laurie Polis, the spa is part of her luxurious doctor's office, giving beauty clients the expertise of a medical pro. The Mezzanine includes five facial rooms and a wet room for rinse-requiring services, such as the volcanic mud treatment. The spa's signature therapy is the Diamond Peel: a device that exfoliates the face using suction and microcrystals.

Prema Nolita

252 Elizabeth St between Houston and Prince Sts (212-226-3972). Subway: F, V, S to Broadway–Lafayette St; 6 to Bleecker St. Call for hours. AmEx, MC, V.
Owned by beauty-biz veteran Celeste Induddi and her two partners, Prema Nolita may be the tiniest spa in the city. In the front of the shop, shelves display cult skin-care lines Jurlique and Anne Semonin. At the back, there's a single treatment room offering a lavish list of services, some of which use the house line Prema Salt Scrubs.

Objects of Desire

Books

There's no shortage of book sources in New York. The city truly is, as the saying goes, book country. Many shops are happy to mail your selections overseas (books shipped out of state don't get charged sales tax). The Barnes & Noble chain has expanded considerably in recent years, but don't overlook the smaller landmark stores, which provide meticulous service. For additional bookstores, see chapter **Books & Poetry** and **Bookshops**, page 280.

Barnes & Noble

33 E 17th St between Broadway and Park Ave South (212-253-0810). Subway: L, N, Q, R, W, 4, 5, 6 to 14th St–Union Sq. 10am–10pm. AmEx, Disc, MC, V.
The nation's largest bookstore and the flagship of this chain (there are 20 Barnes & Nobles in the five boroughs) is a good source for recent hardcovers—some discounted—and the record, tape and CD department has one of the largest classical music selections in the city. Check the phone book for other locations.

Necessities

Borders Books & Music

576 Second Ave at 32nd St (212-685-3938).
Subway: 6 to 33rd St. Mon–Sat 9am–11pm; Sun
9am–9pm. AmEx, Disc MC, V.
Borders seems folksier than Barnes & Noble; there's
an extensive selection of music and videos, and even
if you're searching for an obscure book, staffers usually come through, or try hard to.

Complete Traveller Bookstore

199 Madison Ave at 35th St (212-685-9007).
Subway: 6 to 33rd St. Mon–Fri 9am–6:30pm; Sat
10am–6pm; Sun 11am–5pm. AmEx, Disc, MC, V.
All manner of travel-related texts are available.

St. Mark's Bookshop

31 Third Ave at Stuyvesant St (212-260-7853).
Subway: 6 to Astor Pl. Mon–Sat 10am–midnight;
Sun 11am–midnight. AmEx, Disc, MC, V.
This is the place to go if you're a young intellectual (or
just want to look like one). It's well-stocked with cul-
tural and lit crit, and small- and university-press titles.

Shakespeare & Co.

716 Broadway at Washington Pl (212-529-1330).
Subway: N, R to 8th St–NYU; 6 to Astor Pl. Sun–Thu
10am–11pm; Fri, Sat 10am–midnight. AmEx, Disc,
MC, V.
Some rise by sin, and some by virtue fall, but
Shakespeare & Co. has survived the chain-store
onslaught. See phone book for other locations.

Strand Book Store

828 Broadway at 12th St (212-473-1452). Subway:
L, N, Q, R, W, 4, 5, 6 to 14th St–Union Sq. Mon–Sat
9:30am–10:30pm; Sun 11am–10:30pm. AmEx,
Disc, MC, V.
The Strand, founded in 1927, is reputedly the largest
secondhand bookshop in the country. More than 2.5
million books on all subjects are stocked. Most are
sold at half the list price or less.

Unoppressive Non-Imperialist
Bargain Books

34 Carmine St between Bedford and Bleecker Sts
(212-229-0079). Subway: A, C, E, F, V, S to W 4th St.
Mon–Thu 11am–10pm; Fri 11am–midnight; Sat
noon–midnight; Sun noon–10pm. AmEx, Disc, MC, V.
This ten-year-old bookshop is the only one in the city
that sells new publishers' overstock at bargain
prices. The store has recently expanded and opened
a children's bargain books section next door.

Street of dreams

Slicing through the East Village like a multicultural runway, East 9th Street adds new dimensions to your style repertoire

Before Soho pushed out its galleries to make
way for fashion emporiums, before Nolita—
land of the upscale boutique—even had a
name, and aeons prior to the Meatpacking
District's style-savvy makeover, there was 9th
Street in the East Village, home of the
freethinking and bravely attired. The stretch of
9th Street from Second Avenue to Avenue A
is considered by some to be the most
diversified shopping in the city. In sharp
contrast to the mass-market cheap wares
available just one block south on St. Marks
Place, 9th Street boasts a string of shops
whose goods are either designed by the
proprietors in-store or gleaned from a lifetime
of search and discovery around the world.
Everything from handmade silk Indian
scarves to vintage eyewear is available on
this tree-lined strip, at refreshingly
competitive prices.

Strolling down East 9th Street from Second
Avenue, you'll hit **Katinka** *(303 E 9th St
between First and Second Aves, 212-677-
7897).* The owners, a husband-and-wife team,
handpick all the Indian goods piled high in
this tight space. Bedspreads, clothing,

jewelry, shoes and silk scarves are all well-
selected—and *very* well-priced. If nothing
suits your fancy, the smooth sounds of Billy's
(the hubby's) keyboard music should at least
entertain you. (And yes, that mural out front
is of him.) Another unique shop, **Molode
Zyttia** *(308 E 9th St between First and
Second Aves, 212-673-9530)* imports
Ukrainian goods. The hand-embroidered
peasant blouses are as winsome as the
woman who runs the shop.

On the north side of the block, **Hoshoni**
*(309 E 9th St between First and Second
Aves, 212-674-3120),* named after an
American Indian tribe, is housed in an
adobelike setting. Most jewelry and home
accessories are from New Mexico, or are
crafted by American Indians. Just a few doors
down is **Mostly Bali** *(324 E 9th St between
First and Second Aves, 212-777-9049),*
devoted to all things wooden: hand-carved
statues and masks, solid wood furnishings
and exotic mobiles meant to protect the
intimate corners of your home. The bamboo
chimes and Aja, the owner's pet cockatoo,
make for melodious shopping.

Cameras & electronics

When shopping for cameras and other electronics, it helps if you know exactly what you want before venturing inside a store; if you look lost, you will certainly be given a hard sell. When buying a major item, check newspaper ads for price guidelines (start with the inserts in Sunday's *New York Times*). It pays to go to a well-known shop, but if you're brave, you can get small pieces, such as a Walkman, for cheap in the no-frills spots along Canal Street (just don't expect a warranty). Another reason to go to a more reputable place is to get reliable (and essential) advice about the devices' compatibility with systems in the country where you plan to use them.

Bang & Olufsen

927 Broadway between 21st and 22nd Sts (212-388-9792). Subway: N, R to 23rd St. Mon–Fri 10am–7pm; Sat 10am–6pm; Sun noon–5pm. AmEx, MC, V.
Sleek and Danish-efficient, Bang & Olufsen's upscale home electronics are must-haves for any design-mad techie.

Other location ● *952 Madison Ave at 75th St (212-879-6161). Subway: 6 to 77th St. Mon–Sat 10am–6:30pm; Sun noon–5pm. AmEx, MC, V.*

B&H

420 Ninth Ave between 33rd and 34th Sts (212-444-5040). Subway: A, C, E to 34th St–Penn Station. Mon–Thu 9am–7pm; Fri 9am–1pm; Sun 10am–5pm. AmEx, Disc, MC, V.
If you can deal with the odd hours (B&H is also closed on all Jewish holidays), long lines and a bit of a schlep, this emporium is the ultimate one-stop shop for all your photographic, video and audio needs. This is a favorite of up-and-coming professional photographers.

Harvey

2 W 45th St between Fifth and Sixth Aves (212-575-5000). Subway: B, D, F, V to 42nd St; 7 to Fifth Ave. Mon–Wed, Fri 10am–7pm; Thu 10am–8pm; Sat 10am–6pm; Sun noon–5pm. AmEx, MC, V.
Harvey offers chain-store variety without the lousy warranties and mass-market stereo components. There are lots of high-end products, but plenty of realistically priced items, too.
Other location ● *ABC Carpet & Home, 888 Broadway at 19th St (212-228-5354). Subway: L,*

If vintage is more your thing, **Cobblestones** *(314 E 9th St between First and Second Aves, 212-673-5372)*, is cluttered with well-preserved goodies from the 1930s and '40s. It's been a handbag hot spot for models and fashion mavens for 21 years, but anyone looking for a wallet or an antique cigarette case will be happy too. Staying with the retro theme, **Fabulous Fanny's** *(335 E 9th St between First and Second Aves, 212-533-0637)*, offers eyeglass frames galore. The owners are collectors and sellers of optical oddities from the 1700s to the 1980s. In business for more than ten years, they've acquired a robust stock of 30,000 frames.

Across First Avenue, near Tompkins Square Park, you approach the more risqué side of vintage, courtesy of **Atomic Passion** *(430 E 9th St between First Ave and Ave A, 212-533-0718)*. Dim red lighting casts a mysterious glow over the store's racks of secondhand threads, which date from as far back as the Victorian era and as recently as the 1980s.

Those who perk up at the terms "one of a kind" and "vintage" will also get their fix on 9th Street. For 29 years **Clayworks Pottery** *(332 E 9th St between First and Second Aves, 212-677-8311)* has been the retail shop of one of the few working potters in New York, Helaine Sorgen. Her selection of original

pieces—ranging from decorative vases to functional teapots—is both practical and minimalist.

For the makings of a fairy tale, enter **Dinosaur Hill** *(306 E 9th St between First and Second Aves, 212-473-5850)*. Whether you're 5 years old or 50, you'll marvel at the slew of marionettes and puppets of all sizes. **The Good, the Bad, and the Ugly** *(437 E 9th St between First Ave and Ave A, 212-473-3769)* features handmade clothing designed and sewn by owner Judi Rosen. She describes her corduroy knickers and dolman sleeve–inspired blouses as "urban new frontier."

On another note, the music store **Shrine** *(441 E 9th St between First Ave and Ave A, 212-529-6646)* offers a wide range of secondhand rock records and CDs, not to mention funky Built by Wendy guitar straps.

Before heading back to the hotel, make one last stop at **Flower Power Herbs and Roots Inc.** *(406 E 9th St between First Ave and Ave A, 212-982-6664)*, where organically cultivated flowers, herbs, roots, leaves and seeds are sold—some for medicinal purposes, others for more erotic curatives (the "Love Bath" mixture contains an aphrodisiac blend of damiana, lavender and rose petals). And you thought all that shopping would be the climax of your trip to 9th Street!

I am a camera You'll find knowledgeable service and top-notch electronics at B&H.

N, Q, R, W, 4, 5, 6 to 14th St–Union Sq. Mon–Fri 10am–8pm; Sat 10am–7pm; Sun 11am–6:30pm. AmEx, MC, V.

J&R

23 Park Row between Ann and Beekman Sts (212-238-9000, 800-221-8180). Subway: A, C to Broadway–Nassau St; J, M, Z, 4, 5 to Fulton St; 1, 2 to Park Pl. Mon–Wed, Fri, Sat 9am–7pm; Thu 9am–7:30pm; Sun 10:30am–6:30pm. AmEx, Disc, MC, V.

This block-long row of shops carries every electronic thing you could possibly need (from PCs and TVs to CDs and nose-hair trimmers).

The Wiz

726 Broadway between Washington and Waverly Pls (212-677-4111). Subway: N, R to 8th St–NYU; 6 to Astor Pl. Mon–Fri 10am–9:30pm; Sat 9am–9:30pm; Sun 11am–6pm. AmEx, DC, Disc, MC, V.

Thanks to the Wiz's claim that it will match or beat any advertised price on electronic equipment, even its toughest competitors have a hard time keeping up. Check the phone book for other locations.

Photo processing

Photo-developing services can be found on just about any city block. Most drugstores (Rite Aid and CVS, for example) and megastores, such as Kmart, offer this service, although the best results should be expected from those that develop on the premises.

Duggal

3 W 20th St between Fifth and Sixth Aves (212-242-7000). Subway: F, V, N, R to 23rd St. Mon–Fri 6am–midnight; Sat, Sun 9am–6pm. AmEx, MC, V.

Duggal has amassed a large and dedicated following, ranging from artists such as David LaChapelle to big-name companies, such as American Express and Armani. Started by Indian immigrant Baldev Duggal more than 40 years ago, this around-the-clock shop focuses on the ability to develop any type of film—and to do it flawlessly. The prices reflect that.

Gadget repairs

Computer Solutions Provider

45 W 21st St between Fifth and Sixth Aves, second floor (212-463-9744). Subway: F, V, N, R to 23rd St. Mon–Fri 9am–6pm. AmEx, MC, V.

Specialists in Macs, IBMs and all related peripherals, CSP's staffers can recover your lost data and soothe you through all manner of computer disasters. They perform on-site repairs and sell telephone systems.

Panorama Camera Center

124 W 30th St between Sixth and Seventh Aves (212-563-1651). Subway: 1, 2 to 28th St. Mon–Fri 9am–6pm; Sat 11am–3pm. AmEx, Disc, MC, V.

All kinds of camera and camcorder problems can be solved here, with an eye toward expediency if necessary.

Photo-Tech Repair Service

110 E 13th St between Third and Fourth Aves (212-673-8400). Subway: L, N, Q, R, W, 4, 5, 6 to 14th St–Union Sq. Mon, Tue, Thu, Fri 8am–4:45pm; Wed 8am–6pm; Sat 10am–3pm. AmEx, Disc, MC, V.

Photo-Tech has been servicing the dropped, cracked and drowned since 1959. The shop has 19 on-site technicians and guarantees that all camera wrongs can be righted, regardless of the brand. Expect to pay $5 to replace a battery cover or $100 to get that Canon Elph working. Rush services are available, but repairs usually take one to two weeks.

Children's toys

Enchanted Forest

85 Mercer St between Broome and Spring Sts (212-925-6677). Subway: N, R to Prince St; 6 to Spring St. Mon–Sat 11am–7pm; Sun noon–6pm. AmEx, DC, Disc, MC, V.
Browse through this gallery of beasts, books and handmade toys in a magical forest setting.

FAO Schwarz

767 Fifth Ave between 58th and 59th Sts (212-644-9400). Subway: N, R, W to Fifth Ave–60th St. Mon–Sat 10am–6pm; Sun 11am–6pm. AmEx, DC, Disc, MC, V.
This famous toy emporium, which has been supplying New York kids with playthings since 1862, stocks more stuffed animals than would invade your worst nightmare. There are also kites, dolls, games, miniature cars, toy soldiers, bath toys and so on. The store hosts a number of special events too. Check www.fao.com for listings.

Kidding Around

60 W 15th St between Fifth and Sixth Aves (212-645-6337). Subway: F, V to 14th St; L to Sixth Ave. Mon–Sat 10am–7pm; Sun 11am–6pm. AmEx, Disc, MC, V.
Loyal customers frequent this quaint shop for toys and a small collection of kids' clothing.

Penny Whistle Toys

448 Columbus Ave between 81st and 82nd Sts (212-873-9090). Subway: B, C to 81st St; 1, 2 to 79th St. Mon–Fri 10am–7pm; Sat 10am–6pm; Sun 11am–5pm. AmEx, MC, V.
The bubble-blowing teddy bear stationed outside is a neighborhood favorite. Expect more jigsaw puzzles and Play-Doh than video games.
Other location ● *1283 Madison Ave between 91st and 92nd Sts (212-369-3868). Subway: 6 to 96th St. Mon–Fri 9am–6pm; Sat 10am–6pm; Sun 11am–5pm. AmEx, MC, V.*

Toys R Us

1514 Broadway between 44th and 45th Sts (800-TOYS-R-US). Subway: N, Q, R, W, S, 1, 2, 3, 7 to 42nd St–Times Sq. Mon–Sat 10am–9pm; Sun 11am–8pm. AmEx, Disc, MC, V.
This flagship location is the world's largest toy store. Kids and families are greeted by an animatronic T-Rex dinosaur and can ride a 60-foot Ferris wheel. Eat and drink at the café or snack at Candyland (designed just like the board game), the store's very own sweet shop. Check the phone book for other locations.

Flea markets

For bargain-hungry New Yorkers, rummaging through flea markets qualifies as religious

devotion. There's no better way to walk off that Bloody Mary brunch than to wander among aisles of vinyl records, eight-track tapes, clothes, books and furniture.

Although former mayor Giuliani clamped down on the number of illegal street vendors working in the city, you might still get lucky: East Village vendors are persistent, if unreliable. Try looking below 14th Street along Sixth Avenue or Avenue A at night, or lower Broadway on weekend afternoons, for used clothes, records and magazines. When the weather's nice, there are sidewalk or stoop sales. Although not as common in Manhattan, stoop sales are held on Saturdays in parts of Brooklyn (Park Slope, especially) and Queens. If you have a car, you'll quickly spot the signs attached to trees and posts; if not, local free papers (usually found in grocery stores), provide the hours, dates and addresses. Sidewalk shopping is popular with the natives—and they're serious, so head out early.

Annex Antiques Fair & Flea Market

Sixth Ave between 24th and 26th Sts (212-243-5343). Subway: F, V to 23rd St. Sat, Sun sunrise–sunset. Cash only.
Designer Anna Sui hunts regularly at the Annex, as do plenty of models and the occasional dolled-down celebrity. Divided into scattered sections, one of which charges a $1 admission fee, the market has shrunk a bit because of construction on part of the site. All areas feature heaps of secondhand clothing (some of it actually antique-quality), old bicycles, platform shoes, birdcages, vintage eyeglass frames, funky tools and indispensable accessories: hats, gloves, purses and compacts. Don't miss the Garage: The nearby indoor market—especially heavenly on a cold day—is a trove of unusual items.
Other location ● *The Garage, 112 W 25th St between Sixth and Seventh Aves (212-243-5343). Subway: F, V to 23rd St. Sat, Sun sunrise–sunset. Cash only.*

Antique Flea & Farmers' Market

P.S. 9, W 84th St at Columbus Ave (212-721-0900). Subway: 1, 2 to 86th St. Sat 10am–6pm. AmEx, MC, V accepted by some vendors.
This is a small market, but one that's good for antique lace, silverware and tapestries. Fresh eggs, fish and vegetables are also available.

I.S. 44 Flea Market

Columbus Ave between 76th and 77th Sts (212-721-0900). Subway: B, C to 72nd St; 1, 2 to 79th St. Sun 10am–6pm. AmEx, MC, V accepted by some vendors.
Even though this market isn't what it used to be, you're still likely to find something among the more than 300 stalls.

Florists

Although every corner deli sells flowers—especially carnations—they usually last just a few days. For arrangements that stick around a while and aren't filled with baby's breath, buy from some of Manhattan's better florists.

Blue Ivy
762 Tenth Ave between 51st and 52nd Sts (212-977-8858; 800-448-6355). Subway: C, E to 50th St. Mon–Sat 9am–9:30pm. AmEx, DC, Disc, MC, V.
Simon Naut, a former chief floral designer for the Ritz-Carlton Hotel, joined forces with graphic artist Michael Jackson to open this upscale floral shop. Arrangements start at $50.

City Floral
1661 York Ave between 87th and 88th Sts (212-410-0303). Subway: 4, 5, 6 to 86th St. Mon–Fri 7am–6:15pm; Sat 8am–5pm; Sun 9am–noon. AmEx, DC, Disc, MC, V.
City Floral, a full-service florist specializing in exotic flowers and gourmet fruit baskets, is a member of Interflora, a worldwide delivery network.

Elizabeth Ryan Floral Designs
411 E 9th St between First Ave and Ave A (212-995-1111). Subway: L to First Ave; 6 to Astor Pl. Mon–Fri 9am–6pm; Sat 10am–6pm. AmEx, Disc, MC, V.
Elizabeth Ryan has arranged her shop like one of her gorgeous bouquets, and the result is simply magical. Fork out $40 (or up to whatever you can afford) for an original bouquet, and request your favorite blooms. Ryan's new gift store next door sells candles, picture frames, vases and more.

Gotham Gardens
325 Amsterdam Ave between 75th and 76th Sts (212-877-8908). Tue–Sat 10am–8pm; Sun noon–6pm. AmEx, DC, MC, V.
A birdbath and assorted greenery line the sidewalk out front, which makes Dan Dahl and Kevin Esteban's Upper West Side shop stick out like a green thumb. Their creations use complementary leaves such as galax and lemon, koala and lily grasses, and herbs like Spanish lavender and flowering oregano.

Perriwater Ltd.
960 First Ave at 53rd St (212-759-9313). Subway: E, V to Lexington Ave–53rd St; 6 to 51st St. Mon–Fri 9am–6pm; Sat 10am–6pm. AmEx, MC, V.
Proprietor Patricia Grimley doesn't believe that white flowers should be reserved for weddings; she loves the pure effect of an all-white arrangement for any occasion.

Renny
505 Park Ave at 59th St (212-288-7000). Subway: N, R, W to Lexington Ave–59th St; 4, 5, 6 to 59th St. Mon–Sat 9am–6pm. AmEx, MC, V.
"Exquisite flowers for the discriminating" is the slogan for this florist to the rich and famous.
Other location ● *Renny at the Carlyle, 52 E 77th St at Madison Ave (212-988-5588). Subway: 6 to 77th St. Mon–Sat 9am–6pm. AmEx, MC, V.*

VSF
204 W 10th St between Bleecker and W 4th Sts (212-206-7236). Subway: A, C, E, F, V, S to W 4th St. Mon–Fri 10am–5pm; Sat by appointment only. AmEx, Disc, MC, V.
VSF (for very special flowers) favors Shakespearean-sounding accoutrements such as lady's mantle; soft, green lamb's ears; and waxy, green camellia foliage.

Food & drink

Although New York is urban to the core, there is no shortage of farm-fresh, high-quality produce, meats and grains. Listed below are a few better-known city markets. Pick up a copy of the *Time Out New York Eating & Drinking Guide* for an exhaustive list of markets and everything edible.

A. Zito & Sons Bakery
259 Bleecker St at Seventh Ave South (212-929-6139). Subway: 1, 2 to Christopher St–Sheridan Sq. Mon–Sat 7am–8pm; Sun 7am–3pm. Cash only.
If you're lucky, you'll stop in at Zito when the fresh bread is being brought up from the two 111-year-old brick ovens downstairs. Even if the bread isn't hot, buy two loaves: one for the walk back to your hotel room and the other so you have something to show for your trip to the store. There's a deli area, serving not or cold heros and salads, but Zito's bread is, well, its bread and butter.

Balducci's
424 Sixth Ave at 9th St (212-673-2600). Subway: A, C, E, F, V, S to W 4th St. 7am–8:30pm. AmEx, MC, V.
Solidly rooted in Southern Italian traditions, Balducci's is a New York institution (though it was bought by a corporate chain in 1999). A fraction of the size of your typical suburban megamarket, this gourmet shop is as cramped and bustling as a midtown subway platform during rush hour. Prickly pears, blood oranges and porcini mushrooms overflow crowded bins; $40 bottles of extra-virgin olive oil are racked to the ceiling; and slabs of foie gras and boxes of white truffles at $100 an ounce pack the refrigerated glass cases. Heaven couldn't be better stocked.
Other location ● *Balducci's Lincoln Square, 155A W 66th St between Broadway and Amsterdam Ave (212-653-8320). Subway: 1, 2 to 66th St. 7:30am–9:30pm. AmEx, MC, V.*

Dean & DeLuca
560 Broadway at Prince St (212-431-1691). Subway: N, R to Prince St. Mon–Sat 9am–8pm; Sun 9am–7pm. AmEx, MC, V.
Dean & DeLuca's flagship store (the only one that isn't just a fancy coffee bar) continues to provide the most sophisticated collection of specialty food items in New York City. The grandiose appearance of the place and its epic range of products are reflected in the prices, which are sky-high. But downtown residents and international visitors don't seem to mind. After all, where else can you be

assured that you are choosing from the highest-quality goods on the market?

Dylan's Candy Bar

1011 Third Ave at 60th St (646-735-0078). Mon–Thu 10am–9pm; Fri 10am–11pm; Sat 11am–11pm; Sun 11am–7pm. Subway: N, R, W to Lexington Ave–59th St AmEx, MC, V.

Dylan Lauren, the daughter of Ralph Lauren, opened this sweet dream of a candy shop. You'll find thousands of sugary snacks and a soda fountain.

Foodworks

1C W 19th St between Fifth and Sixth Aves (212-352-9333). Subway: F, V, N, R to 23rd St. Mon–Fri 8am–8:30pm; Sat 11am–6:30pm. AmEx, MC, V.

This is a Flatiron standby for gourmet sandwiches, soups and sushi to go. There's also a nice selection of Japanese candy, as well as a juice bar.

Gourmet Garage

2567 Broadway between 96th and 97th Sts (212-663-0656). Subway: 1, 2, 3 to 96th St. 7am–10pm. AmEx, Disc, MC, V.

Gourmet Garage is the Manhattan version of Trader Joe's, the California-based chain of bargain-basement gourmet markets that has a handful of stores in Westchester and on Long Island. It's not comprehensive: You won't find a dozen different cuts of steak or ten types of mushrooms. What you will find is a select range of produce, meats and fish, and a line of house-brand prepared foods offered at fair prices. Check the phone book for other locations.

Grace's Marketplace

1237 Third Ave at 71st St (212-737-0600). Subway: 6 to 68th St–Hunter College. Mon–Sat 7am–8:30pm; Sun 8am–7pm. AmEx, DC, MC, V.

Grace's Marketplace has been a gourmet stronghold of the Upper East Side since 1985. Grace's core customer is a solidly affluent, high-maintenance society matron, but the store appeals to all fans of high-quality produce, meats and fish. Grace's also stocks the unusual, such as Boutargue pressed carp roe and long flatbreads called Tongue of Mother-in-Law. The bread selection is fab, but Grace herself doesn't do the baking—she chooses the best from 37 selected purveyors.

Greenmarkets

212-477-3220. Information Mon–Fri 9am–6pm.

There are more than 20 open-air markets sponsored by city authorities in various locations and on different days. The most famous is the one at Union Square *(17th St between Broadway and Park Ave South; Mon, Wed, Fri, Sat 8am–6pm)*, where small producers of cheeses, flowers, herbs, honey and vegetables sell their wares from the backs of their flatbed trucks. Arrive early, before the good stuff sells out.

Guss' Pickles

Lower East Side Tenement Museum, 97 Orchard St between Broome and Delancey Sts (212-431-0233). Subway: F to East Broadway. Mon–Thu, Sun 9am–6pm; Fri 9am–3:30pm. MC, V.

Due to a landlord dispute, this Lower East Side legend has found a temporary home at the LES Tenement Museum. So fans can still get the Pickle King's sour or half-sours in several sizes. The sauerkraut and pickled peppers and watermelon rinds are also excellent.

Kam Man Food Products

200 Canal St at Mott St (212-571-0330). Subway: J, M, Z, N, Q, R, W, 6 to Canal St. 9am–9pm. AmEx, MC, V.

This shop has a huge selection of fresh and preserved Chinese, Thai and other Asian foods, as well as utensils and kitchenware.

Kitchen Market

218 Eighth Ave between 21st and 22nd Sts (212-243-4433). Subway: C, E to 23rd St. 9am–10:30pm. AmEx, Disc, MC, V.

This narrow Chelsea storefront is chock-full of Mexican goodies. Kitchen Market sells a selection of *moles*, salsas and tortillas, as well as lots of Mexican knickknacks. Essential ingredients for South-of-the-Border cooking include jicama, *nopales* (cactus leaves), tomatillos and a range of fresh and dried chilies; yuppified treats such as banana soda, chipotle-cheese dip and red-chili honey are also sold.

Li-Lac Chocolates Inc.

120 Christopher St between Bleecker and Hudson Sts (212-242-7374). Subway: 1, 2 to Christopher St–Sheridan Sq. Mon–Fri 10am–8pm; Sat noon–8pm; Sun noon–5pm. AmEx, Disc, MC, V.

Handmade chocolates par excellence are the specialty. Take home an edible Statue of Liberty for $20. **Other location ●** *Grand Central Terminal, Lexington Ave at 43rd St, market hall #24 (212-370-4866). Subway: S, 4, 5, 6, 7 to 42nd St–Grand Central. Mon–Fri 7am–9pm; Sat 10am–7pm; Sun 11am–6pm. AmEx, DC, Disc, MC, V.*

McNulty's Tea and Coffee

109 Christopher St between Bleecker and Hudson Sts (212-242-5351). Subway: 1, 2 to Christopher St–Sheridan Sq. Mon–Sat 10am–9pm; Sun 1–7pm. AmEx, Disc, MC, V.

The original McNulty began selling tea in 1895; in 1980, the shop was taken over by the Wong family. Coffee is sold here, of course, but the real draw is the tea. From the rarest White Flower Pekoe (harvested once a year in China and priced at $25 per quarter pound) or peach-flavored green tea (at $6 per quarter pound) to a basic Darjeeling or Fortnum & Mason box set, this is a tea haven.

Myers of Keswick

634 Hudson St between Horatio and Jane Sts (212-691-4194). Subway: A, C, E to 14th St; L to Eighth Ave. Mon–Fri 10am–7pm; Sat 10am–6pm; Sun noon–5pm. AmEx, MC, V.

This charming English market is a frequent stop for Brits and local Anglophiles. While some come looking for a hint of home or a jolly good meet-and-greet, others flock to the store for Cornish pasties and steak-and-kidney pies. Other specialties include homemade pork bangers and Cumberland sausages. Shelves are lined with jars of clotted cream, PG Tips tea, sweets such as wine gums and Smarties, and "memory cards" emblazoned with the image of Her Majesty Queen Elizabeth II.

Raffeto's Corporation
144 W Houston St at MacDougal St (212-777-1261). Subway: 1, 2 to Houston St. Tue–Fri 9am–6:30pm; Sat 9am–6pm. Cash only.
In business since 1906, Raffeto's is the source of much of the designer pasta that is sold in gourmet shops all over town. The staff cuts noodles to order and sells special fettuccine, gnocchi, manicotti, ravioli and tortellini in any quantity, to anyone who calls in, with no minimum order.

Russ & Daughters
179 E Houston St between Allen and Orchard Sts (212-475-4880). Subway: F, V to Lower East Side–Second Ave. Mon–Sat 9am–7pm; Sun 8am–6pm. AmEx, MC, V.
You'll feel like a circus seal when the jovial men behind the counter of this legendary Lower East Side shop start tossing you bits of lox and gravlax, but who's complaining? Russ & Daughters, open since 1914, sells eight kinds of smoked salmon and many other Jewish foodstuffs, along with Russian and Iranian caviar. A favorite with locals is the herring, soaked in a choice of lemon-ginger sauce, mustard-dill marinade, red wine or schmaltz.

Zabar's
2245 Broadway at 80th St (212-787-2000). Subway: 1, 2 to 79th St. Mon–Fri 9am–7:30pm; Sat 8am–8pm; Sun 9am–6pm. AmEx, MC, V.
Zabar's is more than just a market—it's a New York landmark worthy of campaign stops by would-be elected officials. You won't escape lightly wallet-wise, but you can't argue with the topflight food. Besides the famous smoked fish and rafts of Jewish delicacies, Zabar's has fabulous bread, cheese and coffee selections. Plus, it's the only market of its kind that offers an entire floor of housewares.

Liquor stores

Most supermarkets and corner delis sell beer and aren't too fussy about ID, though you do need to show proof that you are over 21 years old if asked (and don't carry open alcohol containers in the streets—that's a sure bust these days). To buy wine or spirits, you need to go to a liquor store (most don't sell beer), which are closed on Sundays.

Astor Wines & Spirits
12 Astor Pl at Lafayette St (212-674-7500). Subway: N, R to 8th St–NYU; 6 to Astor Pl. Mon–Sat 9am–9pm. AmEx, Disc, MC, V.
This is a modern wine supermarket that would serve as the perfect blueprint for a chain, were it not

for a law preventing liquor stores from branching out. There's a wide range of wines and spirits.

Best Cellars
1291 Lexington Ave between 86th and 87th Sts (212-426-4200). Subway: 4, 5, 6 to 86th St. Mon–Thu 10am–9pm; Fri, Sat 10am–10pm. AmEx, DC, MC, V.
This wine shop stocks only 100 selections, but each one is delicious and has been tasted by the owners (who tested more than 1,500 bottles). The best part is that they're all under $15 (except for "Beyond the best" selections, which are slightly more expensive). A tasting of a wine paired with food is held daily, and the store also offers wine classes.

Sherry-Lehmann
679 Madison Ave at 61st St (212-838-7500). Subway: F to Lexington Ave–63rd St; N, R, W to Fifth Ave–60th St; 4, 5, 6 to 59th St. Mon–Sat 9am–7pm. AmEx, MC, V.
Perhaps the most famous of New York's numerous liquor stores, Sherry-Lehmann has a vast selection of bourbons, brandies, champagnes, ports and Scotches, as well as a superb range of American, French and Italian wines.

Vintage New York
482 Broome St at Wooster St (212-226-9463). Subway C, E to Spring St; 1, 2 to Canal St. Mon–Sat 11am–9pm; Sun noon–5pm. AmEx, Disc, MC, V.
Technically, this place is an outpost of an upstate winery *(see **A toast to Hudson Valley wines**, page 352),* which means it's open for business on Sundays. One catch: It sells wines only from New York vineyards, but you can sample any before buying.

*(see **A toast to Hudson Valley wines**, page 352),*

Home & design

ABC Carpet & Home
888 Broadway at 19th St (212-473-3000). Subway: N, R to 23rd St. Mon–Fri 10am–8pm; Sat 10am–7pm; Sun 11am–6:30pm. AmEx, MC, V.
The selection is unbelievable, and often, so are the steep prices. But this New York shopping landmark really does have it all: accessories, linens, rugs, antique (Western and Asian) and reproduction furniture, plus more (a large selection of carpets is in the store across the street). If you are determined to pay cheaper prices, trek to ABC's warehouse outlet in the Bronx. **Other location ●** *1055 Bronx River Ave between Westchester Ave and Bruckner Blvd, Bronx (718-842-8772). Subway: 6 to Whitlock Ave. Mon–Fri 10am–7pm; Sat 9am–7pm; Sun 11am–6pm. AmEx, MC, V.*

The Apartment
101 Crosby St between Prince and Spring Sts (212-219-3066). Subway: F, V, S to Broadway–Lafayette St; 6 to Bleecker St. Mon–Sat 11am–7pm; Sun noon–6pm. AmEx, MC, V.
If that East Village couch you're crashing on is cramping your style, drop by the Apartment. Owners Gina Alvarez and Stefan Boublil have designed this lifestyle shop to look like the Tribeca loft that the PYT in your office lives in with her perfect boyfriend.

You, the shopper, are meant to lounge on the minimalist Dutch furniture, eat Le Gamin crêpes at the communal dining table and just hang, as if chez *vous*. Everything you see is for sale: the Moderno Lifestyle Emmanuele bed, the Duravit bathroom fixtures by Philippe Starck. The stock changes weekly, so don't debate too long about buying that Trash à Porter sweater or any of the smaller home accessories.

Area I.D. Moderne

262 Elizabeth St between Houston and Prince Sts (212-219-9903). Subway: F, V, S to Broadway–Lafayette St; 6 to Bleecker St. Noon–7pm. AmEx, MC, V.
Area I.D. sells home accessories and furniture from the 1950s, '60s and '70s, both vintage and reproduction. What sets this store apart is that all of its furniture has been reupholstered in luxurious fabrics (Ultrasuede and mohair, for example). The store also carries a wide selection of fur throws and rugs.

Bennison Fabrics

Fine Arts Building, 232 E 59th St between Second and Third Aves, third floor (212-223-0373). Subway: N, R, W to Lexington Ave–59th St; 4, 5, 6 to 59th St. Mon–Fri 9:30am–5:30pm. AmEx, MC, V.
Bennison is an unusual shop that sells a classic yet innovative range of fabrics silk-screened in England. Prices are steep, and the fabrics—usually 70 percent linen, 30 percent cotton—end up in some of the best-dressed homes in town.

Chelsea Garden Center Home Store

435 Hudson St at Morton St (212-727-7100). Subway: 1, 2 to Houston St. 10am–7:30pm. AmEx, MC, V.
The Chelsea Garden Center's 6,000-square-foot sun-filled garden, home and lifestyle store has plenty of books, furniture, indoor plants, pottery and tools that will brighten your host's pad, once winter sets in.
Other location ● *455 W 16th St between Ninth and Tenth Aves (212-929-2477). Subway: A, C, E to 14th St; L to Eighth Ave. 10am–5:30pm. AmEx, MC, V.*

Felissimo

See page 193.

Fishs Eddy

889 Broadway at 19th St (212-420-9020). Subway: N, R to 23rd St. Mon–Sat 10am–9pm; Sun 11am–8pm. AmEx, Disc, MC, V.
Fishs Eddy sells virtually indestructible, well-priced china that you may also find being used in your favorite hotel or diner. Flatware and glassware round out the stock.
Other location ● *2176 Broadway at 77th St (212-873-8819). Subway: 1, 2 to 79th St. Mon–Sat 10am–9pm; Sun 11am–8pm. AmEx, Disc, MC, V.*

Necessities

Fertile ground Chelsea Garden Center Home Store has just about any plant or pot you need.

Gracious Home

1217 and 1220 Third Ave between 70th and 71st Sts (212-988-8990). Subway: 6 to 68th St–Hunter College. Mon–Fri 8am–7pm; Sat 9am–7pm; Sun 10am–6pm. AmEx, DC, MC, V.
If you need a curtain rod, drawer pull, hanger, place mat, sheet—or any other household accessory—this is the place to find it. (Gracious Home will even deliver to your hotel at no charge.)
Other location ● *1992 Broadway at 67th St (212-231-7800). Subway: 1, 2 to 66th St–Lincoln Ctr. Mon–Thu 9am–8pm; Fri, Sat 9am–9pm; Sun 10am–7pm. AmEx, DC, MC, V.*

Ingo Maurer, Making Light

89 Grand St at Greene St (212-965-8817). Subway: A, C, E, J, M, Z, N, Q, R, W, 6 to Canal St. Tue–Sat 11am–7pm; Sun noon–6pm. AmEx, MC, V.
Does the synthesis of language and light make you think of Times Square? Munich native Ingo Maurer wants you to think Soho—not lame-o. His clever lamps and fixtures incorporate neon words and LED phrases. One of his creations hangs in the Library Bar at the Hudson hotel *(see page 121).*

Kartell

45 Greene St between Broome and Grand Sts (212-966-6665). Subway: A, C, E, J, M, Z, N, Q, R, W, 6 to Canal St. Mon–Sat 11am–7pm; Sun noon–6pm. AmEx, MC, V.
If you think "good plastic" is an oxymoron, visit Kartell. Its furniture, crafted from the most durable substances, will set you straight.

MoMA Design Store

44 W 53rd St between Fifth and Sixth Aves (212-767-1050). Subway: E, V to Fifth Ave–53rd St. Sat–Thu 10am–6:30pm; Fri 10am–8pm. AmEx, MC, V.
At the Museum of Modern Art's Design Store, you'll find calendars, coatracks, glasses, jewelry—you name it—in whimsical shapes and colors.
Other locations ● *MoMa Design Store Soho, 81 Spring St at Crosby St (646-613-1367) Subway: 6 to Spring St. Mon–Fri 10am–7pm; Sat 11am–7pm; Sun 11am–6pm. AmEx, MC, V.* ● *MoMA Bookstore, 11 W 53rd St between Fifth and Sixth Aves (212-708-9700). Subway: E, V to Fifth Ave–53rd St. Sat–Thu 10am–6:30pm; Fri 10am–9pm. AmEx, MC, V.*

Moss

146-150 Greene St at Houston (212-226-2190). Subway: N, R to Prince St. Tue–Fri 11am–7pm; Sat noon–7pm; Sun noon–6pm. AmEx, Disc, MC, V.
Do you insist on impeccable design for even the most prosaic objects? Murray Moss's museumlike emporium features the best of what the contemporary design world has to offer, including streamlined clocks, curvy sofas and witty salt and pepper shakers.

Pondicherri

454 Columbus Ave at 82nd St (212-875-1609). Subway: B, C to 81st St–Museum of Natural History. 11am–8pm. AmEx, Disc, MC, V.
Into patchwork duvet covers and multipatterned

throw pillows and table linens? These Indian textiles are all handcrafted and sure to add flavor to any room.

Portico Home

72 Spring St between Broadway and Lafayette St (212-941-7800). Subway: 6 to Spring St. Mon–Sat 10am–7pm; Sun noon–6pm. AmEx, Disc, MC, V.
Portico features country-chic furniture and bed and bath accessories. Check the phone book for other locations.

The Terence Conran Shop

407 E 59th St between First and York Aves (212-755-9079). Subway: N, R, W to Lexington Ave–59th St; 4, 5, 6 to 59th St. Mon–Fri 11am–8pm; Sat 10am–7pm; Sun noon–6pm. AmEx, MC, V.
Sir Terence Conran returned to New York in fall 1999 with this witty design store under the Queensboro Bridge (in the '80s Conran had shops around the city). As in Europe, he offers an overwhelming selection of trendy products—new and vintage—for every room of the house: cabinets, dishes, lighting, rugs, sofas…the list goes on. After your shopping spree, you can fill up at Conran's next-door restaurant Guastavino's *(see page 182).*

Totem Design

71 Franklin St between Broadway and Church St (212-925-5506). Subway: 1, 2 to Franklin St. Mon–Sat 11am–7pm; Sun noon–5pm. AmEx, MC, V.
Totem offers sleek, Scandinavia-inspired, one-of-a-kind furniture (mostly designed by Karim Rashid), lighting fixtures and accessories that will blend seamlessly with your flea market treasures. The Grand Street location stocks similar merchandise, but it's primarily an exhibition space for designers and artists. Totem Design also publishes the quarterly magazine *DSGN.*
Other location ● *83 Grand St between Greene and Wooster Sts (888-519-5587). Subway: A, C, E, J, M, Z, N, Q, R, W, 6 to Canal St. Tue–Sat 11am–7pm; Sun noon–5pm. AmEx, MC, V.*

Urban Archaeology

143 Franklin St between Hudson and Varick Sts (212-431-4646). Subway: A, C, E to Canal St; 1, 2 to Franklin St. Mon–Fri 8am–6pm; Sat 10am–4pm. AmEx, Disc, MC, V.
Old buildings saved! Or rather, picked to pieces and sold for parts. This store carries refurbished architectural artifacts, from Corinthian columns and lobby-size chandeliers to bathtubs and doorknobs, as well as reproductions of favorites. There's a tile showroom on the second floor.
Other location ● *239 E 58th St between Second and Third Aves (212-371-4646). Subway: N, R, W to Lexington Ave–59th St; 4, 5, 6 to 59th St. Mon–Fri 9:30am–5pm. AmEx, MC, V.*

Waterworks Collection

475 Broome St between Greene and Wooster Sts (212-274-8800). Subway: C, E to Spring St. Mon–Fri 9am–6pm; Sat 11am–6pm; Sun noon–5pm. AmEx, MC, V.
Given their awkward shapes and sizes, bathrooms

can be the hardest rooms to furnish. With that in mind, the folks at Waterworks stock an array of items, from secretaries and plumbing accessories to silver-plated shaving brushes and soap dishes that make bathrooms pleasant. The showroom, which offers services for larger bathroom renovations, is located at 469 Broome Street at the corner of Greene Street *(212-966-0605)*.

Wyeth

315 Spring St at Greenwich St (212-243-3661). Subway: C, E to Spring St; 1, 2 to Canal St. Mon–Fri 11am–6pm; Sat noon–5pm. AmEx, DC, MC, V.
This Soho shop is known for its collection of vintage 20th-century pieces, as well as its metal lamps, chairs and tables that have been stripped of old paint, sanded and burnished to a soft finish. The hardware is nickel-plated.

Gift shops

Alphabets

47 Greenwich Ave between Charles and Perry Sts (212-229-2966). Subway: 1, 2 to Christopher St–Sheridan Sq. Mon–Sat noon–8pm; Sun noon–7pm. AmEx, MC, V.
Hilarious postcards, wrapping paper and tiny treasures pack the shelves at Alphabets, along with a range of goofy T-shirts and souvenirs of New York.
Other locations ● *115 Ave A between 7th and 8th Sts (212-475-7250). Subway: L to First Ave; 6 to Astor Pl. Sun–Fri noon–8pm; Sat 11am–8pm. AmEx, MC, V.* ● *2284 Broadway between 82nd and 83rd Sts (212-579-5702). Subway: 1, 2 to 86th St. Mon noon–8pm; Tue–Fri 11am–9pm; Sat 10am–9pm; Sun 11am–7pm. AmEx, MC, V.*

Breukelen

369 Atlantic Ave between Bond and Hoyt Sts, Boerum Hill, Brooklyn (718-246-0024). Subway: A, C, G to Hoyt–Schermerhorn. Tue–Sat noon–7pm; Sun noon–6pm. AmEx, DC, MC, V.
This contemporary-design store crops up unexpectedly in the middle of Atlantic Avenue's popular three-block stretch of antiques stores. While the collection isn't limited to any single style, all the objects—pet dishes, table lamps, tumblers—fit a simple, clean, pared-down aesthetic. The Manhattan branch specializes in furniture and is slightly more expensive.
Other location ● *68 Gansevoort St between Greenwich and Washington Sts (212-645-2216). Subway: A, C, E to 14th St; L to Eighth Ave. Tue–Sat 11am–7pm; Sun noon–6pm. AmEx, MC, V.*

Daily 235

235 Elizabeth St between Houston and Prince Sts (212-334-9728). Subway: F, V, S to Broadway–Lafayette St; 6 to Bleecker St. Mon–Sat 1–8pm; Sun 1–6pm. AmEx, DC, Disc, MC, V.
This store is stocked with stuff you probably don't need but must buy anyway. There are books on photography, condoms, matchbook-size games, soaps, voodoo dolls—and that's just a sampling.

Disney Store

711 Fifth Ave at 55th St (212-702-0702). Subway: E, V to Fifth Ave–53rd St; N, R, W to Fifth Ave–60th St. Mon–Sat 10am–8pm; Sun 11am–6pm. AmEx, Disc, MC, V.
This is where all your favorite Disney characters come to life (in great quantity)—Mickey, Minnie, Goofy, etc. At the Fifth Avenue store, the largest of them all, you can peruse the vast range of Disney's toys and souvenirs. Check the phone book for other locations.

Frenchware

98 Thompson St between Prince and Spring Sts (212-625-3131). Subway: C, E to Spring St. Tue–Sun 11am–7pm. AmEx, DC, MC, V.
If names such as Astérix, Tintin and Le Petit Prince give you a happy jolt, here's a news flash: Frenchware, a *charmant* den for Francophiles, carries *chocolat* bowls bearing those icons, Ricard pitchers and a lot more.

Hammacher Schlemmer

147 E 57th St between Lexington and Third Aves (212-421-9000). Subway: E, V to Lexington Ave–53rd St; N, R, W to Lexington Ave–59th St; 4, 5, 6 to 59th St. Mon–Sat 10am–6pm. AmEx, DC, Disc, MC, V.
Here are two floors of bizarre and ingenious toys and gadgets for car, home, sports and leisure, each one supposedly the best of its kind. It's the perfect place to buy a gift that will permanently attach a smile to anyone's face. In December, the store opens its doors on Sundays for drooling holiday shoppers.

Kar'ikter

19 Prince St between Elizabeth and Mott Sts (212-274-1966). Subway: N, R to Prince St; 6 to Spring St. 11am–7:30pm. AmEx, MC, V.
Babar and Astérix paraphernalia are the main draw at this Nolita housewares shop. But grown-up goodies are also available—the four-foot, $2,200 Tintin rocketship is joined by chic and affordable items such as Philippe Starck–designed flyswatters, colorful Mendolino toilet brushes and interior accessories by Alessi.

Love Saves the Day

119 Second Ave at 7th St (212-228-3802). Subway: 6 to Astor Pl. 1–9pm. AmEx, MC, V.
This shop has more kitschy toys and tacky novelties than you can shake a Yoda doll at. There are Elvis lamps, ant farms, lurid machine-made tapestries of Madonna, glow-in-the-dark crucifixes, collectible toys and Mexican Day of the Dead statues. Vintage clothes and collectible items are peppered throughout the store.

Metropolitan Opera Shop

136 W 65th St at Broadway (212-580-4090). Subway: 1, 2 to 66th St–Lincoln Ctr. Mon–Sat 10am–10pm; Sun noon–6pm. AmEx, Disc, MC, V.
Located in the Metropolitan Opera at Lincoln Center, this shop sells CDs and cassettes of—you guessed it—operas. You can also find a wealth of opera books, memorabilia and DVDs. Kids aren't forgotten

Necessities

either: The store's children's department stocks plenty of educational CDs.

Mxyplyzyk

125 Greenwich Ave at 13th St (212-989-4300). Subway: A, C, E to 14th St; L to Eighth Ave. Mon–Sat 11am–7pm; Sun noon–5pm. AmEx, MC, V.
The name doesn't mean anything, although it's similar to the name of a character from the *Superman* comics. Mxyplyzyk offers a hodgepodge of chic lighting, furniture, housewares, stationery, toys and plenty of novelty books—on topics such as paranoia taxi-driver wisdom.

Pearl River Mart

477 Broadway between Broome and Grand Sts (212-431-4770). Subway: J, M, Z, N, Q, R, W, 6 to Canal St. 10am–7:30pm. AmEx, Disc, MC, V.
This downtown emporium's new location offers 30 percent more space, crammed with all things Chinese—bedroom slippers, clothing, gongs, groceries, medicinal herbs, pots, stationery, teapots, woks and a lot more.
Other location ● *200 Grand St between Mott and Mulberry Sts (212-966-1010). Subway: J, M, Z, N, Q, R, W, 6 to Canal St. 10am–7:30pm. AmEx, MC, V.*

Pop Shop

292 Lafayette St between Houston and Prince Sts (212-219-2784). Subway: F, V, S to Broadway–Lafayette St; 6 to Bleecker St. Mon–Sat noon–7pm; Sun noon–6pm. AmEx, MC, V.
The art of famed pop iconographer Keith Haring lives on in this shop, which sells bags, jigsaw puzzles, pillows and T-shirts—all emblazoned with Haring's famous cartoony, crayon-colored characters.

Shi

233 Elizabeth St between Houston and Prince Sts (212-334-4330). Subway: F, V, S to Broadway–Lafayette St; 6 to Bleecker St. Mon–Sat noon–7pm; Sun noon–6pm. AmEx, MC, V.
At Shi—which means "is" in Chinese—choice finds include bullet-shaped glass hanging vases, crisp Caravane silk bedding, and Liwan glassware and bedding, which is designed in Paris and handmade in Lebanon.

White Trash

304 E 5th St between First and Second Aves (212-598-5956). Subway: F, V to Lower East Side–Second Ave; 6 to Astor Pl. Tue–Sat 2–9pm; Sun 1–8pm. MC, V.
White trash connoisseurs Kim Wurster and Stuart Zamsky opened this popular store, to the delight of those in dire need of Jesus night-lights, Noguchi lamps, 1950s kitchen tables, and designer furniture from the likes of Eames and Saarinen.

Bed knobs and candlesticks Pondicherri specializes in colorful Indian furnishings and accessories.

Music

Superstores

HMV

1280 Lexington Ave at 86th St (212-348-0800). Subway: 4, 5, 6 to 86th St. Mon–Sat 9am–11pm, Sun 10am–10pm. AmEx, Disc, MC, V.
One of the biggest record stores in North America, HMV has a jaw-dropping selection of cassettes, CDs, videos and vinyl. Check the phone book for other locations.

J&R

See page 220.

Tower Records

692 Broadway at 4th St (212-505-1500, 800-648-4844). Subway: N, R to 8th St–NYU. 9am–midnight. AmEx, Disc, MC, V.
Tower Records has all the current sounds on CD and tape. Visit the clearance store down the block on Lafayette Street *(383 Lafayette St at 4th St, 212-*

228-5100) for markdowns in all formats, including vinyl (especially classical). Check the phone book for other locations.

Virgin Megastore

52 E 14th St at Broadway (212-598-4666). Subway: L, N, Q, R, W, 4, 5, 6 to 14th St–Union Sq. Mon–Sat 9am–1am; Sun 10am–midnight. AmEx, Disc, MC, V.
Besides a huge selection of music of all genres, Virgin Megastore has in-store performances and a great selection of U.K.-imported CDs. Check out the Virgin soda machine and the Virgin Megastore Cafe. Books and videos are also available.
Other location ● *1540 Broadway between 45th and 46th Sts (212-921-1020). Subway: N, Q, R, W, S, 1, 2, 3, 7 to 42nd St–Times Sq. Sun–Thu 9am–1am; Fri, Sat 9am–2am. AmEx, Disc, MC, V.*

Multigenre

Bleecker Bob's

118 W 3rd St between MacDougal St and Sixth Ave (212-475-9677). Subway: A, C, E, F, V, S to W 4th St. Sun–Thu noon–1am; Fri, Sat noon–3am. AmEx, MC, V.
Bleecker Bob's is an institution and was named "Best Metal Store" in 2001 by the *Village Voice.* It's the place to go when you can't find what you want anywhere else, especially if it's on vinyl.

Etherea

66 Ave A between 4th and 5th Sts (212-358-1126). Subway: F, V to Lower East Side–Second Ave. Sun–Thu noon–10pm; Fri, Sat noon–11pm. AmEx, DC, Disc, MC, V.
Etherea has taken over the space that used to be Adult Crash. The stock is mostly electronic, experimental, indie and rock.

Mondo Kim's

6 St. Marks Pl between Second and Third Aves (212-598-9985). Subway: 6 to Astor Pl. 9am–midnight. AmEx, MC, V.
This minichain of movie and m

Subway: 6 to Astor Pl. Mon–Thu noon–10:30pm; Fri, Sat noon–11:30pm; Sun noon–9pm. Cash only.
Sounds, consisting of two neighboring stores, is the best bargain on the block. The eastern branch stocks catalog releases, while new releases compose the west. Be advised that the 16 St. Marks location is closed on Tuesdays and Wednesdays.

Subterranean Records

5 Cornelia St between Bleecker and W 4th Sts (212-463-8900). Subway: A, C, E, F, V, S to W 4th St. Noon–8pm. MC, V.
At this just-off-Bleecker shop, you'll find new, used and live recordings, as well as a large selection of imports. Vinyls (LPs and 45s) fill the basement.

Classical

Gryphon Record Shop

233 W 72nd St between Broadway and West End Ave (212-874-1588). Subway: 1, 2, 3 to 72nd St. Mon–Fri 9:30am–7pm; Sat 11am–7pm; Sun noon–6pm. MC, V.
This solidly classical store has traditionally been vinyl only, but the nascent 21st century has swept in a wave of CDs. Gryphon also carries a sprinkling of jazz and show tunes, and drama and film books.

Dance

Dance Tracks

91 E 3rd St at First Ave (212-260-8729). Subway: F, V to Lower East Side–Second Ave. Mon–Thu noon–9pm; Fri noon–10pm; Sat noon–8pm; Sun noon–7pm. AmEx, Disc, MC, V.
Stocked with Europe's imports hot off the plane (which are ne... ...p to buy here), and with racks of... ...angerously enticing bins ...ssics and private decks ...a must.

*...d Stanton Sts (212-
...adway–Lafayette
...n; Sun 1–8pm.*

...ough them and
...ever wanted.

...wntown
...G to Hoyt–
...s St. Mon–Sat
...AmEx, DC, Disc, MC, V.
...asement with two DJ
...go with that phat new
...gamut from dancehall
...e boom shots, 12-inch
...ums that make this the

Necessities

first stop for local DJs seeking killer breakbeats and samples.

Fat Beats

406 Sixth Ave between 8th and 9th Sts, second floor (212-673-3883). Subway: A, C, E, F, V, S to W 4th St. Mon–Thu noon–9pm; Fri, Sat noon–10pm; Sun noon–6pm. MC, V.
Fat Beats is to local hip-hop what church is to gospel music: the foundation. Twin Technics 1200 turntables command the center of this tiny West Village shrine to vinyl. Everyone—Beck, DJ Evil Dee, DJ Premier, Marilyn Manson, Mike D, Q-Tip—shops here regularly for treasured hip-hop, jazz and reggae releases, as well as underground magazines such as *Mass Appeal* and cult flicks such as *Wild Style*.

Jazz

Jazz Record Center

236 W 26th St between Seventh and Eighth Aves, room 804 (212-675-4480). Subway: C, E to 23rd St; 1, 2 to 28th St. Mon–Sat 10am–6pm. Disc, MC, V.
Quite simply, Jazz Record Center is the best jazz store in the city, selling current and out-of-print records, along with books, videos and other jazz-related merchandise. Worldwide shipping is available.

Show tunes

Footlight Records

113 E 12th St between Third and Fourth Aves (212-533-1572). Subway: L, N, Q, R, W, 4, 5, 6 to 14th St–Union Sq. Tue–Fri 11am–7pm; Sat 10am–6pm; Sun noon–5pm. AmEx, DC, MC, V.
This spectacular store specializes in vocalists, Broadway cast recordings and film soundtracks. It also carries DVDs and videos of Broadway shows.

World music

World Music Institute

49 W 27th St between Broadway and Sixth Ave, suite 930 (212-545-7536). Subway: N, R to 28th St. Mon–Fri 10am–6pm. AmEx, MC, V.
The square footage is sparse, but WMI employs experts who can order sounds from any remote corner of the planet, usually within six weeks.

Specialty stores

Arthur Brown & Brothers

2 W 46th St between Fifth and Sixth Aves (212-575-5555). Subway: B, D, F, V to 47–50th Sts–Rockefeller Ctr; 7 to Fifth Ave. Mon–Fri 9am–6:30pm; Sat 10am–6pm. AmEx, DC, Disc, MC, V.
Arthur Brown has one of the largest selections of pens anywhere, including Cartier, Dupont, Mont Blanc, Porsche and Schaeffer.

Big City Kites

1210 Lexington Ave at 82nd St (212-472-2623). Subway: 4, 5, 6 to 86th St. Mon–Wed, Fri 11am–6:30pm; Thu 11am–7:30pm; Sat 10am–6pm. Call for summer hours. AmEx, Disc, MC, V.
Act like a kid again and go fly a kite. There are more than 150 to choose from.

Carrandi Gallery

138 W 18th St between Sixth and Seventh Aves (212-206-0499, 212-242-0710). Subway: 1, 2 to 18th St. Tue–Fri noon–6pm; Sun noon–5pm. AmEx, MC, V.
Carrandi stocks original advertising posters from both sides of the Atlantic, dating as far back as 1880.

Evolution

120 Spring St between Greene and Mercer Sts (212-343-1114). Subway: C, E to Spring St. 11am–7pm. AmEx, DC, Disc, MC, V.
If natural history is an obsession, look no further. Fossils, giraffe skulls, insects mounted behind glass frames and wild boar tusks are among the items for sale in this relatively politically correct store—the animals died of natural causes or were culled.

Fetch

43 Greenwich Ave between Charles and Perry Sts (212-352-8591). Subway: A, C, E, F, V, S to W 4th St; 1, 2 to Christopher St–Sheridan Sq. Mon–Fri noon–8pm; Sat 11am–7pm; Sun noon–6pm. AmEx, Disc, MC, V.
This luxury shop for cats and dogs carries everything from silken coats to aromatherapy perfume for Fido and Fritz. Most of Fetch's specialty foods—such as bone-shaped peanut-butter treats and Kitty Calamari—can be eaten by people too. If you enjoy sharing culinary moments with your pet, *bon appétit!*

Flight 001

96 Greenwich Ave between Seventh and Eighth Aves (212-691-1001). Subway: A, C, E to 14th St; L to Eighth Ave. Mon–Fri 11am–8:30pm; Sat 11am–8pm; Sun noon–6pm. AmEx, DC, MC, V.
This one-stop travel shop in the West Village carries the requisite travel guidebooks and luggage along with products such as vacuum-packed shower-gel pouches and pocket-size aromatherapy kits. Did you forget something? Flight 001's "travel essentials" wall features packets of Woolite, minidominoes and everything in between.

Game Show

1240 Lexington Ave between 83rd and 84th Sts (212-472-8011). Subway: 4, 5, 6 to 86th St. Mon–Sat 11am–6pm; Sun noon–5pm. AmEx, MC, V.
Scads of board games are sold here, including some guaranteed to leave you intrigued or offended (a few are quite naughty).
Other location ● *474 Sixth Ave between 11th and 12th Sts (212-633-6328). Subway: F, V to 14th St; L to Sixth Ave. Mon–Sat noon–7pm; Sun noon–5pm. AmEx, MC, V.*

Jerry Ohlinger's Movie Material Store

242 W 14th St between Seventh and Eighth Aves (212-989-0869). Subway: A, C, E, 1, 2, 3 to 14th St; L to Eighth Ave. 1–7:45pm. AmEx, Disc, MC, V.

Ohlinger has an extensive stock of "paper material" from movies past and present, including photos, posters, programs and fascinating celebrity curios.

Kate Spade Travel

59 Thompson St between Broome and Spring Sts (212-965-8654). Subway: C, E to Spring St. Tue–Sat 11am–7pm; Sun noon–6pm. AmEx, MC, V.

Bag lady Kate Spade's personal calendars and bound agendas come in leather, as well as novelty animal prints and her signature nylon. But the big draw is her full line of luggage. Cosmetics bags, toiletry cases and vintage travel books are also available.

Kate's Paperie

561 Broadway between Prince and Spring Sts (212-941-9816). Subway: N, R to Prince St; 6 to Spring St. Mon–Sat 10am–7pm; Sun 11am–7pm. AmEx, MC, V.

Kate's is the ultimate paper mill—there are more than 5,000 papers to choose from. It's also the best outpost for stationery, custom printing, journals, photo albums, and creative gift wrapping. **Other locations ●** *8 W 13th St between Fifth and Sixth Aves (212-633-0570). Subway: F, V to 14th St; L to Sixth Ave. Mon–Fri 10am–7pm; Sat 10am–6pm; Sun 11am–6pm. AmEx, Disc, MC, V.* **●** *1282 Third Ave between 73rd and 74th Sts (212-396-3670). Subway: 6 to 77th St. Mon–Fri 10am–7pm; Sat, Sun 11am–6pm. AmEx, MC, V.*

Nat Sherman

500 Fifth Ave at 42nd St (212-764-5000). Subway: S, 4, 5, 6, 7 to 42nd St–Grand Central; 7 to Fifth Ave. Mon–Wed 9am–7pm; Thu, Fri 9am–7:30pm; Sat 10am–6pm; Sun 11am–5pm. AmEx, DC, MC, V.

Nat Sherman, located across the street from the New York Public Library, specializes in slow-burning cigarettes, cigars and smoking accoutrements, such as cigar humidors and smoking chairs. Upstairs is the famous smoking room, where you can test your tobacco. Accessorize with the walking sticks and flasks.

Paramount Vending

297 Tenth Ave at 27th St (212-935-9577). Subway: C, E to 23rd St. Mon–Fri 10am–5pm. AmEx, MC, V.

Wondering where to get a new jukebox or a secondhand arcade game? This is the place.

Pearl Paint

308 Canal St between Broadway and Church St (212-431-7932). Subway: A, C, E, J, M, Z, N, Q, R, W, 6 to Canal St. Mon–Fri 9am–7pm; Sat 9am–6:30pm; Sun 9:30am–6pm. AmEx, Disc, MC, V.

This artist's mainstay is bigger than a supermarket and features everything you could possibly need to create your masterpiece—even if it's just in your hotel room. **Other location ●** *207 E 23rd St between Second and Third Aves (212-592-2179). Subway: 6 to 23rd St. Mon–Fri 9am–7pm; Sat 9am–6:30pm; Sun 9:30am–6pm. AmEx, Disc, MC, V.*

Quark International

537 Third Ave between 35th and 36th Sts (212-889-1808). Subway: 6 to 33rd St. Mon–Fri 10am–6:30pm; Sat noon–5pm. AmEx, DC, MC, V.

Quark is a little creepy but worth a visit if you're interested in strapping on some body armor or bugging your ex-spouse's house. The store will even custom bullet-proof your favorite jacket. It's for those with elaborate James Bond fantasies.

Rand McNally Map & Travel Store

150 E 52nd St between Lexington and Third Aves (212-758-7488). Subway: E, V to Lexington Ave–53rd St; 6 to 51st St. Mon–Fri 9am–7pm; Sat 10am–6pm; Sun noon–5pm. AmEx, Disc, MC, V.

Rand McNally stocks atlases, globes and maps, even those from rival publishers. **Other location ●** *555 Seventh Ave between 39th and 40th Sts (212-944-4477). Subway: N, Q, R, W, S, 1, 2, 3, 7 to 42nd St–Times Sq. Mon–Fri 8:30am–6pm. AmEx, Disc, MC, V.*

Sam Ash Music

155, 159, 160 and 163 W 48th St between Sixth and Seventh Aves (212-719-2299). Subway: B, D, F, V to 47–50th Sts–Rockefeller Ctr; N, R, W to 49th St. Mon–Fri 10am–8pm; Sat 10am–7pm; Sun noon–6pm AmEx, Disc, MC, V.

This 78-year-old musical-instrument emporium dominates its midtown block with four neighboring shops. New, vintage and custom guitars are available, along with amps, DJ equipment, drums, keyboards, recording equipment, turntables and all manner of sheet music. **Other locations ●** *2600 Flatbush Ave at Hendrickson Pl, Marine Park, Brooklyn (718-951-3888). Travel: 2, 5 to Flatbush Ave–Brooklyn College, then B41 bus to Kings Plaza. Mon–Fri 11am–8pm; Sat 10am–7pm; Sun noon–5pm. AmEx, Disc, MC, V.* **●** *113-25 Queens Blvd at 76th Rd, Forest Hills, Queens (718-793-7983). Subway: E, F to 75th Ave. Mon–Fri 11am–8pm; Sat 10am–7pm; Sun noon–5pm. AmEx, Disc, MC, V.*

Sony Style

550 Madison Ave between 55th and 56th Sts (212-833-8800). Subway: E, V to Fifth Ave–53rd St; N, R, W to Fifth Ave–60th St. Mon–Sat 10am–7pm; Sun noon–6pm.

For the latest from Sony, including futuristic boom boxes, paper-thin TV screens, innovative earphones and Sony's own VAIO personal computer line (created to interact with other company products), stop by this interactive midtown flagship. Downstairs, watch one of the big-screen TVs with surround sound while lounging on a Polo Ralph Lauren leather couch.

Necessities

Stack's Coin Company

*123 W 57th St between Sixth and Seventh Aves
(212-582-2580). Subway: N, Q, R, W to 57th St.
Mon–Fri 10am–5pm. Cash only.*
The oldest and largest coin dealer in the United
States, Stack's deals in rare and ancient coins from
around the world.

Tender Buttons

*143 E 62nd St between Lexington and Third Aves
(212-758-7004). Subway: F to Lexington Ave–63rd
St; 4, 5, 6 to 59th St. Mon–Fri 10:30am–6pm; Sat
10:30am–5:30pm. Cash or checks only.*
This is probably the best collection of buttons you'll
find on the Eastern seaboard. Search through dozens
of varieties of sailor buttons for your pea coat, or
ask to see the special antique collection upstairs.

Terra Verde

*120 Wooster St between Prince and Spring Sts (212-
925-4533). Subway: N, R to Prince St. Mon–Sat
11am–7pm; Sun noon–6pm. AmEx, MC, V.*
Manhattan's first eco-market combines art and
activism. Architect William McDonough renovated
this Soho space, using nontoxic building materials
and formaldehyde-free paint. Get your earth-
friendly baby stuff, linens, mattresses, organic-cot-
ton towels and solar radios here.

Tiny Doll House

*1179 Lexington Ave between 80th and 81st Sts
(212-744-3719). Subway: 6 to 77th St. Mon–Fri
11am–5:30pm; Sat 11am–5pm. AmEx, MC, V.*
Everything in this shop is tiny: miniature furniture and wares for dollhouses, including beds,
chests, cutlery and kitchen fittings. Even adults
will love it.

Toys in Babeland

*94 Rivington St at Ludlow St (212-375-1701). Subway:
F to Delancey St; J, M, Z Delancey–Essex Sts. Mon–Sat
noon–8pm; Sun noon–8pm. AmEx, MC, V.*
At this Lower East Side shop, which caters to lesbians
but accommodates all lifestyles, you can fondle sample dildos and vibrators on display. Or browse the
shelves of erotic fiction and instruction manuals.

West Marine

*12 W 37th St between Fifth and Sixth Aves (212-594-
6065). Subway: B, D, F, V, N, Q, R, W to 34th St–
Herald Sq. Mon–Fri 9:30am–6pm; Sat, Sun 10am–
2:30pm. AmEx, Disc, MC, V.*
Get basic marine supplies, deck shoes and fishing
gear, or shell out $120 to $2,000 for a Global
Positioning System.

Blades, Board and Skate

*659 Broadway between Bleecker and Bond Sts
(212-477-7350). Subway: F, V, S to Broadway–
Lafayette St; 6 to Bleecker St. Mon–Sat 10am–
9pm; Sun 11am–7pm. AmEx, Disc, MC, V.*
This is where to come for in-line skates, skateboards,

snowboards, and the requisite clothing and gear.
Check the phone book for other locations.

Gerry Cosby & Company

*3 Pennsylvania Plaza, inside Madison Square Garden
(212-563-6464, 800-548-4003). Subway: A, C, E, 1,
2, 3 to 34th St–Penn Station. Mon–Fri 9:30am–
7:30pm; Sat 9:30am–6pm; Sun noon–5pm. AmEx,
Disc, MC, V.*
Cosby features a huge selection of official team wear
and other sporting necessities. The store remains
open during—and until 30 minutes after—evening
Knicks, NY Liberty and Rangers games, just in case
you're feeling celebratory.

Niketown

*6 E 57th St between Fifth and Madison Aves (212-
891-6453, 800-671-6453). Subway: N, R, W to Fifth
Ave–60th St. Mon–Sat 10am–7pm; Sun 11am–6pm.
AmEx, DC, Disc, MC, V.*
Every 23 minutes, a huge screen drops down and
plays a Nike ad at this store, which has 1,200 models of footwear to choose from.

Paragon Sporting Goods

*867 Broadway at 18th St (212-255-8036). Subway:
L, N, Q, R, W, 4, 5, 6 to 14th St–Union Sq. Mon–Sat
10am–8pm; Sun 11:30am–7pm. AmEx, DC, Disc,
MC, V.*
Equipment and clothing for most any sport is available at this three-floor store. There's a good range of
backpacks, bikes, climbing gear, shoes, skis, surf
wear, swimwear and tennis rackets.

Tattooing was made legal in New York in April
1998; piercing is completely unregulated, so
mind your nipples.

Fun City

*94 St. Marks Pl between First Ave and Ave A (212-
353-8282). Subway: L to First Ave; 6 to Astor Pl.
Mon–Fri noon–2am; Sat, Sun noon–4am. Cash only.*
This is no doctor's office, but the folks at Fun City can
be trusted. Tattoos and custom piercings are available.

New York Adorned

*47 Second Ave between 2nd and 3rd Sts (212-473-
0007). Subway: F, V to Lower East Side–Second Ave.
Sun–Thu 1–9pm; Fri, Sat 1–10pm. AmEx, MC, V.*
The waiting area of this beautiful store looks like
the lobby of a clean hipster hotel. Along with piercing and tons of jewelry, Adorned offers tattooing
and mehndi designs.

Venus Modern Body Arts

*199 E 4th St between Aves A and B (212-473-1954).
Subway: F, V to Lower East Side–Second Ave. Sun–
Thu 1–9pm; Fri, Sat 1–10pm. AmEx, Disc, MC, V.*
Venus has been tattooing and piercing New Yorkers
since 1992, before body art became de rigueur. It
offers an enormous selection of jewelry—diamonds
in your navel and platinum in your tongue, anyone?
Piercings range from $15 to $35, plus jewelry.

Arts &
Entertainment

By Season	235
Art Galleries	244
Books & Poetry	257
Cabaret & Comedy	261
Clubs	265
Film & TV	273
Gay & Lesbian	279
Kids' Stuff	290
Music	299
Sports & Fitness	321
Theater & Dance	335

Feature boxes

State of the art	250
Halcyon days	270
Ticket info	275
Crowd pleasers	276
Critics' picks: City cinema	278
Raising the bar	282
Best of the fests	294
A noise grows in Brooklyn	306
Find your groove	313
Diamond dogs	326
You laughing at me?	336
Mark the spot	346

Butt…butt…butt Nancy Davidson's tushified weather balloons stacked up at Chelsea's Robert Miller Gallery.

Visiting NYC?

(A) For a day.

(B) For a weekend.

(C) For a week.

For answers to what to do for all of the above, log on to timeoutny.com and click on ITINERARIES. You'll find ready-made travel plans that take the guesswork out of Gotham.

timeoutny.com

Log on. Find it. Go out.

By Season

Cultural festivals, seasonal celebrations, arts extravaganzas, sports events—
New York City's agenda is jam-packed all year long

New York's mood is closely tied to the seasons. Winter's holiday parties and slushy traffic jams melt into the flowers and in-line skates of spring. Summer is hot, sweaty and slower, as garden restaurants, outdoor concerts and neighborhood fairs (not to mention air-conditioning) provide relief from the sizzling streets. The pace picks up in the fall, when New Yorkers enjoy the last of the sun's long rays and the start of the dance, opera and classical-music seasons.

Following are some of the popular and interesting regularly scheduled happenings.

Each chapter in the **Arts & Entertainment** section lists other seasonal events. Don't forget to confirm an event's cost, or whether it's still being scheduled, before you set out.

Spring

International Artexpo
Jacob K. Javits Convention Center, Eleventh Ave between 34th and 39th Sts, entrance on 37th St (800-331-5706; www.artexpos.com). Subway: A, C, E to 34th St–Penn Station. Mid-March.
The world's largest art exhibition and sale, the Artexpo features original artwork, fine-art prints, limited-edition lithographs and more by thousands of artists, from Picasso to photographer Monte Nagler. More than 40,000 people attend every year.

St. Patrick's Day Parade
Fifth Ave between 44th and 86th Sts (212-484-1222). Mar 17.
New York becomes a sea of green for the annual Irish-American day of days, starting at 11am with the parade up Fifth Avenue and extending late into the night in bars all over the city.

Ringling Bros. and Barnum & Bailey Circus
Madison Square Garden, Seventh Ave at 32nd St (212-465-6741). Subway: A, C, E, 1, 2, 3 to 34th St–Penn Station. Late Mar–mid-Apr.
This famous three-ring circus, "the Greatest Show on Earth," has been performing in New York City since 1919. Don't miss the free midnight parade of animals (through the Queens-Midtown Tunnel and along 34th Street) that traditionally opens and closes the show's run.

Whitney Biennial
Whitney Museum of American Art, 945 Madison Ave at 75th St (212-570-3600). Subway: 6 to 77th St. Late Mar–early Jun.
Every two years, the Whitney showcases what it deems to be the most important recent American art, generating much controversy in the process. The next show will be held March through May 2002.

New York International Auto Show
Jacob K. Javits Convention Center, Eleventh Ave between 34th and 39th Sts; entrance on 35th St (800-282-3336; www.autoshowny.com). Subway: A, C, E to 34th St–Penn Station. April.
More than 1,000 cars, trucks, SUVs and vans from

Body heat Floats like the SheScape make temperatures rise at the Gay Pride Parade.

Hand to mouth Meryl Streep and Kevin Kline get touchy-feely in Chekhov's *The Seagull,* performed at the 2001 New York Shakespeare Festival in Central Park.

the past, present and future are on display during this annual rite of spring.

Easter Parade
Fifth Ave between 47th and 57th Sts (212-484-1222). Subway: E, V to Fifth Ave–53rd St. Easter Sunday.
The annual Easter Parade kicks off at 11am. Try to get a spot around St. Patrick's Cathedral *(see page 74),* which is the best viewing platform—but get there early.

Williamsburg Arts and Culture Festival
Williamsburg Art & Historical Center, 135 Broadway at Bedford Ave, Williamsburg, Brooklyn (718-486-7372). Subway: L to Bedford Ave. Mid-April.

North Brooklyn's artsy neighborhood hosts fashion shows, open studio tours and other happenings at area galleries, restaurants and shops during this weekend-long festival.

New York Antiquarian Book Fair
Park Ave between 66th and 67th Sts (212-777-5218). Subway: 6 to 68th St–Hunter College. Late April.
More than 200 international booksellers exhibit rare books, maps, manuscripts and more.

You Gotta Have Park
Parks throughout the city (212-360-3456). May.
This is an annual celebration of New York's public spaces, with free events in the major parks of all five boroughs. It heralds the start of a busy

schedule of concerts and other events in green places all around the city.

Marijuana March

Starts at Washington Square Park, Washington Sq Park South at Thompson St (212-677-7180; www.cures-not-wars.org). Subway: A, C, E, F, V, S to W 4th St. First Saturday in May.

This annual parade for pot legalization is sponsored by Cures Not Wars, an advocacy group devoted to alternative drug policies. The march usually starts at Washington Square Park, but it's best to visit the Cures Not Wars website for details.

Bike New York: The Great Five Boro Bike Tour

Starts at Battery Park, finishes on Staten Island (212-932-0778; www.bikenewyork.org). Early May.

Every year, thousands of cyclists take over the city for a 42-mile (68km) bike ride through the five boroughs. Traffic is rerouted, and you'll feel like you're in the Tour de France…sort of. You must register in advance.

Bang on a Can Festival

Various venues (212-777-8442; www.bangonacan.org). Starts in early May with events throughout the year.

Think of Bang on a Can as the annual showcase for the rambunctious side of classical music. The festival highlight is the daylong BoaC Marathon, where you might catch art-music heads such as clarinetist Evan Zyporin; Sussan Deyhim, the melodic singer of Persian repertoire; and the Bang on a Can all-stars Michael Gordon, David Lang and Julia Wolfe.

Ninth Avenue International Food Festival

Ninth Ave between 37th and 57th Sts (212-581-7029). Subway: A, C, E to 42nd St–Port Authority. Mid-May.

A glorious mile of gluttony. Hundreds of stalls serve every type of food. Fabulously fattening.

Military Salute Week

See Intrepid Sea-Air-Space Museum, page 44, for listing. Last week in May.

All branches of the military visit New York for this weeklong event honoring the armed forces. U.S. Navy vessels and ships from other countries sail past the Statue of Liberty. Also, expect maneuvers, parachute drops, air displays and various ceremonies. During the week, you can visit some of the ships at Pier 86.

Lower East Side Festival of the Arts

Theater for the New City, 155 First Ave at 10th St (212-254-1109). Subway: L to First Ave; 6 to Astor Pl. Last weekend in May.

This annual arts festival and outdoor carnival celebrates the neighborhood that helped spawn the Beats, Method acting and Pop Art. It features performances by more than 20 theatrical troupes and appearances by local celebrities.

Vision Festival

Venue and festival dates change annually (www.visionfestival.org).

The Lower East Side–based Vision Festival is the only full-fledged avant-garde jazz event in town, but because of newly tight city budgets, city officials have threatened to discontinue the series. The multimedia event brings together some of the biggest talents in jazz (Peter Brøtzmann, Joseph Jarman, Matthew Shipp) with dancers, poets and visual artists.

Summer

New York City Ballet Spring Season

New York State Theater, 20 Lincoln Center Plaza, 65th St at Columbus Ave (212-870-5570). Subway: 1, 2 to 66th St–Lincoln Ctr. Late May–Jul.

The NYCB's late-spring season usually features a new ballet, in addition to repertory classics by George Balanchine and Jerome Robbins, among others *(see also page 344)*.

Metropolitan Opera Parks Concerts

Various locations (212-362-6000). June.

The Metropolitan Opera presents two different operas at open-air evening concerts in Central Park and other parks throughout the five boroughs, New Jersey and Connecticut. The performances are free. To get a good seat, you need to arrive hours early.

The New York Jazz Festival

Knitting Factory and various venues (212-219-3006; www.jazzfest.com). Early June.

This event is guaranteed to be the most sprawling of the year. Knitting Factory owner-impresario Michael Dorf mixes the biggest names in jazz (Ornette Coleman, Charlie Haden, Joe Henderson, Dave Holland, McCoy Tyner and John Zorn) with alterna-draws such as DJ Spooky, Galactic, P-Funk All-Stars, Yoko Ono and Stereolab. That's the difference between this series and that of his mentor/rival George Wein's JVC Jazz Festival *(see page 238)*.

Toyota Comedy Festival

Various locations (888-33-TOYOTA; www.toyotacomedy.com). Early to mid-June.

Hundreds of America's funniest men and women perform at venues around the city. The information line operates from May to mid-June only.

▶ Check the websites **www.timeout.com** and **www.timeout.com/newyork** for more information on seasonal events.
▶ The website of **NYC & Company**, the convention and visitors' bureau, (www.nycvisit.com) has additional info.
▶ For team-sports seasons, see chapter **Sports & Fitness**.

Arts & Entertainment

Puerto Rican Day Parade
Fifth Ave between 44th and 86th Sts (212-484-1222). Second Sunday in June.
Puerto Rican pride is on full display at this annual parade of colorful floats and marching bands.

Museum Mile Festival
Fifth Ave between 82nd and 104th Sts (212-606-2296). Second Tuesday in June.
Several major museums host this open-house festival. Crowds are attracted by the free admission and highbrow street entertainment.

JVC Jazz Festival
Various locations (212-501-1390; www.festival productions.net). Mid-June.
The JVC bash, a direct descendant of the original Newport Jazz Festival, is a city institution. Not only does the festival fill grand halls such as Carnegie and Avery Fisher with big draws (Anita Baker, Ray Charles, Harry Connick Jr., Lena Horne), it also pays tribute to jazz's roots in the city, hosting gigs in Harlem and offering half-price deals at downtown clubs, such as the Village Vanguard.

Summer Restaurant Week
Various locations (212-484-1222; www.nycvisit.com). Mid-June.
You can get a three-course prix-fixe lunch at more than 100 of the city's best restaurants for the bargain price of $20.02 (the price goes up a penny each year, in correspondence with the date).

Gay and Lesbian Pride March
From Columbus Circle, along Fifth Ave to Christopher St (212-807-7433; www.nycpride.org). Late June.
The Heritage of Pride organization rallies New York's gays and lesbians to parade from midtown to Greenwich Village to commemorate the 1969 Stonewall riots. Thousands of visitors come for the week's worth of events, which include a packed club schedule and an open-air dance party on the West Side piers.

Liberty Challenge
Pier 84 at 44th St, south of the USS Intrepid (212-580-0442; www.libertychallenge.org). Third weekend in June.
Top teams from Manhattan and around the world paddle hard in this 15-mile outrigger canoe race from lower Manhattan to the Statue of Liberty and back. Check out buff athletes from Hawaii (where the sport originated), as well as booths selling Hawaiian food and gifts, and paddling gear.

Midsummer Night Swing
Lincoln Center Plaza, Broadway between 64th and 65th Sts (212-875-5766). Subway: 1, 2 to 66th St–Lincoln Ctr. Late Jun–mid-Jul.
Dance under the stars Tuesday through Saturday beside the fountain at Lincoln Center. Each night is devoted to a different style of dance, from swing to square. If you have two left feet, don't worry—performances are preceded by free dance lessons.

Bryant Park Free Summer Season
Bryant Park, Sixth Ave at 42nd St (212-768-4242; www.bryantpark.org). Subway: B, D, F, V to 42nd St; 7 to Fifth Ave. Jun–Aug.
This reclaimed park, a lunchtime oasis for midtown's office population, is the site of a packed season of free classical music, jazz, dance and film. Best of all are the Monday-night open-air movies.

Central Park SummerStage
Rumsey Playfield, Central Park, entrance on Fifth Ave at 72nd St (212-360-2777; www.summerstage.org). Subway: 6 to 77th St. Jun–Aug.
Enjoy free weekend-afternoon concerts featuring top international performers and a wide variety of music; there are a few benefit shows for which admission is charged. Some years, dance and spoken-word events are offered on weeknights as well.

Thursday Night Concert Series
South Street Seaport, South St at Fulton St, Pier 17, main stage (212-732-7678). Subway: A, C to Broadway–Nassau St; J, M, Z, 1, 2, 4, 5 to Fulton St. Jun–Aug.
Free outdoor concerts by emerging artists—performing all types of music—are held on Thursdays throughout the summer at the South Street Seaport. (For more information on the Seaport, *see page 51*).

Celebrate Brooklyn! Performing Arts Festival
Prospect Park Bandshell, 9th St at Prospect Park West, Park Slope, Brooklyn (718-855-7882; www.celebratebrooklyn.org). Subway: F to Seventh Ave. Late Jun–late Aug Thu–Sat.
Nine weeks of free outdoor events—music, dance, film and spoken word—are presented in Brooklyn's answer to Central Park.

Mermaid Parade
Coney Island, Brooklyn (718-372-5159; www.coneyisland.com). Subway: F, Q, W to Coney Island–Stillwell Ave. Saturday after summer solstice.
If your taste runs to the wild and free, don't miss Coney Island's annual showcase of bizarreness, consisting of elaborate floats, paraders dressed as sea creatures, kiddie-costume contests and other kitschy celebrations to kick off the summer. Call for details as parade location varies from year to year.

Macy's Fireworks Display
Locations to be announced (212-494-4495). Jul 4 at 9:15pm.
The highlight of Independence Day is this spectacular fireworks display. Look up in wonder as $1 million worth of pyrotechnics light up the night.

New York Shakespeare Festival
Delacorte Theater, Central Park at 81st St (212-539-8750, 212-539-8500; www.publictheater.org). Subway: B, C to 81st St–Museum of Natural History; 6 to 77th St. Late Jun–Sept.
The free Shakespeare Festival is one of the high-

lights of a Manhattan summer, with big-name stars pulling on their tights for a whack at the Bard. There are two plays each year, with at least one written by Shakespeare *(see also page 336)*.

Nathan's Famous Fourth of July Hot Dog–Eating Contest

Nathan's Famous, 1310 Surf Ave at Stillwell Ave, Coney Island, Brooklyn (718-946-2202). Subway: F, Q, W to Coney Island–Stillwell Ave. Jul 4.
The winner of this Coney Island showdown is the man or woman who can stuff the most wieners down his or her gullet in 12 minutes.

Digital Club Festival

Various venues (www.digitalclubfestival.com). July.
This weeklong affair is organized by Knitting Factory mogul Michael Dorf and Irving Plaza founder Andrew Rasiej. It features hundreds of bands at more than 20 Manhattan venues. While the festival doesn't feature superstar headliners, it's a chance for visitors to check out an array of local talent in one pop.

Lincoln Center Festival

Lincoln Center, 65th St at Columbus Ave (212-875-5928). Subway: 1, 2 to 66th St–Lincoln Ctr. July.
Dance, music, theater, opera, kids' events and more are all part of this ambitious festival held in and around the Lincoln Center arts complex.

Washington Square Music Festival

Washington Square Park, La Guardia Pl at 4th St (212-255-4460). Subway: A, C, E, F, V, S to W 4th St. Tuesdays at 8pm in July.

This open-air concert season, featuring mainly chamber-orchestra and big-band music, has been running in Greenwich Village for years.

New York Philharmonic Concerts

Various locations (212-875-5709; www.newyork philharmonic.org). Jul, Aug
The New York Philharmonic presents a varied program, from Mozart to Weber, in many of New York's larger parks. The bugs are just part of the deal.

Seaside Summer Concert Series

Asser Levy Seaside Park, Sea Breeze Ave at Ocean Pkwy, Brighton Beach, Brooklyn (718-469-1912). Subway: F, Q to W 8th St–NY Aquarium. Jul, Aug.
Funk, soul and gospel acts perform in Brighton Beach beside the ocean during this free music series.

Mostly Mozart

Avery Fisher Hall, Lincoln Center, 65th St at Columbus Ave (212-875-5399). Subway: 1, 2 to 66th St– Lincoln Ctr. Late Jul–Aug.
For more than 35 years, the Mostly Mozart festival has mounted an intensive four-week schedule of works by the genius and his fellow Baroque wig-wearers. There are also lectures and other side attractions.

Lincoln Center Out-of-Doors

Outdoor venues in and around Lincoln Center, 65th St at Columbus Ave (212-875-5108). Subway: 1, 2 to 66th St–Lincoln Ctr. August.
The parks and plazas of Lincoln Center play host to a variety of dance and music performances, special

Music for the people Basement Jaxx ignites the crowd at Central Park's SummerStage.

Arts & Entertainment

Off the beaten path The Fringe Festival hosts avant-garde groups such as Dance in Vein.

Arts & Entertainment

events and children's entertainment during this three-week–long festival.

Central Park Zoo Chill Out Weekend

Central Park Wildlife Center; entrance on Fifth Ave at 64th St (212-861-6030). Subway: N, R, W to Fifth Ave–60th St. Early August.

Stay cool and check up on the polar bears and penguins during Central Park Zoo's annual two-day party.

Harlem Week

Throughout Harlem (212-862-8477). Subway: B, C, 1, 2, 3 to 135th St. Early to mid-August.

The largest black and Latino festival in the world features music, film, dance, fashion, exhibitions and sports. The highlight is the street festival on 135th Street from Fifth Avenue to St. Nicholas Avenue. Don't miss the jazz, gospel, salsa and R&B performances. (For more on Harlem, *see page 84.*)

Hong Kong Dragon Boat Festival

The Meadow Lake at Flushing Meadows–Corona Park, Queens (718-539-8974). Subway: 7 to Flushing–Main St. Mid-August.

This Hong Kong tradition now makes waves here. Teams from the New York area paddle colorful 39-foot teak crafts—with dragon heads at the bow and tails at the stern—to the steady banging of drums.

Fringe Festival

Various locations downtown (212-420-8877). August.

The 12-day Fringe Festival has emerged as a major venue for up-and-coming talent in the performing-arts world. There are more than 1,000 individual performers, and nearly 200 larger-scale productions.

Macy's Tap-o-Mania

Macy's Herald Square, Broadway at 34th St (212-494-5247). Subway: B, D, F, V, N, Q, R, W to 34th St–Herald Sq. Late August.

Thousands of hoofers converge outside Macy's flagship Herald Square store for this annual attempt to break the Guinness World Record for the largest assemblage of tap dancers to dance a single routine.

Panasonic Village Jazz Festival

Throughout Greenwich Village (www.villagejazz festival.com). Late August.

This seven- to ten-day festival features performers at most of the Village's jazz clubs, and includes lectures and films. It culminates in a free concert in Washington Square Park.

U.S. Open

USTA National Tennis Center, Flushing Meadows–Corona Park, Queens (info and tickets 718-760-6200). Subway: 7 to Willets Point–Shea Stadium. Late Aug–early Sept.

The final Grand Slam event of the year, the U.S. Open is also one of the most entertaining tournaments on the international tennis circuit. Tickets are hard to come by for the later rounds.

Richmond County Fair

*See **Historic Richmond Town**, page 106.*

This county fair is held over Labor Day weekend, and is just like the ones in rural America, with arts and crafts, extra-large produce and strange agricultural competitions. Admission is $6, $3 for kids and seniors.

West Indian Day Carnival
Eastern Pkwy from Utica Ave to Grand Army Plaza,
Prospec: Park, Brooklyn (718-625-1515). Subway: 1,
4 to Crown Heights–Utica Ave. Labor Day weekend.
This loud and energetic celebration of Caribbean
culture offers a children's parade on Saturday and
ends with a massive march of flamboyantly cos-
tumed revelers on Labor Day.

Fall

Downtown Arts Festival
Various lower Manhattan locations (212-243-5050;
www.simonsays.org). September.
The former Soho Arts Festival has expanded from
a September block party to a mammoth event of art
exhibitions, gallery tours and critical forums, as well
as performance-art happenings, experimental video
shows and good old-fashioned readings.

Broadway on Broadway
43rd St at Broadway (212-768-1560). Subway: N,
R, W, S, 1, 2, 3, 7 to 42nd St–Times Sq. Sunday
after Labor Day.
For one day at least, Broadway is remarkably affordable, as the season's new productions offer a free
sneak peek at their latest theatrical works right in
the middle of Times Square.

New York City Century Bike Tour
Begins at Harlem Meer, Central Park, 110th St
at Malcolm X Blvd (Lenox Ave) (212-629-8080;
www.transalt.org). Subway: 2, 3 to 110th St–Central
Park North. Early September.
This 100-mile ride through the city benefits (and is
organized by) Transportation Alternatives, a local
group dedicated to promoting cycling and making the
city safe for riders. Shorter routes are also an option.

Brooklyn BeerFest
Outside the Brooklyn Brewery, 79 North 11th St
between Wythe Ave and Berry St, Williamsburg,
Brooklyn (718-486-7422; www.brooklynbrewery.com).
Subway: L to Bedford Ave. Mid-September.
Taste more than 100 beers from around the world at
this annual ale festival hosted by the Craft Brewers
Guild and Total Beer. Industry insiders explain the
finer points of hops and barley.

Mayor's Cup
New York Harbor (212-748-8590). Subway: 4, 5 to
Bowling Green. Mid-September.
Classic schooners and yachts unfurl their sails in
this annual race.

German-American Steuben Parade
Fifth Ave from 63rd to 86th Sts (516-239-0741).
Subway: N, R, W to Fifth Ave–60th St. Sept 22.
This parade celebrates German-American contri-
butions to the American culture.

New York Is Book Country
Various locations (www.nyisbookcountry.com).
Mid- to late September.
This literary festival ends with a massive street fair
on Fifth Avenue from 48th to 57th Streets.

Feast of San Gennaro
Mulberry St from Canal to Houston Sts (212-484-
1222). Subway: J, M, Z, N, Q, R, W, 6 to Canal St.
Third week in September.
Celebrations honoring the patron saint of Naples
last ten days, from 11am to 11pm daily, with fair-
ground booths, stalls and plenty of Italian food.

Atlantic Antic
Atlantic Ave, Brooklyn (718-875-8993). Subway: M,
N, R to Court St; 1, 2, 4, 5 to Borough Hall. Last
Sunday in September.
This multicultural street fair occurs in Boerum Hill,
Brooklyn Heights, Cobble Hill and Downtown
Brooklyn along Atlantic Avenue, and features live
entertainment, vendors and art exhibitions.

BARC's Annual Dog Parade, Show and Fair
Begins at the corner of Wythe Ave and North 1st
St, Williamsburg, Brooklyn (718-486-7489;
www.barcshelter.org/events). Subway: L to Bedford
Ave. Sunday at noon in September or October.
The Brooklyn Animal Resource Coalition and the
BQE Pet Store host this event to heighten adoption
awareness. The day kicks off with a doggie parade
down Bedford Avenue, and ends with a dog show
and fair in McCarren Park. Canines vie for such
awards as "best butt" and "best kisser."

CMJ Music Marathon, MusicFest and FilmFest
Various venues (917-606-1908 ext 241; www.cmj.com).
September or October.
Hundreds of bands play during this four-day industry schmoozefest. *CMJ (College Music Journal)*
publishes trade and consumer mags that track col-
lege-radio airplay, retail sales, etc. The festival books
musicians in genres such as rock, indie rock, hip-hop
and electronica. This is one of the most important
industry showcases for music-biz pros.

New York Film Festival
Alice Tully Hall, Lincoln Center, 65th St at Broadway
(212-875-5610; www.filmlinc.com). Subway: 1, 2 to
66th St–Lincoln Ctr. Late Sept–early Oct.
One of the film world's most prestigious events,
the festival is a showcase for major directors and
new talent from around the world. American and
foreign films are given New York, U.S. or world
premieres, and the festival usually features rarely
seen classics. Tickets for films by known directors
are often hard to come by, but a limited number are
available just before the show—even for sold-out
screenings.

Columbus Day Parade
Fifth Ave between 44th and 79th Sts (212-484-1222).
Columbus Day.
To celebrate the first recorded sighting of America
by Europeans, the country gets an Italian-flavored

Arts & Entertainment

holiday (though not always a day off from work)—and the inevitable parade up Fifth Avenue.

Gotham History Festival

The Graduate Center, City University of New York, 365 Fifth Ave at 34th St (212-817-8474; www.gothamcenter.org). Early October.
Launched in 2001, this biennial celebration of New York features tours, films, exhibitions and talks (Martin Scorsese discussed his film *Gangs of New York*), as well as a conference on topics such as "Brewing and Drinking Life in New York City."

Dumbo: Art Under the Bridge

Various locations in Dumbo, Brooklyn (718-624-3772; www.dumboartscenter.org). Subway: A, C to High St; F to York St. Mid-October.
The Dumbo area of Brooklyn (Down Under the Manhattan Bridge Overpass) becomes one big art happening for a weekend. Open studios, DJs, fashion shows, music, theater, film and dance events are just some of the attractions.

Big Apple Circus

Damrosch Park, Lincoln Center, 62nd St between Broadway and Amsterdam Ave (212-721-6500). Subway: 1, 2 to 66th St–Lincoln Ctr. Late Oct–early Jan.
The audience sits within 50 feet of the lone ring at this long-running classic circus.

Halloween Parade

Starts on Sixth Ave from Broome to Spring Sts, up to 23rd St (www.halloween-nyc.com). Oct 31 at 7pm.
Anyone can participate in this parade (and about 25,000 people do every year)—just wear a costume and line up at the beginning of the route around 6pm with the rest of the fascinating characters. For more information, call *The Village Voice (212-475-3333, ext 4044; operates only in October).*

New York City Marathon

Starts at the Staten Island side of the Verrazano-Narrows Bridge (212-860-4455; www.nyc marathon.org). First Sunday in November at 10:50am.
A crowd of 30,000 marathoners runs through all five boroughs over a 26.2-mile (42km) course. The race finishes at Tavern on the Green *(see page 183)*.

Autumn Blues Festival

Symphony Space, 2537 Broadway at 95th St (212-864-5400; www.symphonyspace.org). Subway: 1, 2, 3 to 96th St. Early November.
New York is by no means a blues town comparable to Memphis or Chicago. But newly renovated Symphony Space invites blues artists—wizened living links to a vanishing rural tradition and new jacks with worldly influences—to show how they connect the dots.

Macy's Thanksgiving Day Parade

From Central Park West at 77th St to Macy's on Broadway at 34th St (212-695-4400). Thanksgiving Day at 9am.
Bring the kids to this one: The parade features enormous inflated cartoon-character balloons, elaborate floats and Santa Claus, who makes his way to Macy's,

where he'll spend the next month in Santaland. Stop by for Inflation Eve the night before to watch the balloons take shape on West 77th and 81st Streets between Central Park West and Columbus Avenue.

Winter

The Nutcracker

New York State Theater, Lincoln Center, 63rd St at Columbus Ave (212-870-5570). Subway: 1, 2 to 66th St–Lincoln Ctr. Thanksgiving–first week of January.
The New York City Ballet's performance of this famous work, assisted by students from the School of American Ballet, is a much-loved Christmas tradition *(see also City Center Theater, page 343).*

Christmas Spectacular

Radio City Music Hall, 1260 Sixth Ave at 50th St (212-247-4777). Subway: B, D, F, V to 47–50th Sts–Rockefeller Ctr. Nov–early Jan.
This famous long-running show features the fabulous high-kicking Rockettes in tableaux and musical numbers that exhaust the thematic possibilities of Christmas.

Christmas Tree Lighting Ceremony

Rockefeller Center, Rockefeller Plaza, near Fifth Ave between 49th and 50th Sts (212-484-1222). Subway: B, D, F, V to 47–50th Sts–Rockefeller Ctr. First week of December.
Five miles of lights festoon a giant evergreen in front of the GE Building. The tree, ice skaters and shimmering statue of Prometheus make this the city's most enchanting Christmas spot.

Messiah Sing-In

Avery Fisher Hall, Lincoln Center, 65th St at Columbus Ave (212-333-5333). Subway: 1, 2 to 66th St–Lincoln Ctr. Mid-December.
Around Christmas—usually a week before—the National Choral Council rounds up 17 conductors to lead huge audiences (sometimes 3,000-strong) in a rehearsal and performance of Handel's *Messiah*. No experience is necessary, and you can buy the score on-site. Call for date and time.

New Year's Eve Ball Drop

Times Square (212-768-1560; www.timessquare bid.org). Subway: N, Q, R, W, S, 1, 2, 3, 7 to 42nd St–Times Sq. Dec 31.
A traditional New York year ends and begins in Times Square, culminating with the dropping of the ball—encrusted with 504 Waterford Crystal triangles, weighing 1,070 pounds and illuminated by 600 multicolored halogen bulbs; it was created specially for the 1999–2000 bash. If teeming hordes of drunken revelers turn you on, by all means go. The surrounding streets are packed by 9pm. Expect very tight security.

New Year's Eve Fireworks

Central Park (212-860-4455). Dec 31.
The best viewing points for this explosive display are Central Park West at 72nd Street, Tavern on the

Nutty buddy The Nutcracker is a
Christmastime favorite for young and old.

Green *(see page 183)* and Fifth Avenue at 90th
Street. The fun and festivities, including hot cider
and food, start at 10:30pm.

New Year's Eve Midnight Run
*Starts at Tavern on the Green, Central Park West at
67th St (212-860-4455). Subway: B, C to 72nd St; 1,
2 to 66th St–Lincoln Ctr. Dec 31.*
A four-mile jaunt through the park, the New York
Road Runners Club's Midnight Run also features
a masquerade parade, a pre- and post-race live
DJ, fireworks *(see above listing)*, prizes and a
champagne toast at the run's halfway mark.

New Year's Day Marathon Poetry Reading
*The Poetry Project at St. Mark's Church in-the-Bowery,
131 E 10th St at Second Ave (212-674-0910;
www.poetryproject.com). Subway: 6 to Astor Pl. Jan 1.*
Big-name bohemians and downtown habitués such
as Patti Smith, Richard Hell and Richard Foreman
traditionally grace the stage for this all-day spectacle of poetry, music, dance and performance art.

Winter Antiques Show
*Seventh Regiment Armory, Park Ave at 67th St
(718-665-5250; www.winterantiquesshow.com).
Subway: 6 to 68th St–Hunter College. Mid-January.*
The city's most prestigious antiques fair has an
eclectic selection of items ranging from ancient
works to Art Nouveau. Owing to the war on terror,
the 2002 show was relocated; call or check the website for details on when it will return to the Armory.

Chinese New Year
*Around Mott St, Chinatown (212-484-1222).
Subway: J, M, Z, N, Q, R, W, 6 to Canal St. First
day of the full moon between Jan 21 and Feb 19.*
The city's Chinese population celebrates the lunar new

year in style, with dragon parades, performers and
delicious food throughout Chinatown. Unfortunately,
private fireworks were banned in 1995, so the celebrations don't have quite the bang they once did.

Outsider Art Fair
*The Puck Building, 295 Lafayette St at Houston St
(212-777-5218). Subway: F, V, S to Broadway–
Lafayette St; 6 to Bleecker St. Late January.*
A highlight of the annual art calendar, this three-
day extravaganza draws buyers and browsers from
all over the world. The fair's 35 dealers exhibit outsider, self-taught and visionary art in all media, at
prices that range from $500 to $350,000.

Winter Restaurant Week
See page 238 for listing. Late January.

Empire State Building Run-Up
*Empire State Building, 350 Fifth Ave at 34th St (212-
860-4455; www.nyrrc.org). Subway: B, D, F, V, N, Q, R,
W to 34th St–Herald Sq; 6 to 33rd St. Early February.*
This New York Road Runners race is up the 1,576
steps from the lobby to the 86th floor, a distance of
.3km. Australian Paul Crake broke his own 2000
record of 9:53 by clocking in 9:37 in 2001.

New York International Children's Film Festival
*Call for location (212-349-0330; www.gkids.com).
Early February.*
This popular festival shows films aimed at children
ages 3 to 18.

New York Independent Film and Video Festival
*Madison Square Garden, Seventh Ave at 32nd St
(212-777-7100; www.nyfilmvideo.com). Subway: A,
C, E, 1, 2, 3 to 34th St–Penn Station. Festivals held
early Feb, early Jul and mid-Sept.*
This cultural extravaganza of film, art and fashion
kicks off with a mammoth event at the Garden.
Then, for nine days, various venues around the city
hold screenings, concerts and fashion shows.

The Armory Show
Call for location (212-777-3338). Late February.
This international art festival is one of the biggest
weekends on the avant-garde calendar. The original
1913 Armory Show introduced Dada art to New
York, and this fair carries on the name and tradition
of showcasing visual groundbreakers from galleries
around the world.

The Art Show
*Seventh Regiment Armory, Park Ave at 67th St (212-
766-9200, ext 248). Subway: 6 to 68th St–Hunter
College. Late February.*
Begun in 1989 and organized by the Art Dealers
Association of America, this is one of New York's
largest art fairs. Exhibitors offer paintings, prints and
sculptures dating from the 17th century to the present.
Proceeds go to the Henry Street Settlement, a Lower
East Side arts and social-services agency.

Arts & Entertainment

Art Galleries

Chelsea may be *the* destination for art-hungry mobs, but inspired work crops up all over, from Madison Avenue to Brooklyn

Blessed with an abundance of galleries that exhibit everything from old and modern masters to contemporary experiments in new media, New York is an art lover's dream. You'll find galleries in postindustrial West Chelsea, amid the refined residences of upper Madison Avenue and among the glossy boutiques of 57th Street. But you'll also find art in areas you might not expect: in scruffy Long Island City, in the Meatpacking hinterland of the West Village—even under the ramps that lead to the Brooklyn Bridge *(see* **State of the art**, *page 250).* Real-estate values have forced relocations and forged a few new partnerships. While uptown galleries remain stable and sedate, occasionally taking on new artists, gallerists in the cast-iron district of Soho—until recently the world capital of the contemporary art market—have had to compete with mushrooming numbers of retail shops, restaurants and hotels. Consequently, all but a few Soho galleries have defected to more spacious (and ever more expensive) quarters in West Chelsea, the former warehouse district now almost entirely dedicated to the exhibition and sale of contemporary art. The few holdouts in Soho are notable though, and on weekends the neighborhood fills with a colorful mix of shoppers, tourists and art enthusiasts—often the same people.

Tribeca has its own odd assortment of small galleries and arty, fine restaurants, and with more artists priced out of Manhattan studios, the Brooklyn neighborhoods of Williamsburg and Dumbo (Down Under the Manhattan Bridge Overpass) have sprouted quirky new artist-run spaces and bona fide galleries. In fact, the New York art world's structure now resembles that of the film industry: uptown corporate studios bear names such as **Gagosian**, **Marlborough** and **PaceWildenstein**; major independent productions in Chelsea and Soho include **Cheim & Read** and **Deitch Projects**; and smaller art-house upstairs and satellite productions, such as **GAle GAtes et al.**, operate on the fringes.

There has also been a curatorial change. A number of galleries have reduced their emphasis on American (particularly New York) artists and shifted to a more global perspective. Photography continues to enjoy a renaissance, along with the emergence of so-called outsider art. And traditional, object-oriented exhibitions share the bill with multidisciplinary, often site-specific artwork that may incorporate several media at once (especially video), adding a theatrical flavor to viewing and collecting.

Gallerygoers should check the monthly notices in such magazines as *Artforum* ($8), *Flash Art* ($7), *Art in America* ($5) and *Art Now Gallery Guide* (free for the asking at most galleries or $3 at museum bookstores). If you are interested in the art market, look to the monthlies *Art and Antiques* ($4.99), *Art & Auction* ($5.95) and *ArtNews* ($6).

Opening times listed are for September to May or June. Summer visitors should keep in mind that from late June to early September, most galleries are open only on weekdays, some close for the month of August. Call before visiting.

Soho

Despite a large number of defections to Chelsea, you can still find something of interest and import on every street in Soho, along with such solid institutions as the downtown branch of the Guggenheim, the Museum for African Art and the New Museum for Contemporary Art. What follows is a selection of the better galleries in the community.

American Fine Arts, Colin deLand

22 Wooster St between Canal and Grand Sts (212-941-0401). Subway: A, C, E, J, M, Z, N, Q, R, W, 6 to Canal St. Tue–Sat noon–6pm.
Dealer Colin deLand mounts what are arguably the most unusual exhibitions in Soho. His shows retain a counter-capitalist, ad-hoc feel that belies the consistently strong quality of the work. Look for work by multimedia artist Mark Dion, filmmaker John Waters and the collective Art Club 2000. *(See also* **American Fine Arts at PHAG**, *page 246.)*

Bronwyn Keenan

3 Crosby St between Grand and Howard Sts, second floor (212-431-5083). Subway: J, M, Z, N, Q, R, W, 6 to Canal St. Sept–Jun Tue–Sat 11am–6pm. Jul, Aug Tue–Fri 11am–6pm.
Among the younger dealers in New York, Keenan may have the sharpest eye for new talent. While work can be inconsistent, shows tend to be greater

than the sum of their parts, making this gallery a worthwhile stop more often than not.

David Zwirner

43 Greene St between Broome and Grand Sts (212-966-9074). Subway: A, C, E, J, M, Z, N, Q, R, W, 6 to Canal St. Sept–May Tue–Sat 10am–6pm. Summer hours Mon–Fri 10am–6pm.

This maverick German expatriate's shop has been the hot spot on Greene Street since it opened in 1993. The shows are a barometer of what's important in art—not just in New York but internationally. The stable of talent includes Stan Douglas, Toba Khedoori, Raymond Pettibon and Jason Rhoades.

Deitch Projects

76 Grand St between Greene and Wooster Sts (212-343-7300). Subway: A, C, E, J, M, Z, N, Q, R, W, 6 to Canal St. Tue–Sat noon–6pm. Closed August.

Jeffrey Deitch is known for spotting new talent and setting trends; his openings attract stellar crowds. He continues to focus on emerging artists who create elaborate, often outrageously provocative multimedia installations. Of late, Deitch's roster of the young and hip has included street artist Barry McGee and the fabulous Vanessa Beecroft. The dealer also recently opened a larger space at 18 Wooster Street between Canal and Grand Streets *(212-941-9475).*

Nolan/Eckman

560 Broadway at Prince St, sixth floor (212-925-6190). Subway: N, R to Prince St; 6 to Spring St. Sept–Jun Tue–Fri 10am–6pm; Sat 11am–6pm. Summer by appointment only.

This small but serious gallery primarily shows works on paper by established contemporary artists from the U.S. and Europe.

Ronald Feldman Fine Arts

31 Mercer St between Canal and Grand Sts (212-226-3232). Subway: J, M, Z, N, Q, R, W, 6 to Canal St. Sept–Jun Tue–Sat 10am–6pm. Jul, Aug Mon–Thu 10am–6pm; Fri 10am–3pm.

Feldman's history in Soho is underscored by landmark shows that include such artists as Ida Applebroog, Leon Golub, Komar & Melamid and Hannah Wilke, but he also puts on more avant-garde installations by Nancy Chunn and Carl Fudge.

Chelsea

The growth of the West Chelsea art district has been nothing short of phenomenal. Until 1993, the **Dia Center for the Arts** *(see page 255)* was the area's only major claim to art. Now new galleries seem to open every month, even in the throes of a sluggish economy. All this activity has inevitably attracted trendy

Good to the last drop You'll enjoy every bit of what you see at the Andrew Kreps Gallery, where the works include Hiroshi Sunairi's psychedelic sculpture.

restaurants and shops such as Comme des Garçons *(see page 195)*, a repercussion that may, in light of Soho's recent history, overthrow art's newfound domination of the neighborhood. Presently, though, West Chelsea is the spot to see the latest in installation, painting, sculpture and video. Some galleries have such distinctive architecture that it's worth the trip just to see the spaces—and to catch the light from the nearby Hudson River. Keep in mind that the subways take you only as far as Eighth Avenue—you'll have to walk at least one long avenue farther to get to the galleries. Otherwise, catch a cab.

AC Project Room

453 W 17th St between Ninth and Tenth Aves, second floor (212-645-4970). Subway: A, C, E to 14th St; L to Eighth Ave; 1, 2 to 18th St. Tue–Sat 10am–6pm. August by appointment only.
This innovative artist-run space attracts a cross-generational mix of New York and international artists working in exciting, diverse forms. To get an insider's take on what's going on, what just happened or what will be next, visit the gallery.

Alexander and Bonin

132 Tenth Ave between 18th and 19th Sts (212-367-7474; www.alexanderandbonin.com). Subway: A, C, E to 14th St; L to Eighth Ave; 1, 2 to 18th St. Tue–Sat 10am–6pm. August by appointment only.
This long, cool drink of an exhibition space features contemporary painting, sculpture, photography and works on paper by an interesting group of international artists, including Eugenio Dittborn, Willie Doherty, Mona Hatoum, Silvia Plimack Mangold, Rita McBride, Doris Salcedo and Paul Thek.

American Fine Arts at PHAG

530 W 22nd St between Tenth and Eleventh Aves (212-727-7366). Subway: C, E to 23rd St. Tue–Sat 11am–6pm.
Vanguard gallerist Pat Hearn, who helped establish the East Village and Soho art scenes before moving to Chelsea, died in August 2000. Her art-savvy husband, Colin deLand, has taken the helm at her gallery and continues to present its roster of fine Abstractionists and Conceptualists. The building, which up until recently was known as Pat Hearn Gallery, has undergone a renovation but still exhibits works by Renee Green, Mary Heilmann, Joan Jonas and Jutta Koettker. *(See also* **American Fine Arts, Colin deLand,** *page 244.)*

Andrea Rosen Gallery

525 W 24th St between Tenth and Eleventh Aves (212-627-6000). Subway: C, E to 23rd St. Sept–Jun Tue–Sat 10am–6pm. Call for summer hours.
Count on this place to show you the young heroes of the past decade; this is where Rita Ackermann's endearing but jarring waifs, John Currin's equally

unsettling young babes, Andrea Zittel's compact model homes and Wolfgang Tillmans's uneasy fashion photos all found their way into the limelight. Recent pickups of Gillian Carnegie, Craig Kalpakjian, Michael Raedecker and Matthew Ritchie promise that the trend will continue into the 21st century.

Andrew Kreps Gallery

516A W 20th St between Tenth and Eleventh Aves (212-741-8849). Subway: C, E to 23rd St. Sept–Jul Tue–Sat 11am–6pm.
Kreps, who started his career working for Paula Cooper, has become one of the best young dealers on the Chelsea scene. Among those in his innovative stable are Ricci Albenda, Meredith Danluck and Ruth Root.

Anton Kern Gallery

532 W 20th St between Tenth and Eleventh Aves (212-965-1706). Subway: C, E to 23rd St. Sept–Jul Tue–Sat 10am–6pm.
The son of artist Georg Baselitz, Gladstone Gallery protégé Kern presents installations by young American and European artists whose futuristic, site-specific installations have provided the New York art world with some of its most visionary shows.

Barbara Gladstone

515 W 24th St between Tenth and Eleventh Aves (212-206-9300). Subway: C, E to 23rd St. Tue–Sat 10am–6pm. Summer hours Mon–Fri 10am–6pm.
Barbara Gladstone is strictly blue-chip. She presents often spectacular shows by established contemporary artists, including Vito Acconci, Matthew Barney and Anish Kapoor, and keeps an eye out for new international work.

Bill Maynes

529 W 20th St between Tenth and Eleventh Aves, eighth floor (212-741-3318). Subway: C, E to 23rd St. Sept–Jun Tue–Sat 11am–6pm. Jul Tue–Fri 11am–6pm. Closed August.
Bill Maynes is an energetic fellow whose gallery has a great view of New York Harbor. He shows painters and sculptors such as Hilary Harkness and Stephen Mueller, who take traditional media to quirky, emotionally affecting new heights.

Brent Sikkema

530 W 22nd St between Tenth and Eleventh Aves (212-929-2262). Subway: C, E to 23rd St. Tue–Sat 10am–6pm.
Formerly the owner of the late Soho gallery Wooster Gardens, Brent Sikkema followed the mass exodus to Chelsea. Here, he mounts evocative, politically charged shows of works by American and European artists, including important contemporary players Burt Barr, Arturo Herrera, Amy Sillman and Kara Walker.

Casey Kaplan

416 W 14th St between Ninth and Tenth Aves (212-645-7335). Subway: A, C, E to 14th St; L to Eighth

Ave. Sept–Jun Tue–Sat 10am–6pm. Jul Mon–Fri 10am–6pm. Closed August.

This gallery has become one of the brightest spots on the downtown art map, introducing work by artists based in New York, Los Angeles and Europe, such as Amy Adler and photographer Anna Gaskell.

Charles Cowles

537 W 24th St between Tenth and Eleventh Aves (212-925-3500; www.charlescowlesgallery.com). Subway: C, E to 23rd St. Sept–Jun Tue–Sat 10am–6pm. Jul, Aug Mon–Fri 10am–5pm.

Charles Cowles has been a defining figure in contemporary art for the past few decades, and his collection proves it. Relocated from Soho, this gallery shows paintings, sculptures, photography and installations by Charles Arnoldi, Edward Burtynsky, Beatrice Caracciolo, Vernon Fisher, Tom Holland, Doug Martin, Al Souza, among others.

Cheim & Read

547 W 25th St between Tenth and Eleventh Aves (212-242-7727). Subway: C, E to 23rd St. Tue–Sat 10am–6pm. Summer hours Mon–Fri 10am–6pm.

Louise Bourgeois and Jenny Holzer are examples of the high-profile artists that John Cheim and Howard Read (formerly of the **Robert Miller Gallery**; see page 250) have put on view in their gallery, which recently relocated from modest digs on 23rd Street. Look for a high concentration of photographers (Adam Fuss, Jack Pierson, August Sander and the like), along with contemporary sculptors and painters such as Lynda Benglis and Louise Fishman.

CRG Gallery

535 W 22nd St between Tenth and Eleventh Aves (212-229-2766; www.crggallery.com). Subway: C, E to 23rd St. Sept–May Tue–Sat 10am–6pm. Jun, Jul Mon–Fri 10am–6pm. August by appointment only.

Carla Chammas, Richard Desroche and Glenn McMillan have moved their gallery from Soho to Chelsea, and they still represent such eminent risk-takers as Robert Beck, Pia Fries, Jim Hodges, Kiki Lamers and Sandra Scolnik.

Cristinerose Gallery

529 W 20th St between Tenth and Eleventh Aves, second floor (212-206-0297). C, E to 23rd St. Tue–Sat 11am–6pm. Closed August.

This gallery consistently mounts engaging shows, spotlighting high-IQ artists whose work focuses on the materials used.

Feigen Contemporary

535 W 20th St between Tenth and Eleventh Aves (212-929-0500). Subway: C, E to 23rd St. Sept–Jun Tue–Sat 10am–6pm.

Feigen's artists include recognizable names such as Shirley Kaneda, but a new generation includes those with a California vibe. Among them are the young painter Yek and the acclaimed digital painter

Jeremy Blake, as well as photographers Peter Garfield and Doug Hall.

Fredericks Freiser

504 W 22nd St between Tenth and Eleventh Aves (212-633-6555). Subway: C, E to 23rd St. Tue–Sat 11am–6pm. August by appointment only.

Jessica Fredericks and her partner-spouse Andrew Freiser work out of this small gallery on the ground floor of townhouse-cum-art gallery. They represent mid-career and emerging artists from New York and Los Angeles; their roster includes Michael Bevilacqua, Christopher Chiappa, Julie Moos, Robert Overby, Marnie Weber and John Wesley.

Friedrich Petzel

535 W 22nd St between Tenth and Eleventh Aves (212-680-9467; www.petzel.com). Subway: C, E to 23rd St. Tue–Sat 10am–6pm. Call for summer hours.

New Yorkers have nicknamed this "the morphing gallery" for its emphasis on the conceptually based art of mutating forms, as seen in work by Jorge Pardo. With painter Richard Phillips and photographer Dana Hoey also on board, Petzel is on the leading edge of his generation of dealers.

Gagosian Chelsea

555 W 24th St between Tenth and Eleventh Aves (212-741-1111). Subway: C, E to 23rd St. Sept–Jun Tue–Sat 10am–6pm. Call for summer hours.

Larry Gagosian's humongous (20,000-square-foot) contribution to 24th Street's row of high-end galleries (for the uptown location, see page 252) was launched in 1999 with a powerful Richard Serra show. Follow-ups have included Damien Hirst and Anselm Kiefer exhibitions. Whatever he shows, you can be sure it will be big, breathtaking and expensive.

Gavin Brown's enterprise

436 W 15th St between Ninth and Tenth Aves (212-627-5258). Subway: A, C, E to 14th St; L to Eighth Ave. Tue–Sat 10am–6pm. Call for summer hours.

Londoner Gavin Brown champions young artists, and has managed to gain mass recognition for exhibitions by Elizabeth Peyton, Rob Pruitt and Rirkrit Tiravanija, while showcasing veteran talents such as Peter Doig and Stephen Pippin. Stop by to view the art and have a drink at Passerby, the gallery's chic bar.

Gorney, Bravin and Lee

534 W 26th St between Tenth and Eleventh Aves (212-352-8372). Subway: C, E to 23rd St. Sept–Jun Tue–Sat 10am–6pm. Jul Tue–Fri 10am–6pm. August by appointment only.

This large new gallery gathers the energies of own-

▶ For weekly reviews and listings, gallerygoers should pick up a copy of *Time Out New York*.

Arts & Entertainment

Direct current The DC Moore Gallery specializes in 20th-century greats, such as African-American painter Jacob Lawrence, whose work was on view in early 2002.

ers Jay Gorney, Karin Bravin and John P. Lee. Its stable of artists includes such established names as Moira Dryer, Kenneth Goldsmith, Emil Lukas, Catherine Opie and Jessica Stockholder.

Greene/Naftali
526 W 26th St between Tenth and Eleventh Aves, eighth floor (212-463-7770). Subway: C, E to 23rd St. Tue–Sat 10am–6pm. Call for summer hours.
Carol Greene's airy aerie has wonderful light, a spectacular view and a history of rock-'em–sock-'em group shows of a Conceptualist nature, as well as fine solo work by international painters and installation specialists. A roster that includes Jaqueline Humphries, Daniel Pflumm and Blake Rayne makes this a gallery that's important to watch.

Henry Urbach Architecture
526 W 26th St between Tenth and Eleventh Aves (212-627-0974). Subway: C, E to 23rd St. Tue–Sat 11am–6pm.
In 2000, this gallery remodeled its space, doubling in size for even larger and more idiosyncratic conceptual shows that usually have a photographic or architectural bent. It's great for architects who like to show their work in offbeat spaces.

Holly Solomon Gallery
Chelsea Hotel, 22 W 23rd St between Seventh and Eighth Aves, room 425 (212-924-1191). Subway: C, E, 1, 2 to 23rd St. Tue–Sat 10am–6pm. By appointment only.
The once-reigning doyenne of the Soho scene has closed her gallery and set up an office in a room at the Chelsea Hotel. Solomon may hold shows in nearby suites or other venues, but for now, viewing her remarkable stock is by appointment only.

Klemens Gasser & Tanja Grunert, Inc.
524 W 19th St between Tenth and Eleventh Aves (212-807-9494). Subway: C, E to 23rd St. Tue–Sat 10am–6pm. Call for summer hours.
Grunert and her husband Grasser ran a gallery in Cologne. Now living in New York, the couple has set up shop in Chelsea, and they continue to present consistently good shows that focus on contemporary American and European artists.

Lehmann Maupin
540 W 26th St between Tenth and Eleventh Aves (212-965-0753). Subway: C, E to 23rd St. Tue–Sat 10am–6pm. Summer hours Tue–Fri 10am–6pm. August by appointment only.

This gallery recently left its Rem Koolhaas–designed space in Soho for digs in a former Chelsea garage. But the work it exhibits remains the same: epic group shows of hip Americans and Europeans.

Luhring Augustine

531 W 24th St between Tenth and Eleventh Aves (212-206-9100). Subway: C, E to 23rd St. Sept–May Tue–Sat 10am–6pm. Jun–Aug Mon–Fri 10am–5pm.
Luhring Augustine's gracious, skylighted Chelsea gallery (designed by the area's architect of choice, Richard Gluckman) features work from an impressive index of artists that includes Americans Janine Antoni, Larry Clark, Jenny Gage, Paul McCarthy and Christopher Wool; Britons Fiona Rae and Rachel Whiteread; Germans Günther Förg and Albert Oehlen; and Swiss Pipilotti Rist.

Marlborough Chelsea

211 W 19th St between Seventh and Eighth Aves (212-463-8634). Subway: C, E to 23rd St; 1, 2 to 18th St. Tue–Sat 10am–5:30pm.
The 57th Street gallery's satellite branch displays contemporary sculpture and painting (for uptown location, see page 252).

Mary Boone

541 W 24th St between Tenth and Eleventh Aves (212-752-2929). Subway: C, E to 23rd St. Tue–Sat 10am–6pm.
See page 252 for review.

Matthew Marks

523 W 24th St between Tenth and Eleventh Aves (212-243-0200). Subway: C, E to 23rd St. Sept–May Tue–Sat 10am–6pm. Jun–Aug Mon–Fri 10am–6pm.
The ambitious Matthew Marks, a driving force behind Chelsea's transformation into an art center, has two galleries. The 24th Street gallery is a 9,000-square-foot, two-story space; the other is a beautifully lit, glass-faced converted garage. Both feature new work by contemporary painters, photographers and sculptors, including Lucian Freud, Nan Goldin, Gary Hume, Ellsworth Kelly, Tracey Moffatt and Sam Taylor-Wood.
Other location ● *522 W 22nd St between Tenth and Eleventh Aves (212-243-1650). Subway: C, E to 23rd St. Sept–May Tue–Sat 11am–6pm. Jun–Aug Mon–Fri 11am–6pm.*

Max Protetch Gallery

511 W 22nd St between Tenth and Eleventh Aves (212-633-6999). Subway: C, E to 23rd St. Sept–Jun Tue–Sat 10am–6pm; Jul Mon–Fri 10am–6pm. August by appointment only.
Max Protetch Gallery has been hosting excellent group shows of contemporary work imported from China and elsewhere. Protetch also shows important new painting, sculpture and ceramics. This is also one of the few galleries that leaves room for architectural drawings and installations.

Metro Pictures

519 W 24th St between Tenth and Eleventh Aves (212-206-7100). Subway: C, E to 23rd St. Sept–May
Tue–Sat 10am–6pm. Jun, Jul Tue–Fri 10am–6pm. August by appointment only.
This artists' playground features the vanguard work of Martin Kippenberger, Cindy Sherman and Fred Wilson, along with Carroll Dunham's wildly polymorphous painting, Mike Kelley's conflation of pathos and perversity, and Tony Oursler's eerie, eye-popping video projections. New artists to be presented here include Olaf Breuning and T.J. Wilcox.

Murray Guy

453 W 17th St between Ninth and Tenth Aves, second floor (212-463-7372; www.murrayguy.com). Subway: A, C, E to 14th St; L to Eighth Ave. Tue–Sat 10am–6pm. August by appointment only.
The dynamic Margaret Murray and Janice Guy mount elegant shows featuring such artists as Fiona Banner, Matthew Buckingham, Francis Cape, Munro Galloway and Beat Streuli.

PaceWildenstein

534 W 25th St between Tenth and Eleventh Aves (212-929-7000). Subway: C, E to 23rd St. Sept–May Tue–Fri 9:30am–6pm; Sat 10am–6pm. Jun, Jul Mon–Thu 10am–5pm; Fri 10am–4pm. Closed August.
This luxurious downtown branch of the famous 57th Street gallery is meant to house grand-scale installations by such big-time contemporaries as George Condo, Philip-Lorca DiCorcia, Sol LeWitt, Julian Schnabel, Joel Shapiro and Robert Whitman, in a plush space designed by artist Robert Irwin. (For the uptown location, see page 252.)

Paula Cooper Gallery

534 W 21st St between Tenth and Eleventh Aves (212-255-1105). Subway: C, E to 23rd St. Tue–Sat 10am–6pm. Jun–Aug Mon–Fri 10am–5pm.
Cooper opened the first art gallery in Soho and, as an early settler in West Chelsea, built one of the more impressive temples of art. Now, perhaps to compete with other big names in the area, she's opened a second space across the street. She is known for showcasing predominantly Minimalist, largely conceptual work. Artists whose careers have flourished under her administration include Carl Andre, Jonathan Borofsky, Sherrie Levine, Rudolf Stingel and Dan Walsh, as well as photographers Zoe Leonard and Andres Serrano.
Other location ● *521 W 21st St between Tenth and Eleventh Aves (212-255-5247). Subway: C, E to 23rd St. Tue–Sat 11am–5pm. Jun–Aug Mon–Fri 10am–5pm.*

Paul Kasmin

293 Tenth Ave at 27th St (212-563-4474). Subway: C, E to 23rd St; 1, 2 to 28th St. Sept–Jun Tue–Sat 10am–6pm. Jul–mid-Aug Mon–Fri 10am–6pm.
Another dealer who fled Soho's shopping hordes, Kasmin puts on group shows involving up-and-

> ▶ If you want to view larger collections of art, see chapter **Museums**.

coming artists and more established names such as Donald Baechler, Caio Fonseca and Mark Innerst. Look for solo exhibitions by James Nares, Elliott Puckette, Aaron Rose, Nancy Rubins and Alessandro Twombly, whose reputations—and prices—increase with each reappearance.

Paul Morris Gallery

465 W 23rd St between Ninth and Tenth Aves (212-727-2752). Subway: C, E to 23rd St. Sept–Jun Tue–Sat 11am–6pm. Jul, Aug Mon–Fri 11am–6pm.
Paul Morris's gallery in Chelsea's London Terrace complex is a shoebox compared to his former digs on 20th Street, but his roster of emerging talent makes the art that's exhibited in the larger neighboring galleries look terribly old-hat.

Postmasters Gallery

459 W 19th St between Ninth and Tenth Aves (212-727-3323). Subway: C, E to 23rd St; 1, 2 to 18th St. Tue–Sat 11am–6pm. Closed August.
Postmasters is an intriguing international gallery run by Magdalena Sawon. She presents techno-savvy art, most of which has Conceptualistic leanings. Artists include E.C. Armstrong, Spencer Finch, Christian Schumann, Wolfgang Staehle and Claude Wampler.

Robert Miller Gallery

524 W 26th St between Tenth and Eleventh Aves (212-366-4774). Subway: C, E to 23rd St. Sept–May Tue–Sat 10am–6pm. Call for summer hours.
This former 57th Street stalwart contracted the Chelsea bug. At Miller's new space, you'll see work you might otherwise expect to see in a museum: Al Held, Lee Krasner, Alice Neel and Philip Pearlstein, as well as photographers such as Diane Arbus, John Clarence Laughlin and Bruce Weber.

Sean Kelly

528 W 29th St between Tenth and Eleventh Aves (212-239-1181). Subway: A, C, E to 34th St–Penn Station. Sept–Jun Tue–Sat 11am–6pm. Jul–mid-Aug Mon–Fri 10am–5pm.
This Brit expat's project-oriented gallery offers exhibitions by established Conceptualists, including Marina Abramovic, Ann Hamilton and Lorna Simpson, and showcases emerging talents such as James Casebere, Cathy de Monchaux and Frank Theil.

Sonnabend Gallery

536 W 22nd St between Tenth and Eleventh Aves (212-627-1018). Subway: C, E to 23rd St. Sept–Jul Tue–Sat 10am–6pm. August by appointment only.

State of the art

Beyond Chelsea, art enclaves are emerging in Harlem, Queens and Brooklyn

For decades, the New York art world has been centered in single neighborhoods: In the 1950s, galleries were found mostly in midtown and on the Upper East Side. In the late 1970s and '80s, a new generation of do-it-yourself dealers started popping up on the Lower East Side before they migrated to the abandoned factories of Soho. More recently, New York galleries began lining the streets of Chelsea (between Tenth and Eleventh Avenues), giving the district the airy glamour of a Hollywood studio lot.

But today, there's the sense that important, innovative galleries and museums might turn up *anywhere*. The scene creating the greatest buzz is uptown, around 125th Street. In particular, the **Studio Museum in Harlem** *(see page 37)* is full of youthful promise, due to the arrival of curator Thelma Golden. Formerly of the Whitney Museum of American Art, Golden made her mark in 2001 with the show "Freestyle," a showcase of artists on the rise—and racial issues were far from the only matter of importance. (Golden introduced the term "postblack" to describe

the artists' work, a slightly tongue-in-cheek term that has been much-discussed ever since.) The vibrant exhibition, accompanied by a catalog of essays by up-and-coming critics, made it clear that any person who wants to know what's happening in contemporary art must visit the museum's galleries. During the summer, the museum exhibits work from its prestigious Artist-in-Residence Program, which has launched the careers of numerous art stars, including Willie Cole, Alison Saar and Nari Ward.

Also in the neighborhood: the nascent gallery **The Project** *(427 W 126th St between Morningside and Amsterdam Aves, 212-662-8610)*, which opened under the direction of writer and dealer Christian Haye. She brings the jet-setting feel of the global art community to Harlem. Among standouts in the gallery's index are digital artist Paul Pfeiffer (who won a prize for his work at the 2000 Whitney Biennial) and painter Julie Mehretu.

Farther uptown, the newly minted **Sugar Hill Arts Center** *(3658 Broadway at 151st St, 212-491-5890)* features four galleries that display everything from French furniture

This elegant old standby has also taken flight from Soho to Chelsea. Look for strong new work from John Baldessari, Ashley Bickerton, Gilbert & George, Haim Steinbach and Matthew Weinstein.

Sperone Westwater

415 W 13th St between Ninth and Tenth Aves, second floor (212-431-3685). Subway: A, C, E to 14th St; L to Eighth Ave. Sept–Jun Tue–Sat 10am–6pm. Jul, Aug Mon–Fri 10am–6pm.
Sperone Westwater has abandoned Soho for a brand-new 15,000-square-foot space in Chelsea. This stronghold of painting shows work by Italian neo-Expressionists Luigi Ontani and Mimmo Paladino, along with other contemporaries such as Jonathan Lasker, Frank Moore, Malcolm Morley, Susan Rothenberg and Richard Tuttle.

Tanya Bonakdar Gallery

521 W 21st St between Tenth and Eleventh Aves (212-414-4144; www.tanyabonakdargallery.com). Subway: C, E to 23rd St. Sept–Jun Tue–Sat 10am–6pm. Jul, Aug Mon–Fri 10am–6pm.
In her dreamy, skylighted Chelsea gallery, Bonakdar presents odd, often disturbing—and just as often distinguished—installations by such vanguard artists as Uta Barth, Mat Collishaw,

Mark Dion, Olafur Eliasson, Sabine Hornig and Ernesto Neto.

303 Gallery

525 W 22nd St between Tenth and Eleventh Aves (212-255-1121). Subway: C, E to 23rd St. Tue–Sat 10am–6pm. Call for summer hours.
This savvy gallery features critically acclaimed international artists working with diverse media. They include photographers Thomas Demand, Maureen Gallace and Collier Schorr; sculptor Daniel Oates; painters Inka Essenhigh, Karen Kilimnik and Sue Williams; and video artist Doug Aitken, winner of the 1999 Venice Biennale Grand Prize. To experience essential contemporary art, one must visit 303.

Venetia Kapernekas Fine Arts, Inc.

526 W 26th St between Tenth and Eleventh Aves, suite 814 (212-462-4150). Subway: C, E to 23rd St. Tue–Sat 11am–6pm.
This gallery adds flair to an already art-packed building, hanging cross-generational shows that mix the work of young New York and Los Angeles artists, such as Glenn Kaino, with that of the more established, such as multimedia artist Meg Cranston.

design to paintings by New York–based artists. Its roof garden and outdoor sculpture garden are open year-round.

The important of Long Island City's **P.S. 1 Contemporary Art Center** continues to grow *(see* **Museum of Modern Art**, *page 35).* Since reopening in 2000 (after being acquired by MoMA), the center has featured exhibitions of artists from around the globe—encouraging New Yorkers to go to Queens for rare looks at such artists as the recent Venice Biennale star Janet Cardiff and Tokyo's video DJ Prince Tongha. P.S. 1 also sponsors experimental architecture projects and deejayed events during the summer as part of its "Warm Up" series *(see* **Culture clubbing**, *page 36).* The art center proved its commitment to younger artists at home with the landmark show, "Greater New York." The exhibition, like many others organized by P.S. 1 (which also has a prestigious studio program), spotlighted many artists who have since gone on to national and international acclaim—Cecily Brown and Rob Pruitt included. The outer-borough energy will be amplified by the arrival of MoMA QNS, which opens in the summer of 2002, while MoMA's headquarters in Manhattan undergoes a major three-year expansion-and-renovation project.

The ever-expanding scene in Brooklyn's Dumbo neighborhood is just as vibrant, if more grass-roots. Its galleries feature artists who haven't even cracked the local Williamsburg scene—but who are definitely ones to watch. Among the nonprofit spaces, there are the **Dumbo Arts Center** *(30 Washington St between Plymouth and Water Sts, 718-694-0831),* which often features group shows, and **GAle GAtes et al.** *(see page 253),* which, while showcasing multimedia theatrical productions and performances, is becoming known in the art world for its "Emerging Curators" series. Also making waves is **Mastel + Mastel** *(70 Washington St between Front and York Sts, seventh floor, 646-452-1300),* a gallery that recently teamed with local new-media studios to present "Digital Dumbo," a festival that offered an insider's view of computer-savvy art and the people who make it. Also watch for summer shows of outdoor sculpture at the nearby **Empire-Fulton-Ferry State Park** *(located under the Brooklyn Bridge at 23 Dock St, 718-858-4708).*

Despite all these art outposts throughout the city, Chelsea remains the elite-art nexus. However, gallerygoers who explore beyond downtown Manhattan will surely be rewarded for their efforts—maybe even beating Chelsea to "the next big thing."

Arts & Entertainment

57th Street

The home of Carnegie Hall, exclusive boutiques and numerous art galleries, 57th Street is a beehive of cultural and commercial activity—ostentatious and expensive, but fun.

DC Moore Gallery

724 Fifth Ave between 56th and 57th Sts, eighth floor (212-247-2111; www.artnet.com/dcmoore.html). Subway: E, V to Fifth Ave–53rd St; N, R, W to Fifth Ave–60th St. Tue–Sat 10am–5:30pm. Closed later half of August.

This airy gallery, overlooking Fifth Avenue, shows prominent 20th-century and contemporary artists, such as Milton Avery, David Bates, Paul Cadmus, Artemis Greenberg, Robert Kushner and Jacob Lawrence.

Marian Goodman

24 W 57th St between Fifth and Sixth Aves, fourth floor (212-977-7160; www.mariangoodman.com). Subway: F to 57th St. Mon–Sat 10am–6pm. Closed August.

Works by acclaimed European contemporary painters, sculptors and conceptualists predominate here, usually in striking installations. The impressive roster of gallery artists includes Christian Boltanski, Maurizio Cattelan and Gerhard Richter, as well as Juan Muñoz, Gabriel Orozco and Jeff Wall. Marian Goodman is one of the savviest dealers in the world, and her gallery is a 57th Street must-see.

Marlborough

40 W 57th St between Fifth and Sixth Aves, second floor (212-541-4900). Subway: F to 57th St. Mid-Sept–mid-Jun Mon–Sat 10am–5:30pm. Late Jun–early Sept Mon–Fri 10am–5:30pm.

Modernist bigwigs are the byword at this monolithic international gallery. On view are works by Fernando Botero, Red Grooms, R.B. Kitaj, Marisol, Larry Rivers and many more. **Marlborough Graphics**, at the same address, is just as splendid. (For the Chelsea location, see page 249.)

Mary Boone

745 Fifth Ave between 57th and 58th Sts, fourth floor (212-752-2929). Subway: E, V to Fifth Ave–53rd St; N, R, W to Fifth Ave–60th St. Tue–Sat 10am–6pm.

This former Soho celeb continues to have hit shows uptown, even though her strongest commitment is to her newly opened gallery in Chelsea, see page 249. Her list of contemporary artists includes Ross Bleckner, Barbara Kruger and hipster Damian Loeb. Boone also occasionally showcases the ideas of independent curators; their stellar group shows include new works in painting, photography and sculpture.

PaceWildenstein

32 E 57th St between Madison and Park Aves (212-421-3292; www.pacewildenstein.com). Subway: N, R, W to Fifth Ave–60th St; 4, 5, 6 to 59th St. Sept–May Tue–Fri 9:30am–6pm; Sat 10am–5:30pm. Call for summer hours.

This gallery giant offers pieces by some of the 20th century's most significant artists: Picasso, Mark Rothko, Ad Reinhardt, Lucas Samaras, Agnes Martin and Chuck Close, along with Julian Schnabel, Kiki Smith and Elizabeth Murray. **Pace Prints and Primitives**, at the same address, publishes prints—from Old Masters to big-name contemporaries—and has a fine collection of African art. (For the Chelsea branch, see page 249.)

Van Doren

730 Fifth Ave at 57th St, seventh floor (212-445-0444). Subway: E, V to Fifth Ave–53rd St; N, R, W to Fifth Ave–60th St. Tue–Sat 10am–6pm. Summer hours Mon–Fri 10am–5:30pm.

The name might sound a little like that of a law firm, but this gallery represents such diverse artists as Roy Lichtenstein and Dorothea Rockburne, plus younger talent that includes on-the-rise painter Benjamin Edwards.

Upper East Side

Most galleries on the Upper East Side are well-established and sell masterpieces priced for millionaires. Still, anyone can look for free, and many works are treasures that could swiftly vanish into someone's private collection. Check the auction-house ads for viewing schedules of important collections before they go on the block.

Gagosian

980 Madison Ave at 76th St (212-744-2313). Subway: 6 to 77th St. Tue–Sat 10am–6pm. Summer hours Mon–Fri 10am–6pm.

The prince of the 1980s scene, Larry Gagosian is still one of New York's major players in contemporary art, showing new work by such artists as Francesco Clemente, Damien Hirst, David Salle, Richard Serra and new star Cecily Brown. He has also been hugely successful in the resale market and has a gigantic new gallery in Chelsea *(see page 247).*

Leo Castelli

59 E 79th St between Madison and Park Aves (212-249-4470). Subway: 6 to 77th St. Tue–Sat 10am–6pm. Summer hours Mon–Sat 11am–5pm.

Castelli returned his operation to its original uptown space shortly before he died in 1999. The world-famous dealer was known for representing such seminal Pop figures as Jasper Johns, Roy Lichtenstein and James Rosenquist, as well as Conceptual artists Joseph Kosuth and Lawrence Weiner. This spot seems more like a museum than a gallery.

Michael Werner

4 E 77th St between Fifth and Madison Aves (212-988-1623). Subway: 6 to 77th St. Sept–May Mon–Sat 10am–6pm. Jun–Aug Mon–Fri 10am–6pm.

In 2000, Werner relocated his gallery to a townhouse slightly grander than the previous one. It's a genteel

Bibliotheque Style makes a statement at Dia Center for the Art's retro-designed bookstore.

addition to his successful operation in Germany, offering finely curated exhibitions of work by such protean European art stars as Georg Baselitz, Marcel Broodthaers and Markus Lupertz.

M. Knoedler & Co.
19 E 70th St between Fifth and Madison Aves (212-794-0550). Subway: 6 to 68th St–Hunter College. Sept–May Mon–Fri 9:30am–5:30pm; Sat 10am–5:30pm. Jun–Aug Mon–Sat 9:30am–5:30pm.
Knoedler represents well-known Abstractionists and Pop artists, including Helen Frankenthaler, Nancy Graves, David Smith, Frank Stella and Donald Sultan, as well as a selection of emerging artists.

Salander-O'Reilly Galleries
20 E 79th St between Fifth and Madison Aves (212-879-6606). Subway: 6 to 77th St. Sept–Jun Mon–Sat 9:30am–5:30pm. Jul Mon–Fri 9:30am–5:30pm. Closed August.
An extensive artist base, including important European and American Realists, makes these museum-quality galleries a must-visit.

Yoshii
17 E 76th St between Fifth and Madison Aves (212-744-5550). Subway: 6 to 77th St. Mon–Fri 10am–6pm by appointment. Call for summer hours.
A recent relocation from 57th Street has not affected the nature of this small gallery. Yoshii presents terrific 20th-century surveys of work by such important Modernists as Giacometti and Picasso, and it occasionally features lively shows by contemporary artists in painting, photography and sculpture.

Zwirner & Wirth
32 E 69th St between Madison and Park Aves (212-517-4178). Subway: 6 to 68th St–Hunter College. Tue–Sat 10am–6pm.
After prospering in Soho, gallerist David Zwirner opened a space uptown in 1999 with a partner from Switzerland. This gallery is devoted to blue-chip contemporary artists such as Dan Flavin, Martin Kippenberger and Bruce Nauman. A recent show, "The Proper Meaning," included the works of 20th-century Surrealists Hans Bellmer, Max Ernst and Robert Gober.

Brooklyn

Artists living and working in the postindustrial blue-collar neighborhoods of Brooklyn have created a new gallery scene. Sponsored by the Dumbo Arts Center, area artists hold group exhibitions in their studios or at art fairs on occasional summer weekends *(see **State of the art**, page 250).* Williamsburg, long known as a flourishing but insular artist's community, has undergone gentrification: One subway stop from Manhattan, the neighborhood offers worthwhile galleries mixed in with the many new restaurants and boutiques. Brooklyn may be the best place to see on-the-verge artists without undue hype and high price tags.

GAle GAtes et al.
37 Main St between Front and Water Sts, Dumbo (718-522-4596). Subway: A, C to High St; F to York St. Wed–Sat noon–6pm.

The first and most energetic gallery to open in Dumbo, this huge nonprofit complex on the Brooklyn waterfront hosts group exhibitions and performances by a wide variety of local and international artists.

Momenta
72 Berry St between North 9th and North 10th Sts, Williamsburg (718-218-8058). Subway: L to Bedford Ave. Mon–Fri noon–6pm.
Arguably the most professional and imaginative organization in Williamsburg, Momenta presents strong solo and group exhibitions by an exhilarating mix of emerging artists. Catch their dynamic work here before it's snapped up by Manhattan dealers.

Pierogi 2000
177 North 9th St between Bedford and Driggs Aves, Williamsburg (718-599-2144). Subway: L to Bedford Ave. Sept–Jul Mon–Fri noon–6pm and by appointment. Closed August.
As one of the first art spaces to open in Williamsburg, this artist-run gallery tends to attract the whole neighborhood.

Roebling Hall
390 Wythe Ave at South 4th St, Williamsburg (718-599-5352). Subway: J, M, Z to Marcy Ave. Sat–Mon noon–6pm.
Directors Joel Beck and Christian Viveros-Fauné cook up provocative shows of emerging artists at this Williamsburg hot spot—a must-see on the Brooklyn gallery circuit. Talents include Adriana Arenas, Sebastiaan Bremer, Christoph Draeger, David Opdyke and Nick O'Shea.

The Rotunda Gallery
33 Clinton St between Cadman Plaza West and Pierrepont St, Brooklyn Heights (718-875-4047; www.brooklynx.org/rotunda). Subway: M, N, R to Court St; 1, 2, 4, 5 to Borough Hall. Tue–Fri noon–5pm; Sat 11am–4pm. Closed Jul, Aug.
This beautiful Brooklyn Heights gallery is the borough's foremost nonprofit exhibition space. Monthly shows feature innovative sculpture, painting, site-specific installation, photography and video by Brooklyn-based artists, always in top-notch presentations.

Nonprofit spaces

Apex Art
291 Church St between Walker and White Sts (212-431-5270). Subway: 1, 2 to Franklin St. Tue–Sat 11am–6pm. Closed August.
At this unconventional gallery, the inspiration comes from independent critics, curators and artists who experiment with a variety of media in cleverly themed shows. Some exhibitions are chosen by anonymous submission to a jury of previous curators. The results are always unpredictable: The work rarely follows prevailing fashions; more often than not, it anticipates them.

Art in General
79 Walker St between Broadway and Lafayette St (212-219-0473; www.artingeneral.org). Subway: J, M, Z, N, Q, R, W, 6 to Canal St. Tue–Sat noon–6pm. Closed Jul, Aug.
Now celebrating its 21st year, Art in General features shows by artists both local and internation-

Pale fire White Columns often shakes up the art world with pieces by young unknowns.

al. One recent key exhibition provided America's first look at the internationally acclaimed Cuban artist Tonel.

Artists Space

38 Greene St between Broome and Grand Sts, third floor (212-226-3970; www.artistsspace.org). Subway: A, C, E, J, M, Z, N, Q, R, W, 6 to Canal St. Tue–Sat 11am–6pm. Closed August.
Director Barbara Hunt has steered this 1970s haunt into the new millennium, with programs discussing digital technology and the business of running a nonprofit art space. Exhibitions are organized by up-and-coming curators.

Dia Center for the Arts

548 W 22nd St between Tenth and Eleventh Aves (212-989-5566; www.diacenter.org). Subway: C, E to 23rd St. Wed–Sun noon–6pm. Closed mid-Jun–Aug. $6, seniors and students $3, children under 10 free.
Dia is about the closest thing New York has to a European-style Kunsthalle. While it isn't a museum, the center offers each of its floors to an especially timely artist, or to an artist who deserves a closer or second look. Among them have been Alfred Jensen, Jorge Pardo and Bridget Riley.

The Drawing Center

35 Wooster St between Broome and Grand Sts (212-219-2166; www.drawingcenter.org). Subway: A, C, E, J, M, Z, N, Q, R, W, 6 to Canal St. Tue–Fri 10am–6pm; Sat 11am–6pm. Closed August.
The Drawing Center has put together exceptionally strong programs over the past five years. One season, it featured a landmark show of Situationist architect Constant; the next, a gorgeous survey of Henri Michaux.

Exit Art: The First World

548 Broadway between Prince and Spring Sts, second floor (212-966-7745). Subway: F, V, S to Broadway–Lafayette St; N, R to Prince St; 6 to Bleecker St. Tue–Fri 10am–6pm; Sat 11am–6pm. Call for summer hours.
Exit Art often features sprawling exhibitions that wrestle with a big topic, whether it's genetic engineering and art, or the history of artist-run spaces. Yet the gallery is also renowned for its surveys of younger artists: a first look at the who's who of tomorrow.

Grey Art Gallery at New York University

100 Washington Sq East between Washington and Waverly Pls (212-998-6780; www.nyu.edu/greyart). Subway: A, C, E, F, V, S to W 4th St; N, R to 8th St–NYU. Tue, Thu, Fri 11am–6pm; Wed 11am–8pm; Sat 11am–5pm. Closed mid-July–Aug. Suggested donation $2.50.
NYU's museum-laboratory has a collection of nearly 6,000 works covering the entire range of visual art. Exhibition subjects run from fine art and cultural trends to offbeat personalities in the history of art.

International Center of Photography

1133 Sixth Ave at 43rd St (212-860-0000; www.icp.org). Subway: B, D, F, V to 42nd St; 7 to Fifth Ave. Tue–Thu 10am–5pm; Fri 10am–8pm; Sat, Sun 10am–6pm. Suggested donation $9, seniors and students $6.
The International Center of Photography is growing along with photography's prestige. Its galleries, once split between midtown and uptown locations, are now consolidated in the expanded and redesigned midtown building, which reopened in November 2000 with shows of work by Annie Leibovitz and Lorie Novak. Having outgrown its uptown landmark building *(1130 Fifth Ave at 94th St)*, the center has moved its school and library containing thousands of biographical and photographic files, as well as back issues of photography magazines, to a new midtown facility. Begun in the 1960s as the International Fund for Concerned Photography, ICP contains work by photojournalists Werner Bischof, Robert Capa, David Seymour and Dan Weiner, all of whom were killed on assignment. Their work was preserved and exhibited by Cornell Capa, Robert's brother, who went on to found the ICP in 1974. It's no surprise that exhibitions are strong on news and documentary photography. Two floors of exhibition space are for retrospectives devoted to single artists, such as the notorious Weegee.

Sculpture Center

44-19 Purves St at Jackson Ave, Long Island City, Queens (718-361-1750). Subway: E, V to 23rd St–Ely Ave. Wed–Sun noon–6pm. Closed mid-Jul–Aug.
Formerly located on the Upper East Side, this gallery remains one of the best places to see work by emerging and mid-career sculptors. Its new digs in Queens will be closed for renovation until September 2002, but you can bet opening exhibitions will be worth the wait.

White Columns

320 W 13th St between Eighth Ave and Hudson St (212-924-4212). Subway: A, C, E to 14th St; L to Eighth Ave. Wed–Sun noon–6pm. Closed August.
Young gallery director Lauren Ross always ensures that the very newest talent and takes on art will appear in the quirkily curated shows at White Columns.

Photography

In the past decade, there has been a renewal of interest in art photography in New York, along with notable strides forward in the medium. For

▶ For more sites in the Brooklyn area, see chapter **The Outer Boroughs, Brooklyn.**
▶ For the best of Brooklyn nightlife, see chapter **Night Train to Brooklyn.**

Buggin' out The ants go marching one by one at the nonprofit gallery Exit Art.

an overview, look for the bimonthly directory *Photography in New York International* ($4).

Ariel Meyerowitz
580 Broadway between Houston and Prince Sts (212-625-3434). Subway: F, V, S to Broadway–Lafayette St; N, R to Prince St; 6 to Spring St. Wed–Sat 11am–6pm; Tuesday by appointment. Call for summer hours.
Ariel Meyerowitz was associate director of the James Danziger Gallery for many years before it closed. Now on her own, she is establishing herself at the forefront of photography gallerists.

Edwynn Houk Gallery
745 Fifth Ave between 57th and 58th Sts, fourth floor (212-750-7070). Subway: N, R, W to Fifth Ave–60th St. Sept–Jul Tue–Sat 11am–6pm. Call for summer hours.
This highly respected specialist in vintage and contemporary photography shows such artists as Brassaï, Lynn Davis, Elliott Erwitt, Dorothea Lange, Annie Leibovitz, Danny Lyon, Sally Mann, Man Ray and Alfred Stieglitz, each commanding top dollar.

Howard Greenberg & 292 Gallery
120 Wooster St between Prince and Spring Sts, second floor (212-334-0010). Subway: C, E, 6 to Spring St; N, R to Prince St. Tue–Sat 10am–6pm. Call for summer hours.
These connecting galleries exhibit one enticing show after another of 20th-century photographers, including Berenice Abbot, Imogen Cunningham, Robert Frank, William Klein and Ralph Eugene Meatyard.

International Center of Photography
See page 255 for review.

Janet Borden
560 Broadway at Prince St, sixth floor (212-431-0166). Subway: N, R to Prince St. Tue–Sat 11am–5pm. Jul Tue–Fri 11am–5pm. Closed August.
No tour of contemporary photography can be complete without a visit to this Soho stalwart, where the latest work by Tina Barney, Jan Groover, Sandy Skoglund and Oliver Wassow, among others, is regularly on view.

Julie Saul Gallery
535 W 22nd St between Tenth and Eleventh Aves (212-431-0747). Subway: C, E to 23rd St. Jul–Jun Tue–Sat 11am–6pm. Jul, Aug Tue–Fri 11am–6pm.
Come here for well-conceived contemporary photography shows featuring clean, smart installations.

Pace/MacGill
32 E 57th St between Madison and Park Aves, ninth floor (212-759-7999). Subway: N, R, W to Lexington Ave–59th St; 4, 5, 6 to 59th St. Sept–late Jun Tue–Fri 9:30am–5:30pm; Sat 10am–6pm. Late Jun–Aug Mon–Thu 9:30am–5:30pm; Fri 9am–4pm.
This gallery never misses. Look for well-known names such as Walker Evans, Robert Frank, Irving Penn and William Wegman, in addition to ground-breaking contemporaries such as Kiki Smith.

Yancey Richardson Gallery
535 W 22nd St between Tenth and Eleventh Aves, third floor (212-343-1255). Subway: C, E to 23rd St. Sept–Jun Tue–Sat 11am–6pm. Jul, Aug Tue–Fri noon–6pm.
This Soho transplant has an impressive range of vintage, contemporary and often experimental American, European and Japanese photography.

Books & Poetry

As the undisputed capital of publishing in the United States, New York has a literary scene that offers lots of entertaining reading and writing

"It's not the easiest place in which to pursue a creative career," says New York novelist and former sex worker Tracy Quan, "but it feels like it is the *only* place."

And indeed it is.

New York has always been a bookish town, a place where the published few are sought-after guests at dinner parties, and where best-selling authors and up-and-comers gather at writers' haunts like the restaurants **Elaine's** *(see page 186)* and **The Half King** to exchange gossip and be seen. "This is a city in which you can reinvent yourself, and it's also a place where people are in each others' faces, up against each other all the time," says Quan, author of *Diary of a Manhattan Call Girl.* "Because of that, opportunities arise where you can make connections."

As the publishing capital of the United States, New York creates literary stars the way Los Angeles creates movie stars. Million-dollar advances and Hollywood options bring fame and gossip-column coverage to select authors (and, in some cases, to their editors). "If you're willing to work very hard and take risks," says Quan, "New York allows you to find success."

But you don't have to be part of the literati to get literary satisfaction in New York. Whether you want to hear high-profile novelists reading from their latest works at **Barnes & Noble**, poets getting iambic at **KGB**, or speakers dazzling (or boring) audiences with intellectual pyrotechnics at the **92nd Street Y**, there's always a literary event going on in New York, often for free. Indeed, these events are among the best entertainment deals in the city.

Spoken word remains a popular New York pastime, even if MTV doesn't care about it anymore and the Gap has retired its spoken-word television commercials. The genre's mainstay events are "slams," in which selected audience members award points to competing poets, and open-mike nights, when would-be Walt Whitmans get five minutes to slam the body electric. Dead poets (and novelists) get an airing too, at marathon readings, a New York tradition. Annual readings often star a stream of big-name personalities. Past readers at **Symphony Space**'s Joycean Bloomsday event *(see Selected Shorts, page 259)* have included Robert MacNeil and Charlotte Moore. You can

also celebrate Good Friday (on Thursday) with a reading of Dante's *Inferno* at the **Cathedral of St. John the Divine**, complete with devil's food cake. Also at St. John is the Muriel Rukeyser Poetry Wall, where all are invited to submit works; and the American Poets' Corner, a celebration of the greatest wordsmiths this country has ever produced. In addition, watch for marathon readings, which are usually held in celebration of a literary anniversary.

New York's bookstores—especially the superstores—have become meccas for anyone seeking a good read, a cappuccino and a comfortable chair. Some of these stores are known among bookishly inclined lonely hearts as pickup spots (a few Barnes & Noble outlets stay open until midnight). Many host author readings, talks and signings, and discussions. **The New York Public Library**, not surprisingly, also hosts readings, which are listed in the brochure *Events for Adults* (available free at all branches). In April, poets read throughout the city for National Poetry Month, and the last Sunday in September is the festival New York Is Book Country *(see page 241).*

Author readings

In today's hypercompetitive publishing climate, where books either make the best-seller lists or die in the remainder bins, authors clamor for the chance to promote their latest titles at bookstores, some of which schedule almost daily events. These are always free, usually in the early evening. At the superstores, events range from low- to

▶ For the most comprehensive listings of book and poetry events, get the monthly **Poetry Calendar,** free at many bookstores, or available online at the Academy of American Poets site *(www.poets.org).*
▶ Check the Books and Around Town sections of **Time Out New York** for weekly listings and reviews.
▶ See chapter **Gay & Lesbian** for more bookstores.

The royal treatment William Norris reads from his latest novel at the Half King in Chelsea.

highbrow: You're as likely to catch Cindy Crawford pushing her children's book as you are Richard Ford reading from his latest work. The following offer frequent author readings, talks and signings.

Barnes & Noble
See page 217 for listing

Calendars of events for each branch (there are **a dozen** in Manhattan alone) are available in-store. Check phone book or website for other locations.

Bluestockings
See page 280 for listing.

Borders Books and Music
See page 217 for listing

Events calendars for each Borders branch are available in-store and on the website.

Cathedral of St. John the Divine
1047 Amsterdam Ave at 112th St (212-316-7490; www.stjohndivine.org). Subway: B, C, 1 to 110th St–Cathedral Pkwy. Mon–Sat 7am–6pm; Sun 7am–8:30pm. Suggested donation: $3.

The cathedral hosts readings throughout the year; check the website for a schedule of events.

Corner Bookstore
1313 Madison Ave at 93rd St (212-831-3554). Subway: 6 to 96th St. Mon–Thu 10am–8pm; Fri 10am–7pm; Sat, Sun 11am–6pm.

Pick up a calendar of upcoming readings—past readers have included the novelist Rebecca Miller.

Rizzoli Bookstore
31 W 57th St between Fifth and Sixth Aves (212-759-2424). Subway: N, Q, R, W to 57th St. Mon–Sat 10am–7:30pm; Sun 11am–7pm.

This arty bookstore is a prime spot for catching high-profile photographers, artists and designers on book tours.

Three Lives & Co.
154 W 10th St at Waverly Pl (212-741-2069; www.threelives.com). Subway: A, C, E, F, V, S to W 4th St; 1, 2 to Christopher St–Sheridan Sq. Mon, Tue noon–8pm; Wed–Sat 11am–8:30pm; Sun noon–7pm.

Hear established novelists at this cozy West Village bookstore; readings are held September through May.

Reading series

The following host fiction and poetry readings; some also offer lectures.

The Algonquin
See page 124 for listing

This literary landmark hosts Spoken Word on Monday nights. At $25 ($50 with dinner), it's a bit steep—but many big names pass through.

The Half King
See page 145 for listing

This bar-restaurant co-owned by Sebastian Junger offers popular, and free, Monday-night readings featuring the likes of novelists Jerry Stahl and William Norris. Arrive about a half-hour early if you want to get a seat—or make a dinner reservation; the readings are at 7pm.

Housing Works Used Books Cafe
126 Crosby St between Houston and Prince Sts (212-334-3324; www.housingworksubc.com). Subway: F, V, S to Broadway–Lafayette St; 6 to Bleecker St. Call or visit website for schedule of events. Free.

If you like a little social consciousness with your literary readings, check out the impressive lineup of writers at this organization dedicated to raising money for the HIV-positive homeless. Housing Works also hosts a series of lectures by the media-watchdog organization Fairness and Accuracy in Reporting.

KGB
85 E 4th St between Second and Third Aves (212-505-3360). Subway: F, V to Lower East Side–Second Ave; 6 to Astor Pl. Mon 7:30pm. Free.
This Soviet-themed East Village bar puts on a weekly reading series featuring literary and poetic luminaries. Some are must-hears. Others will have you reaching for the tomatoes.

Makor
See page 306 for listing.
The mingling scene is marvy at this Jewish-oriented cultural center, though the events have nothing to do with dating per se. Its calendar includes dozens of events from poetry slams and book-discussion groups to gallery talks and yoga workshops. Some events are free; some aren't.

National Arts Club
See page 68 for listing.
This private club in an elegant landmark building opens its doors to the public for free readings by contemporary writers on the publicity circuit, or for, say, devotees of the W.B. Yeats Society. A jacket or business attire is required for many of the events. Call for further information.

New School University
66 W 12th St between Fifth and Sixth Aves (212-229-5488; www.newschool.edu). Subway: F, V to 14th St; L to Sixth Ave. Call or visit website for schedule of events. Admission varies.
The school holds lecture series with lofty themes such as "If War Is Destruction, Is Art the Opposite of War?" Is that a trick question? There are also poetry nights, fiction forums and political discussions. The Academy of American Poets hosts readings by some of the country's best-known writers at the Tishman Auditorium.

92nd Street Y Unterberg Poetry Center
1395 Lexington Ave at 92nd St (212-996-1100; www.92ndsty.org). Subway: 6 to 96th St. Call or visit website for schedule of events. Admission varies.
The Academy of American Poets and the Y cosponsor regular poet, author and playwright readings with such acclaimed scribes as Edward Albee, Athol Fugard and David Mamet. Panel discussions and lectures by high-profile academics are also held.

Selected Shorts: A Celebration of the Short Story
Symphony Space, 2537 Broadway at 95th St (212-864-5400; www.symphonyspace.org). Subway: 1, 2, 3 to 96th St. Early Mar–mid-Jun. Wednesdays at 6:30 or
8pm. *Call or visit website for schedule of events. $18, seniors $15.*
Accomplished Broadway and Hollywood actors tackle short stories at this event, one of the longest-running programs at Symphony Space, a large Art Deco theater that was recently renovated and expanded. The Thalia Book Club, in the downstairs theater (the Leonard Nimoy Thalia Theater), is a new book-discussion series; call for details.

Writer's Voice/West Side YMCA
5 W 63rd St between Central Park West and Broadway (212-875-4124; www.ymcanyc.org/wvoice). Subway: A, C, B, D, 1, 2 to 59th St–Columbus Circle. Call or visit website for schedule of events. $5, under 18 free.
Events include readings by poets, playwrights and novelists, as well as popular open-mike nights. The Y also offers highly regarded writers' workshops.

Spoken word

Dia Center for the Arts
548 W 22nd St between Tenth and Eleventh Aves (212-989-5566; www.diacenter.org). Subway: C, E to 23rd St. One weekend afternoon a month at 4pm. $6, seniors and students $3.
Dia's Readings in Contemporary Poetry series features established American poets and prose writers; past readers have included Paul Auster, Robert Creeley and Sharon Olds.

Dixon Place
Vineyard 26, 309 E 26th St at Second Ave (212-532-1546; www.dixonplace.org). Subway: 6 to 28th St. Call or visit website for schedule of events. Free–$5.
Founder and director Ellie Covan offers open-mike nights on the first Wednesday of each month. There are also regular reading series, such as Homotext (devoted to gay writers), on the second Wednesday of every month. Experiments and Disorders: New Poetic Forms is a curated series that includes poetry, fiction and short plays. The New York Review of Science Fiction reading series relocated from Saturn and is now at Dixon Place on the second Monday of every month.

A Gathering of Tribes
285 E 3rd St between Aves B and C (212-674-3778; www.tribe.org). Subway: F, V to Lower East Side–Second Ave. Sun 5–7pm. Free.
Poetry readings and parties are held on Sunday evenings. A Gathering of Tribes also publishes its own poetry magazine, and is home to an art gallery.

A Little Bit Louder
Thirteen, 35 E 13th St at University Pl (212-979-6677). Subway: L, N, Q, R, W, 4, 5, 6 to 14th St–Union Sq. Mon 7pm. $5, students $4.
Each Monday, the mod lounge Thirteen hosts a stimulating poetry forum; two nights a month, it's dedicated to the slam game. The rest of the time, expect open-mike nights or theme readings,

Verbal workout Playwright Tom Stoppard
exhibits eloquence at the 92nd Street Y.

such as House of Women and featured poets like
Willie Perdomo.

Nuyorican Poets Cafe
*236 E 3rd St between Aves B and C (212-505-8183;
www.nuyorican.org). Subway: F, V to Lower East
Side–Second Ave. Call or visit website for schedule of
events. Admission varies.*
The 27-year-old Nuyorican goes beyond open mikes
and slams with multimedia events, staged readings,
hip-hop poetry, short films and more. Slams are
held Friday nights and the first Wednesday of
every month.

Poetry Project
*St. Mark's Church in-the-Bowery, 131 E 10th St at
Second Ave (212-674-0910; www.poetryproject.com).
Subway: L to Third Ave; 6 to Astor Pl. Call or visit
website for dates and times. $7, seniors and students $4.*
The legendary Poetry Project, whose hallowed
walls first heard the likes of Allen Ginsberg and
Anne Waldman, remains a thriving center for hearing the new and noteworthy. Living legends such
as Jim Carroll and Patti Smith occasionally take the
stage here.

Segue at Double Happiness
*Double Happiness, 173 Mott St between Broome and
Grand Sts (212-941-1282). Subway: S to Grand St;
6 to Spring St. Oct–May Sat 4–6pm. $4.*
The Segue Foundation's long-standing poetry series
now has a home in a bar—Chinatown's funky, cavernous Double Happiness *(see page 144).*

Talks & lectures

Brecht Forum
*122 W 27th St between Sixth and Seventh Aves,
tenth floor (212-242-4201; www.brechtforum.org).
Subway: 1, 2 to 28th St. Call or visit website for
schedule of events. Admission varies.*
This old-style leftist institution offers lectures, forums,
discussions and bilingual poetry readings.

The Brooklyn Public Library
*Grand Army Plaza between Eastern Pkwy and
Flatbush Ave, Prospect Heights, Brooklyn (718-
230-2100; www.brooklynpubliclibrary.org). Subway:
1, 2 to Grand Army Plaza. Call or visit website for
schedule of events. Free.*
Brooklyn's main library branch offers lectures and
readings of impressive scope.

New School University
See page 259 for listing.
The New School University hosts esoteric lectures
by visiting savants.

New York Public Library, Celeste Bartos Forum
*Fifth Ave between 40th and 42nd Sts (212-930-0855;
www.nypl.org). Subway: B, D, F, V to 42nd St; 7 to
Fifth Ave. Call or visit website for schedule of events.
Admission varies.*
Several annual lecture series feature renowned
writers and thinkers in this wonderful room.

92nd Street Y
See page 259 for listing.
The Y offers regular lectures by and dialogues
between top-notch speakers on subjects ranging
from literature and the arts to feminism and
international scandals. The literary likes of Susan
Sontag and Wole Soyinka have spoken here.

Tours

Greenwich Village Literary Pub Crawl
*White Horse Tavern, 567 Hudson St at 11th St
(212-613-5796). Subway: 1, 2 to Christopher St–
Sheridan Sq. Sat 2pm. $12, seniors and students
$9. Reservations recommended.*
This 2.3-mile crawl to four watering holes once frequented by legendary village writers is guided by
actors from the New Ensemble Theatre Company
Inc. These thespians give a history of the establishment and its literary patrons before performing
pieces from each author's work.

Greenwich Village Past and Present
*Washington Square Park, Fifth Ave at Waverly Pl,
Washington Square Arch (212-969-8262). Subway:
A, C, E, F, V, S to W 4th St. Call for schedule of
events. $10.*
This two-hour walk takes you past homes and hang-
outs of Village writers past and present.

Mark Twain Annual Birthday Tour
*Broadway at Spring St. Meet at southwest corner
of Broadway and Spring St (212-873-1944;
www.salwen.com/mtny). Subway: N, R to Prince St.
Late November. $15.*
This tour is led by Twainologist Peter Salwen and
ends with a birthday toast at one of the novelist's
New York City homes.

Cabaret & Comedy

Crooners and comics command the stage at clubs throughout the city

New York is the cabaret capital of the U.S. and, quite possibly, of the world. In what other city can you find a dozen different shows on any given night? The term *cabaret* covers both the venue and the art form. It's the club where songs are sung, generally by one person, but sometimes by a small ensemble; and it is the vocal interpretation of songs, which are usually drawn from what's known as the Great American Songbook, a vast repertoire of the American musical theater—supplemented with the occasional new number by a contemporary composer. More than anything else, cabaret is an act of intimacy: The best singers are able to draw the audience in until each member feels he or she is being personally serenaded.

The Golden Age of cabaret in New York was the 1950s and early 1960s. The advent of rock music and changing tastes has made cabaret an art form for connoisseurs, but plenty of fans and performers keep it alive. Mid-October marks the Cabaret Convention at the Town Hall *(see page 309)*, which attracts the genre's crème de la crème. Today's venues fall into two groups: classic, expensive boîtes such as the Oak Room, Feinstein's and Cafe Carlyle, where you'll hear the likes of Rosemary Clooney, Andrea Marcovicci and Bobby Short; and less formal, less pricey neighborhood clubs such as Don't Tell Mama and Danny's Skylight Room, where up-and-coming singers perform.

Classic nightspots

Cafe Carlyle

The Carlyle Hotel, 35 E 76th St at Madison Ave (212-744-1600, 800-227-5737). Subway: 6 to 77th St. Mon 8:45pm; Tue–Sat 8:45, 10:45pm. Closed Jul–mid-Sept. Cover $75. AmEx, DC, MC, V.
This is the epitome of chic New York, especially when Bobby Short or Eartha Kitt performs. (Woody Allen sometimes sits in as clarinetist with Eddie Davis and his New Orleans Jazz Band on early Monday night shows—call ahead to confirm.) Don't dress down; the Carlyle is a place to plunk down your cash and live the high life. To drink in some atmosphere without spending as much, try **Bemelmans Bar** across the hall, which always features an excellent pianist, such as Barbara Carroll or Peter Mintun *(Tue–Sat, 9:45pm–12:45am, $15 cover).* The playful murals of Ludwig Bemelmans, creator of the lovable *Madeline,* adorn the walls.

The Duplex

61 Christopher St at Seventh Ave South (212-255-5438). Subway: 1, 2 to Christopher St–Sheridan Sq. Show times vary. Piano bar 9pm–4am. Cover $5–$25, two-drink minimum. Free. Cash only.
The Duplex doesn't have that feel of classic cabaret glamour, but it's the city's oldest cabaret. Going strong for 50-plus years, the place sets the pace for

Ripple effect The piano-bar acts spread their love of song at Judy's Chelsea.

Burn, baby, burn Monday nights at Torch feature red-hot songstress Nicole Renaud.

campy, good-natured fun. A mix of regulars and tourists laugh and sing along with classy drag performers, comedians and rising stars.

Feinstein's

The Regency, 540 Park Ave at 61st St (212-339-4095). Subway: N, R, W to Lexington Ave–59th St; 4, 5, 6 to 59th St. Tue–Thu 8:30pm; Fri, Sat 8:30, 11pm. Cover $50–$75, $25–$50 food-and-drink minimum. AmEx, DC, MC, V.

Cabaret's crown prince Michael Feinstein's swanky room in the Regency Hotel draws top performers: Rosemary Clooney, the elegant Ann Hampton Callaway and sexy singer-guitarist John Pizzarelli. Check *Time Out New York*'s weekly listings for bookings of wacky Hollywood footnotes, such as Sally Kellerman, Nell Carter and Tony Danza.

FireBird

363 W 46th St between Eighth and Ninth Aves (212-586-0244). Subway: A, C, E to 42nd St–Port Authority. Show times vary. Cover $20–$35, $15 drink minimum. AmEx, DC, Disc, MC, V.

This classy joint is next door to the regally appointed Russian restaurant of the same name. If the caviar and mosaic reproduction of Klimt's *The Kiss* don't ignite your passions, rely on the first-rate performers, who include Tom Anderson, Steve Ross and genius singer-songwriter John Bucchino.

The Oak Room

Algonquin Hotel, 59 W 44th St between Fifth and Sixth Aves (212-840-6800). Subway: B, D, F, V to 42nd St; 7 to Fifth Ave. Tue–Thu 9pm; Fri, Sat 9, 11:30pm, dinner compulsory at first Fri and Sat shows. Cover $50, $15 drink minimum. AmEx, DC, Disc, MC, V.

This resonant banquette-lined room, overseen by the solicitous Arthur Pomposello, is the place to enjoy the best cabaret performers, among them Andrea Marcovicci, Maureen McGovern, Karen Akers and rising jazz star Jane Monheit. And yes, all you Dorothy Parker fans, it's *that* Algonquin (see page 124).

Standards

Arci's Place

450 Park Ave South between 30th and 31st Sts (212-532-4370). Subway: 6 to 33rd St. Sun, Mon 8pm; Tue–Thu 9pm; Fri, Sat 8:30, 11pm. Cover $25–$30, $15 food-and-drink minimum. AmEx, MC, V.

The Italian food is top-notch at this intimate Park Avenue restaurant, and so is the talent: Karen Mason (of Broadway's *Mamma Mia!* fame), Billy Stritch and *A Chorus Line*'s Donna McKechnie have all played here.

Danny's Skylight Room

Grand Sea Palace, 346 W 46th St between Eighth and Ninth Aves (212-265-8133; www.dannysgsp.com). Subway: A, C, E to 42nd St–Port Authority. Show times vary. Cover $8–$15, $10 food-and-drink minimum. AmEx, DC, MC, V.

A pastel nook in the Grand Sea Palace restaurant, "where Bangkok meets Broadway" on touristy Restaurant Row, Danny's features pop-jazz, pop and cabaret, with the accent on the smooth. In addition to up-and-comers, a few mature cabaret and jazz standbys, such as Blossom Dearie, occasionally perform here.

Don't Tell Mama

343 W 46th St between Eighth and Ninth Aves (212-757-0788). Subway: A, C, E to 42nd St–Port

Authority. 4pm–4am, 4–8 shows per night. Cover $3–$20 in cabaret room, two-drink minimum; no cover for piano bar (no food served). AmEx, MC, V.
Showbiz pros like to visit this Theater District venue. The acts range from strictly amateur to potential stars of tomorrow. The nightly lineup can include pop, jazz or Broadway singers, female impersonators, magicians, comedians or revues.

Judy's Chelsea
169 Eighth Ave between 18th and 19th Sts (212-929-5410). Subway: C, E to 23rd St; 1, 2 to 18th St. Mon–Thu 8:30pm; Fri, Sat 8:30, 11pm; Sun 3, 5:30, 8:30pm. Cover varies, $10 food-and-drink minimum. AmEx, MC, V.
The outré folksinger Go Mahan often performs in this space, and the geek-chic Lounge-O-Leers keep piano-bar patrons laughing with grooved-out versions of Top 40 hits. Co-owner–singer Judy Kreston and pianist David Lahm often perform on Saturdays.

Triad
158 W 72nd St between Columbus Ave and Broadway (212-799-4599). Subway: B, C, 1, 2, 3 to 72nd St. Show times and cover prices vary, two-drink minimum. AmEx, Disc, MC, V ($10 minimum).
This Upper West Side spot has been the launching pad for many revues over the years, several of which *(Forever Plaid, Forbidden Broadway)* have moved on to larger Off Broadway spaces. Dinner is available, and there's an occasional singer or benefit show in the downstairs lounge, which opens at 4:30pm.

Upstairs at Rose's Turn
55 Grove St between Seventh Ave South and Bleecker St (212-366-5438). Subway: 1, 2 to Christopher St–Sheridan Sq. 4pm–4am. Show times vary. Cover $5–$15, two-drink minimum. Cash only.
This dark room with zero atmosphere tends to emphasize comedy or one-act musicals such as *Our Lives & Times*, a hilarious spoof on current events, and *Indigo Rat*, a new spin on life in wartime Berlin.

Alternative venues

Joe's Pub
See page 305 for listing.
This plush club and restaurant in the Public Theater is at once hip and elegant. Performers include chanteuses such as Ute Lemper and Lea DeLaria, and singing sensations as diverse as Mo'Guajiro and Aimee Mann. Show times and cover prices vary.

Torch
137 Ludlow St between Rivington and Stanton Sts (212-228-5151). Subway: F to Delancey St; J, M, Z to Delancey–Essex Sts. Sun–Thu 6pm–2am; Fri, Sat 6pm–4am. Show times vary. No cover. AmEx, DC, MC, V.
On Monday nights, this Lower East Side bar-restaurant is where you'll find Nicole Renaud, an enchanting Parisian songbird. Renaud's crystalline voice, clever playlist (she's been known to break out music from *The Umbrellas of Cherbourg*) and

bizarrely beautiful costumes make for a decidedly charming evening.

Comedy venues

No joke: The business of comedy is booming in New York City. Small, out-of-the-way clubs and bars have been nurturing a new generation of performers who flirt with the avant-garde. A few divey bars on the Lower East Side have helped launched the careers of formerly fringe performers by offering comedy nights. **Luna Lounge**'s Eating It series is on Monday nights *(171 Ludlow St between Houston and Stanton Sts, 212-260-2323)* and **Parkside Lounge** hosts a Tuesday Night Train Wreck series *(317 E Houston St at Attorney St, 212-673-6270)*. Marc Maron, a pioneer of comedy's new wave, makes stand-up appearances on *Late Show with David Letterman*. The Upright Citizens Brigade (whose alumni have made their way to *Saturday Night Live* and *The Daily Show with Jon Stewart*) has its own theater, where the troupe produces shows with up-and-coming talent.

You can still catch offbeat performers at smaller venues, along with established stars such as Colin Quinn, Janeane Garofalo and David Cross. The following clubs offer a range of comedy styles—from traditional stand-up to some very twisted entertainment. Show times vary, so it's best to call ahead.

The Boston Comedy Club
82 W 3rd St between Sullivan and Thompson Sts (212-477-1000; www.thebostoncomedyclub.com). Subway: A, C, E, F, V, S to W 4th St. Mon 8, 10pm; Tue–Thu 9:30pm; Fri, Sat 8, 10pm, 12:15am; Sun 9pm. Cover $5–$7, two-drink minimum. AmEx, MC, V.
This rowdy room is a classic comedy club, with a brick wall behind the stage and hecklers in front of it. The bill can include as many as ten acts.

Carolines on Broadway
1626 Broadway between 49th and 50th Sts (212-757-4100; www.carolines.com). Subway: B, D, E to Seventh Ave; N, R, W to 49th St; 1, 2 to 50th St. Mon–Wed 7:30, 9:30pm; Thu, Sun 8, 10pm; Fri, Sat 8, 10:30pm, 12:30am. Cover $15–$35, two-drink minimum. AmEx, DC, MC, V.
Elbow your way past the crowd of tourists outside this Times Square landmark, and you'll see why people sweat to get tickets to this posh club. Andy Dick, Jay Mohr and Dave Chappelle have all stood and delivered here—as have Wendy Liebman, Billy Crystal and Jay Leno (back when he was funny).

Chicago City Limits Theatre
1105 First Ave between 60th and 61st Sts (212-888-5233; www.chicagocitylimits.com). Subway: N, R, W to Lexington Ave–59th St; 4, 5, 6 to 59th St. Mon, Wed, Thu, Sun 8pm; Fri, Sat 8, 10:30pm. Cover $5–$20; discount with student ID. AmEx, MC, V.
Founded in the Windy City, this popular group

moved to New York in 1979 and has been delighting audiences ever since with topical sketches and audience-inspired improvisation.

Comedy Cellar

117 MacDougal St between Bleecker and W 3rd Sts (212-254-3480; www.comedycellar.com). Subway: A, C, E, F, V, S to W 4th St. Sun–Thu 9, 11pm; Fri 9, 10:45pm, 12:30am; Sat 7:30, 9:15, 11pm, 12:45am. Cover $10–$12, two-drink minimum. AmEx, MC, V.
This well-worn underground lair recalls the counterculture vibe of another era, before the neighborhood was besieged by suburban partyers. Local talent and national headliners perform here.

The Comedy Garden

Madison Square Garden, Seventh Ave at 32nd St (212-307-7171). Subway: A, C, E, 1, 2, 3 to 34th St–Penn Station. Show times and cover prices vary.
The Garden's three different rooms present established performers who have outgrown the small clubs, including Richard Lewis, Steve Harvey, Brett Butler and even Jerry Lewis.

Comic Strip Live

1568 Second Ave between 81st and 82nd Sts (212-861-9386; www.comicstriplive.com). Subway: 4, 5, 6 to 86th St. Mon–Thu 8:30pm; Fri 8:30, 10:30pm, 12:30am; Sat 8, 10:15pm, 12:30am; Sun 8pm. Cover $10–$15, two-drink minimum. AmEx, Disc, MC, V.
This stand-up club with a neighborhood feel doesn't just host the big names, it also offers new hopefuls a chance at the mike every Monday. Aspiring comics can sign up in the first week of May and November.

Dangerfield's

1118 First Ave between 61st and 62nd Sts (212-593-1650). Subway: N, R, W to Lexington Ave–59th St; 4, 5, 6 to 59th St. Sun–Thu 8:45pm; Fri 8:30, 10:30pm; Sat 8, 10:30pm, 12:30am. Cover $12–$20. AmEx, DC, MC, V.
Opened by respect-starved comedian Rodney Dangerfield in 1969, this glitzy lounge is one of New York's oldest and most formidable clubs.

Gladys' Comedy Room

Hamburger Harry's, 145 W 45th St between Sixth Ave and Broadway (212-832-1762). Subway: B, D, F, V to 42nd St; N, Q, R, W, S, 1, 2, 3, 7 to 42nd St–Times Sq. Wed 7:30pm; $6. Thu–Sat 8:30pm; $12, plus $10 table minimum (mention TONY; $7, plus $5 table minimum). Half price for half-pints—five feet tall or under, bring proof of height. Open-mike Wednesday (sign up 6:45–7pm, $5 to perform). AmEx, Disc, MC, V.
Gladys' offers a place for neophyte performers and comedy watchers in a midtown burger joint. In honor of the height-challenged owner, short people get in cut-rate.

Gotham Comedy Club

34 W 22nd St between Fifth and Sixth Aves (212-367-9000). Subway: F, V, N, R to 23rd St. Sun–Thu 8:30pm; Fri, Sat 8:30, 10:30pm. Cover $10–$15, two-drink minimum. AmEx, DC, MC, V.

The most elegant comedy club in town books top comics, including Colin Quinn *(Saturday Night Live)*, living legend Robert Klein and the irascible Lewis Black *(The Daily Show with Jon Stewart)*. Jerry Seinfeld has made rare unannounced appearances (but don't hold your breath).

Gramercy Comedy Club

35 E 21st St between Broadway and Park Ave South (212-254-5709). Subway: F, V, N, R, 6 to 23rd St. Wed, Thu 7:30, 10pm; Fri, Sat 8, 10:30pm. $15, two-drink minimum.
The city's newest comedy venue is a swank affair that features a regular roster of comics who regularly appear on TV (talk shows, sitcoms, commercials).

New York Comedy Club

241 E 24th St between Second and Third Aves (212-696-5233). Subway: 6 to 23rd St. Sun–Thu 9pm; Fri 8, 10, 11pm; Sat 8, 10, 11:30pm, midnight. Cover $7–$10, two-drink minimum. AmEx, MC, V.
This gritty club has two separate rooms, each with a packed lineup and a bargain cover price. Fridays at 11pm and Saturdays at midnight, you can catch the city's top African-American comedians, and Friday's 9pm show offers Latino comics.

PSNBC

HERE, 145 Sixth Ave between Dominick and Spring Sts (212-647-0202; www.here.org). Subway: C, E to Spring St. Show times vary. Free.
You can see the TV stars of tomorrow, today—the NBC network takes up residence in this downtown theater Monday through Thursday to audition new talent for network projects. Shows are free (like TV), and the talent is almost all first-rate (unlike TV).

Stand-Up NY

236 W 78th St at Broadway (212-595-0850). Subway: 1, 2 to 79th St. Sun–Wed 7, 9pm; Thu 7, 9pm; Fri, Sat 8, 10pm, 12:15am. Cover $5–$12, two-item minimum. AmEx, MC, V.
A bare yet intimate place, Stand-Up NY features a mix of club-circuit regulars and new faces.

Surf Reality

172 Allen St between Rivington and Stanton Sts, second floor (212-673-4182; www.surfreality.org). Subway: F, V to Lower East Side–Second Ave. Show times and cover prices vary. Cash only.
The center of the Lower East Side alternative universe, Surf Reality features a lot of comedy—but probably nothing like you've ever seen before. You'll be entertained in new and often alarming ways.

Upright Citizens Brigade Theatre

161 W 22nd St between Sixth and Seventh Aves (212-366-9176; www.uprightcitizens.org). Subway: F, V, 1, 2 to 23rd St. 8pm. Cover $5–$7. Cash only.
The UCB Theatre features excellent sketch comedy and improv every night. Some of the original foursome still perform on Sundays for free; disciples entertain the rest of the week and train aspiring performers in the UCB's improv style.

Clubs

The city's club scene might not be what it was, but there are still plenty of options available to the dedicated night crawler

People (at least those of a certain age) always complain that things were better back in the old days; younger folks are apt to dismiss such talk as tne grumblings of bitter geriatrics. In the case of New York City's club world, though, the old-timers may have a point. The city was once hailed as the world's nightclubbing capital, but few would argue that that's still the case, and the reasons for the perceived decline of nightlife here are many. Because of astronomical Manhattan rents, the hipsters and freaks who color the scene have scattered throughout the boroughs and beyond, and the people who have moved in to replace them are often more interested in their portfolios than in partying. The cost of opening a club has also skyrocketed, making any such venture economically difficult.

The attitude of city officials toward clubs certainly hasn't helped matters. A former deputy mayor infamously labeled the clubs "little buckets of blood" and vowed that the city would try to close them down. To some extent, the effort has been successful. Megaclub Twilo (considered by many to be the best venue in town) was shuttered for good in the spring of 2001, with many others teetering on the edge of closing. Another factor is enforcement of the bizarre, no-dancing-allowed cabaret law. That city code means that frooging is forbidden at many small lounge-type spaces. Despite all the problems, however, there are still kicks to be found during the city's late hours, if you know where to look.

PLAY IT SAFE

Once upon a time, weapons were the only items verboten in nightspots, but the current climate has forced some clubs to police their patrons' drug use as well. If getting high is your cup of E, be careful—drugs are illegal. And leave the guns and knives at home, of course.

While New York isn't nearly as dangerous as it used to be, this is still a city where anything can happen. If you're leaving a club at an ungodly hour, you might want to take a taxi or call a car service as you leave. Here are three of the latter with easily memorizable numbers: **Lower East Side Car Service** *(212-477-7777)*, **A New Day** *(212-228-6666)* and **Tel Aviv** *(212-777-*

Spin city DJ Reid Speed brings jungle to Baktun with her girly brand of drum 'n' bass.

It's all one big blur Britpop fans get down to twee sounds at Don Hill's Tiswas party.

7777). More car services are listed in the chapter **Directory** *(see page 363)*.

Many of the more risqué events shun publicity (and hence may not be listed here), so if you're interested in recreation of a semi-illegal nature, it's best to ask around.

Alcohol is sold until 4am, and some after-hours clubs are open late enough to reopen their bars at 8am (noon on Sunday), the earliest allowed by law. There are also a number of illegal drinking dens (not surprisingly, we can't list these either); query your fellow barflies at last call if you still want another round. Wherever you go, most people don't arrive before midnight. One of the most popular events, **Body & Soul**, is a reaction to that; it's at **Vinyl** *(see page 269)* on Sundays from 3pm until midnight, allowing club dinosaurs and weekday clock-punchers to be in bed at a reasonable hour.

THE SOUND OF NEW YORK

New Yorkers are a cynical, hard-to-impress bunch. But despite the perennial been-there-done-that attitude, New York's club scene is proud of its history and traditions. The birthplace of disco and hip-hop, the city also played a major roll in the development of house music. All of these sounds, along with drum 'n' bass, bleepy IDM, Latin, R&B, reggae, techno, trip-hop and pretty much any other genre you can think of, have a place in the city's clubs and lounges. And while some clubs may seem overly nostalgic for legendary, long-gone nightspots such as the Paradise Garage (the famed gay disco and the source of the term "Garage classics," used to described gospel-influenced vocal house music), the fact that many New York DJs give props to the past helps to connect the musical dots between then and now.

In the past, New York DJs were known for offering a wide-ranging mix of sounds during the course of a night; in recent years, though, dance floors have become musically regimented. Perhaps that's why the crowds at many venues have become segregated by age, race or sexual orientation. There are plenty of exceptions to this trend, of course, and you can still find a mixed crowd at many of the city's parties—for instance, at the aforementioned Body & Soul soiree.

Although the glam clubs do have door policies, these days most are more concerned with how much you have in your wallet than what brand of trousers you've got on. You still want to dress up, however, since door policies can change like the weather. Hetero-heavy venues often refuse entry to groups of men to maintain a desirable gender balance. Thankfully, the bottle-service trend—in which you must purchase an entire bottle of liquor (usually at a few hundred dollars a pop) to be able to sit down at a table—seems to have run its course.

While Friday and Saturday are the biggest nights to go out, many hip locals stick to midweek clubbing to avoid the throngs of suburbanites who overwhelm Manhattan every weekend. Besides, a number of the more interesting events happen during the week.

STAY IN THE KNOW

The club scene is mercurial: Parties move from place to place, and clubs can differ wildly from night to night or change their lineup at a moment's notice. Keeping up can be a challenge. Calling ahead is a good idea, as is consulting the most recent issue of *Time Out New York*, the monthly style magazine *Paper*, or the fun pocket-size clubbing bible *Flyer*. The gay listings magazine *HX (Homo Xtra)* is also good for club reviews, albeit with a gym-queen slant. Another way to keep up with the action is to call the club or check the party's website (we list them below) or sign up for up-to-the-minute e-mailed club guides. DJ Spinoza's underground-electronics–oriented **Beyond Events Calendar** is one of the best (to enroll, send a blank e-mail to nyc_electronic_events_calendar-subscribe@ yahoogroups.com). You can also find flyers for various fiestas at numerous club-oriented clothing and record stores.

Admission prices for the clubs listed below vary according to the night, but usually range from $5 to $30. When no closing time is listed, assume the club stays open until the party fizzles out. FYI, the term *club* is used to describe discos as well as live-music venues (*see chapter* **Music**).

Clubs

Baktun

418 W 14th St between Ninth Ave and Washington St (212-206-1590; www.baktun.com). Subway: A, C, E to 14th St; L to Eighth Ave. Hours vary with event.
This erstwhile meat-processing plant remains a welcome alternative to the upscale joints that have over-

taken the neighborhood, and it's even more desirable now that it has a cabaret license. The smallish club offers an underground-heavy menu of art events, performance, and deejayed and live music (mostly of the electronic variety). On Thursdays, the fabled house/garage veteran Tony Humphries is the DJ for the **Nuttz** party; Friday night is reserved for underground deep- and tech-house sounds, and the long-running **Direct Drive** drum 'n' bass party waffles the woofers on Saturdays.

Centro-Fly

45 W 21st St between Fifth and Sixth Aves (212-627-7770; www.centro-fly.com). Subway: F, N, R to 23rd St. Hours vary with event.
Modeled and named after a late-1960s Italian disco, Centro-Fly is as groovy as its legendary predecessor. The decor is worthy of a *Wallpaper* center spread; the design is ultrahip op art, and there's futuristic furniture and a sunken bar in the round. But the place isn't all show: Two sound systems and a four-turntable DJ booth attract some of the best spinners around. Notable nights include Master At Work Louis Vega's **Dance Ritual** on Wednesdays, the slamming **Subliminal Sessions** on Thursdays and the tech-housey **Plant** affair on Saturdays. If you're hungry, you can grab a bite in the club's Tapioca Room.

Club New York

252 W 43rd St between Broadway and Eighth Ave (212-997-9510). Subway: A, C, E to 42nd St–Port Authority; N, Q, R, W, S, 1, 2, 3, 7 to 42nd St–Times Sq. Hours vary with event.
Famous for the shooting that led to P. Diddy's brush with the law, Club New York is a mainstream Latin-music club, with various DJs spinning merengue, salsa and Spanish rock and pop. Hip-hop, which had a night of its own until the Puffster incident, is now relegated to the smaller VIP room.

Don Hill's

511 Greenwich St at Spring St (212-219-2850). Subway: C, E to Spring St; 1, 2 to Houston St. 9pm–4am.
Part live-music venue, part dance club, loud 'n' divey Don Hill's welcomes gays, lesbians and slick straight types looking to escape the techno scene. The crowd changes nightly: **BeavHer** is a popular Thursday-night routine of punk and new wave, and Saturday, **Tiswas** (a mix of live bands and Britpop records) brings out the black turtlenecks and mop-tops. It's best to call in advance…if only to know what you're getting yourself into.

Exit

610 W 54th St between Eleventh and Twelfth Aves (212-586-9311). Subway: A, C, B, D, 1, 2 to 59th St–Columbus Circle. Hours vary with event.
Despite its fabulous sound system, this mammoth, multiroomed venue is largely the domain of liquored-up, overly aggressive knuckleheads. But Exit is also the home of **Earth** *(see page 286)*, the monthly shindig powered by Junior Vasquez. Although the old fella's not quite what he used to

be as a DJ, dancing to his beats is almost the nightlife equivalent of visiting the American Museum of Natural History.

Filter 14

432 W 14th St at Washington St (212-366-5680). Subway: A, C, E, 1, 2, 3 to 14th St; L to Eighth Ave. 10pm–4am.
Filter 14 is an unassuming little boîte and, as such, is a welcome respite from the trendiness of other venues in its Meatpacking District neighborhood. The club's no-attitude vibe may be matched by its no-frills decor, but it has a secret weapon: a booming sound system, which blasts anything from underground house sounds to yuppie-friendly 1980s material, depending on the night.

Fun

130 Madison St between Market and Pike Sts (212-964-0303). Subway: F to East Broadway. Hours vary with event.
This Chinatown multimedia lounge never really took off the way the owners envisioned when they opened this venue (located in a creepy/cool neighborhood under the Brooklyn Bridge), but it's an interesting space nonetheless, with huge video screens, an industrial feel and a slightly outlaw-party edge.

Lotus

409 W 14th St between Ninth Ave and Washington St (212-242-9710). Subway: A, C, E, 1, 2, 3 to 14th St; L to Eighth Ave. Hours vary with event.
Lotus was one of the first upscale clubs to invade the once scuzzy Meatpacking District, and it immediately attracted legions of celebs, models and gawkers. The venue's patina of trendiness has faded a bit, and that's a good thing. Lotus can be appreciated now for what it is: a well-furnished restaurant-lounge-dance club, with DJs spinning a mainstream mix of sounds.

Luxx

256 Grand St between Driggs Ave and Roebling St, Williamsburg, Brooklyn (718-599-1000). Subway: L to Bedford Ave. Doors open 8pm.
The Brooklyn neighborhood of Williamsburg has long been taken over by bohemian types priced out of the East Village, but Luxx is still the only cabaret-licensed venue in the vicinity. It's a full-on club, with a fairly wide-ranging, ever-changing lineup. Currently, the awkwardly named **Berliniamsburg** *(see page 286)*, longtime club eccentric Larry T's sexually mixed nu-electro Saturday-nighter, is a riot.

▶ An up-close look at queer nightlife can be found in chapter **Gay & Lesbian.**

▶ Discover Brooklyn's club scene in chapter **Night Train to Brooklyn.**

▶ For a listing of nightly club events, pick up a copy of **Time Out New York.**

Nell's

246 W 14th St between Seventh and Eighth Aves (212-675-1567; www.nells.com). Subway: A, C, E, 1, 2, 3 to 14th St; L to Eighth Ave. 10pm–4am.
Nell's has survived its 1980s crowd of champagne-swilling hipsters, young bankers and literary wild children to become a nightlife institution. Its formula is laid-back jazz and funky soul (often with live bands) upstairs, where there's a limited dining menu, and DJ-supplied hip-hop, funk, house, R&B, reggae and classics below. The crowd is straight, multiracial, dressed up and ready to spend.

Ohm

16 W 22nd St between Fifth and Sixth Aves (212-229-2000). Subway: F, N, R to 23rd St. Thu–Sat 8pm–4am.
Although promoters come and go, Ohm is essentially a mainstream, aggressively hetero scene. Expect to hear Euro-house on the main floor, and hip-hop and pop in the basement.

Roxy

515 W 18th St between Tenth and Eleventh Aves (212-645-5156; www.roxynyc.com). Subway: A, C, E to 14th St; L to Eighth Ave. Hours vary with event.
The mammoth Roxy began its long life as a disco-era roller rink, and you can still rent skates and go 'round and 'round on Wednesdays. Other evenings, it's a straight-up dance club. The spot generally hosts one-shot events—live performances as well as DJ nights (mainly of the drum 'n' bass, house and techno varieties). Saturdays, Roxy is home to one of the city's biggest gay (but straight-friendly) dance parties, featuring many of the leading lights of the circuit-DJ scene.

Sapphire

249 Eldridge St between Houston and Stanton Sts (212-777-5153). Subway: F, V to Lower East Side–Second Ave. 7pm–4am.
Sapphire was one of the first trendy Lower East Side DJ bars, and it was unbearable (i.e., crowded). It's a lot better, now that the club has fallen out of fashion. The music is fairly typical during most of the week—disco classics, hip-hop, reggae and R&B. However, Monday's and Wednesday's deep- and tech-house parties, with DJs ranging from local unknowns to superstars such as Roger S, are well worth a visit.

Shine

See page 309 for listing.
Burly bouncers, a brick-lined warehouse space and a metal Statue of Liberty (complete with glowing red eyes and bikini cover-up) create the atmosphere at this surreal and intimidating club. Thursdays, the **Giant Step** organization packs 'em in for its famous showcase of eclectic beats, featuring DJ Ron Trent and various guests (folks such as Gilles Peterson and Rainer Trüby) on the decks. Other nights, the music ranges from progressive house to hip-hop and reggae.

S.O.B.'s
204 Varick St at Houston St (212-243-4940; www.sobs.com). Subway: 1, 2 to Houston St. Hours vary with event.
The venerable S.O.B.'s (the acronym stands for Sounds of Brazil) opened in the mid-1980s as the worldbeat boom began. Although its bread and butter is still the concerts by Latin, Caribbean and African artists, the club is also involved with discotheque-style events. Saturday nights are given over to live Brazilian bands *(see also page 309).*

Sound Factory
518 W 46th St between Eleventh and Twelfth Aves (212-643-0728; www.soundfactory.com). Subway: C, E to 50th St. Hours vary with event.
This reincarnation of the legendary Sound Factory has been open since 1997, and the sound system is even better. However, the club doesn't have Junior Vasquez, and for many, that means it will never be *the* Sound Factory. Unlike the original Factory's streetwise black and Latin gay audience, the new Factory crowd is mostly straight and suburban. Various jocks spin mainstream-leaning megaclub music on Fridays, and Saturdays are ruled by DJ Jonathan Peters, who spins his attack-mode brand of hard house.

Spa
76 E 13th St between Broadway and Fourth Ave (212-388-1062). Subway: L, N, Q, R, W, 4, 5, 6 to 14th St–Union Sq. 10pm–4am.
Spa doesn't attract the limo-riding crowd that it once did, but it does have the fabulous Thursday-night **Ülträ** affair, an always-fun party that hearkens back to club-kid days of yore. On other nights, you can expect a mainly suburban (though not bad-looking) crowd, grooving to hip-hop, house or, at Wednesday's **Shattered**, good old-fashioned rock & roll. The water-themed decor is kind of cool too.

Speeed
20 W 39th St between Fifth and Sixth Aves (212-719-9867). Subway: B, D, F, V to 42nd St; 7 to Fifth Ave. Fri–Sun 10pm–4am.
Speeed opened in late 1997 with much fanfare and then…well. While it never achieved "in" status, it has a full lineup of mostly mainstream parties with hip-hop on the ground floor and house in the basement. The club's best party is the biweekly **Hamsa** affair (ensconced in its own upstairs room), which is sort of a mini Body & Soul.

Thirteen
35 E 13th St at University Pl (212-979-6677). Subway: L, N, Q, R, W, 4, 5, 6 to 14th St–Union Sq. 4pm–4am.
This tiny spot features a variety of nights that offer everything from the usual hip-hop/R&B/classics formula to rock and house music. Parties come and go, but Sunday night's **Shout!** has survived them all by playing Northern soul, 1960s psychedelic rock,

freakbeat and various other genres commonly (but often wrongly) associated with mods.

True
28 E 23rd St between Madison Ave and Park Ave South (212-254-6117). Subway: N, R, 6 to 23rd St. Mon–Fri 5pm–4am; Sat, Sun 10pm–4am.
Although it is one of Manhattan's smaller dance clubs, the somewhat run-down True fills a definite need. The best party is Friday night's **Kitsch Inn** which finds a *very* sexually mixed crowd dancing like loons to 1970s and '80s chestnuts from the likes of ABBA and Soft Cell.

Vinyl
6 Hubert St at Hudson St (212-343-1379). Subway: A, C, E, 1, 2 to Canal St. Hours vary with event.
Even though the revered Shelter party was given the boot in summer of 2001, Vinyl is still a surefire place in which to get lost in music. Danny Tenaglia has his **Be Yourself** party on Fridays, and the Body & Soul tea-dance phenomenon continues to pack 'em in on Sundays with deep house and classics from 3pm to midnight. Even without a liquor license, Vinyl remains one of the city's premier nightspots.

The Warehouse
141 E 140th St between Grand Concourse and Walton Ave, Bronx (718-992-5974). Subway: 4, 5 to 138th St–Grand Concourse. Sat 11pm–6am.
The South Bronx remains one of New York City's—hell, the nation's—most notorious neighborhoods, but it's also the proud home of the Warehouse nightclub. It attracts mostly (but not exclusively) gay black men. They come to hear house or Garage classics in the cavernous top level, and hip-hop or R&B on the smaller ground floor.

Webster Hall
125 E 11th St between Third and Fourth Aves (212-353-1600; www.webster-hall.com). Subway: L, N, Q, R, W, 4, 5, 6 to 14th St–Union Sq. Thu–Sat 10pm–5am.
Webster Hall is a commercial nightclub worth visiting if you're looking for a fun night out with friends. Although the crowd is essentially suburban, there are always a few New York freaks and lots of rampant hetero hormones to amuse newcomers. Choose from various rooms blasting disco, hip-hop/soul, Latin, progressive house or today's pop hits; wherever you turn, you'll see very energetic go-go dancers (male and female).

Lounges

APT
419 W 13th St between Ninth and Tenth Aves (212-414-4245). Subway: A, C, E to 14th St; L to Eighth Ave. Hours vary with event.
APT began life as a pseudosecret snobatorium, but has settled down to become a nice, lushly appointed lounge that occasionally features some pretty good DJs. The best night is Thursday's **Par-Tay** affair, with veteran eccentric $mall ¢hange,

Arts & Entertainment

APT's "musical director" Alec on the ones and twos and Duane (from the great Other Music record shop; *see page 229*). Also worth checking out is **Ursula 1000's Sunday Thing**, with Ursula 1000 (from Thievery Corporation's ESL record label) spinning loungecore, sampledelica, samba and house.

B-Bar
40 E 4th St between Broadway and Lafayette Sts (212-475-2220). Subway: F, V, S to Broadway–Lafayette St; N, R to 8th St–NYU; 6 to Astor Pl. Noon–4am.
Once a watering hole for "celebutants" and models, B-Bar now mainly attracts yuppies. The exception is Tuesday night's gay party, **Beige** *(see page 283)*, with DJs spinning a groovy, just-this-side-of-camp soundtrack that can include everything from show-tune standards to 1980s electro-disco classics. Expect fashionistas, off-duty drag queens and plenty of attitude.

bOb
235 Eldridge St between Houston and Stanton Sts (212-777-0588). Subway: F, V to Lower East Side–Second Ave. 7pm–4am.
bOb is a cramped DJ bar that features everything from the standard hip-hop and classics to exotica and film noir soundtracks. The space doubles as an art gallery.

Frank's Lounge
606 Fulton St at South Elliott Pl, Fort Greene, Brooklyn (718-625-9339). Subway: C to Lafayette Ave; G to Fulton St. 5:30pm–3:30am.
This unassuming Fort Greene bar is the home of E-man and Lori Caval's **Bang the Party** Friday-nighter, one of the least pretentious—and most fun—shindigs that you're likely to find on a weekend. The party features E-man and top-shelf guests spinning NYC-style deep house and Garage classics, and the affair brings out many of the city's old-school club heads, of all races and sexualities. Highly recommended.

Guernica
25 Ave B between 2nd and 3rd Sts (212-674-0984). Subway: F, V to Lower East Side–Second Ave. Hours vary with event.
Guernica is a bi-level restaurant-lounge located in the same space as the much-missed after-hours spot Save the Robots. It currently houses a few absolutely storming affairs. Foremost among them is Monday night's **Tronic Treatment**, a techno party that lures stars such as Derrick May and Richie Hawtin, as well as local luminaries (Christian Smith, John Selway). On other nights, the music ranges from drum 'n' bass to house and two-step.

Halcyon days
The beating heart of NYC's underground club scene is a used-furniture store in Brooklyn

When you enter the space at 227 Smith Street in Brooklyn, the first thing that hits you is the music: a pulsating, electronic wave of sound playing over a booming system. A DJ in a booth near the back furiously works the turntables and mixer. Party people nod their heads to the beat as they enjoy their beverages. What a kickin' lounge, you think—especially for out-of-the-way Carroll Gardens.

But look closer: Most of the patrons aren't boozing it up; rather, they're sipping cappuccinos and chowing down on roasted-veggie–and–tofu sandwiches. And they're settled not into trendy lounge furniture, but comfortable 1950s-era sofas scattered around amoeba-shaped coffee tables. Strangest of all, there are children—children!—here with their moms. And, oh, did I mention it's 3 o'clock on a sunny Sunday afternoon? Just what *is* this place?

Welcome to Halcyon, which has been dishing out music and more to denizens of the club world—and many others—since September 1999. But Halcyon isn't a club at all, nor even a lounge, really: It's a café, record store, board-game parlor, used-furniture store and knickknack shop—with DJs. It does offer beer and wine, but no hard liquor. In fact, the place has a downright wholesome feel. Yet through the efforts of owners Shawn Schwartz, Stephen Schwartz (his cousin), Ben Wild—along with jack-of-all-trades Maggie Stein, DJ-counterman Oliver Vernon and an ace staff—the venue has become an integral part of the city's nightlife (and daylife).

"You feel like you're hanging out in someone's basement," says Margo, a Halcyon regular and confirmed club freak. "The place has absolutely no attitude. Sure, you get weird people in here—like people with baby strollers—but that doesn't kill the vibe, it just adds to it." Of course, the strollers start to disappear as the night grows longer; even without a cabaret license, Halcyon buzzes with underground-music heads on weekend nights, when it stays open until 2am.

How did this oddball entity come to be? The Schwartz cousins and Stein had worked

Liquids

266 E 10th St between First Ave and Ave A (212-677-1717) Subway: L to First Ave. 8pm–4am.
A working fireplace and cozy seating gives this East Village drink spot a bit of a ski-lodge feel. But it's actually a good space to hear state-of-the-art musical musings from some of the local scene's best DJs. Check out the **Tuesday Night Hooka Lounge** party, with a tent, hookah pipes and bubbling tech-house sounds from DJ Dots and guests.

Night Strike

Boulmor Lanes, 110 University Pl between 12th and 13th Sts (212-255-8188). Subway: L, N, Q, R, W, 4, 5, 6 to 14th St–Union Sq. Mon 10pm–4am. $17.
Scenesters exchange their slides for bowling shoes while DJs spin house and techno. There's something humanizing about a crowd of nightcrawlers letting their hair down and hanging out the classic American white-trash way: drinkin', bowlin' and shootin' the shit.

Openair

121 St. Marks Pl between First Ave and Ave A (212-979-1459). Subway: L to First Ave; 6 to Astor Pl. Hours vary with event.
This recently opened lounge is still something of a secret, being nearly invisible and inaudible from the street. Inside is one of the coolest venues in the city. The place is high-tech in style—though not ridiculously so—but what's important is the music: underground house, techno, drum 'n' bass, ambient, etc., all pumped through a sound system that puts others to shame.

The Park

118 Tenth Ave at 17th St (212-352-3313). Subway: A, C, E to 14th St; L to Eighth Ave. 11:30am–1am.
The pastiche style of this Mediterranean restaurant-lounge—equal parts ski chalet, Thai kitsch and 1950s Palm Springs—is a welcome break from minimalism: The ravishing interior is rivaled only by the flash-with-cash crowd that mingles in the gorgeous garage-cum-garden, at the two separate bars and in the "private" Penthouse lounge.

Plant Bar

217 E 3rd St between Aves A and B (212-375-9066). Subway: F, V to Lower East Side–Second Ave. 7pm–4am.
Marcus and Dominique (the men behind Centro-Fly's fab Plant party) are responsible for this always-fun and usually packed DJ space. The pair have used their connections to score international hotshots such as Ian Pooley and Fatboy Slim, but more often, you find local talent doing the business in the booth.

various jobs in the music industry and shared, with their friends Vernon and Wild, a passion for edgy dance music and culture. During the winter of 1997, the seeds of Halcyon were planted at a series of Saturday-afternoon open-turntable get-togethers that the friends tossed in Shawn Schwartz's Cobble Hill apartment. "We started off drinking coffee and playing records, and we'd keep going till midnight," he remembers. "It became a regular monthly event, with people telling their friends, who told more friends, and a lot of them brought records to play. The parties got really big, and the neighbors were buggin' out. We started thinking, 'We've got something here!'"

Thus energized, the crew began searching throughout Manhattan and Brooklyn for an existing bar or club to host its parties, but as Shawn recalls, "No place really had the sort of environment that felt like my apartment; no place felt like home." Just when frustration was beginning to set in, serendipity struck—they stumbled upon a vacated doctor's office in their own neighborhood, and set about re-creating the mid-20th-century style and ambience of his home.

The group quickly established a reputation with DJs, who adore spinning at Halcyon, and not just because of the primo sound system. Halcyon regular and party promoter Lady Miss Diva says, "DJs play true to their sound here, because there's no pressure to bring in the dollars at the bar."

Halcyon hosts a lineup of events that encompasses a wide variety of forward-looking musical styles. Top spinners from NYC's underground scene—the Breakbeat Science, Con-fu-sion and Slam Mode posses, Danny Krivit, DB, Khan, DJ Pathaan and Heather Heart—as well as international hotshots, such as progressive-houser Timo Maas and chill-out king Mixmaster Morris, who frequently stop by to ply their trade.

In New York's largely segregated and oftentimes snobbish club world, Halcyon is the great unifier: This may be the only place in the city where drum 'n' bassers, deep-house heads, technophiles and down-tempo disciples gather under one roof. "It's such an amazing feeling to be involved with a place that people seem to love so much," Stein says. "We've tried so hard to make this place special, and it's really cool to see it all work."

Halcyon

227 Smith St between Butler and Douglass Sts, Carroll Gardens, Brooklyn (718-260-9299). Subway: F, G to Bergen St. Sun–Thu 10am–midnight; Fri, Sat 10am–2am.

The nightly grind Dapper dancers get up close and personal at Club New York.

And it's not just club music here; the bar attracts its share of indie-rocker types, so you're just as likely to hear tunes with a guitar as a Roland 303.

Roving parties

There's something to be said for having a home to call one's own, but there are a number of ongoing soirees that don't stick to one location. The nights vary, as well as the prices and the places, but try to catch one of these peripatetic parties if you can.

Drive By

212-560-0951, or e-mail goldspot@hotmail.com for information.
The hybrid style known as two-step garage (a mishmash of house, breaks, drum 'n' bass and R&B) has been absolutely huge in the U.K. for years, but has only recently begun to make waves across the pond; the Drive By party is largely responsible for the sound's burgeoning acceptance. Resident DJ Dinesh regularly ropes in stars of the scene, such as M.J. Cole and the Artful Dodger as well as local folks such as Greg Poole.

Matter/:Form

www.matter-form.com.
Deep house, tech-house and techno are Matter/:Form's styles of choice, and few do it better than in-house spinner Francis Harris. Renowned for its booming boat parties, the Matter/:Form crew also occasionally takes over a land-based dance floor to get the kids going. The party manages to score cool guests, with folks such as U.K. acid-house stalwart Evil Eddie Richards and California-based deep-house dude Doc Martin working the decks.

Motherfucker

www.motherfuckernyc.com.
The Motherfucker gang celebrates messy, sexually mixed, rock & roll hanky-panky—an endangered form of tomfoolery, considering that the long-running Squeezebox recently breathed its last breath. Michael T. and Justine D. spin power pop, glam, new wave and even some disco in clubs all over Manhattan, usually on those drunken nights before a big national holiday.

Mutiny

212-252-2397; www.mutinysounds.com.
Mutiny's mayhem-makers (DJs Rekha, Siraiki, Navdeep, Anju and Zakhm) wander from venue to venue all over the city in order to rock the Casbah with Near Eastern musical flavaz, along with lots of drum 'n' bass, dub and hip-hop.

Organic Grooves

212-439-1147; www.codek.com.
The Organic Grooves folks throw their parties at any old space (and often at their venue of choice, that lovable floating bucket of bolts, *The Frying Pan*). DJ Sasha Crnobrnja and his coterie of musicians conjure up funky, genre-bending music that combines elements of funk, dub, disco—just about anything danceable—and melds them into a totally off-kilter yet dance-floor–ready sound. The crowd is usually straight, comely and racially mixed.

Scatalogics

www.scatalogics.com.
Plastic City recording artist Ulysses has his finger on the pulse of the way-underground electronic scene, and he's always throwing interesting parties to prove it. You can usually find Ulysses and top-notch guests on the decks, whipping up a machine-made musical storm, in spots ranging from Fun *(see page 268)* to the impressive Lunatarium *(10 Jay St at John St)* loft space in Brooklyn's Dumbo.

Turntables on the Hudson

212-560-5593; www.turntablesonthehudson.com.
This ultrafunky affair pops up all over the place, usually (as the name implies) as close to the Hudson River as it can get. Like Organic Grooves, DJs Nickodemus, Mariano and guests do the dub-funky, worldbeaty thing, but theirs is a more straightforward version of that sound, with live percussionists on hand. And like Organic Grooves, it's one of the city's best parties—the dance floor is packed all night long.

Tsunami

212-439-8124; www.tsunami-trance.com.
The Tsunami crew rides the psychedelic trance wave into town on a semiregular basis, often setting up shop in such unlikely venues as the World (which is, by day, the WWF café located at 1501 Broadway at 43rd Street, 212-398-2563) and the B.B. King Blues Club & Grill *(see page 312)*. Various stars of this scene man the decks, providing a surge of swirly synth action.

Film & TV

New York is ready for its close-up, on the silver screen and the boob tube

Do you ever feel like you're on a movie set when you walk the streets of New York? If the answer is yes, it's no surprise—many corners of the city have added drama to the big and small screens, from Martin Scorsese's Gotham classic *Taxi Driver* to the latest episode of *NYPD Blue*.

The prospect of running into a film or TV shoot is high. The rise in the number of New York–made projects during the past eight years has shot from just 69 in 1993 to 203 movies in 2000. Film-friendly former mayor Rudy Giuliani improved relations between production companies and local labor unions, which led to the business boom. Whether it's a big-name Hollywood movie (such as action flicks *Spider-Man* and *Men in Black 2*) or a small indie picture, there's always some work in progress on location in one of the five boroughs.

Besides providing an urban backdrop, New York allows filmmakers to bypass Hollywood altogether—western Queens has reemerged as a film-production center. It's the location of **Silvercup Studios**, where *Sex and the City* and *The Sopranos* are produced, and **Kaufman Astoria Studios**, where Rudolph Valentino and the Marx Brothers made their hits. The TV show *Sesame Street* and the A&E series *100 Centre Street* are shot there today.

There are also network and cable TV studios scattered around midtown Manhattan. MTV's Times Square studio and NBC's *Today* studio at Rockefeller Center are always mobbed with spectators. Other studios include CBS's *The Early Show*, taped in the GM Building *(767 Fifth Ave between 58th and 59th Sts)*, and ABC's *Good Morning America* studio in Times Square *(1500 Broadway between 43rd and 44th Sts)*. For info on how to be in the studio audience for some popular shows, see **Crowd pleasers**, page 276.

The city is also a great place to pursue behind-the-camera aspirations. Besides New York University's renowned graduate film program, several short-term production courses and workshops are worth investigating, such as those offered by **New York Film Academy** *(212-674-4300)* and the **Reel School** *(212-965-9444)*.

To view the finished product, there are hundreds of screens throughout the city, from the **Landmark Sunshine Cinema** *(143 E Houston St between Eldridge and Forsyth Sts, 212-358-7709)*, a restored 1898 theater that's the city's newest art house, to the **Magic Johnson Harlem USA** multiplex *(Frederick Douglass Blvd [Eighth Ave] at 124th St, 212-665-8742)*. Many movies open in New York before they're shown elsewhere—to build word of mouth or, if it's the end of the year, for Oscar consideration. So catch a flick when you're in town and be part of the buzz machine.

Popular cinemas

Scores of first-run movie theaters pepper the city. New releases come and go relatively quickly; if a film does badly, it might show for only a couple of weeks. Tickets usually cost $10, with discounts for senior citizens and children (often restricted to weekday afternoons). For tips on getting into sought-after screenings, see **Ticket info**, page 275.

AMC Empire 25
234 W 42nd St at Eighth Ave (212-398-3939). Subway: A, C, E to 42nd St–Port Authority; N, Q, R, W, S, 1, 2, 3, 7 to

Street gang The Muppet cast of *Sesame Street* stirs up trouble on the back lots of Kaufman Astoria Studios in Queens.

Foreign affair The Paris Theatre, near the Plaza Hotel, is the place to see European imports.

42nd St–Times Sq. $9.50, seniors and children $6. AmEx, MC, V.
AMC Empire, which incorporates the old 1912 Empire Theater, has 25 screens on 11 floors (the theaters hold 55 to 600 seats). Perfect if you're in Times Square.

Clearview's Ziegfeld
141 W 54th St between Sixth and Seventh Aves (212-765-7600). Subway: E, V to Fifth Ave–53rd St. $9.75, seniors and children $6.25. AmEx, MC, V.
The last truly great movie palace left in New York is synonymous with Hollywood's event pictures, and is often the venue for glitzy New York premieres. It's also a reserved-seating theater, so remember to order tickets in advance or arrive early.

Loews Kips Bay
570 Second Ave at 31st St (212-447-9425). Subway: 6 to 33rd St. $10, seniors and children $6.50. AmEx, MC, V.
Mainstream and slightly off-center Hollywood films are the standards at this megaplex with stadium seating.

Sony Lincoln Square & IMAX Theatre
1992 Broadway at 68th St (212-336-5000). Subway: 1, 2 to 66th St–Lincoln Ctr. $10, seniors and children $6.50; IMAX tickets $10, seniors $7.50, children $6.50. AmEx, MC, V.
Sony's entertainment center, more theme park than dull old movie house, is the biggest and best multiplex on the Upper West Side. A gift shop sells movie memorabilia, and the popcorn vendors are many. There are 12 fairly large screens. The center's eight-

> ▶ For up-to-date movie reviews and cinema listings, check out **www.timeoutny.com**, or pick up a copy of **Time Out New York**.

story IMAX screen shows 3-D films of the usual flaunt-the-technology variety (35 to 45 minutes long). Services for the hearing impaired are available. For another IMAX theater, see page 276.

UA Union Square Stadium 14
Broadway at 13th St (212-253-2225). Subway: L, N, Q, R, W, 4, 5, 6 to 14th St–Union Sq. $9.75, seniors and children $6.25. AmEx, MC, V.
This 14-screen stadium-seating multiplex has some of the Village's best-quality screens and digital sound.

Revival & art houses

New York screens more art films and old movies than any other city in the country. The following are the most popular venues.

Angelika Film Center
18 W Houston St at Mercer St (212-995-2000). Subway: F, V, S to Broadway–Lafayette; N, R to Prince St; 6 to Bleecker St. $9, seniors and children $5.50. Cash only at box office.
The six-screen Angelika features primarily new American independent and foreign films. You can hang out at the espresso-and-pastry bar before the show and bring anything you buy there into the theater (even sandwiches!). It's a zoo on weekends, so come extra early or buy your tickets by phone.

BAM Rose Cinemas
30 Lafayette Ave between Flatbush Ave and Fulton St, Fort Greene, Brooklyn (718-623-2770). Subway: C to Lafayette Ave; G to Fulton St; M, N, R, W to Pacific St; Q, 1, 2, 4, 5 to Atlantic Ave. $9; seniors, students and children $6. Cash only.
Brooklyn's premier art-house theater pulls double duty as a repertory house and a first-run multiplex. The four-screen venue is affiliated with the Brooklyn Academy of Music *(see page 315)*.

Cinema Classics

332 E 11th St between First and Second Aves (212-677-5368; www.cinemaclassics.com). Subway: L to First Ave; N, Q, R, W, 4, 5, 6 to 14th St–Union Sq. $5.50, includes double features. Cash only.

It may be shabby and cramped, but this is where to go for screenings of classic Hollywood, foreign and indie films. The $5.50 double bills can't be beat.

Cinema Village

22 E 12th St between Fifth Ave and University Pl (212-924-3363, box office 212-924-3364). Subway: L, N, Q, R, W, 4, 5, 6 to 14th St–Union Sq. $8.50, children $5.50, students $6.50. Cash only at box office.

Three-screen Cinema Village specializes in American indies and foreign films. The theater also hosts minifestivals and runs midnight horror flicks on weekends.

Film Forum

209 W Houston St between Sixth Ave and Varick St (212-727-8110, box office 212-727-8112). Subway: 1, 2 to Houston St. $9, seniors and children $5. Cash only at box office.

On Soho's edge, the three-screen Film Forum offers some of the best new films, documentaries and art movies around. Series of revivals, usually brilliantly curated, are also shown.

Lincoln Plaza Cinemas

30 Lincoln Plaza, entrance on Broadway between 62nd and 63rd Sts (212-757-2280, box office 212-757-0359). Subway: A, C, B, D, 1, 2 to 59th St–Columbus Circle. $9.50, seniors and children $6. Cash only at box office.

Commercially successful European films can be seen here, along with biggish American independent productions. All six theaters are equipped with assisted-listening devices for the hearing impaired and are wheelchair-accessible.

Paris Theatre

4 W 58th St between Fifth and Sixth Aves (212-688-3800). Subway: F to 57th St; N, R, W to Fifth Ave–60th St. $9.50, seniors and children $6. Cash only at box office.

This posh bijou (named for its original mandate to show only French films) is a de rigueur destination for cinéasts who love foreign-language films.

Quad Cinema

34 W 13th St between Fifth and Sixth Aves (212-255-8800, box office 212-255-2243). Subway: F, V to 14th St; L to Sixth Ave. $9, seniors and children $6. Cash only at box office.

Four small screens show a broad selection of foreign films, American documentaries and independents—many dealing with sexual and political issues. Children under five are not admitted.

Screening Room

54 Varick St at Laight St (212-334-2100). Subway: 1, 2 to Canal St. $9, seniors and children $6. Cash only.

Attached to a swanky bistro, this small three-screen theater is perfect for the ultimate dinner-and-movie date (it has love seats for two). It shows first-run films and revivals—and *Breakfast at Tiffany's* every Sunday.

Two Boots Pioneer Theater

155 E 3rd St between Aves A and B (212-254-3300). Subway: F, V to Lower East Side–Second Ave. First Ave. $8.50; seniors, students and children $6. Cash only.

The pizza chain Two Boots opened the East Village's only first-run alternative film center in 2000, and the programming is as tasty as the pies around the corner. Tickets are half-price with dinner at the nearby Two Boots Restaurant *(see page 166).*

Museums & societies

American Museum of the Moving Image

See page 44 for listing.

The first museum in the U.S. devoted to moving pictures is in Queens. AMMI shows more than 700 films and videos a year, covering everything from Hollywood classics and oddball industrial-safety films to series devoted to a single actor or director.

Anthology Film Archives

32 Second Ave at 2nd St (212-505-5181). Subway: F, V to Lower East Side–Second Ave. $8, seniors and students $5. Cash only.

This New York treasure houses the world's largest collection of written material documenting the his-

Ticket info

On summer weekends, it seems that every movie at every theater sells out hours before show time. To avoid disappointment, call the automated 777-FILM ticket system (which charges a fee of $1.50 per ticket) or visit the websites www.moviefone.com (for no additional charge) or www.fandango.com (additional charge) well in advance. Once at the cinema, go to the ticket machine, swipe your credit card (AmEx, MC, V) and get your tickets.

Note: There are "ticket buyers' lines" and "ticket holders' lines." Know which one you're in. The first showings on Saturday and Sunday (around noon) are less crowded, even for brand-new releases. Finally, a handful of theaters in Manhattan sometimes have reserved seating (such as Clearview's Ziegfeld and Clearview's Chelsea West), so be sure to call ahead.

Arts & Entertainment

tory of independent and experimental film and video. And it has glorious gonzo programming (everything from Maya Deren to Paul Verhoeven).

Brooklyn Museum of Art
See page 33 for listing.
The Brooklyn Museum of Art's intelligent, eclectic roster concentrates primarily on foreign films.

Film Society of Lincoln Center
Walter Reade Theater, Lincoln Center, 165 W 65th St between Broadway and Amsterdam Ave, plaza level above Alice Tully Hall (212-875-5600; www.filmlinc.com). Subway: 1, 2 to 66th St–Lincoln Ctr. $9. Cash only.
The Film Society was founded in 1969 to promote film and support filmmakers. It operates the Walter Reade Theater, a state-of-the-art showcase for contemporary film and video—with the city's most comfortable theater seats. Programs are usually thematic, often with an international perspective. Each autumn, the society hosts the New York Film Festival *(see page 278)*.

Solomon R. Guggenheim Museum
See page 36 for listing.

The Guggenheim programs and series are insightful and provocative. It's worth a look.

IMAX Theater
See **American Museum of Natural History,** *page 33 for listing.*
The IMAX screen is four stories high, and daily programming explores the natural world. The theater is closed through May 2002 for renovations. For another IMAX theater, see page 274.

Metropolitan Museum of Art
See page 35 for listing.
The Met offers a full program of documentary films on art (many of which relate to exhibitions) in the Uris Center Auditorium (near the 81st Street entrance).

Millennium
66 E 4th St between Bowery and Second Ave (212-673-0090). Subway: F, V to Lower East Side–Second Ave; 6 to Astor Pl. $7. Cash only.
This media-arts center screens avant-garde works, sometimes introduced by the films' directors, as part of the Personal Cinema Series *(Sept–Jun Fri, Sat 8pm)*. The center also loans out filmmaking equip-

Crowd pleasers
Drown out the canned laughter with your genuine giggles at these TV shows

Tickets are available to all sorts of TV shows taped in New York studios. If you make requests by mail, be sure to include your name, address, and day and evening telephone numbers.

The Daily Show with Jon Stewart
513 W 54th St between Tenth and Eleventh Aves (212-586-2477; www.comedycentral.com/dailyshow). Subway: A, C, B, D, 1, 2 to 59th St–Columbus Circle. Mon–Thu 5:30pm.
If you're a fan of this Comedy Central series, reserve tickets three months ahead of time by phone (call between 11am and 4pm Monday through Thursday), or call at 11:30am on the Friday before you'd like to attend, to see if there are any unused tickets. You must be at least 18 and have a photo ID.

Late Night with Conan O'Brien
212-664-3056, 212-664-3057; www.nbc.com/conan. Subway: B, D, F, V to 47–50th Sts–Rockefeller Ctr. Tue–Fri 5:30pm.
Call for tickets. A limited number of same-day, standby tickets are distributed at 9am *(30 Rockefeller Plaza, 49th St between Rockefeller Plaza and Sixth Ave, 49th St entrance)*. You must be at least 16 and have a photo ID.

Late Show with David Letterman
Mailing address: Late Show Tickets, c/o Ed Sullivan Theater, 1697 Broadway, New York, NY 10019 (212-975-1003; www.cbs.com/latenight/lateshow). Subway: B, D, E to Seventh Ave; N, R, W to 49th St; 1, 2 to 50th St. Mon–Wed 5:30pm; Thu 5:30, 8pm.
Send a postcard six to eight months in advance, or apply for tickets online; standby tickets are available by calling 212-247-6497 at 11am on the day of taping. You must be at least 16 and have a photo ID.

MTV's TRL
1515 Broadway at 45th St (212-398-8549; www.mtv.com). Subway: N, Q, R, W, S, 1, 2, 3, 7 to 42nd St–Times Sq. Mon–Fri 4pm.
Carson Daly fans stand behind police sawhorses outside the Viacom building, hoping to nab standby spots in the upstairs studio, but few succeed. For tickets, call one month before you'd like to attend the video show. (*TRL* wants you to look between the ages of 16 and 24.) Call 212-258-8000 or watch the music channel for info about being in the audience or participating in other shows.

ment and holds classes and workshops; it can be rented for screenings and has a gallery showing works by and about media artists.

Museum of Modern Art

See page 35 for listing.

MoMA was one of the first museums to recognize film as an art form. Its first director, Alfred H. Barr, believed that film was "the only great art peculiar to the 20th century." Scholars and researchers can delve into the museum's film archives (appointments must be requested in writing). MoMA has roughly 25 screenings each week; typically, they highlight a particular director's work, but they can also be based on other themes. Entry is free with museum admission. An infrared listening system is available for free to the hearing impaired.

The Museum of Television & Radio

See page 44 for listing.

The museum's collection includes more than 100,000 TV programs, which can be viewed at private consoles. Programs are shown daily (noon to closing) in the museum's two screening rooms and its 200-seat MT&R Theater.

Whitney Museum of American Art

See page 37 for listing.

In keeping with its aim of showing the best in contemporary American art, the Whitney runs a varied film-and-video schedule. Exhibitions, including the famous Biennial showcase, often have a strong moving-image component. Entry is free with museum admission.

Foreign-language films

Most of the previous institutions screen films in languages other than English, but the following show only foreign films.

Asia Society

See page 41 for listing.

You can see films from China, India and other Asian countries, as well as Asian-American films.

French Institute–Alliance Française

55 E 59th St between Madison and Park Aves (212-355-6160). Subway: N, R, W to Lexington Ave–59th St; 4, 5, 6 to 59th St. Tue–Fri 11am–

The Rosie O'Donnell Show

212-664-4000, 212-664-3056; www.rosieo.com. Subway: B, D, F, V to 47–50th Sts–Rockefeller Ctr. Mon, Tue, Thu 10am; Wed 10am, 2pm.
Rosie will step down this fall to make way for the *Caroline Rhea Show.* Until then, a ticket lottery is held March through June; call to be entered. You will be notified one to two weeks in advance of taping if you have seats. A few same-day standby seats are available (also by lottery) at 7:30am *(30 Rockefeller Plaza, 49th St between Rockefeller Plaza and Sixth Ave, 49th St entrance).* No children under five admitted.

Saturday Night Live

212-664-4000, 212-644-3056; www.nbc.com/snl. Subway: B, D, F, V to 47–50th Sts–Rockefeller Ctr. Dress rehearsals at 8pm, live at 11:30pm.
A ticket lottery is held in August and only postcards received that month are accepted. You will be notified one to two weeks in advance of taping if you have seats. A few same-day standby tickets, for the dress rehearsal and the live show, are distributed at 9:15am (but people start

Skit parade *SNL* cast members spoof Joan Rivers, Calista Flockhart and Garry Shandling.

lining up at 5am) at 30 Rockefeller Plaza, 49th Street entrance. You must be at least 16.

Who Wants to Be a Millionaire

Mailing address: Who Wants to Be a Millionaire, Columbia University Station, P.O. Box 250225, New York, NY 10025 (212-456-1000; www.abc.com/primetime/ millionaire). Mon–Thu 5pm.
Send postcards or enter online to request tickets. You must be at least 18, and present a valid ID at the taping. Tickets are mailed about two weeks before the scheduled taping.

7pm; Sat, Sun 11am–3pm. $8, students $6. AmEx, MC, V.
The institute shows movies from its homeland. They're usually subtitled (and never dubbed).

Goethe-Institut/ German Cultural Center

See page 42 for listing.
A German cultural and educational organization, the Goethe-Institut shows German films in various locations around the city, as well as in its own opulent auditorium.

Japan Society

333 E 47th St between First and Second Aves (212-752-0824; www.japansociety.org). Subway: E, V to Lexington Ave–53rd St; 6 to 51st St. Call for hours and schedule. $9, seniors and students $5. AmEx, MC, V.
The Japan Society Film Center organizes a full schedule of Japanese films, including two or three big series each year.

Film festivals

Every September and October since 1963, the Film Society of Lincoln Center has hosted the prestigious **New York Film Festival** *(www.filmlinc.com).* The FSLC, with the Museum of Modern Art, also sponsors the highly regarded **New Directors, New Films** each spring, to present works by on-the-cusp filmmakers from around the world.

Smaller but equally anticipated festivals occur throughout the year. January brings the annual **New York Jewish Film Festival** *(212-875-5600).* Held at the Walter Reade Theater *(see* **Film Society of Lincoln Center,** *page 276),* viewers can see works by Jewish filmmakers living abroad. The **Gen Art Film Festival** *(212-290-0312; www.genart.org),* a weeklong late-spring showcase of independent pieces, is followed by the more established **New York Lesbian and Gay Film Festival** in early June *(212-254-7228; www.newfestival.org).* On summer Monday evenings, **Bryant Park** *(Sixth Ave between 40th and 42nd Sts)* offers free classic flicks on a giant screen. In October, the **ResFest Digital Film Festival** *(www.resfest.com)* puts the spotlight on films utilizing new technology and storytelling techniques.

> ▶ Museums and galleries other than those listed here often host special film series and experimental films. See also chapter **Museums**.

City cinema

These are our ten favorite films made in the last 25 years that feature NYC.

After Hours (1985)
Martin Scorsese has built a career out of New York stories; this one, about a mousey yuppie who gets sucked into the downtown art scene, is one of his best.

Bad Lieutenant (1992)
Abel Ferrara pulls no punches in his portrait of a self-destructive cop who wallows in the urban blight that surrounds him.

Do the Right Thing (1989)
The hottest day of the summer leads to a riot in Bedford-Stuyvesant. No other film before or since has portrayed racial tension with such taut, clear-eyed brilliance.

Ghostbusters (1984)
Silly, scary fun—on a massive scale.

I Shot Andy Warhol (1996)
New York's '60s Pop Art scene gets the ultimate homage in this dissection of the city's maniacal obsession with celebrity.

Manhattan (1979)
The ultimate love letter to a city, Woody Allen's Gershwin-drenched b&w masterpiece captures the restless hearts of New Yorkers who ache for a life as majestic as the architecture around them.

Metropolitan (1990)
This endearing comedy of manners is an incisive look at New York's debutante scene, from the ennui of the pampered ultrarich to the amorous longings of the have-nots.

Saturday Night Fever (1977)
Passionate, funky, corny, gritty and soulful, John Badham's throbbing phenomenon of a film (based on a story in *New York* magazine) shows outer-borough yearning for New York's timeless promise of fame, fortune and happiness.

Six Degrees of Separation (1993)
Fred Schepisi's film version of the 1990 John Guare play (from the real-life case of a black teen posing as Sidney Poitier's son) encapsulates the Upper East Side's status-conscious liberal politics.

When Harry Met Sally... (1989)
Rob Reiner's through-the-years friendship-turned-romance between two Manhattanites is a classic portrait of love in the Big Apple.

Gay & Lesbian

Experiencing Gotham's highly visible, much celebrated queer culture is as easy as walking a straight line—to Chelsea, that is

The much-chanted phrase "We're here, we're queer, get used to it" is outdated. It's safe to say that New York is definitely used to its boisterous rainbow contingent. From the floor of the New York Stock Exchange to the big design and fashion houses on Seventh Avenue, it is impossible to ignore the fact that openly gay men and women play a pivotal role in New York's maintaining its status as one of the world's financial and cultural centers. The site of the 1969 Stonewall riots and the birthplace of the American gay-rights movement, New York City is a queer mecca and the headquarters for more than 500 lesbian, gay, bisexual and transgender social and political organizations.

During the annual celebration of **Gay Pride**, which takes place the last weekend in June (although the festivities begin the week prior), the Empire State Building is lit up in glorious lavender. This event draws thousands of visitors to the city. The Pride March, which always takes place on Sunday, attracts up to a half-million spectators. A number of Manhattan businesses fly the rainbow flag in tribute. The march is a great time to visit New York: You'll feel as if everyone is queer.

Arrive during the summer months to sample lesbian and gay resort culture on **Fire Island** *(see page 350)*, which is only a short trip from the center of town, and the stellar lineup of celluloid delights at the increasingly definitive **New York Lesbian & Gay Film Festival** in June *(see page 278)*.

An essential stop for any lesbian or gay visitor to New York is the **Lesbian, Gay, Bisexual & Transgender Community Center** *(see page 281)*, a downtown nexus of information and activity that serves as a meeting place for more than 300 groups and organizations. You can pick up copies of New York's free weekly gay and lesbian publications. And don't miss *Time Out New York*'s lively Gay & Lesbian listings for the latest happenings around town. In 2000, *TONY* received a Media Award from the Gay & Lesbian Alliance Against Defamation, honoring the magazine's overall coverage.

Although the gay and lesbian population of New York is quite diverse, the club and bar scenes don't accurately reflect it; most places are frequently gender-segregated, and like their straight counterparts, tend to attract the single 35-and-under crowd. However, the social alternatives are plentiful—among them, queer coffeebars, bookstores and restaurants, as well as dozens of gay-themed films and plays that are presented in mainstream venues *(see chapters* **Cabaret & Comedy**, **Film & TV** *and* **Theater & Dance**).

Books & media

Publications

New York's gay weekly magazines are *HX (Homo Xtra)* and *Next*—both of which include extensive information on bars, cultural events, dance clubs, group meetings, sex clubs and restaurants…and loads of personals. *HX* also devotes a few pages to lesbian listings. The newspaper *LGNY (Lesbian & Gay New York)* offers feisty political coverage with an activist slant. The *New York Blade News*, a sister publication of *The Washington Blade*, focuses on queer politics and news. All four are free and widely available. *MetroSource* ($4.95) is a bimonthly glossy with a guppie slant, covering interior decorating, designer fashions and exotic travel.

Daniel Hurewitz's *Stepping Out* ($16), which details nine walking tours of gay and lesbian NYC, is another invaluable resource. This book—as well as the above-mentioned magazines—is available at the **Oscar Wilde Memorial Bookshop** *(see page 280)*.

▶ For more information about annual gay events such as the Pride March, see chapter **By Season**.
▶ If you're interested in queer New York's upscale bar scene, see **Raising the bar**, page 282.
▶ For a complete listing of New York's nightlife, check out chapter **Clubs**.
▶ For strictly gay listings, see **Boys' Life**, page 281; for lesbian listings, see **Dyke Life**, page 288.
▶ See chapter **Night Train to Brooklyn** for the highlights of Brooklyn's gay-nightlife scene.

Arts & Entertainment

Television

There's an abundance of gay-related broadcasting, though nearly all of it is amateurishly produced and appears on public-access cable channels. Programming varies by cable company, so you may not be able to watch all these shows on a hotel TV. At night, Channel 35 (in most of Manhattan) switches over to sexually explicit programming that includes the infamous Robin Byrd's *Men for Men* soft-core strip shows. Manhattan Neighborhood Network (channels 34, 56, 57 and 67 on all Manhattan cable systems) has plenty of gay shows, ranging from zany drag queens milking their 15 minutes of fame to serious discussion programs. *HX* and *Next* provide the most current TV listings.

Bookshops

Reflecting a national trend, a number of independent gay bookshops in NYC have closed over the past several years as online purveyors and megastores aggressively pursue the gay market. Most New York bookshops have gay sections (*see chapter* **Books & Poetry**); only a few that cater especially to gays and lesbians continue to hang on.

Bluestockings

172 Allen St at Stanton St (212-777-6028). Subway: F, V to Lower East Side–Second Ave. Tue–Sat noon–8pm; Sun 2–8pm. AmEx, Disc, MC, V.
This funky Lower East Side bookstore devoted to women's literature (it's named after the 18th-century feminist literary society) is a popular cultural center that holds weekly readings and events. Peruse a dyke-hero comic book or a feminist manifesto while having tea and a vegan muffin in the café.

Oscar Wilde Memorial Bookshop

15 Christopher St between Sixth and Seventh Aves (212-255-8097). Subway: 1, 2 to Christopher St–Sheridan Sq. Mon–Sat 11am–8pm; Sun noon–7pm. AmEx, Disc, MC, V.
New York's oldest gay and lesbian bookshop is chock-full of books and magazines, and offers many discounts.

Centers & phone lines

Audre Lorde Project Center

85 S Oxford St between Fulton Street and Lafayette Ave, Fort Greene, Brooklyn (718-596-0342). Subway: C to Lafayette Ave. Mon, Fri 10am–6pm; Tue–Thu 10am–9pm; Sat 1:30–9pm.
Officially known as the Audre Lorde Project Center for Lesbian, Gay, Bisexual, Two-Spirit & Transgender People of Color Communities, this community center is an essential resource for queer people of color. Call for information about events and group meetings.

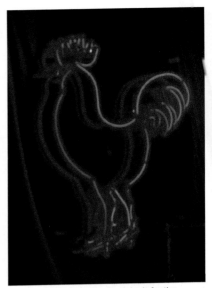

No spring chicken The Cock isn't for the fainthearted, or anyone who's afraid to crow.

Barnard Center for Research on Women

101 Barnard Hall, 3009 Broadway at 117th St (212-854-2067). Subway: 1 to 116th St–Columbia Univ. Mon 9am–8pm; Tue–Fri 9am–5pm.
This academic center is the place to explore scholarly feminism—a calendar of classes, lectures and film screenings is available. The library has an extensive archive of feminist journals and government reports.

Gay & Lesbian Switchboard of New York Project

212-989-0999; www.glnh.org. Mon–Fri 4pm–midnight; Sat noon–5pm.
This is a phone-information service only. Callers who need legal help can be referred to lawyers, and there's information on bars, restaurants and hotels. The switchboard is especially good at giving peer counseling to people who have just come out or who may be considering suicide. There are also details on all sorts of other gay and lesbian organizations. Outside New York (but within the U.S.), callers can contact the switchboard's sister toll-free line, the **Gay & Lesbian National Hotline**, at 888-THE-GLNH.

Gay Men's Health Crisis

119 W 24th St between Sixth and Seventh Aves (212-367-1000, AIDS advice hot line 212-807-6655; www.gmhc.org). Subway: 1, 2 to 23rd St. Advice hot line Mon–Fri 10am–9pm; Sat noon–3pm. Recorded

information in English and Spanish at other times.
Office Mon–Fri 9am–6pm.
This was the world's first organization dedicated to helping people with AIDS. It has a threefold mission: to push for better public policies, to help those who are sick by providing services and counseling to them and their families, and to educate the public to prevent the further spread of HIV. There are 180 staff members and 1,400 volunteers. Support groups usually meet in the evenings.

Lesbian, Gay, Bisexual & Transgender Community Center

208 W 13th St between Seventh and Eighth Aves (212-620-7310; www.gaycenter.org). Subway: F, V, 1, 2, 3 to 14th St; L to Eighth Ave. 9am–11pm.
After being closed almost two years for major renovations, the center is up and running again, this time with a new name that makes it clear that bisexuals and transgender people are vital parts of the community. Founded in 1983, the center provides political, cultural, spiritual and emotional sustenance to the 300-odd groups (this is where ACT UP and GLAAD got started) and individuals who meet here. The center also houses the National Museum and Archive of Lesbian and Gay History, and the Vito Russo lending library.

Lesbian Herstory Archive

P.O. Box 1258, New York, NY 10116 (718-768-3953; www.datalounge.net/lha). By appointment only.
Housed in Brooklyn's Park Slope area (known to some as Dyke Slope for its large lesbian population), the Herstory Archive, started by Joan Nestle and Deb Edel in 1974, includes more than 10,000 books (theory, fiction, poetry, plays), 1,400 periodicals and assorted personal memorabilia. You, too, can donate a treasured possession and become part of Herstory.

Michael Callen–Audre Lorde Community Health Center

356 W 18th St between Eighth and Ninth Aves (212-271-7200; www.callen-lorde.org). Subway: A, C, E to 14th St; L to Eighth Ave. Mon 12:30–8pm; Tue, Thu, Fri 9am–4:30pm; Wed 8:30am–8pm.
Formerly known as Community Health Project, this is the country's largest (and New York's only) health center primarily serving the gay, lesbian, bisexual and transgender community. The center offers a wide range of services, including comprehensive primary care, HIV treatment, free adolescent services (including the youth line *HOTT*: 212-271-7212), STD screening and treatment, mental health services, and peer counseling and education.

NYC Gay & Lesbian Anti-Violence Project

240 W 35th St between Seventh and Eighth Aves, suite 200 (212-714-1184, 24-hour hot line 212-714-1141; www.avp.org). Subway: A, C, E, 1, 2, 3 to 34th St–Penn Station. Mon–Thu 10am–8pm; Fri 10am–6pm.

The project provides support for the victims of antigay and antilesbian crimes. Working with the police department, project volunteers offer advice on seeking police help. Short- and long-term counseling is available.

Boys' Life

The Christopher Street area of the West Village has historical gay sites such as the **Stonewall** *(see page 285),* friendly show-tune piano cabarets and unpretentious stores full of rainbow knickknacks and slogan T-shirts. But over the past several years, the gay epicenter has shifted to Chelsea, which flaunts an attitude that can be intimidating.

The neighborhood's main drag is Eighth Avenue between 16th and 23rd Streets, a strip lined with businesses catering to upwardly mobile gay men: gyms; sexy clothing and trendy home-furnishing stores; tanning and grooming salons; galleries; and cafés, bars and mid-range restaurants for brunch, business lunches and late dinners. The cult of the body reigns in Chelsea, and it's a kick to watch the perfectly toned men strut their stuff down the avenue. True, some of the gym bunnies adopt a creepy pecking order and ignore the existence of all those without bulging muscles. However, the stereotype depicting Chelsea as a vast sea of supermen is exaggerated, and all types of queers converge on the neighborhood to check out the scene.

Most of Manhattan's dance clubs—what's left of them—are either in Chelsea or a hop, skip and jump away from it; many feature a big gay house/techno night during the weekend. At these bacchanals, sybarites can spin and twirl with upwards of thousands of half-naked men until the wee hours *(See chapter Clubs).*

In contrast to Chelsea, a countercultural community of punk-rock glitter-fashion boys and theatrical drag queens thrives in a network of small, divey East Village bars. The scene has an arty, bohemian vibe, and there are many lovely men to be found, ranging from 1970s-style macho butches to Bowie-type androgynes. The crowd tends to be even younger than in Chelsea (although some men may appear to be younger than they are) and is more mixed, both ethnically and sexually.

Some habitués of Chelsea and the East Village do mix. Men of all ages, shapes and sizes frequent the city's leather/fetish bars and clubs, such as the **The Eagle** *(554 W 28th St between Tenth and Eleventh Aves, 646-473-1866)* in Chelsea and **The Lure** in the Meatpacking District *(see page 285).* If you're a devotee of the leather scene, you might want to plan your trip around either the New York Mr. Leather Contest, which takes place in the autumn, or the Black Party at **Saint at Large** *(see page 286)*—a special all-night leather-and-S&M–themed circuit party that attracts thousands of people every March.

For open-air cruising, try the **Ramble** in Central Park, located between the 79th Street transverse and the Lake (but beware of police entrapment). And although the city has made every effort to clean up Times Square and turn it into an extension of Disney World, you can for the moment still find nude male burlesque at the **Gaiety** *(201 W 46th St between Broadway and Eighth Ave, 212-221-8868)*. The adjacent west-midtown area—once known as Hell's Kitchen but now known by the less threatening moniker Clinton—is fast becoming the next hot homo zone. Take a stroll up Ninth Avenue between 42nd and 57th Streets to explore.

Don't worry if you're just an average T-shirt-and-jeans–type gay man. Not only will you feel comfortable in almost any gay space, you'll be surprised at how much cruising happens on the streets while you're walking around town, and how easy it is to turn a glance into a conversation.

Accommodations

Chelsea Mews Guest House

344 W 15th St between Eighth and Ninth Aves (212-255-9174). Subway: A, C, E to 14th St; L to Eighth Ave. Singles and doubles $100–$200. Cash and traveler's checks only.
Built in 1840, this guest house is exclusively for gay men. The rooms are comfortable and well-furnished, and have semiprivate bathrooms. Smoking is not allowed.

Chelsea Pines Inn

317 W 14th St between Eighth and Ninth Aves (212-929-1023; fax 212-620-5646). Subway: A, C, E to 14th St; L to Eighth Ave. Doubles and triples $99–$139 (slightly higher during Gay Pride and holidays). AmEx, DC, Disc, MC, V.
This centrally located inn near the West Village and Chelsea welcomes gay male and female guests. Vintage movie posters set the mood, and the 25 rooms are clean and comfortable; the majority have private bathrooms, and all have radios, televisions, phones, refrigerators and air-conditioning. Continental breakfast is included with your stay.

Colonial House Inn

318 W 22nd St between Eighth and Ninth Aves (212-243-9669, 800-689-3779; www.colonialhouseinn.com).

Raising the bar

Dive bars lose their grip on gay nightlife, as sleek, stylish spots take center stage

Ain't it a shame? Gay New Yorkers, renowned for their stylish flair, are so often stuck with dismal bars, "decorated" with fraying pool tables, crummy furniture and black-painted walls. Sure, a sleazy atmosphere heightens the cruise appeal, but is it too much to ask for a little imagination and taste? Thank goodness a growing number of gay watering holes have realized that a happening habitat can actually lead to happier and more frequent customers (imagine that!).

In the East Village, where most gay bars look like a cross between caves and mildewy rec rooms, there are now a few stylish outposts, including the sister spots **Wonder Bar** *(see page 284)* and **Starlight Bar and Lounge** *(see page 284)*. The owners transformed these former dives into contemporary, minimalist lounges, complete with banquettes and conversation pits. Their civilized allure obviously works: Both joints are superpopular and packed to the

rafters on the weekends. Starlight also has a lively lesbian party, Starlette, on Sundays.

The glamorization of gay nightlife has bypassed the original gay neighborhood—the West Village—where old-school singalong piano bars such as **The Monster** still rule *(see page 285)*. For the newest, most impressive bars, Chelsea is the place to go. The ultraslick **xl Chelsea** *(see page 285)* caused a sensation when it opened in spring 2001; it's the pinnacle of the New York gay scene. Inspired by designer Philippe Starck, the former garbage recycling plant boasts a state-of-the-art lighting system and a dazzling bathroom (an aquarium is installed above the urinals). But don't look for high-stylers in Gucci—the crowd tends to favor basic Banana Republic.

Also in Chelsea is **g** *(see page 285)*, a thriving lounge whose main feature is a circular bar that allows patrons to check each other out from practically all angles. The bare walls and

Subway: C, E to 23rd St. $80–$99 with shared bath; $125–$140 with private bath. Prices higher on weekends (15 percent discount Jan 2–Feb 28 with four-night minimum stay). MC, V.

This beautifully renovated 1880s townhouse sits on a quiet street in the heart of Chelsea. It's run by, and primarily for, gay men. Colonial House is a great place to stay, even if some of the cheaper rooms are small. Major bonuses: free continental breakfast served until noon in the Art Gallery Lounge and a rooftop deck (nude sunbathing allowed!).

Incentra Village House

32 Eighth Ave between Jane and 12th Sts (212-206-0007). Subway: A, C, E to 14th St; L to Eighth Ave. $119–$169, suites $149–$199. AmEx, MC, V.

Two cute 1841 townhouses, perfectly situated in the West Village, make up this guest house run by gay men. The intriguingly decorated rooms (singles, doubles and suites) are spacious and come with private bathrooms and kitchenettes; some have working fireplaces. There's also a 1939 Steinway baby grand piano for snow-tune enthusiasts.

Bars

Most bars in New York offer theme nights, drink specials and happy hours, and the gay ones are no exception. Don't be shy, remember to tip the bartender, and carry plenty of business cards. (*See also* **Raising the bar**, *page 282, and chapters* **Bars** *and* **Cabaret & Comedy**.)

East Village

Beige

B Bar, 40 E 4th St at Bowery (212-475-2220). Subway: F, V, S to Broadway–Lafayette St; 6 to Bleecker St. Tue 10pm–4am. Average drink: $7. AmEx, MC, V.

Considering that hot parties in New York usually last no more than a few seasons, it's truly amazing that Beige is still going strong after a five-year run. By midnight, the sprawling restaurant-lounge is packed, mostly with toned, fashionable young men. It's not the best place to go solo; the scene is more about hanging out with your friends and checking out the occasional celebrity—Calvin Klein, Monica Lewinsky, superstar photographer David LaChapelle, etc. During the summer, the action spills out into the patio area.

Boiler Room

86 E 4th St between First and Second Aves (212-254-7536). Subway: F, V to Lower East Side–Second Ave. 4pm–4am. Average drink: $5. Cash only.

For most self-respecting East Village boys, a weekend stop here isn't just an option—it's a moral imperative.

Wee bit of extravagance The bathrooms at xl Chelsea feature a 30-foot aquarium.

subdued colors make the ideal backdrop for showing off the latest designer outfits.

Hell's Kitchen (*see page 72*), in Manhattan's West 50s, is the latest frontier for homesteading gay professionals, and following their arrival are swanky queer tippling stations, including **Eatery** (*see page 287*) and **Chase** (*see page 285*), where guppies guzzle happy hour cocktails. After the suits go home, martini-sipping fashionistas flock to Chase's tiled bar and lounge on velvety banquettes to admire the pretty-boy parade.

Finally, there's **Splash** (*see page 285*), probably New York's most beloved gay nightclub, which has expanded to mall-like proportions over the past ten years and now includes a dance floor, a basement lounge and a boutique that sells clothing and nightlife trinkets (e.g., poppers and lubricants). The varied crowd includes Europeans, Midwestern farm boys, Chelsea queens and young gyrating Latinos. The vast floor space can be blissfully packed with guys but not feel suffocatingly crowded. On the stage is Splash's most unique design element: a shower, which allows go-go hunks to sensually soak their bodies and clinging underwear. Sure it's cheesy, but, elevated above the crowd and illuminated by spotlights, the stainless-steel nozzle and its glistening streams of water are practically objets d'art. The go-go boys aren't bad either.

Probably the most intensely cruisey of East Village bars, this unassuming joint is busy on weeknights and absolutely mobbed on Friday and Saturday nights. The pool table and renowned jukebox (Dusty Springfield to Rage Against the Machine) keep the neighborhood vibe alive.

The Cock
188 Ave A at 12th St (212-946-1871). Subway: L to First Ave; N, Q, R, W, 4, 5, 6 to 14th St–Union Sq. 9:30pm–4am. Average drink: $7. Cash only.
The Cock is location No. 1 for the East Village's randy, hip crowd, many of whom don't roll into the joint until after 2am. Depending on the night, the music ranges from campy '80s to good old rock & roll.

The Phoenix
447 E 13th St between First Ave and Ave A (212-477-9979) Subway: L to First Ave; N, Q, R, W, 4, 5, 6 to 14th St–Union Sq. 3pm–4am. Average drink: $5. Cash only.
You know the East Village has changed forever when there's a gay bar on what used to be one of its scariest blocks. This unfancy watering hole provides video games, a pool table and lots of men eager to make new friends.

Starlight Bar and Lounge
167 Ave A between 10th and 11th Sts (212-475-2172). Subway: L to First Ave; N, Q, R, W, 4, 5, 6 to 14th St–Union Sq. 9pm–4am. Average drink: $6. Cash only.
On weekends, this bar is almost too popular for its own good, as scores of guys cram into the narrow space. During the week, things are more manageable, and a nice bonus is that Starlight frequently

features top-notch local entertainers performing free shows in the comfy back lounge (usually around 10pm). Sunday night is the bar's very popular lesbian party, Starlette, which attracts all sorts of East Village hipsters.

Wonder Bar
505 E 6th St between Aves A and B (212-777-9105). Subway: F, V to Lower East Side–Second Ave. 6pm–4am. Average drink: $5. Cash only.
East meets West—Village, that is—at Wonder Bar. This smoky Euro-modern lounge is filled with sexy patrons, deep conversations and serious eyewear. The DJ's syncopated spinning defies you not to dance—the walls are lined with benches, but few wallflowers. Glam female bartenders keep the spirits flowing as the smart, young drinkers grope their dates or cruise for fresh action.

West Village

Bar d'O
29 Bedford St at Downing St (212-627-1580). Subway: A, C, E, F, V, S to W 4th St; 1, 2 to Houston St. 7pm–3am. Average drink: $6.50. Cash only.
Thursdays, Saturdays and Sundays at this dark, cozy, candlelit haunt feature intimate cabaret performances by the city's most talented drag queens. The cast varies, but you can almost always count on catching Joey Arias, Raven O or Sade Pendavis—all of whom really sing, not lip-synch. On Mondays, the joint becomes a lesbian lounge called Pleasure. The music (provided by DJ Sharee) is a mellow hip-hop groove, and the place is always full of rap stars who truly believe in "ladies first."

Talking back Drag queens dish out plenty of sass—and serviceable eats—at Lips.

The Lure

409 W 13th St between Ninth and Tenth Aves (212-741-3919). Subway: A, C, E to 14th St; L to Eighth Ave. 8pm–4am. Average drink: $4. Cash only.
Now that the Meatpacking District has been taken over by French bistros and designer boutiques, the Lure is practically the last kink outpost remaining. The newfangled fetish bar attracts a broad, energetic bunch and a few poseurs, many of whom don leather, rubber or manly Levi's and army boots. Pork, a raunchy party for the young set, is on Wednesdays; it features particularly imaginative themes.

The Monster

80 Grove St at Sheridan Sq (212-924-3558). Subway: 1, 2 to Christopher St–Sheridan Sq. Mon–Fri 4pm–4am; Sat, Sun 2pm–4am. Average drink: $5. Cash only.
A Village landmark, this bi-level club offers an old-school piano lounge upstairs, where the locals gather to belt out show tunes. And, honey, you haven't lived until you've experienced a bunch of tipsy queers belting out the best of Broadway. Downstairs is a completely separate environment: a disco that caters to a young and friendly multiracial crowd. Many are from the outer boroughs and itchin' for fun.

The Stonewall

53 Christopher St between Sixth and Seventh Aves (212-463-0950). Subway: 1, 2 to Christopher St–Sheridan Sq. 2:30pm–4am. Average drink: $5. Cash only.
This is a landmark bar, next door to the actual location of the 1969 gay rebellion against police harassment. If you don't already know it, ask the bartender to talk you through the story. Play some pool, chat up the other customers (they're nice), then check out the upstairs bar that frequently features go-go boys. Over the past couple of years, the bar has shed its ho-hum image to become a lively place to linger.

Chelsea

Barracuda

275 W 22nd St between Seventh and Eighth Aves (212-645-8613). Subway: C, E to 23rd St. 4pm–4am. Average drink: $6. Cash only.
This Chelsea bar continues to draw hordes of boys. Friendlier and more comfortable than its neighborhood competition, the space is split in two, with a traditional bar area up front and a frequently redecorated lounge in back, plus a pool table, pinball machine and nightly DJs. Various drag queen celebrities perform shows throughout the week. On Thursdays, Cashetta hosts a star search. Boys on a budget, take note: There's never a cover.

Dusk Lounge

147 W 24th St between Sixth and Seventh Aves (212-924-4490). Subway: F, V, 1, 2 to 23rd St.

Mon–Thu 6pm–2am; Fri 6pm–4am; Sat 8pm–4am. Average drink: $7. AmEx, DC, Disc, MC, V.
In these postironic, post-postmodern days, the emergence of postgay seems inevitable, and Dusk has this nascent market covered: There are no rainbow flags, no disco balls, no dancing…no outward signs of "gayness" whatsoever. Instead, the color scheme is a restrained, cool blue, and there's not a mirror in sight. Dusk is a pressure-free place to meet guys who have the mind-body balance thing all worked out and who don't like shopping at the meat market.

g

223 W 19th St between Seventh and Eighth Aves (212-929-1085). Subway: 1, 2 to 18th St. 4pm–4am. Average drink: $6. Cash only.
This lounge is one of Chelsea's most popular destinations, especially for the well-scrubbed, fresh-faced set. Forgo that Ketel One tonic for something from the juice–power-drink bar. One word of warning: Late in the evening, the space is often filled to capacity, while outside, there's a line of unfortunates waiting to get in. Go early to stake your place at the bar.

Splash

50 W 17th St between Fifth and Sixth Aves (212-691-0073). Subway: F, V to 14th St; L to Sixth Ave; 1, 2 to 18th St. Sun–Thu 4pm–4am; Fri, Sat 4pm–5am. Cover: $10 (Fri, Sat after 10pm). Average drink: $6. Cash only.
You've got to hand it to Splash—for more than ten years now, this Chelsea hot spot has been packing in the guys, who come to dance, cruise and ogle the hunky bartenders, as well as the go-go boys who get all wet and wild under the club's famous onstage shower.

xl Chelsea

357 W 16th St between Eighth and Ninth Aves (212-995-1400). Subway: A, C, E to 14th St; L to Eighth Ave. 4pm–4am. Average drink: $6. Cash only.
This tri-level space is a study in style, from the 30-foot aquarium in the bathroom to the sleek interior design. Fashion divas, muscle men, fag hags and a few trannies all run amok under one roof.

Midtown

Chase

255 W 55th St between Broadway and Eighth Ave (212-333-3400). Subway: A, C, B, D, 1, 2 to 59th St–Columbus Circle. 4pm–4am. Average drink: $5.50. AmEx, MC, V.
Fans call it the g bar of Hell's Kitchen, and like that Chelsea spot, Chase draws an after-work crowd of dapper and professional gay men. Later in the evening, the fashionistas arrive for cocktails and chic ambience (designed with the aid of a feng shui expert). The main bar, a tiled confection of red, orange and yellow, is as pleasing to the eye as the cute boys are to one another.

Stella's

266 W 47th St between Broadway and Eighth Ave (212-575-1680). Subway: A, C, E to 42nd St–Port Authority; N, Q, R, W, S, 1, 2, 3, 7 to 42nd St–Times Sq. Noon–4am. Cover: $5 (Thu–Sun after 8pm). Average drink: $5. Cash only.

One of the last gay vestiges of pre–Disney Times Square, Stella's offers go-go boy floor shows in the basement, starting around 11pm. Connoisseurs of street-smart Latin and African-American homeboys will be especially entertained.

The Townhouse

See page 287.

Uptown

The Works

428 Columbus Ave between 80th and 81st Sts (212-799-7365). Subway: B, C to 81st St; 1, 2 to 79th St. 2pm–4am. Average drink: $5. Cash only.

The major hangout for young gay men on the Upper West Side draws an under-40 guppie crowd. On Sunday evenings, there's a popular beer blast: Between 6pm and 1am, you pay only $1 for a draft beer. Part of the proceeds benefit God's Love We Deliver, a meal-delivery service for homebound AIDS patients.

Clubs

A number of New York clubs have gay nights; many of those we list are one-nighters rather than permanent venues. There's also a large number of fund-raising parties and other events worth looking out for. For more clubs, the majority of which are gay-friendly, plus more information about some of those listed below, see chapter **Clubs**.

Dance clubs

Berliniamsburg

Luxx, 256 Grand St between Driggs Ave and Roebling St, Williamsburg, Brooklyn (718-599-1000). Subway: L to Bedford Ave. Sat 10pm–4am. Cover: $5. Average drink: $3. Cash only.

How did this electronica dance party get its name? It seems promoter Larry Tee heard hot Christian Dior designer Hedi Slimane proclaim groovy Williamsburg the new Berlin. As Mr. Tee spins the sounds of Fisherspooner, Peaches and Chicks on Speed, the artsy crowd (mostly local kids from the 'hood) dances, checks out one another's outfits and absorbs the club's new wave decor.

Earth

Exit, 610 W 56th St between Eleventh and Twelfth Aves (212-582-8282). Subway: A, C, B, D, 1, 2 to 59th St–Columbus Circle. Sat 10pm. Cover: $25. Average drink: $6. MC, V.

Junior Vasquez, the undisputed champ of New York's DJs, has found yet another headquarters to entertain his mobs of manic followers (his previous employer, Twilo, was closed by local authorities). The party is called Earth, and the sheer enormity of the weekly gathering is incredible. Thousands of people—a harmonious mix of muscle men, fashion fags and outer-borough straights—pack the football field–size dance floor, which includes a stage for late-night performances by diva dance artists.

Kitsch Inn

True, 28 E 23rd St between Madison and Park Ave South (212-254-6117). Subway: 6 to 23rd St. Fri 8pm–4am. Cover: $15, with invite $10, before midnight $5. Average drink: $8. AmEx, MC, V.

Fear not, queer rock & rollers, New York's nightlife scene ain't just about house music. At Kitsch Inn, True's Friday-night party, the funky space is devoted to rock, punk, new wave, etc., and includes an evening band showcase. The crowd is mostly gay, but a few straights add to the mix of cute, enthusiastic partiers who love to dance—even though the playlist doesn't really vary much from week to week.

Saint at Large

To get on the mailing list, call 212-674-8541 or visit www.saintatlarge.com.

The now-mythical Saint was one of the first venues where New York's gay men enjoyed dance-floor freedom. The club closed, but the clientele keeps its memory alive with a series of four huge circuit parties each year. The S&M-tinged Black Party, the White Party, Halloween and New Year's Eve each attract muscle-bound, image-conscious gay men from around the U.S.

Bathhouses

Despite the city's crackdown on adult businesses, a few bathhouses for men still exist. Apart from the bar-like **J's Hangout** *(675 Hudson St at 14th St, 212-242-9292)*—which is less blatantly sexual and more of an after-hours desperation cruise—there is the **West Side Club** bathhouse *(27 W 20th St between Fifth and Sixth Aves, 212-691-2700)* in Chelsea and its sister establishment, the **East Side Club** *(227 E 56th St at Second Ave, 212-753-2222 or 212-826-0136)*. For more current details, consult *HX* magazine's Getting Off section.

Restaurants & cafés

Few New York restaurants would bat an eye at a same-sex couple enjoying an intimate dinner. Most of the neighborhoods mentioned above have hundreds of great eating places that are de facto gay restaurants, and many that are gay-owned and -operated. Below are a few of the most obviously gay places in town. For more dining options, see chapter **Restaurants**.

Big Cup

228 Eighth Ave between 21st and 22nd Sts (212-206-0053). Subway: C, E to 23rd St. Mon–Fri 7am–1am; Sat, Sun 8am–2am. Average sandwich: $6.50. Caffè latte: $3.52. Cash only.

Big Cup is as unmistakably Chelsea Boy as a pair of shiny polyester bikini briefs. The cinder block walls are painted with whimsical pastel flowers, the snaky chrome light fixtures are fitted with tinted bulbs, and mainstream club music pumps relentlessly from the sound system. The coffee is fine, as are the snacks—brownies, lemon bars and Rice Krispies treats for $2 a pop, plus sandwiches and soups. But no one pays much attention. Big Cup is one of New York's classic gay meet markets: You don't put a disco ball in a coffee bar and expect patrons to lose themselves in Kierkegaard.

The Dish

201 Eighth Ave between 20th and 21st Sts (212-352-9800). Subway: C, E to 23rd St. Mon–Fri 7am–1am; Sat Sun 8am–2am. Average main course: $12. AmEx, DC, Disc, MC, V.

How do you make diner food *fabulous*? Open a diner in Chelsea and call it the Dish. There's nothing like scarfing a cheeseburger deluxe while gazing at beautiful motorcycles (and their riders) cruising past open French doors. And if you're after sweets, there are cream pies and eye candy aplenty.

Eatery

798 Ninth Ave at 53rd St (212-765-7080). Subway: C, E to 50th St. Sun–Thu noon–4pm, 5pm–midnight; Fri, Sat noon–4pm, 5pm–1am. Average main course: $20. AmEx, DC, MC, V.

A minimalist look helps this small space feel almost as sprawling as the menu. The food ranges from crispy, gingery shrimp spring rolls to macaroni and cheese, but desserts aren't worth the time or money. Instead, turn your attention to the bar, which has a primo house-cocktail menu and is generally packed.

Eighteenth & Eighth

159 Eighth Ave at 18th St (212-242-5000). Subway: A, C, E to 14th St; L to Eighth Ave; 1, 2 to 18th St. Sun–Thu 9am–midnight; Fri, Sat 9am–12:30am. Average main course: $15. AmEx, MC, V.

On warm summer evenings, the sidewalk in front of Eighteenth & Eighth is rife with clinking wine glasses, laughter, and the bare legs of well-sculpted men. Locals revel in the refined breeziness of it all; the inoffensive American food is secondary. The menu ranges from crowd pleasers—chili, meat loaf and half-pound bison burgers—to more upscale entrées.

Foodbar

149 Eighth Ave between 17th and 18th Sts (212-243-2020). Subway: A, C, E to 14th St; L to Eighth Ave; 1, 2 to 18th St. 11am–midnight. Average main course: $17. AmEx, MC, V.

Foodbar's globally influenced American menu will get your mouth watering—if the customers haven't already. Balsamic-glazed roasted chicken, Moroccan salad and steak au poivre are entirely satisfying. Servers are efficient and flirty, not to mention impossibly good looking.

Lips

2 Bank St at Greenwich Ave (212-675-7710). Subway: 1, 2, 3 to 14th St. Mon–Thu 5:30pm–midnight; Fri, Sat 5:30pm–2am; Sun 11:30am–4pm, 5:30pm–midnight. Average main course: $17. AmEx, DC, MC, V.

Like a little entertainment with your dinner? This restaurant certainly provides a spirited time: The drag-queen waitstaff serves tasty meals and performs for very enthusiastic patrons. Weekdays, including Wednesday's Bitchy Bingo, tend to be a lot gayer than the weekends, when scores of shrieking women celebrate bridal showers.

The Townhouse

206 E 58th St at Third Ave (212-826-6241). Subway: N, R, W to Lexington Ave–59th St; 4, 5, 6 to 59th St. Mon–Thu noon–3:30pm, 5–11pm; Fri, Sat noon–3:30pm, 5pm–midnight; Sun noon–4pm, 5–11pm. Average main course: $20. AmEx, DC, MC, V.

If you're a reasonably attractive man under 40, you're likely to be greeted—or at least ogled—by one of the soused middle-aged regulars chatting up the bartenders at this "gentlemen's" restaurant. In the dining room beyond the bar, you'll spot couples in various stages of courtship; the flirty service makes this a good place for solo diners as well.

Gyms

For more fitness facilities, including YMCAs, see page 333.

David Barton

552 Sixth Ave between 15th and 16th Sts (212-727-0004). Subway: F, V to 14th St; L to Sixth Ave. Mon–Fri 6am–midnight; Sat 9am–9pm; Sun 10am–11pm. $20 per day, weekly pass $75. AmEx, MC, V.

David Barton mixes fitness with fashion and nightlife at his gyms. Sleek locker rooms, artfully lit weight rooms and pumping music may make you feel as if you should have a cocktail instead of another set of reps. Besides free weights, Barton offers the three key C's: classes, cardio equipment and cruising—along with scuba diving lessons.

19th Street Gym

22 W 19th St between Fifth and Sixth Aves (212-414-5800). Subway: F, V, N, R to 23rd St. Mon–Fri 5:30am–11pm; Sat, Sun 9am–9pm. $20 per day, weekly passes available. AmEx, Disc, MC, V.

Bulging muscles galore are on display at this popular Chelsea gym. Although it's 16,000 square feet, the place is basically one huge room crammed with all sorts of top-notch athletic equipment. Stretch and ab classes are available, as is personal instruction from staff trainers. After an invigorating workout, you can sip on something healthy at the juice bar and café.

Dyke Life

The most exciting aspect of New York's lesbian life is that the women you'll see—out and about in bars, clubs, restaurants, bookshops, community meetings and lesbian cabarets—defy stereotypes. While lesbian culture in New York is not as visible or geographically concentrated as that of gay men, it is also far less segregated (with some exceptions), either by age or race, and is far more welcoming.

If you're into community activism, you'll find plenty to spark your interest: Just check in at the **Lesbian, Gay, Bisexual & Transgender Community Center** *(see page 281)*. The Center also offers a wide range of support groups and 12-step meetings for people in recovery. But if you're a dyke who's not into the activist or recovery scene and just want to have some unbridled fun, New York City has plenty to offer.

The East Village lesbian bar **Meow Mix** *(see below)* is a popular gathering spot for alternadykes. And the unflappable promoter MegaBoy Kate continues to offer women large-scale dance parties including **Her/SheBar** at La Nueva Escuelita *(see page 289)* and **Lovergirl** *(see page 289)*. The notion that lesbians want more for their money has also given old, standard bars in the West Village a reason to try a little harder. Meanwhile, lesbian disco nights are getting progressively larger and are no longer held only in funky, out-of-the-way dives. Unfortunately, the rising popularity of these club events doesn't guarantee they'll be around for long, so check the lesbian bar guide in *HX* or *Time Out New York* for the most current information. Some women's bars and clubs strive for an all-women environment—better to check ahead if you're planning on bringing your male friends. And if drag king entertainment is your thing, check out the website for Murray Hill *(www.mrmurrayhill.com)*, the gregarious leader of New York's fake-moustache set, who always seems to be organizing a special event.

Outside Manhattan, the Park Slope neighborhood of Brooklyn remains a sort of lesbian residential hub, and is home to the **Lesbian Herstory Archive** *(see page 281)*. The area is lovely, and there is a number of relaxed coffeehouses, cafés and bars to choose from.

If you're staying in Brooklyn and plan to travel into Manhattan to enjoy the dyke nightlife, take a taxi back. While New York isn't quite as dangerous as you might think, it's still not a good idea to ride the subway alone late at night. *(See **Directory**, **Safety**, page 374 or*

NYC Gay & Lesbian Anti-Violence Project, *page 281.)*

Accommodations

For more listings, see **Chelsea Pines Inn**, page 282, **Colonial House Inn**, page 282, and **Incentra Village House**, page 283.

Markle Residence for Women

123 W 13th St between Sixth and Seventh Aves (212-242-2400). Subway: F, V, 1, 2, 3 to 14th St; L to Sixth Ave. $80 per night or $143–$235 per week, including two meals (one-month minimum). MC, V.
Offering women-only Salvation Army accommodations in a pleasant Greenwich Village location, the Markle has clean, comfortable rooms, all of which have telephones and private bathrooms.

Bars

See also **Bar d'O**, page 284, **Beige**, page 283 and **Wonder Bar**, page 284.

Crazy Nanny's

21 Seventh Ave South at Leroy St (212-366-6312). Subway: 1, 2 to Christopher St–Sheridan Sq. Mon–Fri 4pm–4am; Sat, Sun 3pm–4am. Average drink: $5.50. AmEx, Disc, MC, V.
A lesbian bar that's a bit off of the downtown pub crawl circuit, Nanny's is a find. The crowd is unassuming and plentiful at any time of the day. The music runs from soul to Latin, and the weekend DJs keep the small dance floor packed. Bone up on those k.d. lang lyrics for karaoke on Wednesdays and Sundays.

Henrietta Hudson

438 Hudson St at Morton St (212-924-3347). Subway: 1, 2 to Christopher St–Sheridan Sq. Mon–Fri 4pm–4am; Sat, Sun 1pm–4am. Average drink: $6. AmEx, Disc, MC, V.
This very active lesbian watering hole doesn't aspire to be sophisticated or chic; instead, it's a casual bar that's a magnet for women from all over the New York area, many of them quite frisky indeed. Various DJs provide contemporary sounds.

Julie's

305 E 53rd St between First and Second Aves, second floor (212-688-1294). Subway: E, V to Lexington Ave–53rd St; 6 to 51st St. Wed–Sat 5pm–4am; Sun 5pm–2am. Average drink: $5.50. Cash only.
Julie's is a discreet, polished bar for mature, professional, often closeted women in search of the same. Lesbians from all over come to groove on the green-houselike dance floor, or to nuzzle in the romantic lounge area.

Meow Mix

269 Houston St at Suffolk St (212-254-0688). Subway: F, V to Lower East Side–Second Ave. Mon–Fri 5pm–4am; Sat, Sun 3pm–4am. Average drink: $4. Cash only.

Sweet salvation The Markle Residence offers women-only Salvation Army lodging.

This Lower East Side lesbian lair hosts local live acts, mainly of the glam and garage varieties, and DJs typically favor funk, disco, new wave, hip-hop, reggae and R&B. Thursday night is Gloss, which the promoters call the "glammiest girlie night around."

Clubs

Great club nights are the Holy Grail of New York City—something that's fabulous one week sucks or is closed down the next, so the search continues. These are the current lesbian hot spots, but don't panic if they're not around in a few months' time—new nights and venues will already have blossomed. Check the lesbian listings in *HX* or *Time Out New York* for the latest info.

Her/SheBar

La Nueva Escuelita, 301 W 39th St at Eighth Ave (212-631-0588). Subway: A, C, E to 42nd St–Port Authority. Thu–Sat 10pm–5am. Cover: $8. Average drink: $6. AmEx, MC, V.
Extravagant drag floor shows are performed nightly at this Latin showplace, with Sunday reserved for solo performers. Fridays host the mostly lesbian party Her/SheBar, which features everything from whipped cream contests to go-go girls. Steve "Chip

Chop" Gonzalez and Francesca Magliano provide the Latin-flavored tunes.

Lovergirl

True, 28 E 23rd St between Madison Ave and Park Ave South (212-254-6117). Subway: N, R, 6 to 23rd St. Sat 9:30pm–4am. Cover: $8 before midnight, $10 after. Average drink: $8. AmEx, MC, V.
This popular women's party attracts a multiracial crowd that enthusiastically shakes its groove thang to hip-hop, R&B, funk and reggae in the Foreplay Lounge on the ground floor. Latin house, salsa and merengue rule on the second floor. Inspiring the revelers is an array of ultra-sexy go-go gals sporting the latest in fashionable G-strings.

Shescape

To get on the mailing list, call 212-686-5665 or visit www.shescape.com.
For 20 years now, Shescape has been offering lesbian get-togethers and dances at nightclubs all over town. The crowd tends to be a bit on the yuppie side, and not the type of women you'd likely run into on the bar scene. The most popular parties of the year are a mammoth Thanksgiving-eve bash at Tavern on the Green and various events pegged to Gay Pride.

Starlette

Starlight Bar and Lounge, 167 Ave A between 10th and 11th Sts (212-475-2172). Subway: L to First Ave. Sun 9pm–4am. Average drink: $6. AmEx.
By 10pm, this popular lesbian party is in full swing. It has a mix of glamour gals, tomboys, college students, etc., but a cool East Village style prevails. DJ Jolene spins "lush" house.

Restaurants & cafés

Cowgirl Hall of Fame

519 Hudson St at 10th St (212-633-1133). Subway: 1, 2 to Christopher St–Sheridan Sq. 11:30am–4pm; 5–11:30pm. Bar Sun–Thu 5pm–1am; Fri, Sat 5pm–4am. Average main course: $13. AmEx, MC, V.
Cheerful waitresses welcome West Village girls and boys to this retro ranch-hand lounge, where the specialties are trailer-park originals such as pork chops and Frito pie. Yup, it's a bag of corn chips filled with chili; chase it with a margarita served in a mason jar.

Rubyfruit

531 Hudson St between Charles and Washington Sts (212-929-3343). Subway: 1, 2 to Christopher St–Sheridan Sq. Mon–Thu 3pm–2am; Fri, Sat 3pm–4am; Sun 11:30am–2am. Average main course: $20. Average drink: $5. AmEx, DC, MC, V.
A warm and energetic band of women patronizes Rubyfruit, the only dedicated lesbian restaurant and bar in town. Though the food is good, it's not the main selling point. The congenial customers and a varied program of cabaret and music make this a great place for fun-loving old-school dykes.

Arts & Entertainment

Kids' Stuff

Move over, grownups—New York is a fun city for children too. Art, opera, history—and pure play—are a few of the things Junior can get into.

Millions of people visiting New York City for the first time arrive with an image of a gritty, grown-up city, the place already formed in their minds, whether by *Bonfire of the Vanities* or *Breakfast at Tiffany's.* These preconceptions make the city feel both familiar and surprising, because New York *is* its fictitious self—and for kids, the illusion is all the more…real.

Kids have their own set of references for anticipating New York, although they might need to be told that the pond where E.B. White's Stuart Little sailed a mouse-scaled boat is the Conservatory Water in Central Park. There, they'll discover fascinating adults armed with even more fascinating remote controls sailing model boats. None, however, carry mice.

Storybook New York includes the Egyptian rooms at the Metropolitan Museum of Art, where Claudia and Jamie took up residence after running away from home in E.L. Konigsburg's classic tale, *From the Mixed Up Files of Mrs. Basil E. Frankweiler;* the palatial Plaza Hotel, where Eloise instituted a reign of playful terror (and where mildly tongue-in-cheek etiquette workshop/teas for kids are held monthly); the Brooklyn of Maurice Sendak's *In the Night Kitchen* and *The Sign on Rosie's Door;* and the skyline of Faith Ringgold's *Tar Beach,* with its water towers, bridges and tiny dots of incandescent light.

If you never stray from the midtown tourist circuit, New York can seem like a very bland city. The new 42nd Street, which is the old porn strip reinvented as a family-friendly mecca, has little to distinguish it from any other tourist center (in fact, most of what trumpets itself as "family-friendly" in this city is probably worth avoiding).

Head for the outer boroughs to give your kids a taste of New York's colorful grassroots pageantry: In summer, don't miss Brooklyn's **Mermaid Parade** *(see page 238)* and the **West Indian Day Carnival** *(see page 241),* which includes a children's parade.

If you're looking for free, low-key activities to fill an hour or two, pick up a copy of *Events for Children* from any branch of the New York Public Library for listings of storytellings, puppet shows, films and workshops. The **Donnell Library** *(see page 44),* home of the Central Children's Room, is the best place for events; it also houses the original Winnie the Pooh and other toys that belonged to Christopher "Robin" Milne.

Amusement parks

Astroland
1000 Surf Ave at West 8th St, Coney Island, Brooklyn (718-372-0275). Subway: F, Q to W 8th St–NY Aquarium. Mid-Jun–Sept noon–midnight (weather permitting); spring, September weekends only (hours are determined by weather). $2 single kiddie rides, $15 for 10 kiddie rides. Cash only.
Coney Island's amusement park is rather run-down and tacky (to some), but a delight to children nonetheless. In summer, ride the spinning Enterprise or world-famous Cyclone roller coaster ($5). Younger kids will prefer the Tilt-a-Whirl, Pirate Ship or one of the three carousels. If you can navigate among the boom boxes, there's also sun and sand to enjoy.

Nellie Bly Amusement Park
1824 Shore Pkwy, Bensonhurst, Brooklyn (718-996-4002). Subway: M, W to Bay Pkwy, then take the B6 bus. Apr–Jun, Sept–Oct weekends 11am–6pm; Jul, Aug 11am–11pm. Free admission. Each ride ticket 85¢, $15 for 20, $26 for 40 (most rides require two to three tickets). Unlimited-rides admission $9.50 during off-peak hours (call for details).
This low-key amusement park has none of the shriek-inducing excitement of a Great Adventure—but it's accessible, inexpensive, unstressful and totally New York. Families of all ethnicities from the surrounding neighborhoods bring their small children here for a couple of hours of circular activity on buses, trains, Red Baron jets, boats, hopping frogs and other rides. You'll also find bumper cars, a Ferris wheel and mini golf and, of course, ice cream and cotton candy.

Circuses

The animal-free and Vegasy French-Canadian Cirque du Soleil sets up its big top a ferry ride away, in New Jersey, usually in April. Tickets, which are pricey, are snapped up fast. If you're hankering for something more New York, look for free outdoor summer performances by Brooklyn's raucous alternative, Circus Amok.

Big Apple Circus
Damrosch Park, Lincoln Center (212-268-2500, tickets from Centercharge 212-721-6500, Ticketmaster 212-

They're a handful! Kids have a ball watching Em le Carey of the Big Apple Circus.

307-4100). Subway: 1, 2 to 66th St–Lincoln Ctr. Prices vary. AmEx, MC, V.
New York's own traveling circus was founded 23 years ago as a traditional, intimate, one-act-at-a-time answer to the Ringling Bros.' three-ring extravaganza. This nonprofit circus prides itself on being a family affair, with acts that feature the founder's two teenage children and his equestrian wife. Clowns are the highlight, and the focus is on the company rather than star acts. The circus has a regular winter season (October to January) in Damrosch Park and, budget permitting, travels to other city parks in early spring.

Ringling Bros. and Barnum & Bailey Circus
Madison Square Garden, Seventh Ave between 31st and 33rd Sts (212-465-6741; www.ringling.com).

Subway: A, C, E, 1, 2, 3 to 34th St–Penn Station. April. $25–$75. AmEx, DC, Disc, MC, V.
The original and most famous American circus has three rings, lots of glitz and plenty to keep kids glued to their seats, including a menagerie of animals large and small. (Fair warning: Don't be surprised if you are leafleted by animal-rights organizations.) Barnum's famous sideshow was revived in 1998. It's extremely popular, so reserve well in advance.

UniverSoul Big Top Circus
Venue and performance schedule change yearly (info 800-316-7439, Ticketmaster 212-307-7171). $13–$25. AmEx, DC, Disc, MC, V.
This African-American circus has all the requisite clowns, animal acts and hoopla, with a twist: Instead of the usual circus music, you get hip-hop, R&B and salsa.

Museums & exhibitions

Even museums that are not specifically devoted to children provide a wealth of activity. For example, kids will love exploring the revamped dinosaur halls and become starry-eyed at the much-hyped **Rose Center for Earth and Space** at the **American Museum of Natural History**. Kids should also visit the **Liberty Science Center** (don't miss the Touch Tunnel), the **Transit Museum** and the **Intrepid** Sea-Air-Space Museum, which has a collection of military hardware housed on an aircraft carrier. All of the major art museums offer weekly family tours and workshops (the **Guggenheim** has a terrific monthly film program, **CinéKids**, and occasional exhibition-related events for children). Tours at the **Brooklyn Museum of Art** and **Metropolitan Museum** include sketching in the galleries.

ARTime
For a schedule and further information, call 718-797-1573. Oct–Jun first Saturday of the month 11am–12:30pm. $20 per parent-child pair, additional child $5.
ARTime started introducing kids (ages 5 to 10) to contemporary art in Soho galleries three years ago. Art historians with backgrounds in education take children to exhibits in three or four galleries. The shows are chosen to highlight a theme—for example, how artists use unusual materials or technology—and that becomes the focus for lively discussion and the youngsters' own on-site art activities. Kids must be accompanied by an adult; all materials are provided.

Brooklyn Children's Museum
145 Brooklyn Ave at St. Mark's Ave, Crown Heights, Brooklyn (718-735-4400; www.brooklynkids.org). Subway: 1 to Kingston Ave. Winter Wed–Fri 2–5pm; Sat, Sun 10am–5pm. Summer Mon, Wed, Fri–Sun

10am–5pm. Winter and spring school vacations 10am–5pm. Suggested donation $4. Cash only.
Founded in 1899 and redesigned in 1996, BCM was the world's first museum designed specifically for children—it has a fantastic collection of 2,000 artifacts from around the world (children's museums rarely have such extensive hoards). The focus is on opening kids' eyes to world cultures—especially those of the city's immigrant populations—with hands-on exhibits. You reach the displays via a walkway through which a neon-lit stream of water also passes; kids can operate waterwheels and dam the stream with stones. In the music studio, children play synthesizers and instruments from around the globe, and dance on the keys of a walk-on piano. There are special daily workshops and weekly performances (the museum's free summertime rooftop-performance series is on Fridays at 6pm). On weekends, a free shuttle bus runs hourly from the **Brooklyn Museum of Art** *(see page 33)* and Grand Army Plaza subway station to the museum.

Children's Museum of the Arts
182 Lafayette St between Broome and Grand Sts (212-274-0986). Subway: 6 to Spring St. Wed–Sun noon–5pm. $5, Wed 5–7pm voluntary donation. AmEx, MC, V.
The under-7 set loves the low-key Children's Museum of the Arts. It has floor-to-ceiling chalkboards, art computers and vast stores of art supplies—perfect for young travelers pining for their crayons.

Children's Museum of Manhattan
212 W 83rd St between Amsterdam Ave and Broadway (212-721-1234; www.cmom.org). Subway: 1, 2 to 86th St. Wed–Sun 10am–5pm. $6. AmEx, MC, V.
The Children's Museum of Manhattan promotes literacy of every kind through its playful hands-on exhibitions, although in the past couple of years, these have tended to be less carefully conceived and more commercially inspired. Mainstays include "Body Odyssey," which lets kids discover (theoretically, at least) what's going on inside them; and "WordPlay," an exhibition designed to promote verbal (and preverbal) interaction between babies and their caregivers. In the Inventor Center, bigger kids invent stuff using digital imaging and make their own TV shows in the state-of-the-art media lab. Workshops are scheduled for weekends and during school vacations.

▶ For more ideas on where to take the kids, check out chapters **New York by Season; Shopping & Services; Sports & Fitness;** and **Uptown, Central Park.**
▶ Each week, **Time Out New York** magazine lists many family events.
▶ The **Time Out New York Eating & Drinking 2002 Guide** reviews dozens of kid-friendly restaurants.

Lefferts Homestead Children's Museum
Prospect Park, Flatbush Ave near Empire Blvd, Park Slope, Brooklyn (718-965-6505). Subway: Q, S to Prospect Park. Spring–fall, call for hours. Free.
For an entirely different sense of New York, check out Lefferts Homestead, an 18th-century Dutch house that was moved from Flatbush Avenue to Prospect Park and restored as a 19th-century farmhouse. Not far from the park's zoo and carousel, Lefferts gives kids a neighborhood history lesson through its exhibit "Who Lived Here?" Visitors play with cooking utensils in a Dutch kitchen, hunt for barnyard tools in a hay-strewn model barn, play with toys that young residents might have owned and try out the beds—including a Lenape Indian bed made of sapling, straw and animal skin. On summer weekends, there's often storytelling under a tree, as well as hoop games and gardening.

Lower East Side Tenement Museum
See page 40 for listing.
Housed in an old tenement building that was home to successive families of immigrants, this museum offers a weekly interactive children's tour of the Sephardic Confino family's former home. The tour is led by 13-year-old Victoria Confino (actually, a staff member playing her), who teaches visitors about New York in the early 1900s by dancing the fox-trot, playing games with them and forever answering the question "Where does everyone sleep?" The tours are recommended for ages 7 to 14 and are given on weekend afternoons at noon, 1, 2 and 3pm ($9, children $7).

New York Hall of Science
See page 45 for listing.
This museum is situated inside the onetime Space Pavilion of the 1964 New York World's Fair. Director Dr. Alan Friedman is nationally known for his enlightened approach to science education, which he bases on the premise that kids learn by asking questions. Perhaps his biggest contribution to the hall is the 30,000-square-foot outdoor Science Playground (spring through fall, ages 6 and up), where children engage in whole-body science exploration, discovering principles of balance, gravity, energy and so on, as they play on a giant seesaw or turn a huge Archimedes screw to push water uphill. There's plenty to see indoors, too.

Socrates Sculpture Park
Broadway at Vernon Blvd, Long Island City, Queens (718-956-1819). Travel: N to Broadway, then Q104 bus to Vernon Blvd; 10am–sunset. Free.
Unlike most art exhibitions, this outdoor city-owned spread of large-scale contemporary sculpture is devoid of snarling guards and DON'T TOUCH signs. Children can climb on, run through and sit astride works that seem to have been plopped haphazardly on the grounds of this four-acre park. Call for information about Saturday-afternoon

summer art workshops for kids. On weekends, the free Queens A-tlink shuttle runs hourly between the Museum of Modern Art and Socrates (*see* **Go to the art of Queens**, *page 103*).

Sony Wonder Technology Lab

Sony Plaza, 550 Madison Ave between 55th and 56th Sts (212-833-8100). Subway: E, V to Fifth Ave–53rd St; 6 to 51st St. Tue, Wed, Fri, Sat 10am–6pm; Thu 10am–8pm; Sun noon–6pm. Free.

This digital wonderland lets visitors (or "media trainees") experiment with state-of-the art communication technology as they design video games, assist in surgery, crisis-manage an earthquake, edit a TV show, operate robots and play sound engineer. Kids in the 8-and-up age range will probably get the most out of this place, but it's also a great playground for younger children who like pushing buttons and seeing their faces on giant monitors. You should call to make a reservation, preferably one week in advance, during the spring and summer.

Music

Carnegie Hall Family Concerts

See page 316 for listing.

Even kids who profess to hate classical music are usually impressed by a visit to Carnegie Hall (one youngster wrote a postconcert "thank you" letter to "Dear Mr. Hall"). Its thematic Family Concert series, featuring world-class performers, works hard to appeal to youngsters—and only costs $5. Preconcert activities include a workshop and storytelling. The concerts are held monthly, fall through spring, and are recommended for ages 6 and up.

Growing Up with Opera

John Jay Theater, 899 Tenth Ave at 59th St (212-769-7008; www.operaed.org). Subway: A, C, B, D, 1, 2 to 59th St–Columbus Circle. $15–$25. AmEx, MC, V.

Short operas, some written specially for young audiences, are sung in English by the Metropolitan Opera Guild, whose members meet kids after the performance; only three or four concerts are held from fall through spring. The guild has recently added a participatory series for preschoolers (tickets $7–$10), staged in small theaters around the city.

Jazz for Young People

See Alice Tully Hall, page 316, for listing.

These participatory concerts, led by trumpeter and jazz pedagogue Wynton Marsalis, and modeled on the New York Philharmonic Young People's Concerts, help children figure out answers to such eternal questions as "What is jazz?" and "Who is Louis Armstrong?" Tickets are $15; under 18, $10.

Little Orchestra Society

See Avery Fisher Hall, page 317, for listing.

The Little Orchestra Society, founded in 1947, includes the Lolli-Pops concert series—participatory orchestral concerts for children ages 3 to 5, combining classical music with dance, puppetry, theater and mime; tickets for these are available by subscription only. The 21-year-old spectacular *Amahl and the Night Visitors* (complete with live sheep), held in early December, is a New York tradition. Happy Concerts for kids ages 6 to 12 are staged at Avery Fisher Hall about three times a year. Prices vary.

New York Philharmonic Young People's Concerts

See Avery Fisher Hall, page 317, for listing.

Musicians address the audience directly during these legendary educational concerts, made popular by the late composer Leonard Bernstein. Each concert is preceded by an hour-long "Children's Promenade," during which kids meet orchestra members and try out their instruments. Tickets range between $6 and $23. For more children's activities, visit the website.

Outdoor activities

For zoos, see page 297.

Brooklyn Botanic Garden

See page 96 for listing.

The highlight here is the 13,000-square-foot Discovery Garden, where children can play at being botanists, make toys out of natural materials, weave a wall and get their hands dirty.

Nelson Rockefeller Park

Hudson River at Chambers St (212-267-9700). Subway: A, C, 1, 2 to Chambers St. 10am–sunset. Free.

River breezes keep this park several degrees cooler than the rest of the city—a big plus in the summer. There's plenty for kids to do here besides watch the boats. (Saturday is a good day for ocean liners.) They can play on Tom Otterness's quirky sculptures in the picnic area (near the Chambers Street entrance), enjoy one of New York's best playgrounds, and participate in art, sports or street-game activities (call for times and locations). Other activities, such as kite flying and fishing, are scheduled throughout the summer.

New York Botanical Garden

See page 105 for listing.

The immense Everett Children's Adventure Garden is a whimsical "museum of the natural world" with interactive "galleries," both indoors and out ($3 adults, $1 for children). In the Family Garden (late October through early spring), children run under Munchy, a giant topiary; poke around in a touch tank; and plant, weed, water and harvest. If it's too cold to wander outside, ask for a kid's guide and audio tour to the Enid A. Haupt Conservatory ($3.50), the spectacular glass house where you can see papyrus, cocoa and bananas growing all year long.

Arts & Entertainment

Pier 26

North Moore St at West Side Hwy (212-791-2530).
Subway: 1, 2 to Franklin St.
The River Project *(212-941-5901)* on Pier 26 admits
children on weekends; they can examine small creatures under microscopes and feed aquarium fish
culled from the Hudson River—which, children will
realize when they see the sea horses, is briny.

Central Park

Most Manhattanites don't have gardens—they have
parks. The most popular one of all is Central Park,
which offers plenty of places and programs designed
just for children. Go to www.centralparknyc.org for
a calendar of nature programs, art workshops and
other events. **Arts in the Park** *(212-988-5093)*
organizes a summer program of children's arts events
in several parks around the city. Don't miss the
beautiful antique carousel ($1 a ride) and the lively
Heckscher Playground (just one of 20), which
has handball courts, horseshoe pitches, softball
diamonds, a puppet theater, a wading pool and a
crèche (for more on the park, see page 77).

Charles A. Dana Discovery Center

See page 78 for listing.

Conservatory Water

*Central Park at 74th St near Fifth Ave. Subway: 6 to
77th St. Jul–Aug Sun–Fri 11am–7pm; Sat 2–7pm
(weather permitting).*
Stuart Little Pond, named after E.B. White's story-

Best of the fests

Kids can be movers, shakers and art-makers at these
festivals fit for the younger set

Cultural festivals were once the exclusive
provenance of sophisticated adults. Then
came a new generation of fashion-forward
city kids, who order junior portions of
hamachi negimaki without a hitch. These
are not the types to stay home with the
babysitter day after day while their parents
flit around town. No! These kiddies need
social buzz and cultural stimulation,
preferably of the international variety. And for
visitors, arts festivals are ephemeral gems;
they truly are the high points of New York's
kid-oriented culture (just ask the local
children who are participating).

This lineup of festivals spans the calendar
year. Summer events are outdoors,
generally free and, especially if you bring a
picnic, far more relaxed than the indoor
festivals, to which tickets typically sell out
far in advance. If you don't want to join
the crowds of anxious parents and their
offspring on the waiting-list line, purchase
tickets via the festival websites before
you arrive.

BAMkids Film Festival

See **BAM Rose Cinemas**, *page 274, for
listing. April. $5.*
The Brooklyn Academy of Music's
children's film festival is essentially a
shorter, less hip and more edifying version
of the **New York International Children's
Film Festival** *(see page 295).* Like NYICFF,
it screens features and short live-action

and animated films from around the world,
and allows the young audience to pick the
winners by filling out ballots.

Celebrate Brooklyn!
Performing Arts Festival

*Prospect Park Bandshell, 9th St at Prospect
Park West, Park Slope, Brooklyn (718-855-
7882; www.celebratebrooklyn.org). Subway:
F to Seventh Ave. Late Jun–late Aug Thu–Sat.*
Celebrate Brooklyn! outdoes Central Park's
SummerStage festival *(see page 238)* when
it comes to being a kid-friendly location. Here
you can spread a blanket on the grass, lay
out a picnic and let children crawl or boogie,
and still watch the onstage entertainment.
The talent booked is on par with those at
SummerStage as well.

International Children's
Television Festival

See **Museum of Television and Radio**, *page
44, for listing. Weekend afternoons in
November. Free with admission to museum.*
This annual monthlong celebration of the best
children's television from around the world
gives kids and their parents a glimpse of
youngsters' lives in other countries—not to
mention the chance to see some great TV.
Each day includes a pair of thematic
programs, one for grades four and under;
another for grades five and up. The programs
are a mixture of animation, live-action and
documentary.

book mouse, is the city's mecca for model-yacht racing. When the boat master is around, rent one of the remote-controlled vessels ($10 per hour), but be warned—they're not as speedy as Nintendo. Nearby, a large bronze *Alice in Wonderland* statue provides excellent climbing opportunities.

Henry Luce Nature Observatory

See page 78 for listing.
This children's hot spot in Central Park has telescopes, microscopes and simple hands-on exhibits that help teach kids about the plants and animals living (or hiding) in the surrounding area. Weekend afternoon workshops are held spring through fall (1 to 3pm). Kids (with a parent's ID) can borrow a discovery kit—a backpack containing binoculars, a bird-watching guide and cool tools.

North Meadow Recreation Center

Central Park at 79th St (212-348-4867). Subway: B, C to 81st St. Mon–Fri 9am–7pm; Sat, Sun 10am–6pm. Free.
Borrow a fun-in-the-park kit: You'll get a Frisbee, hula hoop, Wiffle ball and bat, jump rope, kickball and other toys. You'll need ID.

Stories at the Hans Christian Andersen Statue

Central Park at Conservatory Water (212-929-6871, 212-340-0906). Subway: 6 to 77th St. Jun–Sept, Sat 11am. Free.
Children 5 and older have gathered for generations near the foot of the Hans Christian Andersen statue to hear master tale-tellers from all over America—a real New York tradition that's not to be missed. On

International Festival of Puppet Theater

Various venues throughout the city (212-794-2400; www.hensonfestival.org). Sept 2002.
Traveling frequently to puppet festivals around the world with his daughter Cheryl, Jim Henson was struck by the sophistication and diversity of the art. Several years later, under the direction of Cheryl Henson, this biennial festival was born. The three-week event focuses on puppet theater for adults, but the kids' component can offer rich theatrical experiences from other countries, as well as a glimpse of the art's breadth.

Lincoln Center Out-of-Doors

Lincoln Center Plaza, Broadway at 65th St (212-875-5108). Subway: 1, 2 to 66th St–Lincoln Ctr. August. Free.
New Yorkers who attend this open-air festival, which started in 1970, know that they're as likely to find a dance company doing hip-hop moves as they are to catch a sitar gig. This type of cross-cultural programming is designed to further one of the goals of Out-of-Doors: introducing New York's many communities to new and unfamiliar forms of expression. Kids' performances and participatory days are scheduled throughout the festival.

New York International Children's Film Festival

Various venues (212-349-0330; www.gkids.com). February or March.
This three-week festival has experienced tremendous growth in its four years and is a hot event in the NYC kids' world. Reserve seats well in advance; the schedule is available in early January. Age-specific programs for tots through teens present an

exciting mix of shorts and full-length features (many of them premieres) from indie filmmakers around the world—and not necessarily those who specialize in kids' flicks. Kids determine the festival winners by filling in ballots after each short-film program. One of the most exciting aspects of the NYICFF is the lively Q&A session with filmmakers and actors after each screening; whenever possible, children who have starred in the films are flown in from around the world to converse with the awed locals. The winning films are screened at an awards ceremony—it's a great party for all ages, with door prizes and a celebrity host.

New York International Fringe Festival: Fringe Jr

Various venues in the East Village and Lower East Side. (212-420-8888, call 888-FRINGE-NYC for schedule; www.fringenyc.org). Three weeks in August. $11, children $7.
Fringe Jr, the kids' component of this downtown theater festival, shrinks and grows from year to year, depending mostly on the number of acceptable submissions received from companies doing children's productions. But there are always a couple of shows just for kids, and several on the adult program that are recommended for older kids. Fort Fringe Jr is a kind of clubhouse at one of the festival's venues, where youngsters can play, create puppets, participate in workshops (e.g., face painting, storytelling) and catch previews of the shows. Most exciting of all is Fringe Al Fresco, the portion of the festival devoted to free outdoor and store-window performance and installations (watch out for human chess games and roving robots). Every year, Fringe Al Fresco kicks off with a blocklong street-theater performance.

Arts & Entertainment

Wednesdays, children's librarians from the New York Public Library read their favorite stories.

NY Skateout

Classes meet at Central Park entrance, Fifth Ave at 72nd St (212-486-1919; www.nyskate.com). Subway: 6 to 68th St–Hunter College. Skate lessons on weekends, call for times. $25 for a two-hour class. Reservations are essential. Kid Skateout Sat 3–4pm (call to confirm). Free.

Classes are offered for beginners and more advanced skaters (ages 5 and up). On Saturdays, children who have the hang of it can join a Kid Skateout group for a social spin around the park's loop road. NY Skateout is dedicated to skating safety: Don't even think of showing up without all the protective gear. Call for information on equipment rental.

Play spaces

For older kids itching to burn some energy, try **Chelsea Piers** *(see pages 330 and 331)* which has a gymnasium, a roller rink and a half-pipe for in-line skating and skateboarding.

Playspace

2473 Broadway at 92nd St (212-769-2300). Subway: 1, 2, 3 to 96th St. 10am–5:30pm. $7.50. Cash only.

In this play space with huge plate glass windows, children ages 6 months to 6 years build in the immense sandbox, ride on toy trucks, dress up and climb on the jungle gym. Play is supervised, and parents can relax in a café off to the side. There are also drop-in games, art classes and storytimes. Mondays through Thursdays at 3:30pm, local folk-rockers from the kiddie circuit give concerts. Admission is for the day: You can leave and come back.

Rain or Shine

202 E 29th St between Second and Third Aves, fourth floor (212-532-4420). Subway: 6 to 28th St. Call for hours; open play is generally daily during school vacations. Play: $6.95 per two-hour session. Trial classes are available in gym, cooking, drama: $20–$30 per two-hour class. Reservations required.

This large, airy place is devoted to imaginative play for kids ages 6 months to 6 years; they'll find a dress-up area, a giant playhouse, ride-on toys and an art room, as well as playmates. During holidays, there may be open hours in the gym, which has a rock-climbing wall for children ages 4 to 12 years. Children must be accompanied by an adult.

Theater

Several small theaters and repertory companies offer weekend-matinee family performances. Most of these are musical productions of questionable value. Check *Time Out New York* or newspaper listings for details. The following are the best of New York's family theaters and series.

Family Matters

Dance Theater Workshop, 219 W 19th St between Seventh and Eighth Aves (212-924-0077). Subway: C, E to 23rd St; 1, 2 to 18th St. Sat 10am–noon. Sept–May, call for schedule. $12, children $8. AmEx, MC, V.

Curated by a pair of choreographer-parents for ages six and up, Family Matters is designed to jump-start children's imaginations and get them to do their own thing. The series blends dance, music, theater and art in a thematic, variety-show format, and features work by experimental artists whose sensibilities and styles are quirky, fun or wild enough to entertain young audiences.

Joyce Theater

See page 343 for listing.

This is the home of Ballet Tech, which was founded by Eliot Feld (you might remember him as Baby John in *West Side Story*). Don't miss Feld's *NoTCRACKER* (its season is the last two weeks of December), a nutty alternative to the traditional tutued thing. Other dance performances are held in late March through the end of April and during the first two weeks of August. Tickets are $35 for evening performances; weekend matinees are $25, $15 for children.

Kids 'n Comedy

Gotham Comedy Club, 34 W 22nd St between Fifth and Sixth Aves (212-877-6115). Subway: F, N, R to 23rd St. Sept–May Sun 4pm. $15.

Kids 'n Comedy has developed a stable of funny kids between the ages of 8 and 16 who know how to handle three minutes in front of a mike; its shows have been featured on American and British TV. The regulars deliver stand-up material they've developed themselves, much of it in the school-food-sucks vein.

Los Kabayitos Children's Theater

CSV Cultural Center, 107 Suffolk St between Delancey and Rivington Sts (212-260-4080, ext 14). Subway: F to Delancey St; J, M, Z to Delancey–Essex Sts. $10.50, children $8.50. Cash only. Call for reservations and show times.

New York's only Latino children's theater was founded in 1999 by the Society of the Educational Arts in a Lower East Side cultural center. English- and Spanish-language performances of traditional and new Latin American musical-theater plays and shows, performed with puppets and actors, alternate every weekend (the theater is dark during school vacations).

New Amsterdam Theater

214 W 42nd St between Seventh and Eighth Aves (212-307-4100). Subway: A, C, E to 42nd St–Port Authority; N, Q, R, W, S, 1, 2, 3, 7 to 42nd St–Times Sq. Wed 2, 8pm; Thu, Fri 8pm; Sat 2pm; Sun 1, 6:30pm. $25–$90. AmEx, DC, Disc, MC, V.

Disney laid claim to 42nd Street by renovating this splendid theater, an Art Deco masterpiece. Its inaugural and perpetually sold-out show, *The Lion King*, is directed by puppetry wizard Julie Taymor.

The New Victory Theater
See page 341 for listing.
New York's only year-round, full-scale young people's theater, the New Victory is a gem that shows the very best in international theater and dance at junior prices (which is why you'll see plenty of adults sans kids in the audience). The theater's winter-holiday season never fails to thrill—and it sells out fast.

Puppetworks
338 Sixth Ave at 4th St, Park Slope, Brooklyn (718-965-3391). Subway: F to Seventh Ave. Sat, Sun 12:30, 2:30pm. $7, children 2–18 $6. Cash only.
This company stages productions based on classic tales, such as *Beauty and the Beast*. The plays are usually performed with marionettes. Puppetworks performs occasional seasons in Greenwich Village; call for information. The company also performs

Get wired Discover hands-on, high-tech fun at the Sony Wonder Technology Lab.

at Macy's Herald Square from Thanksgiving to Christmas ($2.50).

Swedish Cottage Marionette Theater
Central Park West at 81st St (212-988-9093). Subway: B, C to 81st St. Oct–May Tue–Fri 10:30am, noon; Sat 1pm. Jul–Aug Mon–Fri 10:30am, noon. $5, children $4. Cash only.
Reservations are essential for shows at this intimate theater in an old Swedish schoolhouse, which is run by New York's Department of Parks and Recreation.

TADA! Youth Ensemble
120 W 28th St between Sixth and Seventh Aves (212-627-1732). Subway: 1, 2 to 28th St. Jan, Mar, Jul, Aug, Dec; call for times. $15, under 17 $6. AmEx, MC, V.
This group presents musicals performed by and for children. The ensemble casts, ages 8 and up, are drawn from open auditions. The shows are well presented, high-spirited and extremely popular. Reservations are advised; call for details about week-long musical-theater workshops.

Zoos

Bronx Zoo/Wildlife Conservation Society
See page 105 for listing.
Inside the Bronx Zoo is the Bronx Children's Zoo, scaled down for the very young, with lots of domesticated animals to pet, plus exhibits that show you the world from an animal's point of view. Camel and elephant rides are available from April through October. Don't miss the sea-lion feeding (daily at 3pm).

Central Park Wildlife Center
Fifth Ave at 64th St (212-861-6030). Subway: N, R, W to Fifth Ave–60th St. Mon–Fri 10am–5pm; Sat, Sun 10:30am–5:30pm. $3.50, seniors $1.25, children ages 3–12 50¢, under 3 free. Cash only.
This 130-species zoo is one of the highlights of the park. You can watch seals frolic above and below the waterline, crocodiles snap at swinging monkeys and huge polar bears swimming endless laps. Penguins and other cool dudes are celebrated during the Summer Chill-Out party weekend in August.

New York Aquarium for Wildlife Conservation
Surf Ave at W 8th St, Coney Island, Brooklyn (718-265-3400 and 718-265-3474). Subway: F, Q to W 8th St–NY Aquarium. Mon–Fri 10am–5pm; Sat, Sun 10am–5:30pm. $9.75, seniors and children 2–12, $6 under 2 free. Cash only.
Like Coney Island itself, this aquarium is a little shabby, but kids enjoy seeing the famous beluga whale family. There's also an intriguing glimpse of the kinds of things that live in the East River, plus a dolphin show (feedings are weekdays at 11:30am and 3pm; noon, 2 and 4pm on weekends.

New York nightlife is world famous.

(We can help you remember what you heard last night.)
CD, DVD, VHS, Accessories and much more.

Music

Sweet symphonies, heavy-metal thunder, sassy salsa, jazz in its jazillion permutations…New York has all genres covered—live and onstage now!

Proof of how uniquely interwoven New York City and its music are came in the wake of the September 11, 2001 attacks. As the city's inhabitants struggled to make sense of their suddenly altered lives, the first signs of healing were found in the city's music clubs. People found much-needed solace and camaraderie among strangers; tears, hugs and wishes for the future were exchanged beneath the mantle of emotionally soothing music of all kinds. Within days, most every venue in town had lined up benefit concerts with the city's biggest and brightest artists (and also its smallest and most obscure). Clearly, the soul of New York is reflected in its multihued music scene.

To figure out where to go, you need to know what you want, and where to find it. The first part should be simple; the second can be a challenge, because some music spots offer different genres every night. So we've categorized venues according to their primary genre, and cross-referenced where necessary. Because the classical and opera scene is so big and well-defined, its own section starts on page 315.

Popular Music

Separating music clubs from DJ-style lounges has gotten harder, as many clubs with live music also book DJs, and a few lounges also experiment with live music. Of course, DJs themselves are blurring that line *(see Clubs, page 265)*.

Diverse booking policies are well suited for adventurous types, but if you're focused on only one sound, there are plenty of clubs that cater to you. For jazz, try **Iridium** or **Smalls**; if the avant-garde is your bag, the **Knitting Factory** and **Tonic** feature bold programming. Rockers roll to **Brownies**, the **Continental**, Brooklyn's **Northsix** and myriad other clubs. Country-leaning singers and bands fill the schedules at the **Lakeside Lounge** and **Manitoba's**. For Latin rhythms, salsa over to **S.O.B.'s**. For more suggestions, see **Find your groove**, page 313.

Rule No. 1, now and forevermore, is to bring a photo ID (a driver's license or passport is best), as many clubs will ask you to prove that you are over 21, regardless of whether you'll be boozin' it up. The big guy at the door has heard

You can tuna guitar… The Beacon Theatre is the Upper West Side's premier rock & roll room.

your "I forgot my wallet at home" already, so don't waste your breath.

Tickets are generally available from clubs in advance, and at the door. Some small and medium-size clubs also sell advance tickets through local record stores. For larger events, it's wise to buy through **Ticketmaster** over the phone or at one of the outlets located throughout the city. Tickets for some events are also available through **www.ticketweb.com**. You can buy tickets online from websites of specific venues (web addresses are included in venue listings where available). For more ticket details, see page 377. And remember: It's always a good idea to call first for info and show times, which can change without notice.

Arenas

Continental Airlines Arena

East Rutherford, NJ (201-935-3900; www.meadowlands.com). Travel: NJ Transit Meadowlands Sports Complex bus from Port Authority Bus Terminal (212-564-8484), Eighth Ave at 42nd St, $3.25 each way. From $25. Cash only at box office.
New Jersey's answer to Madison Square Garden is the Meadowlands Complex. Not quite as enormous as Giants Stadium, the CAA has recently played host to Britney Spears, the Backstreet Boys and Aerosmith. The arena is also the site of radio-sponsored hip-hop extravaganzas, and hosted Bruce Springsteen and his E Street Band's much bally-hooed 15-night stand a couple of years ago.

Madison Square Garden

Seventh Ave at 32nd St (212-465-6741; www.thegarden.com). Subway: A, C, E, 1, 2, 3 to 34th St–Penn Station. Box office: Mon–Sat noon–6pm. $25–$75. AmEx, DC, Disc, MC, V.
Awright, Noo Yawk! Are you ready to rock & roll? The acoustics may be more suited to the crunch of hockey and the slap of basketball, but MSG is nevertheless the most famous rock venue in the world. U2, Madonna and Bob Dylan are but a few who've sold out the place. Be warned: The cost of good seats is high—tickets for special occasions such as Barbra Streisand's "farewell" concerts sold for more than $1,000; regular shows can top $100.

Nassau Veterans Memorial Coliseum

1255 Hempstead Tpke, Uniondale, Long Island (516-794-9303). Travel: From Penn Station, Seventh Ave at 32nd St, take LIRR (718-217-5477) to Hempstead, then N70, N71 or N72 bus. From $25. AmEx, Disc, MC, V.
Nassau Coliseum doesn't have a lot of character, but that quality isn't usually evident in "enormo-domes," anyway. Many of the same shows that can be heard at MSG and the CAA come here too, and the Coliseum is probably the quintessential place to hear piano man Billy Joel, Long Island's favorite son (sorry, Lou Reed).

Rock, pop & soul

Apollo Theatre

253 W 125th St between Adam Clayton Powell Jr Blvd (Seventh Ave) and Frederick Douglass Blvd (Eighth Ave) (212-749-5838). Subway: A, C, B, D, 1 to 125th St. Box office: Mon, Tue, Thu, Fri 10am–6pm; Wed 10am–8:30pm; Sat noon–6pm. $10–$35. AmEx, MC, V.
It helped launch the careers of Ella Fitzgerald and Michael Jackson, it served as *the* hub for R&B music for years and years, and it continues to house the much-ridiculed *Showtime at the Apollo* TV program. Through good times and bad, this Harlem auditorium remains a handsome place to see a concert (it recently underwent a renovation). It's much smaller than it looks on TV, and just about any seat gives you a good view of the hallowed stage. The weekly Wednesday Amateur Night continues—but when performers such as Maxwell or David Byrne (or even Korn) take the stage, they receive a substantial boost from the appealing Apollo atmosphere.

Arlene Grocery

95 Stanton St between Ludlow and Orchard Sts (212-358-1633). Subway: F, V to Lower East Side–Second Ave. Free–$10. Cash only.
Named for the actual Lower East Side market that it replaced, recently expanded Arlene Grocery runs as many as seven or eight groups a night through its top-notch sound system. As you might expect, lots of them will never make it, but you could also catch worthy local acts such as the Adam Roth Challenge or Sean Altman. And then there are the freak nights, like the time that new-wave icon Midge Ure played…. The Monday metal-and-punk karaoke night remains a popular draw.

Baggot Inn

82 W 3rd St between Sullivan and Thompson Sts (212-477-0622). Subway: A, C, E, F, V, S to W 4th St. $5. AmEx, MC, V.
The Baggot Inn has refurbished its interior as well as its booking policies: Good Irish rock can be heard, but so can the bad bar-band fare that's all too typical of the Bleecker Street scene.

BAMcafé/Brooklyn Academy of Music

See page 315 for listing.
The Brooklyn Academy of Music used to save the funk, jazz and pop-based world music for the fall Next Wave Festival. Now the BAMcafé, a high-ceilinged lounge above the lobby, hosts weekly live-music events. The mix of genres includes cabaret, folk and spoken word. Performers have included poet Carl Hancock Rux and avant-blues griot Mark Anthony Thompson's Chocolate Genius. On select weeks, the Sounds of Praise Sunday Gospel Brunch offers a fine opportunity to hear gospel groups (often local ones from Brooklyn) while feasting on a soul-food buffet. *(See also page 339.)*

Noisy neighbors Local antiheroes Sonic Youth crash through a set at the Knitting Factory.

Beacon Theatre

2124 Broadway at 74th St (212-496-7070). Subway: 1, 2, 3 to 72nd St. Box office: Mon–Fri 11am–7pm, Sat noon–6pm. $15–$175. Cash only at box office.
The Beacon is almost like the legendary Fillmore East, transplanted to the Upper West Side. What else can you say about the site of the Allman Brothers' annual monthlong residency? (Or, for that matter, a multiple-night run by those neo-Allmans, the Black Crowes?) The lovely gilded interior and gigantic statues guarding the stage work perfectly for mature sounds—whether that means the drone of Icelandic band Sigur Rós or the moans of Tori Amos just depends on the night.

The Bitter End

147 Bleecker St at Thompson St (212-673-7030; www.bitterend.com). Subway: A, C, E, F, V, S to W 4th St. $5–$10. AmEx, DC, Disc, MC, V.
The granddaddy of Bleecker Street joints hosts the occasional folk or roots star, such as Ramblin' Jack Elliott, and routinely features benefits for all manner of causes, reflecting the folk community's long-standing dedication to activism. But the Bitter End generally features singer-songwriters who are just jazzed to be on the same stage where Dylan strummed and sang all those years ago.

The Bottom Line

15 W 4th St at Mercer St (212-228-6300). Subway: N, R to 8th St–NYU. Box office: 10am–11pm. $15–$35. Cash only.
This Greenwich Village cabaret is most famous for a run of 1970s Springsteen shows that catapulted the Boss to rock-star status, but this steadfast club remains the city's premier acoustic venue for young folkies and touring classic rockers. Hipper local acts such as the Magnetic Fields and the Harry Smiths stop by too (and almost any performer playing here does two sets a night). Word of warning: After all these years, management still hasn't worked the seating chart to perfection, so the sight lines can suck.

Bowery Ballroom

6 Delancey St between Bowery and Chrystie St (212-533-2111; www.boweryballroom.com). Subway: J, M to Bowery; 6 to Spring St. Box office is at Mercury Lounge (see page 307). $10–$25. AmEx, MC, V (bar only).
Mercury Lounge's roomy outpost is one of the city's best venues. It does, however, have its faults: Bands consistently begin nearly an hour after the club's advertised start time, and the Bowery maintains a strict no-reentry policy, which can be a pain in the ass. The pluses more than compensate: Plenty of space (including one small lounge upstairs and another covering the entire lower level), good sight lines, a big stage and bookings that bring in well-known midsize acts, such as Low and Patti Smith, as well as newer wave makers, such as Goldfrapp and the North Mississippi All Stars.

Brownies

169 Ave A between 10th and 11th Sts (212-420-8392; www.browniesnyc.com). Subway: L to First Ave; 6 to Astor Pl. $7–$10. Cash only.
This East Village bar is drab, stuffy and frequently flooded with hipsters, but it consistently books some of the city's best indie-rock bills and triumphs over the physical drawbacks. Almost every big little band has played here at some point in time—the New Pornographers and Love As Laughter recently stopped by—and one can count on burgeoning local

acts such as Mink Lungs, Radio 4 and Interpol to flesh out the bill.

CBGB

315 Bowery at Bleecker St (212-982-4052; www.cbgb.com). Subway: F, V, S to Broadway–Lafayette St; 6 to Bleecker St. $3–$12. Cash only.
CBGB is becoming a living, breathing museum piece. These days, the progressive spirit and sense of diversity that gave birth to punk rock and made the Ramones, Blondie and Talking Heads tick as one are all but gone, as rote metal and punk bands dominate the stage. Nevertheless, anybody interested in the history of New York rock should check out the venue. From the well-worn walls to the legendary bathrooms, CBGB remains as raunchy as ever. And younger fans of hard-edged rock will no doubt adore its marathon bills, which continue to feature some of the loudest guitars in the city.

CB's 313 Gallery

313 Bowery at Bleecker St (212-677-0455). Subway: F, V, S to Broadway–Lafayette St; 6 to Bleecker St. $6–$10. AmEx, MC, V.
The Gallery is CBGB's more cultivated cousin. Located right next door, it is just as long and narrow, but is festooned with local artists' work instead of graffiti and layers of posters. Acoustic fare and local singer-songwriters dominate.

C-Note

157 Ave C at 10th St (212-677-8142). Subway: F, V to Lower East Side–Second Ave; L to First Ave; 6 to Astor Pl. Free.
This joint has a mix of singer-songwriter offerings, guitar-based pop and jazz; pianist Gil Coggins, who used to play with Sonny Rollins and Max Roach, is a regular. C-Note also occasionally hosts CD release parties for local bands and special events, such as the Women in Music Fest.

Continental

25 Third Ave at St. Marks Pl (212-529-6924). Subway: N, R to 8th St–NYU; 6 to Astor Pl. Free–$6. Cash only.
The Continental's "legendary" status is reflected on its walls, which are lined with photos of past performers, including the Ramones and Wendy O. Williams. What you'll hear is streams of local rock, metal and punk bands, or out-of-town bastards (the Candy Snatchers, Fear and Real Kids). The drink specials are suited to a real rock bar (shot and a beer, dude?), and the sound system can flatten the hardiest of eardrums.

The Ding Dong Lounge

See page 150.

Don Hill's

See page 267 for listing.
Part live-music venue, part dance club, loud and divey Don Hill's sponsors such events as the weekly Röck Cändy party, featuring a mix of glammy, punky bands and glammy, punky onlookers, and special tribute nights (Fire and Ice, dedicated to Pat Benatar, was particularly nutty). Famous groupie, er, muse Bebe Buell is known to perform here as well.

Downtime

251 W 30th St between Seventh and Eighth Aves (212-695-2747). Subway: 1, 2 to 28th St. $5–$12. Cash only.
Downtime seems to be a destination for the old-school NYC rock scenesters. During the week, local rock, pop and jazz up-and-comers play in this vertically spacious bar with an upstairs lounge and pool table. The club also throws Goth and darkwave dance parties on the weekends.

Elbow Room

144 Bleecker St between La Guardia Pl and Thompson St (212-979-8434). Subway: A, C, E, F, V, S to W 4th St. $5–$10. Cash only.
Yet another dive on Bleecker Street, the Elbow Room achieved A-list status a few years ago when its Wednesday-night karaoke parties drew the likes of Courtney Love and Claire Danes to the mike—and inspired a short-lived (thank God) VH1 series in the process. Local music of all stripes rules every other night of the week.

Fez

Inside Time Cafe, 380 Lafayette St at Great Jones St (212-533-2680). Subway: F, V, S to Broadway–Lafayette St; 6 to Bleecker St. $5–$18, two-drink minimum. AmEx, MC, V.
Located downstairs from the restaurant Time Cafe, Fez is one of the city's finest venues for lounge acts, and is great for softer rock bands, too. On Thursdays, the Mingus Big Band introduces a new generation of listeners to the robust, sanctified jazz of the late Charles Mingus. Perhaps best of all, this club has a sweet tooth for gender-bending entertainment: In addition to Hedda Lettuce and Jackie Beat, local favorites Kiki and Herb have sauced up the basement with their wild wit for frequent multiple-week runs. Fez's dinner theater–style seating leaves little standing room, so make reservations and arrive early. (You can hang out in the Fez bar behind the restaurant for free.) Cash only for the cover charge, but credit cards can be used for food and drinks.

Galapagos

70 North 6th St between Kent and Wythe Aves, Williamsburg, Brooklyn (718-782-5188). Subway: L to Bedford Ave. $5–$12. Cash only.

► See chapter **By Season** for listings of annual music festivals and events.

► For more live-music venues, see chapters **Cabaret & Comedy**, **Clubs** and **Gay & Lesbian**.

► Pick up a copy of the current issue of **Time Out New York**, which lists specific shows and upcoming concerts.

Arts & Entertainment

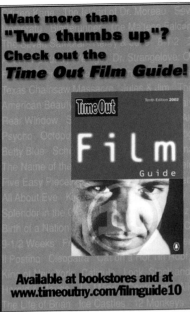

Multiroom Galapagos is both a live-music club and an art space. The trapeze-swinging, lewd-singing Wau Wau Sisters perform in the front room every Monday night (for free), while the other rooms could offer anything from indie faves such as Chris Lee and Cordero to experimental music, theater and spoken-word performances—all with a focus on the deep and diverse community of Williamsburg artists.

Hammerstein Ballroom

Manhattan Center, 311 W 34th St between Eighth and Ninth Aves (212-279-7740, 212-564-4882). Subway: A, C, E to 34th St–Penn Station. Box office: Mon–Sat noon–5pm. $10–$50. AmEx, MC, V.
Built inside the Unification Church–owned Manhattan Center, the Hammerstein Ballroom is a multitiered space that is larger than midsize venues such as Irving Plaza, yet nowhere near as massive as Madison Square Garden. It may not be the best place to see a show—security is a hassle and the sound is fairly crummy—but you can't be faulted for wanting to catch one of the top acts that this venue books: PJ Harvey, Jay-Z and even the Strokes have tackled the mighty Ballroom.

Irving Plaza

17 Irving Pl at 15th St (212-777-6800; www.irvingplaza.com). Subway: L, N, Q, R, W, 4, 5, 6 to 14th St–Union Sq. Box office: Mon–Fri noon–6:30pm; Sat 1–4pm. $10–$30. Cash only.
Irving Plaza, the city's original midsize venue, is often the last stop before big-name locals and nationally touring acts graduate to larger places such as Hammerstein Ballroom. You'll appreciate Irving's elegant decor (no room is swankier for waiting out a suck-ass band than Irving's downstairs lounge), and the plentiful space and a giant screen playing videos complement a sterling booking reputation. Acts run from hoary punks (the Damned, Social Distortion) to a diverse lot of current artists (Blonde Redhead, Femi Kuti, Modest Mouse). You haven't made it in New York City if you haven't played this room.

Izzy Bar

166 First Ave between 10th and 11th Sts (212-228-0444). Subway: L to First Ave; 6 to Astor Pl. $5–$10. AmEx, MC, V.
Izzy Bar is one of NYC's better temples of groove. In addition to smokin' nights geared toward lovers of house and drum 'n' bass, funk bands and jazz-tinged jam sessions keep the party going downstairs.

Joe's Pub

425 Lafayette St between Astor Pl and W 4th St (212-539-8770) Subway: N, R to 8th St–NYU; 6 to Astor Pl. Box office: 1–6pm. $12–$35. AmEx, MC, V.
Named in honor of Public Theater founder Joseph Papp, Joe's Pub features eclectic entertainment (Emmylou Harris, Sandra Bernhard, Kid Koala, Ute Lemper, a DJ series featuring local personalities) in a posh, neocabaret setting. Even when the bar is crowded, this small room maintains its quiet

cool, as downtown hipsters unwind on comfy couches, enjoying the pub's Italian fare before a show. Beware: Seating is limited, and the door policy can be inconsistent (i.e., selectively enforced). *(See also page 263.)*

Knitting Factory/The Old Office/Alterknit Theater

74 Leonard St between Broadway and Church St (212-219-3055; www.knittingfactory.com). Subway: A, C, E to Canal St; 1, 2 to Franklin St. Box office: Mon–Fri 10am–11pm; Sat, Sun 2–11pm $5–$20. AmEx, MC, V ($15 minimum charge).
On some nights, you can traverse entire galaxies of music just by going from one room to another. The main performance space has been known to host well-known rock stars (Lou Reed, Sonic Youth) or indie up-and-comers (Quasi, Kelly Hogan), but genre jumpers (Arto Lindsay, Vinicius Cantuária) are also welcome, as are psychedelic dronesters Bardo Pond. Meanwhile, the smaller Alterknit Theater and Old Office might feature poetry, alternative cinema or jazz artists (Pharoah Sanders, any number of John Zorn protégés). The café and bar are open throughout the day, and the main room holds 250 people.

Lakeside Lounge

162 Ave B between 10th and 11th Sts (212-529-8463; www.lakesidelounge.com). Subway: L to First Ave; N, Q, R, W, 4, 5, 6 to 14th St–Union Sq. Free. AmEx, MC, V.
While flashy electronic-music bars and yuppie hangouts have sprung up around it, the Lakeside remains a great downscale hangout that revels in its scruffiness. A killer jukebox, a photo booth and rockabilly- and roots-loving singers and groups give the club an urban-roadhouse feel. Shows are free, so you can spend more at the bar and get soaked to Michael Shelley, Spike Priggen and the occasional legend from out of town, such as John Sinclair.

L'Amour

1545 63rd St between 15th and 16th Aves, Bay Ridge, Brooklyn (718-837-9506; www.lamourrocks.com). Subway: M, W to 62nd St; N to New Utrecht Ave. $10–$15. Cash only.
Since its 1999 return, L'Amour has brought metal and hard rock back to Brooklyn—and many of the bookings are hair-metal bands that played here in the '80s! Dee Snider (of Twisted Sister) and Kings X will bring you back to the day, while today's hard rock and extreme-metal bands (Type O Negative, Enthroned) will befoul you and your eardrums.

The Living Room

84 Stanton St at Allen St (212-533-7235). Subway: F, V to Lower East Side–Second Ave; J, M, Z to Delancey–Essex Sts. One-drink minimum. Cash only.
As befits its name, the Living Room is a cozy lounge-type space, and its singer-songwriter guests play right up close and personal. The ambience is low-key and friendly, and a hat is often passed around for performers' gas money.

Arts & Entertainment

Luna Lounge

171 Ludlow St between Houston and Stanton Sts (212-260-2323; www.lunalounge.com). Subway: F, V to Lower East Side–Second Ave. Free. Cash only.
This popular Lower East Side hangout's best feature is its cover price: nil. The hectic bar up front directs fans toward the cozy live-music room, where lucky folks might find a soft couch to sink into for the night. As you'd expect from a club that never has a cover, the music can leave a little to be desired. But several of the city's better underground pop artists, such as Nada Surf, Champale and the Irreversible Slacks, frequent the stage, as do a few touring bands (including the Comas).

Luxx

See page 268 for listing.
One of the rooms at the vanguard of Williamsburg's club scene, Luxx splits its time between local and national underground rock bands (Antibalas, the Watchers) and DJ parties, such as DJ Miss Guy's Hellbent for Brooklyn and Larry Tee's Berliniamsburg *(see page 268)*. Reflective wallpaper and a well-designed lighting scheme make Luxx a club to root for.

Makor

35 W 67th St between Central Park West and Columbus Ave (212-601-1000; www.makor.org). Subway: 1, 2 to 66th St–Lincoln Ctr. $5–$12. AmEx, MC, V.

Makor is one of the city's more puzzling venues. A Jewish cultural center located on a fancy Upper West Side street, it transforms its plush basement into an occasionally odd, frequently happening rock club. Past performers have included veteran rockers NRBQ, the sex-obsessed electro-rapper Peaches, a cheeky burlesque show and a range of world music. The audience is always interesting, mixing young downtown music fans with uptown Makor regulars.

Manitoba's

99 Ave B between 6th and 7th Sts (212-982-2511). Subway: F, V to Lower East Side–Second Ave; L to First Ave. Free.
Posted on the rear wall by the floor-level "stage" is a rare photo of the young Bruce Springsteen rocking out in a Dictators T-shirt. That says more about this bar than a thousand words ever could. After all, "Handsome" Dick Manitoba, the self-described "raging bull of rock & roll" and the Dictators' front man, co-owns the boxing-themed joint. Free music is on tap every night—fortified by regulars Tom Clark and Adam Roth—and frequent, spontaneous walk-by performances characterize Manitoba's punch-drunk, freewheeling scene.

Maxwell's

1039 Washington St, Hoboken, NJ (201-798-0406). Travel: PATH train to Hoboken; NJ Transit bus

A noise grows in Brooklyn
Rock & rollers have nested in the county of Kings

If you ever want to trace the migration of a city's rock & roll flock, just follow the flight of the real-estate market, and head in the opposite direction. Musicians are constantly pursuing cheap spaces where they can make loud noises. The catch-22, of course, is that where musicians go, others follow: A sure tip-off to a neighborhood's gentrification-in-progress is the arrival of concert flyers and drum kits. So, while Manhattan has the high-profile history (from the 1920s and '30s Harlem jazz scene to the '70s punk-rock explosion in the East Village) and still hosts most rock shows downtown, many a Gotham guitar-wielder has made tracks to Brooklyn—and the borough has responded with numerous clubs of its own.

MUSICIANS INVADE KINGS COUNTY! isn't exactly headline news—in the 1950s and '60s, for instance, the predominantly Italian neighborhoods of Bay Ridge and Bensonhurst teemed with doo-wop groups, while Alan Freed and DJ Murray "The K"

Kaufman hosted rock and R&B revues at the **Fox Theater** *(Flatbush Ave at Nevins St)*. The borough is the birthplace of such musicians as Neil Diamond, Whitney Houston, 'N Sync's Joey Fatone and the late Aaliyah.

. In other words, music is in the blood of Brooklyn, and since the late '90s, the borough has been experiencing a musical renaissance.

Perhaps the best evidence that Brooklyn is rockin' is the album, *This Is Next Year: A Brooklyn-Based Compilation* (the title refers to a newspaper headline from the day the Brooklyn Dodgers—whose famous rallying cry had been "wait till next year"—finally conquered the Yankees in the 1955 World Series). To Greg Glover, who put out the compilation on his Rock Arena label, not even Manhattan can compete with Brooklyn's whopping 42 acts, which includes Calla, Clem Snide, the Walkmen, Nada Surf and Interpol. "Regardless of bands like the Strokes, I'm hard-pressed to think of any real Manhattan scene," says Glover, whose label is using the proceeds from the comp to benefit the

#126 from Port Authority Bus Terminal. $6–$15. AmEx, MC, V.

Maxwell's has been the most consistently forward-looking rock club in the metropolitan area for the better part of 20 years. Since it's in another state, many visiting acts play a date here as well as at the Bowery Ballroom, Knitting Factory, etc. It can get a little close when it's crowded, but hey, it's a landmark. Music ranges from garage and punk to indie and rocks. The dining room serves edible bar food.

Meow Mix

259 Houston St at Suffolk St (212-254-0688). Subway: F, V to Lower East Side–Second Ave. $5. Cash only.
The music at this brew-fueled neighborhood dyke bar ranges from trashed-up glam to singer-songwriter fare and an anything-goes DJ aesthetic. You can even catch bands on the rise (Sleater-Kinney played once). Meow Mix also features popular tributes, which showcase downtown bands, giving it up for anybody from the Jackson 5 to Kiss. *(See also page 288.)*

Mercury Lounge

217 Houston St at Ave A (212-260-4700; www.mercuryloungenyc.com). Subway: F, V to Lower East Side–Second Ave. Box office: Mon–Fri noon–7pm. $8–$12. Cash only.
Once you've wormed your way past the crowded bar, you'll find the brick-walled room in back that makes Mercury Lounge one of the city's better live-music

venues. The sound is great, you can see from just about any spot, and the staff actually treats you nicely. The bills can seem arbitrary, but there's bound to be at least one artist each night that'll please you, regardless of your taste. That's because the Mercury stays in touch with the local scene, booking the Knoxville Girls and Jerkwater often. The touring acts touch on all genres: Just try fitting Susana Baca, Richard Buckner, Dead Moon, Edith Frost and the James Taylor Quartet into one category.

New Jersey Performing Arts Center

1 Center St at the waterfront, Newark, NJ (888-466-5722). Travel: PATH train to Newark, then Loop shuttle bus two stops to Center. $12–$100. AmEx, DC, MC, V.
NJPAC, the sixth largest performing arts center in the U.S., has hosted everything from the Buena Vista Social Club to Mary J. Blige. *(See also page 316.)*

9C

700 E 9th St at Ave C (212-358-0048). Subway: F, V to Lower East Side–Second Ave; L to First Ave; 6 to Astor Pl. Free–$5. Cash only.
Deep in the heart of Alphabet City, this coolly unassuming watering hole hosts many of New York's underappreciated country-leaning artists, such as Crazee & Heaven and Rebecca Hall.

92nd Street Y

See page 259 for listing.
The Y's popular music schedule extends to gospel,

Brooklyn Animal Resource Coalition. "We live next to the big guy, but have a strong musical community of our own."

"New York City is a hostile place to start a band," adds John Flansburgh of They Might Be Giants, one of Brooklyn's pioneering rock bands. "There's not the kind of local boosterism that one would encounter in a smaller city. But among musicians in Brooklyn, there's a very positive, noncompetitive atmosphere that reminds me of places I've lived outside of New York City."

Brooklyn is a large borough, but its music meccas are concentrated in a few neighborhoods, Williamsburg in particular. Lower Park Slope has a few bars that host local bands (on Fifth Avenue), while Flatbush offers the **Up Over Jazz Cafe**, which regularly welcomes superb players. BAMCafé, part of the Brooklyn Academy of Music, hosts local gospel choirs, visiting bands and lots of multicultural sounds. And Manhattan hipsters cross the river to party at Carroll Gardens' happening DJ haunt, **Halcyon** (see **Halcyon days**, *page 270*).

Whereas Flansburgh "couldn't even convince friends to visit" when he moved to Williamsburg 20 years ago, by the time 20-year-old Ben Kweller relocated from Texas a generation later,

there wasn't much question where he would set up shop. "All of my friends who are in bands live in Brooklyn," says the singer-songwriter, who contributes a harmonica-adorned folk song to *This Is Next Year*.

The neighborhood supports intimate venues, such as **Galapagos** and **Pete's Candy Store**, along with bigger spaces, such as **Northsix**, **Luxx** and **Warsaw at the Polish National Home**, which host local and touring bands alike. Northsix, with its 400-capacity concert space and two smaller rooms, is establishing itself as Brooklyn's answer to Manhattan's Knitting Factory (see page 305). "I've always felt that a medium-size venue would do well in Williamsburg," says club owner Jeff Steinhauser. "National touring bands can play a show in Manhattan, a show at Maxwell's and a show here. There are a lot of [concertgoers] in the neighborhood, and it's easy for people to get here from the city."

"It's always nice not to have to go to Manhattan," adds Karla Schickele, whose group, Ida, appears on *This Is Next Year*. "When I started playing in bands in the early '90s, I was living there, as were a lot of other musicians. These days, I hardly know any who does. Manhattan sucks." ▶

various indigenous folk styles and jazz of the mainstream variety. Jazz in July, the program's centerpiece, entices swingers young and old into the comfy surroundings, as does the Lyrics & Lyricists Series, which celebrates the tunesmiths who wrote the American popular songbook.

Northsix
66 North 6th St between Kent and Wythe Aves, Williamsburg, Brooklyn (718-599-5103). Subway: L to Bedford Ave. Box office: 8pm–midnight. $8–$12. Cash only.
Recently opened on an obscure commercial block in Williamsburg, this bare-bones, 400-capacity club caters largely to the young rock types who have flocked to the neighborhood in recent years. The fledgling club books a lot of Brooklyn-based acts, but it often gets bigger touring bands—like Add N to (X), the Vandermark 5—to hop across the water for a show.

Pete's Candy Store
709 Lorimer St between Frost and Richardson Sts, Williamsburg, Brooklyn (718-302-3770). Subway: G to Metropolitan Ave; L to Lorimer St. Free.
Nestled in the back room of a Brooklyn bar, Pete's is perhaps the city's most charming tiny venue. Shaped something like an old railroad car, the space is smaller than the average American living room, and performances assume the intimacy of a children's puppet show. When a singer stinks, this can get awkward, but alighting in this quirky space on a good night is as sweet as candy.

Radio City Music Hall
1260 Sixth Ave at 50th St (212-247-4777; www.radiocity.com). Subway: B, D, F, V to 47–50th Sts–Rockefeller Ctr. Box office: Mon–Sat 10am–8pm; Sun 11am–8pm. From $25. AmEx, MC, V.
Walking through this awe-inspiring Art Deco hall is almost as exciting as watching the superstars who perform: Even Oasis seems classy on this stage. The hall also hosts the annual Christmas Spectacular *(see page 242)* and has hosted the MTV Video Music Awards.

Roseland
239 W 52nd St between Broadway and Eighth Ave (212-245-5761, concert hot line 212-249-8870). Subway: B, D, E to Seventh Ave; C, 1, 2 to 50th St. Box office open only on the night of the show. From $15. Cash only.
Once upon a time, going to Roseland was a dreadful experience, simply because the 1930s-era ballroom never seemed to cope well with sell-out rock crowds. As part of a major renovation, however, a mezzanine was installed a couple of years ago, so this next-step-before-arenadom is far more palatable. Cake, Slayer and Barenaked Ladies have recently disgraced the stage.

Roxy
See page 268 for listing.

▶ A noise grows in Brooklyn (continued)

In addition to the aforementioned venues, Brooklyn is also home to great record stores and other music-oriented spots.

BAMcafé
See page 300 for listing.

Ear Wax
204 Bedford Ave between North 5th and North 6th Sts, Williamsburg (718-486-3771). Subway: L to Bedford Ave. Tue–Fri 2–8pm; Sat noon–8pm; Sun noon–5pm.
One of the neighborhood's indie-rock hot spots, Ear Wax is such a quintessential record store that it could have served as the set for *High Fidelity*. The selection of new and used CDs and LPs is solid, and as an added bonus, the clerks are generally friendly.

Freddy's Bar
485 Dean St between Flatbush and Sixth Aves, Prospect Heights (718-622-7035). Subway: 1, 2 to Bergen St. 11am–4am.
Located in Prospect Heights, this bar has music almost every night, with nary a cover charge in sight. Eclecticism is the word here: Depending on the night, you'll hear bluegrass, '60s-style psychedelia, singer-songwriters or jug music. Freddy's also hosts open mikes.

Galapagos
See page 303 for listing.

Great Lakes
284 Fifth Ave at 1st St, Park Slope (718-499-3710). Subway: F to Fourth Ave–9th St; M, N, R to Union St. 6pm–4am.
"Just like the East Village—only better," is the mantra at this South Slope club. Blooz, rock, jazz and acoustic acts grace the "stage" (there is no actual stage).

Holy Cow
442 9th St at Seventh Ave, Park Slope (718-788-3631). Subway: F to Seventh Ave. 11am–8pm.
This second-floor walk-up feels a bit like an apartment, with its old living room–like interior. The records could conceivably be one collector's lifetime stash, not straying far from the rock and jazz realms. The store sells current popular CDs (new and used),

Mainly a dance club, and once the cradle of hip-hop, Roxy is now given over to roller skaters one night a week and doesn't regularly host live performances. When it does, bands such as Burning Spear, De La Soul and Moby have taken their bows.

Shine

285 West Broadway at Canal St (212-941-0900; www.shinelive.com). Subway: A, C, E, 1, 2 to Canal St. $10–$20. AmEx, MC, V (for drinks only).
One of Tribeca's hottest nightspots, Shine has a red velvety interior and hosts gigs by local bands of questionable merit and more than a few of yesteryear's one-hit wonders. Shine does have a few tricks up its sleeve, as when Sheryl Crow played an unadvertised series of rambunctious shows in which the likes of Bilal, Stevie Nicks and R.E.M.'s Mike Mills joined her onstage for some rocking covers. British dance act Howie B and Brazilian bossa sensation Bebel Gilberto have also played here, and good DJs are known to come in and mix.

Sidewalk

94 Ave A at 6th St (212-473-7373). Subway: F, V to Lower East Side–Second Ave; 6 to Astor Pl. Free.
They call it "the Fort at Sidewalk," possibly because you have to wend your way through several rooms of diners and drinkers to get to the music space, way in back. Once you're there, anything goes, with the music supplied by host Lach and the bins of vinyl in the back are well worth a look.

Luxx

See page 306 for listing.

Northsix

See page 308 for listing.

Pete's Candy Store

See page 308 for listing.

Rising Café

186 Fifth Ave at Sackett St, Park Slope (718-789-6340). Subway: M, N, R to Union St. Sun–Thu 5pm–1am; Fri, Sat 5pm–2am.
This friendly, cozy café and bar lures the local lesbians, and the booking policy favors singer-songwriters. The cover charge—when there is one—tends to be around $5, making it easy to take a chance on unknown Etheridge-ites.

Up Over Jazz Cafe

See page 312 for listing.

Warsaw at the Polish National Home

See page 310 for listing.

and the "antifolk" scene he spearheads. Open mikes and jam sessions occur frequently, in case you have the mind to drop by with your acoustic guitar, and a passel of antifolkies hit the floor (there's no stage) every night.

S.O.B.'s

See page 269 for listing.
At the city's premier spot for musicians from south of the border, you'll hear samba, reggae, other Caribbean stuff and Afropop. Mondays—La Tropica Nights—are devoted to salsa's biggest names (and free dance lessons). The club has also recently turned into one of the city's prime venues for neosoul and hip-hop acts: Within the past year, it has hosted shows by OutKast, De La Soul, Common, Angie Stone, DJ Hi Tek and Res. How's that for star power?

The Theater at Madison Square Garden

Seventh Ave at 32nd St (212-465-6741). Subway: A, C, E, 1, 2, 3 to 34th St–Penn Station. Box office: Mon–Sat noon–6pm. Prices vary. AmEx, DC, Disc, MC, V.
This is the smaller, classier extension of Madison Square Garden, and since it's not an arena it also sounds better. The theater has hosted various world-music celebrations, medium-size rock shows by String Cheese Incident, Joni Mitchell and a reunited Roxy Music, and a bizarre event in which Elvis Presley's old backing band accompanied giant movie screens of the deceased singer.

The Town Hall

123 W 43rd St between Sixth and Seventh Aves (212-840-2824; www.the-townhall-nyc.org). Subway: B, D, F, V to 42nd St; N, Q, R, W, S, 1, 2, 3, 7 to 42nd St–Times Sq. Box office: Mon–Sat noon–6pm. $15–$85. AmEx, MC, V ($2.50 surcharge for credit card orders).
An 81-year-old theater with ear-pleasing acoustics, The Town Hall was conceived as the "people's auditorium," and its democratic bookings keep that spirit alive. The summer is always slow, but the fall season brings in folk and traditional music artists from around the world (such as Ravi Shankar and Zakir Hussain), as well as a cool mix of American artists (one month could have Laurie Anderson, Tenacious D and Wilco selling out the place). The Town Hall also hosts the annual Mabel Mercer Cabaret Convention in the fall.

Tonic

107 Norfolk St between Delancey and Rivington Sts (212-358-7503; www.tonic107.com). Subway: F to Delancey St; J, M, Z to Delancey–Essex Sts. Box office: 8–11pm. $8–$40. Cash only.
Tonic, a former kosher winery on the Lower East Side, presents avant-garde, creative and experimental music. The venue's artist-curated months, where folks such as John Zorn, Arto Lindsay and Ken Vandermark book the room; its inclusive view of music (jazz, rock, pop, electronic—all are at

Public address system You can really hear what the singers are singing at the Town Hall.

home); and its endless combinations of working jazz musicians hitting the stage together to see what magic happens, make Tonic the best place for the adventurous to begin. The laid-back downstairs Subtonic lounge features DJs (the booths are old wine casks).

Village Underground

130 W 3rd St between Sixth Ave and MacDougal St (212-777-7745). Subway: A, C, E, F, V, S to W 4th St. Box office: 1–8pm. $8–$20. AmEx, MC, V (food and drinks only).

A cozy basement nook where one can stand (albeit awkwardly) or sit (and eat fried food), the Village Underground is a relative newcomer to the city's scene. Its booking leans towards adult-alternative, including loads of roots acts (Amy Rigby, Freedy Johnston) and enticing old-timers (Patti Smith, Ike Turner), who would normally play bigger venues. The club has also hosted Cavestomp!, during which you can catch a mix of veteran '60s garage rockers (? and the Mysterians, the Troggs) and younger combos (the Dirtbombs, the Detroit Cobras) inspired by these rocking elders.

Warsaw at the Polish National Home

261 Driggs Ave at Eckford St, Greenpoint, Brooklyn. (718-387-5252). Subway: G to Nassau Ave. Box office: 5pm. Cash or check only.

The Polish National Home is a spacious, old-fashioned ballroom with a bar in front that serves affordable Polish beers. The cavernous main room with paintings of (presumably) Polish cultural heroes and gigantic mirrors, dubbed Warsaw and run by the bookers of the Village Underground, offers an irregular schedule of touring artists, such as Will Oldham, and local draws with national appeal, such as Luna. It remains to be seen where Warsaw is headed as a live-music venue, but there's no questioning the room's amazing built-in atmosphere.

Jazz & experimental

Birdland

315 W 44th St between Eighth and Ninth Aves (212-581-3080; www.birdlandjazz.com). Subway: A, C, E to 42nd St–Port Authority. $20–$35, $10 food-and-drink minimum. AmEx, MC, V.

The flagship venue for midtown's recent jazz resurgence, Birdland hosts many of jazz's biggest names amid the neon scene of Times Square. The dining area's three tiers allow for maximum visibility while you enjoy pretty fine cuisine. Ron Carter and Dave Holland have made appearances of late, and to compete with the Monday-night big bands in residence elsewhere around town, the club presents the Toshiko Akiyoshi Jazz Orchestra, featuring Lew Tabackin.

Blue Note

131 W 3rd St between Sixth Ave and MacDougal St (212-475-8592; www.bluenote.net). Subway: A, C, E, F, V, S to W 4th St. $10–$65, $5 food-and-drink minimum. AmEx, DC, MC, V.
"The jazz capital of the world" is how this famous club describes itself, and the big names who play are often greeted as if they're visiting heads of state. Recent acts have included Charlie Watts, Roy Haynes and Paquito D'Rivera. All this comes at a price: Dinner will cost you more than $25 a head.

Carnegie Hall

See page 316 for listing.
Although getting the gig at Carnegie Hall remains synonymous with hitting the big time, nowadays many of the venue's showcases are simply reminders that the hall's acoustics were designed for classical music—period. But that didn't stop Carnegie's honchos from launching an annual jazz program, directed by star trumpeter Jon Faddis. Other nights, expect performers such as jazz-congo madman Poncho Sanchez or the singers who appeared on the *O Brother, Where Art Thou?* soundtrack.

Cornelia Street Cafe

29 Cornelia St between Bleecker and W 4th Sts (212-989-9318; corneliastreetcafe.com). Subway: A, C, E, F, V, S to W 4th St. $5–$15, $6 one-drink minimum. AmEx, DC, MC, V.
Cornelia Street Cafe may be avant-garde, but it's accessible too. There's something about walking down the stairs of this Greenwich Village eatery that brings out the calm in some of the scene's most adventurous players, such as Tony Malaby. The result is dinner music with a contemporary edge.

Iridium

1650 Broadway at 51st St (212-582-2121; www.iridiumjazzclub.com). Subway: 1, 2 to 66th St–Lincoln Ctr. $25–$30, $10–$15 food-and-drink minimum. AmEx, DC, Disc, MC, V.
Iridium's new location puts it a step closer to Times Square, but that hasn't changed the club's attitude. It still lures upscale crowds with a mix that's split between household names and those known only by the jazz-savvy—but now both its sight lines and the sound system are truly worthy of celebration. Monday nights belong to the legendary guitarist, inventor and icon Les Paul, who often ends up sharing the stage with one of the guitar heroes who swear by his prize invention, the Gibson solid-body electric guitar that bears his name.

Stanley H. Kaplan Penthouse at Lincoln Center

1650 Broadway at 51st St, tenth floor (212-875-5050). Subway: B, D, E to Seventh Ave; 1, 2 to 50th St. Tickets available from Alice Tully Hall box office 11am–6pm. AmEx, DC, Disc, MC, V.
If you thought Lincoln Center housed only grand concert halls, you should come hear one of the jazz events at the Kaplan Penthouse. A 100-seat room with a terrace that offers a scenic view of the Hudson River, the Penthouse is the specialty room for the Lincoln Center jazz program's series of duets and solo recitals. It's like having Tommy Flanagan while away the evening in your living room.

Knitting Factory/The Old Office/The Alterknit Theater

See page 305 for listing.

Lenox Lounge

288 Lenox Ave (Malcolm X Blvd) between 124th and 125th Sts (212-427-0253). Subway: 2, 3 to 125th St. $15, $5 minimum. AmEx, Disc, MC, V (drinks only).
This is where Malcolm worked before he added the X. The jazz isn't always traditional, but the hardbop outfits that jam at this classy Harlem institution make no bones about carrying on an old tradition.

Merkin Concert Hall

See page 316 for listing.
Just across the street from Lincoln Center, Merkin's elegant digs provide an intimate setting for jazz and experimental music (Matthew Shipp, Robert Ashley, Klezmatics trumpeter Frank London) not likely to be heard at Avery Fisher Hall. Still, the place is open-minded, and you can also hear a classic stylist such as pianist Fred Hersch.

Roulette

228 West Broadway at White St (212-219-8242; www.roulette.org). Subway: C, E to Canal St; 1, 2 to Franklin St. $10. Cash only.
Ever thought you might want live music in your living room? Well, improvising trombonist/Roulette proprietor Jim Staley has saved you the trouble. The atmosphere in his 11-year-old salon is relaxed—until the music starts up. The players, Staley's friends, represent an encyclopedia of world-famous music experimentalists. You're as likely to hear electroacoustic and computer-music pioneers, such as Montreal's Maxime de la Rochefoucauld, as you are avant-jazzers, such as downtown cellist Okkyung Lee.

Smalls

183 W 10th St at Seventh Ave South (212-929-7565; www.smalls.com). Subway: 1, 2 to Christopher St–Sheridan Sq. $10. Cash only.
The spot where new-jazz jacks rub elbows with their college-student counterparts and Beat-era nostalgists, Smalls books high-profile up-and-comers. You'll hear 13 hours of jazz on weekend nights, and pianist Jason Lindner's big band usually plays on Mondays. There's no liquor license, but you can bring your own booze or sample some of the juices and teas at the bar.

St. Nick's Pub

773 St. Nicholas Ave at 149th St (212-283-9728).
Subway: A, C, B, D to 145th St. Free. Cash only.
Up in Harlem's Sugar Hill section, St. Nick's may be
the closest thing to an old-fashioned juke joint you're
likely to find in the city: It has live music six nights a
week, charmingly makeshift decor, a soul-food menu,
and mature Heineken-sipping patrons who take their
hedonistic impulses seriously. The jazz runs from
bebop and vocal-driven to funky. Big names, such as
James Carter, occasionally stop by for the Monday-
night jam. A must-visit for any serious jazz fan.

Swing 46

349 W 46th St between Eighth and Ninth Aves (212-
262-9554; www.swing46.com). Subway: A, C, E to
42nd St–Port Authority. Box office: noon–4pm. Thu–
Sat $12; Sun–Wed $7. MC, V.
You don't have to throw on a zoot suit or a poodle
skirt to make the scene at this midtown bastion of
retro, but it certainly will enhance the vibe. Seven
nights' worth of bands that jump, jive and wail
await you, so be sure to wear your most comfortable
shoes. Regular bands have names such as Nick
Palumbo and the Flipped Fedoras, so you know
what to expect. Live music starts up at 10pm, and
dancing is de rigueur.

Tonic

See page 309 for listing.

Up Over Jazz Cafe

351 Flatbush Ave at Seventh Ave, Park Slope,
Brooklyn (718-398-5413; www.upoverjazz.com).
Subway: F to Seventh Ave; 1, 2 to Grand Army
Plaza. $10–$18. Cash only.
Up Over Jazz Cafe bucks one of the more established
jazz club traditions: It's upstairs rather than in the
basement. The differences stop there. Up Over is one
of Brooklyn's key jazz rooms, mainly because its
good sight lines and warm sound system have lured
name players (John Hicks, Mike LeDonne, Freddie
Hubbard), who usually confine their NYC appearances to Manhattan clubs.

Village Vanguard

178 Seventh Ave South at Perry St (212-255-4037).
Subway: A, C, E, 1, 2, 3 to 14th St; L to Eighth
Ave. Call to reserve tickets. $15–$20, $10 minimum.
Cash only.
This basement club is still blowing strong after 66
years. Its stage—a small but mighty step-up that
has seen the likes of John Coltrane, Bill Evans and
Miles Davis—hosts the crème de la crème of mainstream jazz talent. The Monday-night regular is the
16-piece Vanguard Jazz Orchestra, which has held
the same slot for more than 30 years.

Reggae, world & Latin

Babalu

327 W 44th St between Eighth and Ninth Aves (212-
262-1111; www.babaluny.com). Subway: A, C, E to
42nd St–Port Authority; N, Q, R, W, S, 1, 2, 3, 7 to
42nd St–Times Sq. Tue–Thu, Sat 5:30pm–1am; Fri
5:30pm–3am. $10–$12. AmEx, DC, Disc, MC, V.
This 21st-century version of the Tropicana supper
club featured in *I Love Lucy* features live salsa,
merengue and Latin pop.

S.O.B.'s

See pages 269 and 309 for listing.

Zinc Bar

90 Houston St between La Guardia Pl and Thompson
St (212-477-8337). Subway: A, C, E, F, V, S to W 4th
St. $5. Cash only.
Located in the subnook situated where Noho meets
Soho, Zinc Bar is the place to catch up with the
most die-hard night owls. The after-hours feel
starts well before midnight, and the atmosphere is
enhanced by the cool mix of jazz, Latin, samba,
African and flamenco bands. Cidinho Teixeira's
Brazilian Showfest draws *grande* crowds on
Sundays, while guitarist Ron Affif holds down the
fort on Mondays and Francis M'Bappe's FM Tribe
delivers African funk on Fridays.

Blues, country & folk

B.B. King Blues Club & Grill

237 W 42nd St between Seventh and Eighth Aves
(212-997-4144). Subway: A, C, E to 42nd St–Port
Authority; N, Q, R, W, S, 1, 2, 3, 7 to 42nd St–
Times Sq. Sun–Tue, Thu 11am–midnight; Wed
11am–5am; Fri, Sat 11am–3am. Cover varies.
AmEx, DC, Disc, MC, V.
Praise the lord and pass the bacon—B.B. King's is
shakin' to the beat of J.C., and we don't mean Jim
Croce. Amid the lineup of retread classic rockers,
Southern-rock shitkickers and schlock-and-roll
bookings at this well-appointed 42nd Street club,
there is one dynamite, can't-miss event every week:
The Harlem Gospel Choir buffet brunch on Sunday.
Other stellar soul and blues performers include the
likes of James Brown and Etta James. Can we get a
witness, please!

Kate Kearney's

251 E 50th St between Second and Third Aves (212-
935-2045). Subway: E, V to Lexington Ave–53rd St;
6 to 51st St. Free.
This cozy Irish pub gets a good crowd for its
events: Thursdays, you can see an informal *seisiún*
with Patrick Ourceau and Don Meade, while other
nights feature a variety of Irish-flavored country
and folk.

Paddy Reilly's Music Bar

519 Second Ave at 29th St (212-686-1210;
www.paddyreillys.com). Subway: 6 to 28th St. Fri, Sat
$5–$10. AmEx, MC, V.
The premier local bar for Irish rock hosts nightly
music from the likes of the Prodigals, with *seisiúns*
thrown in as well.

Arts & Entertainment

Music

Rodeo Bar

375 Third Ave at 27th St (212-683-6500). Subway: 6 to 28th St. Free.

Rodeo Bar looks like any other midtown joint—and half of it is, actually. But the sawdust-strewn northern half books local roots outfits and visiting country acts. Ace Austin, Texas, guitarist Rosie Flores often stops by, for instance.

Terra Blues

149 Bleecker St at Thompson St (212-777-7776; www.terrablues.com). Subway: A, C, E, F, V, S to W 4th St. Free–$15. AmEx, MC, V.

You'll hear a wide range of blues-based artists at this otherwise ordinary Bleecker Street bar—from Chicago guitar pickers to NYC's Moe Holmes and the Pioneers.

Tribeca Blues

16 Warren St between Broadway and Church St (212-766-1070). Subway: A, C to Chambers St; N, R to City Hall. $5–$25. AmEx, MC, V.

At Tribeca Blues, you can see local blues acts (such as Wednesday-night jams with Bobby Nathan) and the occasional big name.

Summer venues

The Anchorage

Cadman Plaza West between Hicks and Old Fulton Sts, Dumbo, Brooklyn (212-206-6674; www.creativetime.org). Subway: 2, 3 to Clark St; A, C to High St. Tickets available at Other Music (see page 229). $12–$20. Cash only.

There isn't a more evocative place to catch an avant-rock or electronic event (think Thomas Brinkmann, Sonic Youth, Giant Step) than this arty, Bat Cave–like cavern inside the anchorage of the Brooklyn Bridge. The nonprofit public-art presenter Creative Time organizes the events.

Bryant Park

Sixth Ave between 41st and 42nd Sts (212-983-4142). Subway: B, D, F, V to 42nd St; 7 to Fifth Ave. Free.

Adjacent to the New York Public Library, Bryant

Find your groove

If you like...	Go to...
Ani DiFranco	The Bitter End *(page 301)*, Mercury Lounge *(page 309)* and Sidewalk *(page 309)*
Belle and Sebastian	Bowery Ballroom *(page 301)*, Irving Plaza *(page 305)* and Knitting Factory *(page 305)*
Fatboy Slim	Hammerstein Ballroom *(page 305)*, Roseland *(page 308)* and Shine *(page 309)*
Jill Scott	Irving Plaza *(page 305)*, S.O.B.'s *(page 309)* and Village Underground *(page 310)*
Jay-Z	Irving Plaza *(page 305)*, Madison Square Garden *(page 300)* and Nassau Veterans Memorial Coliseum *(page 300)*
Eddie Palmieri	S.O.B.'s *(page 309)* and Zinc Bar *(page 312)*
Rancid	Brownies *(page 301)*, CBGB *(page 303)*, Continental *(page 303)* and Manitoba's *(page 306)*
Sonny Rollins	Blue Note *(page 311)*, Iridium *(page 311)* and Village Vanguard *(page 312)*
The Roots	Bowery Ballroom *(page 301)*, Irving Plaza *(page 305)* and S.O.B.'s *(page 309)*
The Strokes	Brownies *(page 301)*, Hammerstein Ballroom *(page 305)*, Maxwell's *(page 306)* and Mercury Lounge *(page 307)*
Wilco	Hogs & Heifers Uptown *(page 145)*, Lakeside Lounge *(page 305)* and Rodeo Bar *(see this page)*
John Zorn	Galapagos *(page 303)*, Knitting Factory *(page 305)*, Merkin Concert Hall *(page 311)*, Roulette *(page 311)* and Tonic *(page 309)*

Arts & Entertainment

Eat to the beat The Bobby Blue Band performs for diners at B.B. King's Blues Club & Grill.

Park is a serene and genteel park with a popular free summer concert series.

Castle Clinton
Battery Park, Battery Pl at State St (212-835-2789) Subway: E to World Trade Ctr; N, R to Rector St; 1, 2 to Park Pl; 4, 5 to Bowling Green. Free.
Space is limited at this historic fort in the heart of Battery Park. At the summer Thursday-night concert series, lucky music hounds get an unobstructed view of performers such as the Blind Boys of Alabama and Crash Test Dummies.

Central Park SummerStage
Rumsey Playfield, Central Park entrance on 72nd St at Fifth Ave (212-360-2777; www.summerstage.org). Subway: B, C to 72nd St; N, R, W to Fifth Ave–60th St; 6 to 68th St–Hunter College. Free; benefit concerts $15–$25. Cash only.
On a humid summer weekend, SummerStage is one of New York's great treasures. The number of pricey shows seems to increase every year, but most concerts at this amphitheater are free. The booking policy is remarkably ecumenical, from world music (Cheika Remitti) and soul (Erykah Badu) to country (Lyle Lovett) and dance (Basement Jaxx). Don't forget to show up early—many people had to be turned away from the Manu Chao show.

Giants Stadium
East Rutherford, NJ (201-935-3900; tickets sold through Ticketmaster 212-307-7171). Travel: NJ Transit Meadowlands Sports Complex bus from Port Authority Bus Terminal, Eighth Ave at 42nd St, $3.25 each way (212-564-8484). Box office: Mon–Fri 9am–6pm; Sat 10am–6pm; Sun noon–5pm. $20–$75. AmEx, MC, V.
At Giants Stadium, you can catch biggies such as U2 and 'N Sync, while overhead airliners fly to and from

Newark Airport. Band members look like ants, and you'll wait a long, long time for beer, but the hot dogs aren't that bad. And because it's outdoors, it's the only remaining venue in the Meadowlands complex where you can legally smoke.

Jones Beach
Jones Beach, Long Island (516-221-1000). Travel: LIRR from Penn Station, Seventh Ave at 32nd St, to Freeport, then Jones Beach bus. $18–$65. Cash only.
All right, so getting to Jones Beach from Manhattan isn't the fastest thing in the world if you don't have a car, and once there, the sound isn't that great either. But you can't beat the alfresco setting at this beachside amphitheater. Beware of sand fleas. From July to September, most of the big tours make a pit stop at Jones Beach, so you can catch the likes of Sade, the Deftones, Dido, Paul Simon and Moby.

Lincoln Center Plaza
65th St at Columbus Ave (212-875-5400). Subway: 1, 2 to 66th St–Lincoln Ctr. Free.
The home of Lincoln Center's Midsummer Night Swing *(see page 238)* and Out-of-Door *(see page 239)* festivals, Lincoln Center Plaza hosts many of New York City's sundry cultural communities. In one week, it's possible to hear the world's hottest Latin and African bands (Papa Wemba, the Congolese fashion plate who helped invent *soukous*, recently dropped by) and a concert by tenor-saxophone god Sonny Rollins, or pianists Diane Schuur and Cyrus Chestnut.

Prospect Park Bandshell
Prospect Park, entrance on 9th St at Prospect Park West, Park Slope, Brooklyn (718-965-8969). Subway: F to Seventh Ave; 1, 2 to Grand Army Plaza. Suggested donation $3.

Prospect Park Bandshell is to Brooklynites what Central Park SummerStage is to Manhattan residents: *the* place to hear great music in the great outdoors. Prospect Park may not get as many high-profile acts as its Manhattan counterpart, but that just means you're more likely to discover up-and-coming and local acts in Brooklyn. The shows mirror the borough's great melting pot, and the music runs from *rai* (Khaled) and salsa (Frankie Negron) to Afropop (Baaba Maal) and Louisiana boogie (Marcia Ball). Prospect Park also books excellent modern-dance troupes (where else are you going to see Mark Morris under the stars?) and has started a film series.

Classical Music

The popular press would have you believe that classical music is in a state of crisis in America, but one glance at the listings for concerts in NYC, during any given week, tells another story. The venerable Carnegie Hall plays host to the world's most outstanding orchestras and soloists during the spring and fall, while Lincoln Center (the world's largest performing-arts center) might play host to two operas, an orchestral concert and several chamber-music recitals in a single day. The city's churches, museums and schools add even more musical activity to the mix. Plus, New York has several small—and charming—opera companies to round out the musical offerings happening every night of the week.

Tickets

You can buy tickets directly from most venues, either in-person or online. You can also purchase tickets over the phone for some venues, though a surcharge is added. See page 377 for more ticket information.

CarnegieCharge
212-247-7800. 8am–8pm. AmEx, DC, Disc, MC, V. Surcharge $4.75 per ticket.

Centercharge
212-721-6500. Mon–Sat 10am–8pm; Sun noon–8pm. AmEx, Disc, MC, V. Surcharge $5.50 per ticket.
Centercharge sells tickets for events at Alice Tully Hall, Avery Fisher Hall and the Lincoln Center Festival *(see page 239),* which takes place in July.

New York Philharmonic Ticket Club
212-875-5656. Mon–Fri 10am–5pm; Sat noon–5pm. AmEx, DC, MC, V. Surcharge $5.
In most cases, you can buy discounted tickets ($25) the day of the performance.

Ticketmaster
212-307-4100; www.ticketmaster.com. 6:45am–11pm. AmEx, Disc, MC, V. Surcharges vary by venue.
You can buy tickets for performances at most larger venues, such as the New York State Theater, Town Hall and BAM. The phone line is often busy, and you may be put on hold for ages; go online if possible.

TKTS
See page 377 for listing.
TKTS offers 25 and 50 percent discounts on many Lincoln Center performances, including those by the New York Philharmonic, New York City Opera, Chamber Music Society and Juilliard School musicians (but not the Metropolitan Opera).

Backstage passes

It's possible to go behind the scenes at several of the city's major concert venues. **Backstage at the Met** *(212-769-7020)* takes you around the famous house during opera season (September to May); **Lincoln Center Tours** *(212-875-5350)* escorts you inside Avery Fisher and Alice Tully Halls, and the New York State Theater; **Carnegie Hall** *(212-247-7800)* shepherds you through what is perhaps the world's most famous concert hall. It's also possible to sit in on rehearsals of the **New York Philharmonic**, usually held on the Thursday before a concert, for a small fee.

Concert halls

Brooklyn Academy of Music
30 Lafayette Ave between Flatbush Ave and Fulton St, Fort Greene, Brooklyn (718-636-4100; www.bam.org). Subway: C to Lafayette Ave; G to Fulton St; M, N, R, W to Pacific St; Q, 1, 2, 4, 5 to Atlantic Ave. $17–$95. AmEx, MC, V.
BAM's opera house is America's oldest academy for the performing arts. But the programming is more East Village than, say, Upper West Side: BAM helped launch the likes of Philip Glass (who still performs here regularly) and John Zorn. Current music director Robert Spano has helped refine the resident Brooklyn Philharmonic Orchestra, though the group doesn't get the monetary support its Manhattan counterpart does. Every fall and winter, the **Next Wave Festival** provides an overview of established avant-garde music and theater, while the spring BAM Opera

▶ For information on concerts, times and locations, see *Time Out New York*'s Classical & Opera listings.
▶ The Theater Development Fund *(see page 336)* provides information on all music events, via its **NYC/On Stage** service.

season brings innovative European productions to downtown Brooklyn. *(See also page 339.)*

Carnegie Hall

154 W 57th St at Seventh Ave (212-247-7800; www.carnegiehall.org). Subway: A, C, B, D, 1, 2 to 59th St–Columbus Circle; N, Q, R, W to 57th St. $20–$90. AmEx, DC, Disc, MC, V.
You don't have to practice, practice, practice to get there; you can take the subway to the best of the city's visiting-artist concert venues. A varied roster of American and international stars appears in the two auditoriums: Carnegie Hall itself and the lovely, smaller Weill Recital Hall. This venue is undergoing a massive renovation; a big new subterranean performance space is slated to open in 2003.

Colden Center for the Performing Arts

LeFrak Concert Hall, Queens College, 65-30 Kissena Blvd at 65th Ave, Flushing, Queens (718-793-8080; www.coldencenter.org). Subway: 7 or LIRR to Flushing–Main Street, then Q17, Q25 or Q34 bus to Kissena Blvd. Box office: Mon 10am–4pm; Wed noon–8pm; Fri noon–4pm; Sat 10am–2pm. $10–$30. AmEx, Disc, MC, V.
The home of the Queens Philharmonic, this multipurpose hall also stages concerts by international artists who are in town for Manhattan performances. Due to the Colden Center's "remote" location, tickets are often half the price of the city's other venues.

Florence Gould Hall at the Alliance Française

55 E 59th St between Madison and Park Aves (212-355-6160; www.fiaf.org). Subway: N, R, W to Fifth Ave–60th St; 4, 5, 6 to 59th St. Box office: Tue–Fri 11am–7pm; Sat, Sun 11am–3pm. $10–$35. AmEx, MC, V.
You don't *have* to brush up on your French to attend the recitals and chamber works performed at this small space, but the programming does have a decidedly French accent, in both its artists and repertoire.

Merkin Concert Hall

129 W 67th St between Broadway and Amsterdam Ave (212-501-3330; www.elainekaufmancenter.org). Subway: 1, 2 to 66th St–Lincoln Ctr. $10–$25. AmEx, MC, V (for advance purchases only).
This unattractive theater has rather dry acoustics and is tucked away on a side street in the shadow of Lincoln Center. But its mix of early music and avant-garde programming (heavy on recitals and chamber concerts) can make it a rewarding stop. Merkin also houses the **Lucy Moses School for Music and Dance** and the **Special Music School of America**.

New Jersey Performing Arts Center

See page 307 for listing.
Designed by Los Angeles–based architect Barton Myers, the NJPAC complex is impressive, featuring the oval-shaped, wooden 2,750-seat Prudential Hall and the more institutional-looking 514-seat Victoria

Theater. It may sound far away, but it takes only 15 to 20 minutes to get to NJPAC from midtown. It's a good place to catch big-name acts that may be sold out at Manhattan venues.

92nd Street Y

See page 259 for listing.
The Y emphasizes traditional orchestral, solo and chamber masterworks, but also foments the careers of young musicians.

The Town Hall

See page 309 for listing.
The Town Hall has a wonderful, intimate stage and excellent acoustics. Classical music often shares the programming lineup with New Age speakers, pop concerts and film screenings.

Lincoln Center

This massive arts complex, built in the 1960s, is the center of Manhattan's performing-arts scene. In addition to the main halls—**Alice Tully, Avery Fisher, Metropolitan Opera House, New York State Theater,** the **Vivian Beaumont** and **Mitzi E. Newhouse Theaters** *(see page 339)*—Lincoln Center hosts lectures and symposia in the **Rose Building**. Also on the premises are **The Juilliard School** *(see page 320)* and the **Fiorello La Guardia High School of the Performing Arts** (yes, the *Fame* one, but in a different location), which also occasionally hosts professional performances. The **Mostly Mozart Festival** in August (at Avery Fisher and Alice Tully Halls) used to be the big summer event, but lately it has been upstaged by the larger, multidisciplinary **Lincoln Center Festival** *(see page 239)*, which takes place in July. The big guys (Yo-Yo Ma, Daniel Barenboim, Anne-Sophie Mutter) perform here, but the Center has also been venturing into more adventurous programming in recent years.

Lincoln Center

65th St at Columbus Ave (212-LINCOLN; www.lincolncenter.org). Subway: 1, 2 to 66th St–Lincoln Ctr.
This is the main entry point for Lincoln Center, but the venues that follow are spread out in the square between 62nd and 66th Streets from Amsterdam to Columbus Avenues.

Alice Tully Hall

212-875-5050. Box office: Mon–Sat 11am–6pm; Sun noon–6pm; also open until 30 minutes after the start of performance. Free–$75. AmEx, Disc, MC, V.
Built to house the **Chamber Music Society of Lincoln Center** *(212-875-5788)*, Alice Tully Hall somehow makes its thousand seats feel cozy. It has no central aisle; the rows have extra legroom to compensate. The hall accommodates both music and the

spoken word well; its **Art of the Song** recital series is one of the most extensive in town.

Avery Fisher Hall

212-875-5030; www.nyphilharmonic.org. Box office: Mon–Sat 10am–6pm; Sun noon–6pm. $20–$90. AmEx, Disc, MC, V.

Originally called Philharmonic Hall, this 2,700-seat auditorium used to have unbearable acoustics; it took the largesse of electronics millionaire Avery Fisher, and several major renovations, to improve the sound quality. The venue is now handsome *and* comfortable. This is the headquarters of the **New York Philharmonic** *(212-875-5656)*, the country's oldest orchestra (founded in 1842) and one of the world's finest. It holds free concerts and regular open rehearsals. The hall also hosts concerts by top international ensembles as part of the **Great Performers** series. Every summer, the famous **Mostly Mozart** series is held here.

Metropolitan Opera House

212-362-6000; www.metopera.org. Box office: Mon–Sat 10am–8pm; Sun noon–6pm. $12–$225. AmEx, Disc, MC, V.

Marc Chagall's enormous mystical paintings hang inside its five geometric arches: The Met is the grandest of the Lincoln Center buildings, a spectacular place to see and hear opera. It's home to the Metropolitan Opera from September to May, and it's also where major visiting companies are most likely to appear. Met productions are lavish (though not always tasteful), and cast lists are a who's who of current stars. Under artistic director James Levine, the orchestra has become a true symphonic force. Although the audiences are knowledgeable and fiercely partisan (subscriptions stay in families for generations), the Met has been trying to be more inclusive in recent years, and English-language subtitles on the backs of seats now allow operagoers to laugh in all the right places. Tickets are expensive, and unless you can afford good seats, the view won't be great. Standing-room-only tickets start at $12; you have to wait in line on Saturday mornings to buy them. In recent years, the Met has commissioned productions by the likes of Robert Wilson—to mixed receptions from its conservative audiences; Wilson was booed at the 1998 premiere of his production of *Lohengrin*. Over-the-top Franco Zeffirelli productions of the classics remain the Met's bread and butter.

New York State Theater

212-870-5570; www.nycopera.com. Box office: Mon 10am–7:30pm; Tue–Sat 10am–8:30pm; Sun 11:30am–7:30pm. $25–$100. AmEx, Disc, MC, V.

NYST houses both the **New York City Ballet** and the **New York City Opera**—which has tried to upgrade its "second best" reputation by being defiantly popular and ambitious. That means the opera company has been hiring only American singers, performing many works in English, bringing American musicals into opera houses, giving a more theatrical spin to old favorites and devel-

oping supertitles for foreign-language productions. City Opera has championed modern opera—mixing Tan Dun's *Ghost Opera* with *Madame Butterfly*—resulting in a few great successes and some noble failures. City Opera is ultimately much cooler than its stodgier neighbor, and tickets are about half the price. In 1999, City Opera shocked purists by using a sound-enhancement system in the New York State Theater—but frankly, the acoustics used to suck.

Walter Reade Theater

212-875-5600. Box office: 2–6pm. $12–$15.

Lincoln Center's newest concert hall is a glorified movie house: This is the home for the **Film Society of Lincoln Center** *(see page 276)*, and its acoustics are the driest in the complex—but uniformly perfect sight lines make up for it. The Chamber Music Society uses the space for its **Music of Our Time** series, and the Sunday-morning **Great Performers** concert series is fueled by pastries and hot beverages in the lobby. **Reel to Real**, Lincoln Center's weekend family series, matches silver-screen gems to live performances with audience participation.

Other venues

Bargemusic

Fulton Ferry Landing, next to the Brooklyn Bridge, Brooklyn Heights, Brooklyn (718-624-4061; www.bargemusic.com). Subway: A, C to High St. $15–$27. Cash only.

This former coffee barge offers four chamber concerts a week—and a great view of the Manhattan skyline. It's a magical experience, but dress warmly in winter. When the weather's nice, enjoy a drink on the upper deck during intermission.

CAMI Hall

165 W 57th St between Sixth and Seventh Aves (212-397-6900). Subway: F, N, Q, R, W to 57th St. Prices vary. Cash only.

Located across the street from Carnegie Hall, this 200-seat recital hall is rented out for individual events, mostly by classical artists.

Continental Center

180 Maiden Ln at Front St (212-799-5000, ext 313). Subway: A, C to Broadway–Nassau St; 1, 2, 4, 5 to Wall St. Free.

The **Juilliard Artists in Concert** series offers free lunchtime student recitals on Tuesdays; the schedule expands during the summer.

Frick Collection

See page 34 for listing.

Concerts in this museum's tiny, elegantly appointed concert hall are always a rare treat, featuring lesser-known but world-class performers in an intimate setting (for instance, the Festetics Quartet playing Haydn on period instruments). Tickets are free, but acquiring them can be a bit of a chore:

Written requests must be submitted in advance, and tickets are often gone well before the event. A line for returned tickets forms one hour before each event, and if you still can't get one, at least you can listen to the music through speakers in the museum's outdoor garden.

Kaye Playhouse
Hunter College, 68th St between Park and Lexington Aves (212-772-4448). Subway: 6 to 68th St–Hunter College. Box office: Mon–Sat noon–6pm. Free–$70. AmEx, MC, V.
This refurbished theater, named after comedian Danny Kaye and his wife, offers an eclectic program of professional music and dance.

The Kitchen
512 W 19th St between Tenth and Eleventh Aves (212-255-5793; www.thekitchen.org). Subway: A, C, E to 14th St; L to Eighth Ave. Free–$25. AmEx, MC, V.
Occupying a 19th-century icehouse, the Kitchen has been a meeting place for the avant-garde in music, dance and theater for almost 30 years.

Kosciuszko Foundation House
15 E 65th St at Fifth Ave (212-734-2130; www.kosciuszkofoundation.org). Subway: F to Lexington Ave–63rd St; 6 to 68th St–Hunter College. $15–$25. MC, V.
This East Side townhouse hosts a chamber-music series with a twist: Each program must feature at least one work by a Polish composer. That means you might be choking on Chopin, but there are some unexpected offerings.

Metropolitan Museum of Art
See page 35 for listing.
This is one of the city's best chamber-music venues, so concerts usually sell out quickly.

Miller Theatre at Columbia University
Broadway at 116th St (212-854-7799; www.millertheatre.com). Subway: 1 to 116th St–Columbia Univ. Box office: Mon–Fri noon–6pm. Prices vary. AmEx, MC, V.
Columbia's acoustically excellent space has become the city's most dependable source of contemporary concert music, devoting entire evenings to such composers as Iannis Xenakis, György Ligeti, James Dillon and John Zorn, as well as enterprising surveys of early music and innovative, multidisciplinary events such as "Gogmagogs."

New York Public Library for the Performing Arts
40 Lincoln Center Plaza (212-870-1630). Subway: 1, 2 to 66th St–Lincoln Ctr. Free.
The Bruno Walter Auditorium plays host to recitals, solo performances and lectures.

Symphony Space
*See **Selected Shorts**, page 259, for listing.*
The programming is eclectic; best bets are the annual **Wall to Wall** marathons, which offer a full day of music featuring a composer or theme, from Bach to Miles Davis. The marathons are free, resulting in lines around the block. Symphony Space reopened in March 2002 after a renovation and expansion into a two-venue complex.

John L. Tishman Auditorium
The New School, 66 W 12th St at Sixth Ave (212-229-5689). Subway: F, V, 1, 2, 3 to 14th St; L to Sixth Ave. Free–$12. Cash only.
The New School's modestly priced Schneider chamber-music series runs from April to October and features up-and-coming young musicians as well as more established artists, who play here for a fraction of the prices charged elsewhere.

Churches

An enticing variety of music—sacred to secular—is performed in New York's churches. Many resident choirs are excellent, while superb acoustics and serene surroundings make churches particularly attractive venues. Bonus: Some concerts are free or very cheap.

Cathedral of St. John the Divine
1047 Amsterdam Ave at 112th St (212-662-2133; www.stjohndivine.org). Subway: 1 to 110th St–Cathedral Pkwy. Box office: 10am–6pm. Prices vary. AmEx, MC, V.
The 3,000-seat interior is an acoustical black hole, but the stunning Gothic surroundings provide a heavenly atmosphere for the church's own choir and groups such as the Russian Chamber Chorus. (*See also page 84.*)

Christ and St. Stephen's Church
120 W 69th St between Columbus Ave and Broadway (212-787-2755; www.csschurch.org). Subway: 1, 2, 3 to 72nd St. Prices vary. Cash only.
This West Side church offers one of the most diverse concert rosters in the city.

Church of the Ascension
12 W 11th St (212-254-8553; voicesofascension.org). Subway: N, R to 8th St–NYU. Free–$40. MC, V.
This little Village church has two professional choirs. The Voices of the Ascension choir periodically goes uptown to give concerts at Lincoln Center, but its home turf is much more aesthetically pleasing.

Church of St. Ignatius Loyola
980 Park Ave at 84th St (212-288-2520). Subway: 4, 5, 6 to 86th St. Call to reserve tickets or purchase day or performance. $10–$35. MC, V.
This church's **Sacred Music in a Sacred Space** series is a high point of Upper East Side musical life. In recent seasons, other arts organizations, such as Lincoln Center, have begun to take advantage of the space for choral music concerts as well.

The shipping tunes Bargemusic's chamber-music program will surely float your boat.

Corpus Christi Church

529 W 121st St between Broadway and Amsterdam Ave (212-666-9350). Subway: 1 to 116th St–Columbia Univ. Prices vary. MC, V.
Early-music fans can get their fix from Music Before 1800 *(212-666-9266; www.mb1800.org)*, a series that presents innovative international musical groups as well as resident ensembles.

Riverside Church

490 Riverside Dr at 120th St (212-870-6700; www.theriversidechurchny.org). Subway: 1 to 125th St. Free–$15. AmEx, Disc, MC, V.
Riverside has a fine choir and organ, and hosts visiting guests such as the Orpheus Chamber Orchestra. The 74-bell carillon is a beaut, too (it should be back from a major renovation sometime in 2002).

St. Bartholomew's Church

109 E 50th St between Park and Lexington Aves (212-378-0248; www.stbarts.org). Subway: E, V to Lexington Ave–53rd St; 6 to 51st St. Prices vary. AmEx, MC, V.
Large-scale choral music and occasional chapel recitals fill the magnificent dome behind the church's facade, designed by Stanford White.

St. Paul's Chapel/Trinity Church

Broadway at Wall St (212-602-0747; www.trinitywallstreet.org). Subway: E to World Trade Ctr; N, R to Rector St; 1, 2, 4, 5 to Wall St. Noonday Concert series $2 donation. Choir series $25. AmEx, MC, V.
Historic Trinity, in the heart of the Financial District, schedules individual concerts and the Noonday Concerts series, which are held at 1pm on Mondays at St. Paul's Chapel *(Broadway at Fulton St)* and on Thursdays at Trinity Church.

St. Thomas Church Fifth Avenue

1 W 53rd St at Fifth Ave (212-757-7013; www.saintthomaschurch.org). Subway: B, D, F to 47–50th Sts–Rockefeller Ctr; E, V to Fifth Ave–53rd St. $15–$60. AmEx, MC, V.
Some of the finest choral music in the city can be heard here, performed by the country's only fully accredited choir school for boys. (School head-master Gordon Roland Adams came from the Westminster Abbey Choir School.) The church's annual *Messiah* is a must-see.

Schools

Juilliard, Mannes and the Manhattan School of Music are renowned for their students, faculty and artists-in-residence, all of whom regularly perform for free or at low cost. Noteworthy music and innovative programming can be

Arts & Entertainment

found at several other colleges and schools in the city.

Brooklyn Center for the Performing Arts at Brooklyn College

Campus Rd at Hillel Pl, one block west of the junction of Flatbush and Nostrand Aves, Flatbush, Brooklyn (718-951-4543; www.brooklyncenter.com). Subway: 2, 5 to Flatbush Ave–Brooklyn College. Box office: Tue–Sat 1–6pm. $20–$50. AmEx, MC, V.

While it hosts concerts by mass-appeal pop performers, this hall is also a destination for traveling opera troupes and soloists of international acclaim.

The Juilliard School

60 Lincoln Center Plaza, Broadway at 65th St (212-769-7406; www.juilliard.edu). Subway: 1, 2 to 66th St–Lincoln Ctr. Mostly free.

New York's premier conservatory stages weekly concerts by student soloists, orchestras and chamber ensembles, as well as student opera productions.

Manhattan School of Music

120 Claremont Ave at 122nd St (212-749-2802, ext 4428; www.msmnyc.edu). Subway: 1 to 125th St. Mostly free.

MSM offers master classes, recitals and off-site concerts by its students, faculty and visiting pros. The Augustine Guitar Series, featuring both recitals by top soloists and performances by the American String Quartet (in residence since 1984), is one of the highlights of the school's offerings. The opera program is very adventurous.

Mannes College of Music

150 W 85th St between Columbus and Amsterdam Aves (212-496-8524; www.mannes.edu). Subway: B, C, 1, 2 to 86th St. Free.

This conservatory, a New School affiliate, offers concerts by students, faculty and pro ensembles-in-residence.

Opera

The Metropolitan Opera and New York City Opera may be the big guys, but they're hardly the only arias in town. The following companies perform a varied repertoire—both warhorses and works-in-progress—from Verdi's *Aida* to Wargo's *Chekhov Trilogy*. Call the individual organizations for ticket prices, schedules and venue details. The music schools *(see above)* all have opera programs, too.

Amato Opera Theatre

319 Bowery at 2nd St (212-228-8200; www.amato.org). Subway: F, V, S to Broadway–Lafayette St; 6 to Bleecker St. $25, seniors and children $20. MC, V.

Presented in a theater only 20 feet wide, Anthony Amato's charming, fully staged productions feel like you're watching opera in a cozy living room. Many well-known singers have sung here, but casting can be inconsistent.

American Opera Projects

463 Broome St between Greene and Mercer Sts (718-398-4024). Subway: J, M, Z, N, Q, R, W, 6 to Canal St. Prices vary. Cash only.

AOP is not so much an opera company as a living, breathing workshop. Productions are often a way to follow a work-in-progress.

Bronx Opera Company

Performances take place at different locations in Manhattan and the Bronx (718-365-4209). $15–$30. AmEx, Disc, MC, V.

This 34-year-old company, a training ground for up-and-coming singers, provides a low-key opera alternative. BOC performs lesser-known English-language works along with the classics.

Dicapo Opera Theater

184 E 76th St between Lexington and Third Aves (212-288-9438; www.dicapo.com). Subway: 6 to 77th St. $40. MC, V.

This top-notch chamber-opera troupe benefits from City Opera–quality singers performing on intelligently designed, small-scale sets in the basement of St. Jean Baptiste Church. A real treat.

New York Gilbert & Sullivan Players

See Symphony Space, page 318, and City Center, page 343.

Is Victorian camp your vice? This troupe presents a rotating schedule of the Big Three (*H.M.S. Pinafore, The Mikado* and *The Pirates of Penzance*), plus lesser-known G&S works. The Players will perform at City Center until it returns to its regular home, Symphony Space, which is undergoing an expansion, in May 2002.

Opera Orchestra of New York

Carnegie Hall, 154 W 57th St at Seventh Ave (212-799-1982). Subway: A, C, B, D, 1, 2 to 59th St–Columbus Circle; N, Q, R, W to 57th St. $22–$95. AmEx, Disc, MC, V.

The program organizers unearth forgotten operatic gems and showcase great new talent in semi-staged concert performances at Carnegie Hall.

Operaworks

Raw Space Theater, 529 W 42nd St between Tenth and Eleventh Aves (212-873-9531). Subway: A, C, E to 42nd St–Port Authority. $25, seniors and students $10. Cash only.

This theater-oriented troupe accompanies its modest staged performances of obscure works with synthesizer music.

Regina Opera Company

Regina Hall, Twelfth Ave at 65th St, Bay Ridge, Brooklyn (718-232-3555). Subway: M, W to 62nd St; N to Ft. Hamilton Pkwy. Box office open one hour before show. $12, seniors and students $8. AmEx, Disc, MC, V.

The only year-round opera company in Brooklyn, Regina offers a full orchestra and fully staged productions.

Sports & Fitness

If the action in Times Square doesn't set your pulse racing, take in a Knicks game, cycle around Central Park or kayak the local currents

When it comes to spectator sports, particularly the big four (baseball, basketball, football and hockey), New Yorkers believe they hold a special monopoly on wisdom. This is a place where every third person you meet is convinced that, given enough time and money, he or she could run the local team better than whomever is calling the plays now. Many New Yorkers read the tabloids by starting with the sports pages in the back, and arguments over half-remembered sports trivia can be far more heated than disputes about politics, sex or religion.

The New York metropolitan area has more professional teams than any other city in America: two baseball, two basketball, two football and three hockey, not to mention Major League Soccer, the Women's National Basketball Association and myriad pro and amateur leagues for pretty much any other sport you can name. New Yorkers are passionately devoted to their local heroes; they may grouse about players and condemn owners, but when the home team is in contention for a championship, the city stands up for its own. If the team wins, it's a ticker-tape parade, appearances on *Letterman* and pandemonium in the streets.

When it comes to sports, the city isn't just for those who like to watch. The place is filled with jock-life junkies who get their fix in town and in surrounding areas. Nationally ranked cyclists spin their wheels in Central Park (and take off over the George Washington Bridge on weekends), and swimmers go the distance in the annual Manhattan Marathon Swim in June. Besides satisfying a need to sweat, outdoor activities such as cycling, walking, horseback riding, in-line skating and kayaking are great ways to see the city.

Spectator Sports

With the exception of the *The Wall Street Journal*, all the local papers carry massive amounts of sports analysis and give listings of the day's events and TV coverage. *The New York Times* may have the most literate reporting, but the tabloids—the *Daily News* and the *New York Post*—are best for hyperdetailed information and blunt, insistent opinions. Local broadcasters offer their own takes—the Fox Sports and Madison Square Garden TV networks provide 24-hour events and news, while WFAN radio (AM 660) presents nonstop sports talk.

Baseball

Baseball is very much a product of the five boroughs. The basic rules of the game were drawn up by New York amateur player Alexander Cartwright in 1845, and the first professional leagues originated in the city during the 1870s. Babe Ruth and the **Yankees'** "Murderers' Row" of the 1920s cemented the game's hold on the popular imagination. Joe DiMaggio reinforced it in the 1930s. Today, the American League Yankees are local and national heroes. Trumpeted as "the team of the century" after clinching the World Series an incredible 25 times in the 20th century, they went on to win for a third consecutive year in 2000, defeating none other than the National League **Mets**. Not since battling the Brooklyn Dodgers 44 years ago had the Yanks participated in such an emotional and electrifying "Subway Series" (that's when two local teams square off against one another). The Mets fell off in 2001, but the Yankees again made it to the big show post–September 11, lifting New Yorkers' sagging spirits, even though they lost the series to the Arizona Diamondbacks.

The Yankees-Mets rivalry remains a big draw, and tickets to the teams' annual interleague matchups are usually either unavailable or prohibitively expensive. Most regular-season games for both clubs (April to early October) are more affordable—and it's hard to beat a day at the ballpark for real New York flavor.

▶ **Time Out New York** lists upcoming games played by area teams.
▶ For details on major sporting events, contact **NYC & Company** (212-484-1222; www.nycvisit.com), formerly known as the New York Convention & Visitors Bureau.
▶ Visit **www.nysports.net** for the latest news on all professional sports in the city.
▶ See page 377 for ticketing information.

Arts & Entertainment

New York Mets

*Shea Stadium, 123-01 Roosevelt Ave at 126th St,
Flushing, Queens (718-507-METS; www.mets.com).
Subway: 7 to Willets Point–Shea Stadium. Information
and tickets available Mon–Fri 9am–5:30pm. $12–$43.
AmEx, Disc, MC, V.*

New York Yankees

*Yankee Stadium, River Ave at 161st St, Bronx
(718-293-4300, box office 718-293-6000;
www.yankees.com). Subway: B, D, 4 to 161st St–
Yankee Stadium. Information and tickets available
Mon–Fri 9am–5pm; Sat 10am–3pm and during
games. $15–$55. AmEx, Disc, MC, V.*

Basketball

The local roundball scene is dominated by two
National Basketball Association teams, the
New York Knicks and the **New Jersey
Nets**, with the Knicks reigning supreme in
most New Yorkers' hearts. Tickets range from
expensive to unobtainable. The hottest seat in
town is courtside for Knicks games at Madison
Square Garden, where scene-makers, corporate
types and hard-core fans rub shoulders with
celebrity fixtures such as Spike Lee and Woody
Allen. What draws basketball fanatics is an
on-court mix of pure athleticism, intuition,
improvisation and individual expression not
found in any other team sport; for Knicks
supporters, there's the perennial dream of a
championship, which has been dashed year
after year. In 2001–2002, the Nets actually
began to look respectable.

Exciting court action is also on display at the
WNBA's **New York Liberty**'s games and at
local colleges (St. John's University in Queens
fields a top-tier team), or for free by watching
hoops-hustlers play pickup games on street
courts *(see page 325)*.

New Jersey Nets

*Continental Airlines Arena, East Rutherford, NJ
(201-935-8888, arena box office 201-935-3900,
direct line for Nets tickets 800-7NJ-NETS). Travel:
NJ Transit Meadowlands Sports Complex bus from
Port Authority Bus Terminal (212-564-8484),
Eighth Ave at 42nd St, $3.25 each way. $25–$80.
AmEx, MC, V.*

New York Knickerbockers (Knicks)

*Madison Square Garden, Seventh Ave between
31st and 33rd Sts (box office 212-465-6741;
www.nba.com/knicks). Subway: A, C, E, 1, 2, 3
to 34th St–Penn Station. Box office Mon–Sat
noon–6pm. $25–$265. AmEx, DC, Disc, MC, V.*
Early in the season, it's easy to get seats in the
upper tiers of Madison Square Garden. But closer
to playoff time, official prices are meaningless—
ticket information is usually restricted to "This
game is sold out." You'll need to contact a broker,
know someone with season tickets, or take a risk

with scalped tickets if you want to see Latrell
Sprewell & Co. in action.

New York Liberty

*Madison Square Garden, Seventh Ave between
31st and 33rd Sts (box office 212-465-6741;
www.wnba.com/liberty). Subway: A, C, E, 1, 2, 3 to
34th St–Penn Station. Season Jun–Aug. Box office
Mon–Sat noon–6pm. $8–$57.50. AmEx, DC, Disc,
MC, V.*
The WNBA, launched in 1997, is producing its own
Amazonian stars. The Liberty has established itself
as one of the top women's teams, and the games are
a lot of fun to watch.

St. John's University Red Storm

*Madison Square Garden, Seventh Ave between 31st
and 33rd Sts (box office 212-465-6741). Subway: A,
C, E, 1, 2, 3 to 34th St–Penn Station. Season Nov–
Mar. Box office Mon–Sat noon–6pm. $18–$31.
AmEx, DC, Disc, MC, V.*

Boxing

Church Street Boxing Gym

*25 Park Pl between Broadway and Church St (212-
571-1333; www.nyboxinggym.com). Subway: 4, 5, 6
to Brooklyn Bridge–City Hall; 1, 2 to Park Pl. Fights:
$20. Cash only.*
Church Street is a workout gym and boxing venue
housed in an atmospheric cellar. Amateur fights
(including women's bouts) are staged throughout
the year, as is professional kickboxing. Evander
Holyfield, Mike Tyson, Felix Trinidad and other
heavy hitters practice punches here when in town.

Madison Square Garden

*Seventh Ave between 31st and 33rd Sts (box office 212-
465-6741; www.thegarden.com). Subway: A, C, E, 1, 2,
3 to 34th St–Penn Station. Prices vary. AmEx, DC,
Disc, MC, V.*
After several decades of the biggest bouts being
fought in Atlantic City or Las Vegas, boxing has
punched its way back to the Garden, once considered a mecca for the sport. There are usually a few
major fights here over the course of a year.

Cricket

Thanks to the large populations of Indians,
Pakistanis and West Indians, not to mention
Britons, New York has about 145 cricket teams
and at least two parks where the sound of leather
on willow can be heard. The season runs from
May to September.

Van Cortlandt Park

*Van Cortlandt Park South at Bailey Ave, Bronx.
Subway: 1 to 242nd St–Van Cortlandt Park. There
are 12 pitches here.*
The **Commonwealth Cricket League** *(718-601-
6704)*, the largest league in the nation, plays here on
weekends. The **New York Cricket League** *(201-
343-4544)* also arranges weekend matches.

Swishful thinking Teresa Weatherspoon of the New York Liberty torches the competition.

Walker Park
50 Bard Ave at Delafield Court, Staten Island. Travel: Staten Island Ferry, then S61 or S74 bus to Bard Ave. The **Staten Island Cricket Club** *(718-447-5442)* plays most weekends during the season.

Football

New York is the only city in the country that currently supports two pro teams. Of course, they both play in Giants Stadium, which is in New Jersey, but that's a technicality. From August to December every year—and often longer if the playoffs are involved—New York is as fanatical a football town as any.

The **Giants** have a ten-year waiting list for season tickets, so the only way to see a game is to know someone with season tickets or pay blood money to a broker. The **Jets** situation is no better; there are 13,000 people on the waiting list. When you call for tickets, a recorded announcement explains that tickets have been "sold out since 1979."

New York Giants
Giants Stadium, East Rutherford, NJ (box office 201-935-8222; www.giants.com). Travel: NJ Transit Meadowlands Sports Complex bus from Port Authority Bus Terminal (212-564-8484), Eighth Ave at 42nd St, $3.25 each way.

New York Jets
Giants Stadium, East Rutherford, NJ (box office 516-560-8200). Travel: NJ Transit Meadowlands Sports Complex bus from Port Authority Bus Terminal (212-564-8484), Eighth Ave at 42nd St, $3.25 each way. The Jets play home games at Giants Stadium.

Hockey

A game of speed and skill with the perpetual promise of spectacular violence—it's no wonder hockey is so popular in New York. In recent years, the **New Jersey Devils** have surpassed their competitors, the **New York Islanders** and **Rangers**, but the Rangers remain the hometown favorite. Tickets are available, if tough to come by; they go on sale at the beginning of the season, which runs from October to April.

New Jersey Devils
Continental Airlines Arena, East Rutherford, NJ (201-935-6050, box office 201-935-3900; www.newjerseydevils.com). Travel: NJ Transit Meadowlands Sports Complex bus from Port Authority Bus Terminal (212-564-8484), Eighth Ave at 42nd St, $3.25 each way. $20–$85. AmEx, MC, V.

New York Islanders
Nassau Veterans Memorial Coliseum, 1255 Hempstead Tpke, Uniondale, Long Island (516-501-6700; www.newyorkislanders.com). Travel: From Penn Station, Seventh Ave at 32nd St, take Long Island Railroad (718-217-5477) to Hempstead, then N70, N71 or N72 bus. $15–$85. AmEx, Disc, V.

New York Rangers
Madison Square Garden, Seventh Ave between 31st and 33rd Sts (box office 212-465-6741; www.newyorkrangers.com). Subway: A, C, E, 1, 2, 3 to 34th St–Penn Station. $25–$65. Box office Mon–Sat noon–6:30. AmEx, DC, Disc, MC, V. Single tickets must be purchased through Ticketmaster *(212-307-7171; www.ticketmaster.com)*; there is a limit of four tickets per person.

Horse racing

There are four major racetracks near Manhattan: **Aqueduct**, **Belmont**, the **Meadowlands** and **Yonkers**. If you don't want to trek out to Long Island or New Jersey, head for an Off-Track Betting (OTB) outpost to catch the action and (reliably seedy) atmosphere.

Aqueduct Racetrack
110th St at Rockaway Blvd, Ozone Park, Queens (718-641-4700). Subway: A to Aqueduct Racetrack. Thoroughbred races Oct–May Wed–Sun. Clubhouse $4, grandstand $2. Cash only.
The Wood Memorial, held each April, is a test run

for promising three-year-olds headed for the Kentucky Derby.

Belmont Park
2150 Hempstead Tpke at Plainfield Ave, Elmont, Long Island (718-641-4700). Travel: From Penn Station, Seventh Ave at 32nd St, Pony Express or Belmont Special buses to Belmont Park. Thoroughbred races May–Oct Wed–Sun. Clubhouse $4, grandstand $2. Cash only.
The 1.5-mile Belmont Stakes, the third leg of the Triple Crown, is usually held on the second Saturday in June. In October, the year's best horses run in the $1 million Jockey Gold Cup.

Meadowlands Racetrack
East Rutherford, NJ (201-935-8500; www.thebigm.com). Travel: NJ Transit Meadowlands Sports Complex bus from Port Authority Bus Terminal (212-564-8484), Eighth Ave at 42nd St, $3.25 each way. Meadowlands harness races Jan–Dec; Thoroughbred races Sept–Nov; check website for days. Clubhouse $3, grandstand $1, Pegasus Restaurant $5. Cash only.
Top trotters race for more than $1 million in the prestigious Hambletonian, held the first Saturday in August.

Yonkers Raceway
Central Park Ave, Yonkers, NY (914-968-4200). Travel: 4 to Woodlawn, then #20 bus to the track. Mon, Tue, Thu–Sat 7:40–11:30pm. Cash only.
Harness racing isn't as glamorous as Thoroughbred racing, but you can lose your money here all the same.

Soccer

Soccer (a.k.a. football) is popular in New York, especially in the outer boroughs, where you can catch matches every summer weekend in Italian, Latin American and Polish neighborhood parks. For major-league action, catch a **New York/ New Jersey MetroStars** game at Giants Stadium in New Jersey.

New York/New Jersey MetroStars
Giants Stadium, East Rutherford, NJ (888-4-METRO-TIX; www.metrostars.com). Travel: NJ Transit Meadowlands Sports Complex bus from Port Authority Bus Terminal (212-564-8484), Eighth Ave at 42nd St, $3.25 each way. Season Apr–Sept. $15–$35. Present your bus ticket when you purchase your game ticket to get a $2 discount. AmEx, Disc, MC, V.
The team draws a devoted international crowd.

Tennis

U.S. Open
USTA National Tennis Center, Flushing Meadows–Corona Park, Queens (718-760-6200, tickets 866-673-6849; www.usopen.org). Subway: 7 to Willets Point–Shea Stadium. Late Aug–early Sept. $36–$76 day tickets. AmEx, MC, V.

The tall and short of it A jockey checks his mount at Aqueduct Racetrack.

Tickets go on sale in early June for this Grand Slam thriller, though seats tend to be snapped up by corporate sponsors. As you would expect, the biggest names in tennis hit the hard courts for some of the fastest forehands and blistering backhands of the year.

Active Sports

New York offers plenty for those who define "sports" as something to do, not watch. Central Park *(see page 77)* is an oasis for everybody from skaters to cricket players. Gyms *(see pages 329 and 333)* have practically replaced bars as hip pickup spots, and massive complexes such as Chelsea Piers have brought suburban-style space to the big city.

Department of Parks & Recreation
Call 888-NY-PARKS for a list of scheduled events.

New York Sports Online
www.nysol.com
Visit this site for a comprehensive roundup of recreational sports options in the city. Also call ahead in case there are last-minute changes.

Basketball

They don't call basketball the city game for nothing. The sport's minimal demand for space and equipment makes it ideal for an urban environment, and the level of play on today's street courts is good enough to draw the pros during the off-season. If you have the skills to shoot with the best, check out these public courts.

Asphalt Green
East End Ave at 90th St. Subway: 4, 5, 6 to 86th St.

The Battlegrounds (Carmensville Playground)
Amsterdam Ave at 151st St. Subway: 1 to 145th St.

Marcus Garvey Park
Madison Ave at 121st St. Subway: 4, 5, 6 to 125th St.

West 4th Street Courts (the Cage)
Sixth Ave between 3rd and 4th Sts. Subway: A, C, E, F, V, S to W 4th St.

Bicycling

One of the best ways to tour New York is by bicycle. It's faster than walking—and sometimes cab and subway too—which is why about 100,000 New Yorkers rely on bikes for their daily transportation (at least when the weather is good). And biking is more liberating than a tour bus—you set your own pace and itinerary.

About 120 miles of bike paths lead riders from the bottom to the top of Manhattan. The popular 6.1-mile (9.8km) loop around Central Park is closed to traffic on weekdays from 10am to 3pm and all day on weekends, when the asphalt teems with cyclists, not to mention runners and in-line skaters. Visitors can take a DIY trip using rental bikes and path maps, or go on organized rides.

A word of caution: Unless you stick to Central Park, or Prospect Park in Brooklyn, cycling in the city is serious business. Riders must stay alert and abide by traffic laws—drivers and pedestrians often don't. A few dozen cyclists die in a typical year. This isn't Amsterdam: New York drivers and pedestrians generally treat cyclists as pests, but if you keep your ears and eyes open—and wear a helmet—you can enjoy an adrenaline-pumping ride.

Bike path maps

Department of City Planning Bookstore
22 Reade St between Broadway and Centre St (212-720-3667). Subway: J, M, Z to Chambers St; N, R to City Hall; 4, 5, 6 to Brooklyn Bridge–City Hall. Mon–Fri 10am–1pm, 2–4pm.
The Department of City Planning oversees the bike-

path system. The Bicycle Master Plan has 909 miles of bike lanes. Only 709 to go!

Transportation Alternatives
115 W 30th St between Sixth and Seventh Aves, suite 1207 (212-629-8080; www.transalt.org). Subway: B, D, F, V, N, Q, R, W to 34th St–Herald Sq; 1, 2, 3 to 34th St–Penn Station. Mon–Fri 10am–5pm.
This nonprofit citizens' group lobbies for more bike-friendly streets. You can pop into the office to get free bike-path maps, or you can download them from its website.

Bike rentals

Gotham Bike Shop
112 West Broadway between Duane and Reade Sts (212-732-2453; www.gothambikes.com). Subway: A, C, 1, 2 to Chambers St. Mon, Tue, Thu 9am–6:30pm; Wed, Fri 10:30am–7:30pm; Sat 10am–6:30pm; Sun 10:30am–5pm. $30 for 24 hrs (includes helmet). AmEx, MC, V.
Rent a hybrid or rigid mountain bike from this shop and ride a short way to the Hudson River Esplanade, which runs from Battery Park to 23rd Street.

Larry & Jeff's Bicycles Plus
1690 Second Ave between 87th and 88th Sts (212-722-2201). Subway: 4, 5, 6 to 86th St. Nov–May 10am–7pm; Jun–Oct 10am–8pm. $7.50 per hour; $25 per day. AmEx, MC, V.
This 25-year-old shop rents hybrids, mountain bikes and pure street machines, as well as kids' bikes. Helmets are provided at no additional cost.

Loeb Boathouse
Central Park, entrance on Central Park West at 72nd St (212-517-2233). Subway: B, C to 72nd St. Apr–Nov Mon–Sun 9am–6:30pm (weather permitting). $6–$20 per hour. AmEx, MC, V.
This is the most convenient place to rent a bike for a park cruise. Although the Boathouse has 100 bikes (hybrid 3- and 18-speeds and tandems), reservations are recommended for large groups in summer.

Mr C's Cycles
4622 Seventh Ave between 46th and 47th Sts, Sunset Park, Brooklyn (718-438-7283; www.mrccycles.com). Subway: N, R to 45th St. Mon, Wed–Sat 10am–7pm; Sun 10am–5pm. $15 per four hours, $25 per eight hours (helmet $5 per day). Cash only.
Prospect Park's 3.4-mile loop is usually a lot less crowded than Central Park's. The shop is about 20 blocks from the park and rents hybrids and mountain bikes.

Organized bike rides

Bicycle Habitat
244 Lafayette St between Prince and Spring Sts (212-431-3315; www.bicyclehabitat.com). Subway: N, R to

Prince St; 6 to Spring St. Mon–Thu 10am–7pm; Fri 10am–6:30pm; Sat, Sun 10am–6pm. AmEx, MC, V.
This excellent source for bike gear also has summer mountain-bike excursions to such places as Blue Mountain Park in the Adirondacks. For information, ask for staffer Patrick Dougherty.

Fast and Fabulous
212-567-7160; www.fastnfab.org.
This "queer and queer-friendly" riding group leads tours of various lengths throughout the year, usually meeting in Central Park and heading out of the city. Visit its website for a comprehensive ride calendar.

Five-Borough Bicycle Club
Hosteling International, 891 Amsterdam Ave at 103rd St (212-932-2300, ext 115; www.5bbc.org). Subway: 1 to 103rd St.

The club organizes day and weekend bike rides, as well as the annual Montauk Century Ride in May (a 100-mile trip to the eastern end of Long Island). It also offers bicycle-repair classes. Call for daily ride schedules–all ages and skill levels are welcome to join in.

Time's Up!
212-802-8222; www.times-up.org.
This alternative-transportation advocacy group sponsors rides throughout the year, including "Critical Mass," in which hundreds of cyclists and skaters meet on the steps of Union Square Park at 7pm on the last Friday of every month, then go tearing through Greenwich Village to show the motorists that there's more than one way to get around town. Moonlight Rides through Central Park are the first Friday of the month at 10pm. Visit the website for a complete ride schedule.

Diamond dogs
Minor league baseball gets its moment in the sun…and stadium lights

New Yorkers may get riled up about the Knicks, flirt with the Jets, or even get excited by the Rangers, but Gotham remains, at heart, a baseball town. Since the glory days when the New York Yankees, New York Giants and Brooklyn Dodgers all called this place home, the love of baseball and its lore has run thick and deep through the city's consciousness.

In recent years, as fans across the country have grown disenchanted with the greedy and impersonal major leagues, the minor leagues—with their scrappy play, intimate ballparks and old-fashioned goofy promotions—have exploded in popularity. New York has been no exception; it now fields three minor league teams that play within a short hop of Manhattan.

The newest and most popular addition is the Brooklyn Cyclones. Spiritual heirs to the Dodgers (who, to the eternal anguish of Brooklynites, moved to Los Angeles in 1958; *see chapter* **History**), the Cyclones are a Single A farm team of the big-league Mets. The team's stadium, KeySpan Park, is in the heart of Coney Island: The famous Cyclone roller coaster is visible over the left field wall, the Atlantic Ocean is in center and the famous Parachute Jump (a national landmark) looms down the right field baseline. The Cyclones have been quite successful. In their first season, the team took first place in the New York–Penn League and advanced to the

league championship. (The series was canceled because of the events of September 11, 2001.) It's little wonder that the Cyclones' blue hats have become one of the city's most coveted accessories.

Not to be outdone, the Cyclones' bitter rivals, the Staten Island Yankees, also have a beautiful new stadium, on the shores of New York's most overlooked borough. A 30-minute ferry ride brings you to Richmond County Bank Ballpark and its lovely view of lower Manhattan. The Single A affiliate of the Bronx Bombers (a.k.a. the Major League Yankees), the SI Yanks have had almost as much success as their parent team, winning the league championship in 2000 and making it to the first round of the playoffs in 2001. To the supreme satisfaction of Brooklynites, they lost to the Cyclones.

Across the river, in New Jersey, the Newark Bears play in the independent Atlantic League. In addition to young prospects, the Bears roster features former big leaguers trying to work their way back to the top. For that reason, the level of play is slightly higher than it is in the Cyclones and SI Yankees games, though it's best to catch such stars as Jose Canseco and Jim Leyritz early in the season, before they're snatched up by a needy major league squad.

If you want to go even farther afield, check out the Long Island Ducks, who play in Islip, Long Island *(631-940-DUCK)*; the Hudson

Billiards

Amsterdam Billiard Club

344 Amsterdam Ave at 77th St (212-496-8180; www.amsterdambilliards.com). Subway: 1, 2 to 79th St. Sun–Thu 11am–3am; Fri, Sat 11am–4am. $4.75–$8 per player per hour. Group lessons $8 per person, private $35–$50 per hour. AmEx, MC, V.

Co-owned by comedian David Brenner, Amsterdam was named No. 1 billiard club in the United States by *Billiards Digest* magazine. The classy club features a full bar, a fireplace and several ten-foot television screens.

Other location ● *210 E 86th St between Second and Third Aves (212-570-4545). Subway: 4, 5, 6 to 86th St. Sun–Thu 11am–3am; Fri, Sat 11am–4am. $4.75–$8 per player per hour. Group lessons $8 per person, private $35–$50 per hour. AmEx, DC, MC, V.*

Chelsea Bar & Billiards

54 W 21st St between Fifth and Sixth Aves (212-989-0096). Subway: F, V, N, R to 23rd St. Mon–Thu 11am–5pm $5 per hour for first player, $2 per additional person per hour; 5pm–4am $14 per hour, minimum two players, $3 for each additional player. Fri–Sun 11am–4am $16 per hour, minimum two players, $3 for each additional player. AmEx, MC, V.

Cue up in this swank pool hall, which has 32 pool tables and three full-size snooker tables. There's a full bar with a snack menu, or you can sit down at Slate, the in-hall Mediterranean restaurant.

Bowling

AMF Chelsea Piers Lanes

23rd St at West Side Hwy, between Piers 59 and 60 (212-835-BOWL). Subway: C, E to 23rd St.

Surf and turf The Brooklyn Cyclones and their fans are having a ball in Coney Island.

Valley Renegades, in Fishkill, New York *(914-838-0094)*; or even the Atlantic City Surf *(609-344-8873)*, down the coast in New Jersey. In fact, pretty much any direction you head will bring you to some place where a team is playing the grand old game.

Brooklyn Cyclones

KeySpan Park, 1604 Surf Ave between W 17th and W 19th Sts, Coney Island, Brooklyn (718-449-TIXS). Subway: F, Q, W to Coney Island–Stillwell Ave. Jun–Sept. $6, $8.

Newark Bears

Riverfront Stadium, 10 Bridge St, Newark, NJ (973-483-6900). Travel: NJ Transit (Morris-Essex Line) to Broad St or PATH to Newark Penn Station. May–Sept. $6, $8.

Staten Island Yankees

Richmond County Bank Ballpark, 75 Richmond Terr at Bay St, St. George, Staten Island (718-698-YANKS). Travel: Staten Island Ferry to St. George Terminal. Jun–Sept. $8, $10.

Arts & Entertainment

Sun–Thu 9am–1am; Fri, Sat 9am–2am. $7 per person per game weekdays, $8 weekends, $8 disco bowling; $4 shoe rental. AmEx, Disc, MC, V.
This megacomplex features 40 lanes, a huge arcade and bar, and glow-in-the-dark "disco" bowling every night. Private parties are also available.

Bowlmor Lanes

110 University Pl between 12th and 13th Sts (212-255-8188; www.bowlmor.com). Subway: L, N, Q, R, W, 4, 5, 6 to 14th St–Union Sq. Mon, Fri 10am–4am; Tue, Wed 10am–1am; Thu 10am–2am; Sat 11am–4am; Sun 11am–1am. $5.95 per person per game before 5pm; $6.95 after 5pm and weekends; $4 shoe rental. AmEx, MC, V. Under 21 not admitted after 5pm.
Renovation turned this seedy but historic Greenwich Village alley (Richard Nixon bowled here!) into a hip downtown nightclub. Bowl in your Kenneth Cole ensemble: Monday night's "Nightstrike" features glow-in-the-dark pins action and a techno-spinning DJ, not to mention unlimited bowling from 10pm to 4am, for $17 per scenester.

Leisure Time Recreation

Port Authority Bus Terminal, 625 Eighth Ave at 40th St, second level (212-268-6909). Subway: A, C, E to 42nd St–Port Authority. Sun–Thu 10am–11pm; Fri, Sat 10am–3am. $5 per person per game, $3.50 shoe rental before 5pm; $6 per person per game, $4.50 shoe rental after 5pm and weekends. AmEx, MC, V.
Let fly a few strikes down one of the 30 lanes while you're waiting for your bus. Or sink some shots at the bar.

Climbing

ExtraVertical Climbing Center

Harmony Atrium, 61 W 62nd St at Broadway, entrance on Broadway between 62nd and 63rd Sts (212-586-5382; www.extravertical.com). Subway: A, C, B, D, 1, 2 to 59th St–Columbus Circle. Mon–Fri 4–10pm; Sat–Sun noon–8pm. Call for winter hours. Day pass $20, lessons $55–$110. Equipment rental available. MC, V.
When local rock rats can't get to the Shawangunk Mountains, they keep limber at this public climbing gym inside the atrium of an office building. Climb and rappel on 3,000 square feet of wall, which includes a 50-foot outdoor lead wall (taken from a past X-Games) and 16 top ropes. There's no heating, so it's chilly in winter.

Sports Center at Chelsea Piers

23rd St at West Side Hwy, Pier 60 (212-336-6000; www.chelseapiers.com). Subway: C, E to 23rd St. Mon, Fri noon–10:30pm; Tue, Thu 5–10:30pm; Wed 7–10:30pm; Sat, Sun 9am–8:30pm. $5 shoe rental, $3 harness, $2 chalk bag. AmEx, Disc, MC, V.
A challenging overhang at the top and more than 10,000 square feet of climbing wall means you can play Spider-Man to your heart's content. Call for information on rock-climbing classes. For those who don't like vertigo, check out the tamer 30-foot

high wall at the Field House, Pier 62 *(212-336-6500)* which also houses a gymnastics training center, basketball courts, turf fields, batting cages, a toddler gym, dance studios and locker rooms.

Golf

Golf Club at Chelsea Piers

23rd St at West Side Hwy, Pier 59 (212-336-6400; www.chelseapiers.com). Subway: C, E to 23rd St. Apr–Sept 6am–midnight; Oct–Mar 6:30am–11pm. $15 minimum. AmEx, Disc, MC, V.
The Golf Club has 52 heated and weather-protected driving stalls (stacked four stories high), a 1,000-square-foot practice putting green, an automatic ball transport system, and a 200-yard artificial-turf fairway that extends along the pier. The Golf Academy *(212-336-6444)* offers clinics and lessons with regular trainers or PGA-certified instructors. Call for rates.

Kissena Park Golf Course

164-15 Booth Memorial Ave at 164th St, Flushing, Queens (718-939-4594). Travel: 7 to Flushing–Main St, then Q65 bus. 7am–dusk. Mon–Fri 18 holes $21, after 1pm $18.50, after 3pm $10.50, 9 holes for 1 hour after sunrise $9.75; Sat, Sun 18 holes $24, after 1pm $20.50, after 3pm $11, 9 holes for 1 hour after sunrise $10.75. Club rental $10 per bag. AmEx, MC, V.
The short "executive" course has great views of the Manhattan skyline. Pro lessons cost $35 for 30 minutes. Par 64.

Richard Metz Golf Studio

425 Madison Ave at 49th St, third floor (212-759-6940; www.richardmetzgolf.com). Subway: E, V to Lexington Ave–53rd St; 6 to 51st St. Mon–Fri 9:30am–7pm; Sat 10am–6pm; Sun 10am–5pm. 30-minute lesson $60, five lessons $250, ten lessons $400. Call for special winter rates. AmEx, DC, Disc, MC, V.
PGA pros give lessons that include instant video replay of your swing for movement analysis. There are three nets, several putting areas and a pro shop.

Silver Lake Golf Course

915 Victory Blvd between Forest Ave and Clove Rd, Staten Island (718-447-5686). Travel: Staten Island Ferry, then S67 bus. Dawn–dusk. Mon–Fri $21, after 1pm $18.50, twilight $10.50; Sat, Sun $24, after 1pm $20.50, twilight $11.75; booking fee $2. AmEx, Disc, MC, V.
Narrow fairways, tough hills and a proof-of-residency policy (the out-of-state rate is $6 more) make Silver Lake a difficult course to negotiate. Console yourself by enjoying nature when your ball ends up in the woods again—it's a very picturesque setting. Par 69.

Van Cortlandt Park Golf Course

Van Cortlandt Park South at Bailey Ave, Bronx (718-543-4595). Travel: 1 to 242nd St–Van Cortlandt Park. 30 minutes before sunrise–30 minutes after sunset. Mon–Fri $21, nonresidents $27; Sat, Sun

Arts & Entertainment

$24, nonresidents $30; club rental from $25 per round. AmEx, MC, DC, V.
Created in 1895, the oldest public course in the country is rich in history and easily the most "New York" of the city's 13 public courses. It's quite short but challenging—narrow, tree-filled and hilly. There's also a newly renovated and expanded pro shop. Par 70.

For travelers who just don't feel right without their regular workout, these megagyms offer single-day memberships (some form of photo ID is required). Most have more than one branch:

Call for details about classes and facilities. Towel and locker rentals are usually available. For more gyms, see **YMCAs**, page 333.

Asphalt Green

555 E 90th St between York and East End Aves (212-369-8890; www.asphaltgreen.org). Subway: 4, 5, 6 to 86th St. Fitness center Mon–Fri 5:30am–10pm; Sat, Sun 8am–8pm. Pool Mon–Fri 5:30am–4pm, 8–10pm; Sat 8am–8pm; Sun 11am–8pm. Day membership $20. AmEx, MC, V.
The fee gets you access to either the Olympic-size pool or the fitness center. An additional $5 is required to use both; sauna access is included with the pool.

Pin city Roll a lucky strike in disco style at the AMF Chelsea Piers bowling lanes.

Crunch

*623 Broadway between Bleecker and Houston Sts
(212-420-0507). Subway: F, V, S to Broadway–
Lafayette St; 6 to Bleecker St. Mon–Fri 6am–
midnight; Sat 8am–8pm; Sun 9am–8pm. Day pass
$24. AmEx, DC, Disc, MC, V.*

For a downtown feel without hipster attitude,
Crunch wins hands down. At all eight New York
locations, NetPulse cardio equipment lets you surf
the Web or watch a personal TV while you exercise.
Check phone book for other locations.

New York Sports Club

*151 E 86th St between Lexington and Third Aves
(212-860-8630; www.nysc.com). Subway: 4, 5, 6 to
86th St. Mon–Fri 5:30am–11pm; Sat, Sun 8am–
10pm. Day membership $25. AmEx, MC, V.*

A day membership at New York Sports Club includes
access to the weight room, aerobics classes, squash
courts, cardio machines, studios, steam room and
sauna. For a little extra, you can also get a massage.
Call for gym locations throughout the city.

Sports Center at Chelsea Piers

*23rd St at West Side Hwy, Pier 60 (212-336-6000;
www.chelseapiers.com). Subway: C, E to 23rd St. Mon–
Fri 6am–11pm; Sat, Sun 8am–9pm. Day membership
$50. 16 and older with ID. AmEx, Disc, MC, V.*

The Sports Center comprises a quarter-mile indoor
track, a 25-yard-long swimming pool, a boxing ring,
a weight room, basketball courts, hard and sand volleyball courts, cardio machines, two studios of fitness classes, a steam room, a sauna, an indoor
climbing wall, two outdoor sundecks, a sports
medicine center and the Origins Feel-Good Spa.

World Gym of Greenwich Village

*232 Mercer St between Bleecker and E 3rd Sts (212-
780-7407). Subway: F, V, S to Broadway–Lafayette St;
6 to Bleecker St. Mon–Thu 5am–midnight; Fri 5am–
11pm; Sat 6am–10pm; Sun 7am–10pm. Day
membership $25. AmEx, MC, V.*

At this sparkling clean, blond wood haven, all the
amenities of regular membership (except personal
training) are available, including a weight room, aerobics classes, machines, a boxing gym and steam
rooms in the men's and women's locker rooms.

**Other location ● 65-75 Woodhaven Blvd between
65th and 66th Sts, Rego Park, Queens (718-459-
3248). Subway: G, R, V to Woodhaven Blvd. Mon–
Thu 5am–11pm; Fri 5am–10pm; Sat, Sun 7am–
8pm. Day membership $15. AmEx, MC, V.**

Horseback riding

Claremont Riding Academy

*175 W 89th St between Columbus and Amsterdam
Aves (212-724-5100). Subway: 1, 2 to 86th St. Mon–
Fri 6:30am–10pm; Sat, Sun 8am–5pm. Rental $50 per
hour; lessons $55 per 30 minutes; introductory package
for first 3½ hours $150. MC, V.*

The academy, in an Upper West Side townhouse,
teaches English-style (as opposed to Western-style)
riding. Beginners use an indoor arena; experienced

riders can go for an unguided canter along the six
miles (9.6km) of trails in Central Park. Be prepared
to prove your mounted mettle: Claremont interviews
all riders to determine their level of experience.

Kensington Stables

*51 Caton Pl, Windsor Terrace, Brooklyn (718-972-
4588; www.kensingtonstables.com). Subway: F to Fort
Hamilton Pkwy. 10am–sundown. Guided trail ride
$25 per hour; lessons $45 per hour. AmEx, MC, V.*

The paddock is small, but there are miles of lovely trails
in Prospect Park (*see chapter* **The Outer Boroughs**),
which was designed to be seen by horseback.

Ice skating

Rockefeller Center Ice Rink

*1 Rockefeller Plaza between Fifth and Sixth Aves and
49th and 50th Sts (recorded information 212-332-
7654). Subway: B, D, F, V to 47–50th Sts–Rockefeller
Ctr. Nov–Apr Mon–Fri 8:30–10am, 10:30am–noon,
12:30–2pm, 2:30–4pm, 4:30–6pm, 6:30–8pm,
8:30–10pm, 10:30pm–midnight; Sat, Sun 8–10am,
10:30am–noon, 12:30–2pm, 2:30–4pm, 4:30–6pm,
6:30–8pm, 8:30–10pm, 10:30pm–midnight. Mon–
Fri $13, children under 12 $9; Sat, Sun $15, children
under 12 $10; skate rental $7. Figure skates available
in sizes baby 6 to men's 14. Cash only.*

Rockefeller Center's famous outdoor rink, under the
giant statue of Prometheus, is perfect for atmosphere
but bad for elbow room. The rink generally opens with
an energetic ice show in mid-October, but attracts most
of its visitors when the towering Christmas tree is lit.

Sky Rink at Chelsea Piers

*23rd St at West Side Hwy, Pier 61 (212-336-6100;
www.chelseapiers.com). Subway: C, E to 23rd St. Call
rink for hours. $12, seniors and children $8.50; skate
rental $5.50; helmet rental $3. AmEx, Disc, MC, V.*

This is Manhattan's only year-round indoor ice-skating rink. There are several general skating, figure
skating and ice hockey programs, including lessons
and performances. It often closes for a few hours in
the early evening for ice maintenance.

Wollman Memorial Rink

*Central Park, entrance on 59th St at Fifth or Sixth
Aves (212-439-6900). Subway: F to 57th St; N, R,
W to Fifth Ave–60th St. Mon, Tue 10am–3pm; Wed,
Thu 10am–9:30pm; Fri, Sat 10am–11pm; Sun
10am–9pm. $5.50, seniors and children $3.50; call for
group rates. Skate rental $3.50; lockers $6.75. Open
mid-Oct–Mar 31. Cash only.*

Join the crowds of kids skating to blaring Mariah
Carey tunes. Some practice twirls, and others spray
you with ice shards via hockey-skid stops. The outdoor setting is gorgeous in snowy winters.

In-line skating

An estimated half million in-line skaters have
made that quiet *skish-skish* a familiar sound
on New York streets. It's not unusual to see
the more insane-on-wheels hurtling toward

oncoming traffic at 30 miles per hour. A slightly tamer crowd can be found whirling around Central Park, either on the Park Drive loop (closed to traffic 10am to 3pm during the week and all day on weekends) or near the bandshell at 72nd Street. The "coneheads," or slalomers, strut their stuff near Central Park West at 67th Street, across from Tavern on the Green.

To give it a try, visit Wollman Memorial Rink. If you don't want to be restricted to the rink, rent skates there for $15 a day (plus a $100 deposit). Or try one of the many shops close to the park, such as **Blades, Board and Skate** *120 W 72nd St, 212-787-3911).*

Group skates—some mellow and social, others wild blitzkriegs on wheels—are a popular city pastime. Bring skates, a helmet and a sense of adventure to such events as the **Empire Skate Club's Thursday Evening Roll.**

Your safest bet in Central Park is to stick with the pack and go with the flow of traffic. On weekends from mid-April to mid-October, volunteer skate patrollers (in red T-shirts with white crosses) run free "stopping" clinics for beginners. You'll find them on Saturdays and Sundays from noon to 6pm at the 72nd Street entrances on the east and west sides of the park.

Empire Skate Club of New York

P.O. Box 20070, London Terrace Station, New York, NY 10011 (212-774-1774; www.empireskate.org). This club organizes frequent in-line and roller-skating events throughout the city, including island-hopping tours and nighttime rides, such as the year-round Thursday Evening Roll. Skaters meet at Columbus Circle *(southwest corner of Central Park, 59th Street at Broadway)* at 6:45pm.

Roller Rinks at Chelsea Piers

23rd St at West Side Hwy, Pier 62 (212-336-6200). Subway: C, E to 23rd St. General skating (east and west rinks) Apr–Nov Mon–Fri 3–5pm; Sat, Sun noon–5pm (weather permitting). $6, children $5. Skate Park Mon–Fri 3–7pm; Sat, Sun 10am–7pm. $8 per session. Equipment rental (including protective gear) $15, children $10. AmEx, Disc, MC, V. There are two regulation-size outdoor roller-skating rinks at Chelsea Piers. The Skate Park features an 11½-foot vertical ramp, a six-foot mini vert ramp, a mini vert ramp with spine and a four-way fun box for in-line skating. Call ahead for Skate Park's special hours for "aggressive skaters." Bikes and skateboards are welcome.

Time's Up!

See page 326.

Kayaking

Access to the Hudson River continues to improve with the ongoing development of the Hudson River Park—a 550-acre shoreline play zone running for five miles, from Battery Park to 72nd Street. The project aims to reconnect people with the water, and believe it or not, people are diving in—environmental officials say the city's waters are the cleanest they've been in the past century.

The best way to explore New York Harbor and the Hudson River—and get a loon's-eye view of Manhattan—is by kayak. Between tricky currents, the tide and the sometimes hairy river traffic, navigating the city's waters can be demanding. For this reason, no outfitters rent kayaks for individual use. But you can go on an organized excursion or take a class.

Manhattan Kayak Company

23rd St at West Side Hwy, Pier 63 Maritime (212-924-1788; www.manhattankayak.com). Subway: C, E to 23rd St. Call for schedule and prices. Run by veteran kayaker Eric Stiller, who once paddled halfway around Australia, Manhattan Kayak Company offers beginner to advanced classes and tours. Paddle tours range from a 90-minute "Paddle & Pub" for $50 to the eight-hour circumnavigation of Manhattan for $200. Call before making the trip, as office hours aren't always firm.

New York Kayak

Houston St at West Side Hwy, Pier 40 (212-924-1327; www.nykayak.com). Subway: 1, 2 to Houston St. Mon–Thu 10am–6pm; Fri, Sat 10am–5pm. Call for rates. AmEx, Disc, MC, V. Manhattan's only shop devoted exclusively to kayaking offers beginner to advanced classes and short tours along the Hudson River from mid-May to October. Excursions to destinations such as the Statue of Liberty and Governors Island depend on the day's tides. All instructors are certified by the British Canoe Union. In fact, business has been so brisk, owner Randy Henriksen imports instructors, such as level-five kayaker Len Hartley from the U.K., during the summer.

Running

Join the joggers in Central and Riverside Parks or around Washington Square in the early morning or early evening. It's best—for women especially—to avoid jogging alone. And don't carry or wear anything that's obviously valuable.

New York Road Runners Club

9 E 89th St between Fifth and Madison Aves (212-860-4455; www.nyrrc.org). Subway: 4, 5, 6 to 86th St. Mon–Fri 10am–8pm; Sat 10am–5pm; Sun 10am–3pm. Annual membership $30. AmEx, Disc, MC, V. Hardly a weekend goes by without some sort of run or race sponsored by the NYRRC—they're even responsible for the New York City Marathon. It's the largest running club in the U.S., with almost 34,000 members. Most races take place in Central Park and are open to the public. The club also offers classes and clinics and can help you find a running partner.

Arts & Entertainment

Astral projection Limber locals often stretch with the stars at the Jivamukti Yoga Center.

Squash

New York Sports Clubs

See page 328 for listing.
This uptown branch of the NYSC chain has four newly renovated regulation courts based on international standards and is the epicenter of the New York squash world (as far as public courts go). Its well-rounded coaching staff gives evening and weekend clinics, and caters to all levels of play. But only members can reserve courts, so if you're a nonmember, make friends (nonmember rates are $25 per hour; the peak-hour rate for members is $15 per hour). Two regulation squash courts are also at NYSC's branch on 62nd Street at Broadway *(212-265-0995).*

The Printing House Racquet and Fitness Club

421 Hudson St between Clarkson and Leroy Sts (212-243-7600). Subway: 1, 2 to Houston St. Round-robin for nonmembers. Mon–Fri 6–11pm; Sat, Sun 8–10pm. $25. AmEx, MC, V.
Its five courts are just shy of regulation width, but the Printing House offers the coolest game of squash in the city. Even if you aren't a member of the spectacular, panoramic fitness facility (located on the penthouse floor), you can play in the happy-hour round-robin on Mondays and Fridays. Chris Widney, the squash director and author of *Keep Eye on Ball, Is Most Important One Thing I Tell You,* attracts a steady flow of international players.

Swimming

Municipal Pools

For more information, call New York Parks & Recreation (800-201-PARK; www.nyc.gov/parks.
For adults ages 18 to 54, an annual membership fee of $25 is suggested *(seniors above 55 and teens ages 13 to 17 are asked to pay $10; children under 12 swim for free).* The fee is payable by money order at any recreation center and entitles you to use all of New York's municipal indoor pools for a year. You need proof of your name, an address in the New York City area and a passport-size photograph to register. Outdoor pools are free to all, and open from July to September. Some of the best and most beautifully maintained city-run pools are: **Carmine Street Recreation Center** *(Clarkson St at Seventh Ave South, 212-242-5229);* **Asser Levy Pool** *(23rd St between First Ave and FDR Dr, 212-447-2020);* **East 54th Street Pool** *(348 E 54th St at First Ave, 212-397-3154);* **West 59th Street Pool** *(59th St between Tenth and Eleventh Aves, 212-397-3159).*

Tennis

From April through November, the city maintains excellent municipal courts throughout the five boroughs. Single-play (one-hour) tickets cost $5. The Department of Parks *(212-360-8131)* also issues permits that are valid for unlimited play during the season *($50,* *senior citizens $20, under 17 $10).* For a list of city courts, visit www.nyc.gov/parks.

HRC Tennis

Piers 13 and 14 on the East River (212-422-9300). Subway: J, M, Z to Broad St; 1, 2, 4, 5 to Wall St. 6am–midnight. Court fees $60–$140 per hour. AmEx, MC, V.

This part of the New York Health & Racquet Club is open to nonmembers. There are eight Har-Tru courts under bubbles on twin piers. Ten tennis pros are on hand to give lessons (nonmembers pay $110 per hour; $140 during peak hours). This facility may lose its lease to a proposed Guggenheim Museum satellite designed by Frank Gehry, but it could be a long, drawn-out real-estate battle. To be on the safe side, call to confirm.

Manhattan Plaza Racquet Club

450 W 43rd St between Ninth and Tenth Aves (212-594-0554; www.mprc.com). Subway: A, C, E to 42nd St–Port Authority. 6am–midnight. $55–$80 per court per hour. AmEx, MC, V.

This is primarily a private club, so call for non-member hours and rates. Nonmembers are welcome to play in the singles leagues on Saturday and Sunday nights. The hard-surface outdoor courts are enclosed by a bubble come winter. The club also contains a gym, pool and two climbing walls.

Midtown Tennis Club

341 Eighth Ave at 27th St (212-989-8572; www.midtowntennis.com). Subway: C, E to 23rd St; 1, 2 to 28th St. Mon–Fri 6:30am–11pm; Sat, Sun 8am–8pm. Court fees $40–$75 per hour. AmEx, MC, V.

This club offers eight indoor Har-Tru courts and four outdoor ones when weather permits.

YMCAs

There are Ys throughout the five boroughs, all with a wide range of facilities. Three of the Manhattan sites offer day rates for visitors. Y membership in another country may get you discounts, and if you're already paying for Y accommodations, the sports facilities are free. (*See chapter* **Accommodations, Hostels**).

Harlem YMCA

180 W 135th St at Seventh Ave (212-281-4100). Subway: B, C, 2, 3 to 135th St. Mon–Fri 6am–11pm; Sat 6am–8pm. $12 per day. AmEx, MC, V.

The main attractions include a three-lane swimming pool, basketball court, full gym and sauna.

Vanderbilt YMCA

224 E 47th St between Second and Third Aves (212-756-9600). Subway: S, 4, 5, 7 to 42nd St–Grand Central; 6 to 51st St. Mon 5am–midnight; Tue–Fri 24 hours; Sat 7am–7pm; Sun 7am–9pm. $25 per day. AmEx, MC, V.

The day membership includes use of the two swimming pools, a running track, a sauna and a gym with basketball, handball and volleyball—

plus you can participate in any of the yoga and aerobics classes.

West Side Branch YMCA

5 W 63rd St between Central Park West and Broadway (212-875-4100). Subway: A, C, B, D, 1, 2 to 59th St–Columbus Circle. Mon–Fri 6am–11pm; Sat, Sun 8am–8pm. $15 per day. MC, V.

This Y has two pools and three gyms with all the equipment imaginable. There is also a full range of classes. The day rate provides access to all facilities.

Yoga

Yoga is an increasingly popular way to remain lucid and limber in New York City. Many gyms now add yoga classes to the aerobics and step schedules (*see Gyms, page 329*), and yoga centers are popping up all over the city. The following are three of the best.

Integral Yoga Institute

227 W 13th St between Seventh and Eighth Aves (212-929-0585; www.integralyogaofnewyork.org). Subway: A, C, E, 1, 2, 3 to 14th St; L to Eighth Ave. Call for schedule. $11, Hatha III classes $13. AmEx, Disc, MC, V.

Integral Yoga Institute offers a flexible schedule of classes for beginners and advanced students.

Other location ● *200 W 72nd St at Broadway, fourth floor (212-721-4000). Subway: 1, 2, 3 to 72nd St. Call for schedule. $10, series of classes $45–$150. Cash only.*

Jivamukti Yoga Center

404 Lafayette St between Astor Pl and E 4th St (212-353-0214; www.jivamuktiyoga.com). Subway: 6 to Astor Pl. Mon–Fri 8am–10pm; Sat 9:30am–7pm; Sun 8am–7pm. $17. AmEx, MC, V.

Classes are vigorous Hatha yoga in the Jivamukti style, with an emphasis on ancient yogic teachings and chanting. The place has developed a glamorous following (past patrons include Christy Turlington and Willem Dafoe). Class packages are offered at discount prices, and the center boasts a variety of services, from shiatsu massage to yoga for youngsters.

Other location ● *853 Lexington Ave between 64th and 65th Sts, second floor (212-396-4200). Subway: 6 to 68th St–Hunter College. Call for schedule. $17, series of classes $45–$150. Cash only.*

Yoga Zone

138 Fifth Ave between 18th and 19th Sts, fourth floor (212-647-YOGA; www.yogazone.com). Subway: L, N, Q, R, W, 4, 5, 6 to 14th St–Union Sq. Mon–Thu 7:30am–9pm; Fri 9:30am–7:15pm; Sat 9am–6:15pm; Sun 9:30am–6:30pm. $20 per class, introductory offer of three classes $40. AmEx, DC, Disc, MC, V.

You'll practically trip over all the models and actors, but that's beside the point. Classes here emphasize the less strenuous side of yoga and last at least an hour.

Arts & Entertainment

Theater & Dance

Looking for high drama or avant-garde movements? All the city's a stage...

Theater

The Big Apple is the big cheese when it comes to live theater. There are dozens of venues throughout Manhattan, and many others in the outer boroughs. New York's longtime reputation as an artist's proving ground is intact: This is the only city in the U.S. where superstars regularly tread the boards eight times a week. Big-name players who have recently stuck their necks out on the sometimes unforgiving NYC stages include Sir Ian McKellen, Tom Selleck, Meryl Streep and even the legendary disco band ABBA, which provided the infectious, unforgettable score for the international hit, *Mamma Mia!* The stakes are high, but the gamble remains alluring.

Audiences eager to experience this ephemeral art form pack the city's performance spaces, which range from the landmark palaces of the glittering "Great White Way" of Broadway to more intimate houses along 42nd Street's Theater Row (technically Off Broadway) and the (mostly) downtown nooks and crannies of Off-Off Broadway. The performer-fan relationship is more up close and personal in the New York theater world than in Hollywood. Not only can you watch your favorite actors perform just a few feet away from you, you can also grab their autographs (politely) at the stage door, and maybe even dine at the same restaurant as they do afterward.

BUYING TICKETS

If you have a major credit card, buying Broadway tickets requires little more than picking up a telephone. Almost all Broadway and Off Broadway shows are served by one of the city's 24-hour booking agencies, which are listed in the show's print advertisement or in the capsule reviews that run each week in *Time Out New York*. The venues' information lines can also refer you to ticket agents,

ABBA fab Get your fill of the Swedish foursome's 1970s and '80s hit parade in *Mamma Mia!*

sometimes merely by transfering your call. For additional ticketing info, see page 377.

The cheapest full-price tickets on Broadway are rush tickets (tickets purchased the day of a show at the theater's box office), which cost about $25; but not all theaters offer these. If a show is sold out, it's worth waiting for standby tickets just before show time. Tickets are slightly cheaper for matinees and previews (typically on Wednesdays, Saturdays or Sundays), and for students or groups of 20 or more. Keep an eye out (on campuses, at bookstores, at tourist information centers) for "twofers"—vouchers that allow you to buy two tickets for slightly more than the price of one. These generally promote long-running Broadway shows, and occasionally the larger Off Broadway ones. Some sold-out shows offer good seats at reduced rates (usually $25) after 6pm on the day of performance; those in the know line up hours beforehand.

The best way to obtain discount tickets, however, is to go to **TKTS** *(see page 377)* where you can get as much as 75 percent off the face value of some tickets on the day of the performance. Arrive early to avoid long lines, or show up around 6pm, two hours before most shows start. You can also buy matinee tickets the day before a show at TKTS. (One caveat: Avoid scam artists selling tickets to those waiting in line. The tickets are often fake.) If you are interested in seeing more than one Off-Off Broadway theater,

music or dance event, consider purchasing the **Theater Development Fund**'s book of vouchers.

Theater Development Fund

1501 Broadway between 43rd and 44th Sts (212-221-0013; www.tdf.org). Subway: N, Q, R, W, S, 1, 2, 3, 7 to 42nd St–Times Sq. Check or money order only. TDF offers a book of four vouchers for $28, which can be purchased at its offices only by visitors who bring their passport or out-of-state driver's license, or by students and residents on the TDF mailing list. Each voucher is good for one admission at Off-Off Broadway theater, dance and music events, at venues such as the Joyce, the Kitchen, the Atlantic Theater, La MaMa, P.S. 122 and many more. TDF's NYC/On Stage service *(212-768-1818)* provides information by phone on all theater, dance and music events in town.

New York Shakespeare Festival

The **Delacorte Theater** in Central Park is the fair-weather sister of the **Public Theater** *(see page 341)*. When not producing Shakespeare under its roof, the Public offers the best of the Bard outdoors for free during the *New York Shakespeare Festival (Jun–Sept)*. If you're in the city during the summer, you won't want to miss these innovative alfresco productions. In 2001, *Measure for Measure* and a star-studded (Meryl Streep!) production of Chekhov's *The Seagull* were big draws. Tickets are free (two per person), and are distributed at 1pm on the day of the performance at the Delacorte and at the Public. On some days, the Public also distributes tickets in the outer boroughs. Normally, 11:30am is

You laughing at me?

In a new breed of musical, a little self-mockery goes a long way

Broadway has a long tradition of spoofing itself, of saying: Isn't all this singing and dancing weird? After all, musicals were born out of the raucous and irreverent vaudeville tradition. Then, in the 1960s and '70s, artists such as Leonard Bernstein and Stephen Sondheim brought musical and thematic sophistication to the form. The '80s saw the explosion of the big-budget megashows such as **Les Misérables** and **The Phantom of the Opera** (both still running after all these years; for ticket information, *see page 377*). But recently, there's been a welcome resurgence of big-time silliness. Pushing the boundaries of musical comedy (not to mention taste), several new shows on Broadway seem to have leaped directly from *South Park* and

The Simpsons. We like to call them *spooficals*, but whatever you call them, you're sure to enjoy these ridiculously self-referential blockbusters.

Funnyman Mel Brooks always ribs Broadway in his movies (remember "The Inquisition" number from *The History of the World, Part One*?). In **The Producers**, adapted from Brooks's 1968 movie, an accountant and a crooked producer scheme to cheat investors on a hideously inappropriate show they're sure will flop: *Springtime for Hitler.* Of course, *Hitler* is a hit, thus generating laughs at the expense of our heroes, not to mention schmaltzy Broadway itself. As everyone knows, *The Producers* has been a huge hit—tickets are sold out three months in advance. But you a safe time to line up, but when shows feature box-office giants, the line starts as early as 7am.

Delacorte Theater

A few minutes' walk inside Central Park. Enter the park from either Central Park West at 81st St or Fifth Ave at 79th St, then follow the signs in the park (212-539-8750; www.publictheater.org). Subway: B, C to 81st St; 6 to 77th St.

Broadway

The rumors of its demise were greatly exaggerated—Broadway is booming. In recent years, box-office receipts for newly opened shows have busted records and, by putting movie stars in leading roles, Broadway now competes with Hollywood for its audiences. (Times Square's extensive cleanup hasn't hurt business, either.)

"Broadway," technically speaking, is the theater district around Times Square on either side of Broadway (the street), generally between 41st and 53rd Streets. This is where you'll find the grand theaters, most built in the first 30 years of the 20th century. Officially, 38 of them are designated as being "Broadway," for which full-price tickets cost up to $100. The big shows are hard to ignore; new blockbusters, such as *The Producers, Mamma Mia!,* and the revival of *42nd Street* join long-running shows, such as *The Lion King, Les Misérables* and *Rent,* all of which announce themselves from vast billboards. Still, there's more to Broadway than cartoon-based musicals and flashy Andrew Lloyd Webber spectacles. In recent years, provocative dramas and witty comedies by relative newcomers David Auburn *(Proof)* and Charles Busch *(The Tale of the Allergist's Wife),* have been remarkable successes, as have classics and British imports, such as Michael Frayn's *Copenhagen* and his raucous farce *Noises Off.*

One venue worth a visit is the irrepressible **Roundabout Theater**, the critically acclaimed home of classics played by all-star casts (and the force behind *Cabaret*'s latest incarnation). Its deluxe Broadway space *(American Airlines Theatre, 227 W 42nd St, 212-719-1300)* opened in 2000. You may subscribe to the Roundabout's full season or buy single tickets, if available.

Broadway District

Subway: A, C, E to 42nd St–Port Authority; N, Q, R, W, S, 3, 7 to 42nd St–Times Sq; 1, 2 to 50th St.

Off Broadway

Off Broadway theaters usually have fewer than 500 seats, and have been traditionally located in Greenwich Village. These days, however, they can be found on the Upper West and Upper East Sides, in midtown and in lower Manhattan.

As Broadway increasingly becomes a place of spectacle and crowd-pleasing pop musicals, playwrights who would once have been granted a Broadway production now find themselves in the more risk-taking (and less financially

can line up at the St. James Theatre, Monday through Saturday from 10am to 8pm and score tickets from cancellations.

"An appalling idea, fully realized" is how producers of **Urinetown: The Musical** describe one of Broadway's most unlikely successes. The crazy premise: In an unnamed city, water is so scarce that one must pay to, er, piddle. With excellent tunes and a drop-dead funny script, *Urinetown* asks the tough questions: Can we save the environment? Are corporations evil? Is it, as one song has it, "A Privilege to Pee"?

Does the ABBA-inspired **Mamma Mia!** make the spoofical cut? Abba-solutely! Two dozen unforgettable hits are featured in this light comedy, whose plot is a rather thin excuse for the cast to boogie down memory lane to tunes such as "Dancing Queen," "The Winner Takes it All" and "The Name of the Game." The audience sings along, there's cast winks knowingly, and a good time is had by all.

Mamma Mia!

Winter Garden Theatre, 1634 Broadway at 50th St (212-239-6200). Subway: N, R, W to 49th St; 1 to 50th St. $55–$99. Mon, Tue, Thu, Fri 8pm; Wed, Sat 2, 8pm.

The Producers

St. James Theatre, 246 W 44th St between Broadway and Eighth Ave (212-239-6200). Subway: A, C, E to 42nd St–Port Authority; N, Q, R, W, S, 1, 2, 3, 7 to 42nd St–Times Sq. $30–$100. Tue–Fri 8pm; Sat 2, 8pm; Sun 2, 7:30pm.

Urinetown: The Musical

The Henry Miller, 124 W 43rd St between Sixth Ave and Broadway (212-239-6200). Subway: B, D, F, V to 42nd St; N, Q, R, W, S, 1, 2, 3, 7 to 42nd St–Times Sq. $75. Mon, Tue, Thu, Fri 8pm; Wed 2:15pm; Sat 2, 8pm.

Sometimes well-received Off Broadway shows can move to a Broadway theater. To confirm locations and other information, or to find out about new spooficals, check the Theater section of *Time Out New York.*

DE LA GUARDA

DARYL ROTH THEATRE UNION SQUARE EAST AT 15TH
TELECHARGE 212-239-6200

Bard yard Central Park's Delacorte Theater is the site for Shakespeare in the Park.

demanding) Off Broadway houses, where audiences want plays with something to say.

So if it's brain food and adventure you're after, head Off or Off-Off Broadway—but be prepared for considerable variation in quality. Listed below are some of the most reliable theaters and repertory companies. Tickets typically run from $15 to $60.

Atlantic Theater Company

336 W 20th St between Eighth and Ninth Aves (212-645-1242). Subway: C, E to 23rd St. AmEx, MC, V.
Created in 1985 as an offshoot of the acting workshops taught by David Mamet and actor William H. Macy, this dynamic little theater (in a former church sanctuary on a lovely Chelsea street) has presented nearly 100 plays. Productions have included Mamet's *American Buffalo* (starring Macy), the American premiere of Martin McDonagh's *The Beauty Queen of Leenane*, and the premieres of Jez Butterworth's *Mojo* and Peter Parnell's *The Cider House Rules*.

Brooklyn Academy of Music

See page 315 for listing.
Brooklyn's grand old opera house—along with the Harvey Theater, two blocks away at 651 Fulton Street—stages the famous multidisciplinary Next Wave Festival every October to December. The festival's 2001 theatrical ventures included an eye-popping music-theater collaboration between rocker Lou Reed and director Robert Wilson called *POEtry* (based on the work of Edgar Allan Poe) and German dance legend Pina Bausch's return with *Masurca Fogo*. (For more on BAM, see also page 343.)

Classic Stage Company

136 E 13th St between Third and Fourth Aves (212-677-4210; www.classicstage.org). Subway: L, N, Q, R, W, 4, 5, 6 to 14th St–Union Sq. AmEx, MC, V.
Under the leadership of artistic director Barry Edelstein, the Classic Stage Company has become the best place in town to see movie and TV stars perform the classics in daring new versions. Productions scheduled for spring 2002 include a German satire, *The Underpants* (adapted by comedian-author Steve

Martin) and *Room*, based on Virginia Woolf's writings and directed by Anne Bogart.

Irish Repertory Theatre

132 W 22nd St between Sixth and Seventh Aves (212-727-2737; www.irishrepertorytheatre.com). Subway: F, V, 1, 2 to 23rd St. AmEx, MC, V.
Dedicated to performing works by veteran and contemporary Irish playwrights, this Chelsea company has produced some interesting sold-out shows. Notable productions include Frank McCourt's *The Irish and How They Got That Way* and, more recently, TV legend Charles Nelson Reilly's solo tell-all show *Save It for the Stage: The Life of Reilly.*

Jean Cocteau Repertory

330 Bowery at Bond St (212-677-0060). Subway: F, V, S to Broadway–Lafayette St; 6 to Bleecker St. AmEx, Disc, MC, V.
Housed in the old cast-iron German Exchange Bank, this company, named for the French author and artist, is devoted to producing classics. Recent works include Tom Stoppard's *Night and Day,* Tennessee Williams's *Small Craft Warnings* and Beaumarchais's wonderful French farce *The Marriage of Figaro.*

Lincoln Center

65th St at Columbus Ave (212-362-7600, tickets 212-239-6277; www.lincolncenter.org). Subway: 1, 2 to 66th St–Lincoln Ctr. AmEx, MC, V.
The majestic Lincoln Center complex includes two amphitheater-shaped drama venues: the 1,040-seat **Vivian Beaumont Theater** (considered a Broadway house) and the 290-seat **Mitzi E. Newhouse Theater** (considered Off Broadway). Expect polished productions of new and classic plays, with many a well-known actor. Recent productions include hitmaker Susan Stroman's steamy new musical *Thou Shalt Not* (with music by Harry Connick Jr.) and Richard Greenberg's *Everett Beekin.*

Manhattan Theatre Club

City Center, 131 W 55th St between Sixth and Seventh Aves (212-399-3000; www.manhattantheatreclub.com). Subway: B, D, E to Seventh Ave. AmEx, MC, V.

Manhattan Theatre Club has a reputation for sending young playwrights on to Broadway, as seen in the immense success of David Auburn's *Proof* and Charles Busch's *The Tale of the Allergist's Wife*. The club's two theaters are located in the basement of City Center. The 299-seat **Mainstage Theater** offers four plays a year by new and established playwrights; the **Stage II Theater** serves as an outlet for works-in-progress, workshops and staged readings.

The New Victory Theater

209 W 42nd St between Seventh and Eighth Aves (212-239-6200; www.newvictory.org). Subway: A, C, E to 42nd St–Port Authority; N, Q, R, W, S, 1, 2, 3, 7 to 42nd St–Times Sq. AmEx, DC, Disc, MC, V.
No theater symbolizes the new family-friendly Times Square more than the New Victory. Built in 1900 by Oscar Hammerstein, Manhattan's oldest theater became home to a strip club and XXX cinema in the 1970s and '80s. Renovated by the city in 1995, the building now features a full season of plays geared toward families, including the incredibly popular *Shockheaded Peter*. The New Victory is also a great place to see international shows, such as Australia's *Flying Fruit Fly Circus* or the British import *Arabian Nights*, an adaptation of the Scheherazade stories.

New York Theatre Workshop

79 E 4th St between Bowery and Second Ave (212-460-5475). Subway: F, V to Lower East Side–Second Ave; 6 to Astor Pl. AmEx, MC, V.
Founded in 1979, the New York Theatre Workshop produces new plays with emerging directors who are eager to harness challenging pieces. Besides initiating works by the likes of Claudia Shear *(Dirty Blonde)* and Tony Kushner *(Homebody/Kabul)*, this Off Broadway company is most noted for having premiered *Rent*, Jonathan Larson's Pulitzer Prize–winning musical, which still packs 'em in on Broadway. The Workshop also offers a home to upstart directors through its Just Add Water festival.

Pearl Theatre Company

80 St. Marks Pl between First and Second Aves (212-505-3401; www.pearltheatre.org). Subway: N, R to 8th St–NYU; 6 to Astor Pl. AmEx, MC, V.
Housed on the East Village's punk promenade, this troupe of resident players relies primarily on its actors' ability to present the classics. Besides Shakespeare and the Greeks, Pearl has successfully produced the works of Ionesco, Racine and Shaw, plus lesser-known playwrights such as Alexander Ostrofsky and Thomas Otway—all on a small, minimally dressed stage.

Playwrights Horizons

416 W 42nd St between Ninth and Tenth Aves (Ticket Central 212-279-4200; www.playwrightshorizons.org). Subway: A, C, E to 42nd St–Port Authority. AmEx, MC, V. $4 service charge per phone order.
This power-packed company has premiered more than 300 important contemporary plays, including dramas such as *Driving Miss Daisy* and *The Heidi*

Chronicles, and musicals such as *James Joyce's The Dead*. More recently, the works of newcomers Kenneth Lonergan *(Lobby Hero)*, Kia Corthron *(Breath, Boom)* and the brilliant Christopher Durang *(Betty's Summer Vacation)*, have been staged.

The Public Theater

425 Lafayette St between Astor Pl and 4th St (212-539-8500; www.publictheater.org). Subway: N, R to 8th St–NYU; 6 to Astor Pl. AmEx, MC, V.
This Astor Place landmark is one of the city's most consistently interesting theaters. Founded by Joseph Papp (who bought the building from the city for $1), and dedicated to the work of new American playwrights and performers, the Public also presents new explorations of Shakespeare and the classics *(see* **New York Shakespeare Festival**, *page 336)*. The building houses five stages, a coffee bar and the cabaret space Joe's Pub *(see page 305)*. The Public is under the direction of George C. Wolfe, who directed Suzan-Lori Parks's *Topdog/Underdog* on Broadway and the historic New York premiere of Tony Kushner's *Angels in America*.

Second Stage Theatre

307 W 43rd St at Eighth Ave (212-246-4422; www.secondstagetheatre.com). Subway: A, C, E to 42nd St–Port Authority; N, Q, R, W, S, 1, 2, 3, 7 to 42nd St–Times Sq. MC, V.
Created as a venue for American plays that didn't get the critical reception some thought they deserved, Second Stage now also produces the works of new American playwrights. It staged the New York premieres of Stephen Sondheim's first musical, *Saturday Night*, and August Wilson's *Jitney*. Since 1999, the company has occupied a beautiful Rem Koolhaas–designed space, just off Times Square. Its lineup for 2002 is impressive, including second looks at Wallace Shawn's *Marie and Bruce* and Edward Albee's *Seascape*.

Signature Theatre Company

555 W 42nd St between Tenth and Eleventh Aves (212-244-7529; www.signaturetheatre.org). Subway: A, C, E to 42nd St–Port Authority. AmEx, MC, V.
This unique award-winning company is known for

> ▶ To find out what's playing, see the listings and reviews in *Time Out New York*.
> ▶ For plot synopses, show times and ticket info, call **NYC/On Stage** *(212-768-1818)*, a service of the Theater Development Fund *(see page 336)*. You'll get info about shows on Broadway, Off Broadway and Off-Off Broadway (as well as classical music, dance and opera).
> ▶ If you already know what you want to see, try the **Broadway Line** *(212-302-4111, outside New York 888-276-2392; www.ilovenytheater.com)*, which is limited to Broadway and Off Broadway shows.

focusing on the works of a single playwright in residence each season. (The 2000 scribe was Maria Irene Fornes.) But to celebrate its 10th anniversary, Signature is premiering a new work by each of its past playwrights, such as Edward Albee and Lee Blessing. Signature has delved into the oeuvres of John Guare, Arthur Miller and Horton Foote, whose *The Young Man from Atlanta* originated here, and went on to win the Pulitzer Prize.

The Vineyard Theatre

108 E 15th St at Union Sq East (212-353-3366; www.vineyardtheatre.org). Subway: L, N, Q, R, W, 4, 5, 6 to 14th St–Union Sq. AmEx, MC, V.
This theater near Union Square produces consistently excellent new plays and musicals, and also attempts to revive works that have failed in other arenas. The Vineyard has recently enjoyed a streak of successes, including Paula Vogel's *How I Learned to Drive* and Edward Albee's *Three Tall Women*. The theater is also home to such playwrights as Craig Lucas and the dark wit Doug Wright.

Off-Off Broadway

The technical definition of Off-Off Broadway is a show created by artists who may not be card-carrying pros, presented at a theater with fewer than 100 seats. It's where some of the most innovative and daring writers and performers experiment. Pieces often meld media, including music, dance, film, video and performance monologue—sometimes resulting in an all-too-indulgent marriage of theater and psychotherapy. The New York International Fringe Festival every August (see page 240) is a great place to catch the wackier side of things.

But Off-Off Broadway is not restricted to experimental or solo performance. You can also see classical works and more traditional plays staged by companies such as the **Mint Theater** *(311 W 43rd St between Eighth and Ninth Aves, fifth floor, 212-315-0231)* or the intriguing outfit **Target Margin Theater** *(www.targetmargin. org)* and at venues such as **The Flea Theater**. Tickets usually cost $10 to $25.

The Flea Theater

41 White St between Broadway and Church St (212-226-2407; www.theflea.org). Subway: A, C, E to Canal St; 1, 2 to Franklin St. Cash only.
This lovely Tribeca space is home to the Bat Theater Company, the brainchild of director Jim Simpson, playwright Mac Wellman and designer Kyle Chepulis. The company alternates experimental work (the rock-Kabuki epic *Benten Kozo*) with fresh takes on old chestnuts (the 1906 melodrama *Billy the Kid*).

The Kitchen

512 W 19th St between Tenth and Eleventh Aves (212-255-5793; www.thekitchen.org). Subway: A, C, E to 14th St; L to Eighth Ave. AmEx, MC, V.
Laurie Anderson, David Byrne and Cindy Sherman all started at this small experimental theater, which was founded in 1971. A reputable place to see edgy New York experimentation, the Kitchen presents an eclectic multimedia repertoire of theater, music, dance, video and performance art from September to May.

La MaMa E.T.C.

74A E 4th St between Bowery and Second Ave (212-475-7710; www.lamama.org). Subway: F, V to Lower East Side–Second Ave; 6 to Astor Pl. AmEx, MC, V.
When acclaimed producer Ellen Stewart ("Mama" is her nickname) opened La MaMa in 1961, it was New York's best-kept theater secret. (Did you know, for example, that Harvey Fierstein's *Torch Song Trilogy* started here?) Now with more than 50 Obie Awards under its belt, it's a fixture in the city's dramatic life. If you're looking for traditional theater, skip La MaMa. New ground is routinely broken here, and some of it is rather muddy.

Ontological-Hysteric Theater

St. Mark's Church in-the-Bowery, 131 E 10th St at Second Ave (212-533-4650; www.ontological.com). Subway: L to First Ave; N, R to 8th St–NYU; 6 to Astor Pl. Cash only.
Since the late 1980s, this 100-seat black-box theater has been home to New York's godfather of the avant-garde, Richard Foreman. Every year, the prolific and critically acclaimed auteur presents a humorous new mind-bending spectacle that bedazzles and befuddles. His 2002 production, *Maria del Bosco,* is a surreal meditation on fashion models and race cars. Foreman also opens the door to young directors and fresh talent in such showcases as the Blueprint Series and the Seven Minute Series.

Performance Space 122

150 First Ave at 9th St (212-477-5288; www.ps122.org). Subway: L to First Ave; N, R to 8th St–NYU; 6 to Astor Pl. AmEx, MC, V.
One of New York's most exciting venues, P.S. 122 (as it's casually known) is housed in a former school in the East Village. It's a nonprofit arts center for experimental works, with two theaters presenting dance, performance, music, film and video. Artists develop, practice and present their projects here; P.S. 122 has provided a platform for Eric Bogosian, Whoopi Goldberg, Danny Hoch and John Leguizamo.

The Performing Garage

33 Wooster St between Broome and Grand Sts (212-966-3651). Subway: A, C, E, J, M, Z, N, Q, R, W, 6 to Canal St. Cash only.
The Performing Garage features the inimitable works of the Wooster Group, whose members include Willem Dafoe, Spalding Gray, Elizabeth LeCompte and Kate Valk. In addition to presenting deconstructed versions of theater classics (including a multimedia *Phaedra*), the group sponsors a summer emerging-artists series. This is also where Gray continues to rework his quirky monologues, such as *Swimming to Cambodia*.

Strike a pose Eliot Feld's Ballet Tech is the Joyce Theater's resident company.

Dance

Dance in New York has never been plied with the generous government subsidies that European companies receive. And it's true that the ranks of choreographers have diminished since the 1980s. Yet no other city in the world boasts such a high caliber of established companies and emerging choreographers. Of the two major seasons—October to December and March to June—the spring stretch is decidedly richer. Not only does Paul Taylor regularly present his marvelous troupe each March, but the resident American Ballet Theatre and the New York City Ballet are both onstage in full force. There are usually a couple of dance films and lectures presented each week, and if watching those beautiful bodies onstage inspires you, enroll in a class. New York is jam-packed with wonderful dance schools and teachers. Choose an aggressive rhythm tap class, a retro swing session or a modern dance class—from improvisation to the Martha Graham technique—or drop by a ballet studio for some serious barre work. Call ahead for schedules, but walk-ins are welcome at most schools *(see page 348)*.

(see page 348)

Venues

Brooklyn Academy of Music
See page 315 for listing

See page 315 for listing

BAM, as it's called, turned 140 in 2001, but is hardly old-fashioned—it showcases superb modern and out-of-town companies. The **Howard Gilman Opera House**, with its Federal-style columns and carved marble, is one of the city's most beautiful stages for dance. (The Mark Morris Dance Group and Mikhail Baryshnikov's White Oak Dance Project often perform here.) The 1904 **Harvey Theater** *(651 Fulton St between Ashland and Rockwell Pls)*, has hosted modern troupes such as Chunky Move and the John Jasperse Company. Each fall, BAM's Next Wave Festival showcases experimental and established dance groups; in spring, short festivals focus on ballet, hip-hop, modern dance and tap.

City Center Theater
131 W 55th St between Sixth and Seventh Aves (212-581-7907). Subway: B, D, E to Seventh Ave. $25–$75. AmEx, MC, V. $4 per ticket surcharge.
Before the creation of Lincoln Center changed the cultural geography of New York, this was the home of the American Ballet Theatre, Joffrey Ballet and New York City Ballet (originally known as the Ballet Society). The lavish decor is all golden, and so are the usually established companies that pass through. Seasons to count on are American Ballet Theatre in the fall, Alvin Ailey American Dance Theater in December, and the Paul Taylor Dance Company in the spring.

Joyce Theater
175 Eighth Ave at 19th St (212-242-0800; www.joyce.org). Subway: C, E to 23rd St; 1, 2 to 18th St. $20–$40. AmEx, DC, Disc, MC, V.

The intimate Joyce, once a cinema, is one of the finest theaters in town. Of the 472 seats, there's not a bad one in the house. Ballet Hispanico, David Parsons and Doug Elkins have regularly appeared here. In residence is Eliot Feld's Ballet Tech. Feld, who began his performance career in George Balanchine's *The Nutcracker* and Jerome Robbins's *West Side Story*, presents his company in two monthlong seasons (March and July). The Joyce also hosts out-of-town ensembles, as well as Pilobolus Dance Theatre in June and the Altogether Different Festival in January. In summer, when many theaters are dark, the Joyce may feature almost a dozen companies. The Joyce Soho helps independent choreographers by offering subsidized rehearsal space and a smaller theater in which to perform (emerging companies present work nearly every weekend).

Other location ● *Joyce Soho, 155 Mercer St between Houston and Prince Sts (212-431-9233). Subway: F, V, S to Broadway–Lafayette; N, R to Prince St; 6 to Bleecker St. $10–$15. Cash only.*

Metropolitan Opera House
See page 317 for listing.
The Met hosts a range of top international companies, from the Paris Opéra Ballet to the Kirov Ballet. Each spring, this majestic theater hosts American Ballet Theatre, which presents full-length story classics. The acoustics are wonderful, but the theater is vast, so sit as close as you can afford.

New York State Theater
65th St at Columbus Ave (212-870-5570; www.nycballet.com). Subway: 1, 2 to 66th St–Lincoln Center. $16–$85. AmEx, MC, V.
Both the neoclassical New York City Ballet and the New York City Opera headline at this opulent theater, which Philip Johnson designed to resemble a jewel box. NYCB hosts two seasons: Winter begins just before Thanksgiving and features more than a month of Nutcracker performances that run until early March; the eight-week spring season usually begins in April. The best seats are in the first ring, where the sound is tops, and where one can enjoy the dazzling patterns of the corps de ballet. The repertoire is by George Balanchine (the 89-by-58-foot stage was made to his specifications), Peter Martins,

---

▶ The Theater Development Fund's **NYC/ On Stage** service *(see page 336)* offers information on all dance events in town.
▶ For information on weekly dance performances, see *Time Out New York*, which lists all types of dance, preview shows and dance classes.
▶ *Dance Magazine ($3.95, monthly)* is a good way to find out about a performance well ahead of time.
▶ See page 377 for ticket info.

Jerome Robbins and new resident choreographer, Christopher Wheeldon, among others.

Aaron Davis Hall
City College, 135th St at Convent Ave (212-650-7100). Subway: 1 to 137th St–City College. AmEx, MC, V.
Troupes here often celebrate African-American life and culture. The companies that have appeared include the Bill T. Jones/Arnie Zane Dance Company and the Alvin Ailey Repertory Ensemble.

Brooklyn Arts Exchange
421 Fifth Ave at 8th St, Park Slope, Brooklyn (718-832-0018). Subway: F to Seventh Ave. $6–$12. Cash only.
Brooklyn Arts Exchange (formerly Gowanus Arts Exchange), located in lower Park Slope, presents a variety of dance concerts by emerging choreographers. There are also performances just for children, and theater, music and film that cater to the local community.

Dance Theater Workshop
Bessie Schönberg Theater, 219 W 19th St between Seventh and Eighth Aves (212-691-6500, tickets 212-924-0077; www.dtw.org). Subway: C, E to 23rd St; 1, 2 to 18th St. AmEx, MC, V.
DTW is currently under construction—by fall of 2002, the space will feature a 200-seat theater, two dance studios and an artists' media lab. In the meantime, DTW (where choreographers such as Mark Morris and Bill T. Jones started out) presents Around Town, a series that copresents choreographers at other theaters, including the Duke on 42nd Street.

Danspace Project
St. Mark's Church in-the-Bowery, Second Ave at 10th St (212-674-8194). Subway: L to Third Ave; 6 to Astor Pl. $12–$20. Cash only.
This is a gorgeous, high-ceilinged sanctuary for downtown dance, and it's even more otherworldly when the music is live. Downtown choreographers are selected by the director, Laurie Uprichard, whose preference leans toward pure movement works. Choreographers who semi-regularly perform here are Douglas Dunn, David Gordon and Kevin Wynn.

Galapagos Art and Performance Space
See page 305 for listing. Prices vary.
This Brooklyn club presents monthly dance performances—mainly in the setting of dance cabaret—including Phat Tuesdays and the wildly popular "Terry Dean and Lisa Leann Put on a Dance Show."

The Kitchen
See page 342 for listing.
Best known as an avant-garde theater space, the Kitchen is also a fabulous place to see experimental (and just plain good) dance. Dance/performance

Dance hall BAM's Howard Gilman Opera House is a beautiful place to see a performance.

curator Dean Moss, who is also a choreographer, presents artists who are inventive and, more often than not, provocative (tickets cost $8 to $25).

Merce Cunningham Studio

55 Bethune St between Washington and West Sts, 11th floor (212-691-9751; www.merce.org). Subway: A, C, E to 14th St; L to Eighth Ave. $10–$30. Cash only.

Located in the Westbeth complex on the edge of Greenwich Village, the Cunningham Studio is rented by individual choreographers who self-produce. Performance quality ranges from horrid to surprisingly wonderful. Since the stage and seating area are in Cunningham's large studio, be prepared to take off your shoes. Arrive early too, or you'll have to sit on the floor. For more details, contact the Cunningham Dance Foundation *(212-255-8240)*.

Movement Research at Judson Church

55 Washington Sq South at Thompson St (212-598-0551; www.movementresearch.com). Subway: A, C, E, F, V, S to W 4th St. Free.

Director Catherine Levine carries on the tradition of Monday-night performances at the Judson Church, which originally began in the 1960s. At least two choreographers' works are shown each night, and the series runs from September to June. MR also offers a vast selection of classes and workshops, which are held at various venues, such as Danspace Project *(see page 344)*. Panel discussions are held from time to time.

New Jersey Performing Arts Center

1 Center St between Park Pl and Ronald H. Brown St at the waterfront, Newark, NJ (973-642-8989, box office 888-466-5722; www.njpac.org).

Travel: Call for directions. $12–$64. AmEx, Disc, MC, V.

The New Jersey Performing Arts Center serves as home base for the New Jersey Symphony Orchestra, and has hosted the Alvin Ailey American Dance Theater, Suzanne Farrell Ballet and the Miami City Ballet. Large, open theaters make NJPAC a choice venue for dance.

The New Victory Theater

See page 341 for listing.

The New Victory in Times Square was the first theater on the block to be renovated. Since opening in 1995, this intimate venue has offered exceptional dance programming. What it doesn't present in quantity, it makes up for in quality—among the artists to present seasons here are Suzanne Farrell, Maguy Marin and David Parsons. Tickets are in the $8 to $25 range.

92nd Street Y Harkness Dance Project

The Duke on 42nd Street Theater, 229 W 42nd St between Seventh and Eighth Aves (212-415-5500).

Mark the spot

Mark Morris's new dance center will give you happy feet

Mark Morris lamented for years that he needed a home for his dancers. It wasn't that he didn't deserve one—Morris is one of the most important choreographers working today in modern dance and ballet. Finally, after nearly two years of construction, the Mark Morris Dance Center opened in Brooklyn in September 2001. The building consists of spacious studios, the largest of which—a jaw-dropping 60 by 60 feet—doubles as a performance space. There are also archive, wardrobe and physical therapy rooms; terraces; and a dancers' lounge. But the dressing rooms are perhaps the center's most breathtaking attraction. Modeled after a modern-day stadium locker room, rows of intimate cubicles line the sides of a narrow hallway. The lighting is soft and ambient, and each area, which includes a desk and a closet, is a dancer's dream.

Located in the Fort Greene neighborhood in clear sight of the Brooklyn Academy of Music *(see pages 315, 339 and 343)*, Morris's new HQ could have turned out to be overly sterile, or worse yet, self-consciously funky. But even the choreographer's electric-green office and adjoining red bathroom (he does a lot of thinking while soaking in a tub) are tastefully chic. The only nod to Morris's flamboyance

are two papier-mâché dog heads from Indonesia, which sit on clean wooden shelves ("I wanted 25, but I couldn't carry them all on the plane," Morris notes). The building, inside and out, embodies a word that can also describe the choreographer's work it houses: *magnificent.*

"Well, it's like, do you want to build it nice or do you want to build it crappy?" asks Barry Alterman, the Mark Morris Dance Group's general director. "Really! It cost no more money to build it nice."

But just because it's nice doesn't mean Morris's company is an elitist academy. "This is for the community too; not just the dance community." Morris says. "I want people to come here, to have fun and exposure to dancing." He likens the center to Verla Flowers's Seattle dance school, where he studied as a young boy and learned not just ballet, but the ethnic traditions that inform his choreographic style today.

The MMDC includes a stellar dance academy for children, professionals and adults, directed by founding company member Tina Fehlandt. "I started dancing when I was four or five," she says. "I've been in class for almost 40 years, so I do know something about dancing."

Subway: N, Q, R, W, S, 1, 2, 3, 7 to Times Sq–42nd St. $20. AmEx, MC, V.
This annual monthlong event is presented in early spring at the new Duke theater. Participants in 2002 will include the Nicholas Leichter Dance, Keely Garfield, Chamecki/Lerner, Seán Curran Company and Wil Swanson.

Performance Space 122
See page 342 for listing.
P.S. 122 is the site for all kinds of performance. Executive director Mark Russell presents an appealing range of up-and-coming choreographers (and the occasional established talent) in new and unconventional works ($9–$15). Recent performers include Sarah Michelson, Jim Neuman and Douglas Dunn, and Min Tanaka with Meredith Monk.

Symphony Space
See page 259 for listing.
Located on upper Broadway, this is a center for all the performing arts. The World Music Institute presents many international dance troupes here; tickets are between $10 and $20.

Williamsburg Arts Nexus
205 North 7th St between Driggs and Roebling Aves, Williamsburg, Brooklyn (718-599-7997). Subway: L to Bedford Ave. $10–$20. Cash only.
This Brooklyn venue features dance by local choreographers in a cozy environment. The sight lines are great, and the mix of artists, interesting. Dance is presented nearly every weekend.

Summer performances

Central Park SummerStage
See page 314 for listing.
This outdoor dance series runs on Fridays in July and the first couple of weeks in August. Temperatures can get steamy, but at least you're outside. Count on seeing contemporary dance, but arrive early to secure a seat close to the stage.

Dances for Wave Hill
See page 105 for listing.
This is a lovely setting for outdoor dance. The series, sponsored by Dancing in the Streets, runs in July ($4, cash only).

Ballet of the land You can do or watch at the new Mark Morris Dance Center in Brooklyn.

Since she had no physical school to direct in the beginning, Fehlandt spent all of her free time researching dance programs. "The most important thing I learned was that we had to grow to meet the needs of our community," she says. "I didn't want to make something and then make people fit into it. We want the center to be a neighborhood place for kids and older adults who aren't dancers."

Classes for professional dancers are also an integral part of Fehlandt's program. Morris and members of his company (along with Kraig Patterson and Risa Steinberg) will teach modern technique, and Marjorie Mussman, with whom both Fehlandt and Morris studied in the late '70s, is the school's main advanced-ballet instructor. "Mark and I got to know each other in her class," Fehlandt says. "Actually, the Mark Morris Dance Group was born in Marjorie Mussman's class. When people ask me, 'How did you get into the company?' I'm like, 'Honey, I was there. It didn't exist. Make your own.' In a way, maybe because Mark and I were at the end of the hippie era, we want the same thing to happen here. Not everyone we train is going to get into the company and not everyone wants to. So they should meet here and make their own company."

One letter of inquiry Fehlandt received seems to sum up the Dance Center's mission. On the front of the envelope, a child wrote a message in green cursive: I ♥ BALLET. But the question on the back is even more poignant: "Do you have to be skinny for ballet?"

"And the answer," Fehlandt says with a quick grin, "is no. You don't have to be thin. I'm going to call her right now."

Mark Morris Dance Center
3 Lafayette Ave between Flatbush Ave and Fulton St, Fort Greene, Brooklyn (718-624-8400). Subway: M, N, R, W to Pacific St; Q, 1, 2, 4, 5 to Atlantic Ave. $11. Cash only.

Dance shopping

The New York City Ballet and American Ballet Theatre both have gift shops, open during intermission, that sell everything from autographed pointe shoes to ballet-themed T-shirts, night-lights and jewelry.

Capezio Dance-Theater Shop

1650 Broadway at 51st St, second floor (212-245-2130). Subway: C, E, 1, 2 to 50th St; N, R, W to 49th St. Mon–Fri 9:30am–7pm; Sat 9:30am–6:30pm; Sun 11:30am–5pm. AmEx, MC, V.
Capezio carries an excellent stock of professional-quality shoes and practice-and-performance gear, as well as dance duds that can be worn on the street. **Other locations ● ** *1776 Broadway at 57th St (212-586-5140). Subway: A, C, B, D, 1, 2 to 59th St–Columbus Circle. Mon–Fri 10am–7pm; Sat 10am–6pm; Sun noon–5pm. AmEx, MC, V.* ● *136 E 61st St between Park and Lexington Aves (212-758-8833). Subway: N, R, W to Lexington Ave–59th St; 4, 5, 6 to 59th St. Mon–Fri 10am–7pm; Sat 10am–6pm; Sun noon–5pm. AmEx, MC, V.*

KD Dance

339 Lafayette St at Bleecker St (212-533-1037; www.kddance.com). Subway: F, V, S to Broadway–Lafayette St; 6 to Bleecker St. Mon–Sat noon–8pm; Sun 1–5pm. AmEx, Disc, MC, V.
This shop, owned by Tricia Kaye, former principal dancer and ballet mistress of the Oakland Ballet, and dancer David Lee, features the softest, prettiest dance knits around. Check the bins for sale items.

Dance schools

Most major companies have their own schools. Amateurs are welcome at the following (classes for beginners cost $11 to $22 per session).

The Ailey School

211 W 61st St between Amsterdam and West End Aves, third floor (212-767-0940; www.alvinailey.org). Subway: A, C, B, D, 1, 2 to 59th St–Columbus Circle. From $11. AmEx, MC, V only for 10-class coupon book ($100).
The school of the Alvin Ailey American Dance Theater has a full schedule of classes in modern dance, ballet, tap and even yoga.

American Ballet Theatre

890 Broadway at 19th St, third floor (212-477-3030; www.abt.org). Subway: L, N, Q, R, W, 4, 5, 6 to 14th St–Union Sq. From $12.50. No credit cards.
ABT teacher Diana Cartier (a former Joffrey Ballet principal dancer) leads advanced beginner classical ballet classes.

Broadway Dance Center

221 W 57th St at Broadway, fifth floor (212-582-9304; www.bwydance.com). Subway: A, C, B, D, 1, 2 to 59th St–Columbus Circle; N, Q, R, W to 57th St. From $12.50. Cash only.
The center offers daily classes in ballet, jazz, modern and tap.

Dance Space Inc.

451 Broadway between Grand and Howard Sts, second floor (212-625-8369; www.dancespace.com). Subway: J, M, Z, N, Q, R, W, 6 to Canal St. From $13.50. MC, V ($20 minimum).
Beginner through advanced dancers can take classes in Simonson jazz, modern dance, modern jazz, ballet, stretch, capoeira and yoga. There is a question as to whether this Dance Space will occupy its studio after July 2002, so call ahead.

DanceSport

1845 Broadway at 60th St (212-307-1111; www.dancesport.com). Subway: A, C, B, D, 1, 2 to 59th St–Columbus Circle. $22. AmEx, MC, V ($30 minimum).
At DanceSport, you can learn ballroom and Latin—which includes tango, merengue, salsa, samba and "Cuban motion."

Limón Institute

611 Broadway between Bleecker and Houston Sts, ninth floor (212-777-3353; www.limon.org). Subway: F, V, S to Broadway–Lafayette St; 6 to Bleecker St. $11. Cash only.
Former company members teach classes in the José Limón and Doris Humphrey technique.

Mark Morris Dance Center

See **Mark the spot**, page 346.

Martha Graham School

37 W 26th St between Broadway and Sixth Ave, ninth floor (212-838-5886). Subway: N, R to 28th St. From $12. MC, V.
The Graham technique is taught by former company members such as Stewart Hodes, Sandra Kaufmann and Pearl Lang. This is a temporary space, however, so call ahead.

Merce Cunningham Studio

See page 345 for listing.
You can learn how to "discipline your energy" at Merce Cunningham technique classes ($115 per class).

Paul Taylor School

552 Broadway between Prince and Spring Sts, second floor (212-431-5562; www.paultaylor.org). Subway: F, V, S to Broadway–Lafayette St; N, R to Prince St; 6 to Bleecker St. $12. AmEx, Disc, MC, V (two-class minimum).
This classic company's school offers daily modern technique class.

Steps

2121 Broadway at 74th St (212-874-2410; www.stepsnyc.com). Subway: 1, 2, 3 to 72nd St. $12. Cash only.
Steps holds daily classes in various skill levels of ballet, jazz, modern and tap.

Trips
Out of Town

Beaches   **350**
The Hudson Valley   **355**

Feature box

A toast to Hudson Valley wines   352

Stairway to haven Grand Central
Terminal is a gorgeous embarkation
point for train travelers heading north.

Trips Out of Town

When the city becomes too much of a good thing, it's easy to hit the road (or the rails) to the beach or country

New Yorkers are a funny lot: They'll defend their city to the end—but come Friday, they're scrambling to get the heck out of town. All kinds of getaways, from bustling beaches to tranquil regions with historic import, are within a few hours' reach. But wherever you go, one truism remains: Traffic is absolutely nuts on Fridays and Sundays. Take advantage of your visitor status and plan your retreat for midweek or during off-peak times—or take public transportation.

GENERAL INFORMATION

NYC & Company, the New York visitors and convention bureau *(810 Seventh Ave at 53rd St, 212-484-1222)*, has many brochures on upstate excursions. Look for special packages if you're planning to spend a few days away. *The New York Times* publishes a travel section every Sunday that carries advertisements for resorts and guest houses. *Time Out New York*'s annual Summer Getaways issue can also help point you in the right direction.

GETTING THERE

For all the places listed, we've included information on how to get there from New York City. **Metro-North** and the **Long Island Rail Road** are the two main commuter rail systems. Both offer theme tours in the summer. Call the **Port Authority Bus Terminal** for information on all bus transportation from the city. Car-rental rates in New York are exorbitant; you can save up to 50 percent by renting a car somewhere outside the city, even if it's from the same company. For more information on airports, trains, buses and car rentals, see chapter **Directory**.

Long Island Rail Road (LIRR)

718-217-LIRR, 516-822-LIRR; www.lirr.org.
Trains run from Penn Station in Manhattan and from Flatbush Avenue in Brooklyn; connections and transfers take place at the hub in Jamaica, Queens.

Metro-North

212-532-4900, 800-METRO-INFO; www.mta.info.
Metro-North runs lines from Grand Central Terminal to upstate New York and Connecticut.

Port Authority Bus Terminal

212-564-8484.
Many different bus lines depart from Port Authority.

Beaches

You've heard it before: Manhattan is surrounded by water, but there's nowhere to swim. Luckily, beachfront towns have no shortage of bracing Atlantic waters and fine sand. Of course, it is possible to reach the coast without even leaving the city limits—the grungy carnival known as Coney Island makes for a great day trip, as do the Rockaways. But many urban natives prefer the comparatively serene beaches of Long Island. From Memorial Day (late May) to Labor Day (early September), New Yorkers scramble to get to their summer rentals or day-trip destinations in the Hamptons and on Fire Island.

Nearby

When the city heats up, shore relief doesn't have to mean a long drive. Just 33 miles from Manhattan is **Jones Beach** *(516-785-1600)*. Good for picnicking and sunbathing, this spot attracts plenty of city dwellers and is also the site of big summer music concerts *(see page 314)*. Closer still is **Long Beach**, easily accessible by the Long Island Rail Road and popular for its topless babes and teensy Speedos.

GETTING THERE

Jones Beach: From June 25 to September 3, the LIRR offers an $11 package deal from Penn Station that covers train-and-bus fare and entry to the beach. Take the Babylon line of the LIRR to Freeport, then board the JB24 bus to the beach. Trains leave Penn Station approximately every half-hour. The last bus leaves Jones Beach at 7:40pm.
Long Beach: From June 25 through September 3, the LIRR offers an $11 package deal from Penn Station that covers train fare and entry to the beach. Take the Long Beach line of the LIRR to its terminus; the beach is two blocks south of the train.

Fire Island

Running parallel to the southern coast of Long Island, Fire Island is a thin 30-mile strip of land that separates the Great South Bay from the Atlantic Ocean. Traffic-weary visitors, rejoice: Cars are barred from most of Fire Island, so expect to walk a lot (or take water taxis) and get sand in your shoes (or go barefoot). Since there

Lady of the waves Long Beach, Long Island, offers a freewheeling scene of sun, sand and surf.

are no cars, there are no streets, either, and many places don't have "street" addresses. But everything is fairly easy to find. The season runs from May to October, after which the whole place pretty much shuts down.

Many day-trippers head to **Robert Moses State Park** *(631-669-0449)*, on the western tip of Fire Island. It's only an hour and a half from Penn Station by train and bus. A long stretch of white sand fronts grassy dunes. Head east toward the lighthouse and you'll be able to let it all hang out at a fun and friendly nude beach. A snack bar, public toilets and showers satisfy basic human needs. There's parking for cars as well.

To the east of Robert Moses are the various beach towns of Fire Island, and many short-term visitors find themselves in or around Ocean Beach and the Pines. **Ocean Beach** is a sanctuary for sunbathing, Frisbee-throwing, volleyball-playing families and postcollegiates. The town has neither the frills nor the conveniences of the Hamptons, but nothing will stop an Ocean Beacher from enjoying a day in the sand—not even the fact that it's known as the "Land of NO" (booze and food aren't allowed on the beach, for example). City slickers visiting Ocean Beach tend to share summer rentals with friends or other families, cramming 26 people into a four-bedroom house. For roomier digs, try **Clegg's Hotel** *(631-583-5399)* or **Jerry's Accommodations** *(631-583-8870)*. Burgers and bar food are served at **Albatross** *(Bay Walk, 631-583-5697)*, and anyone with a taste for buttercream-frosted cakes and gooey brownies ends up at **Rachel's**

Bakery *(325 Bay Walk, 631-583-9552)*. You can drink, however, at the **Fair Harbor** dock; on Saturday evenings, sunset cocktails are a tradition. Follow the sand path known as the Burma Road to the enclave, a 20-minute walk to the west from Ocean Beach. Don't forget to bring a bottle of wine or a six-pack in your beach bag—it's a BYO affair.

A mecca for Chelsea boys and other members of New York's gay community, **The Pines** is a world—and a half-hour water-taxi ride—away from Ocean Beach. Modern wood-and-glass houses line this community's carless streets. Pines residents keep a tight social schedule: sunning in the morning, working out in the afternoon and napping before cocktails at sunset. At 8pm, it's the "tea dance" (which involves neither tea nor dancing) outside the famous **Pavilion** *(631-597-6131)*, followed by dinner (never before ten). Then it's back to the Pavilion at 2am for partying until dawn. Guest rooms are available at **Botel** *(631-597-6500)*, an unattractive concrete structure that houses the Pines' heavily used gym, and at the more quaint **Pines Place** *(631-597-6131)*. Wherever you stay, make sure you've got well-honed social skills…and bring plenty of sunblock.

GETTING THERE
Ocean Beach: Take the Babylon line of the LIRR to Bay Shore *($6.50–$9.50)*, then walk or take a cab to the ferry station. **Tommy's Taxi** *(631-665-4800; Mon–Sat $17, Sundays and holidays $20)* runs regular van service from various locations in Manhattan. By car, take the Long Island Expwy to Sagtikos Pkwy. Then take the Southern State Pkwy

eastbound to Exit 42 south *(Fifth Ave in Bay Shore)*; follow the signs for the ferry. From Bay Shore, take the **Fire Island Ferry** *(99 Maple Ave, Bay Shore, 631-665-3600; www.fireislandferries.com; round-trip $11.50, children $5.50)*.

The Pines: Take the Montauk branch of the LIRR to Sayville *($6.50–$9.50, seniors $4.75)*, then walk or take a taxi to the ferry dock. From May to October, **Islander's Horizon Buses** *(212-228-7100, 631-654-2622; www.islanderstravel.com)* run between Manhattan and the Sayville ferry station; Friday and Saturday departure, return Sunday or Monday *($20 one-way)*. By car, take the Long Island Expwy to Exit 59 south, then turn right onto Ocean Ave and continue for 6.5 miles. Turn left on Main St and follow the green-and-white signs to the ferry. From Sayville, take

the **Sayville Ferry** *(41 River Rd, 631-589-0810; round-trip $11, children under 12 $5)* across the bay. **Robert Moses State Park:** From June 25 to September 3, the LIRR offers a $12 train-and-bus package from Penn Station. Take the Babylon line of the LIRR to Babylon and board the S-47 bus. Buses run approximately every half hour on weekends and hourly on weekdays. The last bus leaves the beach at 6:30pm.

The Hamptons

The Hamptons, a series of small towns strung along the South Fork of Long Island, are the ultimate retreat for New York's rich and famous. Socialites, artists and hangers-on drift from

A toast to Hudson Valley wines

New York's vino is primo—really!

The Hudson Valley doesn't produce grapes or wine of the same caliber as, say, the Rhône Valley. But upstate New York is still a desirable destination for adventurous oenophiles—and the Shawangunk Wine Trail makes it easy for you. The "Trail" is a zigzag route that runs roughly parallel to I-87, west of the Hudson River. Plan your trip by visiting www.shawangunkwinetrail.com; for directions to individual wineries, call or check their websites.

What makes this tasting tour interesting is that the makers themselves offer a key intangible: accessibility. So you can not only sample the wine (usually for a small fee) but also learn a bit about how it is made. There is also the opportunity to sample some peculiar potations alongside the grape-based elixirs—such as a ginseng-root blend.

Adair Vineyards

52 Allhusen Rd, New Paltz (845-255-1377; www.cyclepathny.com/adair.htm). Apr–Dec 11am–6pm. AmEx, MC, V.
Sip a sample from this 15-year-old vineyard's lengthy list in the barn tasting room, or take your tipple down by a local stream.

Applewood Winery

82 Four Corners Rd, Warwick (914-986-1684; www.applewoodorchardsandwinery.com). May–Nov Sat, Sun noon–5pm. MC, V.
Fruit wines are the speciality at Applewood, a 120-acre farm that dates back to the 1700s.

Baldwin Vineyards

176 Hardenburgh Rd, Pine Bush (845-744-2226; www.daspin.com/baldwin). Apr–Oct 11am–5:30pm; Nov–Mar Fri–Mon 11:30am–5pm. Disc, MC, V.
Strawberry wine is one of the sweet treats at this winery. There are also apple, cherry and raspberry varietals.

Brimstone Hill Vineyard

61 Brimstone Hill Rd, Pine Bush (845-744-2231). Jan–Apr Sat, Sun 11:30am–5:30pm; Jul–Oct 11:30am–5:30pm; Nov, Dec, May, Jun Mon, Fri–Sun 11:30am–5:30pm. AmEx, Disc, MC, V.
The pinot noir is recommended at this cottage industry, operated out of a garage by two tweedy college professors.

Brotherhood, America's Oldest Winery

100 Brotherhood Plaza, Washingtonville (845-496-9101; www.wines.com/brotherhood). May–Oct Sat, Sun 11am–5pm; Nov–Apr 11am–5pm. AmEx, MC, V.
Brotherhood's other claim to fame is that it skirted Prohibition by claiming that all of its wine was headed for the altar. Try the Rosario, a sangrialike red.

Demarest Hill Winery

81 Pine Island Tpke, Warwick (845-986-4723; www.demaresthillwinery.com). Jun–Oct 11am–6pm; Nov–May 11am–5pm. AmEx, MC, V.
A range of fine reds and whites are available at this winery, which comprises 137 lovely hilltop acres.

Trips Out of Town

benefit bash to benefit bash throughout the summer season, while the locals grimace and bear the vainglorious invasion. In summer 2001, the friction between locals and city slickers became a full-on firestorm when Lizzie Grubman, public-relations princess to the stars, allegedly rammed her father's SUV (of course) into a popular nightclub after an altercation with the doorman. At press time, she was facing multiple felony indictments.

Despite the dust-up, sightseers can still admire the sun-drenched beachfront and superstar estates—Steven Spielberg's palace in East Hampton, for example. For an up-to-date social calendar, pick up the free local rags

Dan's Paper or *Hamptons Country Magazine*, available at retail stores around town. For local news and what remains of "down-home wisdom," the *East Hampton Star* can't be beat.

After Memorial Day, the beaches of **East Hampton** attract celebs looking for rest and relaxation. Still, don't be surprised by the pervasive presence of cell phones and laptops on the beach. **Two-Mile Hollow Beach** is where you might spot the likes of Calvin Klein catching rays.

When it comes to eating, the trends change frequently, but **Della Femina Restaurant** *(99 N Main St, 631-329-6666)* and **Nick and Toni's** *(136 N Main St, 631-324-3550)* are

New York's vinest A harvester at the Whitecliff Vineyard grapples with her grapes.

Rivendell Winery

714 Albany Post Rd, New Paltz (845-255-2494; www.rivendellwine.com). 10am–6pm. AmEx, MC, V.
Bob Ransom and his partner Susan Wine (no, *really*) also run Soho's Vintage New York wine store *(see page 224)*. Wines from around the state are sold at Vintage and Rivendell, along with a selection of cheeses. Picnics on the winery grounds are encouraged.

Warwick Valley Winery

114 Little York Rd, Warwick (914-258-4858; www.wvwinery.com). May–late Aug Sat, Sun 11am–6pm; late Aug–late Oct 11am–6pm;

late Oct–Dec Sat, Sun 11am–6pm. AmEx, MC, V.
Apple and grape wines are made here, and there's a country store, too, filled with gift baskets and Docs Draft, Warwick's hard cider.

Whitecliff Vineyard

331 McKinstry Rd, Gardiner (845-255-4613; www.whitecliffwine.com). May–Oct Thu, Fri, Sun noon–5pm; Sat 11:30am–6pm; May–Dec Sat, Sun noon–5pm. AmEx, MC, V.
The youngest of the region's wineries, Whitecliff opened in 1999 and was the first in the area to grow gamay noir grapes, which are used to create a wine similar to Beaujolais nouveau.

Recipe for success Many renowned chefs have studied at the Culinary Institute of America, on the banks of the mighty Hudson River in upstate New York.

old standbys that promise sophisticated contemporary food and at least one celebrity sighting per night. Keep your eyes peeled for Mr. Long Island, Billy Joel, enjoying a doughnut at **Dreesen's Excelsior Market** *(33 Newtown Ln, 631-324-0465)* or a baseball-capped Jerry Seinfeld strolling the town's tree- and people-lined streets. The **Mill House Inn** *(31 N Main St, 631-324-9766; www.millhouseinn.com)* is a comfortable, if uncomfortably priced, bed-and-breakfast in town.

Over the years, many great painters, including Willem de Kooning and Roy Lichtenstein, have kept studios in **Southampton**. Artists still call the town home—sculptor Larry Rivers among them. Today, the town is just as well known for its antiques shops, galleries…and nightclubs. If you're looking to spend money, wander down

Jobs Lane. If you want to shake your booty, the **Tavern** *(125 Tuckahoe Ln, 631-287-2125)*, **Conscience Point** *(1976 North Sea Rd, 631-204-0600)* and **Jet East** *(1181 North Sea Rd, 631-283-0808)* are beach-town versions of Manhattan's club scene, with VIP lounges, crowded dance floors and lots of pretty faces.

As the locals like to say, **Montauk** is "a drinking town with a fishing problem," and while the seaside village is technically part of the town of East Hampton, it has very little in common with its neighbors—and the locals like to keep their ruffian reputation intact. The **Montauk Point Lighthouse** is New York State's oldest (it was erected in 1795), and historical memorabilia are on display inside. You'll also find surf casters lined up on the rocks; it's one of the most famous surf-fishing spots in the country. In the "fishing village," diners frequent **Gosman's** *(Gosman's Dock, West Lake Dr, 631-668-5330)* or **Dave's** *(468 West Lake Dr, 631-668-9190)*. In town, there is the estimable **Shagwong** *(774 Main St, 631-669-3050)*. The **Montauket** *(88 Firestone Rd, 631-668-5992)* is where you'll find many locals stewing in their steamers, not to mention a beautiful sunset view over Fort Pond Bay.

Despite the down-market, fishing-village feel, rental cottages and hotels can still empty your wallet in the summer season. For the best rates, look for pre- and postseason deals. The **Royal Atlantic Beach Resort** *(South Edgemere St, 631-668-5103)* has family-style cottages set on the water. The **Memory Motel** *(692 Montauk Hwy, 631-668-2702)* was immortalized by the Rolling Stones in a song of the same name. The **Harborside** *(371 West Lake Dr, 631-668-2511)* is a good fishing-village option. From here, it's a short walk to the day boat **Lazybones** *(631-668-5671)*, where reasonably priced half-day fishing excursions are available.

East Hampton Chamber of Commerce

79A Main St, East Hampton, NY 11937 (631-324-0362; www.easthamptonchamber.com).

Montauk Chamber of Commerce

P.O. Box 5029, Montauk, NY 11954 (631-668-2428; www.montaukchamber.com).

Montauk Point Lighthouse

Montauk Pt, Rte 27, 631-668-2544.

Southampton Chamber of Commerce

76 Main St, Southampton, NY 11968 (631-283-0402; www.southamptonchamber.com).

www.ihamptons.com

A project by Hamptons maven Steven Gaines (who wrote the infamous Hamptons tell-all *Philistines at the Hedgerow*), this website has real estate sales and rental listings, services (cleaning, painting, etc.), the iHamptons Emporium (which sells locally made products), and a live cam on the Main Street of every Hamptons community.

GETTING THERE

Take the Montauk line of the LIRR to East Hampton, Southampton or Montauk *($10.25–$15.25)*. The **Hampton Jitney** *(212-936-0440, 631-283-4600, 800-936-0440; one-way $24; Tue–Thu; $15 for seniors and children under 12)* runs regular bus service between Manhattan and the Hamptons. By car, take the Long Island Expwy (I-495) east to Exit 70 (County Rd 111) south. Continue for three miles to Sunrise Hwy (Rte 27) eastbound.

The Hudson Valley

If you want to take in a magical history tour or lush scenery, the **Hudson Valley** in upstate New York will thrill you. The breathtaking summer residences of such famous New York historical figures as John D. Rockefeller Jr. and Franklin D. Roosevelt dot the Hudson River. Most of these sites are maintained by the **Historic Hudson Valley** society and are open to the public for much of the year. The trip to and from the Hudson Valley can be made in a day, but if you have the time, linger a while at a cozy inn and enjoy the area's restaurants, many of which feature the valley's fresh bounty. Metro-North frequently offers discounted rates to the region, and **New York Waterway**, in conjunction with Historic Hudson Valley, runs cruises from Manhattan and New Jersey to several of the grand houses. Wine lovers should plan a trip to a winery or two, see **Wines along the Hudson**, page 352.

Putnam County

Any time of the year, **Cold Spring** is a haven of peace and quiet, and the stunning view from the banks of the Hudson spans the Shawangunk Mountains across the river. The town is only 50 miles (80km) from Manhattan, but light-years away culturally. The best place to crash is the 1832 **Hudson House** *(2 Main St, 845-265-9355; www.hudsonhouseinn.com)*, a peaceful, convenient inn with an excellent contemporary American restaurant. From the inn, follow Main Street into the heart of town, where a number of narrow-frame houses with airy porches and shutters sit alongside the four-story commercial buildings. The tiny town is chock-full of antiques shops, and the popular **Foundry Café** *(55 Main St, 845-265-4504)* serves pastries, salads and sandwiches.

Just a mile away is the town of **Garrison**, where you'll find the **Boscobel Restoration**, a Federal-style mansion built in 1804 by States Morris Dyckman, a wealthy British loyalist.

Boscobel Restoration

1601 Rte 9D, Garrison, NY (845-265-3638; www.boscobel.org). Apr–Oct Mon, Wed–Sun 9:30am–5pm; Nov, Dec Wed–Sun 9:30am–4pm. $8, seniors $7, children 6–14 $5, children under 6 free. Disc, MC, V.

Putnam Visitors Bureau, Cold Spring

110 Old Route 6, building 3, Carmel, NY 10512 (845-225-0381, 800-470-4854; www.visitputnam.org).

About 15 miles north of Garrison is the definitive Hudson Valley estate: **Springwood**, Franklin D. Roosevelt's boyhood home, in **Hyde Park**. The great New Dealer and his iconoclast wife, Eleanor, moved back to Springwood in his later years. The house is just as Roosevelt left it when he died in 1945, filled with family photos and the former president's collections, including one of nautical instruments. In the nearby FDR Library and Museum, you can examine such items as presidential documents and FDR's pony cart. Also in Hyde Park is the **Culinary Institute of America**, whose illustrious alumni include Manhattan celebrity chef and Hudson Valley forager Larry Forgione *(An American Place, 212-888-5650)*. CIA's chefs-in-training prepare French, Italian, American contemporary and American regional cuisine in four different dining rooms. The **Apple Pie Bakery Café** is stocked with baked goods made by pastry majors.

Like many of the valley's towns, Hyde Park has several antiques shops—the **Village Antiques Center** *(4321 Albany Post Rd, 845-229-6600)* and the **Hyde Park Antique Center** *(4192 Albany Post Rd, 845-229-8200)* represent 75 dealers between them. A good place to rest after all of these activities is **Fala House**, a private one-bedroom guest house with a pool—call ahead for reservations *(East Market St, 845-229-5937)*.

Another ten miles north, beyond the reach of Metro-North, is the town of **Rhinebeck**, cherished by history buffs. **Wilderstein**, an 1852 Italianate villa, was rebuilt in Queen Anne style in 1888. The town also boasts the nation's oldest continuously operating hotel, the **Beekman Arms** *(6387 Mill St, 845-876-7077, 800-361-6517; www.beekmanarms.com)*, which is about 300 years old. The Beekman may be historic, but the kitchen is nothing if not of-the-moment. Chef Larry Forgione took over the inn's **Beekman 1766 Tavern** *(845-871-1766)* in 1991, updating the menu with such dishes as roasted Adirondack duck. When you're done eating, check out **Beekman Arms Antique Market and Gallery** *(845-876-3477)*, in a converted barn just steps away. The **Old Rhinebeck Aerodrome**, which houses three hangars' worth of aviation history, hosts weekly air shows on Saturdays and Sundays from 2 to 4pm. You can also ride in a biplane.

Bear Mountain State Park

Palisades Parkway and Rte 9W (914-786-2701). Travel: Short Line Buses from Port Authority bus terminal (212-736-4700).
Hiking can be found across the river in Orange County. The bus will drop you off at a visitors' center that has hundreds of families picnicking on fast food in the parking lot. A quick walk into the wilderness will take you away from it all—there are 66 miles of hiking, biking and cross-country ski trails.

Culinary Institute of America

1946 Campus Dr, Hyde Park, NY (845-471-6608; www.ciachef.edu). AmEx, DC, Disc, MC, V.
Dress to impress here. Reservations are required.

Dutchess County Tourism, Rhinebeck and Hyde Park

3 Neptune Rd, Poughkeepsie, NY 12601 (845-463-4000).

Historic Hudson Valley

150 White Plains Rd, Tarrytown, NY 10591 (914-631-8200; www.hudsonvalley.org).
This historical society maintains several mansions in the area, including John D. Rockefeller Jr.'s **Kykuit**, pronounced "KAI-kut" *(914-631-9491; Apr–Nov; $20, seniors $19, children $17)* and Washington Irving's **Sunnyside** *(914-591-8763; Mar–Dec; $8, seniors $7, children 5–17 $4)*, as well as **Philipsburg Manor** *(914-631-3992; Mar–Dec; $8, seniors $7, children 5–17 $4)*, **Van Cortlandt Manor** *(914-271-8981; Apr–Dec; $8, seniors $7, children 5–17 $4)* and **Montgomery Place** *(845-758-5461; Apr–Dec; $6, seniors $5, children 6–17 $3)*.

Hudson River Heritage

P.O. Box 287, Rhinebeck, NY 12572 (845-876-2474).
This organization is a good resource for anyone interested in the history of the Hudson Valley.

Old Rhinebeck Aerodrome

At Norton and Stone Church Rds, Rhinebeck, NY, off Rte 9 (845-758-8610; www.oldrhinebeck.org). Jun–Oct. $10, children 6–10 $5. Disc, MC, V.

Springwood

U.S. 9, Hyde Park, NY (845-229-2501; www.nps.gov/ hofr). 9am–5pm. $10, under 17 free. MC, V.

Wilderstein

330 Morton Rd, Rhinebeck, NY (845-876-4818). May– Oct Thu–Sun noon–4pm; Thanksgiving weekend–Dec Fri–Sun 1–4pm. $5.

GETTING THERE

Ask about special package rates from **New York Waterway** *(800-53-FERRY)*. Metro-North runs many trains daily to the Hudson Valley *($7.75–$13)*. Unfortunately, the line ends at Poughkeepsie, a 20-minute taxi ride from Rhinebeck (you can also take **Amtrak**, which is more expensive; *see page 359*). **Short Line Buses** *(212-736-4700, 800-631-8405; www.shortlinebus.com; $25.75 round-trip)* also runs regular bus service to Rhinebeck and Hyde Park. By car, take the Saw Mill River Pkwy to the Taconic Pkwy north. For Cold Spring, take Rte 301 west. For Rhinebeck and Hyde Park, take I-84 west, then Rte 9 north.

Directory

Getting to and from NYC	358
Getting Around	361
Resources A to Z	364
Further Reference	379
Index	381
Advertisers' Index	390

Feature boxes

Weather or not	359
Holidays	363
Toilet talk	369
Websites	379
Hot off the press	380

Volume discount Careful reading can save you time and money in New York City.

Directory

These indispensable tips will help you conquer the Naked City

Getting to and from NYC

By air

There are three major airports servicing the New York City area, plus one in Long Island; for details, see page 360. Here are some sources for purchasing airline tickets.

Internet

A few sites to investigate for low fares are **www.airfare.com**, **www.cheaptickets.com**, **www.expedia.com**, **www.travelocity.com** and **www.orbitz.com**.

Newspapers

The best place to get an idea of available fares is the travel section of your local paper. If that's no help, get a Sunday *New York Times*. It usually has plenty of advertisements for discounted fares.

Satellite Airlines Terminal

125 Park Ave between 41st and 42nd Sts (for information 212-986-0888). Subway: S, 4, 5, 6, 7 to 42nd St–Grand Central. Mon–Fri 8am–7pm; Sat 9am–5pm.
Satellite is a one-stop shop for travelers. Major international airlines have ticket counters here. You can exchange frequent-flyer mileage; process passports, birth certificates and driver's licenses; and arrange for transportation and city tours. There are no direct telephone numbers to the centers, so call the carriers individually or the information line listed.
Other locations ● 555 Seventh Ave between 39th and 40th Sts. Subway: N, Q, R, W, S, 1, 2, 3, 7 to 42nd St–Times Sq.● *1 E 59th St at Fifth Ave. Subway: N, R, W to Fifth Ave–60th St.* ● *1843 Broadway at 60th St. Subway: A, C, B, D, 1, 2 to 59th St–Columbus Circle.*

Travel agents

Agents are specialized, so find one who suits your needs. Do you want adventure? Budget? Consolidator? Business? Luxury? Round the world? Student? *(See* **Students**, *page 375).*

Find an agent through word of mouth, newspapers, the yellow pages or the Internet. Knowledgeable travel agents can help you with far more than air tickets, and a good relationship with an agent can be invaluable, especially if you don't like to deal with travel details.

By bus

Buses are an inexpensive means of getting to and from New York City, though the ride is longer and sometimes uncomfortable. They are particularly useful if you want to leave in a hurry, since many bus companies don't require reservations. Most out-of-town buses come and go from the **Port Authority Bus Terminal**.

Bus lines

Greyhound Trailways

800-231-2222; www.greyhound.com. Buses depart 24 hrs. AmEx, Disc, MC, V.
Greyhound offers long-distance bus travel to destinations across North America.

New Jersey Transit

973-762-5100 (6am–midnight); www.njtransit.com. AmEx, MC, V.
NJT provides bus service to most everywhere in the Garden State; buses run around the clock.

Peter Pan

800-343-9999 (6am–midnight); www.peterpanbus.com. Buses depart 24 hrs. AmEx, Disc, MC, V.
Peter Pan runs extensive service to cities across the Northeast, and its tickets are also valid on Greyhound.

Bus stations

George Washington Bridge Bus Station

178th St between Broadway and Fort Washington Ave (bus information

800-221-9903). Subway: A to 175th St; 1 to 181st St.
A few bus lines that serve New Jersey and Rockland County, New York, use this station from 5am to 1am.

Port Authority Bus Terminal

625 Eighth Ave between 40th and 42nd Sts (212-564-8484). Subway: A, C, E to 42nd St–Port Authority.
Many transportation companies serve New York City's commuter and long-distance bus travelers. Call for additional information.

By car

Driving to and from the city can be scenic and fun. However, due to the World Trade Center disaster, you may encounter restrictions at bridges and tunnels (check the sites **www.panynj.gov** and **www.nyc.gov** before driving in). While you're on the road, tune in to **1010 WINS** on the AM dial for up-to-the-minute traffic reports. Expect delays of 15 minutes to 2 hours—plenty of time to get your money out for the toll (they average $5). Note that street parking is very restricted, especially in the summer *(see* **Parking**, *page 361).*

Car rental

If you are interested in heading out of town by auto, car rental is much cheaper on the city's outskirts and in New Jersey and Connecticut; reserve ahead for weekends. New York State honors valid foreign-issued driver's licenses. All car-rental companies listed below add sales tax. Companies located outside of New York State offer a "loss damage waiver" (LDW). This is expensive—almost as much as the rental itself—but without it you are responsible for the cost of repairing even the slightest scratch. If you pay with an AmEx card or a gold Visa or MasterCard, the LDW may be covered by the credit-card company; it might also be covered by a reciprocal agreement with an automotive organization. Personal liability insurance is optional—and recommended (but see if your travel insurance or home policy already covers it). Rental companies in New York are required by law to insure their own cars, so the LDW is not a factor. Instead, the renter is responsible for the first $100 in damage to the vehicle, and the company is accountable for anything beyond that. You will need a credit card (or a large cash deposit) to rent a car, and usually have to be over age 25. If you know you want to rent a car before you travel, ask your travel agent or airline if they can offer any good deals.

Avis
800-331-1212; www.avis.com. 24 hrs. Rates from $70 a day, unlimited mileage. AmEx, DC, Disc, MC, V.

Budget Rent-a-Car
212-807-8700; 800-BUDGET7; www.drivebudget.com. In the city, call for hours; at the airports 5am–2am. Rates from $30 per weekday, $50 per day on weekends, unlimited mileage. AmEx, DC, Disc, MC, V.

Enterprise
800-325-8007; www.enterprise.com. Mon–Fri 7:30am–6pm; Sat 9am–noon. Rates starting from $35 a day outside New York City; around $45 a day in New York City; unlimited mileage restricted to New York, New Jersey and Connecticut. AmEx, DC, Disc, MC, V.
We recommend this inexpensive and reliable service, which has branches that are easily accessible from Manhattan. Try either the Hoboken, New Jersey, location (take the PATH train from 33rd St) or Greenwich, Connecticut (Metro-North from Grand Central). Agents will pick you up at the station. Call for locations within the five boroughs.

Parking

If you drive to NYC, find a garage, park your car and leave it there. Parking on the street is subject to byzantine restrictions (for information on alternate-side-of-the-street parking, call 212-225-5368), ticketing is rampant, and car theft is common. Parking in the outer boroughs is a bit easier, though many restrictions still apply, so if you can't understand the parking signs, find another spot. Garages are plentiful but expensive. If you want to park for less than $15 a day, try a garage outside Manhattan and take public transportation in. Listed below are the best deals in Manhattan. For other options—and there are many—try the yellow pages. *(See also Driving, page 361).*

GMC Park Plaza
407 E 61st St between First and York Aves (212-838-4158; main office 212-888-7400). 7am–2am.

GMC has more than 60 locations in the city; at $22 overnight, including tax, this location is the least expensive.

Kinney System Inc.
212-502-5490.
One of the city's largest parking companies is accessible and reliable, though not the cheapest in town. Rates vary, so call for prices at your location of choice.

Mayor Parking
West St at Houston St, Pier 40 (800-494-7007). 24 hrs.
Mayor Parking offers indoor and outdoor parking. Call for information.

By train

Thanks to Americans' love affair with the automobile, passenger trains are not as common here as in other parts of the world; American rails are used primarily for cargo, and passenger trains from New York are used mostly by commuters. For longer hauls, call **Amtrak**. (*See also chapter* **Trips Out of Town**.)

Weather or not
Rain or shine, New York City is mighty fine

Here are the average high and low temperatures, number of days with precipitation, and the number of sunny days in NYC by month—but remember, there's *always* something to do indoors when it's too nasty to wander around outside.

	Temperature		Rain/Snow	Sun
	Hi °F/°C	Low °F/°C	Days	Days
Jan	37/2	26/-3	11	8
Feb	39/4	27/-2	9	8
Mar	48/9	35/1	11	8
Apr	59/15	44/6	11	8
May	70/21	54/12	11	7
Jun	79/26	63/17	10	8
Jul	84/28	69/20	9	7
Aug	82/27	68/20	9	8
Sep	75/23	61/16	8	10
Oct	64/17	51/10	8	11
Nov	53/11	42/5	10	7
Dec	42/5	31/0	11	8

Source: National Weather Service

Directory

Train service

Amtrak

800-872-7245; www.amtrak.com.
Amtrak provides all long-distance
train service in North America.
Train travel is more comfortable
than busing it, but it's also more
expensive (a sleeper costs more than
flying) and less flexible. All trains
depart from Penn Station.

Long Island Rail Road

718-217-5477; www.lirr.org.
LIRR provides rail service to Long
Island from Penn Station, Brooklyn
and Queens.

Metro-North

*212-532-4900, 800-638-7646;
www.mnr.org.*
Trains leave from Grand Central and
service towns north of Manhattan.

New Jersey Transit

973-762-5100; www.njtransit.com.
Trains based at Penn Station service
New Jersey commuters.

PATH Trains

800-234-7284; www.pathrail.com.
PATH (Port Authority Trans
Hudson) trains run from five
stations in Manhattan to various
places across the Hudson River in
New Jersey, including Hoboken,
Jersey City and Newark. (The World
Trade Center station was destroyed
in the September 2001 attack and is
closed indefinitely; at press time,
supplemental service plans were
being developed.) The system is
fully automated and costs $1.50
per trip. You need change or crisp
bills for the ticket machines,
and trains run 24 hours a day.
Manhattan PATH stations are
marked on the subway map (*see
pages 409–411*).

Train stations

Grand Central Terminal

*42nd–44th Sts between Vanderbilt
and Lexington Aves. Subway: S, 4, 5,
6, 7 to 42nd St–Grand Central.*
Grand Central is home to Metro-
North, which runs trains to more
than 100 stations throughout New
York State and Connecticut. (*See
chapter* **Trips Out of Town**.)

Penn Station

*31st–33rd Sts between Seventh and
Eighth Aves. Subway: A, C, E, 1,
2, 3 to 34th St–Penn Station.*
Amtrak, Long Island Rail Road and
New Jersey Transit trains depart
from this terminal.

To and from the airport

For a list of transportation
services between New York
City and its three airports,
call **800-AIR-RIDE**
(800-247-7433). Public
transportation is the cheapest
method, but the routes can
be frustrating and time-
consuming. Private bus
services are usually the best
budget option. Medallion
(city-licensed) cabs from the
New York airports line up at
designated locations. You can
also reserve a car service in
advance to pick you up or
drop you off (*see* **Taxis
& car services**, *page 362*).
Although it is illegal, many
car-service drivers
and nonlicensed "gypsy
cabs" solicit riders around
the baggage-claim areas.
Avoid them.

Airports

John F. Kennedy International Airport

718-244-4444; www.panynj.gov.
There's a subway link from JFK
(extremely cheap at $1.50), but it
can take up to two hours to get to
Manhattan. Wait for a yellow shuttle
bus to the Howard Beach station
and take the A train to Manhattan.
(Currently, a light rail system called
AirTrain is under construction and
will eventually link the subway with
all terminals.) A private bus service
is a more pleasant and affordable
option (*see listings below*). A
medallion yellow cab from JFK to
Manhattan is a flat $35 fare, plus toll
(depending on route, but usually
$3.50) and tip (if service is fair, give
at least $5). Be advised that this rate
is likely to go up sometime in 2002, to
$49. There is no set fare to JFK from
Manhattan; depending on traffic, it
can be as high as $45. Or try a car
service for around $40.

La Guardia Airport

718-476-5000; www.panynj.gov.
Seasoned New Yorkers take the
M60 bus ($1.50), which runs
between the airport and 106th
Street at Broadway. The ride takes
20 to 40 minutes (depending on
traffic) and runs from 5am to 1am.

The route crosses Manhattan on
125th Street in Harlem; you can
get off at Lexington Avenue for
the 4, 5 and 6 trains; at Malcolm X
Boulevard (Lenox Avenue) for the
2 and 3; or at St. Nicholas Avenue
for the A, C, B and D trains. You
can also disembark on Broadway
at the 116th Street–Columbia
University or 110th Street–
Cathedral Parkway subway
stations for the 1 train. Other
less-time consuming options:
Private bus services cost around
$14 (*see listings below*); taxis or
car services charge about $25 plus
toll and tip.

Newark Airport

973-961-6000; www.panynj.gov.
Though it's a bit far afield, Newark
isn't difficult to get to or from.
The best option is a 40-minute
trip by train and monorail
(*www.airtrainnewark.com*). In
the fall of 2001, the Port Authority
completed a $400 million link that
connects the airport's free monorail,
AirTrain, to the New Jersey Transit
train system. For $11.15, you can
ride to or from Penn Station (*see
above*). Another economical way to
the airport is by bus (*see listings
below*). A car service will run about
$40 and a taxi around $45, plus
tolls and tip.

MacArthur Airport

*631-467-3210; www.macarthur
airport.com.*
This airport is located in Islip on
Long Island. Some flights into this
airport may be cheaper than flying
into those above. Getting to
Manhattan, of course, will take
longer and is more expensive.
Colonial Transportation *(631-589-
3500)* will take four people to
Manhattan for $100, plus tolls and
tip. Visit the airport's website for
other options.

Bus services

Express Shuttle USA/Gray Line

*212-315-3006; 800-451-0455;
www.graylinenewyork.com.*
A minibus service runs from each
of the three area airports to any
address in midtown (from 23rd to
63rd Streets) from early morning
to late at night. On the outbound
journey, the shuttle picks up at
several hotels (you must book in
advance). Fares range from $13
(to Manhattan from La Guardia)
to $19 (from Manhattan to JFK
or Newark).

New York Airport Service

212-875-8200; www.nyairport service.com.

This service operates frequently to and from JFK ($13 one-way, $23 round-trip) and La Guardia ($10 one-way, $17 round-trip) from early morning to late at night, with stops near Grand Central Terminal *(Park Ave between 41st and 42nd Sts)*, near Penn Station *(33rd St at Seventh Ave)*, inside the Port

Authority terminal *(see By bus, page 358)* and outside a number of midtown hotels (for an extra charge).

Olympia Trails

212-964-6233; 877-894-9155; www.olympiabus.com.

Olympia operates between the following: Newark Airport, outside Penn Station *(34th St at Eighth Ave)*, Grand Central Terminal *(41st St between Park and Lexington Aves)* and inside Port Authority *(see page 358)*. The fare is $11 one-way

($21 round-trip) and buses leave every 15 to 20 minutes all day and night.

SuperShuttle

212-258-3826; www.supershuttle.com.

Blue SuperShuttle vans offer 24-hour door-to-door service between NYC and the three airports. Allow extra time when catching a flight, as vans will be picking up other passengers. The fare is $19.50 to airports, $14.50 from airports (exclusive service is $75).

Getting Around

Under normal circumstances, New York City is easy to navigate. However, in light of the terrorist attacks on the World Trade Center and long-term bridge and tunnel reconstruction, subway service in lower Manhattan changes frequently and with short notice, which in turn affects the entire system. Pay attention to service changes posted in stations and listen carefully to any announcements you may hear in trains and on subway platforms. Also, due to heightened security at all Hudson and East River crossings, vehicles entering the city are subject to police search, and noncommercial single-occupant vehicles are prohibited from entering lower Manhattan during certain times of the day, perhaps until fall of 2002. Take mass transit whenever possible and always allow yourself extra time to get to your destination.

Metropolitan Transportation Authority (MTA)

718-330-1234; www.mta.nyc.ny.us.

The MTA runs the subways and buses, as well as a number of commuter services to points outside Manhattan. You can download the most current maps from its website.

MTA buses are fine, but only if you aren't in a hurry. If

your feet hurt from walking around, a bus is a good way to continue your sightseeing. They're white and blue with a route number (in Manhattan, look for the ones that begin with an "M") and a digital destination sign. The fare is $1.50, payable either with a token or **MetroCard** *(see **Subways**, page 362)* or in exact change (silver coins only). Express buses usually head to the outer boroughs; these cost $3.

MetroCards allow automatic transfers from bus to bus and between buses and subways. If you use a token or coins and you're traveling uptown or downtown and want to catch a crosstown bus (or vice versa), ask the driver for a transfer when you get on—you'll be given a ticket for use on the second leg of your journey. You can rely on other passengers for advice, but maps are posted on most buses and at all subway stations; they're also available from **NYC & Company** *(see **Tourist information**, page 378)*. The Manhattan Bus Map is reprinted in this guide, see page 408. Buses make only designated stops, but between 10pm and 5am you can ask the driver to stop anywhere along the route. All buses are equipped with wheelchair lifts. Contact the MTA *(see above)* for further information.

Driving

Manhattan drivers are fearless, and taking to the streets is not for the faint of heart. If you're going to be tooling around the city, try to restrict your driving to evening hours, when traffic is lighter and on-street parking is available. Even then, keep your eyes on the road and stay alert. New York will honor all valid foreign driver's licenses.

Parking

Don't ever park within 15 feet (5 meters) of a fire hydrant, and make sure you read the parking signs. Unless there is metered parking, most streets have alternate-side-of-the-street parking—i.e., each side is off-limits for certain hours every other day. The **New York City Department of Transportation** *(212-225-5368)* provides information on daily changes to parking regulations. If precautions fail, call 212-971-0770 for car towing and impoundment information. *(See also **Parking**, page 359.)*

Towing

Citywide Towing

514 W 39th St between Tenth and Eleventh Aves (212-924-8104). 24 hrs. Repairs 8am–6pm. AmEx, MC, V. All types of repairs are done on foreign and domestic autos.

24-hour gas stations

Amoco
610 Broadway at Houston St (212-473-5924). AmEx, DC, Disc, MC, V.
No repairs.

Hess
502 W 45th St at Tenth Ave (212-245-6594). AmEx, Disc, MC, V.
No repairs.

Shell
2420 Amsterdam Ave at 181st St (212-928-3100). AmEx, Disc, MC, V.
Repairs.

Subways

Subways are the fastest way to get around town during the day, and despite their dangerous, dirty reputation, they're cleaner and safer than they've been in 20 years. The city's system is one of the world's largest and cheapest—$1.50 will get you from the depths of Brooklyn to the northernmost reaches of the Bronx, and anywhere in between. Trains run around the clock, but with sparse service and fewer riders at night, it's advisable (and usually quicker) to take a cab after 10pm.

Several routes in lower Manhattan were affected by the WTC catastrophe, so be aware of service notices posted in stations and on platforms. You can also ask MTA workers in token booths for a map; this guide has the most current one at press time *(see pages 409–411)*. In addition, ongoing system improvements have resulted in several changes. New high-tech subway trains began running in summer 2000 and will eventually replace all of the '60s-era "Red Bird" trains seen mainly on the 1, 2, 3, 4, 5, 6 and 7 lines. Because of long-term Manhattan Bridge repair work, two new subway lines—the V and the W—were recently added, and changes occurred to the B, D and Q trains (in Manhattan, these are

the orange lines along Sixth Avenue and the yellow ones along Broadway).

To ensure safety, don't stand too close to the edge of the platform, and board the train during nonrush hours from the off-peak waiting area, marked at the center of every platform (this area is safer because it's monitored by cameras; it's also where the conductor's car often stops). More advice: Hold your bag with the opening facing you, and don't wear flashy jewelry.

MetroCards & tokens

Entry to the system requires a MetroCard or a token costing $1.50 (both also work on buses), which you can buy from a booth inside the station entrance. Many stations are equipped with brightly colored MetroCard vending machines that accept cash, debit cards and credit cards *(AmEx, Disc, MC, V)*.

If you're planning to use the subway (or buses) a lot, it's worth buying a MetroCard, which is also available at some stores and hotels. Free transfers between subways and buses are available only with the MetroCard. There are two types: **pay-per-use cards** and **unlimited-ride cards**. Any number of passengers can use the pay-per-use cards, which start at $3 for two trips and run as high as $80. A $15 card offers 11 trips for the price of 10. The unlimited-ride MetroCard (an incredible value for frequent users) is offered in three amounts: a 1-day **Fun Pass** ($4, available at station vending machines but not at booths), a **7-day pass** ($17) and a **30-day pass** ($63). These are good for unlimited rides on the subway or buses but can only be used once every 18 minutes (so only one person can use the card at a time).

Subway lines

Trains are known by letters or numbers and are color-coded according to the line on which they run. Stations are named after the street at which they're located. Entrances are marked with a green globe (a red globe marks an entrance that is not always open). Many stations (and most of the local stops) have separate entrances to the uptown and downtown platforms—look before you pay *(see **Walking**, page 363, for an explanation of the city's streets)*. Express trains run between major stops; local trains stop at every station. Check a subway map (posted in all stations; *see also pages 409–411*) before you board. Be sure to look for posted notices indicating temporary changes to a particular line.

Taxis & car services

Taxicabs

Yellow cabs are hardly ever in short supply—except in the rain and at around 4 or 5pm, when rush hour gets going and many cabbies—annoyingly—end their shifts. If the center light on top of the taxi is lit, it means the cab is available and should stop if you flag it down. Jump in and *then* tell the driver where you're going (New Yorkers give cross streets, not building numbers).

Taxis carry up to four people for the same price: $2 plus 30¢ per fifth of a mile, with an extra 50¢ charge after 8pm. This makes the average fare for a three-mile (4.5km) ride $5 to $7, depending on traffic and time of day. Keep in mind that these rates are likely to increase by nearly 25 percent, sometime in 2002. Cabbies rarely allow more than four passengers in a cab (it's illegal), though it may be worth asking. Smoking in cabs is prohibited, but some cabbies won't object.

Some cabbies' knowledge of the further reaches of the city is lamentably meager, so it helps if you know where you're going—and speak up. By law, taxis cannot refuse to take you anywhere inside the city limits (the five boroughs), so don't be duped by a cabbie who is too lazy to drive you to Brooklyn or the airport. In general, tip a buck; if the fare is high, 15 percent. If you have a problem, take down the medallion number and driver's number that are posted on the partition. Or ask for a receipt—there's a meter number on it. To complain or trace lost property, call the **Taxi and Limousine Commission** *(212-692-8294, Mon–Fri 9am–5pm)*.

Late at night, cabbies stick to fast-flowing routes and reliably lucrative areas. Try the avenues and key streets (Canal, Houston, 14th, 23rd, 34th, 42nd, 57th, 86th). Bridge and tunnel exits are also good for a steady flow from the airports, and passengerless cabbies will usually head for nightclubs and big hotels. Otherwise, try the following:

Chinatown

Chatham Square, where Mott St meets the Bowery, is an unofficial taxi stand. You can also try hailing a cab exiting the Manhattan Bridge at the Bowery and Canal St.

Lincoln Center

The crowd heads toward Columbus Circle for a cab; those in the know go to Amsterdam Ave.

Lower East Side

Katz's Deli *(Houston St at Ludlow St)* is a cabbies' hangout; otherwise, try Delancey St, where cabs come in over the Williamsburg Bridge.

Midtown

Penn Station and Grand Central Terminal attract cabs through the night, as does the Port Authority Bus Terminal *(Eighth Ave between 40th and 42nd Sts)*.

Soho

If you're on the west side, try Sixth

Ave; east side, the gas station on Houston St at Broadway.

Times Square

This busy area has 30 taxi stands—look for the yellow globes atop nine-foot poles.

Tribeca

Cabs here (many arriving from the Holland Tunnel) head up Hudson St. Canal St is also a good bet.

Car services

Car services are also regulated by the Taxi and Limousine Commission *(see above)*. What makes them different from a cab is that they aren't yellow and they can only offer prearranged pick-ups. Don't try to hail them and be wary of those that offer you a ride; they may not be licensed or insured and you might get ripped off. (If you see a black Lincoln Town Car, most likely it's a car service; to be sure, look for a license plate that begins with the letter T.)

The following companies will pick you up anywhere in the city, at any time of day or night, for a prearranged fare.

Carmel
212-666-6666

Sabra
212-777-7171

Tel Aviv
212-777-7777

Tri-State Limousine
212-410-7600

Walking

One of the best ways to take in NYC is on foot. Most of the streets are part of a grid system and are relatively easy to navigate. Our maps *(see pages 396–403)* make it even easier. Manhattan is divided into three major sections: **downtown**, or all neighborhoods south of 14th Street; **midtown**, roughly the area from 14th to 59th Street; and **uptown**, or the rest of the island north of 59th Street.

Generally, avenues run along the length of Manhattan from south to north. They are parallel to one another and are logically numbered with a few exceptions (such as Broadway and Columbus and Lexington Avenues). Manhattan's center is Fifth Avenue, so all buildings located east of it will have "East" addresses, with numbers going higher toward the East River, and those west of it will have "West" numbers that go higher toward the Hudson River. Streets also run parallel to each other but they run east to west, or **crosstown**,

Holidays

Although most banks and government offices close on these major U.S. holidays (except Election Day), stores, restaurants and some museums are usually open. If you will be in New York around a holiday, call ahead to check special hours for the venues you want to visit.

New Year's Day
January 1

Martin Luther King Jr. Day
third Monday in January

Presidents' Day
third Monday in February

Memorial Day
last Monday in May

Independence Day
July 4

Labor Day
first Monday in September

Columbus Day
second Monday in October

Election Day
first Tuesday after first Monday in November

Veterans' Day
November 11

Thanksgiving Day
fourth Thursday in November

Christmas Day
December 25

Directory

and are numbered, beginning with 1st Street (a block north of East Houston Street), up to 220th Street. Almost all even-numbered streets run east and odd streets run west (the major crosstown streets, such as 42nd Street, are two-way).

The neighborhoods that define lower Manhattan—the **Financial District**, **Tribeca**, **Chinatown**, **Soho** and **Greenwich Village**—were settled prior to urban planning and can be confusing to walk through

(but it's worth the effort, because they have some of the nicest blocks). These streets lack logical organization, so it is best to use a map *(see pages 396 and 397)*, or to ask a passerby for directions.

Resources A to Z

Age restrictions

In most cases, you must be at least 25 years old to rent a car in the U.S. You must be 18 to buy tobacco products and 21 to buy and be served alcohol. Some bars and clubs will allow admittance to patrons who are at least 18, but you will be removed from the establishment if you are caught drinking alcohol (carry a picture ID at all times to guarantee entrance). The age of consent for both heterosexuals and homosexuals is 17. You must be 18 to purchase pornography and other adult material, and also to play the lottery or gamble (where the law allows).

Baby-sitting

Babysitters' Guild
212-682-0227;
www.babysittersguild. 9am–9pm.
Cash or traveler's checks.
Long or short-term multilingual baby-sitters (four-hour minimum) cost $15 and up per hour.

Avalon Nurse Registry & Child Service
212-245-0250. Mon–Fri 8am–5:30pm; Sat, Sun 9am–8pm. AmEx, MC, V.
Avalon provides baby nurses and sitters (four-hour minimum) for between $16 and $20 per hour, plus travel expenses.

Manhattan Tree House
148 W 83rd St between Central Park West and Columbus Ave (212-712-0113). Subway: B, C to 81st St–Museum of Natural History. 9am–6pm.
Kids ages 6 months and up can have a night out at this drop-off center, which offers dinner and snacks,

movies, face-painting and the like ($38 for three hours and $52 for five).

Pinch Sitters
212-260-6005. Mon–Fri 7am–5pm.
Charges are $14 (four-hour minimum) plus travel expenses after 9pm.

Computers

There are hundreds of computer dealers in Manhattan You might want to buy out of state to avoid the hefty sales tax. Many out-of-state dealers advertise in New York papers and magazines. *(See also* **Cameras & electronics,** *page 219).* Here are reliable places if you're just looking to rent:

Kinko's
240 Central Park South at Broadway (212-258-3750; 800-2-KINKOS). Subway: A, C, B, D, 1, 2 to 59th St–Columbus Circle. 24 hrs. AmEx, Disc, MC, V.
This is a very efficient and friendly place to use computers and copiers. Most branches have Windows and Macintosh workstations and design stations, plus all the major software. Color output is available, as are laptop hookups and Internet connections ($18 per hour, 49¢ per printed page). Check the phone book for other locations.

Fitch Graphics
25 W 45th St between Fifth and Sixth Aves (212-840-3091). Subway: B, D, F, V to 42nd St; 7 to Fifth Ave. Mon–Fri 7:30am–2am. AmEx, MC, V.
Fitch is a full-service desktop-publishing outfit, with color-laser output and prepress facilities. Fitch works on Mac and Windows platforms and has a bulletin board so customers can reach the shop online.

USRental.com
212-594-2222; www.usrental.com. Mon–Fri 8:30am–5pm. Call for appointment. AmEx, MC, V.

Rent by the day, week, month or year. A range of computers, systems and networks, including IBM, Compaq, Macintosh and Hewlett-Packard, is on hand. Rush delivery service (within three hours) is also available.

Consulates

Check the phone book for a complete list of consulates and embassies.

Australia
212-351-6500

Canada
212-596-1700

Great Britain
212-745-0200

Ireland
212-319-2555

New Zealand
212-832-4038

Consumer information

Better Business Bureau
212-533-6200; www.newyork.bbb.org
The BBB offers advice on consumer-related complaints (shopping, services, etc.). Each phone inquiry costs $4.30 (including New York City tax) and must be charged to a credit card; the online version is free.

New York City Department of Consumer Affairs
42 Broadway between Beaver St and Exchange Pl (212-487-4444). Subway: 4, 5 to Bowling Green. Mon–Fri 9:30am–4:30pm.
This is where you go to file complaints on consumer-related matters.

Customs & immigration

When planning your trip, check with a U.S. embassy or consulate to see if you need a visa to enter the country *(see* **Visas**, *page 378).* Standard immigration regulations apply to all visitors arriving from outside the United States, which means you may have to wait at least an hour in customs upon arrival, and due to tightened security at all American airports, expect even slower-moving lines. During your flight, you will be handed an immigration form and a customs declaration form to be presented to an official when you land.

You may be expected to explain your visit, so be polite and prepared. You will usually be granted an entry permit to cover the length of your stay. Work permits are hard to get, and you are not permitted to work without one *(see* **Students**, *page 375).*

U.S. Customs allows foreigners to bring in $100 worth of gifts ($400 for Americans) before paying duty. One carton of 200 cigarettes (or 50 cigars) and one liter of liquor (spirits) are allowed. No plants, fruit, meat or fresh produce can be brought into the country. If you carry more than $10,000 in currency, you will have to fill out a report.

If you must bring prescription drugs into the U.S., make sure the container is clearly marked and that you bring your doctor's statement or a prescription. Marijuana, cocaine and most opiate derivatives and other chemicals are not permitted. Possession of them is punishable by stiff fines and/or imprisonment. Check with the U.S. Customs Service *(www.customs.gov)* before you arrive if you have any

questions about what you can bring. If you lose or need to renew your passport once inside the U.S., contact your country's embassy *(see* **Consulates**, *page 364).*

Student immigration

Upon entering the U.S. as a student, you will need to show a passport, a special visa and proof of your plans to leave (such as a return airline ticket). Even if you have a student visa, you may be asked to show means of support during your stay (cash, credit cards, traveler's checks, etc.).

Before they can apply for a visa, nonnationals who want to study in the U.S. must obtain an I-20 Certificate of Eligibility from the school or university they plan to attend. If you are enrolling in an authorized visitor-exchange program, including a summer course or program, wait until you have been accepted by the course or program before worrying about immigration. You will be guided through the process by the school.

You are admitted as a student for the length of your course, in addition to a limited period for a year's worth of associated (and approved) practical training, plus a 60-day grace period. When your time's up, you must leave the country, or apply to change or extend your immigration status. Requests to extend a visa must be submitted 15 to 60 days before the initial departure date. The rules are strict, and you risk deportation if you break them.

Information on these and all other immigration matters is available from the **U.S. Immigration and Naturalization Service (INS)**. The agency's 24-hour hot line (800-375-5283) is a vast menu of recorded information in English and Spanish; advisers are

available from 8am to 6pm, Monday through Friday. You can visit the INS at its New York office located in the Jacob Javits Federal Building *(26 Federal Plaza, on Broadway between Duane and Worth Sts).* The office is open 7:30am to 3:30pm, Monday through Friday, and cannot be reached directly by telephone.

The **U.S. Embassy** also offers guidance on obtaining student visas *(visa information in the U.S., 202-663-1225; in the U.K., 0-207-499-9000; www.travel.state.gov).* Or, you can write to the Visa Branch of the Embassy of the United States of America, 5 Upper Grosvenor Street, London W1A 2J.

When you apply for your student visa, you'll be expected to prove your ability to support yourself financially (including the payment of school fees), without working, for at least the first full academic year of your studies. After those nine months, you may be eligible to work part-time, but you must have specific permission to do so.

If you are a student from the U.K. who wants to spend a summer vacation working in the States, contact **BUNAC** (British Universities North America Club) for help in arranging a temporary job and the requisite visa *(16 Bowling Green Lane, London EC1R 0QH; 0-20-7251-3472; www.bunac.org/uk).*

Disabled access

Under New York City law, all facilities constructed after 1987 must provide complete access to the disabled—rest rooms and entrances/exits included. In 1990, the Americans with Disabilities Act made the same requirements federal law. In the wake of this legislation, many owners of older

Directory

buildings have voluntarily added disabled-access features. Due to widespread compliance with the law, we have not specifically noted the availability of disabled facilities in our listings. However, it's a good idea to call ahead and check.

Despite its best efforts, New York can be a challenging city for a disabled visitor, but support and guidance are readily available. One useful resource is the **Hospital Audiences Inc.'s** *(212-575-7660)* guide to New York's cultural institutions, *Access for All* (free). The book tells how accessible each place really is, and includes information on the height of telephones and water fountains, hearing and visual aids, passenger-loading zones and alternative entrances. HAI also has a service for the visually impaired that provides descriptions of theater performances on audiocassettes.

All Broadway theaters are equipped with devices for the hearing impaired; call **Sound Associates** *(212-582-7678)* for more information. There are a number of other stage-related resources for the disabled. Call **Telecharge** *(212-239-6200)* to reserve tickets for wheelchair seating in Broadway and Off Broadway venues. **Theater Development Fund's Theater Access Project** (TAP) arranges sign language interpretation and captioning for Broadway and Off Broadway shows *(212-221-1103, 212-719-4537; www.tds.org)*. **Hands On** *(212-822-8550)* does the same.

In addition, the nonprofit organization **Big Apple Greeter** *(see page 109)* will help any person with disabilities enjoy New York City.

Lighthouse International

111 E 59th St between Park and Lexington Aves (212-821-9200, 800-829-0500). Subway: N, R, W to Lexington Ave–59th St; 4, 5, 6 to 59th St. Mon–Fri 10am–6pm; Sat 10am–5pm; Sun 11am–5pm.
In addition to running a store that sells handy items for sight-impaired people, this organization provides the blind with info to help deal with life—or a holiday—in New York City.

Mayor's Office for People with Disabilities

100 Gold St between Frankfort and Spruce Sts, second floor (212-788-2830). Subway: J, M, Z to Chambers St; 4, 5, 6 to Brooklyn Bridge–City Hall. Mon–Fri 9am–5pm.
This municipal office provides a broad range of services for disabled people.

New York Society for the Deaf

817 Broadway at 12th St (212-777-3900). Subway: L, N, Q, R, W, 4, 5, 6 to 14th St–Union Sq. Mon–Thu 8:30am–5pm; Fri 8:30am–4:30pm.
The deaf and hearing-impaired come here for information and services.

The Society for the Advancement of Travel for the Handicapped

347 Fifth Ave between 33rd and 34th Sts, suite 610 (212-447-7284; fax 212-725-8253). Subway: B, D, F, V, N, Q, R, W to 34th St–Herald Sq.
This nonprofit group was founded in 1976 to educate people about travel facilities for the disabled, and to promote travel for the disabled worldwide. Membership is $45 a year ($30 for seniors and students) and includes access to an information service and a quarterly travel magazine. No drop-ins; membership by mail only.

Electricity

Electricity

The U.S. uses 110–120V, 60-cycle AC current, rather than the 220–240V, 50-cycle AC used in Europe and elsewhere. With the exception of a dual voltage, flat-pin plug shaver, any foreign-bought appliance will require an adapter. They're available at airport shops and some pharmacies and department stores.

Emergencies

Ambulance

In an emergency only, dial **911** for an ambulance or call the operator (dial **0**). To complain about slow service or poor treatment, call the **Fire Dept. Complaint Hot Line** *(718-999-2646)*.

Fire

In an emergency only, dial **911**. See above for complaint line.

Police

In an emergency only, dial **911**. For the location of the nearest police precinct, or for general information about police services, call 212-374-5000.

Health & medical facilities

The public health-care system is practically nonexistent in the United States, and costs of private health care are exorbitant. If at all possible, make sure you have comprehensive medical insurance when you travel to New York.

Clinics

Walk-in clinics offer treatment for minor ailments. Most require immediate payment, although some will send their bill directly to your insurance company. You will have to file a claim to recover the cost of prescription medication.

D•O•C•S

55 E 34th St between Madison and Park Aves (212-252-6000). Subway: 6 to 33rd St. Walk-in Mon–Thu 8am–8pm; Fri 8am–7pm; Sat 9am–3pm; Sun 9am–2pm. Extended hours by appointment. Base fee $80–$290. AmEx, Disc, MC, V.
These excellent primary-care facilities, affiliated with Beth Israel Medical Center, offer by-appointment and walk-in services. If you need X rays or lab tests, go as early as possible—no later than 6pm, Monday through Friday.
Other locations ● *202 W 23rd St at Seventh Ave (212-352-2600). Subway: 1, 2 to 23rd St.* ● *1555 Third Ave at 88th St (212-828-2300). Subway: 4, 5, 6 to 86th St.*

Dentists

NYU College of Dentistry

345 E 24th St between First and Second Aves (212-998-9872, off-hours emergency care 212-998-9828). Subwcy: 6 to 23rd St. Mon–Thu 8:30am–6:45pm; Fri 8:30am–4pm. Base fee $90. Disc, MC, V.
If you need your teeth fixed on a budget, you can become a guinea pig for final-year students. They're slow but proficient, and an experienced dentist is always on hand to supervise. Go before 2pm to ensure a same-day visit.

Emergency rooms

You will be billed for emergency treatment. Call your travel insurance company's emergency number before seeking treatment to find out which hospitals accept your insurance. Emergency rooms are always open at:

Bellevue Hospital

462 First Ave at 27th St (212-562-4141). Subway: 6 to 28th St.

Cabrini Medical Center

227 E 19th St between Second and Third Aves (212-995-6000). Subway: L, N, Q, R, W, 4, 5, 6 to 14th St–Union Sq.

Mount Sinai Hospital

Madison Ave at 100th St (212-241-7171). Subway: 6 to 103rd St.

Roosevelt Hospital

1000 Tenth Ave at 59th St (212-523-6800). Subway: A, C, B, D, 1, 2 to 59th St–Columbus Circle.

St. Vincent's Hospital

153 W 11th St at Seventh Ave (212-604-7998). Subway: L to Sixth Ave; 1, 2, 3 to 14th St.

Gay & lesbian health

See chapter **Gay & Lesbian**.

House calls

NY Hotel Urgent Medical Services

3 E 76th St at Fifth Ave (212-737-1212; www.travelmd.com). Subway: 6 to 77th St. 24 hrs. Hotel visit fee $200–$300; office visit fee $55–$155.

Rates increase at night and on weekends.
Dr. Ronald Primas and his partners provide medical attention right in your Manhattan hotel room or private residence. Whether you need a simple prescription or an internal examination, this service can provide a specialist. In-office appointments are also available. Call for office hours.

Pharmacies

See also **Pharmacists**, page 215.

Duane Reade

224 W 57th St at Broadway (212-541-9708). Subway: N, Q, R, W to 57th St. 24 hours. AmEx, MC, V.
This chain operates all over the city, and some stores offer 24-hour service. Check the phone book for additional locations.
Other 24-hour locations ● *378 Sixth Ave at Waverly Pl (212-674-5357). Subway: A, C, E, F, V, S to W 4th St.* ● *661 Eighth Ave at 42nd St (212-977-1562). Subway: A, C, E to 42nd St–Port Authority.* ● *1279 Third Ave at 74th St (212-744-2668). Subway: 6 to 77th St.* ● *2465 Broadway at 91st St (212-799-3172). Subway: 1, 2, 3 to 96th St.*

Rite Aid

303 W 50th St at Eighth Ave (212-247-8736; www.riteaid.com). Subway: C, E to 50th St. 24 hours. AmEx, Disc, MC, V.
Select locations have 24-hour pharmacies. Call 800-RITE-AID for a complete listing.
Other 24-hour locations ● *542 Second Ave at 31st St (212-213-9887). Subway: 6 to 33rd St.* ● *210 Amsterdam Ave between 69th and 70th Sts (212-873-7965). Subway: 1, 2, 3 to 72nd St.* ● *144 E 86th St between Lexington and Third Aves (212-876-0600). Subway: 4, 5, 6 to 86th St.* ● *2833 Broadway at 110th St (212-663-8252). Subway: 1 to 110th St–Cathedral Pkwy.*

Women's health

Liberty Women's Health Care of Queens

37-01 Main St at 37th Ave, Flushing, Queens (718-888-0018). Subway: 7 to Flushing–Main St. By appointment only. AmEx, MC, V.
This facility provides both surgical and nonsurgical abortions for up to 24 weeks of pregnancy. Unlike other clinics, Liberty uses abdominal

ultrasounds before, during and after the abortion to ensure safety.

Park Med Eastern Women's Center

44 E 30th St between Madison Ave and Park Ave South, fifth floor (212-686-6066). Subway: 6 to 33rd St. By appointment only. AmEx, Disc, MC, V.
Urine pregnancy tests are free. Abortions and counseling are also available.

Planned Parenthood of New York City

Margaret Sanger Center, 26 Bleecker St at Mott St (212-274-7200; www.ppnyc.org). Subway: F, V, S to Broadway–Lafayette St; 6 to Bleecker St. Mon 8am–5pm; Tue–Fri 8am–6pm; Sat 7:30am–5pm.
This is the main branch of the best-known, most reasonably priced network of family planning clinics in the U.S. Counseling and treatment are available for a full range of gynecological needs, including abortion, treatment of STDs, HIV testing and contraception. Phone for an appointment or for more information on services. Call 212-965-7000 to make an appointment at any of three centers (the others are in the Bronx and Brooklyn). No walk-ins.

Help lines

Alcohol & drug abuse

Alcoholics Anonymous

212-647-1680. 24 hrs.

Cocaine Anonymous

212-262-2463. 24-hour recorded info.

Drug Abuse Information Line

800-522-5353. 24 hrs.
This program refers callers to recovery programs around the state.

Pills Anonymous

212-874-0700. 24-hour recorded info.
You'll find information on drug-recovery programs for users of marijuana, cocaine, alcohol and other addictive substances, as well as referrals to Narcotics Anonymous meetings. You can also leave a message, if you wish to have a counselor speak to you directly.

Directory

Child abuse

Childhelp USA's National Child Abuse Hotline

800-422-4453. 24 hrs.
Counselors provide general crisis consultation, and can help in an emergency. Callers include abused children, runaways and parents having problems with children.

Health

Visit the **Center for Disease Control** (CDC) website *(www.cdc.gov)* for up-to-date national health information or call one of their toll-free hot lines listed below.

HIV & AIDS Hot Line

800-342-2437. 24 hrs.

STD Hot Line

800-227-8922. 24 hrs.

Travelers' Health

877-FYI-TRIP. 24 hrs.

Psychological services

Center for Inner Resource Development

212-734-5876. 24 hrs.
Therapists will talk to you day or night, and are trained to deal with all kinds of emotional problems, including those resulting from rape.

Help Line

212-532-2400. 24 hrs.
Trained volunteers will talk to anyone contemplating suicide, and will also help with other personal problems.

The Samaritans

212-673-3000. 24 hrs.
People thinking of committing suicide, or suffering from depression, grief, sexual anxiety or alcoholism, can call this organization for advice.

Rape & sex crimes

St. Luke's/Roosevelt Hospital Crime Victims Treatment Center

212-523-4728. Mon–Fri 9am–5pm, recorded referral message at other times.
The Rape Crisis Center provides a trained volunteer who will accompany you through all aspects

of reporting a rape and getting emergency treatment.

Safe Horizon Hotline

212-577-7777. 24 hrs.
SHH offers telephone and one-on-one counseling for any victim of domestic violence, rape or other crimes, as well as practical help with court procedures, compensation and legal aid.

Special Victims Liason Unit of the New York Police Department

212-267-7273, 212-267-7274. 24 hrs.
Reports of sex crimes are handled by a female detective from the Special Victims Liaison Unit. She will inform the appropriate precinct, send an ambulance if requested and provide counseling and medical referrals. Other issues handled: violence against gays and lesbians, child victimization and referrals for the families and friends of crime victims.

Holidays

See **Holidays**, page 363.

Insurance

If you are not an American, it's advisable to take out comprehensive insurance before arriving here; it's almost impossible to arrange in the U.S. Make sure you have adequate health coverage, since medical costs are high. For a list of New York urgent-care facilities, *see* **Emergency rooms**, page 367.

Internet & e-mail

Cyber Café

273 Lafayette St at Prince St (212-334-5140; www.cyber-cafe.com). Subway: F, V, S to Broadway–Lafayette St; N, R to Prince St; 6 to Spring St. Mon–Fri 9am–10pm; Sat, Sun 11am–10pm. $6.40 per half hour, 50¢ per printed page.
This is your standard Internet-connected café, though at least this one serves great coffee.
Other location ● *250 W 49th St between Broadway and Eighth Ave (212-333-4109). Subway: C, E to 50th St; N, R, W to 49th St.*

Easy Everything

234 W 42nd St between Seventh and Eighth Aves (212-398-0775).

Subway: N, Q, R, W, S, 1, 2, 3, 7 to 42nd St–Times Sq. 24 hrs. $1.
International travelers will recognize this giant Internet café. Its Times Square location has more than 700 PCs and costs $1, which will give you a minimum of 30 minutes and a maximum of 4 hours based on computer availability.

Internet Café

82 E 3rd St between First and Second Aves (212-614-0747). Subway: F, V to Lower East Side–Second Ave. 8am–4am. $3 per 15 minutes, 25¢ per printed page.
E-mail your loved ones from this basement café while sipping on a pint.

Kinko's

See **Computers**, page 364.

New York Public Library

188 Madison Ave between 34th and 35th Sts (212-592-7000; www.nypl.org). Subway: 6 to 33rd St. Mon, Fri, Sat 10am–6pm; Tue, Wed, Thu 10am–8pm; Wed 11am–7pm. Free.
The 83 branch libraries scattered throughout the five boroughs are a great place to e-mail and surf the Web for free. A select number of computer stations may make for a long wait, and once you're on, your user time may be limited (this location has the most). Check the yellow pages for the branch nearest you. See also New York Public Library, page 44.

Legal assistance

If you are arrested for a minor violation (disorderly conduct, harassment, loitering, rowdy partying, etc.) and you're very polite to the officer during the arrest (and are carrying proper ID), you'll probably get fingerprinted and photographed at the station and be given a desk-appearance ticket with a date to show up at criminal court. Then you'll most likely get to go home.

Arguing with a police officer or engaging in something more serious (possession of a weapon, drunken driving, gambling or prostitution, for example) might get you processed. In that case, expect to embark on a 24- to 30-hour journey through the system.

If the courts are backed up (and they usually are), you'll be held temporarily at a precinct pen. You can make a phone call after you've been fingerprinted. When you get through central booking, you'll arrive at 100 Centre Street. Arraignment occurs in one of two AR (arraignment courtroom) units, where a judge decides whether you should be released on bail and then sets a court date. If you can't post bail, you'll be held at Rikers Island. Unless a major crime has been committed, a bail bondsman is unnecessary. The bottom line: Try not to get arrested, and if you are, don't act foolishly.

Legal Aid Society

212-577-3300. Mon–Fri 8am–5pm. Legal Aid gives general information and referrals on legal matters.

Sandback, Birnbaum & Michelen Criminal Law

212-517-3200; 800-640-2000. 24 hrs. These are the numbers to have in your head when the cops read you your rights in the middle of the night. If no one in this firm can help you, they'll direct you to lawyers who can.

Libraries

See **New York Public Library**, page 44, and also **Internet & e-mail**, page 368.

Locksmiths

The following emergency locksmiths are open 24 hours. Both require proof of residency or car ownership plus ID.

Champion Locksmiths

16 locations in Manhattan (212-362-7000). $15 service charge day or night, plus $35 minimum to fit a lock. AmEx, Disc, MC, V.

Elite Locksmiths

470 Third Ave between 32nd and 33rd Sts (212-685-1472). Subway: 6 to 33rd St. $45 during the day; $75–$90 at night. Cash and checks only.

Toilet talk

Finding a rest room in the city isn't as easy as finding a hot dog vendor

Visitors to New York—like New Yorkers themselves—are always on the go. But in between all that go, go, go, sometimes you've really got to…go. Contrary to popular belief (and the occasional aroma, especially in summer), the street is no place to drop trou. The real challenge lies in finding a (legal) public place to take care of your business. Though they don't exactly have an open-door policy, the numerous **McDonald's** restaurants, **Starbucks** coffee shops and most of the **Barnes & Noble** bookstores contain (usually clean) rest rooms. If the door to the loo is locked, you may have to ask a cashier for the key. Don't announce that you're not a paying customer, and you should be all right. The same applies to most other fast-food joints (**Au Bon Pain, Wendy's,** etc.) and hotels and bars that don't have a host or maître d' at the door. Here are a few other options around town that can offer sweet relief (although you may have to hold your breath at some places).

Downtown

Kmart
770 Broadway at Astor Pl. Subway: N, R to 8th St–NYU; 6 to Astor Pl.

Tompkins Square Park
Ave A at 9th St. Subway: L to First Ave; 6 to Astor Pl.

Washington Square Park
Thompson St at Washington Sq South. Subway: A, C, E, F, V, S to W 4th St.

Midtown

Grand Central
42nd St at Park Ave, Lower Concourse. Subway: S, 4, 5, 6, 7 to 42nd St–Grand Central.

Macy's
151 W 34th St between Broadway and Seventh Ave. Subway: B, D, F, V, N, Q, R, W to 34th St–Herald Square; 1, 2, 3 to 34th St–Penn Station.

Penn Station
Seventh Ave between 30th and 32nd Sts. Subway: A, C, E, 1, 2, 3 to 34th St–Penn Station.

St. Clement's Church
423 W 46th St between Ninth and Tenth Aves. Subway: A, C, E to 42nd St–Port Authority.

School of Visual Arts
209 E 23rd St between Second and Third Aves. Subway: 6 to 23rd St.

Toys R Us
1514 Broadway at 44th St. Subway: N, Q, R, W, S, 1, 2, 3, 7 to 42nd St–Times Sq.

United Nations
First Ave between 42nd and 50th Sts. Subway: S, 4, 5, 6, 7 to 42nd St–Grand Central.

Uptown

Barneys New York
660 Madison Ave at 61st St. Subway: N, R, W to Fifth Ave–60th St.

Delacorte Theater in Central Park
Mid-park at 81st St. Subway: B, C to 81st St.

Avery Fisher Hall at Lincoln Center
Broadway and 65th St. Subway: 1, 2 to 66th St–Lincoln Ctr.

Directory

Lost property

For property lost in the street, contact the police. For lost credit cards or traveler's checks, see **Money** below.

Buses & subways

New York City Transit Authority, 34th St–Penn Station, near the A train platform (212-712-4500). Mon–Wed, Fri 8am–noon; Thu 11am–6:30pm.

Grand Central Terminal

212-340-2555. Mon–Fri 7am–11pm; Sat, Sun 10am–11pm.
Call if you've left something on a Metro-North train.

JFK Airport

718-244-4444, or contact your airline.

La Guardia Airport

718-533-3400, or contact your airline.

Newark Airport

973-961-6230, or contact your airline.

Penn Station

212-630-7389.
Call for items left on Amtrak, New Jersey Transit or the Long Island Rail Road.

Taxis

212-692-8294; www.nyc.gov/taxi.
Call this number if you leave anything in a cab.

Messenger services

A to Z Couriers

105 Rivington St between Essex and Ludlow Sts (212-253-6500). Subway: F to Delancey St; J, M, Z to Delancey–Essex Sts. Mon–Fri 8am–7pm. AmEx, MC, V.
These cheerful couriers will deliver to anywhere in the city (and Long Island, too).

Breakaway

335 W 35th St between Eighth and Ninth Aves (212-947-4455). Subway: A, C, E to 34th St–Penn Station. Mon–Fri 7am–9pm; Sat 9am–5pm; Sun by arrangement. AmEx, MC, V.
Breakaway is a highly recommended citywide delivery service that promises to pick up and deliver within the hour. The company employs 200 messengers, so you can take this seriously.

Jefron Messenger Service

141 Duane St between Church St and West Broadway (212-964-8441; www.jefron.com). Subway: 1, 2 to Chambers St. Mon–Fri 8am–5pm. Cash, checks, money orders only.
Jefron specializes in transporting import/export documents.

Money

Over the past few years, a lot of American currency has undergone a subtle face-lift—partly as a national celebration and partly to deter increasingly adept counterfeiters. However, the "old" money is still in circulation. One dollar ($) equals 100 cents (¢). Coins range from copper pennies (1¢) to silver nickels (5¢), dimes (10¢), quarters (25¢) and less common half-dollars (50¢).

In 1999, the U.S. Mint began issuing commemorative "state quarters." George Washington's profile still graces the front, but the reverse (or "tails") side is dedicated to one of the 50 states; each coin is stamped with a corresponding design symbolizing the state's history and achievements. These quarters are being issued in segments of five states per year in the order of state entry into the Union—by 2009 all 50 will be in circulation.

The year 2000 marked the introduction of the "golden dollar." The coin is about one inch in diameter and features a portrait of Sacagawea (the Native American woman who helped guide explorers Lewis and Clark on their journey across America). The new gold coin replaces the older Susan B. Anthony silver dollar, and satisfies a growing need for dollar coins in vending and mass transit machines. You might still get a Susan B. on occasion—they're increasingly rare and worth holding onto. For more information on U.S. coins, call 800-USA-MINT or visit www.usmint.gov.

Nothing two-bit about it
The New York State quarter's design is cent-sational.

Paper money is all the same size and color, so make sure you fork over the right bill. It comes in denominations of $1, $2, $5, $10, $20, $50 and $100 (and higher—but you'll never see those). All denominations, except for the $1 and $2 bills, have recently been updated by the U.S. Treasury, which chose a larger portrait placed off-center with extra security features; the new bills also have a large numeral on the back to help the visually impaired identify the denomination. The $2 bills are quite rare and make a smart souvenir. Small shops will rarely break a $50 or $100 bill, so it is best to carry smaller denominations (and cab drivers aren't required to change bills larger than $20). For more information on paper currency, refer to the U.S. Treasury website at www.ustreas.gov.

ATMs

New York City is full of automated teller machines (ATMs). Most accept Visa, MasterCard and AmEx, among other cards, if they have been registered with a personal identification number (PIN). There is a usage fee, although the convenience (and the superior exchange rate) often make ATMs worth the extra charge.

Call the following for ATM locations: **Cirrus** *(800-424-7787)*; **Wells Fargo** *(800-869-3557)*; **Plus Systems** *(800-843-7587)*. Also, look for branch banks or delis, which often have mini ATMs by the front counter (the fees for these machines can be a little odious). If you've lost your number or your card becomes demagnetized, most banks will give cash to card-holders, with proper ID.

Banks & currency exchange

Banks are generally open from 9am to 3pm Monday through Friday, though some have longer hours. You need photo identification, such as a passport, to cash traveler's checks. Many banks will not exchange foreign currency, and the *bureaux de change*, limited to tourist-trap areas, close around 6 or 7pm. It's best to arrive with some dollars in cash but to pay mostly with credit cards or traveler's checks (accepted in most restaurants and larger stores—but ask first, and be prepared to show ID). In emergencies, most large hotels offer 24-hour exchange facilities; the catch is that they charge high commissions and don't give good rates.

Chequepoint USA

22 Central Park South between Fifth and Sixth Aves (212-750-2400). Subway: N, R, W to Fifth Ave–60th St. 8am–8pm.
Foreign currency, traveler's checks and bank drafts are available here.
Other location ● *1568 Broadway at 47th St (212-869-6281). Subway: N, R, W to 49th St; 1, 2 to 50th St.*

People's Foreign Exchange

575 Fifth Ave at 47th St, third floor (212-883-0550). Subway: E, V to Fifth Ave–53rd St; 7 to Fifth Ave. Mon–Fri 9am–6pm; Sat 10am–3pm.
People's provides free foreign exchange on banknotes and traveler's checks of larger

denominations and a nominal fee is applied to smaller amounts.

Travelex

29 Broadway at Morris St (212-363-6206). Subway: 4, 5 to Bowling Green. Mon–Fri 9am–5pm.
A complete foreign exchange service is offered.
Other locations ● *1590 Broadway at 48th St (212-265-6063). Subway: N, R, W to 49th St; 1, 2 to 50th St.* ● *511 Madison Ave at 53rd St (212-753-2595). Subway: E, V to Fifth Ave–53rd St.*

Credit cards

Bring plastic if you have it, or be prepared for a logistical nightmare. It's essential for things like renting cars and booking hotels, and handy for buying tickets over the phone and the Internet. The five major credit cards accepted in the U.S. are American Express, Diners Club, Discover, MasterCard and Visa. If cards are lost or stolen, contact:

American Express
800-528-2122

Diners Club
800-234-6377

Discover
800-347-2683

MasterCard
800-826-2181

Visa
800-336-8472

Traveler's checks

Before your trip, it is wise to buy checks in U.S. currency from a widely recognized company. Traveler's checks are routinely accepted at banks, stores and restaurants throughout the city. Bring your driver's license or passport along for identification. If checks are lost or stolen, contact:

American Express
800-221-7282

Thomas Cook
800-223-7373

Visa
800-336-8472

Wire services

If you run out of cash, don't expect anyone at your embassy or consulate to lend you money—they won't, although they may be persuaded to repatriate you. In an emergency, you can have money wired.

MoneyGram
800-926-9400

Western Union
800-325-6000

Newspapers & magazines

Daily newspapers

Daily News

The *News* has drifted politically from the Neanderthal right to a moderate but tough-minded stance under the ownership of real-estate mogul Mort Zuckerman. Labor-friendly pundit Juan Gonzalez has great street sense (not to mention a Pulitzer).

New York Post

Founded in 1801 by Alexander Hamilton, the *Post* is the nation's oldest daily newspaper. After many decades as a standard-bearer for political liberalism, the *Post* swerved sharply to the right under current owner Rupert Murdoch. The *Post* has more column inches of gossip than any other local paper, and its headlines are often the ones to beat.

The New York Times

Olympian as ever after almost 150 years, the *Times* remains the city's (and the nation's) paper of record. It has the broadest and deepest coverage of world and national events—as the masthead proclaims, it delivers "All the News That's Fit to Print." The mammoth Sunday *Times* can weigh a full five pounds and typically contains hundreds of pages of newsprint, including a magazine, book review, arts, finance, real estate, sports and other sections.

Other dailies

One of the nation's oldest black newspapers, *Amsterdam News*, offers a trenchantly

Directory

African-American viewpoint. New York also supports two Spanish-language dailies, *El Diario* and *Noticias del Mundo*. *Newsday* is the Long Island–based daily with a tabloid format but a sober tone (it has a city edition). *The Wall Street Journal* views the world through a business lens.

Weekly magazines

New York
This magazine is part newsweekly, part lifestyle report and part listings.

The New Yorker
Since the 1920s, *The New Yorker* has been known for its fine wit, elegant prose and sophisticated cartoons. In the postwar era, it established itself as a venue for serious long-form journalism. It usually makes for a lively, intelligent read.

Time Out New York
Of course the best place to find out what's going on in town is *Time Out New York*, launched in 1995. Based on the tried-and-trusted format of its London parent, *TONY* is an indispensable guide to the life of the city (if we do say so ourselves).

Weekly papers

Downtown journalism is a battlefield, pitting the scabrous neocons of the *New York Press* against the unreconstructed hippies of *The Village Voice*. The *Press* uses an all-column format; it's full of youthful energy and irreverence as well as cynicism and self-absorption. *The Voice* is sometimes passionate and ironic, but just as often strident and predictable. Both papers are free. In contrast, *The New York Observer* focuses on the doings of the upper echelons of business, finance, media and politics; it may be on its last legs, however. *Our Town* and *Manhattan Spirit* are on the sidelines; these free sister publications feature neighborhood news and local political gossip, and can be found in street-corner bins around town.

Magazines

Black Book
Since its start in 1996, this quarterly covers New York high fashion and culture with intelligent bravado.

Gotham
From the publisher of the glossy gab-rags *Hamptons* and Miami's *Ocean Drive*, *Gotham* unveiled it's larger-than-life paparrazi-filled pages in 2001.

Paper
Paper covers the city's trend-conscious set with plenty of insider buzz on bars, clubs, downtown boutiques and the people you'll find in them.

Photocopying & printing

Dependable Printing
10 E 22nd St at Broadway (212-533-7560). Subway: N, R to 23rd St. Mon–Fri 8:30am–7pm; Sat 10am–4pm. AmEx, MC, V.
Dependable provides offset and color printing, large-size Xerox copies, color laser printing, binding, rubber stamps, typing, forms, labels, brochures, flyers, newsletters, manuscripts, fax service, transparencies and more.
Other location ● *245 Fifth Ave between 27th and 28th Sts (212-689-2777). Subway: N, R to 28th St.*

Fitch Graphics
See page 364.

Kinko's
See page 364.

Servco
56 W 45th St between Fifth and Sixth Aves (212-575-0991). Subway: B, D, F, V to 42nd St; 7 to Fifth Ave. Mon–Fri 8am–6pm.
Photocopying, offset printing, blueprints and binding services are available here.

Postal services

U.S. Postal Service

Stamps are available at all post offices and from drugstore vending machines.

It costs 34¢ to send a one-ounce (28g) letter within the U.S. (as of July, 2002, it will cost 37¢). Each additional ounce costs 22¢. Postcards mailed within the U.S. cost 21¢ in postage (23¢ beginning in July, 2002); for international postcards, it's 70¢. Airmail letters to anywhere overseas cost 80¢ for the first ounce and 80¢ for each additional ounce.

General Post Office
421 Eighth Ave at 33rd St (212-967-8585; 24-hour postal information 800-275-8777). Subway: A, C, E to 34th St–Penn Station. 24 hrs.
This is the city's main post office; call for the branch nearest you. There are 55 full-service post offices in Manhattan alone; lines are long, but stamps are also available from self-service vending machines. Branches are usually open 9am to 5pm, Monday through Friday; Saturday hours vary from office to office. *(See also page 70.)*

Express Mail
Information: 212-967-8585.
You need to use special envelopes and fill out a form, which can be done either at a post office or by arranging a pickup. You are guaranteed mail delivery within 24 hours to major U.S. cities. International delivery takes two to three days, with no guarantee. Call for more information on various deadlines.

General Delivery
390 Ninth Ave at 30th St (212-330-3099). Subway: A, C, E to 34th St–Penn Station. Mon–Sat 10am–1pm.
U.S. visitors without local addresses can receive their mail here; it should be addressed to recipient's name, General Delivery, New York, NY 10001. You will need to show some form of identification—a passport or ID card—when picking up letters.

Poste Restante
421 Eighth Ave at 33rd St, window 29 (212-330-2912). Subway: A, C, E to 34th St–Penn Station. Mon–Sat 8am–6pm.
Foreign visitors without U.S. addresses can receive mail here; mail should be addressed to General Post Office, Poste Restante, 421 Eighth Avenue, attn: Window 29, New York, NY 10001. Be sure to bring some form of identification to claim your letters.

Couriers

DHL Worldwide Express

Various locations throughout the city; call and give your zip code to find the office nearest you, or get pickup at your door (800-225-5345). AmEx, DC, Disc, MC, V.

DHL will send a courier to pick up packages at any address in New York City, or you can deliver packages to its offices and drop-off points in person. No cash transactions.

FedEx

Various locations throughout the city; call and give your zip code to find the office nearest you, or get pickup at your door (800-247-4747; www.fedex.com). AmEx, DC, Disc, MC, V.

FedEx rates (like those of its main competitor, United Parcel Service) are based on the distance shipped, weight of the package and service chosen. A FedEx envelope to Los Angeles costs about $17; one to London, $30. Packages headed overseas should be dropped off by 6pm for International Priority delivery (depending on destination); packages for most destinations in the U.S., by 9pm (some locations have a later time; call to check).

United Parcel Service

Various locations throughout the city; free pickup at your door (800-742-5877 for 24-hour service; www.ups.com). Hours vary by office; call for locations and times. AmEx, DC, MC, V.

Like DHL and FedEx, UPS will send a courier to pick up parcels at any address in New York City, or you can deliver packages to its offices and drop-off points in person. UPS offers domestic and international service.

Private mail services

Mail Boxes Etc. USA

1173A Second Ave between 61st and 62nd Sts (212-832-1390). Subway: F to Lexington Ave–63rd St; N, R, W to Lexington Ave–59th St; 4, 5, 6 to 59th St. Mon–Fri 9am–7pm; Sat 10am–5pm. AmEx, MC, V.

Mailbox rental, mail forwarding, overnight delivery, packaging and shipping are available. Also available are a phone-message service, photocopying and faxing, typing service and business printing. There are more than 30 branches in Manhattan; check the phone book for locations.

Telegrams

Western Union Telegrams

800-325-6000. 24 hrs.

Telegrams to addresses are taken over the phone at any time of day or night, and charges are added to your phone bill. Service is not available from pay phones.

Radio

There are nearly 100 stations in the New York area. On the AM dial, you can find intriguing talk radio and phone-in shows that attract everyone from priests to sports nuts. Flip to FM for everything from free jazz to the latest No Doubt single. Radio highlights are printed weekly in *Time Out New York,* and daily in the *Daily News.*

College radio

College radio is innovative and free of commercials. However, smaller transmitters mean that reception is often compromised by Manhattan's high-rise topography.

WNYU-FM 89.1 and **WKCR-FM 89.9** (*see* **Jazz**, *below*) are the stations of New York University and Columbia and offer programming that ranges across the musical spectrum.

WFUV-FM 90.7, Fordham University's station, plays mostly folk/Irish music, but also airs a variety of shows, including old-fashioned radio drama on *Classic Radio* every Monday at midnight.

Dance & pop

American commercial radio is rigidly formatted, which makes most pop stations extremely tedious and repetitive during the day. Tune in on evenings and weekends for more interesting programming.

WWRL-AM 1600 features R&B, Caribbean music and oldies. **WPLJ-FM 95.5,** and **WHTZ-FM 100.3** are Top 40 stations. **WQHT-FM 97.1** "Hot 97" is a commercial hip-hop station, with Star and Buc Wild cooking up a breakfast show for the homies; there's rap and R&B throughout the day. **WRKS-FM 98.7** "Kiss FM" has an urban adult-contemporary format, which translates into "unremarkable American pop." But it does have the soulful Isaac Hayes on weekday mornings (6–10am).

WCBS-FM 101.1's playlist is strictly oldies. **WKTU-FM 103.5** is the city's premier dance-music station. **WTJM-FM 105.1,** "Jammin' Oldies," plays a mix drawn from the 1960s, '70s and '80s. **WLTW-FM 106.7,** "Lite FM," plays the kind of music you hear in elevators. **WBLS-FM 107.5** plays classic and contemporary funk, soul and R&B. Highlights include Chuck Mitchell's house and R&B mix on Saturday mornings, plus *Hal Jackson's Sunday Classics* (blues and soul).

Jazz

WCWP-FM 88.1 plays mostly jazz, plus hip-hop, gospel and world music. **WBGO-FM 88.3** is strictly jazz. Branford Marsalis's weekly *JazzSet* program features many legendary artists, and there are also shows devoted to such categories as piano jazz. **WKCR-FM 89.9,** the student-run radio station of Columbia University, is where you'll hear legendary jazz DJ Phil Schaap. **WQCD-FM 101.9** is a soft-jazz station.

Rock

WSOU-FM 89.5, a college station, focuses primarily on heavy metal. **WFMU-FM 91.1** The term *free-form radio* still has some meaning at this Jersey-based station, which offers an eclectic mix of music and other aural oddities. **WXRK-FM 92.3** and **WAXQ-FM 104.3** offer a digest of classic and alternative rock. 92.3 attracts the city's largest group of morning listeners, thanks to Howard Stern's 6 to 10am weekday sleazefest. **WLIR-FM 92.7** plays alternative (indie and Goth) sounds with a British bias.

Other music

Wacky talk shows, sports games and music air on **WEVD-AM 1050.** **WQEW-AM 1560,** "Radio Disney," has kids' programming. On **WNYC-FM 93.9** and **WQXR-FM 96.3** you can hear a varied diet of classical music, WNYC being slightly more progressive. Tune into **WYNY-FM 107.1** for country music.

News & talk

WABC-AM 770, WCBS-AM 880, WINS-AM 1010, and **WBBR-AM 1130** offer news throughout the day, plus traffic and weather reports. **WABC-AM 770** offers a morning show featuring the street-accented demagoguery of Guardian Angels founder Curtis Sliwa and radical attorney Ron Kuby (weekdays 5–9am). Right-winger Rush Limbaugh also airs his views here (noon–3pm), and you can get some therapy from the oh-so-conservative twit Dr. Laura Schlessinger (weekdays 11pm–1am).

WNYC-AM 820/FM 93.9 and **WBAI-FM 99.5** are commercial-free public radio stations providing news and current affairs. Highlights include WNYC's popular *All Things Considered* (weekdays AM: 4–6pm, 7–8pm; FM: 4–6:30pm) and guest-driven talk shows, notably WNYC's *New York & Company* (weekdays noon–2pm) and WNYC-FM's *Fresh Air* (weekdays 7–8pm). WNYC also airs Garrison Keillor's *A Prairie Home Companion* and Ira Glass's *This American Life*. WBAI is a platform for left-wing politics.

WLIB-AM 1190 is the voice of black New York, airing news and talk from an Afrocentric perspective, interspersed with Caribbean music. Former mayor David Dinkins has a show on Wednesdays (noon–1pm).

WNEW-FM 102.7 is primarily talk, with an emphasis on the wacky.

Sports

WFAN-AM 660 airs Giants, Mets, Knicks and Rangers games. In the mornings, talk-radio fixture Don Imus offers his take on whatever's going on in the world.

WABC-AM 770 broadcasts the Yankees and Jets games.

WWRU-AM 1660, "Radio Unica," covers MetroStars soccer games.

Religion

Here are just a few of the many places of worship in New York. Check the yellow pages for a more detailed listing.

Baptist

Abyssinian Baptist Church
See page 87.

Catholic

St. Francis of Assisi
135 W 31st St between Sixth and Seventh Aves (212-736-8500; www.st.francis.org). Subway: B, D, F, V, N, Q, R, W to 34th St–Herald Sq; 1, 2, 3 to 34th St–Penn Station. Services: Mon–Fri 6, 6:30, 7, 7:30,

8, 8:30, 10, 11, 11:45am, 12:15, 1:15, 4:30, 5:30pm; Sat 7:30, 9, 10:30, 11:15am, noon, 4, 5:15, 6:15pm; Sun 7, 8, 9:30, 10 (Korean), 11am, 12:30, 5:15, 6:15pm.

St. Patrick's Cathedral
See page 74.

Episcopal

Cathedral of St. John the Divine
See page 84.

Jewish

UJA-Federation Resource Line
212-753-2288; www.youngleadership.org. 9am–5pm. 24-hour voice mail. This hot line provides referrals to other organizations, groups, temples and synagogues as well as advice on kosher food and restaurants.

Methodist

St. Paul and St. Andrew United Methodist Church
263 W 86th St between Broadway and West End Ave (212-362-3179). Subway: 1, 2 to 86th St. Services: Sun 11am, 6:30pm.

Salem United Methodist Church
2190 Adam Clayton Powell Jr. Blvd (Seventh Ave) at 129th St (212-678-2700). Subway: A, C, B, D, 2, 3 to 125th St. Services: Sept–Jun Sun 11am. Jul, Aug Sun 10am.

Muslim

Islamic Cultural Center of New York
1711 Third Ave between 96th and 97th Sts (212-722-5234). Subway: 6 to 96th St. 9am–8:30pm and for all prayers.

Presbyterian

Fifth Avenue Presbyterian Church
7 W 55th St at Fifth Ave (212-247-0490; www.fapc.org). Subway: E, V to Fifth Ave–53rd St. Services: Sun 9, 11am.

Rest rooms

See **Toilet talk**, page 369.

Safety

Statistics on New York's crime rate, particularly violent crime, have nose-dived over the past decade. More than ever, most crime stays within specific ethnic groups, and occurs late at night in low-income neighborhoods. Don't arrive thinking your safety is at risk wherever you go; it is unlikely that you will ever be bothered.

Still, a bit of common sense won't hurt. If you look comfortable rather than lost, you should deter troublemakers. Do not flaunt your money and valuables. Avoid desolate and poorly lit streets, and if necessary, walk facing the traffic so no one can drive up alongside you. On deserted sidewalks, walk close to the street; muggers prefer to hang back in doorways and shadows. If the worst happens and you find yourself threatened, hand over your wallet or camera at once (your attacker will likely be as anxious to get it over with as you are), then dial **911** as soon as you can (it's a free call).

Be extra alert to pickpockets and street hustlers—especially in busy tourist areas like Times Square—and don't be seduced by cardsharps or other tricksters you may come across. That shrink-wrapped camcorder you bought out of a car trunk for 50 bucks could turn out to be a couple of bricks when you open the box.

New York women are used to the brazenness with which they are stared at by men and usually develop a hardened or dismissive attitude toward it. If unwelcome admirers ever get verbal or start following you, ignoring them is better than responding—unless you are confident about your acid-tongued retorts. Walking into the nearest shop is your best bet to get rid of really persistent offenders. If you've been seriously victimized, see **Emergencies**, page 366, or **Rape & sex crimes**, page 368, for assistance.

Smoking

New Yorkers are the target of some of the strictest antismoking laws on the planet (well, except for California). The 1995 NYC Smoke-Free Air Act makes it illegal to smoke in virtually all public places, including subways, movie theaters and most restaurants—even if a no-smoking sign is not displayed. Bars and restaurants with fewer than 35 indoor seats are the exceptions, although large restaurants can have separate smoking areas. Fines start at $100, so be sure to ask before you light up. Now could be the time to quit.

Students

Student life in NYC is unlike anywhere else in the world. An endless extracurricular education exists right outside the dorm room—the city is both teacher and playground. For further guidance, check the *Time Out New York Student Guide*, available free on campuses in August.

Student identification

Foreign students should get an **International Student Identity Card** (ISIC) as proof of student status and to secure discounts. These can be bought from your local student travel agent (ask at your students' union). If you buy the card in New York, you will also get basic accident insurance—a bargain. The New York branch of the **Council on**

International Educational Exchange can supply one on the spot. It's at 205 East 42nd Street between Second and Third Avenues *(212-822-2700; see* **Student travel***, below)*. Note that a student identity card may not always be accepted as proof of age for drinking (you must be 21).

Student travel

Most agents offer discount fares for those under 26; specialists in student deals include:

Council Travel

205 E 42nd St between Second and Third Aves (212-822-2700; www.counciltravel.com). Subway: S, 4, 5, 6, 7 to 42nd St–Grand Central. Mon, Tue, Thu, Fri 10am–6pm; Wed 11am–6pm; Sat 11am–5pm. Call 800-226-8624 for other locations.

STA Travel

10 Downing St at Sixth Ave (212-627-3111; www.statravel.com). Subway: A, C, E, F, V, S to W 4th St. Mon–Fri 9am–9pm; Sat 10am–6pm; Sun 11am–6pm.
Call 800-777-0112 for other locations.

Telephones

New York, like most of the world's busy cities, is overrun with telephones, cellular phones, pagers and faxes. This increasing dependence on a dial tone accounts for the city's abundance of area codes. As a rule, you must dial 1 + area code before a number if the place you are calling is in a different area code. The area codes for Manhattan are 212 and 646; Brooklyn, Queens, Staten Island and the Bronx are 718 and 347; generally (but not always) 917 is reserved for cellular phones and pagers. The Long Island area codes are 516 and 631, and the codes for New Jersey are 201, 609, 732 856, 908 and 973. Numbers preceded by 800, 877 and 888 are free of charge when dialed from anywhere in the United States. When numbers are listed as letters (e.g., 800-AIR-RIDE) for easy recall, dial the

corresponding numbers on the telephone keypad.

Remember, if you carry a cellular phone, make sure you turn it off on trains and buses, and at restaurants, plays, movies, concerts and museums. New Yorkers are quick to show their annoyance at an ill-timed ring. Some establishments even post signs designating "cellular-free zones."

General information

The yellow pages and white pages directory offer a wealth of useful information in the front, including theater-seating diagrams and maps; the blue pages in the center of the white pages directory list all government numbers and addresses. Hotels will have copies; otherwise, try libraries or Verizon (the local phone company) payment centers.

Collect calls & credit-card calls

Collect calls are also known as reverse charges. Dial 0 followed by the area code and number, or dial AT&T's 800-CALL-ATT, MCI's 800-COLLECT or Sprint's 800-ONE-DIME.

Directory assistance

Dial 411 (free from pay phones). For long-distance directory assistance, dial 1 + area code + 555-1212 (long-distance charges apply). Verizon also offers national 411 directory assistance, but the charges can be high.

Emergency

Dial **911**. All calls are free (including those made on pay and cell phones).

International calls

Dial 011 + country code (U.K. 44; Australia 61; New Zealand 64).

Operator assistance

Dial 0.

Toll-free directory

Dial 1 + 800 + 555-1212 (no charge).

Pagers & cell phones

InTouch USA

212-391-8323; 800-872-7626. Mon–Fri 9am–5:30pm. AmEx, DC, Disc, MC, V.

InTouch, the city's largest cellular phone rental company, rents out equipment by the day, week or month.

Public pay phones & phone cards

Public pay phones are easy to find. Some of them even work. Verizon's phones are the most dependable (those from other phone companies tend to be poorly maintained). If someone's left the receiver dangling, it's often a sign that it doesn't work. Phones take any combination of silver coins: Local calls usually cost 25¢ for three minutes. If you're not used to American phones, know that the ringing tone is long; the "engaged" tone, or busy signal, is short and higher pitched.

If you want to call long-distance or make an international call from a pay phone, you need to use one of the long-distance companies. Most pay phones in New York automatically use AT&T, but phones in and around transportation hubs usually use other long-distance carriers, whose charges can be outrageous. Look in the yellow pages under Telephone Companies. Sprint and MCI are respected brand names *(see* **Collect calls & credit card calls**, *page 375).*

Make the call either by dialing 0 for an operator or by dialing direct (the latter is cheaper). To find out how much a call will cost, dial the number and a computer voice will tell you how much money to deposit. You can pay for calls with your credit card.

The best way to make calls is with a **phone card**, available in various denominations from any post office branch or from chain stores like Duane Reade or Rite Aid *(see* **Pharmacies**, *page 367).* Delis and kiosks sell phone cards, including the New York Exclusive, which has incredible international

rates. Dialing instructions are on the card.

Recorded information

For the exact time and temperature, plus lottery numbers and the New York City weather forecast, call 212-976-2828—a free call 24 hours a day. Other helpful 24-hour information lines, which add extra costs to your phone bill, are listed below. An opening message should tell you how much per minute you are paying.

Horoscopes
900-438-7337

Lottery picks
646-486-6100

Sports scores
900-976-1313

Telephone answering service

Messages Plus
1317 Third Ave between 75th and 76th Sts (212-879-4144). Subway: 6 to 77th St. 24 hrs. AmEx, MC, V. Messages Plus provides telephone answering service, with specialized (medical, bilingual, etc.) receptionists if required, and plenty of ways to deliver your messages. It also offers telemarketing, voice mail and interactive website services.

Television

A visit to New York often includes at least a small dose of cathode radiation and, particularly for British visitors, American TV can inflict culture shock. The TV day is scheduled down to the second, beginning with news and gossipy breakfast magazine programs and segueing into a lobotomizing cycle of soap operas, vintage reruns and game shows—it remains unbroken until around 3pm. Then *Oprah* and *Jerry Springer* take over, broadcasting people's not-so-private problems, with subjects along the lines of "I

married my mother's lesbian lover".

At 5pm, there's showbiz chat and local news, followed by national and international news at 6:30pm. Early evening is the domain of popular reruns *(Friends, Seinfeld, The Simpsons)* and syndicated game shows like *Jeopardy!* Huge audiences tune in at prime time, when action series dramas, sports, movies, game shows and sitcoms battle for ratings. Finally, as sedate viewers go to bed, out come the neon personalities of the various late-night talk shows.

Public television has its own nightly news and a few local productions; its *Frontline* and *P.O.V.* documentaries are often incisive. Public stations receive little money from traditional advertising and rely heavily on "membership" donations garnered during on-air fund drives.

And then there's cable, the 50 or so channels of basic cable, plus premium channels offering uninterrupted movies and sports coverage. Pay-per-view channels provide a menu of recent films, exclusive concerts and sports events at around $5 a pop. Cable also features paid "infomercials" and public-access channels (an eclectic array of weirdos, activists, scenesters and soft-core pornographers).

Time Out New York offers a rundown of weekly television highlights. For full TV schedules, save the Sunday *New York Times* TV section or buy a daily paper.

The networks
Six major networks broadcast nationwide. All offer ratings-led variations on a theme.

CBS (Channel 2 in NYC) has the top investigative show, *60 Minutes,* on Sundays, and its overall programming is geared to a middle-aged demographic *(Citizen Baines, Touched by an Angel).* But check out *Everybody Loves Raymond* (Mondays at 9pm) and *The Late Show with David Letterman* (weeknights at

11:35pm) for some solid humor.
NBC (4) is the home of the long-running sketch-comedy series *Saturday Night Live* (Saturdays at 11:30pm), and hugely popular sitcoms such as *Will & Grace*.

Fox-WNYW (5) is popular with younger audiences for hip shows like *Malcolm in the Middle*, *The Simpsons* and *The X-Files*.

ABC (7) is the king of daytime soaps, working-class sitcoms *(The Drew Carey Show)* and prime-time game shows *(Who Wants to Be a Millionaire)*.

UPN-WWOR (9) and **WB-WPIX** (11) don't attract the huge audiences of other networks, but they feature some offbeat programming, including *Angel*, *Buffy the Vampire Slayer*, *Felicity* and *Roswell*.

WXTV (41) and **WNJU** (47) are Spanish-language channels that offer Mexican dramas and titillating game shows. They're also your best non-cable bet for soccer.

Public TV

Public TV is on channels 13, 21 and 25. Documentaries, arts shows and science series alternate with *Masterpiece Theatre* and reruns of British shows like *Inspector Morse*. Channel 21 broadcasts *BBC World News* daily at 7 and 11pm.

Cable

(Note: All channel numbers listed are for Time Warner Cable in Manhattan. In other locations, or for other cable systems—such as Cablevision and RCN—check listings.)

NY1 (1), **CNN** (10), **MSNBC** (43), **Fox News** (46) are where you'll find news all day, the first with a local focus.

TNT (3), **TBS** (8) and **USA Network** (40) stations show notable reruns *(ER)* and feature films.

Nickelodeon (6) presents programming more suitable for kids and nostalgic fans of shows like *The Brady Bunch* and *Happy Days*.

Lifetime (12) is "television for women."

A&E (16) airs the shallow but popular *Biography* documentary series.

The History Channel (17), **Sci-Fi Channel** (44) and **Weather Channel** (72) are self-explanatory. **Discovery Channel** (18) and **Learning Channel** (52) feature science and nature programs.

VH1 (19), MTV's more mature sibling, airs the popular *Behind the Music* series, which delves into the lives of artists like Vanilla Ice and the Partridge Family.

MTV (20) increasingly offers fewer music videos and more of its

original programming *(Andy Dick Show*, *Jackass* and *The Real World)*.

Court TV (23) scores big ratings when there's a hot trial going on.

E! (24) is "Entertainment Television," a mix of celebrity and movie news. This is where you'll find tabloid segments like the unmissable *E! True Hollywood Story*, which profiles the likes of Mr. T and the Brat Pack.

Fox Sports (26), **MSG** (Madison Square Garden, 27), **ESPN** (28), and **ESPN2** (29) are all-sports stations.

Public Access TV is on channels 34, 56 and 57—surefire sources of bizarre camcorder amusement.

Channel 35 is where you'll find the fun, pornographic *Robin Byrd Show*.

Bravo (38) shows arts programming such as *Inside the Actors Studio*, quality art-house films and classic series, such as *Twin Peaks*.

Comedy Central (45) is all comedy, airing the raunchy cartoon *South Park* (Wednesdays at 10pm), and *The Daily Show with Jon Stewart* (weekdays at 7 and 11pm).

C-SPAN (64) is a forum for governmental affairs programming.

Cinemax, **Disney Channel**, **HBO**, **The Movie Channel** and **Showtime** are premium channels often available for a fee in hotels. They show uninterrupted feature films and exclusive specials.

Tickets

It's always show time somewhere in New York. And depending on what you're after—music, sports, theater—scoring tickets can be a real hassle. Smaller productions usually have their own in-house box office that sells tickets. Larger venues like Madison Square Garden have ticket agencies—and an equal number of devoted spectators. You may have to try more than one tactic to get into a popular or sold-out show.

Box-office tickets

Moviefone

212-777-FILM; www.moviefone.com. 24 hrs. AmEx, MC, V. $1.50 surcharge ($1 charge if purchased online). Use this service to purchase advance movie tickets by credit card over the phone or online and pick them up at an automated teller located in the theater lobby.

Telecharge

212-239-6200; www.telecharge.com. 24 hrs. AmEx, DC, Disc, MC, V. $6 surcharge per Broadway and Off Broadway ticket. Broadway and Off Broadway shows are the ticket here.

Ticket Central

555 W 42nd St between Tenth and Eleventh Aves (212-279-4200); www.ticketcentral.org). Subway: N, Q, R, W, S, 1, 2, 3, 7 to 42nd St–Times Sq. Phone orders Tue–Sat 1–7pm; Sun 1–6pm. AmEx, MC, V. $4 surcharge per order. Off and Off-Off Broadway tickets are available at the office or by phone.

Ticketmaster

212-307-7171; www.ticketmaster.com. Call 212-307-4100 for Broadway productions; call 212-307-4747 for Disney productions. 8am–10pm. AmEx, DC, Disc, MC, V. $3–$8 surcharge per ticket. This reliable service sells tickets to a variety of large-scale attractions including rock concerts, Broadway, and sports events. You can buy tickets by phone, online or at outlets throughout the city—Tower Records, the Wiz, HMV, J&R Music World and Filene's Basement, to name a few.

TKTS

Duffy Square, 47th St at Broadway (212-221-0013; www.tdf.org). Subway: N, Q, R, W, S, 1, 2, 3, 7 to 42nd St–Times Sq. Mon–Sat 3–8pm; Sun 11am–7pm. Wed, Sat 10am–2pm and Sun 11am–2pm for matinee tickets. $3.00 surcharge per ticket. Cash or traveler's checks only. TKTS has become a New York tradition. Broadway and Off Broadway tickets are sold at discounts of 25 and 50 percent (plus a $3.00 service charge per ticket) for same day performances; tickets to other highbrow events are also offered. The line can be long, but it's often worth the wait. The Financial District location is temporary and replaces the TKTS booth that was formerly in 2 World Trade Center. **Other location ● ** *1 Bowling Green at State St. Subway: 4, 5 to Bowling Green. Mon–Fri 11am–5:30pm; Sat 11am–3:30pm.*

Scalpers & standby tickets

You needn't give up all hope when a show sells out. There's always the risky scalper option (it's illegal and you might buy a forged ticket).

Before you part with any cash, make sure the ticket has the correct details. As showtime nears, some scalpers will unload their tickets at bargain prices. But be discreet—the police have been cracking down on scalpers in recent years, particularly outside Madison Square Garden.

Some venues also offer standby tickets right before show time, while others give reduced rates for tickets purchased on the same day as the performance. Those in the know line up hours beforehand.

Ticket brokers

Ticket brokers function like scalpers, although their activities are more regulated. It's illegal in New York State to sell a ticket for more than its face value plus a service charge, so these companies operate by phone from other states. They can almost guarantee tickets for sold-out events, and tend to deal only in better seats. Not surprisingly, this service is costly (Madonna tickets were selling for upwards of $2,000 in the summer of 2001). Look under "Ticket Sales" in the yellow pages for brokers. Listed below are three of the more established outfits.

Apex Tours
800-CITY-TIX; www.tixx.com. Mon–Fri 9am–5pm. AmEx, MC, V.

Prestige Entertainment
800-2GET-TIX; www.prestige entertainment.com. Mon–Fri 9am–6pm; Sat 9am–1pm. AmEx, MC, V.

TicketCity
800-880-8886; www.ticketcity.com. Mon–Fri 8:30am–9pm; Sat 11am–6pm; Sun 11am–3pm. AmEx, Disc, MC, V.

Time & date

New York is on Eastern Standard Time, which extends from the Atlantic coast to the eastern shore of Lake Michigan and south to the Gulf of Mexico. This is five hours behind Greenwich Mean Time. Clocks are set forward one hour in early April and back one hour at the end of October. Going from east to west, Eastern Time is one hour ahead of Central Time, two hours ahead of Mountain Time and three hours ahead of Pacific Time. Call 212-976-2828 for the exact time of day.

In the U.S. the date is written in this order: month, day, year; so 2/5/02 is February 5, 2002.

Tourist information

Hotels are usually full of maps, leaflets and free tourist magazines that give advice about entertainment and events. But be aware: Their advice is not always impartial. Plenty of local magazines (including *Time Out New York*) offer opinionated, yet reliable, info.

NYC & Company
800-NYC-VISIT, 212-397-8222; www.nycvisit.com
This is the city's official tourism marketing organization.
Other location ● 33–34 Carnaby St, London, UK, W1V 1CA (0-207-437-8300).

New York City's Official Visitor Information Center
810 Seventh Ave at 53rd St (212-484-1222; www.nycvisit.com). Subway: B, D, E to Seventh Ave; N, R, W to 49th St; 1, 2 to 50th St. Mon–Fri 8:30am–6pm; Sat, Sun 9am–5pm.
Leaflets on tours, attractions, etc., plus free advice on accommodations and entertainment, discount coupons and free maps are available at this center run by NYC & Company.

Times Square Visitors Center
1560 Broadway between 46th and 47th Sts (212-768-1560). Subway: N, Q, R, W, S, 1, 2, 3, 7 to 42nd St–Times Sq. 8am–8pm.
This center offers discount coupons for Broadway tickets, MetroCards, an Internet station and other useful goods and services.

Translation & language services

All Language Services
545 Fifth Ave at 45th St (212-986-1688; fax 212-986-3396). Subway: S, 4, 5, 6, 7 to 42nd St–Grand Central. 24 hrs. AmEx, MC, V.
ALS will type or translate documents in any of 59 languages and provide interpreters.

Visas

Nearly 30 countries participate in the Visa Waiver Program. Citizens of Andorra, Argentina, Australia, Austria, Belgium, Brunei, Denmark, Finland, France, Germany, Iceland, Ireland, Italy, Japan, Liechtenstein, Luxembourg, Monaco, the Netherlands, New Zealand, Norway, Portugal, San Marino, Singapore, Slovenia, Spain, Sweden, Switzerland, the United Kingdom and Uruguay do not need a visa for stays shorter than 90 days (business or pleasure), as long as they have a passport that is valid for the full 90-day period and a return ticket. An open standby ticket is acceptable.

Canadians and Mexicans don't need visas but must have legal proof of residency. All other travelers must have visas. You can obtain information and application forms from your nearest U.S. embassy or consulate. In general, submit your application at least three weeks before you plan to travel. To apply for a visa on shorter notice, contact your travel agent.

For information on student visas, see page 365.

U.S. Embassy Visa Information
In the U.S. 202-663-1225; in the U.K. 09061-500-590; http://travel.state.gov/visa_services.html.

Websites

See **Websites**, page 379.

Further Reference

In-depth guides

Mindy Bailir: *Fodor's Around New York City with Kids.* A bunch of kid-friendly New York adventures.
Edward F. Bergman: *The Spiritual Traveler, New York City.* This is a guide to sacred and peaceful spaces.
Eleanor Berman: *Away for the Weekend: New York.* Trips within a 200-mile radius of New York City.
Eleanor Berman: *New York Neighborhoods.* Ethnic enclaves abound in this food lover's guide.
Arthur S. Brown: *Vegetarian Dining in New York City.* Includes vegan places.
Eve Claxton: *New York's 100 Best Little Places to Shop.*
William Corbett: *New York Literary Lights.* An encyclopedic collection of info about NYC's literary past.
David Frattini: *The Underground Guide to New York City Subways.*
Alfred Gingold and Helen Rogan: *The New Ultra Cool Parents Guide to All of New York.*
Guide to New York City Landmarks: Produced by the Landmarks Preservation Commission.
Hagstrom: *New York City 5 Borough Pocket Atlas.* You won't get lost with this thorough street map.
Chuck Katz: *Manhattan on Film.* A must for movie buffs who want to scope out the city by foot.
Ruth Leon: *Applause: New York's Guide to the Performing Arts.* Detailed directory of performance venues.
Ann Matthews: *Wild Nights: Nature Returns to the City.* The urban jungle has more than pigeons and people.
OYO Publications: *Sexy New York City 2001.* Discover erotica in the Naked City.
Lyn Skreczko and Virginia Bell: *The Manhattan Health Pages.* Everything from aerobics to Zen.
Earl Steinbicker: *Daytrips New York 2002.*
Linda Tarrant-Reid: *Discovering Black New York.* This guide reveals important black museums and more.
Pamela Thomas: *Romantic Days and Nights in New York City.* Get an insider's look at romantic diversions.
Time Out New York Eating & Drinking 2002: A comprehensive guide to more than 3,000 places to eat and drink in the five boroughs. Written by food critics.
Where to Wear 2001: A fix for shopaholics.
Zagat: *New York City Restaurants.* The popular opinion guide.

Architecture

Margot Gayle: *Cast Iron Architecture in New York.*
Stanley Greenberg: *Invisible New York.* Photographic account of hidden architectural triumphs.
Karl Sabbagh: *Skyscraper.* How the tall ones are built.
Robert A.M. Stern: *New York 1930.* A massive coffee-table slab with stunning pictures.
Robert A.M. Stern: *New York 1960.* Another.
Elliot Willensky and Norval White: *American Institute of Architects Guide to New York City.* A comprehensive directory of important buildings.
Gerard R. Wolfe: *A Guide to the Metropolis.* Historical and architectural walking tours.

Culture & recollections

Candace Bushnell: *Sex and the City.* Smart women, superficial New York.
George Chauncey: *Gay New York.* New York gay life from the 1890s on.
William Cole (ed.): *Quotable New York.*
Martha Cooper and Henry Chalfant: *Subway Art.*
Josh Alan Friedman: *Tales of Times Square.* Sleaze, scum, filth and degradation in Times Square.
Nelson George: *Hip-Hop America.* The history of hip-hop, from Grandmaster Flash to Puffy.
Pat Hackett: *The Andy Warhol Diaries.*
Robert Hendrickson: *New Yawk Tawk.* Dictionary of NYC slang.
A.J. Liebling: *Back Where I Came From.* Personal recollections from the famous *New Yorker* columnist.
Lisa Lovatt-Smith and Alberto Heras: *New York Living.* See some of Gotham's most fabulous digs.
Legs McNeil: *Please Kill Me.* Oral history of the city's 1970s punk scene.
Joseph Mitchell: *Up in the Old Hotel.* An anthology of the late journalist's most colorful reporting.
Frank O'Hara: *The Collected Poems of Frank O'Hara.* The great NYC poet found inspiration in his hometown.
Andrea Wyatt Sexton (ed.): *The Brooklyn Reader.*
Andrés Torres: *Between Melting Pot and Mosaic.* African-American and Puerto Rican life in the city.

Websites

For food-related websites, see **Pulldown menus**, page 185.

www.timeoutny.com
The *Time Out New York* website covers all the city has to offer. When you're planning your trip, check out the New York City Guide section for a variety of itineraries that you can use in conjunction with this guide.
www.council.nyc.ny.us
Learn about local laws and important current events.
www.mta.nyc.ny.us
Subway and bus service changes are always posted here. Plus, an interactive subway map points out sights near each stop.
www.nyc.gov
City Hall's "Official New York City Website" has lots of links.
www.nycvisit.com
This site is run by NYC & Company, the local convention and visitors bureau.
www.ny1.com
NY1 News' site covers local events, news and weather.
www.nytimes.com
"All the News That's Fit to Print" online from *The New York Times.*
www.centralparknyc.org
Find out the nitty-gritty on the city's favorite park.
www.citysearch.com
Online information on entertainment and events.
www.clubplanet.com
Follow the city's nocturnal scene and buy advance tickets to big events.
www.dailycandy.com
Discover tidbits on what's hot in the city.
www.forgotten-ny.com
Remember Old New York here.
www.hipguide.com
A short 'n' sweet site for those looking for what's considered hip.
www.mrbellersneighborhood.com
Locals and literati swap (mostly) true tales about life in the city.
www.nycsubway.org
For fans of the New York underground system.
www.whitehouse.gov
Your connection to the top dogs of the U.S. government.

Fiction

Kurt Andersen: *Turn of the Century.* Millennial Manhattan seen through the eyes of media players.

Paul Auster: *The New York Trilogy.* A search for the madness behind the method of Manhattan's grid.

Kevin Baker: *Dreamland.* A poetic novel about Coney Island's glory days.

James Baldwin: *Another Country.* Racism under the bohemian veneer of the 1960s.

Caleb Carr: *The Alienist.* Hunting a serial killer in New York's turn-of-the-previous-century demimonde.

Bret Easton Ellis: *American Psycho.* A serial killer is loose among the young and fabulous in 1980s Manhattan.

Ralph Ellison: *Invisible Man.* Coming of age as a black man in 1950s New York.

F. Scott Fitzgerald: *The Beautiful and Damned.* A New York City couple squander their fortune during the Jazz Age.

Larry Kramer: *Faggots.* Hilarious gay New York.

Jonathan Lethem: *Motherless Brooklyn.* This cult fave among Brooklyn residents is a rollicking whodunnit romp through the borough.

Toni Morrison: *Jazz.* The music, glamour and grit of 1920s Harlem.

Dawn Powell: *The Locusts Have No King.* A stinging satire of New York's intelligentsia.

Hubert Selby Jr.: *Last Exit to Brooklyn.* Brooklyn dockland degradation, circa the 1950s.

Betty Smith: *A Tree Grows in Brooklyn.* An Irish girl in 1930s Brooklyn.

Edith Wharton: *Old New York.* Four novellas of 19th-century New York, by the author of *The Age of Innocence.*

Tom Wolfe: *The Bonfire of the Vanities.* Rich/poor, black/white. An unmatched slice of 1980s New York.

Time Out Book of New York Short Stories: Of course we like these original short stories by 23 American and British authors.

Writing New York edited by Phillip Lopate. An excellent anthology of short stories, essays and poems set in New York.

Film

See **City cinema**, page 278.

History

Irving Lewis Allen: *The City in Slang.* How New York living has spawned hundreds of new words and phrases.

Patrick Bunyan: *All Around the Town.* A book about fun Manhattan facts and curiosities.

Robert A. Caro: *The Power Broker.* A biography of Robert Moses, the mid-20th-century master builder in New York, and his checkered legacy.

Eric Darton: *Divided We Stand.* A biography of the World Trade Center.

Federal Writers' Project: *The WPA Guide to New York City.* A wonderful snapshot of 1930s New York by writers employed under FDR's New Deal.

Sanna Feirstein: *Naming New York.* An account of how Manhattan places got their names.

Clifton Hood: *722 Miles: The Building of the Subways and How They Transformed New York.*

Kenneth T. Jackson: *The Encyclopedia of New York City.* An ambitious and useful reference guide.

Rem Koolhaas: *Delirious New York.* New York as a terminal city. Urbanism and the culture of congestion.

David Levering Lewis: *When Harlem Was in Vogue.* A study of the 1920s Harlem Renaissance.

Caroline Rennolds Milbank: *New York Fashion: The Evolution of American Style.*

Henry Moscow: *An Encyclopedia of Manhattan Street Names and Their Origins.*

The New York Pop-Up Book: Interactive historical account of NYC.

Shaun O'Connell: *Remarkable, Unspeakable New York.* The history of New York as literary inspiration.

Mitchell Pacelle: *Empire: The Battle for an American Icon.* A tale of the fight for the Empire State Building.

Jacob Riis: *How the Other Half Lives.* A pioneering photojournalistic record of gruesome tenement life.

Roy Rosenzweig and Elizabeth Blackmar: *The Park and the People.* A lengthy history of Central Park.

Luc Sante: *Low Life.* Opium dens, brothels, tenements and suicide salons in New York from the 1840s to the 1920s.

Kim Taylor: *The Great New York City Trivia & Fact Book.* Peculiar facts.

Jennifer Toth: *The Mole People: Life in the Tunnels Beneath New York City.*

Mike Wallace and Edwin G. Burrows: *Gotham: A History of New York City to 1898.* The first volume in a planned mammoth history of NYC.

Hot off the press

These newly published books celebrate the city

James Sanders's *Celluloid Skyline* explores two New Yorks: the real one and the mythic film version. Not a book exactly, Matteo Pericoli's *Manhattan Unfurled* unfolds to reveal two 22-foot-long sketches of the skyline (World Trade Center included). *New York Characters* showcases Gillian Zoe Segal's portraits of "ordinary" New Yorkers, such as Johnnie Footman, the city's oldest cabbie. *Cityscapes* conveys the city's 400-year history through a revealing collection of images. *New York Exposed* features photographs from the *Daily News*, while *The Post's New York* gives a history in headlines. Helen Levitt's *Crosstown* is a coffee-table tome of treasured photos. *Unearthing Gotham* digs through 100 years of excavation to find out more about who we were then and who we are now. *Down 42nd Street* finds Marc Eliot tracing

the transformation of 42nd Street from business district to sex-and-drug den to Disneyland. *Inside the Plaza* Former New York Post columnist Ward Morehouse digs up the dirt about the fabled Plaza Hotel. *It Happened in Manhattan* First-person tales from the likes of Jimmy Breslin recall life here a half-century ago. *Stork Club* This ode to nightlife at the city's celebrity-soaked hot spot is now out in paperback and includes instructions from the daughter of the club's legendary owner, Sherman Billingsley, for throwing your own Stork Club party. *New York September 11* by Magnum photographers, and *The World Trade Center: A Tribute* commemorates that infamous day. Camilo José Vergara, who photographed WTC in its early days, revisits the same vantage points in *Twin Towers Remembered.*

Index

Numbers in **bold** indicate key
information on a topic; *italics*
indicate photographs.

a

Aaron Davis Hall 344
ABC Carpet & Home 64, **224**
ABC No Rio 58
Abyssinian Baptist
Church 84, **87**
Accommodations 115–143
bed-and-breakfast services
142–143
boutique 115, **132–135**
Brooklyn lodging 143
gay & lesbian 282–283, 288
hostels 140–142
hotels **116–140**, 143
Accommodations Express 115
AC Project Room 246
Active Warehouse 202
Ada 181
Adair Vineyards 352
Adventure on a Shoestring
97, **108**
Aesop's Tables 106
African Burial Ground 10, **53**
age restrictions 364
agnès b. 201
African Market 84
agnès b. 201
agnès b. homme 203
A Hospitality Company 142
AIDS and HIV Hot Line 368
Ailey School, The 348
airports 360
transportation to and
from 360–361
AirTrain Newark 360
aKa Café 155
Akwaaba Mansion Bed &
Breakfast 143
Akwaaba Café 143
Alain Ducasse at the Essex
House 179
Alain Mikli Optique 208
Albatross 351
alcohol help lines 367
Alcoholics Anonymous 367
Alcone 213
a. di là 28, **187**
Alexander and Bonin 246
Alexander Hamilton Custom
House 22, 46
Algonquin, The 15, 73, **125**,
258, 262
Alice Tully Hall 316
Alice Underground 205
alife 202
Allan & Suzi 205
All Around the Town 142
All Language Services 378
Alphabet City 63
Alphabet Kitchen 162
Alphabets 227
Amalgamated and Park Reservoir
Houses 102
Amato Opera Theatre 320
ambulance service 366
AMC Empire 25 **273**
American Academy of Arts and
Letters **38**, 87
American Ballet Theatre 348
American Craft Museum **38**, 73
American Express 371
American Fine Arts at
PHAG 246
American Fine Arts, Colin
deLand 246
American Folk Art Museum
20, **38**
American Museum of Natural
History 11, **33**, 82, 291
IMAX Theater 82, **278**

Rose Center for Earth and
Space **33**, 37, 82, 291
Starry Nights: Fridays Under
the Sphere 37
American Museum of the Moving
Image **44**, 97, 275
Artlink 103
American Numismatic
Society 40, 87
American Opera Projects 320
American Park at the
Battery 46, **153**
American Radiator Building 73
Americas Society 79
AMF Chelsea Piers Lanes 327, *329*
Amoco 362
Amsterdam Billiard Club 327
Amsterdam News 371
Amtrak 359–360
amusement parks 95, **290**
Amy Chan 55, **208**
Amy Downs Hats 209
Amy Ruth's 84
An American Place 131
Anchorage, The 90, **313**
Andrade Shoe Repair 208
Andrea Rosen Gallery 246
Andrew Freedman Home 101
Andrew Kreps Gallery *245*, 246
Andy's Colonial 186
Angel 148
Angelica Kitchen 162
Angelika Film Center 274
Angelique Bed & Breakfast 143
Angry Wade's 151
Anna Sui 201
Annex Antiques Fair & Flea
Market 67, **221**
Garage, The 221
Annisa 164, *167*, *167*
Ansonia Hotel 82
answering services 376
Anthology Film Archives 275
Antique Boutique 205
Antique Flea & Farmers'
Market 82, **221**
antiques 221
fairs 236, 243
Anton Kern Gallery 246
AOL Time Warner **21**, 82
Apartment, The 224
Apex Art 254
Apex Tours 378
Apollo Theatre 85, **300**
Appellate Court 66
Apple Pie Bakery Café 356
Applewood Winery 352
APT 61, 144, **269**
AQ Café 44, **176**
Aquavit 44, **176**, *181*
Aqueduct Racetrack 98,
323, *324*
Arabelle 133
Architecture 18–24
Arci's Place 262
Ardsley, The 82
Area I.D. Moderne 225
arenas 300
Continental Airlines Arena 300
Madison Square Garden 300
Nassau Veterans Memorial
Coliseum 300
Ariel Meyerowitz 256
Arlene Grocery 57, **300**
Armory Show, The 243
Arnold Hatters 209
Arraignment Court 53–54
Art Directors Club 67
Art Galleries 244–256
nonprofit 254–255
photography 255–256
Arthur Avenue 102, *104*
Retail Market 102
Arthur Avenue Café 103
Arthur Brown & Brothers 230
ARTime 291

Art in General 254
Artists Space 255
Artlink shuttle bus 96, **103**
Artisanal 174
Art Show, The 243
Asia Society and
Museum **41**, 79, 277
Asphalt Green 325, **329**
Asser Levy Pool 332
Astoria 14, **96–97**
Astor Place 62
Astor Place Hair Stylists 216
Astor Wines & Spirits 224
Astroland Amusement Park
95, **290**
At Home in New York 142
Atlantic Antic 241
Atlantic Avenue 92, *96*
Atlantic Theater Company 339
ATMs 370–371
Atomic Passion 219
A to Z Couriers 370
A.T. Stewart Dry Goods Store 22
Aubette 147
Auction House Bar, The 80
Audre Lorde Project Center 280
Audubon Terrace 87
Austrian Cultural Center 20
Autumn Blues Festival 242
Avalon Nurse Registry & Child
service 364
Aveda 213
Avenue 184
Avery Fisher Hall **317**, 369
Avis 359
Avon Salon & Spa 216
Awesome Bed & Breakfast
142, **143**
Ayurveda Cafe 184
A. Zito & Sons Bakery 222

b

BAAD! 104, **105**
Babbo 164, **166**
Baby Doll Lounge 144
Babysitters' Guild 364
baby-sitting 364
Baggot Inn 300
Bag House 210
Baktun *265*, 267
Baldoria 176
Balducci's 61, **222**
Balthazar 159
BAMcafé **300**, 307
BAMkids Film Festival 294
BAM Rose Cinemas 91, **274**
Bamonte's 187
Banana Republic 54, **195**
B&H 219
Bang & Olufsen 219
Bang on a Can Festival 237
banks 371
Bar, The 29
Bar @ Etats-Unis 150
Baraza 144, *145*
Bar-B 148
Barbara Gladstone 246
Barbizon Hotel 127
BARC's Annual Dog Parade, Show
and Fair 241
Bar Demi 147
Bar d'O 284
Bardolino 184
Bargemusic 90, **317**, *319*
Barking Dog Luncheonette 186
Barnard College 83
Center for Research on
Women 280
Barnes & Noble 64, **217**, 257,
258, 369
Barney Greengrass—The Sturgeon
King 83, **184**
Barneys New York **193**, 203,
211, 369
Co-op 193

Bar Pitti 167
Bar Reis 28
Barracuda 285
Barramundi 149
Barrow's Pub 144
Bars 144–151
age restrictions 364
Brooklyn 28–29, **151**, 270–271
gay & lesbian 29, 281–286,
288–289
Lower East Side 149–150
Bartow-Pell Mansion 104, **105**
baseball **321–322**, 326–327
basketball **322**, 325
Bateaux New York 107
bathhouses 286
Battery Maritime Building 47
Battery Park 46–47, *47*
Battery Park City 48–50
Authority 50
Battlegrounds, The 325
Bayard's 153
Bay Ridge 93
B-Bar 270
B.B. King Blues Club &
Grill 312, *314*
beaches 86–87, **350–355**
Brighton 94
Coney Island 95–96
Orchard 104
Tottenville 106
Beacon Theatre 83, *299*, **301**
Bean 28
Bear Mountain State Park 356
beauty 213–217
Bed & Breakfast (& Books) 142
Bed and Breakfast in
Manhattan 142
Bed & Breakfast Off the
Park 142
bed-and-breakfast services 142–143
Bed, Bath & Beyond 64
Bedford Avenue 28, **92**
Bedford-Stuyvesant 93
Beekman Arms 356
Beekman Arms Antique Market
and Gallery 356
Beekman 1766 Tavern 356
Beekman Tower Hotel 129
Beige 283
Bellevue Hospital 69, **367**
Belmont 102
Belmont Park 324
Bemelmans Bar 116, **261**
Benito One 55
Benjamin, The 129
Bennison Fabrics 225
Bensonhurst 93
Bentley, The 131
Bergdorf Goodman 74,
193, 203
Berliniamsburg 268, **286**
Bernard Kerik Detention
Complex 53
Bessie Schönberg Theater 67
Best Cellars 224
Best Western Manhattan 131
Betsey Johnson 202
Better Business Bureau 364
Beyond Events Calendar 267
Bicycle Habitat 325
bicycling 325
organized rides 325–326
path maps 325
races 237, 241
rentals 325
Big Apple Circus 242, **290**, 291
Big Apple Greeter **109**, 366
Big City Kites 230
Big Cup 287
Big Onion Walking Tours
48–49, **109**
Bike New York: The Great Five
Boro Bike Tour 237
Bike the Big Apple 107
billiards 327

Bill Maynes 246
Billy Martin's 211
Birdland 310
bird-watching 26–27
Bitter End 301
Black Book *372*
Black Duck 135
Black Underground 96
Blades, Board and Skate **232**, 331
Bleecker Bob's 229
Bleecker Street 61
Bleu Evolution 186
Bliss 216
Bliss 57 216
Bloomingdale's 193
Blue Bag 208
Blue Fin 123
Blue Hill 167
Blue Ivy 222
Blue Note 311
Blue Ribbon 168
Blue Ribbon Bakery 168
Blue Ribbon Brooklyn 28, **168**
Blue Ribbon Sushi 168
Bluestockings 280
Blue Water Grill 170
Boat Basin Café, The *85,* 87, **150**
Boathouse in Central Park 78, *184*
Boat Livery 105
b0b 148, **270**
Body & Soul 266, **269**
Body Shop, The 213
Boerum Hill 29
Boiler Room 283
Bond 07 197
Bond St. 161
Bonpoint 204
Books & Poetry 257–260
fairs 236, 241
gay & lesbian 279–281
NYC reference guides 379–380
readings 257–259
spoken word 259–260
talks and lectures 260
tours 260
bookshops **217–218**, 257–258, 280
Borders Books & Music 69, **218**, 258
Borough Hall 91
Borough Park 93
Boscobel Restoration 355
Boston Comedy Club, The 263
Botanica 144
Botel 351
Bottega Veneta 200
Bottom Line, The 301
Bouley Bakery 154
Bowery Ballroom 57, **301**
Bowery Savings Bank 75
Bowery's Whitehouse Hotel of New York 140
bowling 327–328
Bowlmor Lanes 146, **328**
Bowne House 98
boxing 322
Brasserie 180
Brasserie 8½ 179, *179*
Breakaway 370
Brecht Forum 260
Brent Sikkema 246
Bronwyn Keenan 244
Bronx 99–105
restaurants 190
Bronx Academy of Arts & Dance (BAAD!) 104, **105**
Bronx County Historical Society Museum 105

Bronx Museum of the Arts 100, **105**
Bronx Opera Company 320
Bronx Zoo/Wildlife Conservation Facility 102, **105**, 297
Brooklyn 28–29, **90–96**
art galleries 244, 251, 253–254
bars 28–29, 151, 270–271
destinations 95–96
lodging 143
music scene 306–309
neighborhoods 90–95
restaurants 28–29, 187–189
tours 93
Brooklyn Academy of Music (BAM) 29, 91, **315**, 339, 343, *345*
BAMcafé 300, 307
BAMkids Film Festival 294
BAM Rose Cinemas 91, 274
Brooklyn Arts Exchange 344
Brooklyn BeerFest 241
Brooklyn Botanic Garden 95, **96**
Cherry Blossom Esplanade 95
Cranford Rose Garden 95
Japanese Hill-and-Pond Garden 95
Steinhardt Pavilion 95
Brooklyn Bridge 11, 90, **94**
Anchorage, The 90, 313
Brooklyn Center for the Performing Arts at Brooklyn College 320
Brooklyn Children's Museum 291
Brooklyn Cyclones 326–327, *327*
Brooklyn Dodgers 16, *16*
Brooklyn Heights 90–91
Promenade 90, 94
Brooklyn Historical Society **40**, 90
Brooklyn Information and Culture 94
Brooklyn Museum of Art 32, **33**, 95, 276, 291
First Saturdays 36
Brooks Brothers 203
Brotherhood, America's Oldest Winery 352
Brownies 63, 299, **301**
Brownstone, The 85
Brownstoners of Bedford-Stuyvesant Tour 93
Bryant Park 69, 73, *76,* **314**
Free Summer Season 238
Bryant Park, The 73, **132**, *134,* 177
Bryant Park Cafe and Grill 73
Bubby's 154
Budget Rent-a-Car 359
Bulgari 209
Bulgin' Waffles 162
BUNAC 365
Burberry 200
buses **352**, 358
city 361
fares 361
lines 358
lost property 370
services to and from airports 360–361
stations 358
Butta' Cup Lounge 29

C

Cabaret & Comedy 261–264
Cabrini Medical Center 367
Café Boulud 182
Cafe Carlyle 116, **261**
Cafe Edison 134, **177**
Cafe Gitane 56
Cafe Habana 56
Café La Fortuna 82
Café La Grolla 185
Café Mogador *162,* 163
Café Sabarsky 32
Café Steinhof 189
Café Weissman 32
Cafe Wha? 61
Caffè Roma 55
Calvin Klein 200
Calypso Enfants 204
Calypso on Broome *194,* 197
cameras 219–220
CAMI Hall 317
Campbell Apartment 75, **147**

Camper 211
Canal Jean Company 202
Canal Street 56
Cannon's Pub 150
Canton 157
Capezio Dance-Theater Shop 348
Caputo Bakery 91
Caputo's Fine Foods 91
Carapan 217
Carla Dawn Behrle 199
Carlton Arms Hotel 138
Carlyle Hotel 116
Carmel 363
Carmensville Playgrounds 325
Carmine Street Recreation Center 332
Carnegie Club 147
Carnegie Deli 72, **177**
Carnegie Hall 11, 22, 72, 311, 315, **316**
CarnegieCharge 315
Family Concerts 293
tours 315
Caroline Distribution 67
Carolines on Broadway 263
Carrandi Gallery 230
car rental 358–359
age restrictions 364
car services 265–266, **363**
to and from airports 360
Cartier 54, 74, **209**
Casablanca Hotel 133
Casey Kaplan 246
Casimir 163
Castle Clinton 13, 46, **314**
Cathedral of St. John the Divine 83, 84, 87, 257, 258, 318
Catherine 195
CBGB 17, 62, **303**
CB's 313 Gallery 303
Ceci-Cela 160
Cedar Tavern 59
Celebrate Brooklyn! Performing Arts Festival 238
Celine 200
Cellar Bar 73, 132, **147**
Cello 165
cemeteries
First Shearith Israel Graveyard 57, **59**
Flushing 101
Green-Wood 95, **96**
Quaker Friends 95
St. Michaels 101
Woodlawn 26
Centercharge 315
Center for Disease Control 368
Center for Inner Resource Development 368
Central Library 90
Central Park 11, 25–27, *27,* **77–79**, 294–296
Arts in the Park 294
Belvedere Castle 78
Bethesda Fountain and Terrace 78
bicycle tours 107
Bow Bridge 78
Carousel 77, **78**, 294
Charles A. Dana Discovery Center 78
Chill Out Weekend 240
Conservatory Garden 78
Conservatory Water 78, **294**
Dairy, The 78
Delacorte Theater 78, **337**, *339,* 369
Great Lawn 78
Harlem Meer 78
Heckscher Playground 294
Henry Luce Nature Observatory **78**, 295
Jacqueline Kennedy Onassis Reservoir 26, **78**
Lake 78
Loeb Boathouse 78, **79**, 325
loop 325
Mall, The 77
Naumburg Bandshell 77
North Meadow Recreation Center 295
Ramble **78**, 282
Sheep Meadow 77

Strawberry Fields 77
Stories at the Hans Christian Andersen Statue 295
SummerStage 78, 238, *239,* **314**, 347
Wildlife Center 297
Wollman Memorial Rink 77, **330**
Central Park Bicycle Tours 107
Central Park Hostel 139, **141**
Central Park West 82
Central Reservation Service 135
Centro-Fly 267
Century, The 82
Century 21 193, **202**
Chamber Music Society of Lincoln Center 316
Chambers *117,* 119
Champion Locksmiths 369
Chanel 200
Chanel Gardens 73
Chanin Building 75
Charles Cowles 247
Charles' Southern Style Kitchen 187
Charlton-King-Vandam Historic District 21
Chase 283, **285**
cheap eats 172
Cheim & Read 244, **247**
Chelsea 66–67
art galleries 244, 245–251
flower district 66
Chelsea Bar & Billiards 327
Chelsea Center 141
Chelsea Garden Center Home Store 225, *225*
Chelsea Historic District 66, **67**
Chelsea Hotel 67, **131**
Chelsea Lodge *136,* 138
Chelsea Market 67
Chelsea Mews Guest House 282
Chelsea Piers 67, **296**
AMF Lanes 327, *329*
Golf Club 328
Roller Rinks 331
Sky Rink 330
Sports Center 328, **330**
Chelsea Pines Inn 282
Chelsea Screamer 107
Chelsea Star Hotel 138
Chequepoint USA 371
Chicago City Limits Theatre 263
Chicama 170
child abuse help line 368
children 290–297
clothing stores 204–205
literature 88, 290
toy stores 221
Children's Museum of the Arts 292
Children's Museum of Manhattan 83, **292**
Child USA's National Child Abuse Hotline 368
China Institute **42**, 79
Chinatown 55, **56–57**, 364
restaurants 157–159
snacks 157
taxis 363
Chinatown Fair 56
Chinatown Ice Cream Factory 57
ChinatownNYC.com Walking Tours 109
Chinese New Year 56, **243**
Chip Shop 29
Chloé 200
Christ and St. Stephen's Church 318
Christian Dior 200
Christian Louboutin 211
Christie's 73
Christmas Spectacular 242
Christmas Tree Lighting Ceremony 242
Chrysler Building 15, 23, **75**
Chrysler Trylons 75
Chuckie's 211
Chumley's 62, **144**
Church Lounge 144
churches 374
performances in 318–319
Church of St. Ignatius Loyola 318
Church of the Ascension 318
Church Street Boxing Gym 322
Churrascaria Plataforma 177

Chu Shing 56
CineKids 291
Cinema Classics 275
cinemas 273–278
  foreign-language
    films 277–278
  museums and
    societies 275–277
  popular 273–274
  revival and art-house 274–275
Cinema Village 275
Circle Line 72, **107**
circuses 235, 242, **290–291**
Cirque du Soleil 290
Cirrus 370
Citarella 83
Citicorp Center 2₅
City Bakery 170, *173*
City Center Theater 343
City Club Hotel **121**, *129*, 132
City College 86
City Floral 222
City Hall 21, **52–53**
City Hospital 81
City Island 104–105
City Lights Bed and
  Breakfast 143
CitySonnet 143
Citywide Towing 361
Civic Center 52–54
Civil War Memorial Arch 91
Claremont Riding
  Academy 83, **330**
Clarion Hotel Fifth
  Avenue 132
Clarion Park Avenue 138
Classic Stage Company 339
Clayworks Pottery 219
Clearview's Chelsea West 275
Clearview's Ziegfeld **274**, 275
Clegg's Hotel 351
climbing 328
clinics 366
Clinton 72
  restaurants 179–180
Cloisters, The **33**, 88
clothing
  rental 206
  repair 207
  stores 193–207
Club Guastavino 182
Club New York 267, *272*
Clubs 265–272
  age restrictions 364
  gay & lesbian 93, 286, 289
CMJ Music Marathon, MusicFest
  and FilmFest 241
C-Note 303
Coach 190
Cobblestones 219
C.O. Bigelow Apothecaries
  215, *217*
Cocaine Anonymous 367
Cock,The *280*, 284
Cocktail Room, The 150
Cold Spring 355
Colden Center for the Performing
  Arts 316
Colonial House Inn 282
Colonial Transportation 360
Colonnade Row **22**, 62
Columbia University 83, **84**
  Miller Theatre 318
Columbus Avenue 82
Columbus Centre 82
Columbus Circle 21, **82**
Columbus Day Parade 241
Comedy Cellar 264
comedy clubs 263–264
Comedy Garden, The 264
Comfort Inn Manhattan 132
Comic Strip Live 264
Comme des Garçons **195**, 246
Commissary 182
Commonwealth Cricket
  League 322
Complete Traveller
  Bookstore 218
computers 220, **364**
Computer Solutions
  Provider 220
concert halls 315–317
Concord Baptist Church of
  Christ 93, **94**

Condé Nast Building 71
Coney Island 94, **95–96**, 238,
  326–327, *327*
  Fourth of July Hot Dog–Eating
    Contest 95, **239**
  Mermaid Parade 238
  New York Aquarium for Wildlife
    Conservation **96**, 297
  Sideshows by the Seashore
    95, **96**
Conference House (Billop
  House) 8, **106**
Confucius Plaza 56
Congee Village 155
Conscience Point 354
Conservatory Café 137
consulates 364
consumer information 364
Continental 63, 299, **303**
Continental Airlines Arena 300
Continental Center 317
Cook's Corner 185
Co-op City 102, **104**
Cooper-Hewitt, National Design
  Museum 11, **34**, 79
Cooper Union 10, **62**
Cornelia Street Cafe 311
Cornel's Garden Romanian 97
Corner Bistro 168
Corpus Christi Church 319
Corpus Christi Monastery
  104, **105**
Cosmopolitan 137
Costume National 202
Cotton Club 14, **86**
Council on International
  Educational Exchange 375
Council Travel 375
couriers 373
Cowgirl Hall of Fame 289
Craft 171
Crazy Nanny's 288
credit cards 371
Creed 215
CRG Gallery 247
cricket 322–323
Cristinerose Gallery 247
Cristoforo Colombo
  Boulevard 93
Critics' Picks
  chefs 166
  Chinatown snacks 57
  city cinema 278
  eat out 157
  hotels 125
  landmark restaurants 177
  museums 40
  shopping 207
Croton Gatehouse 86
Crown Heights 17, **93**
C3 138
Culinary Institute of
  America 356
  Apple Pie Bakery Café 356
currency 370
  exchange 371
Curry Hill 69
Curry in a Hurry 171
Cushman Row 66
customs 365
Cyber Café 368
Cyclo 163
Cynthia Rowley 202

Daffy's 202
Dahesh Museum 38
Daily News Building, The 75
Daily News 16, **371**
Daily Show with Jon Stewart
  276, 377
Daily 235 **227**
Dakota, The 77, 78
dance 343–348
  schools 346, 348
  shopping 348
Dance Magazine 344
Dance Space Inc. 348
DanceSport 348
Dances for Wave Hill 347
Dance Theater Workshop 344
Dance Tracks 229
D&G 195

Dangerfield's 264
Daniel 182
Danny's Skylight Room 262
Dano Restaurant 171
Danspace Project 344
Danube 54, **154**
D'Artagnan—The
  Rotisserie 180
Daryl K 202
Da Silvano 167
date and time 378
Dave's 144
David Barton 287
David Zwirner 245
Dazies 97
d.b.a. 144
db bistro moderne **177**, 182
DC Moore Gallery *248*, 252
DDC Lab 197
Dean & DeLuca 222
Decibel Sake Bar 144
Deitch Projects 245
Delacorte Theater 78, **336**,
  339, 369
Delhi Palace 97, **190**
Della Femina Restaurant 353
Demarest Hill Winery 352
Demeter 215
Denino's 106
dentists 367
Department of City Planning
  Bookstore 325
Department of Parks &
  Recreation **324**, 332
department stores 193–195
Dependable Printing 372
De Robertis 63
De Salvio Playground 55
DHL Worldwide Express 373
Dia Center for the Arts 66,
  253, **255**
Diamond Row 73
Diane von Furstenburg, the
  Shop 195, *205*
Dicapo Opera Theater 320
Diesel 195
Digital Club Festival 239
Diner 187
Dinerbar 186
Diners Club 371
Ding Dong Lounge, The 150
Dinosaur Hill 219
DiPaulo Fine Foods 55
Directory 358–380
disabled 365–366
Discover 371
Dish, The 187
Disney Store 85, **227**
District 135, 163
Dive 75 150
Dixon Place 259
Djema Imports 85
D/L Cerney 204
D.O.C.S. 366
Do Hwa 163
Dok Suni's 163
Dolce & Gabanna 201
Dominick's 190
Domsey's Warehouse 205
Don Hill's *266*, 267, **303**
Donna Karan 201
Donnell Library Center 44
  Central Children's Room 290
Don't Tell Mama 262
Double Happiness 56, **144**
Downtime 303
Downtown 46–63
  restaurants 153–169
  rest rooms 369
Downtown Arts Festival 241
Draft Riots, The 10
Drawing Center, The 255
Dreesen's Excelsior Market 354
Dressing Room 197
Drip Cafe 185
Drive By 272
driver's licenses 358
driving 358–359
  breakdowns 361
  car rental 359–360
  parking 359, 361
  towing 361
drug abuse help lines 367

Drug Abuse Information
  Line 367
dry cleaners 206
Duane Reade 367
Duggal 220
Dumbo
  art galleries 244, 251
Dumbo Arts Center **251**, 253
Dumbo: Art Under the
  Bridge 242
DuMont 187
Duplex, The 261
Dusk Lounge 285
Dutchess County 356
Dyckman Farmhouse Museum
  21, **88**
Dylan bar 144
Dylan hotel 121
Dylan's Candy Bar 223

e

Eagle, The 281
Earl Jeans, 195
Earth 267, **286**
Ear Wax 308
Easter Parade 236
Eastern States Buddhist
  Temple of America 56, **57**
East 54th Street Pool 332
East Hampton 353–355
  Chamber of Commerce 355
East Side Club 286
East Village **62–63**, 218
  restaurants 162
Easy Everything 368
Eatery 283, **287**
Ecowash 207
Edgar Allan Poe Cottage
  102, **105**
Edwynn Houk Gallery 256
Eighteenth & Eighth 287
888 Grand Concourse 100
85 Leonard Street 54
Elaine's 80, **186**
Elbow Room 303
El Diario 372
Eldorado, The 82
Eldridge Street Synagogue
  57, **58**
Electric Lady Studios 61
electricity 366
electronics 219–220
1150 Grand Concourse 101
Elias Corner 97, **190**
Elite Locksmiths 369
Elizabeth Ryan Floral
  Designs 222
Elk Candy Company 80
Ellis Island Immigration Museum
  13, 41, 46, **47**
  Registry Room 76
El Museo del Barrio **42**, 79, 84
emergencies 366–367
emergency rooms 367
Empire Diner 66
Empire Hotel 136
Empire Skate Club of New
  York 331
Empire State Building 15, 22, 23,
  26, 51, 73, **74–75**
  Run-Up 243
Emporio Armani 64
Enchanted Forest 221
Enelra 200
Enid's 151
Enoteca i Trulli 147
Enterprise 359
Épices du Traiteur 183
Equitable Building 50
Esca 167
Esposito and Son 85
Ess-a-Bagel **171**, 180
Essex Street Markets 58
Etats-Unis 186
Etherea 229
Eugenia Kim 209
Evolution 230
Excelsior Hotel 136
Executive Towers 100
Exit 267
Exit Art: The First World 255, *256*
Express Hotel Reservations 115
Express Mail 372

Express Shuttle/USA Gray
Line 360
ExtraVertical Climbing Center 328
eyewear 208

f

Fabulous Fanny's 219
Face Stockholm 213
Fair Harbor 351
Fairway 83
Fala House 356
Family Matters 296
FAO Schwarz 74, **221**
Fashion Institute of Technology
(FIT) 70, *72*
Museum 38
Fast and Fabulous 326
Fat Beats 230
Feast of San Gennaro 55, 94, **241**
Federal Hall National
Memorial 21, **51**
Federal Reserve Bank 51
FedEx 373
Feeding Tree, The 190
Feigen Contemporary 247
Feinstein's 262
Felissimo 193
Fendi 201
Ferdinando's Focaccaria 187
Festa of St. Rosalia 93
festivals
art 235–238, 241–243
boat 240
children's 294–295
comedy 237
film 241, 243, 278, 319
food 237–239, 241, 243
music 237–243
parks 236, 238, 240
performance 237–242
Fetch 230
Fez 145, **303**
Up Over the Time Cafe 150
Fifth Avenue 73–74
Fifth Avenue Presbyterian
Church 374
55 Central Park West 82
55 Wall Street 129
Film & TV 273–278
festivals 241, 243, 278, 319
Film Forum 275
Film Society of Lincoln Center
276, 278
Filter 14 **268**
Filthmart 206
Final Home 202
FireBird 262
Fire Dept. Complaint Hot Line 366
Fire Island 279, **350–352**
Ferry 352
Fireman's Memorial Garden 27
First 163
First Shearith Israel
Graveyard 57, **59**
Fishs Eddy 225
Fitch Graphics 364
Fitzpatrick Grand Central
Hotel 125
Fitzpatrick Manhattan 125
Five-Borough Bicycle Club 326
Five Points 161
Flatbush 93, 95
Flatiron Building *7,* 22, 64, *65,* **66**
Flatiron District 64–66
restaurants 170–174
flea markets 221
Flea Theater, The 342
Flight 001 230
Flor de Mayo 185
Florence Gould Hall at the
Alliance Française 316
Florent 61, **168**
florists 221–222
Fleur de Sel 171
Flower Power Herbs and Roots
Inc. 219
Flushing 97
Council on Culture and the
Arts 98
Main Street 97
Town Hall 98

World's Fairgrounds 15
Flushing Meadows–Corona
Park 98
Foley Square 52
Foodbar 287
Foods of New York Walking and
Tasting Tours 109
food stores 83, 91, 92, **222–224**
Bronx 102–103
Brooklyn 91–95
Little Italy 55
Soho 55
Foodworks 223
football 323
Footlight Records 230
Forbes Magazine Galleries 38
Fordham University 101
Fort Greene 29, **92**
Fort Hamilton 93
42nd Street **71–72,** 75
40 Wall Street 51
Founders Hall 80
Foundry Café 355
Four Seasons, The 76, **181**
Four Seasons Hotel 107
Fragments 45, **209**
Franklin, The 123
Frank's Lounge 270
Fraunces Tavern Museum 9, 21,
42, 46
Frédéric Fekkai Beauté de
Provence 215
Fredericks Freiser 247
Freddy's Bar 308
French Institute–Alliance
Française **40,** 277
Florence Gould Hall 316
Frenchware 227
Fresh 213
Frick Collection 32, **34,** 79, 317
Friedrich Petzel 247
Friends' Meeting House 98
Fringe Festival 240, *240*
Fulton Fish Market 52
Fulton Landing 90
Fulton Market 52
Fun 56, **268**
Fun City 62, **232**
Further Reading 379

g

g 282, **285**
Gagosian 79, 244, **252**
Gagosian Chelsea 247
Gaiety 282
Galapagos 28, *28,* 151, **305,**
307, 344
GAle GAtes et al. 244, 251, **253**
Gallagher's Steak House 177
Gallery M 85
Gallery X 85
Game Show 230
Garibaldi-Meucci Museum 42
Garment District 70
restaurants 175–176
gas stations 362
Gathering of Tribes, A 259
Gavin Brown's enterprise 247
Gay & Lesbian 279–289
accommodations 282–283, 288
bars 29, 281–286, 288–289
bathhouses 286
books and media 279–280
centers and phone lines 280–281
clubs 286, 289
gyms 287
Pride March *235,* **238,** 279
restaurants and cafés
286–287, 289
Switchboard of New York
Project 280
Gay Men's Health Crisis 280
GE Building 73
Gen Art Film Festival 278
General Delivery 372
General Grant National Memorial
83, **84,** 87
General Post Office 22, 70, **372**
General Theological
Seminary 66, **67**
George Washington Bridge 86, **88**
Bus Station 358

German-American Steuben
Parade 241
Gerry Cosby & Company 232
Gershwin Hotel, The 138
Ghenet 159
Giants Stadium 323
gift shops 227–228
Ginger Man, The 147
Ginger's 29
Giorgio Armani 201
Giraffe, The 134, **135**
Givenchy 201
Gladys' Comedy Room 264
GMC Park Plaza 359
Godiva Chocolatier 49
Goethe-Institut/German Cultural
Center **42,** 79, 278
golf 328
Golf Club at Chelsea Piers 328
Good, the Bad, and the Ugly,
The 219
Goody's 157
Gorham New York, The 133
Gorney, Bravin and Lee 247
Gosman's 355
Gotham 372
Gotham Bar and Grill 167
Gotham Bike Shop 325
Gotham Comedy Club 264
Gotham Gardens 222
Gotham History Festival 242
Gourmet Garage 223
Governors Island 46, **48–49**
Grace's Marketplace 223
Gracie Mansion 80
Gracious Home 226
Graffiti Hall of Fame 84
Gramercy Comedy Club 264
Gramercy Park *66,* 67–69
restaurants 170–174
Gramercy Park Hotel 66–68, **133**
Gramercy Tavern 164, **171**
Grand Army Plaza, Brooklyn *91*
Grand Army Plaza, Manhattan 74
Grand Central Market 75
Grand Central Oyster Bar &
Restaurant 76, **181**
Grand Central Partnership 109
Grand Central Terminal 22, 75, **76,**
360, 369
lost property 370
Grand Concourse 100, **105**
Grand Ferry Park 92
Grand Sichuan 157
Grand Sichuan International 169
Grand Sichuan International
Midtown 179
Grant's Tomb 83, **84,** 87
Gravesend 93–94
Gray Line 108
Great Lakes 29, **308**
Greeley Square 69, 70
Green Apple 25–27
Greene/Naftali 248
Greenmarkets 223
Greenwich Village 15, 59–61
restaurants 166–167
Greenwich Village Literary Pub
Crawl 109, **260**
Greenwich Village Past and
Present tour 260
Grey Art Gallery at New York
University 255
Greyhound Trailways 358
Grocery, The 92, **188**
Ground Zero 18–19, 48–49
Growing Up with Opera 293
Gryphon Record Shop 229
Guastavino's Restaurant 76
Gucci 34, **201**
Guernica 145, **270**
Guggenheim Museum,
Solomon R. 32, **36,** 77, 276
CinéKids 293
Soho 36, 54
Worldbeat Jazz 37
Guss' Pickles 58, **223**
gyms 287, **329–330**

h

Habitat Hotel 140
Halcyon 29, **270–271,** 307
Half King, The **145,** 258, *259*

Hallo Berlin 177, **179**
Hall of Fame of Great
Americans 101, **105**
Halloween Parade 242
Halo 145
Hamilton Grange 86, **87**
Hamilton Heights 86
Hammacher Schlemmer 227
Hampton Jitney 355
Hamptons, The 352–355
handbags 199, **208–209**
H&H Bagels 83
H&M 70, 74, **194**
Hands On 366
Harborside 355
Harkness Dance Project 346
Harlem 84–88
art galleries 85, 250–251
restaurants 85, 186–187
Harlem Business Improvement
District 86
Harlem Heritage Tours 109
Harlem Spirituals 109
Harlem USA Mall 85
Harlem Week 240
Harlem YMCA 333
Harrison, The 154
Harvey 219
Hassidic Tours 93, **109**
hats 209
Hat Shop, The 209
Haughwout Building 22
health and medical
facilities 366–367
health help lines 368
Heartbeat 123
Hedra Prue 197
Helena Rubinstein 217
Hell 145
Hell's Angels 63
Hell's Kitchen 72
Hell's Kitchen restaurant 180
Helmut Lang 202
Help Line 368
help lines 367–368
Henderson Place Historic
District 80
Henri Bendel 194
Henrietta Hudson 288
Henry Urbach Architecture 248
Herald Square 69, **70**
Herald Square Hotel, The
70, **138**
Herban Kitchen 160
Her/SheBar 288, **289**
Hess 362
High Bridge 88
hiking 86
Hicks-Platt House 93
Hinsch's Confectionary 93
Hispanic Society of America
42, 88
Historic Hudson Valley 355, **356**
Historic Richmond Town 106
History 6–16
American Revolution 7–9
British occupation 7–9
Commissioners' Plan 10
Dutch settlement 6–7
Civil War–era 10
Federal Works Progress
Administration (WPA) 15
immigrant poverty 13
Industrialization 10–11
Jazz Age 14
literary 14, 15
Rudolph Giuliani's term 17
Tammany Hall 12–13
theater 14, 15–16
time line 8–9
HIV & AIDS Hot Line 368
HMV 228
hockey 323
Hog Pit Barbecue NYC 168
Hogs & Heifers 145
Hogs & Heifers North 150
Holiday Inn Wall Street 127
holidays 74–75, **363**
museums closed 33
Holly Solomon Gallery 248
Holy Basil 163
Holy Cow 308
home & design stores 224–227

Hong Kong Dragon Boat
Festival 24●
Honmura An 160
horoscopes 376
horseback riding 330
horse racing 323–324
Hoshoni 218
Hospital Audiences Inc. 366
hospitals 367
Hosteling International New
York 141
hostels 140–142
Hotel Association of New York
City 115
Hotel Beacon 137
Hotel Edison 135
Hotel Elysée 125
Hotel Grand Union 139
Hotel Metro 134
Hotel Plaza Athénée 133
hotel reservation agencies 115
Hotel Reservations
Network 115
hotels 115–143
amenities 116
boutique 115, **132–135**
budget 137–140
business 127–131
comfortable 131–137
deluxe 116–119
first-class 125–127
gay & lesbian 282–283, 288
stylish 119–125
Hotel 17 *139*
Hotel Venus 199
Hotel Wales, The 123
HotRes.com 115
house calls 367
Housing Works Used Books
Cafe 258
Howard E. and Jessi Jones
House 93
Howard Greenberg & 292
Gallery 256
Hoyt & Bond 204
HRC Tennis 333
Hub, The *108*, 111
Hudson, The **121**, 132
Bar 121
Cafeteria 121
Hudson House 355
Hudson River Greenway 87
Hudson River Piers 67
Hudson Valley 355–356
Hungarian Pastry Shop 185
Hunts Point 103
Cooperative Market 103
Hyde Park 356
Hyde Park Antique Center 356

IBM Building 24
ice skating 330
Ideya 160
Idlewild 148
Iglesia Pentecostal Camino
Damasco 63
www.ihamptons.com 355
Il Cortile 55
Ilias Lalacunis 209
I'll Take Manhattan Tours 110
Ilo 73, 132, **177**
IMAX Theater 33, 274, **276**
immigration 365
INA 206
INA.Men 206
Incentra Village House 283
Independence Avenue 102
Infrared Lounge, The 149
Inge Mauer, Making Light 226
in-line skating 330–331
Innat Irving Place 133
Innovation Luggage 211
insurance
car rental 358–359
personal 368
Integral Yoga Institute 333
Intermix 197
International Artexpo 235
International Building 73
International Center of
Photography 32, **255**

International Children's Television
Festival 294
International Festival of Puppet
Theater 295
International House 141
International Salsa Museum 42
International Student Identity
Card 375
Internet and e-mail 368
Internet Café 368
InTouch USA 375
Intrepid Sea-Air-Space
Museum **44**, 72
Inwood 86–88
Iridium 299, **311**
Irish Repertory Theatre 339
Iroquois, The 115
Irving Place 68
Irving Plaza 68, **305**
Isamu Noguchi Garden
Museum **38**, 96
Artlink 103
I.S. 44 Flea Market 221
Islamic Cultural Center of New
York 374
Islander's Horizon Buses 352
Issey Miyake 20, 200, **201**
Italian Food Center 55
Izzy Bar 305

Jack's Bar 117
Jackson Heights **97**, 101
Beautification Group 97
Jack Spade 209
Jacob Javits Federal Building 365
INS office 365
Jacob K. Javits Convention
Center 72
Jacques Marchais Museum of
Tibetan Art 41
Jamaica Bay Wildlife
Refuge 25–27, *25*, **98**
Jamin Puech 209
J&R Electronics 220
Janet Borden 256
Japan Society *39*, **41**, 278
Jaques Marchais Museum for
Tibetan Art **42**, 106
Jazz for Young People 293
Jazz on the Park Hostel 141
Jazz Record Center 230
Jazz Standard, The 147
JCB 371
Jean Claude 160
Jean Cocteau Repertory 339
Jean-Georges 82, 119, **183**
Jean Louis David 216
Jefferson Market Library *60*, 61
Jeffrey New York 61, **194**, 211
Jefron Messenger Service 370
Jerry Ohlinger's Movie Material
Store 230
Jerry's Accommodations 351
Jet East 354
Jewel Bako 163
jewelry
repair 207
stores 209–210
Jewish Museum 32, **49**, 79
Jill Stuart 202
Jimmy Choo *210*, 211
Jimmy's Bronx Cafe 102
Jimmy's Corner 148
Jivamukti Yoga Center 333
J.M. Weston 211
Job Lane 354
Joe's Bar 145
Joe's Dairy 55
Joe's of Avenue U **94**, 153
Joe's Pub 62, 145, 263, **305**
Joe's Shanghai 165
John F. Kennedy International
Airport 360
lost property 370
John H. Finley Walk 80
John Masters Salon and Spa 215
Johnny's Famous Reef
Restaurant 105
John's Deli 93
Jo-Jo 183
Jones Beach 15, **314**, 350
Jones Diner 162

Joseph 201
Joya 188
Joyce Gold History Tours of New
York 110
Joyce Theater 67, **343**
Joyce Soho 344
Kids Dance 296
J's Hangout 286
Judy's Chelsea **261**, 263
Juilliard School of Music 320
Jules Bistro 165
Julie's 288
Julie Saul Gallery 256
Jussara Lee 61
Jutta Neumann 199
JVC Jazz Festival 238

Kam Man Food Products 223
Karam 93, **188**
Kara Varian Baker 209
Kari'kter 227
Kartell 54, **226**
Katayone Adeli 195
Kate Kearney's 312
Kate's Joint 163
Kate Spade 209
Kate Spade Travel 230
Kate's Paperie 231
Katinka 218
Katz's Delicatessen 58, *58*, **155**
Kaufman Astoria Studios **97**,
273, *273*
kayaking 331
Kaye Playhouse 317
Kazuyo Nakano 209
KB Garden 97
KD Dance 348
Kelly Christy 209
Keni Valenti Retro-Couture 206
Kensington Stables 95, **330**
Key Sites 412
KeySpan Park 95, **326–327**
KGB 258
Kidding Around 221
Kids 'n Comedy 96
Kids' Stuff 290–297
amusement parks 290
arts festivals 294–295
circuses 290–291
museums 291–293
music 293
outdoors 293–296
play spaces 296
theater 296–297
zoos 297
Kiehl's 213
"King and Queen of Green
Street" 54
King Cole Bar 148
Kingsland House 98, **99**
Kinko's 364
Kinney Systems Inc. 359
Kips Bay 69–70
Kirna Zabête 197
Kissena Park Golf Course 328
Kitano, The 127
Kitchen, The 67, 318, **342**, 344
Kitchen Market 223
Kitsch Inn 269, **286**
Klemens Gasser & Tanja Grunert
Inc. 248
Kmart 369
Knitting Factory/The Old Office/
Alterknit Theater 54, 209,
301, 305
Kosciuszko Foundation House 318
Kum Gang San 98, **175**, 190
Kush 148

La Chinita Linda 169
Ladd Road 102
Ladies' Mile 64
Lady Mendl's 134
Lafayette Avenue Presbyterian
Church 92, **95**
La Focacceria 163
La Guardia Airport 360
lost property 370
Lakeside Lounge 145, 299, **305**
La MaMa E.T.C. 342

L'Amour 305
La Marqueta 84
Landmark Tavern 148
Language 197
Lansky Lounge & Grill 58
La Perla 199
La Petite Coquette 199
Larchmont Hotel 137
Larry & Jeff's Bicycles Plus 325
Late Great Pennsylvania Tour 110
L'Atelier 210
*Late Night with Conan
O'Brien* 276
*Late Show with David
Letterman* 276
L-Cafe 188
Le Bernardin 164, **178**
Le Cirque 2000 116
Le Corset by Selima 201
Lefferts Homestead 21
Children's Museum 292
Le Figaro Cafe 59
Legal Aid Society 369
legal assistance 368
Le Gamin Cafe 160, 164, **168**, 169
Lehmann Maupin 248
Leisure Time Recreation 328
Le Jardin Bistro 157
Lenox Lounge 84, 150, **311**
Leo Castelli 252
Le Pain Quotidien 184
Le Parker Meridien 117
Lesbian & Gay Community
Services Center **281**, 288
Lesbian Herstory
Archive **281**, 288
Les Deux Gamins 168
Les Halles 172
Les Halles Downtown **153**, 173
Lever House **23**, 76
Lexington Avenue 80
Le Zinc 154
Liberty Challenge 238
Liberty Helicopter Tours 211
Liberty Science Center **45**, 291
Liberty Women's Health Care of
Queens 367
Library Hotel 133, **134**
Lighthouse International 366
Li-Lac Chocolate Inc. 223
Lilliput 204
Limón Institute 348
Lincoln Center 15, 82, 315,
316–317, 339
Alice Tully Hall 316
area restaurants 183–184
Avery Fisher Hall **317**, 369
Centercharge 315
Festival **239**, 316
Fiorello H. La Guardia High
School of the Performing
Arts 316
Juilliard School of Music 320
Kaplan, Stanley H.
Penthouse 311
Metropolitan Opera House 317
Mitzi E. Newhouse
Theater 316, **339**
Mostly Mozart Festival 316
Midsummer Night Swing 238
New York State Theater 317
Out-of-Doors **239**, 295
Plaza 314
Rose Building 316
taxis 363
tours 315
Vivian Beaumont
Theater 316, **339**
Walter Reade Theater 276, **317**
Lincoln Plaza Cinemas 82, **275**
lingerie 200–201
Lingerie & Co. 201
Ling Skin Care 217
Lips **284**, 287
"lipstick building" 24
Liquids 145, **271**
Liquors 29
liquor stores 224
Little Basil 168
Little Bit Louder, A 259
Little India 63
Little Italy 56–57
restaurants 157–159
Little Orchestra Society 293

Little Red Lighthouse 86
Living Room, The 148, **306**
Liz Lange Maternity 205
Local 138 *146*, 149
L'Occitane 213
locksmiths 369
Loeb Boathouse 78, 79, **325**
Loews Kips Bay 69, **274**
Lombardi's 157
Londel's Supper Club 87
Long Beach 350, *351*
Long Island City **96–97**, 103, 244, 251
Long Island Rail Road 350, **360**
Lord & Taylor 194
Los Dos Rancheros Mexicanos 175
Los Kabayitos Children's Theater 296
lost property 370
lottery picks 376
Lotus 268
Lotus Club 149
Louie 197
Louis Armstrong Archives 100–101
Louis Licari 215
Louis Vuitton 201
Loulou 29
Lovergirl 288, **289**
Love Saves the Day 227
Lowell Hotel 135
Lower East Side 13, **57–59**
restaurants 155–157
taxis 363
Lower East Side Car Service 265
Lower East Side Festival of the Arts 237
Lower East Side Tenement Museum 13, **42**, 57, 292
Lower Manhattan Cultural Council 50
Lucerne, The 137
Lucien 164
Ludlow Bar 148
luggage 210–211
luggage lockers 369
Luhring Augustine 249
Luna Lounge 148, **306**
Luna Park 64
Lunettes et Chocolate 208
Lupa 167
Lure, The 281, **285**
Luxx **268**, 306, 307
LVMH Tower 20, **76**

M.A.C. 213
MacArthur Airport 360
Macy's 70, **194**, 369
Fireworks Display 238
Tap-o-Mania 240
Thanksgiving Day Parade 242
Madame Paulette Custom Couture Cleaners 206
Madame Tussaud's New York 71, **72**, *73*
Madiba 188
Madison Square 64–66, **69**
Madison Square Garden 70, **300**, 322
Comedy Garden, The 264
Theater 309
magazines 372
Magic Johnson Harlem USA 273
Mahayana Temple Buddhist Association 56, **57**
Mail Boxes Etc. USA 373
Mainly Manhattan Tours 110
Majestic, The 82
Make Up Forever 213
Makor 259, **306**
Malia Mills 201
Malibu Studios Hotel 140
Mamma Mia! 335, 337
Mamoun's Falafel 167
M&G Soul Food Diner 187
M&I International 94
Mandoo Bar 175
Manhattan Carriage Company 111
Manhattan Kayak Company 331
Manhattan Plaza Racquet Club 333

Manhattan Rickshaw Company 111
Manhattan School of Music 320
Manhattan Spirit 372
Manhattan Theatre Club 339
Manhattan Tree House 364
Manitoba's 306
Mannes College of Music 320
Manny Winick & Son 210
Manolo Blahnik 211
Man Ray 169
Mansfield, The 122
Maps 391–411
Marcel, The 69, **134**
Marc Jacobs 54, **202**
Mare Chiaro 55, **146**
Margherita Cafe 103
Margon 178
Marian Goodman 252
Marijuana March 237
Mark, The 117
Market Cafe 175
Markle Residence for Women 288
Mark Morris Dance Center 346–347
Mark's 117
Mark's Bar 117
Mark Twain Annual Birthday Tour 260
Marlborough 252
Marlborough Chelsea 249
Marlborough Graphics 252
Marmalade 206
Martha Graham School 348
Mart 1-2-5 85
Marseille 178
Mary Boone 249, **252**
Masjid Malcolm Shabazz 84
Mastel + Mastel 251
MasterCard 371
maternity wear 205
Matter/:Form 272
Matthew Marks 249
Max 164
Max & Moritz 189
Max Fish 148
Max Protetch Gallery 249
Max Soha 187
Maxwell's 306
Marbridge Building 70
Mayflower Hotel 137
Mayle 195
May May 57
Mayor Parking 359
Mayor's Cup 241
Mayor's Office for People with Disabilities 366
M Bar *121*, 123
McCreedy & Schreiber 211
McKim, Mead & White **22**, 70
McNulty's Tea and Coffee 223
McSorley's Old Ale House 63, **146**
Meadowlands Racetrack 324
medical facilities 366–367
Me & Ro 210
Meatpacking District 61
Medi 178
Meditation Steps 81
Mei Lei Wah 57
Memes 202
Memory Motel 355
Menswear 203–204
Meow Mix 288, **288**, 307
Merce Cunningham Studio **345**, 348
Mercer, The 54, **119**
Mercer Kitchen 183
Merchants' Exchange 50
Merchant's House Museum 40
Mercury Lounge 63, **307**
Merge 163
Merkin Concert Hall 311, **316**
Mermaid Parade 238
Messages Plus 376
messenger services 370
Messiah Sing-In 242
Met Life Building **24**, 76
Métrazur 75
MetroCard 361, **362**
Metro Grill 148, *151*
Metro-North 350, **360**
Metro Pictures 249
Metropolitan Hotel 131

Metropolitan Life Insurance Company Building 66
Metropolitan Museum of Art 11, 22, 32, **35**, 79, 276, 291, 318, 412
Metropolitan Opera 11, **317**
House **317**, 344
Parks Concerts 237
Shop 227
Tours 315
Metropolitan Transportation Authority (MTA) 361
buses 361
fares 361, 362
subways 362
MetroTech Center 91
Mets, New York 321, **322**, 326
Meurice Garment Care 206
Mexicana Mama 168
Mexican Radio *155*, 157
Mezzanine Spa at Soho Integrative Health Center 217
Miano Viel Salon and Spa 215
Michael Callen–Audre Lorde Community Health Center 281
Michael Jordan's—The Steak House NYC 75, **181**
Michael Kors 201
Michael Werner 252
Michelangelo, The 127
Midnight Express Cleaners 207
Midsummer Night Swing 82, **238**
Midtown 64–76
restaurants 169–183
restrooms 369
taxis 363
Midtown East 75–76
restaurants 180–181
Midtown Tennis Club 333
Mike's Deli 102
Milk & Honey 149
Military Salute Week 237
Millennium 276
Miller Theatre at Columbia University 318
Mill House Inn 354
Minette 208
Min-K 199
Minton's Playhouse 86
Mint Theater 342
Miramax 54
Miss Mamie's Spoonbread Too 83
Miss Maude's Spoonbread Too 187
Miu Miu 202
M. Knoedler & Co. 79, **253**
Modell's 85
Moe's 151
Molode Zyttia 218
Molyvos 136, **180**
MoMA Design Store 226
MoMA QNS 95, 96, *103*
Artlink 103
Momenta 254
Mondel Chocolates 83
Mondo Kim's 226
money 370–371
MoneyGram 371
Monkey Bar 125
Montauk 354
Chamber of Commerce 355
Montauket, The 355
Montauk Point Lighthouse 354, **355**
Moon Curser Records 105
Morgan Library, The 22,32, **35**, 70
Morgans 15, **121**, 132
Morningside Heights 83–84
Morris-Jumel Mansion 8, **88**
Morris, Mark 346–347
Moschino 201
Moses, Robert 15, 19
Moss 54, **226**
Mostly Bali 218
Mostly Mozart Festival **239**, 316
Motherfucker 272
Motor City Bar 149
Mount Sinai Hospital 367
Mount Vernon Hotel Museum and Garden **40**, 80
Moustache **165**, 169
Movement Research at Judson Church 346
Moviefone 275, **377**
Mr C's Cycles 325
Mr. Joe 203

Mt. Morris Park Community Association 85
MTV 71, **276**
Municipal Art Society 38
Tours 110
Municipal Building 22, **52**
Municipal Pools 332
Murray Guy 249
Murray Hill 69–70
restaurants 179–180
Murray Hill Inn 139
Muse, The 135
Museum at FIT 38
Museum Café 32
Museum for African Art **43**, 54
Museum Mile 79
Festival 238
Museum of American Financial History 41
Museum of Chinese in the Americas **43**, 56
Museum of Jewish Heritage: A Living Memorial to the Holocaust 32, **43**, 50
Museum of Modern Art 15, 21,32, **35**, 73, 277
Artlink 103
Design Store 226
MoMA QNS 96
P.S. 1 Contemporary Art Center
Summer Warm Up 37
Museum of Television & Radio 44, 73, 277
International Children's Television Festival 294
Museum of the City of New York **41**, 79
Museums 32–45
museums, children's 291–293
Music 299–320
music, children's 293
music, classical and opera 315–320
churches and other venues 317–319
concert halls 315–317
record stores 228–230
schools 319–320
tickets 315
tours 315
music, popular 299–315
arenas 300
blues, country & folk 312–313
Brooklyn scene 306–309
clubs and lounges 267–272
"Find your groove" 313
jazz & experimental 310–312
radio 373
record stores **228–230**
reggae, world & Latin 312
roving parties 272
summer venues 313–315
music stores 228–230, 231
Mutiny 272
Mxyplyzyk 228
Myers of Keswick 223
Myoptics 208

Nadaman Hakubai 127
Nascimento 182
Nasdaq MarketSite 71
Nassau Veterans Memorial Coliseum 300
Nathan's Famous 95
Fourth of July Hot Dog–Eating Contest 239
National Academy of Design **39**, 79
National Arts Club **68**, 259
National Museum of the American Indian 22, **35**, 46
Nat Sherman 231
nature 25–27
Nazar Turkish Cuisine 97
NBC 73, **74**, 273
NBC Experience Store 74
Nellie Bly Amusement Park 290
Nelson Rockefeller Park 293
Nell's 268
Neue Galerie 32, **39**
New Amsterdam Theatre 14, 71, **296**
Newark Airport 360

lost property 370
Newark Bears 326–327
New Day, A 265
New Directors, New Films 278
New Indonesia & Malaysia
 Restaurant 159
New Jersey Devils 323
New Jersey Nets 323
New Jersey Performing Arts
 Center 307, 316, 346
 AirTrain Newark 360
New Museum of Contemporary
 Art 34, 36, 54
New School University 259, 260
 John L. Tishman Auditorium 318
 Mannes College of Music 320
Newsday 372
newspapers 371–372
New Victory Theater 297, 341
New Year's Day Marathon Poetry
 Reading 243
New Year's Eve
 Ball Drop 242
 Fireworks 242
 Midnight Run 243
New York magazine 372
New York Adorned 232
New York Airport Service 361
New York Antiquarian Book
 Fair 236
New York Aquarium for Wildlife
 Conservation 96, 297
New York Botanical Garden 27,
 102, 105, 293
 Enid A. Haupt Conservatory 102
**New York by Season
 235–243**
New York City Ballet 344
 Nutcracker 242
 Spring Season 237
New York City Century Bike
 Tour 241
New York City Cultural Walking
 Tours 110
New York City Custom
 Leather 200
New York City Department of
 Consumer Affairs 364
New York City Department of
 Transportation 361
New York City Fire Museum 43,
 45, 54
New York City Marathon 242
New York City Opera 317
New York City's Official Visitor
 Information Center 72, 378
New York Comedy Club 264
New York County Courthouse 53
New York County Supreme
 Court 91
New York Cricket League 322
New York Curmudgeon Tours 110
New Yorker 372
New York Film Academy 68, 273
New York Film Festival 241, 278
New York Gilbert & Sullivan
 Players 320
New York Hall of Science 45,
 98, 292
New-York Historical Society 11,
 32, 41, 82
New York Hospital/Cornell
 Medical Center 80
New York Independent Film and
 Video Festival 243
New York International Auto
 Show 235
New York International Children's
 Film Festival 243, 295
New York International Fringe
 Festival 240, 240, 342
 Fringe Jr 295
New York Is Book Country 241
New York Islanders 323
New York Jazz Festival 237
New York Jets 323
New York Jewish Film Festival 278
New York Kayak 331
New York Knicks 322
New York Lesbian and Gay Film
 Festival 278, 279
New York Life Insurance Company
 Building 66

New York Liberty 322
New York Marriott Brooklyn 143
New York Mercantile
 Exchange 50, 51
New York Mets 321, 322, 326
New York/New Jersey
 MetroStars 324
New York Noodle Town 159
New York Observer, The 372
New York Palace 116, 150
New York Philharmonic 317
 open rehearsals 315
 summer concerts 239
 Ticket Club 315
 Young People's Concerts 293
New York Police Museum 45
New York Post 371
New York Press 372
New York Public Library 11, 22,
 44–45, 69, 73, 74, 368, 412
 Celeste Bartos Forum 260
 Central Children's Room 290
 Donnell Library Center 44
 Humanities and Social Sciences
 Library 44, 412
 Library for the Performing
 Arts 44, 318
 Rose Main Reading Room 44, 73
 Schomburg Center for Research
 in Black Culture 32, 45, 85, 88
 Science, Industry and Business
 Library 45
New York Rangers 323
New York Road Runners Club 331
New York Shakespeare Festival 62,
 236, 238, 336, 341
New York Society for the
 Deaf 366
New York Sports Club 330, 332
New York Sports Online 324
New York State Theater 317, 344
New York Stock Exchange 51
New York Theatre Workshop 341
New York Times, The 70–71, 350,
 358, 371, 376
New York Transit
 Museum 45, 291
New York Unearthed 46, 47
New York University 59–61
 College of Dentistry 367
 Medical Center 69
New York Yankees 16, 321,
 322, 326
New Victory Theater, The
 341, 346
Next Door Nobu 155
Next Wave Festival 91, 315
Nha Trang 159
Nicholas Roerich Museum 39
Nick and Toni's 353
Nicole Farhi 201
Night Strike 271
Night Train to Brooklyn 28–29
Niketown 232
9C 307
19th Street Gym 287
92nd Street Y 80, 260, 260,
 316, 346
 de Hirsch Residence 142
 Harkness Dance Project 346
 Tours with 111
 Unterberg Poetry Center 259
Ninth Avenue International Food
 Festival 237
Nobu 54, 154
Nolan/Eckman 245
Nolita 55–56
North Lawn 50
Northsix 299, 308
North Wind Undersea
 Institute 105
Nostalgias 190
Noticias del Mundo 372
Nutcracker, The 242
Nuyorican Poets Cafe 63, 260
NYC & Company 361, 378
NYC Discovery Tours 111
NYC Gay & Lesbian Anti-Violence
 Project 281
NYC/On Stage 341, 344
NY Hotel Urgent Medical
 Services 367
Nylonsquid 203
Nyonya 159

NY Skateout 296
NY Skyride 75
NY Waterway 100, 108, 110, 355

O

Oak Bar 149
Oak Room, The 125, 262
Ocean Beach 351
Octagon Tower 81
Odeon 155
Off Broadway 337–342
Off-Off Broadway 342
Off-Soho Suites Hotel 137
Ohm 268
Old Homestead 170
Old Navy 195
Old Rhinebeck Aerodrome 356
Oliva 155
Olive & Bette's 199
Olives NY 64, 172, 175
Olympia Trails 361
OMO Norma Kamali 201
One c.p.s.119
One Night Out/Mom's Night
 Out 206
One Penn Plaza 69
One Times Square 70
Only Hearts 201
On the Ave 123
125th Street 85
Ontological-Hysteric Theater 342
Openair 271
opera 320
Opera Orchestra of New York 320
Operaworks 320
Orchard Bar 149
Orchard Beach 104
Orchard Street Bargain District 58
Organic Grooves 272
Oscar Wilde Memorial
 Bookshop 280
Other Music 229
Otto Tootsi Plohound 211
Ouest 185
Our Town 342
Outer Boroughs, The 90–106
 restaurants 187–190
Outsider Art Fair 243

P

Pace/MacGill 256
Pace Prints and Primitives 252
PaceWildenstein 244, 252
Paddy Reilly's Music Bar 312
Palacinka 160
Paladar 155
Palm Room, The 135
Panasonic Village Jazz Festival 240
Panorama Camera Center 220
Paper 372
Paragon Sporting Goods 232
Paramount, The 121, 123, 132
Paramount Vending 231
Paris Theatre 274, 275
Park, The 66, 271
Park Bistro 172
Parkchester 104
parking 359, 361
 garages 359
 restrictions 359
Park Med Eastern Women's
 Center 367
Park Plaza Apartments 100
Park Row 52
parks
 Bear Mountain State 356
 Blackwell 80
 Carl Schurz 80
 City Hall 52
 Clement Clark Moore 68
 Cunningham 26
 Columbus 56
 De Witt Clinton 72
 Dr. Gertrude B. Kelly
 Playground 68
 Empire-Fulton-Ferry State 251
 Floral 98
 Fort Greene 92
 Fort Tryon 88
 Greenacre 69
 Hudson River 50, 331
 Inwood Hill 86, 88, 89

Isham 86
Marcus Garvey 85, 325
Marine 26
Morningside 83
Nelson A. Rockefeller 50, 293
Paley 69
Pelham Bay 26, 104, 105
Riverdale 102
Riverfront State 87
Riverside 83, 87
Robert F. Wagner Jr. 50
Robert Moses State 351, 352
St. Nicholas 86
Stuyvesant Square 68
Van Cortlandt 26, 102, 105, 322
Walker 323
Weeping Beach 99
 See also Battery; Bryant;
 Central; Flushing Meadows–
 Corona; Gramercy; Madison
 Square; Prospect; Tompkins
 Square; Washington Square
Park Slope 28
Park South Hotel 135
Park View Hotel 141
Parlor 216
passports 365
Pastis 61, 165
PATH Trains 360
Patria 173
Patricia Field 199
 Hotel Venus 199
Paula Cooper Gallery 249
Paul Kasmin 249
Paul Morris Gallery 250
Paul Smith 204
Paul Taylor School 348
Pavilion 351
Peace Gardens 76
Pearl Oyster Bar 169
Pearl Paint 231
Pearl River Mart 56, 228
Pearl Theatre Company 341
Penn Station 22, 70, 360, 369
 lost property 370
Penny Whistle Toys 221
People's Foreign Exchange 371
Pepe Giallo to Go 170
Pepe Rosso to Go 160
peregrine falcons 25–26, 76
Performance Space 122 342, 347
Performing Garage, The 342
perfumeries 215
Periyali 173
Perriwater Ltd. 222
Peter Coppola Salon 215
Peter Luger 165, 186, 189
Peter Pan Bus Service 358
Pete's Candy Store 307, 308
Pete's Tavern 68
pharmacists 215, 367
Phat Farm 203
Phillips Club 131
Philosophy di Alberta Ferretti 195
Phoenix, The 284
photocopying and printing 372
photography 255–256
photo processing 220
Photo-Tech Repair Service 220
Piaget 210
Pickwick Arms 139
Pier A 46
piercing 232
Pierogi 2000 28, 92, 254
Pierre Hotel 117
Pier 17 52
Pier 26 294
Pieter Claesen Wyckoff House
 Museum 21
Pills Anonymous 367
Pinch Sitters 364
Pines, the 351, 352
Pines Place 351
Ping's Restaurant 159
Pink Pony 164
Pink Tea Cup 169
Pino's Prime Meat Market 55
Pipa 173, 176
P.J. Clarke's 149, 183
Planned Parenthood of New York
 City 367
Plant Bar 271
Players, The 67
Playspace 296

play spaces 296
Playwrights Horizons 341
Plaza Hotel 74, 115, **117**
Plein Sud 197
Plus Systems 371
Plymouth Church of the Pilgrims 10, 90, **95**
Poetry Project 260
Point, The 103
police 366
Police Headquarters Building 56
Polytechnic University 91
  Wunsch Student Center 91
Pomander Walk 83
Pondicherri 226, 228
Pongal 173
Pop Shop 228
Port Authority Bus Terminal 72, 350, **358**
Portico Home 226
postal services 372–373
  couriers 373
  private mail services 373
  telegrams 373
  U.S. Postal Service 372
Postmasters Gallery 250
Prada 202
Prema Nolita 217
Pressure 146
Prestige Entertainment 378
Printing House Racquet and Fitness Club 332
Prison Ship Martyr's Monument 92
private mail service 373
Privé 216
Producers, The 336–337
Product 197
Project, The 85, 250
Prospect Park 95, **96**
  Bandshell 314
  Carousel 95
  Celebrate Brooklyn! Performing Arts Festival 238
  Drummers Grove 95
  Quaker Friends Cemetery 95
  Ravine 95
  R. H. Macy's Fishing Contest 95
  Wildlife Center 95
PSNBC 264
P.S. 1 Contemporary Art Center 33, **35**, 37, 96, 251
  Artlink 103
  Summer Warm Up 37
psychological services help lines 368
Public Theater 336, **341**
Puck Fair 146
Puerto Rican Day Parade 238
Pug Bros. Popcorn 82
Pumpkin Maternity 205
Puppetworks 297
Push 210
Putnam County 355
  Visitors Bureau 355

q
Q, a Thai Bistro *188*, 190
Quad Cinema 275
Quality Hotel and Suites Midtown 139
Quark International 231
Queens 96–99, 100–101, 103
  addresses 97
  Artlink 96, **103**
  restaurants 190
  tours 97
Queensboro Bridge 76
Queens Botanical Garden 98, **99**
Queens Council on the Arts 99
Queens County Farm Museum 98, **99**
Queens Historical Society 99
Queens Jazz Trail tour 98, **100–101**
Queens Museum of Art **39**, 98
Queens Theatre in the Park 98, **99**
Queens Zoo 98, **99**

r
Rachel's Bakery 351
Radical Walking Tours 111
radio 358, **373–374**

  college 373
  dance and pop 373
  history of 14
  jazz 373
  news and talk 373–374
  rock 373
  sports 374
  traffic 358
Radio City Music Hall 14, **73**, 74, **308**
  Christmas Spectacular 242
Raffeto's Corporation 224
Rainbow Grill 178
Rain or Shine 296
Ralph Lauren 201
Ramon's Tailor Shop 207
R & S Cleaners 207
Rand McNally Map & Travel Store 231
Raoul's 161
rape and sex crimes help lines 368
Rasputin 189
Ratner's 58
Ravenite Social Club 55
reading series 258–259
Recon 203
Red Cat, The 66, **170**
Red Roof Inn 139
Reel School 273
Regency, The 262
Regent Wall Street 50, **129**
Regina Opera Company 320
Reinstein/Ross 210
religious services 374
Religious Sex 201
Renaissance Ballroom 86
Renny 222
  at the Carlyle 222
repairs
  clothing 207
  gadget 220
  jewelry & watch 207
  shoe 208
Republic 193
Rescue 216
  Beauty Lounge 216
ResFest Digital Film Festival 278
Restaurant Above 72, **176**
Restaurant Row 71
Restaurants 153–191
  Bronx 190
  Brooklyn 28–29, 187–189
  by cuisine 191
  cheap eats 172
  Chinatown snacks 57
  critics' picks 157, 166, 177
  downtown 153–169
  gay & lesbian 286–287, 289
  landmark 177
  midtown 169–183
  Queens 190
  tax and tipping 161
  uptown 183–187
  websites 185
  Week **238**, 243
restrooms 369
Resurrection 206
Rhinebeck 356
Rhône 146
Richard Metz Golf Studio 328
Richmond County Bank Ballpark 106, 326–327
Richmond County Fair 240
Rick's Café 133
Ricky's 213
Ringling Bros. and Barnum & Bailey Circus 235, **291**
Rising Café 309
Rite Aid 367
Ritz-Carlton New York
  Battery Park 50, **116**
  Central Park 119
River Café 90, **189**
Rivendell Winery 353
Riverdale 102
Riverfront State Park 87
Riverside Church 83, **84**, 319
Riverside Towers Hotel 140
Rizzoli Bookstore 258
Robert Lee Morris 210
Robert Miller Gallery 250
Robert Moses State Park 351–352
Robin des Bois 29
Rock & Roll Walking Tour 111

Rockefeller Center 15, 73, **74**, 412
  Christmas Tree Lighting Ceremony 242
  Ice Rink 73, **330**
Rockefeller University, The 80
  Founders Hall 80
Rodeo Bar 69, 313
Roebling Hall 254
Roger Smith, The 127
Roger Williams, The 123
Roller Rinks at Chelsea Piers 331
Ronald Feldman Fine Arts 245
Roosevelt Hospital 367
Roosevelt Hotel, The 135
Roosevelt Island 80
  Operating Corporation 81
Roosevelt Island Tramway 81, *81*
Rose Building 316
Rose Center for Earth and Space **33**, 82, 291
Roseland 308
Rose Main Reading Room 73
Rosie O'Donnell Show 277
Rotunda Gallery 254
Roulette 311
Roundabout Theater 337
roving parties 272
"Row," the 22
Roxy **268**, 309
Royalton, The 121, **123**, 132
Ruben's Empanadas 154, **161**
Ruby Foo's **178**, 185
Rubyfruit 289
Rudy's Bar & Grill 149
running 331
Russ & Daughters 224
Russian Samovar 178
Russian Tea Room 183

s
Sabra 363
Safe Horizon Hotline 368
safety 374
S'Agapo 97
Sahadi Importing Company 92
Saint at Large 282, **286**
Saints 150
Saint's Alp Teahouse 57, 159, **165**, 189
Saks Fifth Avenue 74, **194**, 211
Salander-O'Reilly Galleries 253
Salem United Methodist Church 374
Salmagundi Club 59, **61**
salons 215–216
Samaritans, The 368
Sam Ash Music 231
Sammy's Roumanian 58
Sandback, Birnbaum & Michelen Criminal Law 369
S & B Report 193
Sandwich Planet 176
San Isidro y San Leandro 63
San Remo 82
Sapphire 149, **268**
Satellite Airlines Terminal 358
Satellite Records 229
Saturday Night Live 277, *277*
Sayville Ferry 352
Scandinavia House: The Nordic Center in America 43
Scatalogics 272
Schaller & Weber 80
Schermerhorn Row 52
Scholastic Books Headquarters 20, *20*
Schomburg Center for Research in Black Culture 32, **45**, 85, 88
  See also New York Public Library
School of Visual Arts 369
Scopa 165
Scoop 199
Scratcher, The 146
Screaming Mimi's 206
Screening Room 54, **275**
Sculpture Center 255
SEA 165
Seagram Building 24, 76, 180
Sean 204
Sean Kelly 250
Seaside Summer Concert Series 239
Second Avenue Deli 166

Second Stage Theatre 341
Segue at Double Happiness 260
Seize sur Vingt 204
Selected Shorts: A Celebration of the Short Story 259
Self-service laundry 207
Selima Optique 208
  Lunettes et Chocolat 208
Seneca Village 77
Sephora 215
Serena 67, **149**
Servco 372
Sesame Street 97, *273*
17 East 126th Street 86
750 Lexington Avenue 24
Seventh Regiment Armory 79, **80**
79th Street Boat Basin 83
72nd Street subway station 8
Sex Crimes Report Line NYPD 368
S'Agapo 97
Shagwong 355
Shakespeare & Company 218
Shallots NY 183
Shanghai Cuisine 165
Shanghai Tide **161**, 190
Shea Stadium 15, 98
Shell 362
Sherman Square 82
Sherry-Lehmann 224
Shescape 289
Shi 228
Shine 268, **309**
Shiseido Studio 215
shoe
  repair 208
  stores 211
Shoe Service Plus 208
Shopping & Services 193–232
  accessories 208–211
  books 217–218
  cameras and electronics 219–221
  children's clothes 204–205
  dance 348
  designer 200–202
  discount 202
  department stores 193–195
  eyewear 208
  fashion 195–206
  fashion services 206–208
  flea markets 221
  florists 221–222
  food and drink 222–224
  gifts 227–228
  handbags 208–209
  hats 209
  health and beauty 213–217
  home & design 224–227
  jewelry 209–210
  leather goods 199–200
  lingerie 200-201
  luggage 210–211
  maternity wear 205
  menswear 203–204
  music **228–230**, 231
  national chains 195
  shoes 211
  specialty 231–232
  sports 232
  streetwear 202–203
  swimwear 201
  tattoos & piercing 232
  toys 221
  vintage clothes 205–206
Short Waves 58
Showman's 86
Show World 71, **72**
Shrine 219
Shrine of Elizabeth Ann Seton 46, **47**
Shun Lee Palace 183
Shun Lee West 183
Shu Uemura 215
Siberia 149
Sidewalk 309
Sigerson Morrison 211
Signature Theatre Company 341
Silicon Alley 66
Silvercup Studios 97, 273
Silver Lake Golf Course 328
Singer Building 22
Sisters Cuisine 84
65 Mott Street 56

69th Regiment Armory 68
60 Thompson 54, 119
Sky Rink at Chelsea Piers 330
Skyscraper Museum 41
Slipper Room 119
Smallpox Hospital 81
Small's 62, 299, **311**
Small's Paradise 86
Smith Street 25
smoking 375
   age restrictions 364
Sniffen Court 69
Snug Harbor Cultural Center 106
S.O.B.'s 269, 299, **309**
soccer 324
Society for the Advancement of
   Travel for th. Handicapped 366
Socrates Sculpture Park 96,
   99, 292
   Artlink 103
Sofitel 131
Soha 150
Soho 54–55
   art galleries 244–245
   restaurants 159–161
   taxis 362–363
Soho Grand Hotel 54, **119**
Soldiers' and Sailors'
   Monument 83, 87
Sol Moscot Opticians 208
Sonnabend Gallery 250
Sony Building 24, 75
Sony Lincoln Square & IMAX
   Theatre 82, 274
Sony Style 231
Sony Wonder Technology Lab 76,
   293, **297**
Sophie's Restaurant 154
Sosinna's 159
Sound Factory 269
Southampton 354
   Chamber of Commerce 355
South Cove 50
South Street Seaport 51, 52
   Museum 41
   Music of the Sea 36
   Thursday Night Concert
      Series 238
SouthWestNY 49
Spa 269
Spanish Harlem 84
Sparky's Ale House 151
spas 216–217
Spaulding Lane 102
specialty stores 230–232
Special Victims Liason Unit of the
   New York Police Department 368
Spectrum 93
Speed 269
Sperone Westwater 251
spoken word 259–260
Sports Center at Chelsea
   Piers 328, **330**
Sports & Fitness 321–333
   active sports 324–333
   media 321
   radio 374
   scores 376
   spectator sports 321–324
   stores 232
Spread 69, 185
Springwood 56
squash 332
SSS Sample Sales 193
SSUR 203
Stack's Coin Company 232
Stand-Up NY 264
Starlette 282, 284, 289
Starlight Bar and Lounge 282, 284
Starret-Lehigh Building 67
Staten Island 106
   Cricket Club 323
Staten Island Ferry **108**, 412
Staten Island Yankees 106,
   326–327
Staten Island Zoo 106
STA Travel 375
Statue of Liberty 41, 43, **47**,
   110, 412
St. Bartholomew's Church 319
St. Clement's Church 369
STD Hot Line 368
Steinway Piano Factory 97, **99**
Stella's 286

Steps 348
Steven Alan 199
St. Francis of Assisi Roman
   Catholic Church 374
St. George Ferry Terminal 106
St. George's Ukrainian Catholic
   Church 63
Stinger Club 28
St. John's University Red
   Storm 322
St. Lucy's Roman Catholic
   Church, Our Lady of
   Lourdes Grotto 103
St. Luke's/Roosevelt Hospital
   Crime Victims Treatment
      Center 368
St. Mark's Bookshop 218
St. Mark's Church in-the-
   Bowery 63
St. Marks Place 62
St. Marks Sounds 229
St. Nick's Pub 87, **312**
Stonewall 62, **285**
Stone Street Historic District 47
Stone Street Tavern 47
St. Patrick's Cathedral 69, 73, 74
St. Patrick's Day Parade 235
St. Patrick's Old Cathedral 55
St. Paul and St. Andrew United
   Methodist Church 374
St. Paul's Chapel 51, **312**
Strand Bookstore 218
Street Smarts N.Y. 111
Strivers' Row 87
St. Thomas Church Fifth
   Avenue 319
students 375
   identification 375
   immigration 365
   travel 375
Studio Museum in Harlem **37**,
   85, 250
Stüssy 203
Stuyvesant Town 68
St. Vincent's Hospital 367
Subterranean Records 229
Subway Inn 151
subways 13–14, 92, 362
   fares 362
   lost property 370
   to and from airports 360
Sugar Hill Arts Center 250
suicide help lines 368
Suite 303 316
Suite 16 146
Summer Restaurant Week 238
Sunshine Cinema 273
Sunnyside 97
Sunnyside Gardens 97
SuperShuttle 361
Supreme 203
Sur 92
Surf Reality 264
Sushi Samba 174
Sushi Samba 7 169
Sushisay 116, **181**
Sway 146
Swedish Cottage Marionette
   Theater 297
Swift Hibernian Lounge 147
swimming 332
swimwear 201
Swinburne Island 26
Swing 46 312
Sybil's 93
Sylvan Terrace 88
Sylvia's 84
Symphony Space 83, 257, **259**,
   318, 347

t
Tabla 66, **174**
TADA! Youth Ensemble 297
Takashimaya 195
talks and lectures 260
Tamarind 174
Tamarind Tea Room 174
Tammany Hall 12–13
TanDa 174
Tanger Outlet Center 198
Tanya Bonakdar Gallery 251
Tappo 164
Target Margin Theater 342

tattoos and piercing 232
Tavern, The 354
Tavern on the Green 77, **183**
tax 161
Taxi and Limousine
   Commission 363
taxis 362–363
   lost property 370
   to and from the airports 360
Ted Muehling 210
Tel Aviv car service 266, 363
Telecharge 366, **377**
telegrams 373
telephones 375–376
   answering service 376
   cellular phone rental 375
   general information 375
   phone cards 376
   public pay phones 375–376
television 280, **376–377**
   shows taped in NYC 276–277
Temple Bar 147
Tender Buttons 232
tennis 240, **324**, 332–333
Terence Conran Shop 76, **226**
Terminal Market 103
Terra Blues 313
Terra Verde 232
TG-170 199
Thali 169
Thalia Spanish Theater 97, **99**
Theater & Dance 335–348
   Broadway 337
   children's 296–297
   history 14, 15–16
   Off Broadway 337–342
   Off-Off Broadway 342
   tickets 335–337, 341
Theater at Madison Square
   Garden, The 309
Theater Development Fund 336
   Theater Access Project
      (TAP) 366
Theater District **71**, 412
   restaurants 176–179
Theodore Roosevelt
   Birthplace 68
Theresa Towers 85
Thirteen 269
13th Street Presbyterian
   Church 22
ThirtyThirty New York City 139
32 Mott Street General Store 56
This Is Next Year: A Brooklyn-
   Based Compilation 306–307
Thomas Cook 371
Thomas Pink 204
Three Lives & Co. 258
303 Gallery 251
Ticket Central 377
TicketCity 378
Ticketmaster 300, 315, **377**
www.ticketweb.com 300
tickets 300, **377–378**
   airline 358
   box office 377
   brokers 378
   classical music 315
   film 275
   museum 35
   online 300
   scalpers 377–378
   standby 377–378
   theater 335–337, 341
   TV shows 276–277
Tiffany & Co. 74, **210**
Tiki Room 150
Time, The 123
time and date 378
time line of New York City 8–9
Time Out 151
Time Out New York 193, 279, 350,
   372, 376
   *Eating & Drinking
      Guide 2002* 153
   Student Guide 375
timeoutny.com 116
Times Square 16, 17, 70, 72, 412
   New Year's Eve 242
   taxis 362
   Visitors Center 378
Time's Up! 326
Tin Pan Alley 71
Tiny Doll House 232

tipping 161
Tishman Auditorium, John L. 318
Titanic Memorial Lighthouse 52
TKTS 315, 336, **377**
Today 73, 74, 273
Tommy's Taxi 351
Tompkins Square Park 60,
   63, 369
Tonic 57, 149, 299, **309**
Top of the Tower, The 129
Torch 262, 263
Totem Design 226
Totonno Pizzeria
   Napolitano **186**, 189
Tottenville Beach 106
Tottenville Inn 106
tourist information 378
Tours 107–112
   bicycle 107
   boat 107
   Brooklyn 93
   bus 108
   concert halls 315
   jazz 98, **100–101**
   literary 260
   Queens 97, 98, **100–101**
   walking 108–111
   other 111
Tours with the 92nd Street Y 111
Tower Records 228
Town, The 121, **180**
Town Hall, The **310**, 310, 316
Townhouse, The 287
Toyota Comedy Festival 237
toy stores 221
Toys in Babeland 232
Toys R Us 221, 369
Tracy Feith 199
trains 359–360
   service 360
   stations 360
Transit 211
translation services 378
Transportation 358–363
   airplane 358
   bus 359, 358, 360–361
   car 358–359, 361–362
   car service 265–266, 363
   ferry **108**, 352, 412
   Metropolitan Transit
      Authority 361
   subway 362
   taxi 362–363
   to and from airports 360–361
   train 350, 359–360
   walking 363–364
Transportation Alternatives 325
   New York City Century Bike
      Tour 241
Trash & Vaudeville 199
Trata 184
Trattoria dell'Arte 180
travel agents 358
traveler's checks 371
Traveler's Health 368
Travelex 371
Treadwell Farm Historic
   District 80
Triad 263
Triangle Shirtwaist Factory 13
Tribeca **54**, 364
   restaurants 154–155
   taxis 363
Tribeca Blues 313
Tribeca Film Center 54
Tribeca Grand Hotel 119
Tribeca Grill 54
Trinity Church 21, 51, **52**, 319
   Museum 52
Triomphe 127
Triple Five Soul 203
Trips Out of Town 350–356
TRL 276
True 269
Trump International Hotel and
   Tower 82, **119**
Trump Tower 24, 74
Trump World Tower 76
Tsunami 272
Turntables on the Hudson 272
Turtle Bay 76
Tuscan Steak 174
Tweed Courthouse 13, 53, 53
'21' 73, **178**

Two Boots Pioneer Theater 275
Two Boots Restaurant 166
  Park Slope 189
  Pizzeria 166, 175
  Rock Center 178
  to Go-Go 162
  to Go West 169
Two Mile Hollow Beach 353
230 Park Avenue 76

U

UA Union Square
  Stadium 14 274
UJA-Federation Resource Line 374
Ukrainian Institute 79
Ultra 216
Umberto's Clam House 55
Union 203
Union Pacific 174
Union Square 64
  Greenmarket 64
Union Square Cafe 64, 164
Union Square Inn **137**, 139
Union Square Theater 68
United Nations 16, 23, 23, 76
  Secretariat 76
United Parcel Service 373
United States Courthouse 53
United States National Tennis
  Center 98
UniverSoul Big Top Circus 291
Unoppressive Non-Imperialist
  Bargain Books 218
Up Over Jazz Café 307, **312**
Upper East Side 79–80
  art galleries 252–253
  restaurants 184, 186
Upper West Side 81–83

restaurants 183–186
Upright Citizens Brigade
  Theatre 264
Upstairs at Rose's Turn 263
Uptown 77–89
  restaurants 184–187
  restrooms 369
Urban Archeology 226
Urban Jem Guest House, The
  85, **143**
Urban Park Rangers 26, 79, **111**
Urban Wild Life 25–27
Urinetown: The Musical 337
U.S. Customs 365
  Service 365
U.S. Embassy 365
  student visas 365
  visa information 378
U.S. Immigration and
  Naturalization Service (INS) 365
U.S. Open 98, 240, **324**
U.S. Post Office 91
USRental.com 364

V

Valentino 201
Van Cortlandt House
  Museum 102, **105**
Van Cortlandt Park 26, **322**
  Golf Course 328
Van Cortland Village 102
Vanderbuilt YMCA 333
Van Doren 252
Venetia Kapernekas Fine Arts,
  Inc. 251
Veniero's Pasticceria and Caffe 63
Venus Modern Body Arts 232
Vera Wang 201

Verdi Square 82
Veritas 174
Verrazano-Narrows Bridge 15,
  26, **93**
Versace 74, 201
Veselka 166
Victoria's Secret 195
Victor's Cafe 179
Victory Kitchen 189
Vietnam Restaurant 159
Villabate Pasticceria and Bakery 93
Village Antiques Center 356
Village Gate 61
Village Underground 310
Village Vanguard 312
Village Voice, The 372
Villard Bar & Lounge 150
vineyards 352–353
Vineyard Theatre, The 342
vintage clothes 205–206
Vintage New York 224
Vinyl 266, **269**
Virgil's Real BBQ 179
Virgin Megastore **64**, 229
Visa 371
visas 378
Vision Festival 237
Vivienne Tam 202
Vivienne Westwood 202
Von Bar 147
Vong 183
VSF 222

W

Waldorf-Astoria Hotel 76, **116**
Walker Park 323
Wall Street 7, 46, **50–51**
Wall Street Inn 129
Wall Street Journal, The 372
Wall Street Walking Tour 111
Walter Reade Theater 276, **317**
Warehouse, The 269
Warsaw at the National Polish
  Home 307, **310**
Warwick New York, The 127
Warwick Valley Winery 353
Washington Heights 17, 88
Washington Square Park 59, *59*,
  61, 369
  Arch 59
  Music Festival 239
Washington Square Hotel 137
Waterfront Museum 41
Waterworks Collection 226
Wave Hill 102, 105
weather 359
websites 379
Webster Hall 289
Weeksville Society/Hunterfly Road
  Houses 93, 95
Welcome to the Johnsons 149
Wellington Hotel 136
Well's Fargo 371
Westbeth 61
Westbeth Theatre Center 62
West End, The 83
Western Union 371, 373
West 59th Street Pool 332
West 4th Street Courts 325
West Indian Day Carnival 93,
  241, 290
West Marine 232
West Side Club 286
West Side Branch YMCA 333
West Village **61–62**, 244
  restaurants 167–169
Wheel Tapper Pub, The 125
Whiskey Blue 123
White Cliff Vineyard 353, *353*
White Columns *254*, 255
White Horse Tavern 62, **147**
White Trash 228
Whitney Museum of American
  Art 32, **37**, 79
  at Philip Morris 37
  Biennial 79, 235
  Fab Fridays 36
Who Wants to Be a Millionaire 277
Wilderstein 356
Wild Lily Tea Room 170, *171*
Williamsburg 28, 92, 307–309
Williamsburg Art & Historical
  Center 92, 95

Williamsburg Arts and Culture
  Festival 236
Williamsburg Art Nexus 247
Wing Fat Shopping 56
Winter Antiques Show 79, **243**
Winter Garden 49, **50**
Winter Restaurant Week 243
W New York 123
  The Court 123
  Times Square 123
  The Tuscany 123
  Union Square 123
wire services 371
Wiz, The 220
Wolcott Hotel 140, *140*
Wollman Memorial Rink,
  The 77, **330**
women's health 367
Wonder Bar 282, **284**
Wong Kee 57
Woodbury Common Premium
  Outlets 202
Woodside 97
Woolworth Building 15, 25, 52
Works, The 286
work permits 365
World Financial Center 48–49, **50**
  Winter Garden 49, 50
World Gym of Greenwich
  Village 330
World Music Institute 230
World Trade Center 17, *18*, 18–23,
  48–50, 106
  Viewing Platform 49, **50**
Writer's Voice/West Side
  YMCA 259
WWF New York 71–72
Wyckoff, Pieter Claesen House
  Museum 21
Wyeth 227
Wyndham Hotel 136

X

X-Large 203
xl Chelsea 282, 283, 285

Y

Yancey Richardson Gallery 256
Yankee Stadium 100
Yeshiva University 84
  Museum 44
YMCAs 333
  Harlem 333
  Vanderbilt **141**, 333
  West Side 141, 259, 333, **334**
YMHA (de Hirsch Residence at the
  92nd Street Y) 142
yoga 333
Yoga Zone 333
Yohji Yamamoto 202
Yonkers Raceway 324
York Avenue 80
Yorkville 80
Yoshi 253
You Gotta Have Park 236
Yves Saint Laurent 201

Z

Zabar's 83, **224**
Zao 199
Z'Baby Company 205
Zeckendorf Towers 64
Zeitlin Optik 208
Zeller Tuxedos 206
Zen Palate 174, **179**, 184
Zig Zag Jewelers 207
Zinc Bar 312
Zitomer 215
Zoë 161
zoos 297
  Bronx 102, **105**, 412
  Central Park 240
  New York Aquarium for Wildlife
    Conservation 96
  Staten Island 106
Zum Schneider 147
Zwirner & Wirth 253

Advertisers' Index

Aladdin Hotel 122
Blue Man Group .... Inside front cover
Bowery's Whitehouse Hotel of New York 126
Central Park Summer Stage 304
The Chelsea Center 130
Chelsea Star Hotel 126
De La Guarda 338
Ettia Holistic Day Spa 214
Gramercy Park Hotel 128
Grand Central Partnership 196
Heartland Brewery & Chophouse 156
HMV 192, 298
Hostelling International 114
Hotel Beacon 128
Hotel Conxions 128, 198, 304
The Hotel Wolcott iv
The Inns of New York 130
The Marmara Manhattan 120
Jazz on the Park 118
Jutta Newmann New York Inc. 198
Les Halles 156
Mamma Mia! 334
Maximus Spa Salon 212
Metro Dwellings 130
New York City Opera 302
92 St. Y 30
Oasis Day Spa 212
1800usahotels.com 124
Parkview Hotel 122
Pearl Paint 198
Telephone Bar & Grill 156
Virgin Megastore .... Inside back cover
WWF New York 152

Maps

Street Index 392
Manhattan 396
Brooklyn 404
Queens 406
Trips Out of Town 407
Manhattan Bus 408
Manhattan Subway 409
New York City Subway 410

Key Sites 412

Ticket to ride Subways are the fastest way to travel—especially with a MetroCard.

Street Index

MANHATTAN

65th St Transverse Rd: N2–N3
79th St Transverse Rd: L2–M3
86th St Transverse Rd: L2–L3
97th St Transverse Rd: K2–K3
196th St: B1–C1

Abraham A Kazan St: S6
Academy St: B1–2
Adam Clayton Powell Jr Blvd: F3–J3
Albany St: T3
Alexander Hamilton Bridge: D2
Allen St: R5–S5
Amsterdam Ave: C2–N2
Ann St: T4
Arden St: B1
Asser Levy Pl: Q5
Astor Pl: R4
Attorney St: R5–S5
Audubon Ave: C2, D2
Audubon Terr: E1–2
Ave of the Finest: T4
Ave A: Q5–R5
Ave B: Q5–R5
Ave C: Q5–R5
Ave D: Q6–R6
Ave of the Americas (Sixth Ave): N3–S3

Bogardus St: C2
Bank St: R2–3
Barclay St: T3–T4
Barrow St: R2–3
Battery Pl: U3–4
Baxter St: S4–T4
Bayard St: S4
Beach St: S3
Beak St: B1
Beaver St: U4
Bedford St: R3
Beekman Pl: O5
Beekman St: T4
Bennett Ave: C1–D1
Bethune St: R2
Bleecker St: R2–4
Bond St: R4
The Bowery: R4–S4
Bridge St: U4
Broad St: U4
Broadhurst Ave: F2–G2
Broadway Terr: C1
Broadway: A2, A1–K1, K2–N2, N3–Q3, Q4–U4
Brooklyn Bridge: T4–5
Brooklyn–Battery Tunnel: U4
Broome St: S3–6

Cabrini Blvd: C1–D1
Canal St: S3–5
Cardinal Hayes Pl: T4
Cardinal Stepinac Pl: O2
Carlisle St: U3
Carmine St: R3
Cathedral Pkwy: J1–2

Catherine St: T5
Cedar St: T3–4, T4–U4
Central Park North: J2–3
Central Park South: N2–N3
Central Park West: J2–N2
Centre St: S4–T4
Chambers St: T3–4
Charles St: R2–3
Charlton St: S3
Cherokee Pl: M5
Cherry St: S5–6, T5
Chisum Pl: G3
Chittenden Ave: C1
Christopher St: R2–3
Chrystie St: R4–S4
Church St: S3–U3
Claremont Ave: H1–J1
Clarkson St: R2–3, S2
Clinton St: R5, S5–6
Coenties Slip: U4
Collister St: S3
Columbia St: R6–S6
Columbus Ave: J2– N2
Convent Ave: F2–H2
Cooper St: A2–B2
Cornelia St: R3
Cortland St: T4
Cortland Al: S4–5
Crosby St: R4–S4
Cumming St: B1
Cuyler's Slip: U4

Delancey St: S5–6
Delancey St North: S5–6
Delancey St South: S5–6
Depeyster St: U4
Desbrosses St: S3
Dey St: T4
Division St: S4–5
Dominick St: S3
Dongan St: B1
Dover St: T4–5
Downing St: R3
Duane St: T3–4
Dyckman St: B1–2

E 1st St: R4–5
E 2nd St: R4–6
E 3rd St: R4–6
E 4th St: R4–6
E 5th St: R4–6
E 6th St: R4–6
E 7th St: R4–6
E 8th St: R4–6
E 9th St: R4–6
E 10th St: R4–6
E 11th St: R4–6
E 12th St: R3–6
E 13th St: Q3–6
E 14th St: Q3–6
E 15th St: Q3–6
E 16th St: Q3–6
E 17th St: Q3–5
E 18th St: Q3–5
E 19th St: Q3–5
E 20th St: Q3–5
E 21st St: Q3–5
E 22nd St: Q3–5
E 23rd St: Q3–5
E 24th St: Q4–5
E 26th St: P3–5
E 28th St: P3–5

E 30th St: P3–5
E 32nd St: P3–5
E 34th St: P3–5
E 36th St: P3–5
E 38th St: P3–5
E 40th St: O3–5
E 42nd St: O3–5
E 44th St: O3–5
E 46th St: O3–5
E 48th St: O3–5
E 50th St: O3–5
E 52nd St: O3–5
E 54th St: N3–5
E 56th St: N3–5
E 58th St: N3–5
E 60th St: N3–5
E 62nd St: N3–5
E 64th St: N3–5
E 66th St: N3–5
E 68th St: M3–5
E 70th St: M3–5
E 72nd St: M3–5
E 74th St: M3–5
E 76th St: M3–5
E 78th St: M3–5
E 79th St: M3–5
E 80th St: L3–5
E 82nd St: L3–5
E 84th St: L3–5
E 86th St: L3–5
E 88th St: L3–5
E 90th St: L3–5
E 92nd St: L3–5
E 94th St: K3–5
E 96th St: K3–5
E 98th St: K3–4
E 100th St: K4–5
E 102nd St: K3–5
E 103rd St: K3–5
E 105th St: K3–5
E 109th St: J3–5
E 111th St: J3–5
E 113th St: J4
E 114th St: J5
E 115th St: J3–5
E 117th St: J3–5
E 118th St: J3–5
E 119th St: H4–5
E 120th St: H4–5
E 121st St: H4
E 123rd St: H4
E 124th St: H3–5
E 125th St: H3–5
E 127th St: H3–4
E 129th St: H3–H4
E 131st St: H3–4
E 132nd St: G3–4
E 135th St: G3–4
East Broadway: S5–6
East Dr: J3–N3
East End Ave: L5–M5
Edgecombe Ave: E2–G2
Eighth Ave: L2–Q2
Eldridge St: R5–S5
Eleventh Ave: N1–Q1
Elizabeth St: R4–S4
Ellwood St: B2–C2
Erickson Pl: S3
Essex St: R5–S5
Exchange Pl: U4
Exterior St: B2

Fairview Ave: C1
Fifth Ave: G3–R3
First Ave: H5–R5
First Pl: U3
Fletcher St: T4
Foley Sq: T4
Forsyth St: R4–S4, S4–5
Fort George Hill: B2, B1–C1
Fort Washington Ave: D1–E1
Frankfort St: T4
Franklin D Roosevelt Dr: J5–Q5, Q6–S6, S6–5, S5–T5, T5–4, T4–U4
Franklin St: S3
Frederick Douglass Blvd: G2–J2
Freedom Pl: M1–N1
Front St: T4–U4
Fulton St: T4

Galvin Ave: O2–P2
Gansevoort St: Q2–R2
George Washington Bridge: D1
Gold St: T4
Gouverneur La: U4
Gouverneur St: S6
Gracie Sq: L5
Gracie Terr: L5
Grand St: S3–6
Great Jones St: R4
Greene St: R3–S3
Greenwich Ave: Q2–3, R3
Greenwich St: R2–S2, S2–S3, S3–U3
Grove St: R3

Hamill Pl: T4
Hamilton Pl: G1–G2
Hamilton Terr: F2–G2
Hanover Sq: U4
Hanover St: U4
Harlem River Dr: C2–E2, E2–3, E3–F3, F3–G3, G4–H4
Harrison St: S3–T3
Haven Ave: D1–E1
Henry Hudson Bridge: A1
Henry Hudson Pkwy: A1–M1
Henry St: S6–5, S5–T5
Henshaw St: B1
Hester St: S4–5
Hillside Ave: B1–C1
Horatio St: Q2–R2
Houston St: S2–3, S3–R3, R3–6
Howard St: S4
Hubert St: S3
Hudson St: R2–3, R3–T3

Indian Rd: A1
Irving Pl: Q4
Isham St: A1–2

Jackson St: S6
Jane St: R2
Jay St: T3
Jefferson St: S5
Joe DiMaggio Hwy (West

Side Hwy): N1–Q_, Q2–S2, S3
John St: T4
Jones St: R3

Kenmare St: S4–5
King St: R3–S3

La Salle St: H1–2
Lafayette Plaza: D1
Lafayette St: R4–S4
La Guardia Pl: R3
Laight St: S3
Laurel Hill Terr: C2–D2
Lenox Ave: F3–J3
Leonard St: S3–4
Leroy St: R2–3
Lewis St: S6
Lexington Ave: H4–Q4
Liberty St: T3
Lincoln Tunnel: O1
Lispenard St: S3–4
Little West 12th St: Q2
Ludlow St: R5–S5
Luis Munoz Marin Blvd: J4–5

MacDougal St: R3–S3
Macombs Pl: F2–3
Madison Ave: G4–P4
Madison Ave Bridge: G4
Madison St: S5–T5
Maiden Ln: T4
Maker Circle: F2
Malcolm X Blvd (Lenox Ave): F3–J3
Manhattan Ave: H2–K2
Manhattan Bridge: T5–6
Margaret Corbin Dr: B1–C1
Market St: S5–T5
Marketfield St: U4
Martin Luther King Jr Blvd: H1–2
Mercer St: R4–S4
Mitchell Pl: O5
Monroe St: T4
Montgomery St: S5–6
Moore St: U4
Morningside Ave: H2–J2
Morningside Dr: H2–J2
Morris St: U3
Mott St: R4–T4
Mt Carmel Pl: P5
Mt Morris Park West: H3
Mulberry St: R4–T4
Murray St: T3

Nagle Ave: B2, B1–C1
Nassau St: T4–U4
Nathan D Perlman Pl: Q4
New St: U4
Ninth Ave: A2–B2, N2–Q2
Norfolk St: R5–S5
North End Ave: T3
North Moore St: S3

Odell M Clark Pl: G3
Old Broadway: G1–H1
Old Slip: U4
Oliver St: T4–5
Orchard St: R5–S5
Overlook Terr: C1

Paladino Ave: H5
Park Ave: G4–O4
Park Ave South: O4–Q4
Park Pl: T3–4
Park Pl West: T5
Park St: S4–T4
Park Terr East: A2
Park Terr West: A1–2
Payson Av: B1
Pearl St: T4–U4
Peck Slip: T4–5
Pell St: S4
Perry St: R2–3
Pike St: S5–T5
Pine St: U4
Pitt St: R5–SE, S6
Platt St: T4
Pleasant Ave: H5–J5
Post Ave: B2–C2
Prince St: S3–4
Public Pl: T3

Queensboro Bridge: N5

Reade St: T3–4
Rector Pl: U3
Reinhold Niebuhr Pl: H1–2
Renwick St: S3
Ridge St: R5–S5
River Terr: T3
Riverside Dr: B1–L1
Riverside Dr East: E1
Riverside Dr West: E1
Rivington St: S5
Rockefeller Plaza: O3
Rutgers St: S5
Rutherford Pl: Q4

Seaman Ave: A1–B1
Second Ave: H4–R4
Second Pl: U3
Seventh Ave: N3–Q3
Seventh Ave South: R3
Sherman Ave: B1–2
Sickles St: B1
Sixth Ave (Ave of the
    Americas): N3–S3
South End Ave: T3–U3
South St: U4
South William St: U4
Spring St: S3–4
Spruce St: T4
Staff St: B1
St. Andrews Plaza: T4
Staple St: T3
State St: U4
St. James Pl: T4
St. John's Ln: S3
St. Lukes Pl: R3
St. Marks Pl: R4–5
St. Nicholas Ave: C2–H2
St. Nicholas Pl: F2
St. Nicholas Terr: G2–H2
Stanton St: R5–S5
Stone St: U4
Stuyvesant St: R4
Suffolk St: R5–S5
Sullivan St: R3–S3
Sutton Pl: N5
Sutton Pl South: N5–O5
Szold Pl: R6

Tenth Ave: A2–B2, N2–Q2
Thames St: T3
Thayer St: B1
Third Ave: H4–R4
Third Ave Bridge: G4–H4
Third Pl: U3

Thomas St: T3–4
Thompson St: R3–S3
Tiemann Pl: H1
Trans Manhattan Expwy:
    D1–2
Tudor City Pl: O5
Twelfth Ave: G1, N1–Q1

Union Sq East: Q4
Union Sq West: Q4
United Nations Plaza: O5
University Pl: Q4–R4

Vandam St: S3
Vanderbilt Ave: O4
Varick St: R3–S3
Verdi Sq: J1
Vermilyea Ave: B1–2
Vesey Pl: T3
Vesey St: T3–4
Vestry St: S3

W 3rd St: R3–4
W 4th St: R2–4
W 8th St: R3
W 9th St: R3
W 10th St: R2–3
W 11th St: R2–3
W 12th St: R2
W 13th St: Q2–3
W 14th St: Q2–3
W 15th St: Q2–3
W 16th St: Q2–3
W 17th St: Q2–3
W 18th St: Q2–3
W 19th St: Q2–3
W 20th St: Q1–3
W 21st St: Q1–3
W 22nd St: Q1–3
W 23rd St: Q1–3
W 24th St: Q1–3
W 25th St: Q1–3
W 26th St: P1–3
W 28th St: P1–3
W 30th St: P1–3
W 32nd St: P1–P3
W 34th St: P1–3
W 36th St: P1–3
W 38th St: P1–3
W 40th St: O1–3
W 42nd St: O1–3
W 44th St: O1–3
W 46th St: O1–3
W 48th St: O1–3
W 50th St: O1–3
W 52nd St: O1–3
W 54th St: N1–3
W 56th St: N1–3
W 57th St: N1–5
W 58th St: N1–3
W 59th St: N1–2
W 60th St: N1–2
W 62nd St: N2
W 64th St: N1–2
W 66th St: N1–2
W 68th St: M2
W 70th St: M1–2
W 72nd St: M1–2
W 74th St: M1–2
W 76th St: M1–2
W 78th St: M1–2
W 79th St: M1–3
W 80th St: L1–2
W 82nd St: L1–2
W 84th St: L1–2
W 86th St: L1–2
W 88th St: L1–2
W 90th St: L2–3
W 92nd St: L1–2

W 94th St: K1–2
W 96th St: K1–2
W 98th St: K1–2
W 100th St: K1–2
W 102nd St: K1–2
W 103rd St: K1–2
W 105th St: K1–2
W 107th St: J1–2
W 109th St: J1–3
W 111th St: J1–3
W 113th St: J1–3
W 114th St: J3
W 115th St: J1–3
W 119th St: H1–3
W 121st St: H1–3
W 123rd St: H1–3
W 125th St: H2–3
W 126th St: H1–3
W 129th St: H1–3
W 131st St: H1–3
W 133rd St: G1–3
W 135th St: G1–3
W 137th St: G1–3
W 139th St: G1–3
W 141st St: G1–3
W 142nd St: G1–3
W 143rd St: G1–3
W 145th St: F1–3
W 147th St: F1–3
W 149th St: F1–3
W 151st St: F1–3
W 153rd St: F1–3
W 155th St: F1–3
W 157th St: E1–2
W 159th St: E1–2
W 161st St: E1–2
W 163rd St: E1–2
W 165th St: E1–2
W 167th St: E2
W 169th St: E1–2
W 171st St: D1–2
W 173rd St: D1–2
W 175th St: D1–2
W 176th St: D1–2
W 177th St: D1–2
W 179th St: D1–2
W 180th St: D1–2
W 181st St: D1–2
W 183rd St: D1–2
W 186th St: C1
W 187th St: C1–2
W 189th St: C1–2
W 190th St: C1–2
W 191st St: C1–2
W 192nd St: C1–2
W 193rd St: C1–2
W 196th St: B1–C1
W 201st St: B2
W 203rd St: B2
W 204th St: B1–2
W 205th St: B2
W 207th St: A1–B1, B1–2
W 208th St: B2
W 211th St: A2
W 213th St: A2
W 215th St: A1–2
W 216th St: A2
W 217th St: A2
W 218th St: A1–2
W 219th St: A2
W 220th St: A2
Wadsworth Ave: C1–E1
Wadsworth Terr: C1
Wagner Pl: T4–5
Walker St: S3–4
Wall St: U4
Warren St: T3–4
Washington Ave: C1–D1
Washington Pl: R3

Washington Sq East: R4
Washington Sq North: R3
Washington Sq West: R3
Washington St: Q2–S2,
    S3–U3
Water St: S6–5, S5–T5,
    T5–4, T4–U4
Watts St: S3
Waverly Pl: R3–4
West Broadway: R3–T3
West Dr: J2–3, J3–M3,
    M2–3, N3–2
West End Ave: J2–N2
West Side Hwy: N1–Q1,
    Q2–S2, S3–U3
West St: S3–U3
West Thames St: U3
White St: S3–4
Whitehall St: U4
Williamsburg Bridge: S5–6
Wooster St: R4–S4, S3
Worth St: T3–4

York Ave: K5–N5

BROOKLYN

1st Ave: T10
1st Pl: U8
1st St: U8–9, U9–V9
2nd Ave: T10–9, T9–U9
2nd Pl: U8
2nd St: U8–U9, U9–V9
3rd Ave: T10–9, T9–U9,
    U9–8
3rd Pl: U8
3rd St: U8–9, U9–V9
4th Ave: T10–U10,
    U10–8, U8–V8
4th Pl: U8
4th St: U8–9, U9–V9
5th Ave: V9–V8
5th St: U8–9, U9–V9
6th Ave: T10–U10,
    U10–9, U9–V9, V9–8
6th St: U9–V9
7th Ave: T10–U10,
    U10–9, U9–V9, V9–8
7th St: U9–V9
8th Ave: U10–9, U9–V9
8th St: U9–V9
9th Ave: U10
9th St: U9–V9
10th Ave: U10–V10,
    V10–V9
10th St: U9–V9
11th Ave: V10
11th St: U9–V9
12th St: U9–V9
13th St: U9–V9
14th St: U9–V9
15th St: U9–V9
16th St: U9–V9, V9–10
17th St: U9–10,
    U10–V10
18th St: U9–10,
    U10–V10
19th St: U9–10,
    U10–V10
20th St: U9–10,
    U10–V10
21st St: U9–10
22nd St: U9–10
23rd St: U9–10
24th St: U9–10
25th St: U9–10
26th St: U9–10
27th St: U9–10
28th St: U9–10

29th St: T9–U9, U9–10
30th St: T9–10, T10–U10
31st St: T9–10, T10–U10
32nd St: T9–10, T10–U10
33rd St: T9–10, T10–U10
34th St: T10–U10
35th St: T10–U10
36th St: T10–U10
37th St: T10–U10
38th St: T10–U10
39th St: T10–U10
40th St: T10–U10
41st St: T10–U10
42nd St: T10–U10
43rd St: T10–U10
44th St: T10–U10
45th St: T10–U10
46th St: T10–U10
47th St: T10–U10
48th St: T10
49th St: T10
50th St: T10
51st St: T10
52nd St: T10
53rd St: T10
54th St: T10
55th St: T10
56th St: T10
57th St: T10
58th St: T10

Adams St: U7
Adelphi St: V7–8
Ainslie St: W6
Albany Ave: X8–10
Albee Sq: U7–8
Albemarle Rd: V10–W10
Amity St: U8–V8
Anthony St: X6
Apollo St: X5–6
Argyle Rd: V10
Ashland Pl: V8
Atlantic Ave: U8–X8

Bainbridge St: X8
Baltic St: U8–V8
Banker St: W5–6
Bartlett St: W7
Bay St: T9–U9
Beadel St: X6
Beard St: T9
Beaver St: X7
Bedford Ave: W6–V6,
    V6–V7, V7–W7, W7–10
Bergen St: W8–X8, X8–9
Berkeley Pl: V8–9
Berry St: V7–6, V6–W6
Beverley Rd: V10–X10
Boerum Pl: U8
Boerum St: W7–X7
Bogart St: X6–7
Bond St: U8
Bowne St: T8
Bridge St: U7–8
Bridgewater St: X5–6
Broadway: V6–W6, W6–7,
    W7–X7, X7–8
Brooklyn Ave: W8–10
Brooklyn Bridge: U7
Brooklyn-Queens Expwy:
    W7–6, W6–X6, X6–5
Brooklyn–Battery Tunnel:
    T7–8
Buckingham Rd: V10
Buffalo Ave: X8–9
Bush St: T9–U9
Bushwick Ave: W6–X6,
    X6–7
Butler St: U8–V8

Calyer St: W5
Cambridge Pl: V8
Carlton Ave: V8
Carroll St: T8–U8, U8–9,
 U9–X9
Caton Ave: V10
Central Ave: X7
Centre St: T9–U9
Chauncey St: X8
Cherry St: X5–6
Chester Ave: U10
Church Ave: V10–X10
Clarendon Rd: W10–X10
Clark St: U7
Clarkson Ave: W10–X10
Classon Ave: V7–W7,
 W7–8
Claver Pl: W8
Clay St: W5
Clermont Ave: V7–8
Clifton Pl: V8–W8
Clinton Ave: V7–8
Clinton St: T9–U9, U9–8,
 V8–7
Clymer St: V7
Coffey St: T8–9
Columbia St: T9–8, T8–U8
Commerce St: T8
Commercial St: W5
Concord St: U7–V7
Congress St: U8–V8
Conover St: T8–9
Conselyea St: W6
Cook St: X7
Cortelyou Rd: W10–X10
Court St: U8–9
Cranberry St: U7
Creamer St: U9
Crooke Ave: V10–W10
Crown St: W9–X9
Cumberland St: V7–8

Dahill Rd: V10
Dean St: V8–X8
Decatur St: W8–X8
DeGraw St: T8–V8
Dekalb Ave: V8–W8,
 W8–7, W7–X7
Delavan St: T8
Devoe St: W6–X6
Diamond St: W5–6
Dikeman St: T8–9
Division Ave: V7
Division Pl: X6
Dobbin St: W5–6
Douglass St: U8–V8
Downing St: W8
Driggs Ave: V7–6, V6–X6
Duffield St: U7–8
Dupont St: W5
Dwight St: T8–9

E 2nd St: V10
E 3rd St: V10
E 4th St: V10
E 5th St: V10
E 7th St: V10
E 8th St: V10
E 19th St: W10
E 21st St: W10
E 22nd St: W10
E 28th St: W10
E 29th St: W10
E 31st St: W10
E 32nd St: W10
E 34th St: W10
E 35th St: W10
E 37th St: W10
E 38th St: W10

E 39th St: W10–X10
E 40th St: X10
E 42nd St: X10
E 43rd St: X10
E 45th St: X9–10
E 46th St: X10
E 48th St: X10
E 49th St: X9–10
E 51st St: X9–10
E 52nd St: X9–10
E 53rd St: X9–10
E 54th St: X10
E 55th St: X10
E 56th St: X10
E 57th St: X10
E 58th St: X10
E 59th St: X10
E 91st St: X9–10
E 93rd St: X9–10
E 95th St: X9
E 96th St: X9
E 98th St: X9
Eagle St: W5
East New York Ave:
 W9–X9
Eastern Pkwy: V9–X9
Eckford St: W5–6
Ellery St: W7
Empire Blvd: W9–X9
Engert Ave: W6
Erasmus St: W10
Evergreen Ave: X7

Fairview Pl: W10
Fenimore St: W10
Ferris St: T8
Flatbush Ave: V8–9,
 V9–W9, W9–10
Flushing Ave: W7–X7,
 X7–6
Ford St: X9
Fort Greene Pl: V8
Fort Hamilton Pkwy:
 U10–V10
Franklin Ave: W7–9
Franklin St: W7
Freeman St: W5
Frost St: W6
Fulton St: U8–X8
Furman St: U7

Gardner Ave: X5–6
Garfield Pl: U9–V9
Garnet St: T9–10
Gates Ave: W8–X8
George St: X7
Gerry St: W7
Gold St: U7
Gowanus Expwy: U9
Graham Ave: W6–7
Grand Ave: V7–8, V8–W8
Grand St: X6
Grand Street Ext: W6–X6
Grattan St: X7
Green St: W5
Greene Ave: V8–X8, X8–7
Greenpoint Ave: W5–X5
Greenwood Ave: V10
Guernsey St: W5–6

Hall St: V7–8
Halleck St: T9–U9
Halsey St: W8–X8
Hamilton Ave: T8–U8,
 U8–9
Hancock St: W8–X8
Hanson Pl: V8
Harrison Ave: W7
Harrison Pl: X7

Hart St: W7–X7
Hausman St: X5–6
Havemeyer St: W6
Hawthorne St: W10
Henry St: T9–8, T8–U8
Herkimer St: W8–X8
Hewes St: W7
Heyward St: W7
Hicks St: T8–U8, U8–7
Hooper St: V7–W7, W7–6
Hopkins St: W7
Howard Ave: X8
Hoyt St: U8
Hudson Ave: V8
Humboldt St: W5–7,
 W7–X7
Huntington St: U8–9
Huron St: W5

Imlay St: T8
India St: W5
Ingraham St: X7
Irving Pl: W8
Irving St: T8–U8

Jackson St: W6
Java St: W5
Jay St: U7
Jefferson Ave: W8–X8
Jefferson St: X7
Jewel St: W5
John St: U7–V7
Johnson Ave: X6–7
Johnson St: U7

Kane St: T8–U8
Keap St: W6–7
Kent Ave: V7–W7, W7–8
Kent St: W5
King St: T8
Kings Hwy: X9–10
Kingsland Ave: W5–7,
 W6–7
Kingston Ave: V8–X8
Knickerbocker Ave: X7
Kosciusko St: W8–X8,
 X8–7
Kosciuszko Bridge: X5
Kossuth Pl: X7

Lafayette Ave: V8–X8,
 X8–7
Lawrence St: U7–8
Lee Ave: W7
Lefferts Ave: W9–X9
Lefferts Pl: V8–W8
Lenox Rd: W10–X10
Leonard St: W6–7
Lewis Ave: X7–8
Lexington Ave: V8–X8
Lincoln Pl: V8–9, V9–X9
Lincoln Rd: W9
Linden Blvd: W10–X10
Livingston St: U8–V8
Lombardy St: X6
Lorimer St: W6–7
Lorraine St: T9–U9
Lott St: W10
Luquer St: U8
Lynch St: W7

Macdonough St: W8–X8
Macon St: W8–X8
Madison St: W8–X8
Malcolm X Blvd: X7–8
Manhattan Ave: W5
Manhattan Bridge: U7
Maple St: W9–X9
Marcy Ave: W6–8

Marginal St East: T9–10
Marion St: X8
Marlborough Rd: V10
Marshall St: V7
Martense St: W10
Maspeth Ave: X6
Maujer St: W6–X6
McGuinness Blvd: W5–6
McKeever Pl: W9
McKibbin St: W7–X7
Meadow St: X6
Melrose St: X7
Meserole Ave: W5
Meserole St: W7–X7,
 X7–X6
Metropolitan Ave: V6–X6
Middagh St: U7
Middleton St: W7
Midwood St: W9–X9
Milton St: W5
Minna St: U10–V10
Monitor St: W5–6
Monroe St: W8–X8
Montague St: U7
Montgomery St: W9–X9
Montrose Ave: W7–X7
Moore St: W7–X7
Morgan Ave: X6
Moultrie St: W5
Myrtle Ave: U7–X7

Nassau Ave: W6–5,
 W5–X5
Nassau St: U7–V7
Navy St: V7–8
Nelson St: U8–9
Nevins St: U8–V8
New York Ave: W9–10
Newell St: W5–6
Noble St: W5
Noll St: X7
Norman Ave: W6–5,
 W5–X5
North 1st St: V6–W6
North 3rd St: V6–W6
North 4th St: V6–W6
North 5th St: V6–W6
North 6th St: V6–W6
North 7th St: W6
North 8th St: W6
North 9th St: W6
North 10th St: W6
North 11th St: W6
North 12th St: W6
North 13th St: W6
North 14th St: W6
North 15th St: W6
North Oxford St: V7
North Portland Ave: V7
Nostrand Ave: W7–10

Oak St: W5
Ocean Pkwy: V10
Onderdonk Ave: X6
Orange St: U7
Orient Ave: X6
Otsego St: T9

Pacific St: U8–X8
Paidge Ave: W5
Parade Pl: V10
Park Ave: V7–W7
Park Pl: V8–9, V9–X9
Parkside Ave: V10–W10
Patchen Ave: X8
Pearl St: U7
Penn St: W7
Pierrepont St: U7
Pineapple St: U7

Pioneer St: T8
Plymouth St: U7–V7
Poplar St: U7
Porter Ave: X6
Powers St: W6–X6
President St: T8–8,
 V8–9, V9–X9
Prince St: U7–8
Prospect Ave: U9–10,
 U10–V10
Prospect Expwy: U9–10,
 U10–V10
Prospect Park SW: V10
Prospect Park W: V9–10
Prospect Pl: V8–W8,
 W8–9, W9–X9
Provost St: W5
Pulaski Bridge: W5
Pulaski St: W7–X7
Putnam Ave: W8–X8

Quincy St: W8–X8

Raleigh Pl: W10
Ralph Ave: X8–9
Randolph St: X6
Reed St: T9
Remsen Ave: X9–10
Remsen St: U7
Rewe St: X6
Richards St: T8–9
Richardson St: W6
River St: V6
Rochester Ave: X8–9
Rock St: X7
Rockaway Pkwy: X9
Rockwell Pl: V8
Rodney St: W6–7
Roebling St: W6
Rogers Ave: W8–10
Ross St: V7–W7
Rugby Rd: V10
Russell St: W5–6
Rutland Rd: W10–9,
 W9–X9
Rutledge St: W7
Ryerson St: V7

Sackett St: T8–V8
Sandford St: W7
Sands St: U7–V7
Schenectady Ave: X8–10
Schermerhorn St: U8–V8
Scholes St: W7–6,
 W6–X6
Scott Ave: X5–6
Seabring St: T8
Sedgwick St: T8–U8
Seeley St: V10
Seigel St: W7–X7
Sharon St: X6
Sherman St: V10
Skillman Ave: W6
Skillman St: W7–8
Smith St: U8–9
Snyder Ave: W10–X10
South 1st St: V6–W6
South 2nd St: V6–W6
South 3rd St: V6–W6
South 4th St: V6–W6
South 5th St: V6–W6,
 W6–7
South 6th St: V6
South 8th St: V6–W6
South 9th St: V6–7,
 V7–W7
South 10th St: V7
South 11th St: V7
South Elliott Pl: V8

South Oxford St: V8
South Portland Ave: V8
Spencer St: W7–8
Stagg St: W6–X6
Starr St: X7
State St: U8–V8
St. Edwards St: V7
Sterling Pl: V9–X9
Sterling St: W9
Steuben St: V7
Stewart Ave: X6–7
St. Felix St: V8
St. James Pl: V8
St. Johns Pl: V8–9, V9–X9
St. Marks Ave: V8–W8, W8–9, W9–X9
St. Marks Pl: V8
St. Nicholas Ave: X7
Stockholm St: X7
St. Pauls Pl: V10
Stratford Rd: V10
Stuyvesant Ave: X7–8
Sullivan Pl: W9
Sullivan St: T8
Summit St: T8–U8
Sumner Ave: W7–X7, X7–8
Sutton St: X5–6
Suydam St: X7

Taaffe Pl: W7–8
Taylor St: V7
Tehama St: U10–V10
Ten Eyck St: W6–X6
Terrace Pl: V10
Thames St: X7
Throop Ave: W7–8, W8–X8
Tilden Ave: W10–X10
Tompkins Ave: W7–8
Troutman St: X6–7
Troy Ave: X8–10

Underhill Ave: V8–9
Union Ave: W6–7
Union St: T8–V8, V8–9, V9–X9
Utica Ave: X8–10

Van Brunt St: T8–9
Van Buren St: W8–X8, X8–7
Van Dyke St: T8–9
Vandam St: X5
Vanderbilt Ave: V8
Vanderbilt St: V10
Vandervoort Ave: X6
Varet St: W7–X7
Varick Ave: X6–7
Vernon Ave: W7–X7
Verona St: T8
Veronica Pl: W10

Wallabout St: W7
Walton St: W7
Walworth St: W7–8
Warren St: U8–V8
Washington Ave: V7–9, V9–W9
Water St: U7
Waterbury St: X6
Waverly Ave: V7–8
West St: W5
Westminster Rd: V10
Whipple St: W7
White St: X7
Williamsburg Bridge: V6
Willoughby Ave: V7–X7
Willow St: U7
Wilson Ave: X7
Wilson St: V7–W7

Windsor Pl: U9–V9, V9–10
Winthrop St: W10–X10
Withers St: W6
Wolcott St: T8–9
Woodruff Ave: V10–W10
Wyckoff Ave: U8
Wyckoff St: X7
Wythe Ave: W7

York St: U7–V7

QUEENS

1st St: X2–3
2nd St: W4–3, W3–X3, X3–2
4th St : X2
5th St : W4–5
8th St: X3
9th St: W4–3, W3–X3, X3–2
10th St: W4–3, W3–X3
11th St: W5–3, W3–X3
12th St: W4–3, W3–X3
13th St: X3–4
14th St: X2–3
18th St: X3–2, X2–Y2
19th Ave: Y2–Z2
19th Rd: Z3
19th St: X2–Y2
20th Ave: Y2–Z2, Z2–3
20th Rd: Y2–3
20th St: Y2
21st Ave: Y2–3
21st Rd: Y2
21st St: W4–X4, X4–2, X2–Y2
22nd Dr: X2–Y2
22nd Rd: Y2
22nd St: W4–X4, X4–3
23rd Ave: Y2–3, Y3–Z3
23rd Rd: X2–Y2
23rd St: W4–X4, X4–3
24th Ave: X2–Y2, Y2–3, Y3–Z3
24th Rd: X2
24th St: W4–X4, X4–2, X2–Y2
25th Ave: Y3–Z3
26th Ave: X2
26th St: Y2–3
27th Ave: X2–3
27th St: Y2–3
28th Ave: X3–Y3
28th St: X4–3, X3–Y3, Y3–2
29th Ave: X3
29th St: W5–X5, X5–3, X3–Y3, Y3–2
30th Ave: X3–Z3
30th Dr: X3
30th Rd: X3–Y3
30th St: X3–5
31st Ave: X3–Y3, Y3–4, Z3
31st Dr: X3
31st Rd: X3
31st St: X5–3, X3–Y3, Y3–2
32nd St: X4–3, X3–Y3
33rd Ave: X3
33rd Rd: X3
33rd St: X5–3, Y3–2
34th Ave: X3–4, X4–Z4
34th St: X5–3, X3–Y3, Y3–2
35th Ave: W3–X3, X3–4, X4–Z4
35th St: X5–3, X3–Y3, X3–2

36th Ave: W3–X3, X3–4
36th St: X5–3, X3–Y3, Y3–2
37th Ave: W3–X3, X3–4, X4–Z4
37th St: X5–3, X3–Y3, Y3–2
38th Ave: W3–4, Z4
38th St: X5–3, X3–Y3, Y3–2
39th Ave: X4–Y4
39th Dr: Y4
39th St: X4–5
40th Ave: W4–Y4
40th St: X4–5
41st Ave: W4–Z4
41st St: X5–4, X4–Y4, Y4–2, Y2–Z2
42nd Pl: X4
42nd St: X5–4, X4–Y4, Y4–2, Y2–Z2
43rd Ave: W4–Z4
43rd Rd: W4
43rd St: X5–4, X4–Y4. Y4–2, Y2–Z2
44th Ave: W4, Y4, Z5–4
44th St: X5–4, X4–Y4, Y4–2, Y2–Z2
45th Ave: W4–Y4, Y4–5, Y5–Z5
45th St: X5–4, X4–Y4, Y4–Y2, Y2–Z2
46th Ave: W4
46th St: X5–Y5, Y5–3, Y3–2, Y2–Z2
47th Ave: W4–X4, X4–5 X5–Z5
47th St: X6–5, X5–Y5, Y5–3, Y3–Z3, Z3–2
48th Ave: W4–5, W5–Z5
48th St: W4, X5–Z5
49th Ave: W4–5, W5–X5
49th Pl: Y6
49th St: Y5–3, Y3–2
50th Ave: X5–Z5
50th St: Y5–3
51st Ave: W4–5, Y5
51st St: Y4
52nd Ave: Y5–Z5
52nd Dr: Z5
52nd Rd: Y5–Z5
52nd St: Y4
53rd Ave: X5–Z5
53rd Dr: Y5
53rd Pl: Y4
54th Ave: Y5
54th Rd: X5–Y5
54th St: Y4, Y6
55th Ave: W5–Y5
55th St: Y4–6
56th Ave: X5–Y5, Y5–6
56th Dr: X5
56th Rd: Y6
56th St: Y4–6
57th Ave: X5
57th Dr: Y6
57th Rd: Y6–Z6
57th St: Y4, Y6
58th Ave: Y6–Z6
58th Dr: Y6
58th Rd: X6–Z6
58th St: Y4–6
59th Ave: Y6–Z6
59th Rd: Y6–Z6
59th St: Y4–6
60th Ave: Y6–Z6
60th Pl: Y6–7
60th Rd: Y6–Z6

60th St: Y3–7
61st St: Y4–6, Y6–Z6, Z6–7
62nd Ave: Z6
62nd Rd: Y6–Z6
62nd St: Y4–6, Y6–Z6, Z6–7
63rd Ave: Z6
63rd St: Y4–6
64th St: Z4–Y4, Y4–6, Y6–Z6, Z6–7
66th Rd: Z6
66th St: Y5–Z5, Z5–6
67th St: Z5–6
68th Rd: Y7–Z7
68th St: Z4–6
69th Pl: Z5
69th St: Z3–6
70th Ave: Y7–Z7
70th St: Z3–6
71st St: Z3–6
72nd Pl: Z5
72nd St: Z3–6
73rd St: Z3–5
74th St: Z3–6
75th St: Z3–6
76th St: Z3–6
78th St: Z3–6
79th St: Z3–5
80th St: Z3–4
81st St: Z3–4
82nd St: Z3–4
84th St: Z3–4
86th St: Z3–4

Admiral Ave: Z6
Astoria Blvd: X3–Z3

Baxter Ave: Z4
Berrian Blvd: Z2
Bleecker St: Y6–7
Borough Pl: Y3
Broadway: X3–Y3, Y3–4, Y4–Z4, Z4–5
Brooklyn-Queens Expwy East: Y4–3, Y3–Z3
Brooklyn-Queens Expwy West: Y3

Caldwell Ave: Z6
Catalpa Ave: Y7–Z7
Central Ave: Z6
Clinton Ave: Y6
Cornelia St: Y7–Z7
Crescent St: W4–X4, X4–3
Cypress Ave: Y7

Dekalb Ave: X7–Y7, Y7–6
Ditmars Blvd: X2–Y2, Y2–3, Y3–Z3

Eliot Ave: Y6–Z6

Fairview Ave: Y6–7
Flushing Ave: X7–6, X6–Y6
Forest Ave: Y6–7
Fresh Pond Rd: Y6–Z6, Z6–7

Galasso Pl: X6–Y6
Garfield Ave: Z5
Gates Ave: Y7
Gorsline St: Z5
Grand Ave: Z5
Greene Ave: Y6–7
Greenpoint Ave: W5–X5, X5–4, X4–Y4
Grove St: Y6–7

Hamilton Pl: Y5
Harman St: Y6–7
Hazen St: Y3–Z3
Henry Ave: Z5
Hillyer St: Z5
Himrod St: Y6–7
Honeywell St: X4
Hull Ave: Y5–Z5
Hunter St: W4–X4

Ireland St: Z5

Jackson Ave: W4–X4
Jacobus St: Z5
Jay Ave: Y5–Z5

Kneeland Ave: Z5

Linden St: Y6–7

Madison St: Y7–Z7
Main Ave: X3
Manilla St: Z5
Maurice Ave: Y6–5, Y5–Z5
Menahan St: Y6–7
Metropolitan Ave: W6–Z6
Mount Olivet Cres: Z6–Z6

Newtown Ave: X3
Newtown Rd: Y3–4
North Henry St: W5–6
Northern Blvd: Y4–Z4
Nurge Ave: Y6

Page Pl: Y6
Palmetto St: Y7–Z7, Z7–6
Perry Ave: Y6
Pleasant View St: Z6
Pulaski Bridge: W5

Queens Blvd: X4–Y4, Y4–5, Y5–Z5
Queens–Midtown Tunnel: W4
Queensboro Bridge: W3–W4

Rene Ct: Y6
Review Ave: X5
Rikers Island Bridge: Z2
Roosevelt Ave: Z4

Seneca Ave: Y7
Shore Blvd: Y2
Skillman Ave: W6, W4–Y4
Stanhope St: Y6–7
Starr St: X7–Y7, Y7–6
Steinway Pl: Y2–Z2
Steinway St: Y3–2, Y2–Z2

Thomson Ave: W4–X4
Traffic St: Z6
Triborough Bridge: Y1–X1, X1–2
Troutman St: X7–6, X6–Y6
Tyler Ave: Y5

Van Dam St: X4–5
Vernon Blvd: W5–3, W3–X3

West St: W5
Willoughby Ave: X7–Y7, Y7–6
Woodbine St: Y7–Z7, Z7–6
Woodside Ave: Y4–Z4
Woodward Ave: Y6–7
Wyckoff Ave: X7–Y7

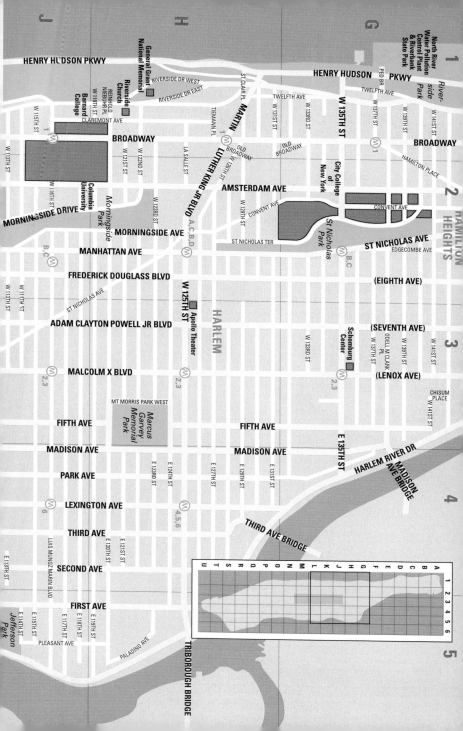

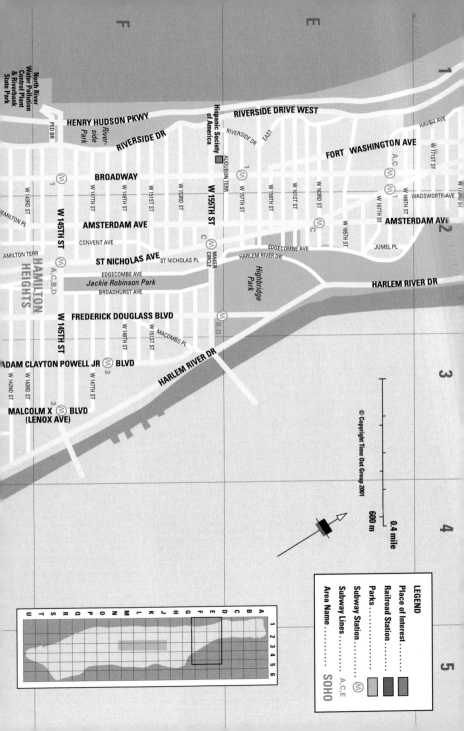

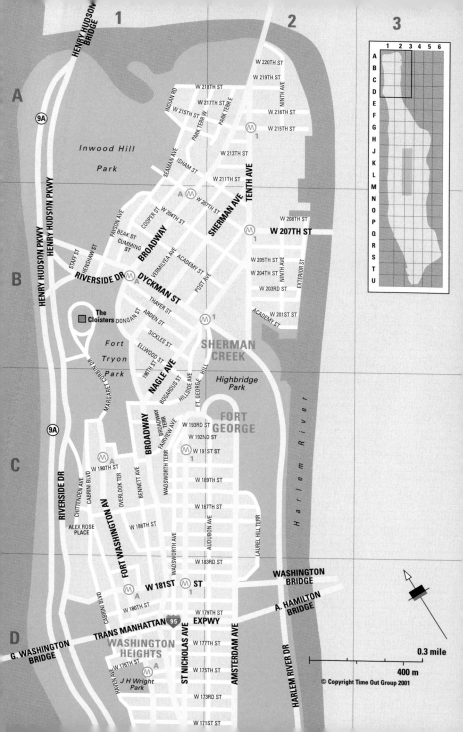

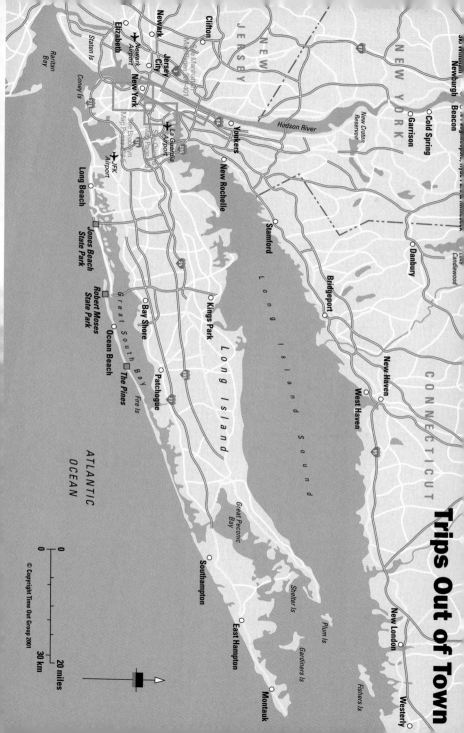

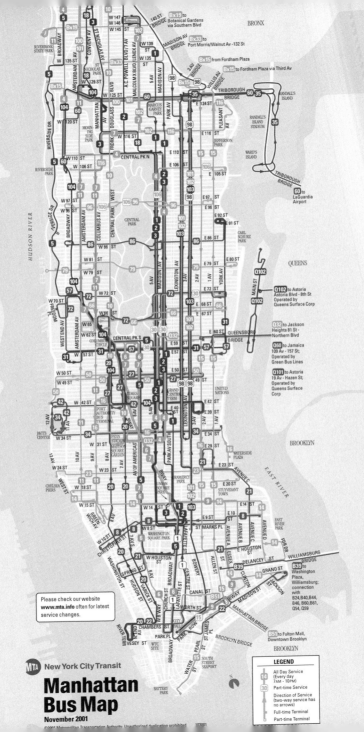

Manhattan Bus Map

MTA New York City Transit

November 2001

©2001 Metropolitan Transportation Authority. Unauthorized duplication prohibited.   103001

LEGEND

14 — All Day Service (Every day 7AM – 10PM)

30 — Part-time Service

Direction of Service (two-way service has no arrows)

Full-time Terminal

Part-time Terminal

Please check our website **www.mta.info** often for latest service changes.

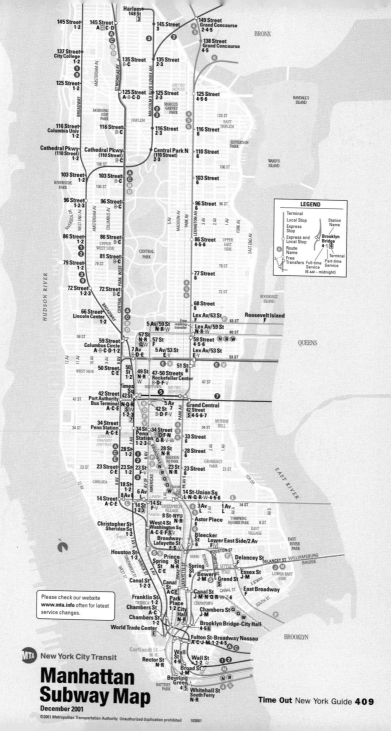

LEGEND

New York City Transit

Manhattan
Subway Map

December 2001

©2001 Metropolitan Transportation Authority Unauthorized duplication prohibited   103001

Time Out New York Guide **409**

Key Sights

Any trip to New York, New York, should include a stop at one of these fave places—maybe even all!

American Museum of Natural History
Central Park West at 79th St (212-769-5000, recorded information 212-769-5100). Subway: B, C to 81st St; 1, 2 to 79th St. See page 33.

Apollo Theatre
253 W 125th St between Adam Clayton Powell Jr. Blvd (Seventh Ave) and Frederick Douglass Blvd (Eighth Ave) (212-749-5838). Subway: A, C, B, D, 1 to 125th St. See page 300.

Bronx Zoo/Wildlife Conservation Society
Bronx River Pkwy at Fordham Rd, Bronx (718-367-1010). Subway: 2, 5 to Bronx Park East. See pages 105 and 297.

Brooklyn Botanic Garden
900 Washington Ave between Eastern Pkwy and Empire Blvd, Prospect Park, Brooklyn (718-623-
7200). Subway: C to Franklin Ave, then S to Botanic Garden; 1, 2 to Eastern Pkwy–Brooklyn Museum. See pages 96 and 293.

Brooklyn Bridge
Subway: J, M, Z to Chambers St; 4, 5, 6 to Brooklyn Bridge–City Hall. See page 94.

Central Park
59th to 110th Sts between Fifth Ave and Central Park West. (212-360-3456). See page 77.

Chinatown
Subway: J, M, Z, N, Q, R, W, 6 to Canal St. See page 56.

Coney Island
Subway: B, Q, W to Coney Island–Stillwell Ave. See pages 95 and 96.

Empire State Building
350 Fifth Ave between 33rd and 34th Sts (212-736-3100). Subway: B, D, F, V, N, Q, R, W to 34th St–Herald Sq; 6 to 33rd St. See pages 23, 74 and 76.

Metropolitan Museum of Art
1000 Fifth Ave at 82nd St (212-535-7710). Subway: 4, 5, 6 to 86th St. See page 35.

New York Public Library Center for the Humanities
Fifth Ave between 40th and 42nd Sts (212-930-0830). Subway: B, D, F, V to 42nd St; 7 to Fifth Ave. See pages 73 and 74.

Rockefeller Center
48th to 51st Sts between Fifth and Sixth Aves (212-632-3975). Subway: B, D, F, V to 47–50th Sts–Rockefeller Ctr. See pages 73 and 74.

Staten Island Ferry
South St at Whitehall St (718-727-2508). Subway: N, R to Whitehall St; 4, 5 to Bowling Green. See pages 46 and 108.

Statue of Liberty and Ellis Island Immigration Museum
Liberty Island and Ellis Island (212-363-3200). Travel: N, R to Whitehall St; 4, 5 to Bowling Green, then ferry from Battery Park to Liberty Island and Ellis Island. See pages 41 and 47.

Times Square/Theater District
Broadway at 42nd St. Subway: N, Q, R, W, S, 1, 2, 3, 7 to 42nd St–Times Sq. See page 70.

Suspend belief A walk across the Brooklyn Bridge offers a great perspective on the city.